W9-AAN-222

Thailand's
Islands & Beaches

Joe Cummings
Nicko Goncharoff

Thailand's Islands & Beaches

1st edition

Published by
 Lonely Planet Publications
 Head Office: PO Box 617, Hawthorn, Vic 3122, Australia
 Branches: 155 Filbert St, Suite 251, Oakland, CA 94607, USA
 10 Barley Mow Passage, Chiswick, London W4 4PH, UK
 71 bis rue du Cardinal Lemoine, 75005 Paris, France

Printed by
 SNP Printing Pte Ltd, Singapore

Photographs by

Jerry Alexander	Richard I'Anson
Paul Beinssen	Bernard Napthine
Joe Cummings	Richard Nebesky
Nicko Goncharoff	Mark Strickland/Oceanic Impressions

Front Cover: Traditional Thai fishing boat at Ko Phi Phi (Nevada Wier, The Image Bank)

First Published
 January 1998

Although the authors and publisher have tried to make the information as accurate as possible, they accept no responsibility for any loss, injury or inconvenience sustained by any person using this book.

National Library of Australia Cataloguing in Publication Data

Cummings, Joe.
 Thailand's islands & beaches.

1st ed.
 Includes index.
 ISBN 0 86442 540 6.

1. Thailand - Guidebooks. I. Goncharoff, Nicko. II. Title.

915.930444

text & maps © Lonely Planet 1998
 photos © photographers as indicated 1998
 The Surat Thani climate chart was compiled from information supplied by Patrick J Tyson, © Patrick J Tyson, 1998

All rights reserved. No part of this publication may be reproduced, stored in a retrieval system or transmitted in any form by any means, electronic, mechanical, photocopying, recording or otherwise, except brief extracts for the purpose of review, without the written permission of the publisher and copyright owner.

Joe Cummings

Joe has travelled extensively in Thailand since 1977. Before travel writing became a full-time job, he was a Peace Corps volunteer in Thailand, an extra in the Indochina War film *The Deer Hunter*, a translator/interpreter of Thai, a graduate student of Thai language and Asian art history at the University of California at Berkeley, a columnist for *The Asia Record*, an East-West Center Scholar in Hawaii, a university lecturer in Malaysia, and a bilingual studies consultant in the USA and Taiwan.

Fluent in Thai, Joe has travelled through all 76 of the kingdom's provinces. Joe is the author of Lonely Planet's *Thai phrasebook*, the *Thailand, Bangkok* and *Laos* guides, and a contributor to LP guides to *South-East Asia* and *Myanmar*. He occasionally writes for *Geographical, World & I, Outside, Worldview, BBC Holidays, The Independent, Bangkok Post, The Nation, Suwasdee, South China Morning Post, Ambassador, Asia Magazine* and other periodicals.

Nicko Goncharoff

Born and raised in New York, Nicko headed for the mountains (and university) in Colorado at age 17, where he learned there was more to life than pavement and partying. After graduating he moved to Taiwan for a brief stint in Asia that ended up lasting eight years. In 1995 Nicko joined the Lonely Planet team to work on the 5th edition of the *China* guide and has since written *Hong Kong city guide*, and co-authored guides to *Japan* and the *Rocky Mountain States*. At the time of writing he was living out of his backpack, still in search of a home.

From Joe

Thanks to the following people in Thailand who assisted along the way: Nicole Altclass, Rachel Foord, Andrew Forbes, David Henley, Sarah Lynch, Jennifer Bartlett, John DeModena, Mark Strickland, Noah Shepherd, Steve Rosse, Uthit Sawat, Nanthirat Prasertzup, Nuansri Vongchanyakul and Max & Tick.

From Nicko

Thanks must go to Sandra Moore, Chris Taylor, Sarah Rooney and Paula, all of whom helped smooth the way for me in Bangkok. A special tip of the hat to Ellen Cowhey for her time, generosity and company. Byron and Chris were invaluable nightlife co-researchers in Phuket, where Karl Theisen, Jaroen, Anna Boellaad and Sean Duncan also lent a hand. Mary and Jung gave me a great place to work and regroup in Krabi, as did Karin and Hassan on Ko Lanta. Also on Ko Lanta, thanks to Patrick, Tik, Toby and Jin for showing me a few excellent 'blue fish' nights. Stefan and Birte were fine travelling companions, and Wasanna helped make my brief stay on Ko Bulon Leh far more pleasant than it might otherwise have been. Chachimai was generous with both time and information in Trang, as was Olaf at Poseidon. Jessica and Chris were great people with whom to share the boat back from Ko Adang, and Nancy Hoffman was an outstanding drinking partner on the Trang-Bangkok train. And last, but never least, special thanks to Rieko.

From the Publisher

This 1st edition of *Thailand's Islands & Beaches* was produced in LP's Melbourne office. The book was edited by Emma Miller and designed by Glenn Beanland. Chris Love drew the maps and proofreading was done by Greg Alford, Kristin Odijk and Linda Suttie. Lindsay Brown researched and wrote the text for the Thailand's Marine Environment colour section. Dan Levin mastered the Thai fonts and David Kemp and Adam McCrow designed the front cover. Thanks also to Sally Gerdan for helping out, and to avid Thailand diver Fiona Thomson for her tips.

Warning & Request

Things change – prices go up, schedules change, good places go bad and bad places go bankrupt – nothing stays the same. So, if you find things better or worse, recently opened or long since closed, please tell us and help make the next edition even more accurate and useful.

We value all of the feedback we receive from travellers. Julie Young coordinates a small team who read and acknowledge every letter, postcard and email, and ensure that every morsel of information makes its way to the appropriate authors, editors and publishers.

Everyone who writes to us will find their name in the next edition of the appropriate guide and will also receive a free subscription to our quarterly newsletter, *Planet Talk*. The very best contributions will be rewarded with a free Lonely Planet guide.

Excerpts from your correspondence may appear in new editions of this guide; in our newsletter, *Planet Talk*; or in updates on our Web site – so please let us know if you don't want your letter published or your name acknowledged.

Contents

Map Index

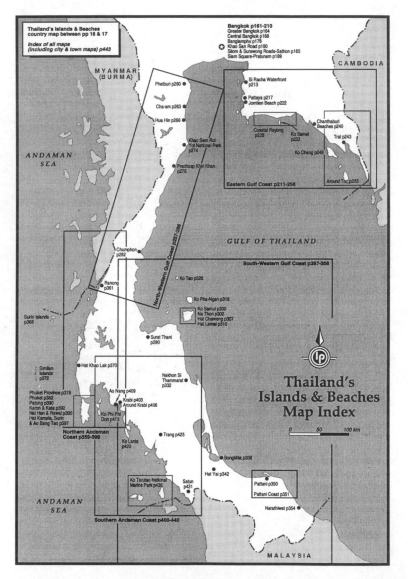

Thailand's Islands & Beaches country map between pp 16 & 17

Index of all maps (including city & town maps) p443

Bangkok p161-210
Greater Bangkok p164
Central Bangkok p168
Banglamphu p178
Khao San Road p180
Silom & Surawong Roads-Sathon p185
Siam Square-Pratunam p189

CAMBODIA

MYANMAR (BURMA)

Phetburi p260

Cha-am p263

Hua Hin p266

Khao Sam Roi Yot National Park p274

Prachuap Khiri Khan p276

ANDAMAN SEA

Si Racha Waterfront p213

Pattaya p217
Jomtien Beach p222

Coastal Rayong p228

Ko Samet p233

Chanthaburi Beaches p240

Trat p243

Ko Chang p248

Eastern Gulf Coast p211-256

Around Trat p255

GULF OF THAILAND

Chumphon p282

South-Western Gulf Coast p287-358

Ranong p361

Ko Tao p326

Ko Pha-Ngan p316

Ko Samui p300
Na Thon p302
Hat Chaweng p307
Hat Lamai p310

Surin Islands p368

North-Western Gulf Coast p357-398

Surat Thani p290

Hat Khao Lak p370

Nakhon Si Thammarat p332

Similan Islands p372

Ao Nang p409

Krabi p403
Around Krabi p406

Phuket Province p378
Phuket p382
Patong p390
Karon & Kata p392
Nai Han & Rawai p395
Hat Kamala, Surin & Ao Bang Tao p397

Ko Phi Phi Don p413

Northern Andaman Coast p359-399

Ko Lanta p420

Trang p425

Songkhla p338

Hat Yai p342

Ko Tarutao National Marine Park p435

Satun p431

Pattani p350
Pattani Coast p351

ANDAMAN SEA

Narathiwat p354

Southern Andaman Coast p400-440

Thailand's Islands & Beaches Map Index

0   50   100 km

MALAYSIA

Map Legend

BOUNDARIES

.... International Boundary
.... Provincial Boundary
.... Disputed Boundary

ROUTES

..... Freeway, with Route Number — A25
.... Major Road
.... Minor Road
.... Minor Road - Unsealed
.... City Road
.... City Street
.... City Lane
.... Train Route, with Station
.... Metro Route, with Station
.... Cable Car or Chairlift
.... Ferry Route
.... Walking Track

AREA FEATURES

.... Building
.... Cemetery
.... Beach
.... Market
.... Park, Gardens
.... Pedestrian Mall
.... Reef
.... Urban Area

HYDROGRAPHIC FEATURES

.... Canal
.... Coastline
.... Creek, River
.... Lake, Intermittent Lake
.... Rapids, Waterfalls
.... Salt Lake
.... Swamp

SYMBOLS

✈ .... Airport	⟶ .... One Way Street	
⌒⌒ ... Ancient or City Wall	🅿 .... Parking	
⊖ .... Bank	)(........................ Pass	
🏖 .... Beach	⛽ .... Petrol Station	
⌒ .... Cave	★ .... Police Station	
🏛 📌 .... Church	✉ .... Post Office	
⌢⌢⌢ .... Cliff or Escarpment	∴ .... Ruins	
◰ .... Dive Site	❖ .... Shopping Centre	
○ .... Embassy	◎ .... Spring	
⌐ .... Golf Course	🏄 .... Surf Beach	
⊕ .... Hospital	🏊 .... Swimming Pool	
☀ .... Lookout	☎ .... Telephone	
⊥ .... Monument	🈁 .... Temple	
ⓒ .... Mosque	☐ .... Tomb	
▲ .... Mountain or Hill	❶ ..... Tourist Information	
🏛 .... Museum	⊖ .... Transport	
☂ .... National Park	🐘 .... Zoo	

○ CAPITAL .... National Capital
◎ CAPITAL .... Provincial Capital
● CITY .... City
● Town .... Town
● Village .... Village

■ .... Place to Stay
Å .... Camping Ground
⌂ .... Caravan Park
⌂ .... Hut or Chalet

▼ .... Place to Eat
🍺 .... Pub or Bar
☕ .... Cafe

Note: not all symbols displayed above appear in this book

Introduction

Once known only to a trickle of backpacking hedonists plying the beach circuit between Crete and Bali, the beauty and bargains of Thailand's seaside resorts are now enjoyed by visitors of every ilk. In terms of variety and sheer attractiveness, and in many cases, cost, Thailand's islands and beaches more than hold their own against sun-and-sand offerings anywhere in the world.

Tropical Thailand offers the gentlest introduction to the Orient, combining images of the exotic – sparkling temple spires, sarong-clad farmers bending over rice shoots – with high standards of hygiene (including the best medical facilities in mainland South-East Asia) and most of the comforts of home. The country's 2710km dual coastline, rimming the Andaman Sea and Gulf of Thailand, includes many of Asia's finest stretches of sand and marine recreation spots. The friendly and relaxed nature of the Thai people is also infectious: it doesn't take long for most visitors to slow their pace and move to the calmer rhythms of tropical Thai life.

Only a relatively small portion of coastline has been seriously developed for tourism. Travellers to these areas can choose from a variety of environments, from very casual palm-thatch and bamboo beach huts to luxurious Mediterranean-style idylls perched on sea cliffs. Seafood feasts, prepared as only the Thais know how, form a major part of coastal Thai culture and are available for every budget. Away from the tourist resorts and beach huts, a lesser known world of sand, rock, palm and salt water awaits discovery. Among the country's innumerable

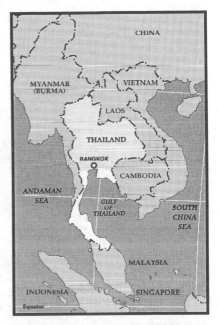

oceanic islands are many that no foreigner has yet stepped upon. Other beaches and islands – including several marine areas which enjoy national park status – receive only the occasional beachcomber, scuba diver, rock-climber or kayaker. Whatever your style, whatever type of marine experience you may enjoy, Thailand's islands and beaches should fit the bill.

Facts about the Country

HISTORY

Prehistory

The Maekhong River Valley and Khorat Plateau areas of what today encompasses much of Thailand were inhabited as far back as 10,000 years ago. Modern linguistic theory and recent archaeological finds in Thailand show a culture that was among the world's earliest agrarian societies. According to world-renowned scholar Paul Benedict (author of *Austro-Thai Language & Culture*), 'it now seems likely that the first true agriculturists anywhere, perhaps also the first true metalworkers, were Austro-Thai speakers'.

The ancestors of today's Thais were scattered amid a vast, non-unified zone of Austro-Thai influence that involved periodic migrations along several geographic lines. The early Thais proliferated over all South-East Asia, including the islands of Indonesia, and some later settled in south and southwest China, later to 're-migrate' to northern Thailand to establish the first Thai kingdom in the 13th century.

Early Kingdoms

With no surviving written records or chronologies, it is difficult to say with certainty what kind of cultures lived in Thailand before the middle of the first millennium AD. However, by the 6th century an important network of agricultural communities was thriving as far south as modern-day Pattani and Yala, and as far north and north-east as Lamphun and Muang Fa Daet (near Khon Kaen).

Khmer conquests of the 7th to 11th centuries brought their cultural influence in the form of art, language and religion. A number of Thais became mercenaries for the Khmer armies in the early 12th century, as depicted on the walls of Angkor Wat. The Khmers called the Thais 'Syam', possibly from the Sanskrit *shyama* meaning 'golden' or 'swarthy', because of their relatively deeper skin colour at the time. Another theory claims the word means 'free'. Whatever the meaning, this was how the Thai kingdom came to be called Sayam or Syam. In northwestern Thailand and Myanmar (Burma) the pronunciation of Syam became 'Shan'. English trader James Lancaster penned the first known English transliteration of the name as 'Siam' in 1592.

Meanwhile southern Thailand – the upper Malay peninsula – was under the control of the Srivijaya empire, the headquarters of which may have been in Palembang, Sumatra, between the 8th and 13th centuries. The regional centre for Srivijaya was Chaiya, near the modern town of Surat Thani. Srivijaya art remains can still be seen in Chaiya and its environs.

Several Thai principalities in the Maekhong Valley united in the 13th and 14th centuries, when Thai princes wrested the lower north from the Khmers – whose Angkor government was fast declining – and created Sukhothai or 'Rising of Happiness'. They later took Hariphunchai from the Mon to form Lan Na Thai (literally, 'million Thai rice fields').

The Sukhothai kingdom declared its independence in 1238 under King Si Intharathit and quickly expanded its sphere of influence, taking advantage not only of the declining Khmer power but the weakening Srivijaya domain in the south. Thais consider Sukhothai the first true Thai kingdom. Although it was annexed by Ayuthaya in 1376, a national identity of sorts had already been forged. Many Thais today view the Sukhothai period sentimentally, seeing it as a golden age of politics, religion and culture – an egalitarian, noble period when everyone had enough to eat and the kingdom was unconquerable.

Among other accomplishments, the third Sukhothai king, Ram Khamhaeng, sponsored a fledgling Thai writing system that became the basis for modern Thai; he also codified the Thai form of Theravada Buddhism, as borrowed from the Sinhalese. Under Ram Khamhaeng, the Sukhothai kingdom extended as far as Nakhon Si Thammarat in the south, to the upper Maekhong River Valley in Laos and to Bago (Pegu) in southern Myanmar. For a short time (1448-86), the Sukhothai capital was moved to Phitsanulok.

The Thai kings of Ayuthaya grew very powerful in the 14th and 15th centuries, taking over U Thong and Lopburi, former Khmer strongholds, and moving east until Angkor was defeated in 1431. Even though the Khmers were their adversaries in battle, the Ayuthaya kings incorporated large portions of Khmer court customs and language.

Ayuthaya was one of the greatest and wealthiest cities in Asia, a thriving seaport envied not only by the Burmese but by the Europeans who were in great awe of the city. It has been said that London, at the time, was a mere village in comparison. The kingdom sustained an unbroken monarchical succession through 34 reigns, from King U Thong (1350-69) to King Ekathat (1758-67), over a period of 400 years.

By the early 16th century Ayuthaya was receiving European visitors, and a Portuguese embassy was established in 1511. The Portuguese were followed by the Dutch in 1605, the English in 1612, the Danes in 1621 and the French in 1662. In the mid-16th century Ayuthaya and the independent kingdom of Lanna came under the control of the Burmese, but the Thais regained rule of both by the end of the century. In 1690 Londoner Engelbert Campfer proclaimed, 'Among the Asian nations, the Kingdom of Siam is the greatest. The magnificence of the Ayuthaya Court is incomparable'.

The Burmese again invaded Ayuthaya in 1765 and the capital fell after two years of fierce battle. This time the Burmese destroyed everything sacred to the Thais, including manuscripts, temples and religious sculpture. The Burmese, despite their effectiveness in sacking Ayuthaya, could not maintain a foothold in the kingdom, and Phaya Taksin, a half-Chinese, half-Thai general, made himself king in 1769, ruling from the new capital of Thonburi on the banks of the Chao Phraya River, opposite Bangkok. The Thais regained control of their country and further united the disparate provinces to the north with central Siam.

Taksin eventually came to regard himself as the next Buddha; his ministers, who did not approve of his religious fantasies, deposed and then executed him in the custom reserved for royalty – by beating him to death in a velvet sack so that no royal blood touched the ground.

Bangkok Rule

Another general, Chao Phaya Chakri, came to power and was crowned in 1782 under the title Phraphutthayotfa Chulalok. He moved the royal capital across the river to Bangkok and ruled as the first king of the Chakri dynasty. He and his heir, Loet La (1809-24), assumed the task of restoring the culture so severely damaged decades earlier by the Burmese.

The third Chakri king, Phra Nang Klao (1824-51), went beyond reviving tradition and developed trade with China while increasing domestic agricultural production. He also established a new royal title system, posthumously conferring 'Rama I' and 'Rama II' upon his predecessors and taking the title 'Rama III' for himself.

Rama IV, commonly known as King Mongkut (Phra Chom Klao to the Thais), was one of the more colourful and innovative of the early Chakri kings. He originally missed out on the throne in deference to his half-brother Rama III and lived as a Buddhist monk for 27 years. During his long monastic term he became adept in Sanskrit, Pali, Latin and English, studied western sciences and adopted the strict discipline of local Mon monks. He kept an eye on the outside world and when he took the throne in 1851 he immediately courted diplomatic relations with European nations, while avoiding colonialisation.

Thai trade restrictions were loosened and many western powers signed trade agreements with the monarch. He also established

Siam's first printing press and instituted educational reforms, developing a school system along European lines. Although the king courted the west, he did so with caution and warned his subjects: 'Whatever they have invented or done which we should know of and do, we can imitate and learn from them, but do not wholeheartedly believe in them'. Mongkut was the first monarch to show Thai commoners his face in public; he died of malaria in 1868.

His son, King Chulalongkorn (known to the Thais as Chulachomklao or Rama V, 1868-1910), continued Mongkut's tradition of reform, especially in the legal and administrative realm. Educated by European tutors, Chula abolished prostration before the king as well as slavery and corvée (state labour). Thailand further benefited from relations with European nations and the USA: railways were built, a civil service established and the legal code restructured. Though Siam still managed to avoid colonialisation, the king was compelled to con-

A spirit cult has emerged in veneration of King Chulalongkorn (1868-1910), considered a champion of the common man and a strident nationalist. In Bangkok, devotees worship nightly at a statue of Rama V at Royal Plaza.

cede territory to French Indochina (Laos in 1893, Cambodia in 1907) and British Burma (three Malayan states in 1909) during his reign.

In 1912 a group of Thai military officers unsuccessfully attempted to overthrow the monarchy – the first in a series of 20th century coup attempts that continues to the present day.

Revolution & Succession

While King Prajadhipok (Pokklao or Rama VII, 1925-35) ruled, a group of Thai students living in Paris became so enamoured of democratic ideology that they mounted a successful coup d'état against absolute monarchy in Siam. This bloodless revolution led to the development of a constitutional monarchy along British lines, with a mixed military-civilian group in power.

In 1935 the king abdicated without naming a successor and retired to Britain. The cabinet named his nephew, 10-year-old Ananda Mahidol, to the throne as Rama VIII, though Ananda didn't return to Thailand from school in Switzerland until 1945. Phibul (Phibun) Songkhram, a key military leader in the 1932 coup, maintained an effective position of power from 1938 until the end of WWII.

Under the influence of Phibul's government, the country's name was officially changed in 1939 from 'Siam' to 'Thailand' – rendered in Thai as 'Prathêt Thai'. 'Prathêt' is derived from the Sanskrit *pradesha* or 'country'. 'Thai' is considered to have the connotation of 'free', though in actual usage it simply refers to the Thai, Tai or T'ai peoples, who are found as far east as Tonkin, as far west as Assam, as far north as south China and as far south as north Malaysia.

Ananda Mahidol ascended the throne in 1945, but was shot dead in his bedroom under mysterious circumstances in 1946. His brother, Bhumibol Adulyadej, succeeded him as Rama IX. Nowadays no one ever speaks or writes publicly about Ananda's death. Even as recently as 1993, a chapter in David Wyatt's *A Short History of Thailand* chronicling the known circumstances surrounding the event had to be excised before the Thai publisher would print and distribute the title in Thailand.

WWII & Postwar Periods

During their invasion of South-East Asia in 1941, the Japanese outflanked Allied troops in Malaya and Myanmar. The Phibul government complied with the Japanese in this action by allowing them into the Gulf of Thailand; consequently the Japanese troops occupied a portion of Thailand itself. Phibul declared war on the USA and Great Britain in 1942 but Seni Pramoj, the Thai ambassador in Washington, refused to deliver the declaration. Phibul resigned in 1944 under pressure from the Thai underground resistance (Thai Seri), and, after V-J Day in 1945, Seni became premier.

In 1946, the year King Ananda was shot dead, Seni and his brother Kukrit were unseated in a general election and a democratic civilian group took power under Pridi Phanomyong, a law professor who had been instrumental in the 1932 revolution. Pridi's civilian government, which changed the country's name back to Siam, ruled for a short time, only to be overthrown by Phibul in 1947. Two years later Phibul suspended the constitution and reinstated 'Thailand' as the country's official name. Under Phibul the government took an extreme anti-communist stance, refused to recognise the People's Republic of China and became a loyal supporter of French and US foreign policy in South-East Asia.

In 1951 power was wrested from Phibul by General Sarit Thanarat, who continued the tradition of military dictatorship. However, Phibul somehow retained the actual title of premier until 1957 when Sarit finally had him exiled. Elections that same year forced Sarit to resign and go abroad for 'medical treatment'; he returned in 1958 to launch another coup. This time he abolished the constitution, dissolved the parliament and banned all political parties, maintaining effective power until he died of cirrhosis in 1963. From 1964 to 1973 the Thai nation was ruled by army officers Thanom Kittikachorn

and Praphat Charusathien, during which time Thailand allowed the USA to develop several military bases within its borders in support of the US campaign in Vietnam.

Reacting to political repression, 10,000 students publicly demanded a real constitution in June 1973. In October that year the military brutally suppressed a large demonstration at Thammasat University in Bangkok, but General Krit Sivara and King Bhumibol refused to support further bloodshed, forcing Thanom and Praphat to leave Thailand. Oxford-educated Kukrit Pramoj took charge of a 14 party coalition government and steered a leftist agenda past a conservative parliament. Among his lasting successes were a national minimum wage, the repeal of anti-communist laws and the ejection of US forces from Thailand.

Polarisation & Stabilisation

Kukrit's elected, constitutional government ruled until October 1976 when students demonstrated again, this time protesting Thanom's return to Thailand as a monk. Thammasat University again became a battlefield as border patrol police, along with right-wing, paramilitary civilian groups, assaulted a group of 2000 students holding a sit-in. Hundreds of students were killed and injured; more than a thousand were arrested. Using public disorder as an excuse, the military stepped in and installed a new right-wing government with Thanin Kraivichien as premier.

This bloody incident disillusioned many Thai students and older intellectuals not directly involved with the demonstrations, the result being that numerous idealists 'dropped out' of Thai society and joined the People's Liberation Army of Thailand (PLAT) – armed communist insurgents, based in the hills of northern and southern Thailand, who had been active since the 1930s.

In October 1977 the military replaced Thanin with the more moderate General Kriangsak Chomanand in an effort to conciliate anti-government factions. When this failed, the military-backed position changed hands again in 1980, leaving Prem Tinsulanonda at the helm. By this time the PLAT had reached a peak force of around 10,000.

Prem served as prime minister until 1988 and is credited with the political and economic stabilisation of Thailand in the post-Indochina War years (only one coup attempt in the 1980s!). The major accomplishment of the Prem years was a complete dismantling of the Communist Party of Thailand and PLAT through an effective combination of amnesty programs (which brought the students back from the forests) and military action. His administration is also considered responsible for the gradual democratisation of Thailand, culminating in the 1988 election of his successor, Chatichai Choonhavan.

Approximately 60% of Chatichai's cabinet were former business executives rather than ex-military officers, as compared to 38% in the previous cabinet. Thailand seemed to be entering a new era in which the country's double-digit economic boom coincided with democratisation. Critics praised the political maturation of Thailand, even if they grumbled that corruption seemed as rife as ever. By the end of the 1980s, however, certain high-ranking military officers had become increasingly disappointed with this *coup d'argent*, complaining that Thailand was being run by a plutocracy.

February 1991 Coup

On 23 February 1991, in a move that shocked Thailand observers around the world, the military overthrew the Chatichai administration in a bloodless coup (*pàtìwát*) and handed power to the newly formed National Peace-Keeping Council (NPKC), led by General Suchinda Kraprayoon. It was Thailand's 19th coup attempt and one of 10 successful coups since 1932; however, it was only the second coup to overthrow a democratically elected civilian government. Charging Chatichai's civilian government with corruption and vote-buying, the NPKC abolished the 1978 constitution and dissolved the parliament. Rights of public assembly were curtailed but the press was closed down for only one day.

Following the coup, the NPKC handpicked the civilian prime minister, Anand Panyarachun, a former ambassador to the USA, Germany, Canada and the UN, to dispel public fears that the junta was planning a return to 100% military rule. Anand claimed to be his own man, but like his predecessors – elected or not – he was allowed the freedom to make his own decisions only insofar as they didn't affect the military. In spite of obvious constraints, many observers felt Anand's temporary premiership and cabinet were the best Thailand had ever had.

In December 1991 Thailand's national assembly passed a new constitution that guaranteed an NPKC-biased parliament. Under this constitution, regardless of who was chosen as the next prime minister or which political parties filled the lower house, the government would remain largely in the hands of the military. The new charter included a provisional clause allowing for a 'four year transitional period' to full democracy.

Elections & Demonstrations

A general election in March 1992 ushered in a five party coalition government with Narong Wongwan, whose Samakkhitham (Justice Unity) Party received the most votes, as premier. But amid allegations that Narong was involved in Thailand's drug trade, the military exercised its constitutional prerogative and immediately replaced Narong with (surprise, surprise) General Suchinda in April.

Back in power again, the NPKC promised to eradicate corruption and build democracy, a claim that was difficult to accept since they had previously done little on either score. Thailand's independent political pundits agreed there was more oppression under the NPKC than under any administration since pre-1981 days.

In May 1992 several huge demonstrations demanding Suchinda's resignation – led by charismatic Bangkok governor Chamlong Srimuang – rocked Bangkok and larger provincial capitals. After street confrontations between protesters and the military

RICHARD NEBESKY

Traditional southern Thai fishing boats are adorned with coloured strips of homage cloth *(phâa wái phrá)* to placate the sea spirits, Hat Rin Nai, Ko Pha-Ngan.

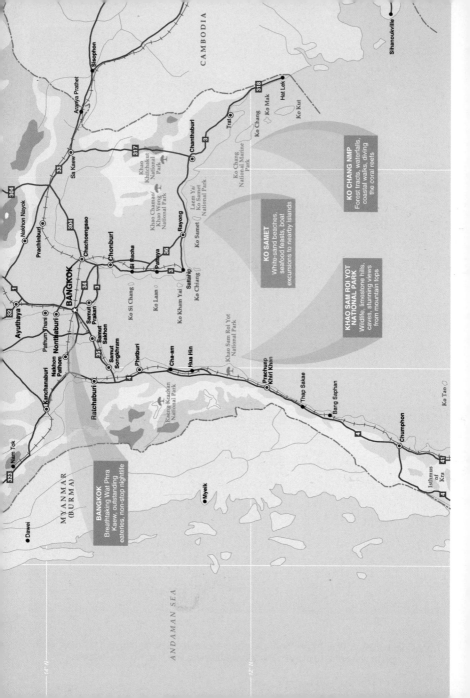

CAMBODIA

Sihanoukville

Sisophon

Aranya Prathet

Sa Kaew

33

304

Nakhon Nayok

Prachinburi

317

Khao Khitchakut National Park

Chanthaburi

318

Ko Mak

Hat Lek

Ko Chang

Ko Kut

3

Trat

Ko Chang National Marine Park

KO CHANG NMP
Forest tracts, waterfalls, coastal walks, diving the coral reefs

304

Chachoengsao

Chonburi

Si Racha

Pattaya

36

3

Khao Chamao/ Khao Wong National Park

Rayong

Laem Ya/ Ko Samet National Park

Ko Samet

KO SAMET
White-sand beaches, seafood feasts, boat excursions to nearby islands

Ayuthaya

32

Pathum Thani

34

3

BANGKOK

Nonthaburi

Nakhon Pathom

Samut Prakan

Ko Si Chang

Ko Laan

Ko Kham Yai

Sattahip

Ko Chang

Kanchanaburi

35

Samut Sakhon

Samut Songkhram

Phetburi

Cha-am

Hua Hin

Khao Sam Roi Yot National Park

KHAO SAM ROI YOT NATIONAL PARK
Wildlife, limestone hills, caves, stunning views from mountain tops

Nam Tok

323

Ratchaburi

4

Kaeng Krachan National Park

Prachuap Khiri Khan

Thap Sakae

Bang Saphan

BANGKOK
Breathtaking Wat Phra Kaew, outstanding eateries, non-stop nightlife

MYANMAR (BURMA)

Dawei

Myeik

Ko Tan

Chumphon

4

Isthmus of Kra

ANDAMAN SEA

14° N

12° N

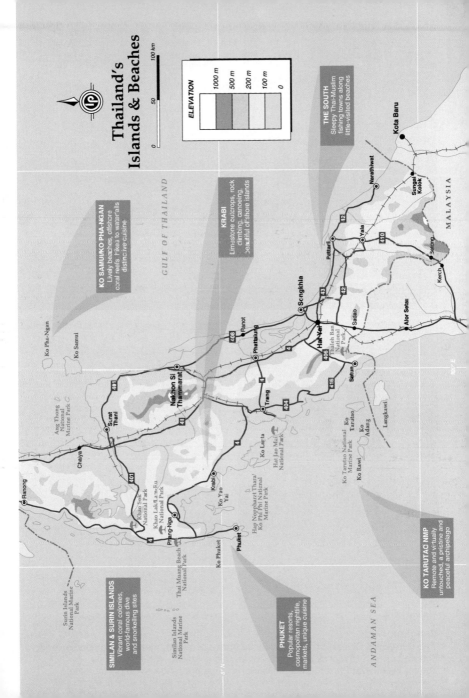

Thailand's Islands & Beaches

ELEVATION
- 1000 m
- 500 m
- 200 m
- 100 m
- 0

0   50   100 km

SIMILAN & SURIN ISLANDS
Vibrant coral colonies, world-famous dive and snorkelling sites

PHUKET
Popular resorts, cosmopolitan nightlife, markets, unique cuisine

KO TARUTAO NMP
Remote and virtually untouched, a pristine and peaceful archipelago

KO SAMUI KO PHA-NGAN
Lively beaches, offshore coral reefs. Hikes to waterfalls, distinctive cuisine

KRABI
Limestone outcrops, rock climbing, canoeing, beautiful offshore islands

THE SOUTH
Sleepy Thai-Muslim fishing towns along little-visited beaches

GULF OF THAILAND

ANDAMAN SEA

MALAYSIA

Surin Islands National Marine Park

Similan Islands National Marine Park

Ranong

Chaiya

Khao Sok National Park

Khao Lak/Lam Ru National Park

Thai Muang Beach National Park

Phang-Nga

Ko Phuket

Phuket

Krabi

Ko Yao Yai

Hap Nopparat Thara/ Ko Phi Phi National Marine Park

Surat Thani

Ang Thong National Marine Park

Ko Pha-Ngan

Ko Samui

Nakhon Si Thammarat

Ranot

Phatthalung

Ko Lanta

Trang

Hat Jao Mai National Park

Ko Tarutao National Marine Park

Ko Tarutao

Ko Adang

Ko Rawi

Langkawi

Satun

Thaleh Ban National Park

Hat Yai

Songkhla

Pattani

Yala

Betong

Sadao

Alor Setar

Kroh

Narathiwat

Sungai Kolok

Kota Baru

401
41
4
4
401
4
404
416
406
43
42
42
410
12
408

100° E
9° N

RICHARD I'ANSON

RICHARD NEBESKY

RICHARD NEBESKY

Bangkok

Top: Bangkok's Chinatown is a maddening maze of shops, markets and noodle vendors.
Bottom Left: A mythical *kinnari* figure covered in gold leaf, Wat Phra Kaew.
Bottom Right: Wat Phra Kaew's mosaic-encrusted pillars are strikingly intricate.

near Bangkok's Democracy Monument resulted in nearly 50 deaths and hundreds of injuries, Suchinda resigned after less than six weeks as premier. The military-backed government also agreed to institute a constitutional amendment requiring that Thailand's prime minister come from the ranks of elected MPs. Anand Panyarachun was reinstated as interim premier for a four month term, once again winning praise from several circles for his even-handed and efficient administration.

The September 1992 elections squeezed in veteran Democrats Party leader Chuan Leekpai with a five seat majority. Chuan led a coalition government consisting of the Democrats, New Aspiration, Palang Dharma and Solidarity parties. Though well regarded for his honesty and high morals, Chuan accomplished little in the areas of concern to the majority of Thais – most pointedly Bangkok traffic, national infrastructure and the undemocratic NPKC constitution.

Chuan never completed his four year term, and a new general election ushered in a seven party coalition led by the Chart Thai (Thai Nationality) Party. At the helm was 63-year-old billionaire Banharn Silapa-archa, whom the Thai press called a 'walking ATM'. Two of the largest partners in the coalition, the Palang Dharma and New Aspiration parties, were former participants from the Chuan coalition. Barnharn wasn't very popular with the Thai media, who immediately attacked his tendency to appoint from a pool of rural politicians known to be heavily involved in money politics. In September 1996 the Barnharn government collapsed amid a spate of corruption scandals and a crisis of confidence. The November national election, marked by violence and accusations of vote-buying, saw former deputy prime minister and army commander Chavalit Yongchaiyudh of the New Aspiration Party secure the premiership with a dubious mix of coalition parties.

In most ways since the coup/counter-coup events of 1991 and 1992, Thailand has seen 'business as usual'. Thai cynics will tell you that things *never* change – it depends on how closely you observe politics. The temporary military takeover undoubtedly hurt Thailand's international image, especially among those observers who had seen Thailand moving towards increased democratisation.

Optimists now see Suchinda's hasty resignation as a sign that the coup was only a minor detour on the country's road towards a more responsive and democratic national government. Others say the democratic Chatichai, Chuan and Banharn governments may merely be short-lived deviations from the norm of military rule. Widespread vote-buying makes a joke of democracy in Thailand at any rate. Hardened cynics might hold the view that Thailand's 20th century coups, counter-coups and poll corruption are mere extensions of the warlordism of early Thai kingdoms. Some even warned that Thailand's attempts to draft a new constitution that lays down clear rules for parliamentary succession will not sit well with the military. At the time of writing, some political observers doubted the constitution would be ready by the scheduled August 1997 target. As long as the military and bureaucracy work to hamper this progress, and until election reform is effected, Thailand's claims to democratic status and political stability will remain as shaky as ever.

GEOGRAPHY

Thailand has an area of 517,000 sq km, making it slightly smaller than the US state of Texas, or about the size of France. Its shape on the map has been compared to the head of an elephant, with its trunk extending down the Malay peninsula. The centre of Thailand, Bangkok, is at about 14° north latitude, putting it on a level with Madras, Manila, Guatemala and Khartoum.

The country's longest north-to-south distance is about 1860km, but its shape makes distances in any other direction a thousand kilometres or less. Because the north-south reach spans roughly 16 latitudinal degrees, Thailand has perhaps the most diverse climate in South-East Asia. The topography varies from high mountains in the north – the southernmost extreme of a series of ranges that extends across northern Myanmar and south-west China to the south-eastern edges of the Tibetan Plateau – to the limestone-encrusted tropical islands in the south that are part of the Malay archipelago. The rivers and tributaries of northern and central Thailand drain into the Gulf of Thailand via the Chao Phraya Delta near Bangkok; those of the Mun River and other north-eastern waterways exit into the South China Sea via the Maekhong River.

These broad geographic characteristics divide the country into four main zones: the fertile centre region, dominated by the Chao Phraya River; the north-east plateau, rising some 300m above the central plain; northern Thailand, a region of mountains and fertile valleys; and the southern peninsular region, which extends to the Malaysian frontier and is predominantly rainforest. The southern region receives the most annual rainfall and the north-east the least, although the north is less humid.

Seacoasts & Islands

Extending from the east coast of Peninsular Malaysia to Vietnam, the Sunda Shelf separates the Gulf of Thailand from the South China Sea. The gulf is relatively flat and shallow, with an average depth of 30m, up to 85m at its deepest points. Most of Thailand's major rivers drain into the gulf, tempering the water's surface salinity significantly.

On the opposite side of the Thai-Malay peninsula, the much deeper Andaman Sea – over a hundred metres deep in offshore areas – encompasses that part of the Indian Ocean east of India's Andaman and Nicobar islands. Together Thailand's Andaman Sea and Gulf of Thailand coastlines form 2710km of beaches, hard shores and wetlands.

Hundreds of oceanic and continental islands are found offshore on both sides. Those with tourist facilities constitute only a fraction. The two broad types of island geography in Thai waters are gently sloped, granitic islands, such as those of the Surin and Similan island groups, and the more dramatic limestone islands which charac-

terise marine karst topography, often with steep cliffs, overhangs, and caverns above and below the tideline. Abundant examples of such limestone islands can be found in Ao Phang-Nga (Phang-Nga Bay, also known as the Sea of Phuket).

CLIMATE
Rainfall

Thailand's climate is ruled by monsoons which produce three seasons in northern, north-eastern and central Thailand, and two in southern Thailand. The three season zone, which extends roughly from the country's northernmost reaches to Phetburi Province on the southern peninsula, experiences a 'dry and wet' monsoon climate, with the south-west monsoon arriving between May and July and lasting into November. This is followed by a dry period from November to May, a period that begins with lower relative temperatures until mid-February (because of the influences of the north-east monsoon, which bypasses this part of Thailand but results in cool breezes), followed by much higher relative temperatures from March to May.

It rains more and for longer along the Thai-Malay peninsula south of Phetburi, an area subject to the north-east monsoon from November to January, as well as the countrywide south-west monsoon. Because of this dual monsoon pattern, and because it is located closer to the equator, most of southern Thailand has only two seasons, a wet and a dry, with smaller temperature differences between the two.

Although the rains officially begin in July (according to the Thai agricultural calendar), they actually depend on the monsoons in any given year. As a rule of thumb, the dry season is shorter the further south you go. From Chiang Mai north, the dry season may last six months (mid-November to May); in most of central and north-east Thailand five months (December to May); on the upper peninsula three months (February to May); and below Surat Thani only two months (March and April). Occasional rains in the dry season are known as 'mango showers'.

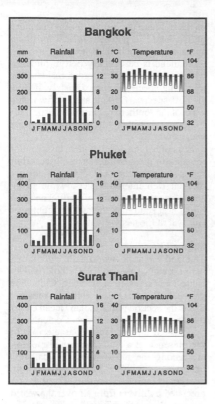

be determined by the time of year. Both sides are mostly rain-free from January to April, both are more or less equally rainy from June to November, while the gulf is drier than the Andaman coast from November to January, May and June. The South-west monsoon affects the Andaman Sea coast the most, while only the southern gulf coast – south of Phetburi – generally receives rain from the north-east monsoon. There is some rain year-round in the south, while it's very dry along the northern and eastern gulf coast areas from November to May.

In general, monsoon rains in southern Thailand last only a couple of hours a day, occasionally longer. Travelling in the rainy season is usually not unpleasant, but un-paved roads may become impassable. 'Monsoon' comes from the Arabic *mausim*, which means 'season', and is not a reference to any type of tropical storm as is mistakenly believed by many outside tropical Asia. In the last half-century only one typhoon has entered the Gulf of Thailand, though some generated along the Vietnamese coast may produce heavier than usual wind and rain conditions in the Gulf of Thailand from time to time. For climate detail as it affects divers, see the Dive Seasons section of Facts for the Visitor. See also When to Go in the same chapter for more climate information.

Temperature

Most of Thailand is very humid, with an overall average humidity of 66 to 82%, depending on the season and time of day. The dry season reaches its hottest along the north-east plain, and temperatures easily soar to 39°C in the daytime, dropping only a few degrees at night.

Temperatures south of Phetburi are more stable year-round. When it is 35°C in Bangkok, it may be only 30 to 32°C on Phuket or Ko Samui.

The Eastern Gulf Coast, stretching from Bangkok to Trat, can be uncomfortably warm (over 35°C) during the months of March, April and May, although sea breezes moderate interior mainland temperatures to some degree.

In central Thailand it rains most during August and September, though there may be floods in October since the ground has reached full saturation by then. If you are in Bangkok in early October don't be surprised if you find yourself in hip-deep water in certain parts of the city. Along the Andaman coast it rains most in May and October, as this area undergoes both monsoons.

Coastal Conditions

Having two curving coastlines to choose from means you can usually find good beach or island weather somewhere in Thailand virtually any month of the year. Hence, which seacoast you choose – the Gulf of Thailand or the Andaman Sea – might best

ECOLOGY & ENVIRONMENT
Flora
Unique in South-East Asia because its north-south axis extends some 1800km from mainland to peninsular South-East Asia, Thailand provides potential habitats for an astounding variety of flora and fauna. As in the rest of tropical Asia, most indigenous vegetation in Thailand is associated with two basic types of tropical forest: monsoon forest (with a distinctive dry season of three months or more) and rainforest (where rain falls more than nine months per year).

Monsoon forests amount to about a quarter of all remaining natural forest cover in the country; they are marked by deciduous tree varieties which shed their leaves during the dry season to conserve water. Rainforests account for about half of all forest cover; they are typically evergreen. Central, north, eastern and north-eastern Thailand mainly contain monsoon forests, while southern Thailand is predominantly a rainforest zone. There is much overlap – some forest zones support a mix of monsoon forest and rainforest vegetation.

The country's most famous flora includes an incredible array of fruit trees (see the Cuisine of Coastal Thailand section in the Facts for the Visitor chapter), bamboo (more species than any country outside China), tropical hardwoods and over 27,000 flowering species, including Thailand's national floral symbol, the orchid.

Fauna
As with plant life, the variation in the animal kingdom is closely affiliated with geographic and climatic differences. Hence the indigenous animals of Thailand's northern half are mostly of Indochinese origin, while those of the south are generally Sundaic (ie typical of Malaysia, Sumatra, Borneo and Java). The invisible dividing line between the two zoogeographical zones runs across the Isthmus of Kra, about halfway down the southern peninsula. The large overlap area between zoogeographical and vegetative zones – extending from Uthai Thani in the lower north to around Prachuap Khiri Khan on the southern peninsula – means that much of Thailand is a potential habitat for plants and animals from both zones.

Thailand is particularly rich in bird life, with more than 1000 recorded resident and migrating species – approximately 10% of all bird species. Coastal and inland waterways of the southern peninsula are especially important habitats for South-East Asian waterfowl.

Loss of habitat due to human intervention remains the greatest threat to birdlife; shrimp farms along the coast are robbing waterfowl of their rich intertidal diets, while in the south the overharvesting of swiftlet nests for bird's nest soup may threaten the continued survival of the nests' creators.

Marine Life
Thailand's marine world falls within two major oceanic spheres. The Gulf of Thailand is itself an extension of the South China Sea, part of the Pacific Ocean, while the Andaman Sea is the section of the Indian Ocean east of the Andaman-Nicobar Ridge. Coelenterates – a class of marine fauna characterised by the presence of a tentacle-rimmed mouth – are among the most exotic of Thailand's underwater life. They include jellyfish, sea anemones and the colourful corals appreciated by divers from all over the world. Among the most commonly seen are gorgonians, sea fans and sea whips.

Coral reefs may contain hundreds of thousands of species of flora and fauna; after tropical rainforests they are the most productive life habitat on the planet. A true coral reef develops on a substratum made up of the calcified 'skeletons' of hard coral. Most coral formations in Thai waters have established themselves on clusters of rock or on artificial structures such as shipwrecks. Over 200 hard coral species have been identified in the Andaman Sea, and around 60 in the gulf. Coral generally isn't found below 30m, as its survival requires sufficient sunlight for the photosynthesis of algae.

Molluscs, another easily identified part of the Thai waterscape, comprise clams, oysters, mussels, scallops, sea snails, sea slugs, squids and octopuses – all important parts of Thai gastronomy. Less commonly seen underwater than on seafood platters are crustaceans such as crabs, lobster and shrimp, many of which are nocturnal and hard to spot. The barnacle, however, is more likely found on coastal rocks and boat bottoms than in restaurants. Spiny organisms or echinoderms like sea urchins, sea cucumbers and sea stars are often seen in sandy areas near coral and rock reefs. See the Hazardous Marine Life boxed aside under Health in the Facts for the Visitor chapter for cautionary notes on sea urchins and the like.

Although they have yet to be properly catalogued, there are hundreds of species of fish in Thailand, from tiny gobies, the world's smallest fish (only around 20mm), to gargantuan whale sharks, the world's largest fish (up to 18m and 3600kg). Reef fish, camouflaged among the colourful corals, provide endless hours of underwater entertainment for human observers. They include clownfish, parrotfish, wrasses, angelfish, soldierfish, rabbitfish, sweetlip, cardinalfish, triggerfish, tang, butterflyfish and lionfish. Deeper waters are home to larger species like snapper, jack, grouper, barracuda, mackerel and shark, or even larger pelagics like marlin, sailfish, tuna and wahoo.

Rays are quite common in the warmer offshore-to-inshore waters of coastal Thailand. Divers in deeper waters may come across large manta rays, which can measure up to 7m across their wing-like fins and weigh nearly 2 tonnes. See the Hazardous Marine Life boxed aside in the Health section of the Facts for the Visitor chapter for details on how to avoid (and treat if necessary) the ray's painful sting.

The most common sharks in Thai waters – the leopard shark, nurse shark, whitetip reef shark and blacktip reef shark – tend to be under 2m long and are quite timid. Out at the Burma Banks in the Andaman Sea, divers may see larger hammerhead and tiger sharks.

Four of the world's six sea turtle species swim in the Andaman Sea and the Gulf of Thailand: the Pacific ridley, green turtle, leatherback turtle and hawksbill turtle. All are endangered species because their eggs, meat and shells are highly valued among coastal Thais. Hunted to extinction in Thai waters, the loggerhead turtle once brought the list to five. The Thai government has declared turtle hunting and turtle egg collecting illegal; the destruction of the turtles has slowed considerably but hasn't yet stopped. The main culprit in recent times has been Japan, the world's largest importer of sea turtles (including the endangered ridley and hawksbill), both of which the Japanese use for meat, leather and turtle-shell fashion accessories.

Thailand's warm waters attract whales and dolphins, around 25 species of which are known to frequent either or both the Andaman Sea and the Gulf of Thailand. Whales which frequently visit Thai seas or make them their year-round habitat include Bryde's, false killer and pilot. Commonly seen dolphins are the Pacific white-sided, bottle-nosed, spotted, Risso's, spinner and the under-threat Irrawaddy. Another marine mammal of note, the endangered dugong (also called manatee or sea cow), is occasionally spotted off the coast of Trang Province in southern Thailand. Sacred to southern Thais, the dugong is now protected by law from all molestation.

National Parks & Wildlife Sanctuaries

Despite Thailand's rich diversity of flora and fauna, only in recent years have most of the 79 national parks (only 50 of which receive an annual budget), 89 'non-hunting areas' and wildlife sanctuaries, and 35 forest reserves been established.

Eighteen of the national parks are marine parks that protect coastal, insular and open-sea areas. The majority of these are well maintained by the Forestry Department, but a few have allowed rampant tourism to threaten the natural environment, most notably on the islands of Ko Samet and Ko Phi Phi. Poaching, illegal logging and shifting cultivation have also taken their toll on protected lands, but since 1990 the government has cracked down with some success.

Marine national parks offer very basic visitor facilities. There is usually somewhere to stay for a reasonable fee, and sometimes meals are provided, but it's a good idea to take your own sleeping bag or mat; basic camping gear is useful for parks without fixed accommodation. You should also take a torch (flashlight), rain gear, insect repellent, a water container and a small medical kit.

Most parks charge a small fee to visit (typically 3 to 5B for Thais, 5 to 25B for foreigners). For more information on staying in national parks, see Accommodation in the Facts for the Visitor chapter.

Environmental Policy

Like all countries with a high population density, Thailand has put enormous pressure on its fragile ecosystems. Fifty years ago the countryside was around 70% forest; as of 1995 an estimated 25% of the natural forest cover remained. The loss of forest cover has been accompanied by dwindling wildlife populations. Logging and agriculture are mainly to blame for the decline.

In response to environmental degradation, the Thai government has created a large number of protected lands since the 1970s, and has enacted legislation to protect specific plant and animal species. The government hopes to raise total forest cover to 40% by the middle of next century. Thailand has also become a signatory to the UN Convention on International Trade in Endangered Species (CITES).

In 1989 logging was banned following a 1988 disaster in which hundreds of tonnes of cut timber washed down deforested slopes in Surat Thani Province, killing more than a hundred people and burying a number of villages. These days builders even need government permission to use timber salvaged from old houses. This has helped curb illegal logging in the interior (unfortunately, Thai timber brokers are now turning their attention to Laos and Myanmar – neither of which are CITES signatories), but corruption remains a problem.

Corruption also impedes government at-tempts to shelter 'exotic' species from the illicit global wildlife trade and to preserve Thailand's sensitive coastal areas. The Forestry Department is currently under pressure to take immediate action where preservation laws are unenforced, including coastal zones where illegal tourist accommodation has flourished. There has also been a crackdown on restaurants serving 'jungle food' (aahãan pàa), which consists of exotic and often endangered animals like barking deer, bear, pangolin, civet and gaur.

The tiger is one of the most endangered of Thailand's large mammals. Although tiger hunting or trapping is illegal, poachers continue to kill them for the lucrative Chinese pharmaceutical market; among the Chinese, the ingestion of tiger penis and bone is thought to have curative effects. In Taipei, the world centre for Thai tiger consumption, at least two-thirds of the pharmacies deal in tiger parts (in spite of the fact that such trade is forbidden by Taiwanese law). Around 200 to 300 wild tigers are thought to be hanging on in the national parks of Khao Yai, Kaeng Krachan, Thap Lan, Mae Wong and Khao Sok.

Forestry Department efforts are limited by lack of personnel and funds. The average ranger is paid only 75B a day – some aren't paid at all but receive food and lodging – to face down armed poachers backed by the rich and powerful godfathers who control illicit timber and wildlife businesses.

Marine resources are also threatened by a lack of long-term conservation goals. The upper portion of the Gulf of Thailand between Rayong and Prachuap Khiri Khan was once one of the most fertile marine areas in the world. Now it is virtually dead due to overfishing and the release of mainland pollutants.

Experts say it's not too late to rehabilitate the upper gulf by reducing pollution and the number of trawlers, and by restricting commercial fishing to certain zones. A ban on the harvest of plaa tuu (mackerel) at the spawning stage has brought this fish back from the brink of total depletion. The Bangkok Metropolitan Administration (BMA) is also establishing a system of sewage treatment plants in the Chao Phraya Delta area, with the intention of halting all large-scale dumping of sewage into gulf waters. Similar action needs to be taken along the entire eastern seaboard, which is rapidly becoming Thailand's new industrial centre.

Overdevelopment on Ko Phuket and Ko Phi Phi is starving the surrounding coral reefs by blocking nutrient-rich run-off from the islands' interiors, as well as smothering the reefs with pollutants. Ko Samui and Ko Samet face a similar fate if growth isn't controlled and waste-disposal standards improved.

One encouraging sign was the passing of the 1992 Environmental Act, which sets environment standards and designates conservation and pollution control areas. Pattaya and Phuket were the first locales decreed pollution control areas, making them eligible for government cleanup funds. With such assistance, officials in Pattaya claim they'll be able to restore Pattaya Bay – exposed to improper waste disposal for at least the past 20 years – to its original state by the end of this decade.

A large number of Thais remain ignorant of the value of taking a pro-environment stance in everyday life or in encouraging ecologically sound tourism. The director of a certain regional Tourism Authority of Thailand (TAT) office was recently heard to complain that eco-tourism was *lambàak* (inconvenient or bothersome) for Thai people but there was little she could do about it because 'that's national policy'. Fortunately such attitudes are steadily changing, especially among the young, who have grown up in relative affluence but who have begun to perceive the dangers of environmental neglect.

Even though environmentalism is national policy, only with strong popular support can protective laws which are already plentiful but often ignored be enforced. Current examples of 'people power' include the hundreds of forest monasteries that voluntarily protect chunks of forest. When one such *wat* (temple) was forcibly removed by

the military in Buriram Province, thousands of Thais around the country rallied behind the abbot, Phra Prachak, and the wat's protectorship was re-established. On the other hand, wats with less ecologically minded trustees have sold off virgin land to developers.

Non-governmental organisations play a large role surveying and designating threatened areas and educating the public about the environment. In 1983 Wildlife Fund Thailand (WFT) was created under Queen Sirikit's patronage as an affiliate of the World-Wide Fund for Nature (WWF). The main function of the WFT is to raise consciousness about the illegal trade in endangered wildlife. A list of several other groups is included in the following section. Citing the country's free press as a major incentive, the international watchdog organisation Greenpeace – known for its campaigns against whale hunting and nuclear weapons testing – may soon be opening a regional office in Thailand.

Tourism & the Environment

In some instances tourism has had positive effects on conservation in Thailand. Conscious that the country's natural beauty is a major tourist attraction for both residents and foreigners – and that tourism is a major revenue earner – the government has stepped up efforts to protect wilderness areas and to add more acreage to the park system. In Khao Yai National Park, for example, all hotel and golf course facilities were removed to reduce damage to the park environment and upgrade the wilderness. Under government and private sector pressure, the fishing industry has all but eliminated coral dynamiting in the Similan and Surin islands.

Of course, tourism has also caused environmental damage. Eager to make fistfuls of cash, hotel developers and tour operators have rushed to provide ecologically inappropriate services in areas which are unable to sustain high-profile tourism. Concerns about this has prompted the government to look more closely at Ko Phi Phi and Ko Samet – two national park islands notorious for overdevelopment. Part of the problem is that it's not always clear which lands are protected and which are privately owned.

Common problems in marine areas include the anchoring of tour boats on coral reefs and the dumping of rubbish into the sea. Coral and seashells are also illegally collected and sold in tourist shops. 'Jungle food' restaurants – with endangered species on the menu – flourish near inland national parks. Perhaps the most visible abuses occur in areas without basic garbage and sewage services, where there are piles of rotting garbage, mountains of plastic and open sewage run-off.

One of the saddest sights is the piles of discarded plastic water bottles on popular beaches. Those seen floating in the sea or in rivers are sometimes ingested by marine or riparian wildlife with fatal results. Many of these bottles started out on a beach only to be washed into the sea during the monsoon season.

What can the average visitor to Thailand do to minimise the impact of tourism on the environment? First off, avoid all restaurants serving 'exotic' wildlife species (eg barking deer, pangolin, bear). Visitors should also consider taking down the names of any restaurants serving or advertising such fare and filing a letter of complaint with the TAT, the WFT and the Forestry Department (addresses are further in this section). The main patrons of this cuisine are the Thais themselves, along with visiting Chinese from Hong Kong and Taiwan. Municipal markets selling endangered species, such as Bangkok's Chatuchak Market, should also be duly noted – consider enclosing photographs to support your complaints. For a list of endangered species in Thailand, contact the WFT.

When using hired boats near coral reefs, urge boat operators not to lower anchors onto coral formations. This is becoming less of a problem with established boating outfits – some of whom mark off sensitive areas with blue-flagged buoys – but is common among small-time pilots. Perhaps volunteer to collect (and later dispose of) rubbish if it's

obvious that the usual mode is to throw everything overboard.

Obviously, you shouldn't buy coral or shells, or items made from coral or shells, while in Thailand. Thai law forbids the collection of coral or seashells anywhere in the country – report any observed violations in tourist or marine park areas to the TAT and Forestry Department, or in other places to the WFT.

One of the difficulties in dealing with rubbish and sewage problems in tourist areas is that many Thais don't understand why tourists should expect different methods of disposal than are used elsewhere in the country. In urban areas or populated rural areas, piles of rotting rubbish and open sewage lines are frequently the norm – after all, Thailand is still a 'developing' country. Thais sensitive to western paternalism are quick to point out that on a global scale the so-called 'developed' countries cause far more environmental damage than Thailand does (eg per capita greenhouse emissions for Australia, Canada or the USA average over 5 tonnes each, while ASEAN countries contribute less than half a tonne per capita).

Hence, when making environmental complaints or suggestions to Thais in the tourist industry, it's important to emphasise that you want to work *with* them rather than against them.

Whether on land or at sea, refrain from purchasing or accepting drinking water offered in plastic bottles wherever possible. When there's a choice, request glass water bottles, which are recyclable in Thailand. The 4B deposit is refundable when you return the bottle to any vendor who sells drinking water in glass bottles. When only plastic-bottled water is available, consider transferring the water to your own reusable container and leave the plastic bottle with the vendor or dispose of it yourself later at a dumpster or other legitimate collection site.

A few guesthouses now offer drinking water from large, reusable plastic containers as an alternative to the individual disposable containers. This service is available in most areas of Thailand (even relatively remote areas like Ko Chang) and is certainly available wherever the disposable plastic bottles are. Encourage hotel and guesthouse staff to switch from disposable plastic to either glass or reusable plastic.

In outdoor areas where rubbish has accumulated, consider organising an impromptu cleanup crew to collect plastic, styrofoam and other non-biodegradables for delivery to a regular rubbish pick-up point. If there isn't a pick-up nearby, enquire about the nearest collection point and deliver the refuse yourself.

By expressing your desire to use environmentally friendly materials – and by taking direct action to avoid the use and indiscriminate disposal of plastic – you can provide an example of environmental consciousness not only for the Thais but for other international visitors.

Write to the following organisations to offer your support for stricter environmental policies or to air complaints or suggestions:

Asian Society for Environmental Protection – c/o CDG-SEAPO, Asian Institute of Technology, GPO 2754, Bangkok 10501

Bird Conservation Society of Thailand – PO Box 13, Ratchathewi Post Office, Bangkok 10401

Community Ecological Development Programme – PO Box 140, Chiang Rai 57000

Friends of Nature – 670/437 Charansavatwong Rd, Bangkok 10700

Magic Eyes – 15th floor, Bangkok Bank Bldg, 333 Silom Rd, Bangkok 10400

Office of the National Environment Board – 60/1 Soi Prachasumphan 4, Rama IV Rd, Bangkok 10400

Project for Ecological Recovery – 77/3 Soi Nomjit, Naret Rd, Bangkok 10500

Raindrop Association – 105-7 Ban Pho Rd, Thapthiang, Trang 92000

Royal Forestry Department – 61 Phahonyothin Rd, Bangkhen, Bangkok 10900

Siam Environmental Club – Chulalongkorn University, Phayathai Rd, Bangkok 10330

The Siam Society – 131 Soi Asoke, Sukhumvit Rd, Bangkok 10110

Thailand Information Centre of Environmental Foundation – 58/1 Sakol Land, Chaeng Wattana Rd, Pak Kret, Nonthaburi

Tourism Authority of Thailand – 372 Bamrung Meuang Rd, Bangkok 10100

Wildlife Fund Thailand – 251/88-90 Phahonyothin Rd, Bangkhen, Bangkok 10220;
255 Soi Asoke, Sukhumvit 21, Bangkok 10110

GOVERNMENT & POLITICS
The 1991 Constitution

Since 1932, the government of the Kingdom of Thailand has nominally been a constitutional monarchy inspired by the bicameral British model but with myriad subtle differences. Thailand's 15th constitution, enacted on 9 December 1991 by the coup regime's now-defunct National Peace-Keeping Council (NPKC), replaced the one promulgated in December 1978 and allows for limited public participation in the choosing of government officials. National polls elect the 360 member lower house and prime minister, but the 260 senators of the upper house are appointed by the prime minister. In Thailand the upper house or Senate is not as powerful as the elected House of Representatives; the latter writes and approves legislation, while the Senate votes on constitutional changes.

Administrative Divisions

For administrative purposes, Thailand is divided into 76 *jangwàat* or provinces. Each province is subdivided into *amphoe* or districts, which are further subdivided into *king-amphoe* (subdistricts), *tambon* (communes or village groups), *mùu-bâan* (villages), *sukhăaphibaan* (sanitation districts) and *thêtsàbaan* (municipalities). Urban areas with more than 50,000 inhabitants and a population density of over 3000 per sq km are designated *nákhon*; those with populations of 10,000 to 50,000 with not less than 3000 per sq km are *meuang* (usually spelt 'muang' on roman-script highway signs). The term 'meuang' is also used loosely to mean metropolitan area (as opposed to an area within strict municipal limits).

A provincial capital is an *amphoe meuang*. An amphoe meuang takes the same name as the province of which it is capital, eg amphoe meuang Chiang Mai (often abbreviated as 'meuang Chiang Mai') means the city of Chiang Mai, capital of Chiang Mai Province.

Except for Krungthep Mahanakhon (Metropolitan Bangkok), provincial governors *(phûu wâa râatchakaan)* are appointed to their four year terms by the Ministry of the Interior – a system that leaves much room for corruption.

The Monarchy

His Majesty Bhumibol Adulyadej (pronounced 'Phumíphon Adunyádèt') is the ninth king of the Chakri Dynasty (founded in 1782) and, as of 1988, the longest reigning king in Thai history. Born in the USA in 1927 and schooled in Bangkok and Switzerland, King Bhumibol was a nephew of King Rama VII (King Prajadhipok, 1925-35) as well as the younger brother of King Rama VIII (King Ananda Mahidol). His full name – including royal title – is Phrabaatsomdet Boramintaramahaphumiphonadunyadet.

The current king, His Majesty Bhumibol Adulyadej (Rama IX), is the ninth king of the Chakri Dynasty and the longest reigning monarch in Thai history.

His Majesty ascended the throne in 1946 following the death of Rama VIII, who had reigned as king for only one year (Ananda served as regent for 10 years after his uncle's abdication in 1035 – see History earlier).

A jazz composer and saxophonist, King Bhumibol wrote the royal anthem, *Falling Rain*, which accompanies photos of the royal family shown before every film at cinemas across the country. His royal motorcade is occasionally seen passing along Ratchadamnoen (Royal Promenade) Rd in Bangkok's Banglamphu district; the king is usually seated in a vintage yellow Rolls Royce or a 1950s Cadillac.

The king has his own privy council composed of up to 14 royal appointees who assist with his formal duties; the president of the privy council serves as interim regent until an heir is throned.

The king and his wife, Queen Sirikit, have four children: Princess Ubol Ratana (born 1951), Crown Prince Maha Vajiralongkorn (1952), Princess Mahachakri Sirindhorn (1955) and Princess Chulabhorn (1957). A royal decree issued by King Trailok (1448-88) to standardise succession in a polygamous dynasty makes the king's senior son or full brother his *uparaja* (Thai: *ùpàrâat*) or heir apparent. Thus Prince Maha Vajiralongkorn was officially designated as crown prince and heir when he reached 20 years of age in 1972; if he were to decline the crown or be unable to ascend the throne due to incurable illness or death, the senior princess (Ubol Ratana) would be next in line.

Princess Ubol Ratana married American Peter Jensen in 1972 against palace wishes, thus forfeiting her royal rank, but was reinstated as Princess a few years ago. The Crown Prince has married twice, most recently to an ex-actress. His son Prince Juthavachara is the eldest male of the next Chakri generation.

Though Thailand's political system is officially classified as a constitutional monarchy, the constitution stipulates that the king be 'enthroned in a position of revered worship' and not be exposed 'to any sort of accusation or action'. With or without legal writ, the vast majority of Thai citizens regard King Bhumibol as a sort of demigod, partly in deference to tradition but also because of his impressive public works record.

It is often repeated that the Thai king has no political power (by law his position is strictly titular and ceremonial) but in times of national political crisis, Thais have often looked to the king for leadership. Two attempted coups d'état in the 1980s may have failed because they received tacit royal disapproval. By implication, the successful military coup of February 1991 must have had palace approval, whether *post facto* or *a priori*.

Along with nation and religion, the monarchy is very highly regarded in Thai society – negative comment about the king or any member of the royal family is a social as well as legal taboo. See the Society & Conduct section in this chapter for details.

ECONOMY

During the 1980s, Thailand maintained a steady GNP growth rate which by 1988 had reached 13% per annum. Thailand in the 90s finds itself on the threshold of attaining the exclusive rank of NIC or 'newly industrialised country'. Soon, economic experts say, Thailand will join Asia's 'little dragons', also known as the Four Tigers – South Korea, Taiwan, Hong Kong and Singapore – in becoming a leader in the Pacific Rim economic boom.

The Thai currency took a beating in mid-1997 when assaults by currency traders, combined with an already somewhat weakened economy, forced a 20% decrease in the value of the baht in relation to the US dollar and many other currencies. If the devaluation doesn't progress any further, the drop should fuel exports and possibly aid economic growth. The Thai government, along with other ASEAN governments in the region, is taking steps to shore up its currency, since a dramatic devaluation of the baht could adversely affect the Malaysian ringgit, Singaporean dollar, Philippine peso and so on.

Sixty per cent of Thailand's exports are agricultural; the country ranks first in the world for rice (followed by the USA and Vietnam), second in tapioca (after Brazil) and fifth in coconut (following Indonesia, the Philippines, India and Sri Lanka). Since 1991 Thailand has been the world's largest producer of natural rubber, although it still ranks behind Malaysia in total rubber exports. Other important agricultural exports include sugar, maize, pineapple, cotton, jute, green bean, soybean and palm oil. Processed food and beverages – especially canned shrimp, tuna and pineapple – also account for significant export earnings. Thailand's top export markets are the USA, Japan and Singapore.

About 60% of the Thai labour force is engaged in agriculture, 10% each in commerce and services, and 20% in manufacturing. Manufactured goods have become an increasingly important source of foreign exchange revenue and now account for at least 30% of Thailand's exports. Cement, textiles and electronics lead the way, with car and truck manufacture coming up fast. The country also has substantial natural resources, including tin, petroleum and natural gas.

Since 1987 tourism has become a leading earner of foreign exchange, occasionally outdistancing Thailand's largest single export, textiles. The government's economic strategy remains focused, however, on export-led growth through the development of light industries such as textiles and electronics, backed by rich reserves of natural resources and a large, inexpensive labour force.

Raw average per capita income by 1996 was US$2680 per year; if measured using the 'purchasing power parity' method (which takes into account price differences between countries), the Thais average US$6870 per capita annually. With an average net escalation of 11.2% per annum since 1985, Thailand has ranked highest in Asia in terms of real GDP growth per employee in Asia over the last decade. Regional inequities, however, mean that annual income averages range from US$400 in the north-east to US$3000 in Bangkok. An estimated 20% of Thai citizens – most of them in Bangkok or

Phuket – control 63% of the wealth. The minimum wage in Bangkok and surrounding provinces is 145B (US$5.80) per day; it can be as low as 95B a day in the outer provinces.

Thailand's annual inflation rate was an estimated 4.8 % in 1996, down from around 7% in the early 90s. Unemployment hovers at around 1.4%, tied with Taiwan for the lowest in Asia; 56.5% of the population – the highest percentage in Asia – participate in the general labour force.

Regional Economies

Southern Thailand is the richest region outside Bangkok, due to abundant agricultural (fruit, rubber, rice), fishing and mineral (tin and oil) resources along with burgeoning beach tourism. Central Thailand, including the Eastern Gulf Coast, grows fruit (especially pineapples), sugar cane and rice for export, and supports most of the ever-growing industry (textiles, food processing and cement).

The north-east has the lowest inflation rate and cost of living. Hand-woven textiles and farming remain the primary means of livelihood, though Nakhon Ratchasima (Khorat) is an emerging centre for metals and automotive industry. In the south, fishing, tin mining and rubber production keep the local economy fairly stable, with tourism a seasonal runner-up.

North Thailand produces mountain or dry rice (as opposed to water rice, the bulk of the crop produced in Thailand) for domestic use, maize, tea, various fruits and flowers, and is very dependent on tourism.

Tourism

According to figures from the TAT, the country averages about seven million tourists per year, a 64-fold increase since 1960 when the government first began keeping statistics. In the first nine months of 1996 – the most recent period for which data are available – 61% of all visitors (5.2 million of total) came from East and South-East Asia, with Malaysians leading the way with 758,000, then Japanese (709,000), Koreans (376,000), Taiwanese (342,000) and Chinese

(339,000). Europeans made up approximately 1.2 million of the total, with Britons at the top (257,000), followed by Germans (236,000), French (162,000) and Italians (91,000). US visitors accounted for 246,000 of the total, Australians 161,000.

Tourist revenue amounts to between US$5 billion and US$6 billion a year. A recent study carried out by the Thailand Development Research Institute confirms that 'although the average daily expenditure of typical guesthouse tourists may not be as high as that of hotel dwellers, they do, in fact, normally spend more because they usually stay in the country much longer. Income generated by these tourists is thought to penetrate more deeply and widely to the poorer segments of the industry'.

Spurred by steady economic growth, an estimated 40 million Thais per year are now taking domestic leisure trips. Ten years ago western tourists often outnumbered Thais at some of the nation's most famous tourist attractions. Now the opposite is true; except at major international beach destinations like Phuket and Ko Samui, Thai tourists tend to outnumber foreign tourists in most places at a rate of more than five to one.

POPULATION & PEOPLE

The population of Thailand is about 61 million and currently growing at a rate of 1.5% per annum (as opposed to 2.5% in 1979), thanks to a highly successful nationwide family-planning campaign.

Over a third of all Thais live in urban areas. Bangkok is by far the largest city in the kingdom, with a population of over six million (more than 10% of the total population) – too many for the scope of its public services and what little 'city planning' exists. Ranking the nation's other cities by population depends on whether you look at thetsabaan (municipal district) limits or at meuang (metropolitan district) limits. By the former measure, the four most populated cities in descending order (not counting the densely populated 'suburb' provinces of Samut Prakan and Nonthaburi, which would rank second and third if considered separately from Bangkok) are Nakhon Ratchasima (Khorat), Chiang Mai, Hat Yai and Khon Kaen. Using the rather misleading meuang measure, the ranking runs Udon Thani, Lopburi, Nakhon Rachasima and Khon Kaen. Most of the other towns in Thailand have populations of well below 100,000.

The average life expectancy in Thailand is 69, the highest in mainland South-East Asia. Yet only an estimated 59% of people have access to local health services; in this the nation ranks 75th worldwide, behind countries with lower national incomes such as Sudan and Guatemala. There is only one doctor per 4316 people, and infant mortality figures are 26 per 1000 births (figures for neighbouring countries vary from 110 per 1000 in Cambodia to 12 in Malaysia). Thailand as a whole has a relatively youthful population; only about 12% are older than 50.

The Thai Majority
About 75% of the citizenry are ethnic Thais, who can be divided into the central Thais or Siamese of the Chao Phraya Delta (the most densely populated region of the country); the Thai Lao of north-east Thailand; the Thai Pak Tai of southern Thailand; and the northern Thais. Each of these groups speak their own Thai dialect and to a certain extent practise customs unique to their region. Politically and economically the central Thais are the dominant group, although they barely outnumber the Thai Lao of the north-east.

Smaller groups with their own Thai dialects include the Shan (Mae Hong Son), the Thai Lü (Nan, Chiang Rai), the Lao Song (Phetburi and Ratchaburi), the Phuan (Chaiyaphum, Phetburi, Prachinburi), the Thai Khorat or Sawoei (Nakhon Ratchasima), the Phu Thai (Mukdahan, Sakon Nakhon), the Yaw (Nakhon Phanom, Sakon Nakhon) and the Thai-Malay (Satun, Trang, Krabi).

The Chinese
People of Chinese ancestry make up 11% of the population, most of whom are second or third-generation Hokkien (Hakka), Tae Jiu (Chao Zhou/Chiu Chao) or Cantonese.

Ethnic Chinese probably enjoy better relations with the majority population here than in any other country in South-East Asia, due partly to historical reasons and partly to traditional Thai tolerance of other cultures (although there was a brief spell of anti-Chinese sentiment during the reign of Rama VI). King Rama V used Chinese businesspeople to infiltrate European trading houses, a manoeuvre that helped defeat European colonial designs on Siam. Wealthy Chinese also introduced their daughters to the royal court as consorts, developing royal connections and adding a Chinese bloodline that extends to the current king.

Minorities
The second largest ethnic minority group living in Thailand are the Malays (3.5%), most of whom reside in the southern Thai provinces of Songkhla, Yala, Pattani and Narathiwat. The remaining 10.5% of the population are divided among smaller non-Thai-speaking groups like the Vietnamese, Khmer, Mon, Semang (Sakai), Moken (chao leh or 'sea gypsies'), Htin, Mabri, Khamu and a variety of hill tribes in the north.

A small number of Europeans and other non-Asians live in Bangkok and the provinces – their total numbers aren't recorded since very few have immigrant status.

ARTS
Traditional Sculpture & Architecture
The following scheme is the latest one used by Thai art historians to categorise historical styles of Thai art, principally sculpture and architecture (since very little painting prior to the 19th century has survived).

A good way to acquaint yourself with these styles is to visit Bangkok's National Museum, where works from each of these periods are on display. Then, as you travel and view old monuments and sculpture, you'll know what you're seeing, as well as what to look for.

Areas in coastal Thailand of historical interest for art and architecture include Thonburi, Phetburi, Chaiya and Nakhon Si Thammarat. Some of the monuments at these sites have been restored by the Fine Arts Department and/or by local interests. For

Thai Art Styles

Style	Duration	Centred in	Characteristics
Mon Art (formerly Dvaravati)	6th to 13th C	central Thailand, also north and north-east	adaptation of Indian styles, principally Gupta
Khmer Art	7th to 13th C	central and north-east Thailand	post-classic Khmer styles accompanying spread of Khmer empires
Peninsular Art	(formerly Srivijaya period)	Chaiya and Nakhon Si Thammarat	Indian influence 3rd to 5th C, Mon and local influence 5th to 13th C, Khmer influence 11th to 14th C
Lan Na (formerly Chiang Saen)	13th to 14th C	Chiang Mai, Chiang Rai, Phayao, Lamphun, Lampang	Shan/Burmese and Lao traditions mixed with local styles
Sukhothai	13th to 15th C	Sukhothai, Si Satchanalai, Kamphaeng Phet, Phitsanulok	unique to Thailand
Lopburi	10th to 13th C	central Thailand	mix of Khmer, Pala and local styles
Suphanburi-Sangkhlaburi (formerly U Thong)	13th to 15th C	central Thailand	mix of Mon, Khmer and local styles; prototype for Ayuthaya style
Ayuthaya A	1350-1488	central Thailand	Khmer influences gradually replaced by revived Sukhothai influences
Ayuthaya B	1488-1630	central Thailand	ornamentation distinctive of Ayuthaya style, eg crowns and jewels on Buddhas
Ayuthaya C	1630-1767	central Thailand	baroque stage and decline
Ratanakosin	19th C to present	Bangkok	return to simpler designs, beginning of European influences

more detail on historical sites, see the relevant regional sections in this book.

Recommended books on Thai art are AB Griswold's classic *Arts of Thailand* (Indiana University Press, 1960), the similarly titled *The Arts of Thailand* (Thames & Hudson, 1991) by Steve Van Beek and *A Concise History of Buddhist Art in Siam* (Tokyo, 1963) by Reginald Le May. There are several decent English-language books on various aspects of Thai art for sale at the national museums around Thailand (particularly at the Bangkok National Museum) and at the Ancient City (Muang Boran) office on Ratchadamnoen Klang Rd in Bangkok.

For information about the export of antiques or objects of art from Thailand see Antiques & Art in the Customs section of the Facts for the Visitor chapter.

Modern Architecture

Modern Thai architects are among the most daring in South-East Asia, as even a short visit to Bangkok will confirm. Thais began mixing traditional Thai with European forms in the late 19th and early 20th centuries, as exemplified by Bangkok's Vimanmek Palace, the Author's Wing of the Oriental Hotel, the Chakri Mahaprasat next to Wat Phra Kaew, the Thai-Chinese Chamber of Commerce on Sathon Tai Rd and any number of older residences and shophouses in Bangkok or provincial capitals throughout Thailand. This style is usually referred to as 'old Bangkok' or 'Ratanakosin'. The recently completed Old Siam Plaza shopping centre, adjacent to Bangkok's Chalermkrung Royal Theatre, is an attempt to revive the old Bangkok school.

Buildings of mixed heritage in the south typically show Portuguese influence. Shophouses throughout the country, whether 100 years or 100 days old, share the basic Chinese shophouse (*hâwng tháew* in Thai) design in which the ground floor is reserved for trading purposes while the upper floors contain offices or residences.

During most of the post-WWII era, the trend in modern Thai architecture – inspired by the European Bauhaus movement – was towards a boring functionalism in which the average building looked like a giant egg carton turned on its side. The Thai aesthetic, so vibrant in prewar eras, almost entirely disappeared in this characterless style of architecture.

When Thai architects finally began experimenting again during the building boom of the mid-1980s, it was to provide high-tech designs like Sumet Jumsai's famous robot-shaped Bank of Asia on Sathon Tai Rd in Bangkok. Few people seemed to find the space-age look endearing, but at least it was different. Another trend affixed gaudy Roman and Greek-style columns to rectangular Art Deco boxes in what was almost a parody of western classical architecture. One of the outcomes of this fashion has been the widespread use of curvilinear banisters on the balconies of almost every new shophouse, apartment or condominium throughout Thailand, often with visually disturbing results.

A good book on Thai residential design, interior or exterior, is William Warren's *Thai Style* (Asia Books), a coffee-table tome with excellent photography by Luca Invernizzi Tettoni.

Painting

Except for prehistoric and historic cave or rock-wall murals found throughout the country, not much formal painting predating the 18th century exists in Thailand. Presumably there were a great number of temple murals in Ayuthaya that were destroyed by the Burmese invasion of 1767. The earliest surviving temple examples are found at Ayuthaya's Wat Ratburana (1424), Wat Chong Nonsii in Bangkok (1657-1707) and Phetburi's Wat Yai Suwannaram (late 17th century).

Nineteenth century religious painting has fared better. Ratanakosin-style temple art is in fact more highly esteemed for painting than for sculpture or architecture. Typical temple murals feature rich colours and lively detail. Some of the finest are found in Wat Phra Kaew's Wihan Buddhaisawan (Phutthaisawan) Chapel in Bangkok and at Wat Suwannaram in Thonburi.

Music

Traditional Music The classical, central Thai music is spicy, like Thai food, and features an incredible array of textures and subtleties, hair-raising tempos and pastoral melodies. The classical orchestra is called the *pìi-phâat* and can include as few as five players or more than 20. Among the more common instruments is the *pìi*, a woodwind instrument which has a reed mouthpiece; it is heard prominently at Thai boxing matches. The pìi is a relative of a similar Indian instrument, while the *phin*, a banjo-like stringed instrument whose name comes from the Indian *vina*, is considered native to Thailand. A bowed instrument similar to ones played in China and Japan is aptly called the *saw*. The *ranâat èk* is a bamboo-keyed percussion instrument resembling the western xylophone, while the *khlui* is a wooden flute.

One of the more amazing Thai instruments is the *khawng wong yài*, tuned gongs arranged in a semicircle. There are also several different kinds of drums, some played with the hands, some with sticks. The most important Thai percussion instrument is the *tà-phon* (or *thon*), a double-headed hand drum which sets the tempo for the ensemble. Prior to a performance, the players make offerings of incense and flowers to the tà-phon, which is considered to be the 'conductor' of the music's spiritual content.

The pìi-phâat ensemble was originally developed to accompany classical dance-drama and shadow theatre but can be heard in straightforward performance these days, in temple fairs as well as concerts. One reason classical Thai music may sound strange to the western ear is that it does not use the tempered scale we have been accustomed to hearing since Bach's time. The standard Thai scale does feature an eight note octave but it is arranged in seven full-tone intervals, with no semi-tones. Thai scales were first transcribed by Thai-German composer Peter Feit (Phra Chen Duriyanga), who also composed Thailand's national anthem in 1932.

Recommended books on the subject are *The Traditional Music of Thailand* by David Morton and *Thai Music* by Phra Chen Duriyanga (Peter Feit).

Modern Music Popular Thai music has borrowed much from western music, particularly its instruments, but still retains a distinct flavour of its own. Although Bangkok bar bands can play fair imitations of everything from Hank Williams to Madonna, there is a growing preference among Thais for a blend of Thai and international styles.

The best example of this is Thailand's famous rock group Carabao. Recording and performing for nearly 20 years now, Carabao is by far the most popular musical group in Thailand, and has even scored hits in Malaysia, Singapore, Indonesia and the Philippines with songs like 'Made in Thailand' (the chorus is in English). This band and others have crafted an exciting fusion of Thai classical and lûuk thûng forms with heavy metal. These days almost every other Thai pop group sounds like a Carabao clone, and members of the original band are putting out solo albums using the now classic Carabao sound.

Another major influence on Thai pop was a 1970s group called Caravan, which created a modern Thai folk style known as *phleng phêua chii-wít* or 'songs for life'. Songs of this nature have political and environmental topics rather than the usual moonstruck love themes; during the authoritarian dictatorships of the 1970s many of Caravan's songs were banned by the government. Though they dissolved in the early 1980s, Caravan re-form for the occasional live concert. The group's most gifted songwriter, Surachai, continues to record and release solo efforts.

Yet another inspiring movement in modern Thai music is the fusion of international jazz with Thai classical and folk motifs. The leading exponent of this newer genre is the composer and instrumentalist Tewan Sapsanyakorn (also known as Tong Tewan), whose performances mix western and Thai instruments. The melodies of his compositions are often Thai-based but the improvisations and rhythms are drawn from such heady sources as Sonny Rollins and Jean-Luc Ponty. Tewan plays soprano and alto sax, violin and khlui with equal virtuosity.

Other notable groups fusing international jazz and indigenous Thai music include Kangsadarn and Boy Thai; the latter adds Brazilian *samba* to the mix. Thai instrumentation in world music settings are specialities of Todd Lavelle and Nupap Savantrachas, each of whom has had a steady flow of recent hits. Fong Nam, a Thai orchestra led by American composer Bruce Gaston, performs an inspiring blend of western and Thai classical motifs.

Cassette tapes of Thai music are readily available in department stores, cassette shops and street vendors. The average price for a Thai music cassette is 55 to 75B. Western tapes are cheaper (about 30B each) if bootlegged, but the days of pirate tapes in Thailand are numbered now that the US music industry is enforcing international copyright laws. Licensed western music tapes cost 90 to 110B, still a good deal by the pricing standards of most western nations.

Arts section continued on page 46

Thailand's Marine Environment

Photographs by Mark Strickland/Oceanic Impressions

Thailand's underwater wonders can be conveniently accessed from island and beach resorts – there is easy snorkelling and, for those who wish to venture deeper, scuba courses and beginner dives, as well as adventurous live-aboard charters for the hard-core diver. Even the relatively shallow and busy Gulf of Thailand offers coral gardens around its offshore islands, but across the Isthmus of Kra the Andaman Sea beckons divers from all around the world with its first class diving. The Similan and Surin Islands, the Burma Banks and numerous deserted limestone islands can be accessed from popular resort centres such as Phuket and Krabi.

Soft corals and their relatives the gorgonians and sea whips do not develop the limestone skeleton of the more familiar reef-building hard corals. Also unlike their hard cousins, soft corals do not contain light-dependent algae within their tissues and so are free to grow at greater depths away from sunlight. These graceful corals develop an amazing variety of form in order to strain their microscopic food from the currents, and because the individual polyps of soft corals are not encased in a limestone cup, they are more visible, giving the colony its vivid colour.

Title Page: A seahorse perches among the coral, sponges and weed using its prehensile tail – a rare and rewarding sight in Thailand's famous coral reefs.

Right: Delicate soft corals and sea whips dominate the reef bottom here at the Similan Islands. A diver must exercise buoyancy control and great care not to damage these habitats.

*M*olluscs, in their immense variety of form, inhabit all parts of the coral reef; among the most dramatic are the nudibranchs, or sea-slugs, unrivalled in the animal kingdom for elaborate shape and vibrant colour. Other molluscs of the reef include the snails, which encompass cowries and cone shells; bivalves, such as clams and oysters; and perhaps the most interesting of all, the cephalopods – octopus, squid and cuttlefish. The octopus is the master of stealth and camouflage, squeezing and contorting its colour-coded body and arms through impossible crevices to pounce on unwary crustaceans, particularly crabs. Squid and cuttlefish are superb swimming carnivores and can often be seen swimming in schools. Along with the octopus they possess unrivalled intelligence in the invertebrate world.

Above Left: Many species of nudibranch are bad tasting or poisonous – concentrating in their own tissues the stinging cells from their coral prey – and it pays to advertise such traits with vibrant colours. (Similan Islands)

Left: Rapid colour changes enable the cuttlefish to blend with its immediate surroundings and to communicate mood swings or alarm. The diver may be left watching a pool of ink and a rapidly retreating cuttlefish.

*C*rabs, shrimps and other crustaceans abound on the coral reef, but it will take more than a cursory glance to spot them. Many are minute, spindly, almost transparent, others are masters of disguise – some crabs paste weeds and reef debris onto their carapace. Many of the small shrimps and crabs play a vital role in the reef ecosystem, removing detritus, dead tissue and parasites from their hosts, which may be a coral, sponge, fish or other reef creature.

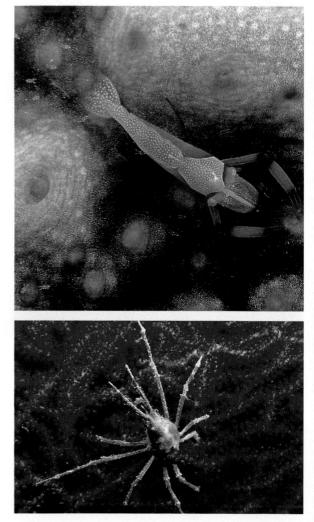

Above Right: The tiny imperial shrimp explores the lumpy surface of a sea cucumber in search of food. The shrimp will probably spend most of its life on the one host. (Andaman Sea)

Right: A twin-prong spider crab, a slow-moving scavenger, crawls over a brilliant red gorgonian coral. (Similan Islands)

*L*ooking more like a plant than an animal, the featherstar, or crinoid, is a primitive echinoderm, a group which also includes starfish, brittlestars, sea urchins and sea cucumbers. Featherstars, sometimes seen in 'rainbow' clusters of different species, grip onto coral outcrops with their claw-like cirri, and wave their brightly coloured arms in the current to trap water-borne food. Of the many starfish species, the most easy to recognise is the crown-of-thorns. Notorious for destroying large areas of reef when their populations periodically boom, the crown-of-thorns is, nevertheless, an integral part of the reef ecosystem.

Above Left: A featherstar nestles among soft coral in the Andaman Sea. Although appearing to have numerous arms, these are actually branches of just five arms – the five part body plan is common to all echinoderms.

Left: The crown-of-thorns starfish feeds at night, everting its stomach over a hard coral, digesting the polyps to leave behind a bleached-white coral skeleton. (Burma Banks, Andaman Sea)

*S*hark encounters in Thailand are usually limited to the passive leopard and nurse shark, which shelter during the day in gutters and crevices, and the white-tip reef shark – easily excited predators, often baited to 'perform' for visiting divers. Along with the leopard shark, stingrays inhabit the sand and mud bottom adjacent to the reefs, feeding on molluscs and echinoderms which they find with acute senses of touch and taste. Stingrays mostly rest during the day, partially burying themselves in the substrate, and so posing a potential danger to unwary divers. Should a stingray be stepped on, its reflex action is to strike upwards with its poison-barbed tail.

Above Right: A marbled stingray glides to the reef floor where it will partially bury its mottled form and all but disappear.

Right: The leopard shark is a large (up to 3m), docile seafloor dweller. Their sluggish nature and size has made them a target for harassment by divers. Such behaviour is now actively discouraged by conscientious dive operators. (Ko Tachai, Andaman Sea)

*M*orays and other eels usually hunt at night, when they can be seen sliding in and around coral cavities and crevices searching for food, which, for them, is virtually any animal, dead or alive. Morays must swallow their food quickly to re-establish sufficient water flow through the mouth and over the gills for breathing. During the day morays retire to a coral grotto, their large heads and fang-filled mouths all that is visible as they gape and 'pant' water. At a few popular dive sites in the Andaman Sea, morays have been accustomed to hand feeding to the point where they will leave their protective lairs at the first sign of an approaching diver and beg for hand-outs.

Above Left: A gaping moray eel in its coral cave – a common sight on day trips from Phuket. In lacking a swim-bladder, and thus much in the way of buoyancy control, morays must rest among the reef crevices during the day after spending the night hunting and scavenging.

Left: Growing to over a metre long, though more usually seen at half that size, the blue ribbon eel starts life as a mostly black male, changing later into the blue-and-yellow female form. (Similan Islands)

*T*o live among the riot of colour and shapes of the coral reef, many animals have evolved elaborate camouflage for protection and to aid hunting. Scorpionfish, stonefish and lionfish are related masters of camouflage, hunting by stealth and ambush. The scorpionfish lies motionless in the coral and reef rubble awaiting the approach of small fish; after a few small adjustments in position the strike will be a lightening-swift gulp. The lionfish uses a different tactic, slowly sneaking up on its prey before rapidly opening a cavernous mouth, sucking in a great volume of water and, if successful, the meal.

Above Right: Festooned with fleshy fringes, protrusions and mottled skin, the scorpionfish ingeniously blends into its surroundings.(Richelieu Rock, Andaman Sea)

Right: Spotfin lionfish (also known as firefish) hunt by stealth. Their elaborate, elongate spines and contrasting markings confuse the prey; the familiar body shape of a predator does not register – until it is too late. (Similan Islands)

*R*elentless competition for food and a place to shelter has led to the amazing variety of shape, size, colour and behaviour of coral reef fish. There are algal grazers, coral grinders and large-mouthed gulpers and sievers. There are countless ecological niches in the reef ecosystem, and often when a species rests, either during the day or night, another species will start its shift in that same niche.

Top Left: This splendid coral grouper, normally a voracious and opportunistic feeder, patiently allows a cleaner wrasse to clean its gills.

Middle Left: Facial markings are common among angelfish species. The yellow mask angelfish is a rare but memorable sight on Thai reefs. (Similan Islands)

Bottom Left: This ember parrotfish retreats to a small cave at night, after a day of scraping and grazing coral surfaces. Occasionally parrotfish secrete a clear mucous membrane in which they become encased while sleeping – perhaps as protection against predators that hunt using smell.

*I*n Thailand and all over the tropics, certain fish species have evolved a close relationship with sea anemones. These fish are able to move freely among the stinging tentacles which would quickly paralyse other fish on contact. Although the anemone fish gains protection, and indeed is always found in proximity to an anemone, the anemone does not need the anemone fish and probably gains very little out of the deal.

Above Right: Clown anemone fish never venture far from their host anemone. A typical group consists of a large dominant female, a single mature male and several immature males. When the female dies, the largest male will change sex and one of the smaller males will mature. (Phuket)

Right: Anemone fish, such as this saddle back anemone fish at the Similan Islands, are not born immune to the anemone's stinging tentacles. The fish acquire immunity by gradually covering themselves in the anemone's own mucous. Chemicals in the mucous stop the anemone from stinging itself and this feature is put to use by the anemone fish.

*M*any fish choose to feed at the edge of the reef where the plankton-rich waters of the open sea meet the reef. But away from the confines of the reef there is the increased danger of being eaten, so often fish will feed in tightly packed schools for protection. Along with common reef sharks and the occasional visit from larger oceanic sharks, other predators of the reef edge include turtles. Not great migrators like other turtles, hawksbill turtles are usually seen close to their feeding and breeding grounds, the coral reefs and tropical islands.

Above Left: Fusiliers are among the most common schooling fish in Thailand's tropical waters. At night they disband and individuals find shelter in the nooks and crannies of the reef. (Similan Islands)

Left: The hawksbill turtle is losing the battle for survival in South-East Asia. Not only is it still hunted for its 'tortoiseshell', but the quiet, sandy beaches it requires for nesting are disappearing under human encroachment. (Ko Surin National Park)

*T*he largest animals likely to be encountered at Thailand's offshore dive locations are the magnificent whale shark, the largest living fish, and the manta ray, perhaps the most graceful and majestic of fishes. These docile plankton feeders are entirely harmless and amazingly patient in the presence of over-friendly divers, but their true wonder is best appreciated from a respectful distance while they do what comes naturally.

Above Right: Dwarfing a diver, the immense bulk of a whale shark is an unforgettable sight. Such encounters, though rare, can be had on day trips from Phuket.

Right: Manta rays are relatively common in the reef waters of Thailand. This manta at Ko Tachai is using its 'horns', modified from part of the pectoral fins, to feed by directing plankton-carrying water through its cavernous mouth.

Amid swirling schools of tiny baitfish, a diver explores a reef outcrop adorned with lush soft coral. (Similan Islands)

Arts section continued from page 32

Theatre & Dance

Traditional Thai theatre consists of six dramatic forms: *khŏn*, formal masked dance-drama depicting scenes from the *Ramakian* (the Thai version of India's *Ramayana)* and originally performed only for the royal court; *lákhon*, a general term covering several types of dance-dramas (usually for non-royal occasions) as well as western theatre; *lí-khe* (likay), a partly improvised, often bawdy folk play featuring dancing, comedy, melo-drama and music; *mánohra*, the southern Thai equivalent of lí-khe, but based on a 2000-year-old Indian story; *năng* or shadow plays, limited to southern Thailand; and *hùn lŭang* or *lákhon lék* – puppet theatre.

Manohra Also known simply as *nora*, this is southern Thailand's equivalent to líkhe and the oldest surviving Thai dance-drama. The basic story line bears some similarities to the *Ramayana*. In this case the protagonist, Prince Suthon (Sudhana in Pali), sets off to rescue the kidnapped Manohra, a *kinnari* or woman-bird princess. As in lí-khe, performers add extemporaneous comic rhymed commentary – famed nora masters sometimes compete at local festivals to determine who's the best rapper.

Nang Shadow-puppet theatre – in which two dimensional figures are manipulated between a cloth screen and light source at night-time performances – has been a South-East Asian tradition for perhaps five centuries. Originally brought to the Malay peninsula by Middle Eastern traders, the technique eventually spread to all parts of mainland and peninsular South-East Asia; in Thailand it is mostly found only in the south. As in Malaysia and Indonesia, shadow puppets in Thailand are carved from dried buffalo or cow hides *(năng* in Thai).

Two distinct shadow-play traditions survive in Thailand. The most common, *năng thálung*, is named after Phattalung Province, where it developed based on Malay models. Like their Malay-Indonesian counterparts,

the Thai shadow puppets represent an array of characters from classical and folk drama, principally the *Ramakian* and *Phra Aphai-mani* in Thailand. A single puppet master manipulates the cutouts, which are bound to the ends of buffalo-horn handles. Năng thálung is still occasionally seen at temple fairs in the south, mostly in Songkhla and Nakhon Si Thammarat provinces. Performances are also held periodically for tour groups or visiting dignitaries from Bangkok.

The second tradition, *năng yài* (literally, 'big hide'), uses much larger cutouts, each bound to two wooden poles held by a puppet master; several masters (almost always male) may participate in a single performance. Năng yài is rarely performed nowadays because of the lack of trained năng masters and the expense of the shadow puppets. Most năng yài made today are sold to interior decorators or tourists – a well-crafted hide puppet may cost as much as 5000B.

In 1994, in order to celebrate the King's 50th year on the throne, the Fine Arts Department initiated a project to restore the original 180-year-old set of năng yài figures used by the Thai royal court. The project required the refurbishing of 352 puppets along with the creation of 100 new ones to complete the royal set, known as Phra Nakhon Wai ('City-Shaking') – a tribute to the impact they had on audiences nearly two centuries ago. In addition to the occasional performance in Nakhon Si Thammarat or Bangkok, năng yài can be seen at Wat Khanon in Ratburi Province, where năng yài master Khru Chalat is passing the art on to younger men.

Literature

Of all classical Thai literature, the *Ramakian* is the most pervasive and influential in Thai culture. The Indian source – the *Ramayana* – came to Thailand with the Khmers 900 years ago, first appearing as stone reliefs on Prasat Hin Phimai and other Angkor-period temples in the north-east. Oral and written versions may also have been available; eventually, though, the Thais developed their own version of the epic, first written down during the reign of Rama I (1782-1809). This version contained 60,000 stanzas, about 25% longer than the Sanskrit original.

Although the main theme remains the same, the Thais embroidered the *Ramayana* by providing much more biographical detail on arch-villain Ravana (Dasakantha, called Thótsàkan or '10-necked' in the *Ramakian)* and his wife Montho. Hanuman the monkey-god differs substantially in the Thai version insofar as he is very flirtatious with females (in the Hindu version he follows a strict vow of chastity). One of the classic *Ramakian* reliefs at Bangkok's Wat Pho depicts Hanuman clasping a maiden's bared breast as if it were an apple.

Also passed on from Indian tradition are the many *jatakas* or life stories of the Buddha *(chaa-tòk* in Thai). Of the 547 jataka tales in the Pali *tripitaka* (Buddhist canon) – each one chronicling a different past life – most appear in Thailand almost word-for-word as they were first written down in Sri Lanka. A group of 50 'extra' stories, based on Thai folk tales of the time, were added by Pali scholars in Chiang Mai 300 to 400 years ago. The most popular jataka in Thailand is one of the Pali originals known as the Mahajati or Mahavessandara (Mahaa-Wetsandon in Thai), the story of the Buddha's penultimate life. Interior murals in the *bòt* (ordination chapel) of Thai wats typically depict this jataka and nine others: Temiya, Mahaachanaka, Suwannasama, Nemiraja, Mahaasotha, Bhuritat, Chantakumara, Nartha and Vithura.

The 30,000 line *Phra Aphaimani*, composed by poet Sunthorn Phu in the late 18th century and set on the island of Ko Samet, is Thailand's most famous classical literary work. Like many of its epic predecessors around the world, it tells the story of an exiled prince who must complete an odyssey of love and war before returning to his kingdom in victory.

SOCIETY & CONDUCT

Citizens of the only South-East Asian country never to be colonised by a foreign power, the Thais are independent-minded yet steeped in a tradition of friendliness toward visitors. Although the pressures of modern develop-

ment (Thailand enjoyed double-digit growth throughout the 80s) have brought a changing set of national values – not always for the better – the travel-poster epithet 'Land of Smiles' still applies to the treatment most visitors receive. The influence of Buddhism, arguably the most tolerant of the world's major religions, is said to be largely responsible for the Thais' easy friendliness.

When outsiders speak of 'Thai culture' they're referring to a complex of behavioural modes rooted in the history of Thai migration throughout South-East Asia, with many commonalities shared by the Lao of neighbouring Laos, the Shan of north-eastern Myanmar and the numerous tribal Thais found in isolated pockets from Dien Bien Phu, Vietnam, all the way to Assam, India. Nowhere are such norms more generalised than in Thailand, the largest of the Thai homelands.

Practically every ethnicity represented in Thailand, whether of Thai ancestry or not, has to a greater or lesser degree been assimilated into the Thai mainstream. Although Thailand is the most 'modernised' of the existing Thai (more precisely, Austro-Thai) societies, the cultural underpinnings are evident in virtually every facet of everyday life. Those aspects that might be deemed 'westernisation' – eg the wearing of trousers instead of *phâkhamãa*, the presence of cars, cinema and 7-Elevens – show how Thailand has adopted and adapted tools invented elsewhere.

Such adaptations do not necessarily represent cultural loss. Ekawit Na Talang, a scholar of Thai culture and head of the government's National Culture Commission, defines culture as 'the system of thought and behaviour of a particular society – something which is dynamic and never static'. Talang and other world culture experts agree that it's paradoxical to try to protect a culture from foreign influences as cultures cannot exist in a vacuum. Culture evolves naturally as outside influences undergo processes of naturalisation. From this perspective, cultures which don't change, die. As Talang has said, 'Anything obsolete, people will reject and anything that has a relevant role in life, people will adopt and make it part of their culture'.

Nevertheless there are certain aspects of Thai society that virtually everyone recognises as 'Thai' cultural markers. The Thais themselves don't really have a word that corresponds to the English term 'culture'. The nearest equivalent, *wátánátham*, emphasises fine arts and ceremonies over other aspects usually covered by the concept. So if you ask Thais to define their culture, they'll often talk about architecture, food, dance, festivals and the like. Religion – obviously a big influence on culture as defined in the western sense – is considered more or less separate from wátánátham.

Sanùk

The Thai word *sanùk* means 'fun'. In Thailand anything worth doing – even work – should have an element of sanùk, otherwise it becomes drudgery. This doesn't mean Thais don't want to work or strive, they just tend to approach tasks with a sense of playfulness. Nothing condemns an activity more than the description *mâi sanùk*, 'not fun'. Sit down beside a rice field and watch workers planting, transplanting or harvesting rice; it's obviously back-breaking work, but participants generally inject the activity with lots of sanùk – flirtation, singing, trading insults and cracking jokes. The same goes in an office or a bank, or other white-collar work – at least when the office is predominantly Thai (businesses run by non-Thais don't necessarily exhibit sanùk). The famous Thai smile comes partially out of this desire to make sanùk.

Face

Thais believe strongly in the concept of 'saving face', that is, avoiding confrontation and trying not to embarrass themselves or other people (except when it's sanùk to do so!). The ideal face-saver doesn't bring up negative topics in everyday conversation, and when they notice stress in another's life, they usually won't say anything unless that person complains or asks for help. Laughing at minor accidents – like when someone trips

and falls – may seem callous to outsiders but it's really just an attempt to save face on behalf of the person suffering the mishap. This is another source of the Thai smile – it's the best possible face to put on in almost any situation.

Phûu Yài-Phûu Náwy & Phîi-Náwng

All relationships in traditional Thai society – and virtually all relationships in the modern milieu as well – are governed by connections between *phûu yài* (literally, 'big person') and *phûu náwy* ('little person'). Phûu náwy are supposed to defer to phûu yài following simple lines of social rank defined by age, wealth, status, and personal and political power. Examples of 'automatic' phûu yài status include adults (vs children), bosses (vs employees), elder classmates (vs younger classmates), elder siblings (vs younger siblings), teachers (vs pupils), military (vs civilian), Thai (vs non-Thai) and so on.

While this tendency toward social ranking is to some degree shared by many societies around the world, the Thai twist lies in the set of mutual obligations linking phûu yài to phûu náwy. Sociologists have referred to this phenomenon as the 'patron-client relationship'. Phûu náwy are supposed to show a degree of obedience and respect (together these concepts are covered by the term *'kreng jai'*) toward phûu yài, but in return phûu yài are obligated to care for or 'sponsor' the phûu náwy they have frequent contact with. In such relationships phûu náwy can, for example, ask phûu yài for favours involving money or job opportunities. Phûu yài reaffirm their rank by granting such requests when possible; to refuse would be to risk loss of face and status.

Age is a large determinant where other factors are absent or weak. In such cases the terms *phîi* (elder sibling) and *náwng* (younger sibling) apply more than phûu yài/phûu náwy, although the intertwined obligations remain the same. Even people unrelated by blood quickly establish who's phîi and who's náwng; this is why one of the first questions Thais ask new acquaintances is 'How old are you?'.

When dining, touring or entertaining, the phûu yài always picks up the tab; if a group is involved, the person with most social rank pays the check for everyone, even if it empties his or her wallet. For a phûu náwy to try and pay would risk loss of face. Money plays a large role in defining phûu yài status in most situations. A person who turned out to be successful in his or her post-school career would never think of allowing an ex-classmate of lesser success – even if they were once on an equal social footing – to pay the bill. Likewise a young, successful executive will pay an older person's way in spite of the age difference.

The implication is that whatever wealth you come into is to be shared – at least partially – with those who have been less fortunate. This doesn't apply to strangers – the average Thai isn't big on charity but always comes into play with friends and relatives.

Foreigners often feel offended when they encounter such phenomena as two tiered pricing for hotels or sightseeing attractions – one price for Thais, a higher price for foreigners. But this is simply just another expression of the traditional patron-client relationship. On the one hand foreigners who can afford to travel to Thailand from abroad are seen to have more wealth than Thai citizens (on average this is true), hence they're expected to help subsidise Thai enjoyment of these commodities; and at the same time, paradoxically, the Thais feel they are due certain special privileges as homelanders – what might be termed the 'home-town discount'. Another example: in a post office line, Thais get served first as part of their national privilege.

Comportment

Personal power (baará-mii, sometimes mistranslated as 'charisma') also has a bearing on one's social status, and can be gained by cleaving as close as possible to the ideal 'Thai' behaviour. 'Thai-ness' is first and foremost defined, as might be expected, by the ability to speak Thai. It doesn't matter which dialect, although southern Thai – with its Malay/Yawi influences – is slightly more

suspect, mainly due to the region's association with the 'foreign' religion of Islam.

Other hallmarks of the Thai ideal – heavily influenced by Thai Buddhism – include discretion toward the opposite sex, modest dress, a neat and clean appearance, and modes of expression and comportment that value the quiet, subtle and indirect rather than the loud, obvious and direct.

The degree to which Thais conform to these ideals matches the degree of respect they receive from most of their associates. Although high rank – age-related, civil, military or clerical – will exempt certain individuals from chastisement by their social 'inferiors', it doesn't exempt them from the way they are perceived by other Thais. This goes for foreigners as well, even though most first-time visitors can hardly be expected to speak idiomatic Thai. But if you do learn some Thai, and you make an effort to respect Thai social ideals, you'll come closer to enjoying some of the perks awarded for Thai-ness.

Dos & Don'ts

Monarchy and religion are the two sacred cows in Thailand. Thais are tolerant of most kinds of behaviour as long as it doesn't insult one of these.

King & Country The monarchy is held in considerable respect in Thailand and visitors should be respectful too – avoid making disparaging remarks about the king, queen or anyone in the royal family. One of Thailand's leading intellectuals, Sulak Sivaraksa, was arrested in the early 1980s for lese-majesty because of a passing reference to the king's fondness for yachting (Sulak referred to His Majesty as 'the skipper') and again in 1991 when he referred to the royal family as 'ordinary people'. Although on the first occasion he received a royal pardon, in 1991 Sulak had to flee the country to avoid prosecution again for alleged remarks made at Thammasat University about the ruling military junta, with reference to the king (Sulak has since returned under a suspended sentence). The penalty for lese-majesty is seven years imprisonment.

While it's OK to criticise the Thai government and even Thai culture openly, it's considered a grave insult to Thai nationhood, as well as to the monarchy, not to stand when you hear the national or royal anthems. Radio and TV stations in Thailand broadcast the national anthem daily at 8 am and 6 pm. In towns and villages (and even in some Bangkok neighbourhoods) the anthem is broadcast over public loudspeakers in the streets. The Thais stop whatever they're doing to stand during the anthem (except in Bangkok where nobody can hear above the din of the street) and visitors are expected to do likewise. The royal anthem is played just before films are shown in cinemas; again, the audience always stands until it's over.

Religion Correct behaviour in temples entails several considerations, the most important of which is to dress neatly and take your shoes off when you enter any building that contains a Buddha image. Buddha images are sacred, so don't pose in front of them for pictures and definitely do not clamber on them.

Shorts or sleeveless shirts are considered improper for both men and women when visiting temples. Locals wearing either would be turned away by monastic authorities, but except for the most sacred temples in the country (eg Wat Phra Kaew, Wat Phra That Doi Suthep), Thais are often too polite to refuse entry to improperly clad foreigners. Some wats hire trousers or long sarongs so that shorts-wearing tourists can enter the compound.

Monks are not supposed to touch or be touched by women. If a woman wants to hand something to a monk, the object should be placed within reach of the monk, not handed directly to him.

When sitting in a religious edifice, keep your feet pointed away from any Buddha images. The usual way to do this is to sit in the 'mermaid' pose in which your legs are folded to the side, with the feet pointing backwards.

Social Gestures & Attitudes Traditionally, Thais greet each other not with a handshake but with a prayer-like palms-together gesture known as a *wâi*. If someone wâis you, you should wâi back (unless wâi-ed by a child). Most urban Thais are familiar with the western-style handshake and will offer the same to a foreigner, although a wâi is always appreciated.

Thais are often addressed by their first name with the honorific *khun* or other title preceding it. Other formal terms of address include *Nai* (Mr) and *Naang* (Miss or Mrs). Friends often use nicknames or kinship terms like *phîi* (elder sibling), *náwng* (younger sibling), *mâe* (mother) or *lung* (uncle), depending on the age differential.

A smile and *sawàt-dii khráp/khâ* (the all-purpose Thai greeting) goes a long way towards calming the trepidation locals may initially feel upon seeing a foreigner, whether in the city or the countryside.

When encounters take a turn for the worse, don't get angry – losing one's temper means loss of face for everyone present. Remember that this is Asia, where keeping your cool is paramount. Talking loudly is seen as rude by cultured Thais, whatever the situation. Remember, the pushy foreigner often gets served last.

The feet are the lowest part of the body (spiritually as well as physically) so don't point them at people or at things. Even when sitting crossed-legged, for example, it's good to make sure you're not inadvertently aiming your lowliest body part at your neighbour.

The head is regarded as the highest part of the body, so don't touch Thais there. Don't sit on pillows meant for sleeping, as this represents a variant of the taboo against head-touching.

When handing things to people you should use both hands or your right hand only, never the left hand (reserved for toilet ablutions). Books and other written material are given a special status over other secular objects. Hence you shouldn't slide books or documents across a table or counter-top and never put them on the floor – use a chair if table space isn't available.

Dress & Nudity Shorts (except knee-length walking shorts), sleeveless shirts, tank tops (singlets) and other beach-style attire are not considered appropriate dress in Thailand for anything other than sport. Such dress is especially counterproductive if worn to government offices (eg when applying for a visa extension). Having an attitude of 'This is how I dress at home and no-one is going to stop me' gains nothing but contempt or disrespect from the Thais.

Sandals or slip-on shoes are OK for all but the most formal occasions. Short-sleeved shirts and blouses with capped sleeves are quite acceptable. Regardless of what the Thais may (or may not) have been accustomed to centuries ago, they are quite offended by public nudity today. Bathing nude at beaches in Thailand is illegal. If you are at a truly deserted beach and are sure no Thais may come along, there's nothing stopping you; however, at most beaches travellers should dress suitably. Topless bathing for women is frowned upon. Likewise, except when on the beach, men should keep a shirt on; entering a shop or (particularly) a restaurant half naked looks barbaric to the Thais. Many Thais say nudity on the beach is what bothers them most about foreign travellers. Thais often take nudity as a sign of disrespect for the locals, rather than as a libertarian symbol or modern custom and are extremely modest (despite racy billboards in Bangkok).

RELIGION
Buddhism

Approximately 95% of the Thai citizenry are Theravada Buddhists. The Theravada school (literally, 'teaching of the elders') is an earlier and, according to its followers, less corrupted form of Buddhism than the Mahayana schools found in East Asia or in the Himalayan lands. Also called the 'southern' school, it took a southern route from India, its place of origin, through South-East Asia (Myanmar, Thailand, Laos and Cambodia), while the 'northern' school proceeded north into Nepal, Tibet, China, Korea, Mongolia, Vietnam and Japan. Because the Theravada school tried to preserve or limit the Buddhist doctrines to only those canons codified in the early Buddhist era, the Mahayana school gave Theravada Buddhism the name Hina-yana, or the 'lesser vehicle'. The Mahayana school was the 'great vehicle', because it built upon the earlier teachings, 'expanding' the doctrine in such a way as to respond more to the needs of lay people, or so it is claimed.

Theravada or Hinayana doctrine stresses three principal aspects of existence: *dukkha* (stress, unsatisfactoriness, 'dis-ease'), *anicca* (impermanence, transience of all things) and *anatta* (non-substantiality or non-essentiality of reality – no permanent 'soul'). The truth of anicca reveals that no experience, no state of mind, no physical object lasts; trying to hold onto experience, states of mind and objects that are constantly changing creates dukkha; anatta is the understanding that we cannot point to any part of the changing world and say 'This is me' or 'This is God' or 'This is the soul'. These three concepts, when 'discovered' by Siddhartha Gautama in the 6th century BC, were in direct contrast to the Hindu belief in an eternal, blissful self (para-matman), hence Buddhism was originally a 'heresy' against India's Brahmanic religion.

Gautama, an Indian prince-turned-ascetic, subjected himself to many years of severe austerity before he realised that yoga and self-mortification were not the way to reach the end of suffering. He then turned his attention to investigating the arising and passing away of the mind and body in the present moment. Seeing that even the most blissful and refined states of mind were subject to decay, he abandoned all desire for what he now saw as unreliable and unsatisfying. He then became known as Buddha, 'the enlightened' or 'the awakened'. Gautama Buddha spoke of four noble truths which had the power to liberate any human being who could realise them. These four noble truths are:

1. The truth of dukkha: 'All forms of existence are subject to dukkha (dis-ease, unsatisfactoriness, stress, imperfection)'
2. The truth of the cause of dukkha: 'Dukkha is caused by tanha (desire)'
3. The truth of the cessation of dukkha: 'Eliminate the cause of dukkha (ie desire) and dukkha will cease to arise'
4. The truth of the path: 'The Eightfold Path is the way to eliminate desire/extinguish dukkha'

The Eightfold Path (Atthangika-Magga), which if followed will put an end to dukkha, consists of:

1. Right understanding
'2. Right mindedness (right thought)
3. Right speech
4. Right bodily conduct
5. Right livelihood
6. Right effort
7. Right attentiveness
8. Right concentration

These eight limbs belong to three different 'pillars' of practice: wisdom or *pañña* (1 and 2), morality or *sila* (3 to 5) and concentration or *samadhi* (6 to 8). The path is also called the Middle Way, since ideally it avoids both extreme austerity and extreme sensuality. Some Buddhists believe it is to be taken in successive stages, while others say the pillars and/or limbs are interdependent. Another key point is that the word 'right' can also be translated as 'complete' or 'full'.

The ultimate end of Theravada Buddhism is *nibbana* (Sanskrit: *nirvana)*, which literally means the 'blowing out' or extinction of all desire and thus of all suffering (dukkha). Effectively, it is also an end to the cycle of rebirths (both moment to moment and life to life) that is existence. In reality, most Thai Buddhists aim for rebirth in a 'better' existence rather than the supramundane goal of nibbana, which is highly misunderstood by Asians as well as westerners.

Many Thais express the feeling that they are somehow unworthy of nibbana. By feeding monks, giving donations to temples and performing regular worship at the local wat they hope to improve their lot, acquiring enough merit (Pali: *puñña*; Thai: *bun)* to prevent or at least lessen the number of rebirths. The making of merit *(tham bun)* is an important social and religious activity in Thailand. The concept of reincarnation is almost universally accepted, even by non-Buddhists, and the Buddhist theory of karma is well expressed in the Thai proverb *tham dii, dâi dii; tham chûa, dâi chûa* – 'do good and receive good; do evil and receive evil'.

Thai Buddhism has no particular 'sabbath' or day of the week to make temple visits. Nor is there anything corresponding to a liturgy or mass over which a priest presides. Instead Thai Buddhists visit the wat whenever they feel like it, most often on *wan phrá* (literally, 'excellent days'), which occur every full and new moon, ie every 15 days. On such a visit lotus buds, incense and candles are offered at various altars, and bone reliquaries are placed around the wat compound. Other activities include offering food to the temple Sangha (monks, nuns and lay residents – monks always eat first), meditating (individually or in groups), listening to monks chanting *suttas* or Buddhist discourse, and attending a *thêt* or dhamma talk by the abbot or other respected teacher. Visitors may also seek counsel from monks or nuns regarding new or ongoing life problems.

Monks & Nuns Socially, every Thai male is expected to become a monk for a short period, optimally between the time he finishes school and the time he starts a career or marries. Men or boys under 20 may enter the Sangha as novices – this is not unusual since a family earns great merit when one of its sons takes robe and bowl. Traditionally, three months is spent in the wat during the Buddhist lent *(phansãa)*, which begins in July and coincides with the rainy season. However, nowadays men may spend as little as a week or 15 days to accrue merit as a monk. There are about 32,000 monasteries in Thailand and 200,000 monks; many of them ordain for life. Of these a large percentage become scholars and teachers, while some specialise in healing and/or folk magic.

At one time the Theravada Buddhist world had a separate monastic lineage for females, who called themselves *bhikkhuni* and observed more vows than monks did – 311 precepts as opposed to the 227 followed by monks. Started in Sri Lanka around two centuries after the Buddha's lifetime by the daughter of King Asoka (a Buddhist king in India), the bhikkhuni tradition in Sri Lanka eventually died out and was unfortunately never restored.

In Thailand, the modern equivalent is the *mâe chii* (Thai for 'nun'; literally, 'mother priest') – women who live the monastic life as *atthasila* or 'Eight-Precept' nuns. Thai nuns shave their heads, wear white robes and take vows in an ordination procedure similar to that undergone by monks. Generally speaking, nunhood in Thailand isn't considered as 'prestigious' as monkhood. The average Thai Buddhist makes a great show of offering new robes and household items to the monks at their local wat but pay much less attention to the nuns. This is mainly due to the fact that nuns generally don't perform ceremonies on behalf of laypeople, so there is less incentive to make offerings to them. Furthermore, many Thais equate the number of precepts observed with the total Buddhist merit achieved, hence nunhood is seen as less 'meritorious' than monkhood since mâe chiis keep only eight precepts.

This difference in prestige represents social Buddhism, however, and is not how those with a serious interest regard the mâe chii. Nuns engage in the same fundamental eremitic activities – meditation and dhamma study – as monks do, activities which are the core of monastic life. The reality is that wats which draw sizeable contingents of mâe chiis are highly respected, since women don't choose temples for reasons of clerical status. When more than a few nuns reside at one temple, it's usually a sign that the teachings there are particularly strong.

An increasing number of foreigners are coming to Thailand to ordain as Buddhist monks or nuns, especially to study with the famed meditation masters of the forest wats in southern and north-eastern Thailand.

Further Information If you wish to find out more about Buddhism you can contact the World Fellowship of Buddhists (☎ (2) 251-1188), 33 Sukhumvit Rd (between sois 1 and 3), Bangkok. Senior farang monks hold English-language dhamma/meditation classes there on the first Sunday of each month from 2 to 6 pm; all are welcome.

A Buddhist bookshop across the street from the north entrance to Wat Bovornives (Bowonniwet) in Bangkok sells a variety of English-language books on Buddhism. Asia Books and DK Book House also stock Buddhist literature.

For more information on meditation study in southern Thailand see the sections on Chaiya's Wat Suan Mokkhaphalaram and also Wat Khao Tham on Ko Pha-Ngan in the South-Western Gulf Coast chapter.

Recommended books about Buddhism include:

Buddhism Explained – by Phra Khantipalo
Buddhism, Imperialism, and War – by Trevor Ling
Buddhism in the Modern World – edited by Heinrich Dumoulin
Buddhism in Transition – by Donald K Swearer
Buddhist Dictionary – by Mahathera Nyanatiloka
The Buddhist World of Southeast Asia – by Donald K Swearer
The Central Conception of Buddhism – by Th Stcherbatsky
Heartwood of the Bodhi Tree – by Buddhasa Bhikku
In This Very Life: The Liberation Teachings of the Buddha – by Sayadaw U Pandita
Living Buddhist Masters – by Jack Kornfield
The Mind and the Way – by Ajaan Sumedho
A Still Forest Pool: the Teaching of Ajaan Chaa at Wat Paa Pong – compiled by Jack Kornfield & Paul Breiter
What the Buddha Never Taught – by Timothy Ward
What the Buddha Taught – by Walpola Rahula
World Conqueror and World Renouncer – by Stanley Tambiah

Other Religions
A small percentage of Thais and most of the Malays in the south, amounting to about 4% of the population, are followers of Islam. Half a percent of the population – primarily missionised hill tribes and Vietnamese immigrants – profess Christianity, while the remaining half percent are Confucianists, Taoists, Mahayana Buddhists and Hindus. Mosques (in the south) and Chinese temples are both common enough that you will probably come across some in your travels in Thailand. Before entering *any* temple, sanctuary or mosque you must remove your shoes, and in a mosque your head must be covered.

LANGUAGE

Learning some Thai is indispensable for travelling in the kingdom; naturally, the more language you pick up, the closer you get to Thailand's culture and people. Foreigners who speak Thai are so rare in Thailand that it doesn't take much to impress most Thais with a few words in their own language.

Your first attempts to speak the language will probably meet with mixed success, but keep trying. When learning new words or phrases, listen closely to the way the Thais themselves use the various tones – you'll catch on quickly. Don't let laughter at your linguistic forays discourage you; this amusement is an expression of their appreciation.

I would particularly urge travellers, young and old, to make the effort to meet Thai college and university students. Thai students are, by and large, eager to meet visitors from other countries. They will often know some English, so communication is not as difficult as it may be with shop owners, civil servants etc, plus they are generally willing to teach you useful Thai words and phrases.

For a complete selection of phrases, basic vocabulary and grammar for travel in Thailand, see the fully updated and expanded 3rd edition of Lonely Planet's *Thai phrasebook*.

Many people have reported modest success with *Robertson's Practical English-Thai Dictionary* (Charles E Tuttle Co, Tokyo), which has a phonetic guide to pronunciation with tones and is compact in size. It may be difficult to find, so write to the publisher at 2-6 Suido 1-chome, Bunkyo-ku, Tokyo, Japan.

More serious learners of the Thai language should get Mary Haas' *Thai-English Student's Dictionary* (Stanford University Press, Stanford, California) and George McFarland's *Thai-English Dictionary* (also Stanford University Press) – the cream of the crop. Both of these require that you know the Thai script. The US State Department's *Thai Reference Grammar* by RB Noss (Foreign Service Institute, Washington, DC, 1964) is good for an in-depth look at Thai syntax.

Other learning texts worth seeking out include:

AUA Language Center Thai Course: Reading & Writing (two volumes) – AUA Language Center (Bangkok), 1979

AUA Language Center Thai Course (three volumes) – AUA Language Center (Bangkok), 1969

Foundations of Thai (two volumes) – by EM Anthony, University of Michigan Press, 1973

A Programmed Course in Reading Thai Syllables – by EM Anthony, University of Hawaii, 1979

Teaching Grammar of Thai – by William Kuo, University of California at Berkeley, 1982

Thai Basic Reader – by Gething & Bilmes, University of Hawaii, 1977

Thai Cultural Reader (two volumes) – by RB Jones, Cornell University, 1969

Thai Reader – by Mary Haas, American Council of Learned Societies, Program in Oriental Languages, 1954

The Thai System of Writing – by Mary Haas, American Council of Learned Societies, Program in Oriental Languages, 1954

A Workbook for Writing Thai – by William Kuo, University of California at Berkeley, 1979

Dialects

Thailand's official language is Thai as spoken and written in central Thailand. This dialect has successfully become the lingua franca of all Thai and non-Thai ethnic groups in the kingdom. Of course, native Thai is spoken with differing tonal accents and with slightly differing vocabularies as you move from one part of the country to the next, especially in a north to south direction. But it is the Central Thai dialect that is most widely understood.

All Thai dialects are members of the Thai half of the Thai-Kadai family of languages and are closely related to languages spoken in Laos (Lao, Northern Thai, Thai Lü), northern Myanmar (Shan, Northern Thai), north-western Vietnam (Nung, Tho), Assam (Ahom) and pockets of south China (Zhuang, Thai Lü).

Modern Thai linguists recognise four basic dialects within Thailand: Central Thai (spoken as a first dialect through central Thailand and throughout the country as a second dialect); Northern Thai (spoken from Tak Province north to the Myanmar border); North-Eastern Thai (north-eastern provinces towards the Lao and Cambodian borders);

and Southern Thai (from Chumphon Province south to the Malaysian border). Each of these can be further divided into subdialects; North-Eastern Thai, for example, has nine regional variations easily distinguished by those who know Thai well. There are also a number of Thai minority dialects such as those spoken by the Phu Thai, Thai Dam, Thai Daeng, Phu Noi, Phuan and other tribal Thai groups, most of whom reside in the north and north-east.

Vocabulary Differences

Like most languages, Thai makes distinctions between 'vulgar' and 'polite' vocabulary, so that *thaan*, for example, is a more polite everyday word for 'eat' than *kin*, and *sǔi-sà* for 'head' is more polite than *hǔa*. When given a choice, foreigners are better off learning and using the polite terms since these are less likely to lead to unconscious offence.

A special set of words, collectively called *kham râatchaasàp* (royal vocabulary), is set aside for use with Thai royalty within the semantic fields of kinship, body parts, physical and mental actions, clothing and housing. For example, in everyday language Thais use the word *kin* or *thaan* for 'eat', while with reference to the royal family they say *ráppràthaan*. For the most part these terms are used only when speaking to or referring to the king, queen and their children, hence as a foreigner you will have little need to learn them.

Script

The Thai script, a fairly recent development in comparison with the spoken language, consists of 44 consonants (but only 21 separate sounds) and 48 vowel and diphthong possibilities (32 separate signs). Experts disagree as to the exact origins of the script, but it was apparently developed around 800 years ago using Mon and possibly Khmer models, both of which were in turn inspired by south Indian scripts. Like these languages, written Thai proceeds from left to right, though vowel signs may be written before, above, below, 'around' (before, above *and* after), *or* after consonants, depending on the sign.

Though learning the alphabet is not difficult, the writing system itself is fairly complex, so unless you are planning a lengthy stay in Thailand it should perhaps be foregone in favour of learning to actually speak the language.

Tones & Pronunciation

In Thai the meaning of a single syllable may be altered by means of five different tones (in standard Central Thai): level or mid tone, low tone, falling tone, high tone and rising tone. Consequently, the syllable *mai*, for example, can mean, depending on the tone, 'new', 'burn', 'wood', 'not?' or 'not', eg *Mái mài mâi mâi mǎi* ('New wood doesn't burn, does it?'). This makes it rather tricky to learn at first, especially for those of us who come from non-tonal language traditions. Even when we 'know' what the correct tone in Thai should be, our tendency to denote emotion, verbal stress, the interrogative etc through tone modulation often interferes with speaking the correct tone. Therefore the first rule in learning to speak Thai is to divorce emotions from your speech, at least until you have learned the Thai way to express them without changing essential tone value.

The following is a brief attempt to explain the tones. The only way to really understand the differences is by listening to a native or fluent non-native speaker. The range of all five tones is relative to each speaker's vocal range so there is no fixed 'pitch' intrinsic to the language.

1. The level or mid tone is pronounced 'flat', at the relative middle of the speaker's vocal range. Eg: *dii* means good. (No tone mark used.)
2. The low tone is 'flat' like the mid tone, but pronounced at the relative *bottom* of one's vocal range. It is low, level and with no inflection. Eg: *bàat* means baht (the Thai currency).
3. The falling tone is pronounced as if you were emphasising a word, or calling someone's name from afar. Eg: *mâi* means 'no' or 'not'.
4. The high tone is usually the most difficult for westerners. It is pronounced near the relative top of the vocal range, as level as possible. Eg: *níi* means 'this'.
5. The rising tone sounds like the inflection generally given by English speakers to a question – 'Yes?'. Eg: *sǎam* means 'three'.

If the tones were to be represented on a visual curve they might look like this:

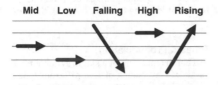

Words in Thai that appear to have more than one syllable are usually compounds made up of two or more word units, each with its own tone. They may be words taken directly from Sanskrit, Pali or English, in which case each syllable must still have its own tone. Sometimes the tone of the first syllable is not as important as that of the last, so for these I am omitting the tone mark.

Here is a guide to the phonetic system which has been used in the Language and special Cuisine of Coastal Thailand sections, as well as throughout the book when transcribing directly from Thai. It is based on the Royal Thai General System of transcription (RTGS), except that it distinguishes between: vowels of short and long duration (eg 'i' and 'ii'; 'a' and 'aa'; 'e' and 'eh'; 'o' and 'oh'); between 'o' and 'aw' (both would be 'o' in the RTGS); between 'u' and 'eu' (both 'u' in the RTGS); and between 'ch' and 'j' (both 'ch' in the RTGS).

Consonants

th	as the 't' in 'tea'
ph	as the 'p' in 'put' (never as the 'ph' in 'phone')
kh	as the 'k' in 'kite'
k	as the 'k' in 'skin'; similar to 'g' in 'good', but unaspirated (no accompanying puff of air) and unvoiced
t	as the 't' in 'forty', unaspirated; similar to 'd' but unvoiced
p	as the 'p' in 'stopper', unvoiced and unaspirated (not like the 'p' in 'put')
ng	as the 'ng' in 'sing'; used as an initial consonant in Thai (practise by saying 'sing' without the 'si')
r	similar to the 'r' in 'run' but flapped (tongue touches palate); in everyday speech often pronounced like 'l'

All the remaining consonants correspond closely to their English counterparts.

Vowels

i	as the 'i' in 'it'
ii	as the 'ee' in 'feet'
ai	as the 'i' in 'pipe'
aa	as the 'a' in 'father'
a	half as long as *aa*
ae	as the 'a' in 'bat' or 'tab' (for British English speakers, as in 'there')
e	as the 'e' in 'hen'
eh	as the 'a' in 'hate'
oe	as the 'u' in 'hut' but more closed
u	as the 'u' in 'flute'
uu	as the 'oo' in 'food', longer than *u*
eu	as the 'eu' in French 'deux', or the 'i' in 'sir'
ao	as the 'ow' in 'now'
aw	as the 'aw' in 'jaw' or 'prawn'
o	as the 'o' in 'bone'
oh	as the 'o' in 'toe'
eua	diphthong, or combination, of *eu* and *a*
ia	as 'ee-ya', or as the 'ie' in French *rien*
ua	as the 'ou' in 'tour'
uay	as the 'ewy' in 'Dewey'
iu	as the 'ew' in 'yew'
iaw	as the 'io' in 'Rio' or Italian *mio* or *dio*

Here are a few extra hints to help you with the alphabetic tangle.

- Remember that 'ph' is not meant to be pronounced like the 'ph' in phone but like the 'p' in 'pound' (the 'h' is added to distinguish this consonant sound from the Thai 'p' which is closer to the English 'b'). This can be seen written as 'p', 'ph', and even 'bh'.

- There is no 'v' sound in Thai; Sukhumvit is pronounced Sukhumwit and Vieng is really Wieng.

- 'L' or 'r' at the end of a word is always pronounced like an 'n'; hence, Satul is pronounced Satun, Wihar is really Wihan. The exception to this is when 'er' or 'ur' are used to indicate the sound 'oe', as in 'ampher' *(amphoe)*. In the same way 'or' is sometimes used for the sound 'aw' as in 'Porn' *(phawn)*.

- 'L' and 'r' are often used interchangeably in speech and this shows up in some transliterations. For example, *naliga* (clock) may appear as 'nariga' and *râat nâa* (a type of noodle dish) might be rendered 'laat naa' or 'lat na'.
- 'U' is often used to represent the short 'a' sound, as in *tam* or *nam*, which may appear as 'tum' and 'num'. It is also used to represent the 'eu' sound, as when *beung* (swamp) is spelt 'bung'.
- Phonetically all Thai words end in a vowel (a, e, i, o, u), semi-vowel (y, w), nasal (m, n or ng) or one of three stops: p, t and k. That's it. Words transcribed with 'ch', 'j', 's' or 'd' endings – like Panich, Raj, Chuanpis and Had – should be pronounced as if they end in 't', as in Panit, Rat, Chuanpit and Hat. Likewise 'g' becomes 'k' (Ralug is actually Raluk) and 'b' becomes 'p' (Thab becomes Thap).
- Finally, the 'r' in 'sri' is *always* silent, so that word should be pronounced 'sii' (extended 'i' sound, too).

Transliteration

Writing Thai in roman script is a perennial problem – no truly satisfactory system has yet been devised to assure both consistency and readability. The Thai government uses the Royal Thai General System of transcription for official government documents in English and for most highway signs. However, local variations crop up on hotel signs, city street signs, menus and so on in such a way that visitors often become confused. Add to this the fact that even the government system has its flaws. For example, 'o' is used for two very different sounds ('o' and the 'aw' in the Vowels section above), as is 'u' ('u' and 'eu' above). Likewise for 'ch', which is used to represent two different consonant sounds ('ch' and 'j'). The government transcription system also does not distinguish between short and long vowel sounds, which affect the tonal value of every word.

To top it off, many Thai words (especially people and place names) have Sanskrit and Pali spellings but the actual pronunciation bears little relation to that spelling if romanised strictly according to the original Sanskrit/Pali. Thus Nakhon Si Thammarat, if transliterated literally, becomes 'Nagara Sri Dhammaraja'. If you tried to pronounce

it using this Pali transcription, very few Thais would be able to understand you.

Generally, names in this book follow the most common practice or, in the case of hotels for example, simply copy their roman script name, no matter what devious process was used in its transliteration! When this transliteration is especially distant from actual pronunciation, I've included the pronunciation (following the system outlined in this section) in parentheses after the transliteration. Where no roman model was available, names were transliterated phonetically directly from Thai. Of course, this will only be helpful to readers who bother to acquaint themselves with the language – I'm constantly amazed at how many people manage to stay for great lengths of time in Thailand without learning a word of Thai.

Problems often arise when a name is transliterated differently, even at the same place. 'Thawi', for example, can be Tavi, Thawee, Thavi, Tavee or various other versions. Outside the International Phonetic Alphabet, there is no 'proper' way to transliterate Thai – only wrong ways. The Thais themselves are incredibly inconsistent in this matter, often using English letters that have no equivalent sound in Thai: Faisal for Phaisan, Bhumibol for Phumiphon, Vanich for Wanit, Vibhavadi for Wiphawadi. Sometimes they even mix literal Sanskrit transcription with Thai pronunciation, as in King Bhumibol (which is pronounced Phumiphon and if transliterated according to the Sanskrit would be Bhumibala).

Here are a few words that are commonly spelt in a way that encourages mispronunciation among native English speakers:

Common Spelling	Pronunciation	Meaning
bung	beung	pond or swamp
ko or koh	kàw	island
muang	meuang	city
nakhon or nakorn	nákhawn	large city
raja	usually râatch if at the beginning of a word, râat at the end of a word	royal

Greetings & Civilities

When being polite, the speaker ends his or her sentence with *khráp* (for men) or *khâ* (for women). It is the gender of the *speaker* that is being expressed here; it is also the common way to answer 'yes' to a question or show agreement.

Greetings/Hello.
  sawàt-dii (khráp/khâ) สวัสดี (ครับ/ค่ะ)
How are you?
  pen yangai? เป็นยังไง?
I'm fine.
  sabàay dii สบายดี
Thank you.
  khàwp khun ขอบคุณ
Excuse me.
  khãw thôht ขอโทษ

Small Talk

you
  khun (for peers) คุณ
  thâan (for elders, people in authority) ท่าน
  phõm (for men) ผม (ผู้ชาย)
  dii chãn (for women) ดีฉัน (ผู้หญิง)
What is your name?
  khun chêu arai? คุณชื่ออะไร?
My name is ...
  phõm chêu ... (men) ผมชื่อ...
  dii chãn chêu ... (women) ดีฉันชื่อ...
Do you have ...?
  mii ... mãi/... mii mãi? มี...ไหม?
  (..มีไหม?)
No
  mâi châi ไม่ใช่
No?
  mãi/châi mãi? ไหมฝ่า/ใช่ไหม?

go
  pai ไป
come
  maa มา
(I) like ...
  châwp ... ชอบ...

(I) do not like ...
  mâi châwp ... ไม่ชอบ...
(I) would like ... (+ verb)
  yàak jà ... อยากจะ...
(I) would like ... (+ noun)
  yàak dâi ... อยากได้...
when
  mêu-arai เมื่อไร
It doesn't matter.
  mâi pen rai ไม่เป็นไร
What is this?
  níi arai? นี่อะไร?

Language Difficulties

I understand.
  khâo jai เข้าใจ
I don't understand.
  mâi khâo jai ไม่เข้าใจ
Do you understand?
  khâo jai mãi? เข้าใจไหม?
a little
  nít nàwy นิดหน่อย
What do you call this in Thai?
  níi phaasãa thai rîak wâa arai? นี่ภาษาไทยเรียกว่าอะไร?

Getting Around

I would like to go ...
  yàak jà pai ... อยากจะไป...
Where is (the) ...?
  ... yùu thîi nãi? ...อยู่ที่ไหน?
airport
  sanãam bin สนามบิน
bus station
  sathãanii rót meh สถานีรถเมล์
bus stop
  thîi jàwt rót pràjam ที่จอดรถประจำ
railway station
  sathãanii rót fai สถานีรถไฟ
taxi stand
  thîi jàwt rót tháek-sîi ที่จอดรถแท็กซี่
I would like a ticket.
  yàak dâi tũa อยากได้ตั๋ว
What time will the train leave?
  kìi mohng rót jà àwk? กี่โมงรถจะออก?

motorcycle
rót maw-toe-sai รถมอเตอร์ไซ
train
rót fai รถไฟ
bus
rót meh/rót bát รถเมล์/รถบัส
car
rót yon รถยนต์
straight ahead
trong pai ตรงไป
left
sáai ซ้าย
right
khwāa ขวา
far/not far
klai/mâi klai ใกล/ไม่ใกล

Accommodation
hotel
rohng raem โรงแรม
guesthouse
bâan phák (kèt háo) บ้านพัก
(เกสต์ฮาส์)

Do you have a room?
mii hâwng māi? มีห้องไหม?
How much per night?
kheun-lá thâo rai? คืนละเท่าไร?
bathroom
hâwng náam ห้องน้ำ
toilet
hâwng sûam ห้องส้วม
room
hâwng ห้อง
hot
ráwn ร้อน
cold
não หนาว
bath/shower
àap náam อาบน้ำ
towel
phâa chét tua ผ้าเช็ดตัว

Around Town
Can (I/we) change money
here?
lâek ngoen thîi nîi แลกเงินที่นี้ได้ไห
dâi māi? ม?

What time does it open/
close?
raan poed muea ร้านเปิดเมื่อไร/ปิดเม
rai/pit muea rai? ื่อไร
bank
thanaakhaan ธนาคาร
beach
hàat หาด
hospital
rohng phayaabaan โรงพยาบาล
market
talàat ตลาด
museum
phíphíth phan พิพิธภัณฑ์
post office
praisanii ไปรษณีย์
restaurant
ráan aahãan ร้านอาหาร
tourist office
sãmnák-ngaan สำนักงานท่อง
thâwng thîaw เที่ยว

Shopping
How much?
thâo raí? เท่าไร?
How much is this?
níi thâo rai/kìi bàat? นี่เท่าไร (กี่บาท)
too expensive
phaeng pai แพงไป
cheap, inexpensive
thùuk ถูก

Health & Emergencies
(I) need a doctor.
tâwng-kaan māw ต้องการหมอ
chemist/pharmacy
ráan khãai yaa ร้านขายยา
Help!
chûay dûay ช่วยด้วย
Stop!
yàt หยุด
Go away!
bai sí ไปซิ
I'm lost.
chãn lõng thaang ฉันหลงทาง

Time
What's the time?
kìi mohng láew? กี่โมงแล้ว?

today
  wan níi วันนี้
tomorrow
  phrûng níi พรุ่งนี้
yesterday
  mêua waan เมื่อวาน

Days of the Week
Sunday
  wan aathít วันอาทิตย์
Monday
  wan jan วันจันทร์
Tuesday
  wan angkhaan วันอังคาร
Wednesday
  wan phút วันพุธ
Thursday
  wan phréuhàt วันพฤหัส
Friday
  wan sùk วันศุกร์
Saturday
  wan sáo วันเสาร์

Numbers

0	*sǔun*	ศูนย์
1	*nèung*	หนึ่ง
2	*sǎwng*	สอง
3	*sǎam*	สาม
4	*sìi*	สี่
5	*hâa*	ห้า

6	*hòk*	หก
7	*jèt*	เจ็ด
8	*pàet*	แปด
9	*kâo*	เก้า
10	*sìp*	สิบ
11	*sìp-èt*	สิบเอ็ด
12	*sìp-sǎwng*	สิบสอง
13	*sìp-sǎam*	สิบสาม
14	*sìp-sìi*	สิบสี่
20	*yîi-sìp*	ยี่ สิบ
21	*yîi-sìp-èt*	ยี่ สิบเอ็ด
22	*yîi-sìp-sǎwng*	ยี่ สิบสอง
23	*yîi-sìp-sǎam*	ยี่ สิบสาม
30	*sǎam-sìp*	สามสิบ
40	*sìi-sìp*	สี่ สิบ
50	*hâa-sìp*	ห้าสิบ
100	*ráwy*	ร้อย
200	*sǎwng ráwy*	สองร้อย
300	*sǎam ráwy*	สามร้อย
1000	*phan*	พัน
10,0000	*mèun*	หมื่น
100,000	*sǎen*	แสน
1,000,000	*láan*	ล้าน
billion	*phan láan*	พันล้าน

Facts for the Visitor

PLANNING
When to Go
The best overall time for visiting coastal Thailand vis-à-vis climate falls between November and March – during these months it rains least and is not so hot. Temperatures are more steady in the south, making it a good refuge when the heat peaks in the rest of Thailand (April to June). Both the Gulf of Thailand and Andaman Sea coastlines are mostly rain-free from March to May, both are somewhat rainy from June to November, while the gulf side is drier than the Andaman side from November to January. See Climate in the Facts about the Country chapter for more detail on seasons, which can vary significantly from one part of the country to another.

The peak tourist months are November, December, February, March and August, with secondary peaks in January and July. Consider travelling during the least crowded months of April, May, June, September and October if you want to avoid crowds and take advantage of discounted rooms and other low-season rates.

Who Goes Where
These days in Thailand you're liable to meet people from all walks of life and from just about any country in the world, but when it comes to beaches and islands, certain types of visitors tend to favour certain areas. Phuket and nearby Hat Khao Lak attract a well-heeled, middle-aged singles and couples crowd of Australians and Europeans who are most numerous in August, December and January. They tend to stay for a week or less.

Older Europeans, Russians and families on short-stay budget packages tend to frequent Pattaya and, to an increasing extent, Hua Hin and Cha-am. Since these areas are within an easy afternoon's drive of Bangkok, both resort areas tend to be more crowded on weekends and holidays than at other times.

Despite the upscaling of tourist facilities in recent years, Ko Samui continues to attract a younger, if slightly more wealthy, group of international beachgoers who like to party nightly. Peak seasons on Ko Samui are July to August and November to February.

Krabi, Ko Lanta and other Ao Phang-Nga beach areas draw a younger, more adventurous bunch, who are typically on a more long-term search for low-cost, less discovered Asian beaches. The winter tourist season is a bit longer here, extending from mid-November through early March.

Rustic Ko Pha-Ngan and Ko Chang are favoured by backpackers who spend less but stay longer than any of the aforementioned groups. The peak season on these islands more or less corresponds with that in Ao Phang-Nga.

Maps
Lonely Planet publishes the 1:1,150,000 scale *Thailand travel atlas*, an accurate 44 page country map booklet. It has place names in both Thai and roman script, topographic shading and a complete geographic index.

Nelles Maps and Bartholomew Maps each publish good 1:500,000 scale maps of Thailand with general topographic shading. The Bartholomew map tends to be a bit more up-to-date and accurate than the Nelles.

Also good, though bulky, is the Roads Association of Thailand's large-format, 48 page, bilingual road atlas called *Thailand Highway Map*. In addition to up-to-date, 1:1,000,000 scale maps, the atlas contains dozens of city maps and driving distances. It costs 100 to 120B depending on the vendor, but beware of inferior knock-offs.

Regional Maps Several companies in Thailand publish 'guide maps' to Phuket, Krabi and the Samui archipelago. Most accurate and current are those published by V Hongsombud, such as the *Guide Map of Koh Samui, Koh Pha-Ngan & Koh Tao*. Periplus

Editions' *Ko Samui Southern Thailand Travel Map* contains maps of the Samui archipelago, southern Thailand, the Tarutao archipelago and a city plan for Hat Yai.

The beaches and islands of the Eastern Gulf Coast, save for the area around Pattaya, have so far been neglected by regional map publishers.

Prannok Witthaya publishes individual maps of most of the provinces along the coast. These include English and Thai script, and can be found in most Thai bookshops. The maps are often a bit dated and not always accurate, but are of a larger scale than the regional and country maps.

What to Bring

Pack light, tropical-weight clothes, along with a light parka or windbreaker for occasional breezy or rainy evenings. Sunglasses are important, and slip-on shoes or sandals are highly recommended – besides being cooler than lace-up shoes, they are easily removed before entering a Thai home or temple.

You might also think about picking up a *phâakhamã* (short Thai-style sarong for men) or a *phâasîn* (a longer sarong for women) to wear in your room, on the beach or when bathing outdoors. These can be bought at any local market (different patterns/colours in different parts of the country) and the vendors will show you how to tie them.

The sarong is a very handy item; it can be used to sleep on or as a light bedspread, as a makeshift 'shopping bag', as a turban/scarf to keep off the sun and absorb perspiration, as a towel, as a small hammock and as a device with which to climb coconut palms – to name just a few of its many functions. It is not considered proper street attire, however.

A small torch (flashlight) is a good idea, as it makes it easier to find your way back to your bungalow at night if you are staying at the beach or at a remote guesthouse. Other handy items include a compass, a plastic lighter for lighting candles and mosquito coils, and foam ear plugs for noisy nights.

Toothpaste, soap and most other toiletries can be purchased anywhere in Thailand. Sun block and mosquito repellent (except high-percentage DEET – see the Health section in this chapter) are available, although they can be expensive and the quality of both is generally substandard. If you want to wash your own clothes, bring a universal sink plug, a few plastic pegs and 3m of plastic cord or plastic hangers for hanging wet clothes out to dry.

If you're a keen snorkeller, you might want to bring your own equipment (see Diving & Snorkelling in the Highlights & Activities of Coastal Thailand section of this chapter). This would save you having to rent gear and would also assure a proper fit. Shoes designed for water sports, eg aquasocks, are great for wearing in the water whether you're diving or not. They protect your feet from coral cuts, which easily become infected.

If you require computer modem communications in Thailand, see the Online Services section later in this chapter for items you might want to add to your mobile kit.

TOURIST OFFICES

The Tourism Authority of Thailand (TAT) is a government-operated tourist information/promotion service attached to the prime minister's office, with several offices within the country and overseas. In 1991 TAT was granted regulatory power to monitor tourism-related businesses throughout Thailand, including hotels, tour operators, travel agencies and transport companies, in an effort to upgrade the quality of these services and prosecute unscrupulous operators.

Local TAT Offices

Bangkok Head Office – 4 Ratchadamnoen Nok Rd, Pomprap, Bangkok 10100 (☎ (2) 281-0422); Temporary Office (despite the name the office shouldn't move until 1999 at the earliest) – 372 Bamrung Meuang Rd, Bangkok 10100 (☎ (2) 226-0060/72; fax 224-6221)

Cha-am – 500/51 Phetkasem Rd, Amphoe Cha-am, Phetburi 76120 (☎ (32) 471005/6; fax 471502)

Hat Yai – 1/1 Soi 2, Niphat Uthit 3 Rd, Hat Yai, Songkhla 90110 (☎ (74) 243747; fax 245986)

Nakhon Si Thammarat – Sanam Na Meuang, Ratchadamnoen Rd, Nakhon Si Thammarat 80000 (☎ (75) 346515/6; fax 346517)

Narathiwat (Sungai Kolok) – Sungai Kolok Tourist Information Centre, Asia 18 Rd (temporary office), Sungai Kolok, Narathiwat 96120 (☎ (73) 612126; fax 615230)

Pattaya – 382/1 Chai Hat Rd, Pattaya City, Amphoe Bang Lamung, Chonburi 20260 (☎ (38) 427667; fax 429113)

Phuket – 73-5 Phuket Rd, Phuket 83000 (☎ (76) 212213, 211036; fax 213582)

Rayong – 153/4 Sukhumvit Rd, Rayong 21000 (☎/fax (38) 655420/1; fax 655422)

Surat Thani – 5 Talaat Mai Rd, Ban Don, Surat Thani 84000 (☎ (77) 288818/9; fax 282828)

Trat (Laem Ngop) – 100 Muu 1, Trat-Laem Ngop Rd, Tambon Laem Ngop, Trat 23120 (☎/fax (38) 597255)

Overseas TAT Offices

Australia – Level 2, National Australia Bank House, 255 George St, Sydney, NSW 2000 (☎ (02) 9247-7549; fax 9251-2465)

France – 90 Avenue des Champs Elysées, 75008 Paris (☎ 01.45.62.86.56; fax 01.45.63.78.88)

Germany – Bethmannstrasse 58, 60311 Frankfurt/Main (☎ (069) 295-704/804; fax 281-468)

Hong Kong – Rm 401, Fairmont House, 8 Cotton Tree Drive, Central (☎ 2868-0732; fax 2868-4585)

Italy – Via Barberini 50, 00187 Rome (☎ (06) 487-3479; fax 487-3500)

Japan – 2nd floor, South Tower, Yurakucho Denki Bldg, 1-7-1 Yurakucho, Chiyoda-ku, Tokyo 100 (☎ (03) 3218-0337; fax 3218-0655); 3rd floor, Technoble Yosubashi Bldg, 1-6-8 Kitahorie, Nishi-ku, Osaka (☎ (06) 543-6654; fax 543-6660)

Korea – 10th floor, Coryo Daeyungek Center Bldg 25-5, 1-ka, Chungmu-Ro, Chung-Ku, Seoul 100-706 (☎ (02) 779-5417; fax 779-5419)

Malaysia – c/o Royal Thai Embassy, 206 Jalan Ampang, Kuala Lumpur (☎ (03) 248-0958; fax 241-3002)

Singapore – c/o Royal Thai Embassy, 370 Orchard Rd, 238870 (☎ 235-7694; fax 733-5653)

Taiwan – 13th floor, Boss Tower, 109-111 Sung Chiang Rd, Taipei 104 (☎ (02) 502-1600; fax 502-1603)

UK – 49 Albemarle St, London W1X 3FE (☎ (0171) 499-7679; fax 629-5519)

USA – Suite 3443, 5 World Trade Center, New York, NY 10048 (☎ (212) 432-0433; fax 912-0920); Suite 1100, 3440 Wilshire Blvd, Los Angeles, CA 90010 (☎ (213) 382-2353/5; fax 389-7544); Suite 400, 303 East Wacker Drive, Chicago, IL 60601 (☎ (312) 819-3990/5; fax 565-0359)

VISAS & DOCUMENTS
Passport

Entry into Thailand requires a passport valid for at least three months from the time of entry. If you anticipate your passport may expire while you're in Thailand, you should obtain a new one before arrival or enquire from your government whether your embassy in Thailand (if one exists – see the Embassies section further on) can issue a new one after arrival.

Visas

Transit & Tourist Visas The Thai government allows 56 different nationalities to enter the country without a visa for 30 days at no charge. Shining exceptions are visitors with New Zealand, Swedish or South Korean passports, who may enter Thailand for up to 90 days without a visa!

Seventy-six other nationalities – those from smaller European countries like Andorra or Liechtenstein, or from West Africa, South Asia or Latin America – can obtain a 15 day transit visa on arrival for a 300B fee. Some visitors, such as those from eastern European countries, have found that on-arrival visas can only be obtained if they fly into Bangkok, and can't be arranged at land border crossings.

A few nationalities must obtain a visa before arriving or they'll be turned back. Check with a Thai embassy or consulate to be sure if you plan to try arriving without a visa.

Without proof of an onward ticket and sufficient funds for one's projected stay any visitor can be denied entry, but in practice your ticket and funds are rarely checked if you're dressed neatly for the immigration check. See Exchange Control in the Money section in this chapter for officially required amounts for each visa type.

Next in its length of validity is the tourist visa, which is good for 60 days and costs US$15. Up to three passport photos may be needed with your application, depending on the individual consulate or embassy.

Non-Immigrant Visas The non-immigrant visa is good for 90 days, must be applied for in your home country, costs US$20 and is not difficult to obtain if you can offer a good reason for your visit. Business, study, retirement and extended family visits are among the purposes considered valid.

Visa Extensions Sixty day tourist visas may be extended for up to 30 days at the discretion of Thai immigration authorities. The Bangkok office (☎ (2) 287-3101) is on Soi Suan Phlu, Sathon Tai Rd, but you can apply at any immigration office in the country – every province that borders a neighbouring country has at least one. The usual fee for extension of a tourist visa is 500B. Bring along one photo and one copy each of the photo and visa pages of your passport. Normally only one 30 day extension is granted.

The 30 day, no-visa stay can be extended by seven to 10 days (depending on the immigration office) for 500B. You can also leave the country and return immediately to obtain another 30 day stay. There is no limit on the number of times you can do this, nor is there a minimum interval you must spend outside the country.

Extension of the 15 day, on-arrival transit visa is only allowed if you hold a passport from a country that has no Thai embassy.

If you overstay your visa, the usual penalty is a fine of 100B per day of your overstay, with a 20,000B limit; fines can be paid at the airport or in advance at the Investigation Unit (☎ (2) 287-3129, ext 2204), Immigration Bureau, Rm 416, 4th floor, Old Building, Soi Suan Phlu, Sathon Tai Rd, Bangkok.

Extending a non-immigrant visa very much depends on how the officials feel about you – if they like you then they will extend it. Other than the 500B extension fee, money doesn't usually come into it; neat appearance and polite behaviour count for more. Typically, one must collect various signatures and go through various interviews which result in a 'provisional' extension. You may then have to report to a local immigration office every 10 to 14 days for the next three months until the actual extension comes through.

Retirees 55 years of age or older can actually extend the 90 day non-immigrant visa to a yearly visa. To do this you will need to bring the following documents to the Immigration Bureau: a copy of your passport's personal details pages, one photo, 500B extension fee, proof of financial status or pension. The requirement for the latter is that foreigners aged 60 or older must show proof of an income of not less than 200,000B per year (or 20,000B per month for extensions of less than a year); for those aged 55 to 59 the minimum is raised to 500,000B/50,000B. According to immigration regulations, however, 'If the alien is ill, or has weak health and is sensitive to colder climates, or has resided in Thailand for a long period, and is 55-59 years of age, special considerations will be granted'.

Foreigners with non-immigrant visas who have resided in Thailand continuously for three years – on one year extensions – may apply for permanent residency at Section 1, Subdivision 1, Immigration Division 1, Rm 301, 3rd floor, Immigration Bureau, Soi Suan Phlu (☎ (2) 287-3117/01). Foreigners who receive permanent residence must carry an 'alien identification card' at all times.

Re-Entry & Multiple-Entry Visas If you need to leave and re-enter the kingdom before your visa expires, say for a return trip to Laos or the like, apply at the immigration office on Soi Suan Phlu, Sathon Tai Rd, Bangkok. The cost is 500B; you'll need to supply one passport photo. There is no limit to the number of re-entry permits you can apply for and use during the validity of your visa.

Thailand does not issue multiple-entry visas. If you want a visa that enables you to leave the country and then return, obtain a visa permitting two entries; this will cost double the single-entry visa. For example, a two-entry 90 day non-immigrant visa will cost US$40 and will allow you six months in the country, as long as you cross a border with immigration facilities by the end of your first three months. The second half of your visa is validated as soon as you recross the Thai border, so there is no need to go to a Thai embassy/consulate abroad. All visas acquired in advance of entry are valid for 90 days from the date of issue.

Visas & Documents continued on page 76

Highlights & Activities of Coastal Thailand

JERRY ALEXANDER

RICHARD NEBESKY

Title Page: A traditional wooden long-tail boat bobs on the shore at Ao Maya, Ko Phi Phi Leh. (photo by Mark Strickland/Oceanic Impressions)

Top Right: Typical Thai-style beach umbrellas, Phuket.

Middle Right: Sunset at Ban Mae Hat, Ko Tao, where the inter-island boats land.

Bottom Right: The coral reefs around the remote and undeveloped Similan Islands are world-renowned for their magnificent diving and snorkelling.

MARK STRICKLAND/OCEANIC IMPRESSIONS

Highlights

The country's unique geography offers three starkly different coastal settings.

The Eastern Gulf Coast, stretching south-east from Bangkok to the Cambodian border, is a succession of beaches and offshore islands which face south-west and thus escape one of the two major monsoons that sweep across mainland South-East Asia each year. The oldest and most well established of the resorts along this coast is densely developed Pattaya, although gulf alternatives nearby are expanding with each passing season. The main advantage of the eastern gulf resorts is their proximity to Bangkok; except for some of the islands, such as Ko Samet and Ko Chang (in Thai, 'ko' means 'island'), the beaches aren't all that spectacular.

The Malay peninsula extends 1600km south-east from Bangkok, creating a slender land barrier between the South China Sea and the Indian Ocean. Lined on either side by sandy bays, lagoons, mangroves, islands and islets, over half the length of this peninsula falls within Thailand's borders.

The west side of this peninsula, referred to in this book as the Andaman Coast, faces the Andaman Sea (the part of the Indian Ocean that lies between the Andaman islands and Thailand's west coast). This coastline is characterised by craggy cliffs and islands composed of a chalky limestone that dissolves to impart a deep turquoise hue to coastal shallows. Diving among the coral reefs in this area can be superb.

Phuket, Thailand's largest island, is the Andaman Coast's most popular resort, followed by Ko Phi Phi and a number of up-and-coming beaches and islands, including Ko Lanta to the south and Hat Khao Lak to the north. Travel to the more remote island groups is seasonal, since during the height of the south-west monsoon (May to October) the Andaman Sea becomes too rough for offshore navigation.

Waters along the gulf coast of the Malay peninsula are calmer year-round. This coast remains the most undeveloped, with the bulk of the tourist activity focused on Ko Samui, Thailand's third largest island. The opening of Samui's airport in the late 1980s spurred the island's already rapid development, while other islands nearby remain favoured destinations for those with more time than money.

Which side of the peninsula you choose – the Gulf of Thailand (for Prachuap Khiri Khan, Ko Samui, Songkhla) or the Andaman Sea (Phuket, Krabi, Trang) – might be determined by the time of year. See When to Go earlier in this chapter and Climate in the previous chapter for more information on seasonal considerations.

If time is an issue, check out the beaches and islands along the Eastern Gulf Coast of central Thailand (Pattaya, Ko Samet, Ko Chang) or upper peninsular gulf (Cha-am, Hua Hin) for shorter beach excursions. Head to southern Thailand if you have a week or more and will be using ground transport. Or fly to one of the airports in the southern beach resort areas (eg Ko Samui, Phuket).

One of the main highlights of Thai travel is soaking up the general cultural ambience, which can be done just about anywhere away from the resorts. You won't experience much if you spend most of your time sitting around in guesthouse cafes, hanging out on the beach or diving with your own kind. At least once during your trip, try going to a small to medium-sized town well off the main tourist circuit, staying at a local hotel, and eating in Thai curry shops and noodle stands. It's not as easy as going with the crowd but you'll learn a lot more about Thailand, and the experiences you have will likely be the ones you remember best years later.

Resorts & Convenient Escapes

Pattaya This bay is near Bangkok on the eastern Gulf of Thailand coast. Golf, go-karting, parasailing, wave-running, sailboarding, high-style dining and a notorious nightlife attracts those interested in an active, urbanised beach vacation. Pattaya Bay is far from Thailand's cleanest resort – beaches at nearby Jomtien and Naklua are a bit better – though there is fair to good snorkelling and diving at nearby islands (including shipwrecks). Prices: moderate to expensive (see Costs in the Money section later of this chapter). Accessible by rail and road.

Ko Samet Off the Eastern Gulf Coast, and only three hours from Bangkok by road and boat, this island can be quite over-run on weekends and holidays. The fine white sand and clear waters attract a cross-section of expats, Thais and tourists. There's some decent snorkelling at nearby islets. Prices: inexpensive to moderate. Accessible by boat only.

Cha-am On the gulf, south-east of the provincial capital of Phetburi and less than four hours from Bangkok, Cha-am is a small but well-developed beach town more favoured by Thais than foreigners. The beach is clean, straight and fringed with casuarina trees. Crowded on holidays. Prices: moderate. Accessible by road.

Hua Hin & Prachuap Khiri Khan The upper peninsula province of Prachuap Khiri Khan, facing the gulf, offers sandy beaches of medium quality along much of its length, from the well-touristed Hua Hin in the north to little known Thai resorts near Ao Manao and Bang Saphan. Most accommodation is in medium-priced hotels. Not much in the way of diving, but seafood is superb and economical. Crowded on holidays. Prices: inexpensive to moderate. Accessible by air (Hua Hin only), rail and road.

Ko Samui In the Gulf of Thailand, off the coast of Surat Thani, this is the third largest island in the country and quite heavily developed. Once a haven for backpackers on the Asia Trail, it is for the most part now given over to middle-class hotels and guesthouses, though dirt-cheap digs can still be found. Snorkelling and diving are fair, beaches superb. Prices: inexpensive to moderate, with a few luxury resorts. Accessible by ferry from Surat Thani, air from Bangkok or by train/bus/ferry combo from Bangkok.

Phuket In the Andaman Sea, Thailand's largest and most geographically varied island was the first to develop a tourist industry. Nowadays it has become a fairly sophisticated international resort, albeit one with the highest number of 'green' hotel developments as well as two well-respected national parks. Good diving at nearby islands and reefs of the Andaman Sea and Ao Phang-Nga (Sea of Phuket). Best Thai cuisine of any of the islands. Prices: moderate to expensive. Accessible by air and road (via a causeway).

More Remote Beach & Island Areas

Ko Chang & Ko Kut In the Gulf of Thailand, near the Cambodian border, these islands are relatively undertouristed. Though part of a national park, both islands have coastal zones where development is permitted but so far high-profile development has been kept at bay by their distance from Bangkok and mountainous geography. Attracts those looking for quiet, economical beach stays, with some spillover from Ko

Pha-Ngan. Waterfalls and hiking trails on Ko Chang add to the attraction. Prices: inexpensive, save for a couple of moderate to expensive beach resorts. Accessible by boat only from Trat.

Ko Pha-Ngan Just north of Ko Samui in the Gulf of Thailand, this is the main backpackers beach headquarters at the moment as beach accommodation is among the least expensive in the country, though some posh places are now popping up. Good snorkelling and diving at some parts of the island, plus waterfalls and hiking trails. Very little in the way of nightlife except at Hat Rin on the island's south-east tip, famous for its 'full moon parties' (now on the wane). Prices: inexpensive. Accessible by boat only from Ko Samui, Ko Tao or Surat Thani.

Ko Tao A small crescent-shaped island north of Ko Pha-Ngan with the best diving in the gulf. Development here has outpaced Ko Pha-Ngan mostly due to the diving industry; virtually every beach bungalow development on the island offers diving trips and/or instruction. Many beaches are too shallow for swimming. Prices: moderate. Accessible by boat only from Ko Samui, Ko Pha-Ngan or Chumphon.

Songkhla, Pattani & Narathiwat Southernmost Gulf of Thailand, these deep south provinces near Malaysia offer hundreds of kilometres of deserted beach. During the north-east monsoon (November to March), the water tends to be murky due to cross-currents. Culturally these are some of the most interesting coastal areas in the country due to Islamic Malay influences. Good for regional handicrafts, including cotton prints, sarongs and batik. Very little is available in the way of beach accommodation, though village housing is a possibility for those with initiative and who can speak some Thai. Prices: inexpensive. Accessible by rail (parts of Narathiwat and Songkhla only) and road. Hat Yai is the nearest air hub.

Ko Similan, Ko Surin & Ko Tarutao National Marine Parks These Andaman island groups enjoy some of the best park protection in Thailand. There is fantastic diving and snorkelling at all three; Similan and Surin are rated among the world's top 10 dive destinations. Accommodation is limited to park bungalows and camping, except for one private island in Tarutao. Prices: inexpensive. Accessible by boat only, and only during the non-monsoon months (November to April), from Phuket and the mainland.

Krabi This province facing Ao Phang-Nga, opposite Phuket, offers a range of beaches and islands ringed with striking limestone formations. Rock climbing, snorkelling, diving, boating and fishing provide opportunities for active holidays. Generally quiet, though accommodation tends to book out from December to February, while during months of lower visitation (May, June, September, October) it can be nearly deserted. Prices: inexpensive to moderate (or luxurious at the Dusit Rayavadee Resort). Provincial capital accessible by half-day boat or bus trip from Phuket; overnight bus from Bangkok. Islands, and some beaches, accessible by boat only.

Ko Lanta Actually part of Krabi Province, this slender island is a perennial winter favourite among low-budget travellers; it's practically deserted from April to November when lashed by south-west monsoon rains. Some snorkelling and diving; good seafood. Crowded on holidays. Prices: inexpensive. Accessible by boat from Krabi and Ko Phi Phi, by road and ferry from nearby coastal towns.

Trang The next province south of Krabi, facing the Andaman Sea, Trang is largely undiscovered, but the beaches and islands aren't as pretty as Krabi's. Good diving but you'll have to bring your own gear. Prices: inexpensive to moderate. Islands accessible by boat only, mainland by road and air.

National Parks in Coastal Areas

Thailand boasts nearly 80 national parks, a number expected to exceed 100 by the end of the century. See the National Parks & Wildlife Sanctuaries section under Ecology & Environment in the Facts about the Country chapter for general information about the country's protected areas, and the destination chapters for complete details on each of the parks covered in this book. The book *National Parks of Thailand* by Denis Gray, Collin Piprell & Mark Graham is the most comprehensive source of English-language material on the parklands.

Ko Chang National Marine Park, Trat Province The mountainous Ko Chang archipelago encompasses around 50 islands, all but three of which are almost completely undeveloped. Beaches and interiors tend to be pristine, though transport among them can be problematic (except for Ko Chang, where boat transport is regular). Good any time of year, although the June to October south-west monsoon strikes here with more force than elsewhere on the gulf coast.

Khao Laem Ya/Ko Samet National Park, Rayong Province It's difficult to find this park under all the private development that has been allowed to take place. The main feature is beautiful Ko Samet, which is often crowded but still boasts some of Thailand's nicest, whitest beaches. Drier than most destinations, even during the June to October rainy season, this area is good to visit year-round.

Khao Sam Roi Yot National Park, Prachuap Khiri Khan Province This 98 sq km park on the coast near Hua Hin is one of the country's most scenic due to a blend of mountains and seacoast. Good trails and camping. Best visited November to July, though it's relatively protected from the south-west monsoon so don't rule out other months.

Khao Sok National Park, Surat Thani Province Limestone crags, rainforests and jungle streams provide the perfect environment for the remnants of Thailand's threatened tiger and clouded leopard populations, as well as two species of *Rafflesia*. Tree-house accommodation protects the forest floor and gives visitors an opportunity to experience one of the country's most important ecosystems. Best visited December to February.

Laem Son Wildlife & Forest Preserve, Ranong & Phang-Nga Provinces This area includes some 100km of Andaman Sea coastline, and consists mainly of mangrove swamps, home to various species of birds, fish, deer and monkeys, including crab-eating macaques. Accommodation available at Hat Bang Ben beach. Best visited November to April.

Ko Surin National Marine Park, Phang-Nga Province The five oceanic islands that make up this park are well known for excellent diving and snorkelling, but also offer some opportunities for hikers and viewing wildlife. Camping and bungalows found on one island only. Best visited November to April

Khao Lak/Lam Ru National Park, Phang-Nga Province This 125 sq km park combines sea cliffs and beaches with 1000m peaks, original rainforest and mangroves. Good hiking and the chance to see wildlife, including gibbons and (less likely) the Asiatic black bear. Bungalow accommodation at visitor centre and private resorts nearby. Best visited November to April.

Ko Similan National Marine Park, Phang-Nga Province Although relatively small, this remote, nine island archipelago has become one of Thailand's better known dive destinations due its profusion of hard corals growing on huge rock reefs. Sea turtles are known to nest here. Camping and bungalows found on one island only. Best visited November to April.

Ao Phang-Nga National Marine Park, Phang-Nga Province The coastline is marked by stunning karst topography, with steep-sided, verdant limestone islets dropping straight into deep, turquoise waters. Over 40 islands are included in this park near Phuket. Best visited November to April.

Hat Noppharat Thara/Ko Phi Phi National Marine Park, Krabi Province Although this huge marine park in the southern half of Ao Phang-Nga is unevenly protected, many designated park islands are still pristine. Ko Phi Phi is the glaring exception as it has become crowded with illegal beach accommodation and is probably a lost cause (as a parkland) at this point. Great kayaking, diving and snorkelling. No park accommodation, though there is private accommodation on Ko Phi Phi. Typical marine karst topography as elsewhere in Ao Phang-Nga. Best visited November to April.

Sirinat National Marine Park, Phuket Province This new park in the north-west corner of the island of Phuket comprises two smaller, formerly separate national parks and Thailand's longest beach for a total of 22km along the shoreline. Sea turtles nest here, and there is a coral reef offshore. A visitor centre, toilets and picnic tables are the only facilities provided. Best visited November to April.

Ko Tarutao National Marine Park, Satun Province This archipelago of 51 islands is one of the most pristine coastal areas in Thailand, and offers great snorkelling and hiking to those willing to make the effort to get there. Limited bungalows and camping space are available within the park, as well as some privately run options at nearby islands outside park jurisdiction. Best visited November to April.

Cultural Pursuits

Those who would like to temper beach time with cultural and spiritual diversions can do so in southern Thailand, though less so along the Eastern Gulf Coast. Below are a few recommended sights; greater detail can be found in the relevant destination chapters.

Historic Temples Although the Eastern Gulf Coast is predominantly Buddhist, there are virtually no temples of particular historic value in the region. Southern Thailand, despite its heavily Muslim character (predominantly so in the deep south), does have several Buddhist centres with significant temple sites.

The provincial capital of Phetburi on the north-western gulf coast contains numerous older wats, including a few with some of the best preserved Ayuthaya-period temple murals in the country.

In Chaiya, Surat Thani Province, a highly venerated stupa at Wat Phra Boromathat dates to the Srivijaya era (8th to 13th centuries).

Nakhon Si Thammarat boasts Wat Phra Mahathat, one of the oldest Buddhist temples in Thailand, in a large 13th century compound which also contains an exhibit of antique religious objects.

Museums Coastal Thailand isn't known for the outstanding quality of its museums, but there are a few worth looking out for. Nakhon Si Thammarat's national museum features a room dedicated to works of religious art and handicrafts which originated in southern Thailand.

The Songkhla National Museum is a work of art in itself, an old Sino-Portuguese mansion converted into exhibit space for historic artefacts from around the south and beyond.

The Southern Thai Folklore Museum on Ko Yo, near Songkhla, contains an impressive array of southern Thai religious and folk art, while Nakhon Si Thammarat National Museum features the country's best collection of southern Thai religious art, plus Dong-Son bronze drums, Dvaravati Buddha images and Pallava (south Indian) Hindu sculpture.

If you're coming through Bangkok, a visit to the National Museum, Vimanmek Teak Mansion and Jim Thompson's House can be recommended for their displays of art and artefacts from centuries past.

Activities

Diving & Snorkelling

Thailand's two coastlines and countless islands are popular among divers from all over the globe for their mild waters and colourful marine life. Sandy coves, coral reefs, limestone outcroppings, rock reefs, seamounts and pinnacles, undersea caverns and tunnels, and sunken ships provide a wide variety of dive sites. Water temperature hovers at 27 to 29°C year-round, ideal for recreational divers, not to mention coral and tropical fish.

Guided dives and diving instruction have become sizeable industries in Thailand, especially during the high tourist season, November to April. The biggest diving centre – in terms of the number of participants, but not the number of dive operations – is still Pattaya, simply because it's less than two hours drive from Bangkok and has a year-round dive season. There are several islands with reefs within a short boat ride from Pattaya and the little town is packed with dive shops.

Phuket is the second biggest jumping-off point, or largest if you count dive operations. It has the advantage of offering the largest variety of dive sites to choose from, including small offshore islands less than an hour away, Ao Phang-Nga (a one to two hour boat ride) with its unusual rock formations and clear green waters, and the world-famous Similan and Surin islands in the Andaman Sea (about four hours away by fast boat). Reef dives in the Andaman are particularly rewarding – some 210 hard corals and 108 reef fish have so far been catalogued in this under-studied marine zone, where probably thousands more species of reef organisms live.

In recent years dive operations have multiplied rapidly on the palmy islands of Ko Samui, Ko Pha-Ngan and Ko Tao in the Gulf of Thailand off Surat Thani. Chumphon Province, just north of Surat Thani, is another up-and-coming area where there are a dozen or so islands with undisturbed reefs. Newer frontiers include the so-called Burma Banks (north-west of the Surin archipelago), Hat Khao Lak (on the mainland north of Phuket), Ko Chang and islands off the coast of Krabi and Trang provinces. All of these places, with the possible exception of the Burma Banks, have areas that are suitable for snorkelling as well as scuba diving, since many reefs are no deeper than 2m.

Dive Centres Most dive centres rent equipment at reasonable rates and offer instruction and NAUI or PADI qualification for first-timers – PADI is by far the most prevalent. The average four day, full-certification course costs around 5000 to 8000B, including instruction, equipment and several open-water dives. Shorter, less expensive 'resort' courses are also available, including half-day 'introductory' dives. Speciality courses may include dive master certification and underwater photography. It's a good idea to shop around for courses, not just to compare prices but to suss out the types of instruction, the condition of the equipment and the personalities of the instructors.

The minimum age for PADI or NAUI certification is 12 years; children aged 12 and 15 are classified 'junior divers' and must be accompanied by an adult. There are no maximum age limits. Beginners should note that courses are usually only available at the larger areas: for example, you can't take an open water course at the remote Similan Islands.

German and English are the most common languages of instruction, but French and Italian courses are also available at a few places. See the relevant destination sections of this book for names and locations of established diving centres.

Equipment Virtually every dive operation rents ample gear and air compressors. The better ones provide high-quality equipment, while cheaper places may offer sub-standard gear – inspect carefully before renting. Tanks, regulators and Buoyancy Compensation Devices (BCDs) are especially critical.

Masks, fins and snorkels are readily available not only at dive centres but also at guesthouses in beach areas. If you're fussy about the quality and condition of the equipment you use, you might be better off bringing your own mask and snorkel – some of the stuff for rent is second-rate. And people with large heads may have difficulty finding masks that fit since most of the masks are made or imported for Thai heads.

Wetsuits are not usually required except for deeper Andaman Sea dives where cold water upwellings and/or thermoclines occur, but a lycra suit or 'skin' does serve as protection against scrapes and jellyfish. These are available from most dive shops, but if you're unusually tall or large they may have trouble fitting you – in which case bring your own.

Because divers and anglers occasionally frequent the same areas, a good diving knife is essential for dealing with a wayward fishing line or net. Bring two knives so you'll have a spare. Include extra O-rings, CO_2 cartridges for flotation vests and a wetsuit patching kit if you plan to dive away from resort areas.

Dependable air for scuba tanks is available in Pattaya, Ko Chang, Ko Samui, Ko Tao, Khao Lak and Phuket. Always check the compressor first to make sure it's well maintained and running clean. Divers with extensive experience usually carry a portable compressor, not only to avoid contaminated air but to use in areas where tank refills aren't available.

Dive Seasons Generally speaking, the Gulf of Thailand has a year-round dive season, although tropical storms sometimes blow out visibility temporarily. The south-west monsoon seems to affect the Ko Chang archipelago more than the rest of the Eastern Gulf Coast dive sites, hence November to May is the ideal season for these islands.

On the Andaman Coast the best diving conditions – calm surf and good visibility – fall between December and April; from May to November monsoon conditions prevail. However, there are still many calm days even during the south-west monsoon season – it's largely a matter of luck. Whale sharks and manta rays in the offshore Andaman Sea (eg Similan and Surin Islands) can be spotted during the March and April planktonic blooms.

Considerations for Responsible Diving

The popularity of diving is placing immense pressure on many sites. Please consider the following tips when diving and help preserve the ecology and beauty of reefs:

- Do not use anchors on the reef, and take care not to ground boats on coral. Encourage dive operators and regulatory bodies to establish permanent moorings at popular dive sites.

- Avoid touching living marine organisms with your body, or dragging computer consoles and gauges across the reef. Polyps can be damaged by even the gentlest contact. Never stand on coral, even if they look solid and robust. If you must secure yourself to the reef, only hold fast to exposed rock or dead coral.

- Be conscious of your fins. Even without contact the surge from heavy fin strokes near the reef can damage delicate organisms. When treading water in shallow reef areas, take care not to kick up clouds of sand. Settling sand can easily smother the delicate organisms of the reef.

PAUL BEINSSEN
An open-decked diving boat explores the coral reefs around Ko Tao.

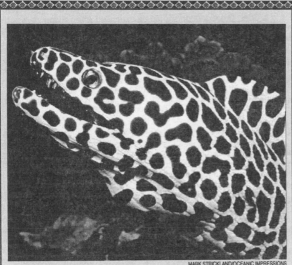

MARK STRICKLAND/OCEANIC IMPRESSIONS

A reticulated moray eel at the Burma Banks, Northern Andaman Coast.

- Practise and maintain proper buoyancy control. Major damage can be done by divers descending too fast and colliding with the reef. Make sure you are correctly weighted and that your weight belt is positioned so that you stay horizontal. If you have not dived for a while, have a practice dive in a pool before taking to the reef. Be aware that buoyancy can change over the period of an extended trip; initially you may breath harder and need more weighting, a few days later you may breath more easily and need less weight.

- Take great care in underwater caves. Spend as little time in them as possible as your air bubbles may be caught within the roof and thereby leave previously submerged organisms high and dry. Taking turns to inspect the interior of a small cave will lessen the chances of damaging contact.

- Respect the integrity of marine archaeological sites (mainly ship-wrecks); they may even be protected by law from looting.

- Ensure that you take home all your rubbish, and any litter you may find as well. Plastics are a particularly serious threat to marine life. Turtles will mistake plastic for jelly fish and eat it.

- Resist the temptation to feed fish. You may disturb their normal eating habits, encourage aggressive behaviour or feed them food that is detrimental to their health.

- Minimise your disturbance of marine animals. In particular, do not ride on the backs of turtles as this causes them great anxiety.

Dive Medicine Due to the overall lack of medical facilities oriented toward diving injuries, great caution should be exercised when diving anywhere in Thailand. Recompression chambers are located at three permanent facilities:

Apakorn Kiatiwong Naval Hospital – Sattahip, Chonburi (☎ (38) 601185); 26km east of Pattaya; urgent care available 24 hours
Dept of Underwater & Aviation Medicine – Phra Pinklao Naval Hospital, Taksin Rd, Thonburi, Bangkok (☎ (2) 460-0000/19, ext 341, 460-1105); open 24 hours
Dive Safe Asia – 113/6 Song Roi Pi Rd, Patong beach, Phuket (☎ (76) 342-518; fax 342-519, mobile phone (for emergencies) 01-606-1869)

Guidebooks *Diving in Thailand* (Asia Books, 1994), by Collin Piprell & Ashley J Boyd, contains well-researched, well-organised information on diving throughout the country. *ScubaGuide Thailand* (1994), published by *Asian Diver* magazine, is also helpful. Both guides are illustrated with colour photos; *Diving in Thailand* has many more maps, plus a detailed section on underwater photography.

Environmental Issues To preserve Thailand's impressive marine environment for the future, it is imperative than divers take care not to disrupt the fragile ecosystems beneath the seas. This means, first and foremost, not touching corals, fish or other marine life. It includes refraining from hitching rides on fish, dolphins or turtles by grabbing onto their fins or shells, practices that are thought to frighten them and cause undue stress. Such contact can also adversely affect the health of marine life by scraping away mucous coverings that protect the creatures against infection.

Spearfishing is not appropriate on a recreational dive as it reduces the number of larger fish necessary to the marine ecosystem. Errant spears also often damage coral. It is also absolutely illegal in national marine parks.

Resist the temptation to collect or buy corals or shells. Aside from the ecological damage, taking home marine souvenirs depletes the beauty of a site and spoils the site for others.

See the Tourism & the Environment section in the Facts about the Country chapter for important recommendations on boat anchoring and waste disposal. See also the boxed aside titled Considerations for Responsible Diving in this section for more tips.

Windsurfing

The best combination of rental facilities and wind conditions are found on Pattaya and Jomtien beaches in Chonburi Province, on Ko Samet, on the west coast of Phuket and on Chaweng beach on Ko Samui. To a lesser extent you'll also find rental equipment on Hat Khao Lak (north of Phuket), Ko Pha-Ngan, Ko Tao and Ko Chang. Rental windsurfing gear found at Thai resorts is generally not the most complete and up-to-date. Original parts may be missing, or may have been replaced by improvised Thai-made parts. For the novice windsurfer this probably won't matter, but hot-doggers may be disappointed by the selection. Bring your own if you have it. In Thailand's year-round tropical climate, wetsuits aren't necessary.

If you have your own equipment you can set out anywhere you find a coastal breeze. If you're looking for something 'undiscovered', you might check out the cape running north from Narathiwat's provincial capital in southern Thailand. In general, the windier months on the Gulf of Thailand are mid-February to April. On the Andaman Sea side of the Thai-Malay peninsula, winds are strongest from September to December.

Sea Canoeing & Kayaking

Paddling your own watercraft is one of the best ways to experience Thailand's magnificent coastline, yet as a recreational pastime it has barely begun. Touring the islands and coastal limestone formations around Phuket and Ao Phang-Nga by inflatable canoe or kayak, however, has become an increasingly popular activity over the past five years. The typical sea canoe tour seeks out half-submerged caves called 'hongs' *(hâwng,* meaning 'room'), timing the trips so they can paddle into and out of caverns at low tide. Several outfits in Phuket and Krabi hire equipment and guides – see the relevant destination sections for details.

You might also consider bringing your own craft. Inflatable or folding kayaks make the most sense for travellers, though hardshell kayaks track better. In Thailand's tropical waters an open-top or open-deck kayak – whether hardshell, folding or inflatable – is more comfortable and practical than the closed-deck type with spray skirt and other sealing paraphernalia, which only transforms your kayak into a floating sauna. As the paddler sits on top of the deck rather than beneath it, the open-top is much easier to exit and thus a bit safer overall. Open-cockpit kayaks are also easier to paddle and more stable than traditional kayaks – almost anyone can paddle one with little or no practice. But they do manoeuvre a bit more slowly due to a wider beam and higher centre of gravity.

Surfing

This sport has never really taken off in Thailand, mainly as there don't seem to be any sizeable, annually dependable breaks (tell us if you find any). Phuket's west coast occasionally kicks up some surfable waves during the south-west monsoon from May to November, as does the west coast of Ko Chang. Ko Samet's east coast gets some waves during the dry season (November to February).

Low-quality boards can be rented in Pattaya and on Phuket's Patong beach (but bigger surf is usually found on nearby Laem Singh and Hat Surin). Coastal Trang is reputed to receive large waves during the south-west monsoon, but there aren't many tales of surfers hitting the breaks out there.

Hiking

You can hike in southern Thailand's larger national parks – Kaeng Krachan, Khao Sam Roi Yot, Khao Sok, Khao Lak and Thalehban – where park rangers may be hired as guides/cooks for a few days. Rates are reasonable; see the respective park descriptions later in this book.

Parks suitable for hiking without guide – because they contain marked trails – include Khao Sam Roi Yot and Ko Tarutao. Inter-village footpaths on southern Ko Chang can also easily be hiked without guides, though paths in the island's hilly interior can be challenging due to steep grades and undergrowth.

When hiking without a guide, it is recommended that you always hike with at least one other person and that you let someone in the local community know where you're headed and for how long. Always take plenty of water and insect repellent.

Leeches can be a hindrance during the monsoon seasons, particularly in Khao Sok National Park; see the Health section of this chapter.

Cycling

Details on pedalling your way around Thailand can be found in the Getting Around chapter.

Visas & Documents continued from page 64

Warning Whichever type of visa you have, be sure to check your passport immediately after stamping. Overworked officials sometimes stamp 15 or 30 days on arrival even when you hold a longer visa; if you point out the error before you've left the immigration area at your port of entry, officials will make the necessary corrections. If you don't notice this until you've left the port of entry, go to Bangkok and plead your case at the central immigration office.

Similarly, if you plan to come back to Thailand at some point, make sure your visa is stamped when you leave the country. One poor fellow, who had last left Thailand via an unmanned checkpoint at the Malaysian border, flew in from London for a return visit only to be refused entry and put on the next flight back home! All because he didn't have the proper exit stamp.

Once a visa is issued, it must be used (ie you must enter Thailand) within 90 days.

Photocopies

It's a good idea to keep photocopies of all vital documents – passport data page, all credit card numbers, airline tickets, travellers cheque serial numbers and so on – in a separate place from the originals. Replacement will be much easier to arrange if you can provide issuing agencies with copies. You might consider leaving extra copies of these documents with someone at home or in a safe place in Bangkok or other entry point.

Tax Clearance

Anyone who receives income while in Thailand must obtain a tax clearance certificate, before they leave the country, from the Revenue Department (☎ (2) 216-5331) at Soi Samsen 2 in Bangkok. There are also Revenue Department offices in every provincial capital.

Old Thai hands note: The tax clearance requirement no longer applies to those who have simply stayed in Thailand beyond a cumulative 90 days within one calendar year – this regulation was abolished in 1991. This makes it much easier for expats or other long-termers who live in Thailand on nonimmigrant visas – as long as they don't receive income. Hence there's no more hustling for tax clearance every visa trip to Penang or Vientiane.

Travel Insurance

A travel insurance policy to cover theft, loss and medical problems is strongly recommended. Though Thailand is generally safe, sickness, accidents and theft do happen. Travel agents can make recommendations on a wide variety of policies. Check the small print to see if the policy covers any potentially dangerous sporting activities you may do, such as diving or trekking, and make sure that it adequately covers your valuables. A few credit cards offer limited, sometimes full, travel insurance to the holder. See the Health section later in this chapter for more information on health insurance.

Driving Licence & Permits

An international driving permit is necessary for any visitor who intends to drive a motorised vehicle in Thailand. These are usually available from motoring organisations such as AAA (US) or BAA (UK) in your home country. If you'd like to obtain a Thai driving licence, see the Driving Permits section of the Getting Around chapter for details.

EMBASSIES
Thai Embassies

To apply for a visa, contact one of Thailand's diplomatic missions in any of the following countries. In many cases, if you apply in person you may receive a tourist or nonimmigrant visa on the day of application; by mail it generally takes anywhere from two to six weeks.

Australia – 111 Empire Circuit, Yarralumla, Canberra, ACT 2600 (☎ (02) 6273-1149/2937)
Canada – 180 Island Park Drive, Ottawa, Ontario K1Y OA2 (☎ (613) 722-4444)
China – 40 Guanghua Lu, Beijing 100600 (☎ (010) 532-1903)
France – 8 Rue Greuze, 75116 Paris (☎ 01.47.27.80.79, 01.47.24.32.22)

Germany – Ubierstrasse 65, 53173 Bonn (☎ (0228) 355-065/8)

Hong Kong – 8th floor, Fairmont House, 8 Cotton Tree Drive, Central (☎ 2521-6481/2)

India – 56-N Nyaya Marg, Chanakyapuri, New Delhi, 110021 (☎ (11) 60-5679, 60-7289)

Indonesia – Jalan Imam Bonjol 74, Jakarta (☎ (021) 390-4052/3/4)

Italy – Via Bertoloni 26 B, 00197 Rome (☎ (06) 807-8955)

Japan – 3-14-6 Kami-Osaki, Shinagawa-ku, Tokyo 141 (☎ (03) 3441-1386/7)

Laos – Route Phonkheng, Vientiane Poste 128 (☎ (21) 214582/3)

Malaysia – 206 Jalan Ampang, Kuala Lumpur (☎ (03) 248-8222/350)

Myanmar (Burma) – 91 Pyi Rd, Yangon (☎ (01) 282471, 276555)

Nepal – Jyoti Kendra Bldg, Thapathali, Kathmandu (☎ (01) 213-910/2)

Netherlands – Buitenrustweg 1, 2517 KD The Hague (☎ (070) 345-2088/9703)

New Zealand – 2 Cook St, Karori, Wellington 5 (☎ (04) 476-8618/9)

Philippines – 107/B Rada St, Legaspi Village, Makati, Metro Manila (☎ (02) 810-3833, 815-4219)

Singapore – 370 Orchard Rd (☎ 235-4175, 737-2158/3372)

Sweden – 5th floor, Sandhamnsgatan 36, Stockholm (☎ (08) 667-2160/8090)

Switzerland – 3rd floor, Eigerstrasse 60, 3007 Bern (☎ (031) 372-2281/2)

UK – 29-30 Queen's Gate, London SW7 5JB (☎ (0171) 589-0173/2944)

USA – 1024 Wisconsin Ave NW, Washington, DC 20007 (☎ (202) 944-3600)

Vietnam – 63-5 Hoang Dieu St, Hanoi (☎ (04) 235-092/94)

Foreign Embassies in Thailand

Bangkok is a good place to collect visas for onward travel, and most countries have diplomatic representation in Bangkok. The visa sections of most embassies and consulates are open from around 8.30 to 11.30 am, Monday to Friday only (but call first to be sure).

Countries with diplomatic representation in Bangkok include:

Australia – 37 Sathon Tai Rd (☎ (2) 287-2680)

Bangladesh – 727 Soi 55, Sukhumvit Rd (☎ (2) 391-8069)

Canada – 11/12th floor, Boonmitr Bldg, 138 Silom Rd (☎ (2) 238-4452)

China – 57 Ratchadaphisek Rd (☎ (2) 245-7032)

France – 35 Customs House Lane, Charoen Krung Rd (☎ (2) 234-0950/6); consular section (visas): 29 Sathon Tai Rd (☎ (2) 213-2181/4)

Germany – 9 Sathon Tai Rd (☎ (2) 213-2331/6)

India – 46 Soi Prasanmit (Soi 23), Sukhumvit Rd (☎ (2) 258-0300/6)

Indonesia – 600-2 Phetburi Rd (☎ (2) 252-3135/40)

Ireland – 205 United Flour Mill Bldg, Ratchawong Rd (☎ (2) 223-0876)

Israel – 31 Soi Lang Suan, Ploenchit Rd (☎ (2) 252-3131/4)

Italy – 399 Nang Linchi Rd (☎ (2) 2872054/6)

Japan – 1674 New Phetburi Rd (☎ (2) 252-6151/ 9); consular sections (visas): 9th floor, Soemmit Tower, Soi 21, Sukhumvit Rd (☎ 259-0444)

Korea (South) – 23 Thiam-Ruammit Rd, Huay Khwang, Sam Saen Nok (☎ (2) 247-7535)

Laos – 520/1-3 Soi Ramkhamhang 39, Bangkapi (☎ (2) 538-3696)

Malaysia – 35 Sathon Tai Rd (☎ (2) 286-1390/2)

Myanmar (Burma) – 132 Sathon Neua Rd (☎ (2) 233-2237, 234-4698)

Nepal – 189 Soi Phuengsuk (Soi 71), Sukhumvit Rd (☎ (2) 391-7240)

New Zealand – 93 Withayu Rd (☎ (2) 251-8165)

Pakistan – 31 Soi Nana Neua (Soi 3), Sukhumvit Rd (☎ (2) 253-0288/9)

Philippines – 760 Sukhumvit Rd (☎ (2) 259-0139)

Singapore – 129 Sathon Tai Rd (☎ (2) 286-2111/ 1434)

Sri Lanka – 89/3 Soi 15, Sukhumvit Rd (☎ (2) 251-2788/9)

Taiwan – 10th floor, Taipei Economic & Trade Office, Kian Gwan Bldg, 140 Withayu Rd (☎ (2) 251-9393)

UK – 1031 Ploenchit Rd (☎ (2) 253-0191/9)

USA – 95 Withayu Rd (☎ (2) 252-5040/9)

Vietnam – 83/1 Withayu Rd (☎ (2) 251-5835/8)

CUSTOMS

Like most countries, Thailand prohibits the import of illegal drugs, firearms and ammunition (unless registered in advance with the police), and pornographic media. A reasonable amount of clothing for personal use, toiletries and professional instruments are allowed in duty free, as are one still or one movie/video camera with five rolls of still film or three rolls of movie film or videotape. Up to 200 cigarettes can be brought into the country without paying duty, or for other smoking materials a total of up to 250g. One litre of wine or spirits is allowed in duty free.

Electronic goods like stereos, calculators

and computers can be a problem if the Customs officials have reason to believe you're bringing them in for resale. As long as you don't carry more than one of each, you should be OK. Occasionally, Customs will require you to leave a hefty deposit for big-ticket items (eg a lap-top computer or midi-component stereo) which is refunded when you leave the country with the item in question. If you make the mistake of saying you're just passing through and don't plan to use the item in Thailand, they may ask you to leave it with Customs until you leave the country.

For information on currency import or export, see Exchange Control in the Money section.

Antiques & Art

Upon leaving Thailand, you must obtain an export licence for any antiques or objects of art you want to take with you. An antique is any 'archaic movable property, whether produced by man or by nature, any part of ancient structure, human skeleton or animal carcass, which by its age or characteristic of production or historical evidence is useful in the field of art, history or archaeology'. An art object is a 'thing produced by craftsmanship and appreciated as being valuable in the field of art'. Obviously these are very sweeping definitions, so if in doubt go to the Fine Arts Department for inspection and licensing.

Applications can be made by submitting two front-view photos of the object(s) (no more than five objects to a photo) and a photocopy of your passport, along with the object(s) in question, to one of three locations: the Bangkok National Museum, the Chiang Mai National Museum or the Songkhla National Museum. Allow three to five days for the process to be completed.

Thailand has special regulations for taking a Buddha or other deity image (or any part thereof) out of the country. These require not only a licence from the Fine Arts Department but a permit from the Ministry of Commerce as well. The one exception to this are the small Buddha images (*phrá phim* or *phrá*

khreûang) that are meant to be worn on a chain around the neck; these may be exported without a licence as long as the reported purpose is religious.

Temporary Vehicle Importation

A passenger vehicle (car, van, truck or motorcycle) can be brought into Thailand for tourist purposes for up to six months. Documents needed are a valid international driving permit, passport vehicle registration papers (in the case of a borrowed or hired vehicle, authorisation from the owner) and a cash or bank guarantee equal to the value of the vehicle plus 20%. (For entry through Khlong Toey port or Bangkok international airport, this means a letter of bank credit; for overland crossings via Malaysia a 'self-guarantee' filled in at the border is sufficient.)

Home Country Customs

Be sure to check the import regulations in your home country before bringing in or sending back a large quantity of (or high value) Thai goods. The limit varies from country to country; the USA, for example, allows US$400 worth of foreign-purchased goods to enter without duty (with no limit on handicrafts and unset gems), while in Australia the total value is limited to A$400.

MONEY
Costs

For most visitors the major expense of a Thai beach holiday is getting there. Comfortable beach or island accommodation is inexpensive by international standards, and a full day's worth of world-class Thai cuisine usually costs less than a standard lunch back home.

Outside major beach resorts, budget-squeezers should be able to get by on 200B per day. This estimate includes basic guesthouse accommodation, food, nonalcoholic beverages and local transport, but not film, souvenirs, tours, long-distance transport or vehicle hire. Add another 50 to 75B per day for every large beer you drink (25 to 35B for small bottles)!

Expenses vary from place to place; where

The Baht

As we went to press, economic conditions in Thailand forced a devaluation of the baht such that it was trading at about 30B per US$1. So far this devaluation is not enough to cause a rapid increase in prices, and we don't expect dramatic price changes for anything quoted in this book. If the baht's value were to drop further, however, prices may increase to keep up with foreign exchange rates. ■

there are high concentrations of budget travellers (Ko Pha-Ngan, for example), accommodation tends to be cheaper and food more expensive.

For around 350 to 500B per day, life can be quite comfortable: cleaner and quieter accommodation is easier to find once you pass the 200B-a-night zone in room rates. Of course, a 50B guesthouse room with a mattress on the floor and responsive management is better than a poorly maintained 350B room with air-con that won't turn off and a noisy all-night card game next door.

In Bangkok, Phuket and Ko Samui there's almost no limit to the amount you *could* spend, but if you live frugally, avoid the tourist ghettos and make use of public transport, you can get by on only a little more than what you would spend in more remote areas. Where you stay on the resort beaches or in Bangkok is of primary concern, as accommodation can cost more than 300B per day when it includes air-con (in a twin room).

Those seeking international-class accommodation and food will spend at least 1500B a day for a room with all the modern amenities – International Direct Dialling (IDD) phone, 24 hour hot water, air-conditioning, carpeting, fitness centre and all-night room service. Such hotels are found only in major cities and resort areas.

Food, likewise, is more expensive in Bangkok and on resort beaches than elsewhere. Western food (especially beef) costs significantly more than Thai and Chinese food. Seafood – particularly shrimp and lobster – also increases the tab considerably. Still, when you consider that Thailand has possibly the best seafood cuisine in the world, it's often a bargain.

Carrying Money

Give some thought to how you're going to carry your money – whether it's travellers cheques, cash, credit and debit cards, or a combination of these. Many travellers favour hidden pouches that can be worn beneath clothing. Hip-pocket wallets are easy marks for thieves. Pickpockets work markets and crowded buses throughout the country, so keep your money concealed. See the Dangers & Annoyances section later in this chapter for more on petty crime.

It's a good idea not to keep all your money in one place; keep an 'emergency' stash well concealed in a piece of luggage separate from other money. Long-term travellers might even consider renting a safety deposit box at a local bank (see following Safety Deposit Boxes entry). Keep your onward tickets, a copy of your passport, a list of all credit card numbers and some money in the box just in case all your belongings are stolen while you're on the road. It's not likely, but it does happen.

Safety Deposit Boxes

Travellers can rent safety deposit boxes at Bangkok's Safety Deposit Centre, 3rd floor, Chan Issara Tower, 942/81 Rama IV Rd (near the Silom Rd intersection). It costs 150B a month plus 2000B for a refundable key deposit. The centre is open from 10 am to 7 pm Monday to Friday, and until 6 pm on weekends and public holidays. A few banks rent safety deposit boxes, but generally you need to open an account with them first.

ATMs & Credit/Debit Cards

An alternative to carrying around large amounts of cash or travellers cheques is to

Living Costs in Thailand

		Average daily cost per person	
	Low Budget	Medium Budget	High Budget
accommodation	60 to 100B	250 to 500B	600B up
food	75 to 100B	300B	1500B up
local transport	25B	75 to 100B	500B up
incidentals (admission fees, personal items)	40B	100B	200B up

open an account at a Thai bank and get an Automatic Teller Machine (ATM) card. Most major banks in Thailand now have ATMs in provincial capitals and in many smaller towns as well, open 24 hours. You can then withdraw cash at ATMs throughout Thailand, whether they belong to your bank or another Thai bank. ATM cards issued by Thai Farmers Bank or Bangkok Bank can be used with the ATMs of 14 major banks – there are at least 2500 machines nationwide. A 10B transaction charge is usually deducted for using another bank's ATM. Opening an account only costs around 150 to 200B and some banks, such as Thai Farmers, will give you an ATM card right away.

Plastic money is becoming increasingly popular in Thailand, and many shops, hotels and restaurants now accept credit and debit cards. The most commonly accepted cards are Visa and MasterCard, followed by Diner's Club and Japan Card Bureau (JCB). American Express (Amex) and Carte Blanche are of much more limited use.

Visa and MasterCard credit card holders can get cash advances of up to US$500 per day (in baht only) through some branches of the Thai Farmers Bank, Bangkok Bank and Siam Commercial Bank (and also at the night-time exchange windows in well-touristed spots like Banglamphu, Ko Samui, Phuket and so on). Amex card holders can also get advances, but only in travellers cheques. The Amex agent is SEA Tours (☎ (2) 216-5757), Suite 88-92, 8th floor, Payathai Plaza, 128 Phayathai Rd, Bangkok.

Debit cards (also known as cash cards or cheque cards) issued by a bank in your own country can also be used at several Thai banks to withdraw cash (in baht only) directly from your cheque or savings account back home, thus avoiding all commissions and finance charges. You can use MasterCard debit cards to buy baht at foreign exchange booths or desks at either Bangkok Bank or Siam Commercial Bank. Visa debit cards can buy cash though Thai Farmers Bank exchange services.

Debit cards can also be used at many Thai ATMs, though a surcharge of around US$1 is usually subtracted from your home account each time you complete a machine transaction. As a general rule, debit cards issued under the MasterCard name work best at Bangkok Bank ATMs, while Visa debit cards work best with Thai Farmers Bank machines. (It's still a good idea to bring along an emergency travellers cheque fund in case you lose your card.)

Card Problems Occasionally when you try to use a Visa or MasterCard at rural hotels or shops, the staff may say that only cards issued by Thai Farmers Bank or Siam Commercial Bank are accepted. With a little patience, you should be able to explain that Thai Farmers Bank or Siam Commercial Bank will pay them and that your bank will pay Thai Farmers Bank or Siam Commercial Bank – and that any Visa or MasterCard issued anywhere in the world is indeed acceptable.

It's against Thai law to pass on the 3% credit card surcharge to the customer, but almost all merchants do it anyway. Some even ask 4 or 5%! The only exception seems to be hotels (although even a few hotels will hit you with a credit card surcharge). If you don't agree to the surcharge they'll simply refuse to accept your card. Begging and pleading or pointing out the law doesn't seem to help. The best way to get around the illegal surcharge is to politely ask that the credit card receipt be itemised with cost of product or service and the surcharge listed separately. Then when you pay your bill, photocopy all receipts showing the surcharge and request a 'charge back' from your card issuer. Not all banks in all countries will offer such refunds – banks in the UK, for example, refuse to issue such refunds, while banks in the USA usually will.

To report a lost or stolen credit/debit card, call the following hotlines in Bangkok: Amex (☎ (2) 273-0022/44), Diners Club (☎ (2) 238-3660), MasterCard (☎ (2) 299-1990), Visa (☎ (2) 273-1199/7449). See Dangers & Annoyances in this chapter for important warnings on credit card theft and fraud.

International Transfers

If you have a reliable place to get mail in Thailand, one of the safest and cheapest ways to receive money from overseas is to have an international cashier cheque (or international money order) sent by courier. It usually takes no more than four days for courier mail to reach Thailand from anywhere in the world.

If you have a bank account in Thailand or your home bank has a branch in Bangkok, you can have money wired direct via a telegraphic transfer. This costs a bit more than having a cheque sent; telegraphic transfers take anywhere from two days to a week to arrive. International banks with branches in Bangkok include Hongkong Bank, Standard Chartered Bank, The Sakura Bank, Bank of America, Banque Indosuez, Citibank, Banque Nationale de Paris, Chase Manhattan Bank, Bank of Tokyo, Deutsche Bank, Merrill Lynch International Bank, Hongkong & Shanghai Bank and United Malayan Bank.

Currency

The basic unit of Thai currency is the baht. There are 100 satang in one baht; coins include 25 satang and 50 satang pieces, and baht in 1B, 5B and 10B coins.

Paper currency comes in denominations of 10B (brown), 20B (green), 50B (blue), 100B (red), 500B (purple) and 1000B (beige). A 10,000B bill is on the way. The 10B bills are being phased out in favour of the 10B coin and have become rather uncommon. Fortunately for newcomers to Thailand, numerals are printed in their western as well as Thai forms. Notes are also scaled in size; the larger the denomination, the larger the note. Large denominations – 500B and especially 1000B bills – can be hard to change in small towns, but banks will always change them.

Currency Exchange

Australia	A$1	=	25.53
Canada	C$1	=	25.37
France	FF1	=	5.7
Germany	DM1	=	19.27
Japan	¥100	=	28.9
Malaysia	M$1	=	11.86
New Zealand	NZ$1	=	22.27
Singapore	S$1	=	23.13
UK	UK£1	=	55.83
USA	US$1	=	35.1

Changing Money

There is no black-market money exchange for baht, so there's no reason to bring in any Thai currency. Banks or legal money-changers offer the best exchange rate within the country.

Exchange rates are listed in the *Bangkok Post* and *The Nation* every day. For buying baht, US dollars are the most readily accepted currency and travellers cheques get better rates than cash. Since banks charge 10B commission and duty for each travellers cheque cashed, you will save on commissions if you use larger cheque denominations (eg a US$50 cheque will only cost 10B, while five US$10 cheques will cost 50B).

Exchange Control

Legally, any traveller arriving in Thailand must have at least the following amounts of money in cash, travellers cheques, bank draft or letter of credit, based on visa category: non-immigrant visa, US$500 per person or US$1000 per family; tourist visa, US$250 per person or US$500 per family; and transit visa or no visa, US$125 per person or US$250 per family. This may be checked if you arrive on a one way ticket or if you look as if you're at 'the end of the road'.

According to 1991 regulations, there are no limits on the amount of Thai or foreign currency you may bring into the country. Upon leaving Thailand, you're permitted to take no more than 50,000B per person without special authorisation; exportation of foreign currencies is unrestricted.

It's legal to open a foreign currency account at any commercial bank in Thailand. As long as the funds originate from abroad, there are no restrictions on their maintenance or withdrawal.

Bargaining & Tipping

Good bargaining, which takes practice, is another way to cut costs. Anything bought in a market should be bargained for; prices in department stores and most non-tourist shops are fixed. Sometimes accommodation rates can be bargained down. Bargain hard in heavily touristed areas as the one week, all-air-con type of visitor often pays whatever's asked, creating an artificial price zone between the local and tourist market that the budgeteer must deal with.

On the other hand, the Thais aren't *always* trying to rip you off, so use some discretion when going for the bone on a price. Draw the line between bargaining and niggling – getting hot under the collar over 5B makes both seller and buyer lose face, and wastes everyone's time. Some more specific suggestions concerning costs can be found in the Accommodation and Things to Buy sections later in this chapter.

The cost of transport between cities and within them is very reasonable; again, bargaining (when hiring a vehicle) can save you a lot of baht. See the Getting Around chapter.

Tipping is not normal practice in Thailand, although they're getting used to it in expensive hotels and restaurants. Elsewhere don't bother. In taxis where you have to bargain the fare, it certainly isn't necessary.

Consumer Taxes

The Thai government collects a 7% Value-Added Tax (VAT) for certain goods and services. This doesn't mean that consumers are to be charged 7% over retail – the tax is supposed to be applied to a retailer's cost for the product. For example, if a merchant's wholesale price is 100B for an item that retails at 200B, the maximum adjusted retail price, including VAT, should be 207B, not 214B. In practice, the tax is supposed to have caused a net decrease in prices for most goods and services as the VAT replaced a pre-1992 graduated business tax that averaged 9%. But this doesn't always stop Thai merchants from trying to add 'VAT' surcharges to their sales. Like the credit card surcharge, a direct VAT surcharge is illegal and should be reported to the TAT tourist police.

Tourist hotels add a 7 to 11% hotel tax, and sometimes an 8 to 10% service charge as well, to your room bill.

POST & COMMUNICATIONS

Thailand has an efficient postal service and within the country postage is very cheap.

Bangkok's GPO on Charoen Krung (New) Rd is open from 8 am to 8 pm Monday to Friday, and until 1 pm weekends and holidays. A 24 hour international telecommunications service (including telephone, fax, telex and telegram) is in a separate building behind and to the right of the main GPO building.

Outside Bangkok the typical provincial GPO is open from 8.30 am to 4.30 pm Monday to Friday, and from 9 am to noon Saturday. Larger GPOs in provincial capitals may also be open for a half day on Sunday.

Parcel Postage Rates

Destination		1kg	5kg	10kg	20kg
Australia	surface	270B	430B	610B	1000B
	air	400B	1400B	2650B	5150B
Canada	surface	220B	380B	560B	920B
	air	450B	1570B	2970B	3770B
France	surface	330B	550B	770B	1210B
	air	500B	1500B	2750B	5250B
Germany	surface	330B	550B	770B	1210B
	air	500B	1500B	2750B	5250B
Japan	surface	370B	530B	690B	1010B
	air	400B	920B	1550B	2870B
New Zealand	surface	330B	550B	770B	1210B
	air	500B	1500B	2750B	5250B
UK	surface	330B	550B	770B	1210B
	air	500B	1500B	2750B	5250B
USA	surface	180B	550B	1080B	2080B
	air	500B	1500B	2750B	5250B

Postal Rates

Air mail letters weighing 10g or less cost 13B to Europe, Australia and New Zealand, and 16B to the Americas. Aerograms cost 10B regardless of the destination, while postcards are 9B.

Letters sent by registered mail cost 20B in addition to regular air mail postage. International Express Mail (EMS) fees vary according to country of destination. Sample rates for items weighing 100 to 250g are: Australia, Germany and the UK 215B; France, Canada and the USA 235B; and Japan 250B. Within Thailand, this service costs only 20B (100 to 250g) in addition to regular postage.

The rates for parcels shipped by post vary according to weight (rising in 1kg increments), country of destination and whether they're shipped by surface (up to two months) or air (one to two weeks). See the Parcel Postage Rates table above for sample prices.

Most provincial post offices sell do-it-yourself packing boxes (11 sizes!) costing 5 to 35B; tape and string are provided free. Some offices even have packing services, which cost 4 to 10B per parcel depending on size. Private packing services may also be available near large provincial post offices.

You can insure a package's contents – it costs 8.50B for each 1740B of the goods' value.

Receiving Mail

Thailand's poste restante service is reliable, though during high tourist months (December to February, July, August) you may have to wait in line at post offices in Bangkok and on Ko Samui. There is a fee of 1B for every piece of mail collected, 2B for each parcel. As with many Asian countries, confusion at poste restante offices is most likely to arise over given names and surnames. Ask people writing to you to print your surname clearly and to underline it. If you're certain a letter should be waiting for you and it cannot be found, it's always wise to check if it has been filed under your given name. You can collect poste restante at almost any post office in Thailand.

The Amex office (☎ (2) 216-5757), Suite 88-92, 8th floor, Payathai Plaza, 128 Phayathai Rd, Bangkok, also takes mail on behalf of Amex card holders. The hours are from 8.30 am to noon and 1 to 4.30 pm Monday to Friday, and until 11.30 am Saturday. Amex won't accept courier packets that require your signature. The mail window staff have had a well-deserved reputation for rude service – one employee has been known to shut the window on patrons' fingers!

Couriers

Several companies in Thailand offer courier

services. The main ones, headquartered in Bangkok, include:

DHL Worldwide – 22nd floor, Grand Amarin Tower, New Phetburi Rd (☎ (2) 207-0600)
Federal Express – 8th floor, Green Tower, Rama IV Rd (☎ (2) 367-3222)
TNT Express – 599 Chong Non Sii Rd, Khlong Toey (☎ (2) 249-0242)

Two international courier services also have offices in Phuket:

DHL Worldwide – 145 Phang-Nga Rd (☎ (76) 219-005)
UPS – Phuket Business Service, 9/44 Chao Fa Rd (☎ (76) 218-719)

Telephone

The telephone system in Thailand, operated by the government-subsidised Telephone Organization of Thailand (TOT) under the Communications Authority of Thailand (CAT), is quite efficient and from Bangkok you can usually direct dial most major centres with little difficulty.

The country code for Thailand is ☎ 66. See the Thai Area Codes table below for listings of domestic area codes.

Telephone Office Hours GPO phone centres in most provincial capitals are open daily from 7 am to 11 pm; smaller provincial phone offices may be open from 8 am to 8 or 10 pm. Bangkok's international CAT phone

office at the Charoen Krung Rd GPO is open 24 hours.

Pay Phones In most places there are two kinds of public pay phones, 'red' and 'blue'. The red phones are for local city calls and the blue are for long-distance calls (within Thailand). Local calls from pay phones cost 1B. Although there are three different 1B coins in circulation, only the middle-sized coin fits the slots. Some hotels and guesthouses have private pay phones that cost 5B per call; these take only nine-sided 5B coins.

Card phones are available at most Thai airports as well as major shopping centres and other public areas. Telephone cards come in 25B, 50B, 100B, 200B and 240B denominations, all roughly the same size as a credit card. They can be purchased at any TOT office or at the information counter or at a gift shop in airports.

Directory Assistance If you're trying to find a phone number within Thailand, you can try ringing English-language directory assistance: ☎ 13 for the Bangkok area and ☎ 183 for provincial locations. The operators aren't always exactly fluent, so be patient and speak clearly.

International Calls To direct dial an international number (except those in Malaysia and Laos, see later this section) from a

---

Thai Area Codes

The area codes for coastal Thailand's major cities are presented below. See the relevant destination chapters for the area codes of smaller towns not listed here. Note that zeros aren't needed in area codes, whether dialling domestically or from overseas. To dial a long-distance, domestic phone number (eg to call the THAI office in Bangkok from Surat Thani) dial ☎ (2)+ 513-0121.

2	Bangkok, Thonburi, Nonthaburi, Pathum Thani, Samut Prakan
32	Phetburi, Cha-am, Prachuap Khiri Khan, Pranburi, Ratchaburi
38	Chachoengsao, Chonburi, Pattaya, Rayong, Si Racha
39	Chanthaburi, Trat
73	Narathiwat, Sungai Kolok, Pattani, Yala
74	Hat Yai, Phattalung, Satun, Songkhla
75	Krabi, Nakhon Si Thammarat, Trang
76	Phang-Nga, Phuket
77	Chumphon, Ranong, Surat Thani, Chaiya, Ko Samui

private phone, simply dial ☎ 001 before the number. For operator-assisted international calls, dial ☎ 100.

A service called Home Direct is available at Bangkok's GPO (Charoen Krung Rd), at airports in Bangkok, Phuket, Hat Yai and Surat Thani, and at post office CAT centres in Bangkok, Hat Yai, Phuket, Surat Thani, Pattaya and Hua Hin. Home Direct phones offer easy one button connection with international operators in 20-odd countries around the world. You can also direct dial Home Direct access numbers from any private phone (most hotel phones won't work) in Thailand.

For Home Direct service, dial ☎ 001-999 followed by:

Australia	61-1000
Canada	15-1000
Denmark	45-1000
Germany	49-1000
Hawaii	14414
Hong Kong	852-1086
Indonesia	62-1000
Italy	39-1000
Japan	81-0051
Korea	82-1000
Netherlands	31-1035
New Zealand	64-1066
Norway	47-1000
Philippines	63-1000
Singapore	351-1000
Taiwan	886-1000
UK	44-1066
USA	(AT&T) 1111
USA	(MCI) 12001
USA	(Sprint) 13877

Hotels generally add surcharges (sometimes as much as 30% more than the TOT rate) for international calls; it's always cheaper to call abroad from a CAT telephone office. These offices are almost always attached to a city's GPO, often on the building's 2nd floor, around the side or just behind the GPO. There may also be a separate TOT office down the road, used only for residential or business service (eg billing or installation), not public calls. Even when public phone services are offered, TOT offices accept only cash payments – reverse-charge and credit

card calls aren't permitted. Hence the CAT office is generally your best choice.

To make an international call *(thorásàp ráwàang pràthêt)* you must fill out a bilingual form with your name and details of the call's destination. Except for reverse-charge calls *(kèp plai-thaang)*, you must estimate in advance the time you'll be on the phone and pay a deposit equal to the time/distance rate. There is always a minimum three minute charge, refunded if your call doesn't go through.

Usually, only cash or international phone credit cards are acceptable for payment at CAT offices; some provincial CAT offices also accept Amex and a few take Visa/MasterCard.

If the call doesn't go through you must pay a 30B service charge anyway – except for reverse-charge calls, for which you pay the 30B charge only if the call goes through. Depending on where you're calling, reimbursing someone later for a reverse-charge call to your home country may be less expensive than paying CAT/TOT rates – it pays to compare at source and destination. For calls between the USA and Thailand, for example, AT&T collect rates are less than TOT's direct rates.

Private long-distance telephone offices operate in most towns, but sometimes these are only for calls within Thailand. Often they're just a desk or a couple of booths in the rear of a shop. These private offices typically collect a 10B surcharge for long-distance domestic calls, 50B for international calls. The vast majority accept only cash.

Whichever type of phone service you use, the least expensive time of day to make calls is from 10 pm to 7 am (66% discount), followed by 6 to 10 pm (50% discount). You pay full price from 7 am to 6 pm.

Malaysia & Laos CAT does not offer long-distance service to Malaysia or Laos. To call these countries you must go through TOT. For Vientiane, dial ☎ 101 to arrange a TOT operator-assisted call. Malaysia can be dialled direct by prefixing the Malaysian number (including area code) with the code ☎ 09.

Fax, Telex & Telegraph

GPO telephone offices throughout the country offer fax, telegraph and telex services. There's no need to bring your own paper, as the post offices supply their own forms. A few TOT offices also offer fax services. International faxes typically cost a steep 100 to 140B for the first page, and 65 to 110B per page for the remaining pages, depending on size of the paper and destination.

Larger hotels with business centres offer the same services but always at higher rates.

BOOKS

Most books are published in different editions by different publishers in different countries. As a result, a book might be a hardcover rarity in one country while it's readily available in paperback in another. Fortunately, bookshops and libraries search by title or author, so your local bookshop or library is best placed to advise you on the availability of the following recommendations.

Lonely Planet

Lonely Planet publishes several other books to Thailand: the *Thailand* guidebook, *Bangkok city guide*, *Thailand travel atlas*, *Thai phrasebook* and *Thai Hill Tribes phrasebook*. For diving books, see Diving & Snorkelling in the Highlights & Activities of Coastal Thailand section earlier in this chapter.

Description & Travel

The earliest western literature of note on Thailand, Guy Tachard's *A Relation of the Voyage to Siam*, recounts a 1680s French expedition through parts of the country with little literary flair. Shortly thereafter, Simon de la Loubére's 1693 *New Historical Relation of the Kingdom of Siam* chronicled the French mission to the Ayuthaya court in great detail. Maurice Collis novelised this period with a focus on the unusual political relationship between King Narai and his Greek minister, Constantin Phaulkon, in *Siamese White*.

Joseph Conrad evoked Thailand in several of his pre-WWII novels and short stories, most notably in his 1920s *The Secret Sharer* and *Falk: A Reminiscence*.

Pico Iyer, Robert Anson Hall and several other well known and not-so-well known authors have contributed travel essays of varying style to *Travelers' Tales Thailand* (edited by James O'Reilly & Larry Habegger, 1994). It was the first title in a relatively new series that assembles travel articles and chapters from various sources into a single anthology devoted to a particular country. Savvy travel tips are sprinkled through the text.

A more serious collection of literature is available in *Traveller's Literary Companion: South-East Asia*, edited by Alastair Dingwall. The Thailand chapter, edited by scholar Thomas John Hudak, is packed with hard-to-find information on the history of literature in Thailand and includes extracts from various works by Thai as well as foreign authors.

Temple buffs will find plenty to chew on in *Guide to Thailand* by Achille Clarac, edited and translated by Michael Smithies. Studded with descriptions of obscure temple ruins, Clarac's guide originally appeared in English in 1971 as *Discovering Thailand*; it hasn't been updated since 1977 but was a pioneering work in its day.

People, Culture & Society

Culture Shock! Thailand by Robert & Nanthapa Cooper is an interesting book about adapting to the Thai way of life, although it's heavily oriented toward Bangkok life. *Letters from Thailand* by Botan (translated by Susan Fulop Kepner) and Carol Hollinger's *Mai Pen Rai Means Never Mind* can also be recommended for their insights into traditional Thai culture. *Bangkok Post* reporter Denis Segaller's *Thai Ways* and *More Thai Ways* present further expat insights into Thai culture.

Behind the Smile: Voices of Thailand (1990) by Sanitsuda Ekachai is a very enlightening collection of interviews with Thai peasants from all over the country. *In the Mirror* (1985) is an excellent collection of translated modern Thai short stories from the 1960s and 70s. The Siam Society's *Culture & Environment in Thailand* is a collection of scholarly papers by Thai and foreign authors delivered at a 1988 symposium which examined the relationship between Thai culture and the natural world; topics range from the oceanic origins of the Thai race and nature motifs in Thai art to evolving Thai attitudes toward the environment.

Siam in Crisis by Sulak Sivaraksa, one of Thailand's leading intellectuals, analyses modern Thai politics from his unique Buddhist-nationalist perspective. Sivaraksa has written several other worthwhile titles on Thai culture which have been translated into English. Essays by this contrary and contradictory character posit an ideal that neither Thailand nor any other country will likely ever achieve, and his attempts to use western-style academic argument to discredit western thinking can be exasperating and inspiring.

The Lioness in Bloom, translated by Susan Fulop Kepner, is an eye-opening collection of 11 short stories written by or about Thai women.

For books on Buddhism and Buddhism in Thailand, see the Religion section of the Facts about the Country chapter.

History & Politics

George Coedes' classic prewar work on South-East Asian history, *The Indianised States of South-East Asia*, contains groundbreaking historical material on early Thai history, as does WAR Wood's *A History of Siam*, published in the same era. One of the more readable general histories written in the latter half of the 20th century is David Wyatt's *Thailand: A Short History* (Trasvin Publications, Chiang Mai).

Concentrating on post-revolutionary Thailand, *The Balancing Act: A History of Modern Thailand* (Asia Books, 1991), by Joseph Wright Jr, starts with the 1932 revolution and ends with the February 1991 Coup. Wright's semi-academic chronicle concludes that Thai history demonstrates a continuous circulation of elites governed by

certain 'natural laws' and that, despite the 1932 revolution, democracy has never gained a firm foothold in Thai society.

Although it's fiction, ex-prime minister Kukrit Pramoj's 1961 *Red Bamboo* vividly portrays and predicts the conflict between the Thai Communist movement and the establishment during the 1960s and 70s. His book *Si Phaendin: Four Reigns* (1981), the most widely read novel ever published in Thailand, covers the Ayuthaya era. Both novels are available in English-language versions.

Natural History

Complete with sketches, photos and maps, *The Mammals of Thailand* (Association for the Conservation of Wildlife, 1988), by Boonsong Lekagul & Jeffrey McNeely, remains the classic on Thai wildlife in spite of a few out-of-date references (it was first published in 1977). Birdlovers should seek out the *Bird Guide of Thailand* (Association for the Conservation of Wildlife, 1972) by Boonsong Lekagul & EW Cronin for comprehensive descriptions of Thailand's avian species.

Detailed summaries of 77 of Thailand's national parks, along with an objective assessment of current park conditions, are available in *National Parks of Thailand* (Communication Resources, Bangkok, 1994) by Gray, Piprell & Graham.

Bookshops

Bangkok probably has the largest selection of English-language books and bookshops in South-East Asia. The principal chains are Asia Books (headquarters on Sukhumvit Rd near Soi 15) and DK Book House (Siam Square); each has branch shops in half a dozen street locations around Bangkok as well as in Hat Yai and Phuket. See the Bookshop entries under the relevant cities for further details.

Asia and DK offer a wide variety of fiction and periodicals as well as books on Asia. Some of Thailand's larger tourist hotels also have bookshops with English-language books and periodicals.

ONLINE SERVICES

A growing number of online service providers offer information on Thailand. Many of these World Wide Web (WWW) sites are commercial sites established by tour operators or hotels; the ratio of commercial to noncommercial sites is liable to increase over time if current Internet trends continue. Remember that all Universal Resource Locators (URL's) mentioned below are subject to change without notice.

The TAT has its own WWW site at (www.tat.or.th); like many Web sites these days, it contains only basic info crowded with lots of ad-style propaganda. Another Web site sourced from Thailand is one carried by Siam Net (www.siam.net). Pages include general information, a list of tour operators in Thailand, a limited hotel directory and a golf directory.

Lonely Planet's own Web site (www.lonelyplanet.com) contains Thailand updates from travellers, occasional author updates and other salient info; there's a direct link to Thailand-related material also (www.lonelyplanet.com.au/dest/sea/thai.htm). Indochina.net (www.icn.net/icn/) links to many Thailand-related Web pages. Mahidol University in Bangkok maintains a very useful site (mahidol.ac.th/Thailand/Thailand-main.html) that's searchable by keyword.

Online in Thailand

If you're bringing a computer and modem to Thailand with hopes of staying on the info highway's fast lane, keep in mind that online options are still quite limited and that baud rates are very slow – generally 9600 or less (2400 was the overall practical norm as of mid-1996). Higher baud rates are bottlenecked by low bandwidth and can be very unreliable. This will change rapidly with time, and as more global providers are allowed into the market. One big bureaucratic impasse stands in the way: the Communication Authority of Thailand (CAT), which classifies digital telecommunications as a 'premium' service requiring a surcharge. In early 1997 CAT announced it would start lowering access charges for both domestic and international data circuits, but even if the reductions go through, logging on will still be relatively expensive.

AOL, CompuServe and IBM Global are among the international providers that thus far have Bangkok nodes. AT&T and MCI have promised to catch up.

For the moment all dial-ups go through Bangkok, which means you must add long-distance charges to your online costs if you plug in outside the capital. A nonprofit group in Phuket is petitioning the government to establish a local Internet Service Provider (ISP), efforts which will probably bear fruit very soon. For the latest news on a possible ISP in Phuket, email Phuket Computer Services at @phuket.com (despite the name, this domain works off a Bangkok number at the moment).

RJ11 phone jacks are becoming the standard in new hotels, but in older hotels and guesthouses the phones may still be hardwired. A pocketknife and pair of alligator clips are useful for stripping and attaching wires, or bring along an acoustic coupler.

NEWSPAPERS

Thailand's 1991 constitution guarantees freedom of the press, though the National Police Department reserves the power to suspend publishing licences for national security reasons. Editors nevertheless exercise self-censorship in certain realms, particularly with regard to the monarchy. But overall, Thailand is widely considered to have the freest print media in South-East Asia.

Two English-language newspapers are published daily in Thailand and distributed in most provincial capitals throughout the country – the *Bangkok Post* in the morning and *The Nation* in the afternoon. *The Nation* is almost entirely staffed by Thais and presents, obviously, a Thai perspective, while the *Post*, which was Thailand's first English daily (established 1946), has a mixed Thai and international staff and represents a more international view. *The Nation*, on the other hand, has better and more objective regional coverage – particularly with regard to Myanmar and former Indochina, and the paper is to be commended for taking a harder anti-NPKC stance during the 1991 coup.

The Singapore edition of the *International Herald Tribune* is widely available in Bangkok, Pattaya and Phuket.

The most popular Thai-language newspapers are *Thai Rath* and *Daily News*, but they're mostly full of blood-and-guts stories. The best Thai journalism is found in the somewhat less popular *Matichon* and *Siam Rath* dailies. The *Bangkok Post* also publishes a Thai-language version of the popular English daily.

MAGAZINES

English-language magazine publishing in Thailand continues to grow, although the lifespan of individual titles tends to be short. Though mostly devoted to domestic and regional business, the English-language *Manager* occasionally prints very astute, very up-to-date cultural pieces. *Bangkok Metro*, a slick lifestyle magazine introduced in 1995, brings a new sophistication to Bangkok publications concerned with art, culture and music. *Samui* and *Phuket* are among several tourist-oriented magazines published by expat photographer John Everingham's ArtAsia Press.

Many popular magazines from the UK, USA, Australia and Europe – particularly those concerned with computer technology, autos, fashion, music and business – are available in bookstores which specialise in English-language publications (see Bookshops under Books earlier in this chapter).

RADIO

Thailand has more than 400 radio stations, with 41 FM and 35 AM stations in Bangkok alone. Of these, two have English-language programming. FMX, at 95.5 FM, offers pop music and news on the half hour. Bangkok's national public radio station, Radio Thailand (Sathãanii Wítháyú Hàeng Pràthêt Thai), also uses 95.5 FM to air government-slanted English-language news broadcasts at 7 am, and 12.30, 7 and 8 pm.

The other English-language alternative is Smooth 105 FM, an easy listening station. If you're in search of classical music, tune in to Digital Classic FM 95, which broadcasts 24 hours a day. For the latest from the Thai pop music scene try 88 FM, Radio 'No Problem', or 98 FM.

TV

Thailand has five TV networks based in Bangkok, each owned by a government ministry. Programming, however, is often contracted out to private firms. Channel 7 draws the largest viewership, mainly due to its slew of popular soap operas. Channel 9, run by the military, is not surprisingly one of the more conservative of the lot, and Channel 11 runs mainly educational programs.

Satellite & Cable TV

As elsewhere in Asia, satellite and cable TV services are swiftly multiplying in Thailand, and competition for the largely untapped market is keen – especially since satellite telecasts can be received anywhere in Thailand, not just in Bangkok. Of the many regional satellite operations aimed at Thailand, the most successful so far is Satellite Television Asian Region (STAR), beamed from Hong Kong via AsiaSat 1 & 2. STAR offers five 24 hour channels, covering music, sports, movies and news plus other subscription-based channels.

Thailand has launched its own ThaiCom 1 & 2 as an uplink for AsiaSat and as carriers for the standard Thai networks, as well as for International Broadcasting Corporation (IBC; focussing on news and entertainment), Vietnam Television and Thai Sky.

Turner Broadcasting (CNN International), ESPN, HBO, and various telecasts from Indonesia, Malaysia, the Philippines, Brunei and Australia are available in Thailand via Indonesia's Palapa C1 satellite.

VIDEO SYSTEMS

The predominant video format in Thailand is PAL, a system compatible with that used in most of Europe (France's SECAM format is a notable exception) as well as in Australia.

This means if you're bringing videotapes from the USA or Japan, which use the NTSC format, you'll have to bring your own VCR to play them! Some video shops (especially those which carry pirated or unlicensed tapes) sell NTSC as well as PAL and SECAM tapes. A 'multi-system' VCR has the capacity to play both NTSC and PAL, but not SECAM.

PHOTOGRAPHY & VIDEO
Photography
Print film is fairly inexpensive and widely available in Thailand. Japanese print film costs 65 to 70B per 36 exposures, US print film 75 to 90B. Fujichrome Velvia and Provia slide films costs around 160B per roll, Kodak Ektachrome Elite is 140B and Ektachrome 200 about 200B. Slide film, especially Kodachrome, can be hard to find outside Bangkok, Pattaya and Phuket, so stock up before heading out. Film processing is generally quite good in the larger cities in Thailand and also quite inexpensive. Dependable E6 processing is available at several labs in Bangkok and Phuket.

Pack some silica gel with your camera to prevent mould growing on the inside of your lenses. A polarising filter could be useful to cut down on tropical glare at certain times of day, particularly around water, wide expanses of sand or highly polished glazed-tile work.

Outdoor photography is best between sunrise and 10 am or from 4 pm to sunset, when sunlight illuminates subjects from the side rather than overhead. If you're using natural light, the best time for undersea photography is 10 am to 2 pm, when the sun is directly overhead; at other times of day flash gear is usually necessary.

Video
Properly used, a video camera can give a fascinating record of your holiday. As well as videoing the obvious things – sunsets, spectacular views – remember to record some of the ordinary everyday details of life in the country. Often the most interesting things occur when you're actually intent on filming something else. Remember too that, unlike still photography, video 'flows' – so, for example, you can shoot scenes of countryside rolling past the train window to give an overall impression that isn't possible with ordinary photos.

Video cameras these days have amazingly sensitive microphones, and you might be surprised how much sound will be picked up. This can also be a problem if there is a lot of ambient noise – filming by the side of a busy road might seem OK when you do it, but viewing it back home might simply give you a deafening cacophony of traffic noise. One good rule to follow for beginners is to try to film in long takes, and don't move the camera around too much. Otherwise, your video could well make your viewers seasick! If your camera has a stabiliser, you can use it to obtain good footage while travelling on various means of transport, even on bumpy roads. And remember, you're on holiday – don't let the video take over your life, and turn your trip into a Cecil B de Mille production.

Make sure you keep the batteries charged, and have the necessary charger, plugs and transformer for the country you are visiting. In most countries, it is possible to obtain video cartridges easily in large towns and cities, but make sure you buy the correct format. It is usually worth buying at least a few cartridges duty free to start off your trip.

Finally, remember to follow the same rules regarding people's sensitivities as for still photography – having a video camera shoved in their face is probably even more annoying and offensive for locals than a still camera. Always ask permission first.

Airport Security
The X-ray baggage inspection machines at Thailand's airports are all deemed film safe. Nevertheless, if you're travelling with high-speed film (ISO 400 or above), you may want to have your film hand-inspected rather than X-rayed. Security inspectors are usually happy to comply. Packing your film in see-through plastic bags generally speeds up the hand inspection process. Some photographers pack their film in lead-lined bags to ward off potentially harmful rays.

TIME

Time Zone

Thailand's time zone is seven hours ahead of GMT/UTC (London). Thus, noon in Bangkok is 10 pm the previous day in Los Angeles, 1 am in New York, 5 am in London, 6 am in Paris, 1 pm in Perth and 3 pm in Sydney.

Thai Calendar

The official year in Thailand is reckoned from 543 BC, the beginning of the Buddhist Era, so 1997 AD is 2540 BE.

ELECTRICITY

Electric current is 220V, 50 cycles. Electrical wall outlets are usually of the round, two pole type; some outlets also accept flat, two bladed terminals, and some will accept either flat or round terminals. Any electrical supply shop will carry adapters for any international plug shape as well as voltage converters.

WEIGHTS & MEASURES

Dimensions and weight are usually expressed using the metric system in Thailand. The exception is land measure, which is often quoted using the traditional Thai system of *waa*, *ngaan* and *râi*. Old-timers in the provinces will occasionally use the traditional Thai system of weights and measures in speech, as will boat-builders, carpenters and other craftspeople when talking about their work. Here are some conversions to use for such occasions:

1 sq *waa*	=	4 sq m
1 *ngaan* (100 sq waa)	=	400 sq m
1 *râi* (4 ngaan)	=	1600 sq m
1 *bàht*	=	15g
1 *taleung* or *tamleung* (4 bàht)	=	60g
1 *châng* (20 taleung)	=	1.2kg
1 *hàap* (50 châng)	=	60kg
1 *níu*	=	about 2cm (or 1 inch)
1 *khêup* (12 níu)	=	25cm
1 *sàwk* (2 khêup)	=	50cm
1 *waa* (4 sàwk)	=	2m
1 *sén* (20 waa)	=	40m
1 *yôht* (400 sén)	=	16km

LAUNDRY

Virtually every hotel and guesthouse in Thailand offers a laundry service. Rates are generally geared to room rates; the cheaper the accommodation, the cheaper the washing and ironing. Cheapest of all are public laundries, where you pay by the kg.

Many Thai hotels and guesthouses also have laundry areas where you can wash your clothes at no charge; sometimes there's even a hanging area for drying. Laundry detergent is readily available in general mercantile shops and supermarkets.

For dry-cleaning, be aware that laundries advertising dry-cleaning often don't really dry-clean (they just boil everything!) or do it badly. Luxury hotels usually have dependable dry-cleaning services.

HEALTH

Good travel health depends on your pre-departure preparations, your day-to-day health care while travelling and how you handle any medical problem or emergency that does develop. While the list of potential dangers can seem quite frightening, with a little luck, some basic precautions and adequate information few travellers experience more than upset stomachs.

Travel Health Guides

There are a number of books on travel health:

Staying Healthy in Asia, Africa & Latin America – Moon Publications, 1994. Probably the best all-round guide to carry, as it's compact but very detailed and well organised.

Travellers' Health – Dr Richard Dawood, Oxford University Press, 1995. Comprehensive, easy to read, authoritative and also highly recommended, although it is reasonably large to lug around.

Where There Is No Doctor – David Werner, Macmillan, 1994. A very detailed guide intended for someone (such as a Peace Corps volunteer) going to work in an undeveloped country, rather than for the average traveller.

Travel with Children – Maureen Wheeler, Lonely Planet Publications, 1995. Includes basic advice on travel health for younger children.

Guide to Healthy Living in Thailand – published jointly by the Thai Red Cross Society and US embassy. Available from the 'Snake Farm' (Queen Saovabha Memorial Institute) for 100B, this booklet is rich in practical health advice on safe eating, child care, tropical heat, immunisations and local hospitals.

Predeparture Preparations

Health Insurance Some policies offer lower and higher medical-expense options but the higher ones are chiefly for countries like the USA which have extremely high medical costs. Check the small print.

- Some policies specifically exclude 'dangerous activities' which can include scuba diving, motorcycling, even trekking. If such activities are on your agenda you don't want that sort of policy. A locally acquired motorcycle licence may not be valid under your policy.
- You may prefer a policy which pays doctors or hospitals direct rather than one which requires you to pay on the spot and claim later. If you have to claim later, make sure you keep all documentation. Some policies ask you to call back (reverse charges) to a centre in your home country where an immediate assessment of your problem is made.
- Check if the policy covers ambulances or an emergency flight home. If you have to stretch out you will need two seats and somebody will have to pay for them!

Medical Kit A small, basic medical kit is a wise thing to carry. A kit could include:

- Aspirin or paracetamol (acetaminophen in the USA) – for pain or fever.
- Antihistamine (such as Benadryl) – useful as a decongestant for colds and allergies, to ease the itch from insect bites or stings and to help prevent motion sickness. There are several antihistamines on the market, all with different pros and cons, so it's worth discussing your requirements with a pharmacist or doctor. Antihistamines may cause sedation and interact with alcohol so take care when using them.
- Antibiotics – useful if you're travelling well off the beaten track, but they must be prescribed and you should carry the prescription with you.
- Loperamide (eg Imodium) or Lomotil – for diarrhoea. Antidiarrhoea medication should not be given to children under the age of 12.
- Rehydration mixture – for treatment of severe diarrhoea. This is particularly important if travelling with children, but is recommended for everyone.

- Antiseptic such as povidone-iodine (eg Betadine) for cuts and grazes.
- Multivitamins – a worthwhile consideration, especially for long trips when dietary vitamin intake may be inadequate.
- Calamine lotion or Stingose spray – to ease irritation from bites or stings.
- Bandages and Band-aids – for minor injuries.
- Scissors, tweezers and a thermometer (note that mercury thermometers are prohibited by airlines).
- Cold and flu tablets and throat lozenges.
- Insect repellent, sunscreen, lip balm and water purification tablets.
- A couple of syringes, in case you need injections. Ask your doctor for a note explaining why they have been prescribed.

Ideally, antibiotics should be administered only under medical supervision and should never be taken indiscriminately. Take only the recommended dose at the prescribed intervals and continue using the antibiotic for the prescribed period, even if the illness seems to be cured earlier. Antibiotics are quite specific to the infections they can treat. Stop immediately if there are any serious reactions and don't use the antibiotic at all if you are unsure that you have the correct one.

In Thailand medicine is generally available over the counter and the price will be much cheaper than in the west. However, be careful when buying drugs, particularly where the expiry date may have passed or correct storage conditions may not have been followed. Bogus drugs are not uncommon and it's possible that drugs which are no longer recommended, or have even been banned, in the west are still being dispensed in Thailand.

Health Preparations Make sure you're healthy before you start travelling. If you are embarking on a long trip make sure your teeth are OK and if you wear glasses, take a spare pair and your prescription.

If you require a particular medication take an adequate supply, as it may not be available locally. Take the prescription or, better still, part of the packaging showing the generic rather than the brand name (which may not be locally available), as it will make getting replacements easier. It's a wise idea to have a legible prescription with you to show you legally use the medication.

Immunisations Vaccinations provide protection against diseases you might meet along the way. However, there are no health requirements for Thailand in terms of required vaccinations unless you are coming from an infected area (eg Africa).

Any vaccinations that you have should be recorded on an International Health Certificate.

Plan ahead for getting your vaccinations; some of them require an initial shot followed by a booster, while some vaccinations should not be given together. Try to seek medical advice at least six weeks prior to travel.

Most travellers will have been immunised against various diseases during childhood but your doctor may still recommend booster shots against measles or polio. The period of protection offered by vaccinations differs widely and some are contraindicated if you are pregnant.

In Thailand immunisations are available from a number of sources, including public hospitals and private clinics. Bangkok is your best bet in terms of locating less common or more expensive vaccines. Vaccinations you should consider having for Thailand are:

Tetanus & Diphtheria – Boosters are necessary every 10 years and protection is highly recommended.
Typhoid – Available either as an injection or oral capsules. Protection lasts from one to five years and is useful if you are travelling for long periods in rural, tropical areas.
Hepatitis A – The most common travel-acquired illness which can be prevented by vaccination. Protection can be provided in two ways – either with the antibody gamma globulin or with a vaccine called Havrix 1440.
Hepatitis B – Travellers at risk of contact are strongly advised to be vaccinated, especially if they are children or will have close contact with children.
Rabies – Pre-travel rabies vaccination involves having three injections over 21 to 28 days and should be considered by those who will spend a month or longer in an area where rabies is common, especially if they are cycling, handling animals, caving or travelling to remote areas. Consider it too for children (who may not report a bite).

Japanese Encephalitis – A good idea for those who think they may be at moderate or high risk while in Thailand.

See the relevant entries later on in this section for further information.

Basic Rules

Care in what you eat and drink is the most important health rule; stomach upsets are the most likely travel health problem (between 30 and 50% of travellers in a two week stay experience this) but the majority of these upsets will be relatively minor. Don't become paranoid; trying the local food is part of the experience of travel, after all.

Water If you don't know for certain that the water is safe always assume the worst. Reputable brands of Thai bottled water or soft drink are generally fine, although in some places bottles refilled with tap water are not unknown. Only use water from containers with a serrated seal – not tops or corks. Take care with fruit juice, particularly if water may have been added. Chinese tea served in most restaurants is safe.

Ice is produced from purified water under hygienic conditions and is therefore theoretically safe. During transit to the local restaurant, however, conditions are not so hygienic (you may see blocks of ice being dragged along the street), but it's very difficult to resist in the hot season. The rule of thumb is that if it's chipped ice, it probably came from an ice block (which may not have been handled well) but if it's ice cubes or 'tubes', it was delivered from the ice factory in sealed plastic. In rural areas, villagers mostly drink collected rainwater. Most travellers can drink this without problems, but some people can't tolerate it.

In Thailand, virtually no-one bothers with filters, tablets or iodine since bottled water is so cheap and readily available. Try to purchase the glass water bottles, however, as these are recyclable (unlike the plastic disposable ones).

Food Salads and fruit should be washed with purified water or peeled where possible. Ice cream is usually OK if it is a reputable brand name, but beware of street vendors and of ice cream that has melted and been refrozen. Thoroughly cooked food is safest but not if it has been left to cool or if it has been reheated. Uncooked shellfish such as mussels, oysters and clams should be avoided as well as undercooked meat, particularly in the form of mince. Steaming does not make shellfish safe for eating.

If a place looks clean and well run and if the vendor also looks clean and healthy, then the food is probably safe. In general, places that are packed with travellers or locals will be fine, while empty restaurants are questionable. Busy restaurants mean the food is being cooked and eaten quite quickly with little standing around and is probably not being reheated.

Everyday Health A normal body temperature is 37°C (or 98.6°F); more than 2°C (4°F) higher is a 'high' fever. A normal adult pulse rate is 60 to 100 per minute (children 80 to 100, babies 100 to 140). You should know how to take a temperature and a pulse rate. As a general rule the pulse increases about 20 beats per minute for each °C (2°F) rise in fever.

Respiration (breathing) rate is also an indicator of illness. Count the number of breaths per minute: between 12 and 20 is normal for adults and older children (up to 30 for younger children, 40 for babies). People with a high fever or serious respiratory illness (like pneumonia) breathe more quickly than normal. More than 40 shallow breaths a minute usually means pneumonia.

In hot weather make sure you drink enough – don't rely on feeling thirsty to indicate when you should drink. Not needing to urinate or very dark yellow urine is a danger sign. Always carry a water bottle with you on long trips. Excessive sweating can lead to loss of salt and muscle cramping. Salt tablets are not a good idea as a preventative, but in places where salt is not used much adding salt to food can help.

Clean your teeth with purified water rather than straight from the tap. You can get worm infections by walking barefoot or dangerous coral cuts by walking barefoot over coral. You can avoid insect bites by covering bare skin when insects are around, by screening windows or beds or by using insect repellents.

Medical Problems & Treatment

Self-diagnosis and treatment can be risky, so wherever possible seek qualified help. Although we do give treatment dosages in this section, they are for emergency use only. Medical advice should be sought where possible before administering any drugs.

An embassy or consulate can usually recommend a good place to go for such advice. So can five star hotels, although they often recommend doctors with five star prices. (This is when that medical insurance really comes in useful!) In some places the standard of medical attention is so low that for some ailments the best advice is to get on a plane and go somewhere else.

Environmental Hazards

Sunburn In the tropics you can get sunburnt surprisingly quickly, even through cloud. Use a sunscreen and take extra care to cover areas which don't normally see sun – eg your feet. A hat provides added protection, and you should also use zinc cream or some other barrier cream for your nose and lips. Calamine lotion is good for mild sunburn.

Prickly Heat Prickly heat is an itchy rash caused by excessive perspiration trapped under the skin. It usually strikes people who have just arrived in a hot climate and whose pores have not yet opened sufficiently to cope with greater sweating. Keeping cool and bathing often, using a mild talcum powder or even resorting to air-conditioning may help until you acclimatise.

Heat Exhaustion Dehydration or salt deficiency can cause heat exhaustion. Take time to acclimatise to high temperatures and make sure you get sufficient liquids. Salt deficiency is characterised by fatigue, lethargy, headaches, giddiness and muscle cramps, and in this case salt tablets may help. Vomiting or diarrhoea can deplete your liquid and salt levels.

Heat Stroke This serious, sometimes fatal, condition can occur if the body's heat-regulating mechanism breaks down and the body temperature rises to dangerous levels. Long, continuous periods of exposure to high temperatures can leave you vulnerable to heat stroke. You should avoid excessive alcohol or strenuous activity when you first arrive in a hot climate.

The symptoms are feeling unwell, not sweating very much or at all and a high body temperature (39°C to 41°C, or 102°F to 106°F). Where sweating has ceased the skin becomes flushed and red. Severe, throbbing headaches and lack of coordination will also occur, and the sufferer may be confused or aggressive. Eventually the victim will become delirious or convulse. Hospitalisation is essential, but meanwhile get victims out of the sun, remove their clothing, cover them with a wet sheet or towel and then fan continually.

Fungal Infections Hot-weather fungal infections are most likely to occur on the scalp, between the toes or fingers, in the groin and on the body. You get ringworm (which is a fungal infection, not a worm) from infected animals or by walking on damp areas, like shower floors.

To prevent fungal infections wear loose, comfortable clothes, avoid artificial fibres, wash frequently and dry carefully. If you do get an infection, wash the infected area daily with a disinfectant or medicated soap and water, and rinse and dry well. Apply an antifungal powder like Tinaderm. Try to expose the infected area to air or sunlight as much as possible, and wash all towels and underwear in hot water as well as changing them often.

Motion Sickness Eating lightly before and during a trip will reduce the chances of motion sickness. If you are prone to motion sickness try to find a place that minimises disturbance – near the wing on aircraft, close to midships on boats, near the centre on buses. Fresh air usually helps, reading or cigarette smoke doesn't. Commercial anti-motion-sickness preparations, which can cause drowsiness, have to be taken before the trip; when you're feeling sick it's too late. Ginger (available in capsule form) and peppermint (including mint-flavoured sweets) are natural preventives.

Infectious Diseases
Diarrhoea A change of water, food or climate can all cause the runs; diarrhoea caused by contaminated food or water is more serious. You may get a bout of mild travellers' diarrhoea but a few rushed toilet trips with no other symptoms is not indicative of a serious problem. Dehydration is the main danger with any diarrhoea, particularly for children who can dehydrate quickly. Fluid replacement remains the mainstay of management. Weak black tea with a little sugar, soda water, or soft drinks allowed to go flat and diluted 50% with water are all good. With severe diarrhoea a rehydrating solution is necessary to replace minerals and salts. Commercially available oral rehydration salts (ORS) is very useful; add the contents of one sachet to a litre of boiled or bottled water. In an emergency you can make up a solution of eight teaspoons of sugar to a litre of boiled water. You should stick to a bland diet as you recover.

Lomotil or Imodium can be used to bring relief from the symptoms, although they do not actually cure the problem. Only use these drugs if absolutely necessary – eg if you *must* travel. For children under 12 years, Lomotil and Imodium are not recommended. Under all circumstances fluid replacement is vital. Do not use these drugs if the person has a high fever or is severely dehydrated.

In certain situations the need for antibiotics may be indicated by: diarrhoea with blood and mucous (gut-paralysing drugs like Imodium or Lomotil should be avoided in this situation); watery diarrhoea with fever and lethargy; persistent diarrhoea for more than five days; and severe diarrhoea, if it is logistically difficult to stay in one place.

The recommended drugs (adults only) are either norfloxacin 400mg twice daily for three days or ciprofloxacin 500mg twice daily for five days.

The drug of choice for children is co-trimoxazole (Bactrim, Septrin, Resprim), with dosage dependent on the person's weight. A five day course is given.

Amoebic Dysentery Amoebic dysentery is more gradual in the onset of symptoms, with cramping abdominal pain and vomiting less likely; fever may not be present. It is not a self-limiting disease: it will persist until treated and can recur and cause long-term health problems.

A stool test is necessary to diagnose which kind of dysentery you have, so you should seek medical help urgently.

Giardiasis The parasite causing this intestinal disorder is present in contaminated water. The symptoms are stomach cramps, nausea, a bloated stomach, watery and foul-smelling diarrhoea and frequent gas. Giardiasis can appear several weeks after you have been exposed to the parasite. The symptoms may disappear for a few days and then return; this can go on for several weeks. Tinidazole (known as Fasigyn) or metronidazole (Flagyl) are the recommended drugs for treatment.

Hepatitis Hepatitis A is a very common problem among travellers to areas with poor sanitation, such as Thailand. With good water and adequate sewage disposal in most industrialised countries since the 1940s, very few young adults today have any natural immunity and must be protected.

The disease is spread by contaminated food or water. The symptoms are fever, chills, headache, fatigue, feelings of weakness, and aches and pains, followed by loss of appetite, nausea, vomiting, abdominal pain, dark urine, light coloured faeces, jaundiced skin and the whites of the eyes may turn yellow. In some cases you may feel unwell, tired, have no appetite, have aches and pains, and be jaundiced. You should seek medical advice, but in general there is not much you can do apart from rest, drink lots of fluids, eat lightly and avoid fatty foods. As hepatitis attacks the liver, sufferers must forgo alcohol for six months to fully recover.

Hepatitis B, which used to be called serum hepatitis, is spread through contact with infected blood, blood products or bodily fluids, eg through sexual contact, unsterilised needles and blood transfusions. Other risk situations include having a shave or tattoo in a local shop, or having your body pierced. The symptoms of type B are much the same as type A, except that they are more severe and may lead to irreparable liver damage or even liver cancer. Although there is no treatment for hepatitis B, an effective prophylactic vaccine is readily available in most countries. The immunisation schedule requires two injections at least a month apart followed by a third dose five months after the second. Persons who should receive a hepatitis B vaccination include anyone who anticipates contact with blood or other bodily secretions, either as a health care worker or through sexual contact with the local population, particularly those who intend to stay in the country for a long period.

Hepatitis C is similar to B but is less common. Hepatitis D (the 'delta particle') is also similar to B and always occurs in concert with it; its occurrence is currently limited to IV drug users. Hepatitis E, however, is similar to A and is spread in the same manner, by water or food contamination. Hepatitis E is common in Thailand.

Tests are available for these strands, but are very expensive. Travellers shouldn't be too paranoid about this apparent proliferation of hepatitis strains; following the same precautions as for A and B should be all that's necessary to avoid them.

Health section continued on page 114

Cuisine of Coastal Thailand

TAT

Title Page: Crisp-fried whole fish garnished in the traditional way with chilli, garlic and shallots and presented on a bed of banana leaves. (photo by Bernard Napthine)

Above Right: Inspired by the foods common to the region, southern Thai soups, curries and condiments feature a tantalising array of fresh seafood, flavoured using the milk, oil and grated flesh of coconuts, as well as lime, lemon grass and chillies.

Right: At many coastal and island destinations food vendors serve up incredible meals from simple beachside kitchens for the hungry hoards of vacationers.

RICHARD NEBESKY

Food

In a 1991 study that surveyed 1450 travel agencies in 26 countries, Thailand ranked fourth after France, Italy and Hong Kong in the perceived excellence of cuisine. Still, some people take to the food in Thailand immediately while others don't; Thai dishes can be pungent and spicy. Lots of garlic and chillies are used, especially *phrík khîi nŭu* (literally, 'mouse-shit peppers' – these are the small torpedo-shaped devils which can be pushed aside if you are timid about red-hot curries). Almost all Thai food is cooked with fresh ingredients, including vegetables, fish, poultry, pork and some beef. Of course, in coastal Thailand seafood predominates. Plenty of lime juice, lemon grass and fresh coriander leaf are added to give the food its characteristic tang, and fish sauce *(náam plaa,* generally made from anchovies) or shrimp paste *(kà-pi)* to make it salty.

Other common seasonings include 'laos' or galanga root *(khàa),* black pepper, three kinds of basil, ground peanuts (more often a condiment), tamarind juice *(náam makhăam),* ginger *(khĭng)* and coconut milk *(kà-tí).* The Thais eat a lot of what could be called Chinese food, which is generally, but not always, less spicy.

Rice *(khâo)* is eaten with most meals; 'to eat' in Thai is literally 'eat rice' or *kin khâo.* Thais can be very picky about their rice, insisting on the right temperature and cooking times. Ordinary white rice is called *khâo jâo* and there are many varieties and grades. The finest quality Thai rice is known as *khâo hăwm máli* or 'jasmine fragrant rice' for its sweet, inviting smell when cooked. 'Sticky' or glutinous rice *(khâo nĭaw),* a staple in northern and north-eastern Thailand, is sometimes found in other regions.

Regional Food Differences

For the most part people living along the eastern and northern coasts of the Gulf of Thailand eat standard, central Thai cuisine as found in Bangkok and the surrounding Chao Phraya River Valley. From Chumphon Province south, on both sides of the Thai-Malay peninsula, you'll find yourself in the domain of southern Thai cuisine – *aahăan pàk tâi.* One of the major hallmarks of this style of cooking is that curries are generally hotter – sometimes much hotter, sometimes only a little hotter – than their counterparts elsewhere in the country. One of the most notorious is *kaeng tai plaa,* a thick yellow fish curry which, when prepared in the most typical style, will leave all but the most chilli-habituated farangs weeping.

Another southern Thai speciality – particularly in Trang and Phuket – is *khănom jiin náam yaa,* a thin, yellowish fish curry served over white wheat noodles. Several Malay and Indian-style curries are also available in the south, and these tend to be milder than most Thai curries. In the four southernmost, Muslim-dominated provinces you may come across *roti kaeng,* a breakfast dish that consists of *roti* – a fried flatbread similar to India's *paratha* – dipped in a mild curry gravy *(kaeng).* Served with jam, chocolate or fruit fillings, roti is also a common street vendor food throughout the south – Nakhon Si Thammarat is known to have the best sweet roti.

For breakfast the most typical southern Thai dish is *khâo yam,* a delicious concoction of room-temperature rice, chopped lemongrass and lime leaves, bean sprouts, dried shrimp, toasted coconut and powdered red chilli served with a salty-sour-sweet tamarind sauce – sort of a southern-style rice salad. ■

What to Eat

Thai food is served with a variety of condiments and sauces, including ground red pepper *(phrík bon)*, ground peanuts *(thùa bon)*, vinegar with sliced chillies *(náam sôm phrík)*, fish sauce with chillies *(náam plaa phrík)*, a spicy orange-red sauce called *náam phrík sĭi raachaa* (from coastal Si Racha, of course) and any number of dipping sauces *(náam jîm)* for particular dishes. Soy sauce *(náam sĭi-yú)* can be requested, though this is normally used as a condiment for Chinese food only.

Except for the 'rice plates' and noodle dishes, Thai meals are usually ordered family style, ie two or more people order together, sharing different dishes. Traditionally, the party orders one of each kind of dish, eg one chicken, one fish, one soup etc. One dish is generally large enough for two people. One or two extras may be ordered for a large party. If you come to eat at a Thai restaurant alone and order one of these 'entrees', you had better be hungry or know enough Thai to order a small portion. This latter alternative is not really acceptable socially; Thais generally consider eating alone in a restaurant unusual – but then as a farang you're an exception anyway.

The Green Bowl

Sponsored by the famous oil company, Thai food critic Thanad Sri bestows his favourite dishes at restaurants around the country with the 'Shell Chuan Chim' (Shell's Invitation to Taste) designation. Look for a sign bearing the outline of a green bowl next to the familiar Shell symbol posted somewhere on the outside of the restaurant. Though such a designation usually means the food is good at such places, it's not a foolproof guarantee; some restaurants hang onto their Chuan Chim signs long after the kitchen has lowered its standards. ∎

A cheaper alternative is to order dishes 'over rice' or *râat khâo*. Curry *(kaeng)* over rice is called *khâo kaeng*; in a standard curry shop khâo kaeng is only 10 to 15B a plate. Another category of Thai food is called *kàp klâem* – dishes meant to be eaten while drinking alcoholic beverages. On some menus these are translated as 'snacks' or 'appetisers'. Typical kàp klâem include *thùa thâwt* (fried peanuts), *kài săam yàang* (literally 'three kinds of chicken', a plate of chopped ginger, peanuts, mouse-shit peppers and bits of lime – to be mixed and eaten by hand) and various kinds of *yam*, Thai-style salads made with lots of chillies and lime juice.

To end a meal with something sweet, the Thais overwhelmingly prefer to nibble from the country's seemingly infinite variety of tropical fruits. Thai pineapples, available year-round, are among the world's sweetest and juiciest. Bananas come in over 20 varieties, from the tiny, slender 'princess fingernail' bananas (eaten by the bunch) to the pendulous 'fragrant' bananas more familiar in the west. Rambutan – a succulent grape-like orb surrounded by a thick, soft hull with bright red tendrils poking in all directions – quickly becomes a favourite with many visitors. Definitely an acquired taste is the large, spiky durian fruit that is in season only a couple of months a year. Protected by a formidable, mace-like exterior, the slippery yellow segments inside the fruit exude a musky odour that has been described as a cross between peaches and onions. Aficionados claim that if you can get past the smell, you're more than amply rewarded by a rich, toothsome flavour that has earned the durian its 'king of fruits' reputation in Asia.

Where to Eat

Many smaller restaurants and food stalls do not have menus, so it is worthwhile memorising a standard 'repertoire' of dishes. Most provinces have their own local specialities in addition to the standards and you might try asking for 'whatever is good', allowing the proprietors to choose for you. Of course, you might get stuck with a large bill this way, but with a little practice in Thai social relations you may get some very pleasing results. The most economical places to eat – and the most dependable – are noodle shops *(ráan kǔaytǐaw)*, curry-and-rice shops *(ráan khâo kaeng)* and night markets *(talàat tǒh rûng)*. Most towns and villages have at least one night market and a few noodle and/or curry shops. Curry shops are generally open for breakfast and lunch only, and are a cheap source of nutritious food.

Another common eatery in larger cities is the *ráan khâo tôm*, literally 'boiled rice shop', a type of Chinese-Thai restaurant that offers not just boiled rice soups *(khâo tôm)* but an assortment of *aahǎan taam sàng*, 'food according to order'. In the better places cooks pride themselves on being able to fix any Thai or Chinese dish you name. One attraction of the ráan khâo tôm is that they tend to stay open late – some are even open 24 hours.

In larger cities you may also come across 'food centres' where hawkers serve their specialities from rented stalls in a large room. These are often attached to department stores. You typically purchase a meal via a coupon system – you buy, say, 50B worth of paper coupons printed in denominations of 5B, 10B, 20B etc, and then exchange these coupons for dishes you select.

Vegetarian Visitors who wish to avoid eating meat while in Thailand can be accommodated with some effort. Vegetarian restaurants are increasing in number throughout the country, thanks largely to Bangkok's ex-Governor Chamlong Srimuang, whose strict vegetarianism has inspired a nonprofit chain of vegetarian restaurants *(ráan aahǎan mangsàwírát)* in Bangkok and several provincial capitals. Many of these are sponsored by the Asoke Foundation, an ascetic (some would say heretic) Theravada Buddhist sect that finds justification for vegetarianism in the Buddhist suttas. Look for the green sign out the front featuring large Thai numerals – each restaurant is numbered according to the order in which it was established. The food at these restaurants is usually served buffet style and is very inexpensive – typically 5 to 8B per dish. Most are open only from 7 or 8 am until noon.

Other easy, though less widespread, sources of vegetarian meals are Indian restaurants, which usually feature a vegetarian section on the menu. Cooks here also understand what 'vegetarian' really means (some Thai restaurants don't). Currently Indian restaurants are most prevalent in Bangkok, Pattaya and Phuket's Patong beach. Chinese restaurants are also a good bet since many Chinese Buddhists eat vegetarian food during Buddhist festivals, especially in southern Thailand.

More often than not, however, vegetarians are left to their own devices at the average Thai restaurant. In Thai the magic words are *phǒm kin jeh* (for men) or *dii-chǎn kin jeh* (women). Like other Thai phrases, getting the tones right makes all the difference – the key word, *jeh*, should rhyme with the English 'jay' without the 'y'. Loosely translated this phrase means 'I eat only vegetarian food'. It might also be necessary to follow with the explanation *phǒm/dii-chǎn kin tàe phàk*, 'I eat only vegetables'. Don't worry – this won't be interpreted to mean no rice, herbs or fruit. For other useful food phrases, see the Useful Food Words list later in this section. In Thai culture, 'brown' (unpolished) rice is said to be reserved for pigs and prisoners! Look for it at the local feed store.

Those interested in tapping into the Thai vegetarian movement can phone the Vegetarian Society of Bangkok (☎ (2) 254-5444, 254-3502) for information. The society usually meets monthly to share a vegetarian feast, swap recipes and discuss the whys and wherefores of vegetarianism.

Table Etiquette

Using the correct utensils and eating gestures will garner much respect from the Thais, who are of the general opinion that western table manners are rather coarse. Thais eat most dishes with a fork and tablespoon except for noodles, which are eaten with chopsticks *(tà-kìap)*; noodle soups are eaten with a spoon and chopsticks. Another exception to the fork-and-spoon routine is sticky rice (common in the north and north-east), which is rolled into balls and eaten with the right hand, along with the food accompanying it.

The fork *(sáwm)* is held in the left hand and used as a probe to push food onto the spoon *(cháwn)*; you eat from the spoon. To many Thais, pushing a fork into one's mouth is akin to putting a knife into one's mouth in western countries. When serving yourself from a common platter, put no more than one or two spoonfuls onto your own plate at a time. It's customary at the start of a shared meal to eat a spoonful of plain rice first – a gesture recognising rice as the most important part of the meal. If you're being hosted by Thais, they'll undoubtedly encourage you to eat less rice and more curries, seafood etc as a gesture of their generosity (since rice costs comparatively little). The humble guest, however, takes rice with every spoonful.

Always leave some food on the serving platters as well as on your plate. To clean your plate and leave nothing on the serving platters would be a grave insult to your hosts. This is why Thais tend to 'over-order' at social meal occasions – the more food is left on the table, the more generous the host appears. ■

Food Glossary

The following list gives standard dishes in Thai script with a transliterated pronunciation guide, using the system outlined in the Language section of the Facts about the Country chapter.

Curries (*kaeng*) แกง

hot Thai curry with chicken/beef/pork
    kaeng phèt kài/néua/mŭu
    แกงเผ็ดไก่/เนื้อ/หมู

'green' curry, with fish/chicken/beef
    kaeng khĭaw-wăan plaa/kài/néua
    แกงเขียวหวานปลา/ไก่/เนื้อ

rich and spicy Muslim-style curry with chicken/beef & potatoes
    kaeng mátsàman kài/néua
    แกงมัสมั่นไก่/เนื้อ

savoury curry with chicken/beef
    kaeng phánaeng kài/néua
    แกงพะแนงไก่/เนื้อ

mild, Indian-style curry with chicken
    kaeng kari kài
    แกงกะหรี่ไก่

chicken curry with bamboo shoots
    kaeng kài nàw mái
    แกงไก่หน่อไม้

hot & sour fish & vegetable ragout
    kaeng sôm
    แกงส้ม

catfish curry
    kaeng plaa dùk
    แกงปลาดุก

Soups (*súp*) ซุป

mild soup with vegetables & pork
  kaeng jèut
  แกงจืด

mild soup with vegetables, pork &
bean curd
  kaeng jèut tâo-hûu
  แกงจืดเต้าหู้

soup with chicken, galanga root
& coconut
  tôm khàa kài
  ต้มข่าไก่

prawn & lemon grass soup with
mushrooms
  tôm yam kûng
  ต้มยำกุ้ง

fish ball soup
  kaeng jèut lûuk chín
  แกงจืดลูกชิ้น

rice soup with fish/chicken/shrimp
  khâo tôm plaa/kài/kûng
  ข้าวต้มปลา/ไก่/กุ้ง

Egg (*khài*) ไข่

hard-boiled egg
  khài tôm
  ไข่ต้ม

fried egg
  khài dao
  ไข่ดาว

plain omelette
  khài jiaw
  ไข่เจียว

scrambled egg
  khài kuan
  ไข่กวน

omelette stuffed with
vegetables & pork
  khài yát sài
  ไข่ยัดไส้

Rice Dishes (*khâo râat nâa*) ข้าวราดหน้า

fried rice with pork/chicken/shrimp
  khâo phàt mũu/kài/kûng
  ข้าวผัดหมู/ไก่/กุ้ง

boned, sliced Hainan-style chicken
with marinated rice
  khâo man kài
  ข้าวมันไก่

chicken with sauce over rice
  khâo nâa kài
  ข้าวหน้าไก่

roast duck over rice
  khâo nâa pèt
  ข้าวหน้าเป็ด

'red' pork (char siu) with rice
  khâo mũu daeng
  ข้าวหมูแดง

curry over rice
  khâo kaeng
  ข้าวแกง

Noodles (*kũaytĩaw/bà-mìi*) ก๋วยเตี๋ยว/บะหมี่

wide rice noodle soup with
vegetables & meat
  kũaytĩaw náam
  ก๋วยเตี๋ยวน้ำ

wide rice noodles with
vegetables & meat
  kũaytĩaw hâeng
  ก๋วยเตี๋ยวแห้ง

Fresh from the Sea

Thailand has a well-deserved reputation for its seafood cuisine, which many gourmets agree ranks among the world's very best. The Thais consume more protein via fish than from any other single source. With two lengthy seacoasts from which to harvest marine food products, plus an intricate spice pantry that draws from indigenous, Indian and Chinese cooking traditions, the menu possibilities are virtually limitless.

Thai chefs are masters at employing quick-cooking techniques to maintain the delicate flavours of fresh seafood. Shrimp and crab are year-round favourites no matter how far inland one wanders; spiny lobster is abundant along the Andaman Coast. Other common fruits of the sea include cuttlefish, oysters, cockles, sea perch, kingfish, shark and pompano.

Thais seem to have a particular genius for preparing molluscs such as shrimp, lobster, mussels and squid so that they remain tender and succulent – no easy task when the difference between undercooking and overcooking is often only a matter of seconds. The liberal use of lime juice, fresh coriander leaf and preserved Chinese plums eliminates or tempers the 'fishy' taste many westerners object to.

Dipping sauces *(náam jîm)* served in small saucers with Thai seafood can be very simple or very intricate. One of the most typical sauces combines salty *náam plaa* (a thin sauce made from anchovies), tangy *náam mánao* (lime juice), plenty of fresh minced *kràtiam* (garlic), a little *náam-taan* (sugar) and a healthy portion of fresh sliced *phrík* (chillies).

The most common forms of seafood preparation include:

dìp – raw; usually served with a variety of dipping sauces

nêung – steamed

phǎo – grilled

phàt – sliced, filleted and fried

râat phrík – smothered in garlic and chillies

thâwt – fried whole; the Thai style is to make the edges of the fish very crisp

chúp pâeng thâwt – batter-fried, a popular way to prepare shrimp

tôm yam – in a hot and tangy broth made with lemon grass and chillies

yâang – roast (squid only)

The following is a list of common seafood dishes found throughout coastal Thailand:

Seafood *(aahǎan tháleh)*

อาหารทะเล

steamed crab *puu nêung* ปูนึ่ง	crisp-fried fish *plaa thâwt* ปลาทอด
steamed crab claws *kâam puu nêung* ก้ามปูนึ่ง	fried prawns *kûng thâwt* กุ้งทอด

batter-fried prawns
kûng chúp pâeng thâwt
กุ้งชุบแป้งทอด

grilled prawns
kûng phão
กุ้งเผา

steamed fish
plaa nêung
ปลานึ่ง

grilled fish
plaa phão
ปลาเผา

whole fish cooked in ginger, onions
& soy sauce
plaa jīan
ปลาเจี๋ยน

sweet & sour fish
plaa prîaw wãan
ปลาเปรี้ยวหวาน

cellophane noodles baked with
crab
wûn-sên òp puu
วุ้นเส้นอบปู

spicy fried squid
plaa mèuk phàt phèt
ปลาหมึกผัดเผ็ด

roast squid
plaa mèuk yâang
ปลาหมึกย่าง

oysters fried in egg batter
hãwy thâwt
หอยทอด

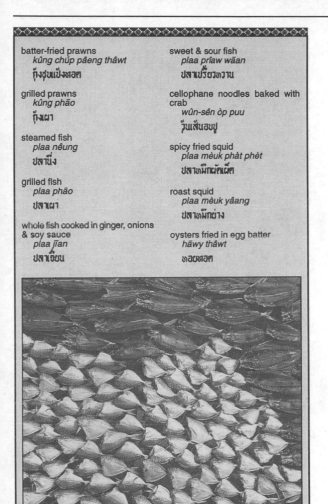

RICHARD NEBESKY

BERNARD NAPTHINE

squid	spiny lobster
plaa mèuk	*kûng mangkawn*
ปลาหมึก	กุ้งมังกร
shrimp	green mussel
kûng	*hāwy malaeng phùu*
กุ้ง	หอยแมลงภู่
fish	scallop
plaa	*hāwy phát*
ปลา	หอยพัด
saltwater eel	oyster
plaa lòt	*hāwy naang rom*
ปลาหลด	หอยนางรม

wide rice noodles with gravy
râat nâa
ราดหน้า

thin rice noodles fried with tofu, vegetables, egg & peanuts
phàt thai

ผัดไทย

fried thin noodles with soy sauce
phàt sii-yíw
ผัดซีอิ๊ว

Miscellaneous

stir-fried mixed vegetables
phàt phàk lǎi yàang

ผัดผักหลายอย่าง

spring rolls
pàw-pía
เปาะปิย

beef in oyster sauce
néua phàt náam-man hǎwy
เนื้อผัดน้ำมันหอย

duck soup
pèt tǔn
เป็ดตุ๋น

roast duck
pèt yâang
เป็ดย่าง

fried chicken
kài thâwt
ไก่ทอด

chicken fried in holy basil
kài phàt bai kà-phrao
ไก่ผัดใบกะเพรา

grilled chicken
kài yâang
ไก่ย่าง

chicken fried with chillies
kài phàt phrík
ไก่ผัดพริก

chicken fried with cashews
kài phàt mét má-mûang
ไก่ผัดเม็ดมะม่วง

wheat noodles in broth, with vegetables & meat
bà-mìi náam
บะหมี่น้ำ

wheat noodles with vegetables & meat
bà-mìi hâeng
บะหมี่แห้ง

morning-glory vine fried in garlic, chilli & bean sauce
phàk bûng fai daeng
ผักบุ้งไฟแดง

'satay' or skewers of barbecued meat, sold on the street
sà-té
สะเต๊ะ

spicy green papaya salad (northeast speciality)
sôm-tam
ส้มตำ

noodles with fish curry
khānom jiin náam yaa
ขนมจีนน้ำยา

prawns fried with chillies
kûng phàt phrík phǎo
กุ้งผัดพริกเผา

chicken fried with ginger
kài phàt khǐng
ไก่ผัดขิง

fried wonton
kíaw kràwp
เกี๊ยวกรอบ

cellophane noodle salad
yam wún sên
ยำวุ้นเส้น

spicy chicken or beef salad
lâap kài/néua
ลาบไก่/เนื้อ

hot & sour grilled beef salad
yam néua
ยำเนื้อ

chicken with bean sprouts
kài sàp thùa ngâwk
ไก่สับถั่วงอก

fried fish cakes with
cucumber sauce
thâwt man plaa
ทอดมันปลา

Southern Thailand Specialities

flatbread (roti)
roh-tii
โรตี

roti with bananas
roh-tii klûay
โรตีกล้วย

roti with curry dip
roh-tii kaeng
โรตีแกง

strong Hokkien-style coffee
koh-pîi
โกปี้

chicken briyani
khâo mòk kài
ข้าวหมกไก่

rice salad (with toasted coconut,
dried shrimp, lime leaves)
khâo yam
ข้าวยำ

southern fish curry (very hot)
kaeng tai plaa
แกงไตปลา

noodles with mild fish curry
khanŏm jiin náam yaa
ขนมจีนน้ำยา

Vegetables (*phàk*) ผัก

angle bean
thùa phuu
ถั่วภู

bitter melon
márá-jiin
มะระขึน

brinjal (round eggplant)
mákhĕua pràw
มะเขือเปราะ

cabbage
phàk kà-làm or *kà-làm plii*
ผักกะหล่ำ กะหล่ำปลี

cauliflower
dàwk kà-làm
ดอกกะหล่ำ

Chinese radish (daikon)
phàk kàat hŭa
ผักกาดหัว

corn
khâo phôht
ข้าวโพด

cucumber
taeng kwaa
แตงกวา

eggplant
mákhĕua mûang
มะเขือม่วง

garlic
kràtiam
กระเทียม

lettuce
phàk kàat
ผักกาด

long bean
thùa fák yao
ถั่วฝักยาว

okra (ladyfingers)
krà-jíap
กระเจี๊ยบ

onion (bulb)
hŭa hāwm
หัวหอม

onion (green, 'scallions')
tôn hāwm
ต้นหอม

peanuts (groundnuts)
tùa lísŏng
ถั่วลิสง

potato
man faràng
มันฝรั่ง

pumpkin
fák thawng
ฟักทอง

taro
pheùak
เผือก

tomato
mákhēua thêt
มะเขือเทศ

Fruit (*phŏn-lá-mái*) ผลไม้

mandarin orange (year-round)
sôm
ส้ม

watermelon (year-round)
taeng moh
แตงโม

guava (year-round)
fa-ràng
ฝรั่ง

lime (year-round)
má-nao
มะนาว

mangosteen – round, purple fruit
with juicy white flesh (April to September)
mang-khút
มังคุด

coconut – grated for cooking when
mature, eaten from the shell with
a spoon when young; juice is
sweetest and most plentiful in
young coconuts (year-round)
máphráo
มะพร้าว

rose-apple – small, apple-like texture, very fragrant (April to July)
chom-phûu
ชมพู่

tamarind – comes in sweet as well
as tart varieties (year-round)
mákhāam
มะขาม

sapodilla – small, brown, oval,
sweet but pungent-smelling (July
to September)
lámút
ละมุด

pineapple (year-round)
sàp-pàrót
สับปะรด

mango – several varieties
& seasons
má-mûang
มะม่วง

custard-apple (July to October)
náwy naa
น้อยหน่า

rambeh – small, reddish-
brown, sweet, apricot-like
(April to May)
máfai
มะไฟ

pomelo – large citrus similar to
grapefruit (year-round)
sôm oh
ส้มโอ

papaya (year-round)
málákaw

มะละกอ

jackfruit – similar in appearance to durian but much easier to take (year-round)
kha-nŭn

ขนุน

durian – held in high esteem by the Thais, but most westerners dislike this fruit. There are several varieties and seasons, so keep trying.
thúrian

ทุเรียน

banana – over 20 varieties (year-round)
klûay

กล้วย

rambutan – red, hairy-skinned fruit with grape-like interior (July to September)
ngáw

เงาะ

longan – 'dragon's eyes', small, brown, spherical, similar to rambutan (July to October)
lam yài

ลำใย

Sweets (*khăwng wăan*) ของหวาน

Thai custard
săngkha-yaa

สังขยา

'Indian-style' banana, fried
klûay khàek

กล้วยแขก

coconut custard
săngkha-yaa ma-phráo

สังขยามะพร้าว

sweet palm kernels
lûuk taan chêuam

ลูกตาลเชื่อม

sweet shredded egg yolk
făwy thawng

ฝอยทอง

Thai jelly with coconut cream
ta-kôh

ตะโก้

egg custard
mâw kaeng

หม้อแกง

sticky rice with coconut cream
khâo nĩaw daeng

ข้าวเหนียวแดง

banana in coconut milk
klûay bùat chii

กล้วยบวชชี

sticky rice in coconut cream with ripe mango
khâo nĩaw má-mûang

ข้าวเหนียวมะม่วง

Useful Food Words

For 'I' men use *phŏm*; women use *dii-chăn*

I eat only vegetarian food.
Phŏm/dii-chăn kin jeh.

ผม/ดีฉัน กินเจ

I can't eat pork.
Phŏm/dii-chăn kin mŭu mâi dâi.

ผม/ดีฉัน   กินหมูไม่ได้

I can't eat beef.
Phŏm/dii-chăn kin néua mâi dâi.

ผม/ดีฉัน กินเนื้อไม่ได้

(I) don't like it hot & spicy.
Mâi châwp phèt.

ไม่ชอบเผ็ด

(I) like it hot & spicy.
Châwp phèt.
ชอบเผ็ด

(I) can eat Thai food.
Kin aahāan thai pen.
กินอาหารไทยเป็น

What do you have that's special?
Mii a-rai phí-sèt?
มีอะไรพิเศษ?

I didn't order this.
*Níi phõm/dii-chãn
mâi dâi sàng.*
นี้ ผม/ดิฉัน ไม่ได้สั่ง

Do you have ...?
Mii ... mãi?
มี...ไหม?

Drinks

Nonalcoholic Drinks

Fruit Juices & Shakes The incredible variety of fruits in Thailand means an abundance of nutritious juices and shakes. The all-purpose term for fruit juice is *náam phõn-lá-mái*. Put *náam* (water or juice) together with the name of any fruit and you can get anything from *náam sôm* (orange juice) to *náam taeng moh* (watermelon juice). When a blender or extractor is used, fruit juices may be called *náam khán* or 'squeezed juice' (eg *náam sàppàrót khán*, pineapple juice). When mixed in a blender with ice the result is *náam pon* (literally, 'mixed juice') as in *náam málákaw pon*, a papaya 'smoothie' or 'shake'. Night markets will often have vendors specialising in juices and shakes.

Thais prefer to drink most fruit juices with a little salt mixed in. Unless a vendor is used to serving farangs, your fruit juice or shake will come slightly salted. If you prefer unsalted fruit juices, specify *mâi sài kleua* (without salt). Sugar cane juice *(náam âwy)* is a Thai favourite and a very refreshing accompaniment to curry and rice plates. Many small restaurants or food stalls that don't offer any other juices will have a supply of freshly squeezed náam âwy on hand.

Coffee Over the past 10 years or so, Nescafé and other instant coffee producers have sadly made deep inroads into Thai coffee culture at the expense of freshly ground coffee. The typical Thai restaurant – especially those in hotels, guesthouses and other tourist-oriented establishments – serves instant coffee with packets of artificial, non-dairy creamer on the side. Up-market hotels and coffee shops sometimes also offer filtered and espresso coffees at premium prices.

Traditionally, coffee in Thailand is locally grown (mostly in hilly areas of northern and southern Thailand), roasted by wholesalers, ground by vendors and filtered just before serving. Thai-grown coffee may not be as full and rich-tasting as gourmet Sumatran, Jamaican or Kona beans but it's still considerably tastier than Nescafé or other instant coffees. To get real Thai coffee ask for *kafae thũng* (literally, 'bag coffee'), which refers to the traditional method of preparing a cup of coffee by filtering hot water through a bag-shaped cloth filter. Thailand's best coffee of this sort is served in Hokkien-style cafes in the southern provinces. Elsewhere in Thailand outdoor morning markets are the best place to find kafae thũng. The usual kafae thũng is served mixed with sugar and sweetened condensed milk – if you don't want either ask for *kafae dam* (black coffee) followed with *mâi sài náam-taan* (without sugar). Kafae thũng is often served in a glass instead of a ceramic cup – to pick up a glass of hot coffee, grasp it along the top rim.

Tea Both Indian-style (black) and Chinese-style (green or semi-cured) teas are commonly served in Thailand. The latter predominates in Chinese restaurants and is the usual ingredient in *náam chaa*, the weak, often lukewarm tea-water traditionally served free in Thai restaurants. The aluminium teapots seen on every table in the average restaurant are filled with náam chaa; ask for a plain glass *(kâew plào)* and you can drink as much as you like at no charge. For iced náam chaa ask for a glass of ice (usually 1B) and pour your own; for fresh, undiluted Chinese tea request *chaa jiin*.

Black tea, both imported and Thai-grown, is usually available in the same restaurants or food stalls that serve real coffee. An order of *chaa ráwn* (hot tea) almost always results in a cup (or glass) of black tea with sugar and condensed milk. As with coffee you must specify as you order if you want black tea without milk and/or sugar.

A favourite thirst quencher, especially for those adventuring among the more chilli-laden dishes, is Thai iced tea. This frothy orange potion – a blend of Thai-grown tea seasoned with ground tamarind seed and mixed with a healthy dollop of palm sugar and condensed milk over ice – is extremely refreshing.

Water Purified water is simply called *náam dèum* (drinking water), whether boiled or filtered. *All* water offered to customers in restaurants or to guests in an office or home will be purified, so you needn't fret about the safety of taking a sip (for more information on water safety, see the Health section in this chapter). In restaurants you can ask for *náam plào* (plain water), which is always either boiled or taken from a purified source; it's served by the glass at no charge or you can order by the bottle. A bottle of carbonated water (soda) costs about the same as a bottle of plain purified water, but the bottles are smaller.

Drinks Glossary

Beverages *(khreûang dèum)* เครื่องดื่ม

plain water
náam plào
น้ำเปล่า

Chinese tea
chaa jiin
ชาจีน

hot water
náam ráwn
น้ำร้อน

weak Chinese tea
náam chaa
น้ำชา

boiled water
náam tôm
น้ำต้ม

iced Thai tea with milk & sugar
chaa yen
ชาเย็น

cold water
náam yen
น้ำเย็น

iced Thai tea with sugar only
chaa dam yen
ชาดำเย็น

ice
náam khãeng
น้ำแข็ง

no sugar (command)
mâi sài náam-taan
ไม่ใส่น้ำตาล

hot Thai tea with sugar
chaa dam ráwn

ชาดำร้อน

hot Thai tea with milk & sugar
chaa ráwn

ชาร้อน

hot coffee with milk & sugar
kafae ráwn

กาแฟร้อน

traditional filtered coffee with milk
& sugar
kafae thũng (ko-pĩi in southern
Thailand)

กาแฟถุง/โกปี๊

iced coffee with sugar, no milk
oh-liang

โอเลี้ยง

Ovaltine
oh-wantin

โอวันติน

orange soda
náam sôm

น้ำส้ม

plain milk
nom jèut

นมจืด

iced lime juice with sugar (usually
with salt too)
náam manao

น้ำมะนาว

no salt (command)
mâi sài kleua

ไม่ใส่เกลือ

soda water
náam sõh-daa

น้ำโซดา

bottled drinking water
náam dèum khùat

น้ำดื่มขวด

bottle
khùat

ขวด

glass
kâew

แก้ว

Alcoholic Drinks

Drinking in Thailand can be quite expensive in relation to the cost of other
consumer activities. The Thai government has placed increasingly heavy
taxes on liquor and beer, so that it accounts for about 30B out of the 50
to 70B that you pay for a large beer. One large bottle (630ml) of Singha
beer costs more than half the minimum daily wage of a Bangkok worker.

Beer Three brands of beer are brewed in Thailand by Thai-owned
breweries: Singha, Amarit and Kloster. Singha (pronounced 'Sĩng' by the
Thais) is by far the most common beer in Thailand, holding some 66%
of the domestic market. Singha is a strong, hoppy-tasting brew thought
by some to be the best beer produced in Asia. The barley for Singha is
grown in Thailand, the hops are imported from Germany and the alcohol
content is 6%. Singha is sometimes available on tap in pubs and
restaurants.

Kloster is quite a bit smoother and lighter than Singha and generally
costs about 5B more per bottle, but it is a good-tasting brew often
favoured by western visitors, expats and upwardly mobile Thais who view
it as somewhat of a status symbol. Amarit NB (the initials stand for
'naturally brewed', though who knows whether it is or not) is similar in
taste to Singha but a bit smoother, and is brewed by Thai Amarit, the
same company that produces Kloster. Like Kloster it costs a few baht
more than the national brew. Together Amarit and Kloster claim only 7%

of Thailand's beer consumption. Alcoholic content for each is 4.7%. Boon Rawd Breweries, makers of Singha, also produce a lighter beer called Singha Gold which comes only in small bottles; most people seem to prefer either Kloster or regular Singha to Singha Gold, which is a little on the bland side. Better is Singha's new canned 'draft beer' – if you like cans.

Carlsberg, jointly owned by Danish and Thai interests, is a strong newcomer to Thailand. As elsewhere in South-East Asia, Carlsberg has used an aggressive promotion campaign (backed by the makers of Mekong whisky) to grab around 25% of the Thai market in only two years. The company adjusted its recipe to come closer to Singha's 6% alcohol content, which may be one reason they've surpassed Kloster and Amarit so quickly.

Singha has retaliated with advertisements suggesting that drinking Carlsberg is unpatriotic. Carlsberg responded by creating 'Beer Chang' (Elephant Beer), which matches the hoppy taste of Singha but ratchets the alcohol content up to 7%. Dutch giant Heineken opened a plant in Nonthaburi in 1995, but so far the little green bottles have failed to inundate the market.

The Thai word for beer is *bia*. Draught beer is *bia sòt* (literally, 'fresh beer').

Spirits The more adventurous can tipple the Thai workingman's drink, Mekong-brand whisky. Distilled from rice at a strength of around 70 proof (35% alcohol), Mekong goes well mixed with any number of fruit juices, with Coke or served in the manner preferred by traditionally minded Thai whisky drinkers – swirled with carbonated soda water (one measure of Mekong to two measures of soda) and a wedge of lime over ice. Mekong is pronounced 'Mâe-khŏng', not 'Meekong'. It costs around 120B for a large bottle *(klom)* or 60B for the flask-sized bottle *(baen)*.

More expensive Thai whiskies appealing to the pre-Johnnie Walker set include Singharaj blended whisky (240B a bottle) and VO Royal Thai whisky (260B), each with 40% alcohol. One company in Thailand produces a true rum, that is, a distilled liquor made from sugar cane, called Sang Thip (formerly Sang Som). Alcohol content is 40% and the stock is supposedly aged. Sang Thip costs several baht more than the rice whiskies, but for those who find Mekong and the like unpalatable, it is an alternative worth trying.

Other Liquor A cheaper alternative to whisky is *lâo khăo*, or 'white liquor', of which there are two broad categories: legal and contraband. The legal kind is generally made from sticky rice and is produced for regional consumption. Like Mekong and its competitors, it is 35% alcohol, but sells for 50 to 60B per klom, or roughly half the price. It tastes sweet and raw and much more aromatic than the amber stuff – no amount of mixer will disguise the distinctive taste.

The illegal kinds are made from various agricultural products, including sugar palm sap, coconut milk, sugar cane, taro and rice. Alcohol content may vary from as little as 10 or 12% to as much as 95%. Generally this *lâo thèuan* (jungle liquor) is weaker in the south and stronger in the north and north-east. This is the choice of the many Thais who can't afford to pay the heavy government liquor taxes; prices vary but 10 to 15B worth of the stronger concoctions will intoxicate three or four people.

These types of home-brew or moonshine are generally taken straight with water as a chaser. In smaller towns, almost every garage-type restaurant (except, of course, Muslim restaurants) keeps some under the counter for sale. Sometimes roots and herbs are added to jungle liquor to enhance flavour and colour.

Thai Whisky

As dusk falls on the beaches of Thailand, orange-labelled flat bottles filled with amber fluid start popping up everywhere: it's whisky time. Especially in the more Thai-style resorts, the beaches sport rows of open-air and thatched hut drinking places. Here, Thai rice whisky is more often than not the drink of choice.

As in the rest of Thailand, whisky is usually served with several bottles of soda water, a few slices of lime and a dripping bucket of ice. Often there's a waiter or waitress hovering nearby to regularly replenish the glasses, taking care to ensure that the mixture retains a consistent light amber colour. With self-serve groups (usually male), the drinks get darker and stonger over time as the ratio of whisky to soda gradually increases.

The most popular (and cheapest) brand of rice whisky is Mekong, though Sang Thip 'rum', which actually tastes quite similar, can also be seen gracing seaside bamboo tables. Turn a Mekong bottle over and you'll see a purple date, stamped in Thai, on the back of the label. Rarely is the stuff more than a few weeks or months old, though some proprietors keep a pricier 'aged' stock behind the counter for special customers. Still, it's a working class drink and many well-to-do young urban Thais prefer beer or imported whisky, foregoing what some see as a cultural birthright.

Mekong has a very mild sweet taste, and although some drinkers mix it with Coke or other flavoured drinks, the only way to really appreciate it is to drink it with water – either plain or carbonated. Foreign opinion on Mekong is quite mixed; some visitors can't stand it, while others find it almost dangerously appealing. With its mild taste, Mekong and soda can go down all too easily.

You may hear people saying that because you drink whisky with so much water, you rarely get a hangover from Mekong or Sang Thip. But years of research have shown us that, in excess, Mekong is just as capable as any other whisky of making the morning after a living hell.

One other note: if you find yourself making drinking buddies with the locals, be alert for signs of an impending whisky-chugging contest. Thais are just as susceptible to drunkenness and hangovers as foreigners, but some will gladly take the pain if they know they can bring you along for the ride. In the end, you may have to choose between pride and a quiet exit out the back door.

Nicko Goncharoff

Herbal liquors are somewhat fashionable throughout the country and can be found at roadside vendors, small pubs and in a few guesthouses. These liquors are made by soaking various herbs, roots, seeds, fruit and bark in lâo khão to produce a range of concoctions called yàa dong. Many of the yàa dong preparations are purported to have specific health-enhancing qualities. Some of them taste fabulous while others are rank.

Wine Thais are becoming increasingly interested in wine drinking, but still manage to average a minuscule one glass per capita per year. Various enterprises have attempted to produce wine in Thailand, most often with disastrous results. The latest is a winery called Chateau de Loei, near Phu Reua in Loei Province. Dr Chaiyut, the owner, spent a lot of money and time studying western wine-making methods, and his first vintage, a Chenin Blanc, is a quite drinkable wine. It's available at many of the finer restaurants in Bangkok and Phuket. If you're a wine connoisseur, note that Thailand's best restaurant wine collection can be found at The Boathouse Wine & Grill on Phuket (see Kata & Karon beach in the Phuket Province section of the Northern Andaman Coast chapter for details).

Health section continued from page 96

Typhoid Typhoid fever is one of the most dangerous infections, so seek medical help .

In its early stages typhoid resembles many other illnesses: sufferers may feel like they have a bad cold or flu on the way, as early symptoms are a headache, sore throat and a fever which rises a little each day until it is around 40°C (104°F) or more. The victim's pulse is often slow relative to the degree of fever present and gets slower as the fever rises – unlike a normal fever where the pulse increases. There may also be vomiting, diarrhoea or constipation.

In the second week the high fever and slow pulse continue and a few pink spots may appear on the body; trembling, delirium, weakness, weight loss and dehydration are other symptoms. If there are no further complications, the fever and other symptoms will slowly dissipate during the third week. However, you must get medical help before this because pneumonia (acute infection of the lungs) or peritonitis (perforated bowel) are common complications, and because typhoid is very infectious. The fever should be treated by keeping the victim cool, and dehydration should also be watched for.

The drug of choice is ciprofloxacin at a dose of 1g daily for 14 days. It is quite expensive and may not be available. The alternative, chloramphenicol, has been the mainstay of treatment for many years. In many countries it is still the recommended antibiotic but there are fewer side effects with Ampicillin. The adult dosage is two 250mg capsules, four times a day. Children aged between eight and 12 years should have half the adult dose; younger children should have one-third the adult dose.

People who are allergic to penicillin should not be given Ampicillin.

Worms These parasites are most common in rural, tropical areas and a stool test when you return home is not a bad idea. They can be present on unwashed vegetables or in undercooked meat and you can pick them up through your skin by walking in bare feet.

Infestations may not show up for some time and, although they are generally not serious, if left untreated they can cause severe health problems. A stool test is necessary to pinpoint the problem and medication is often available over the counter.

Tetanus This potentially fatal disease is found in undeveloped tropical areas. It is difficult to treat but is preventable with immunisation. Tetanus occurs when a wound becomes infected by a germ which lives in soil and in the faeces of horses and other animals, so clean all cuts, punctures or animal bites. Tetanus is also known as lockjaw, and the first symptom may be discomfort in swallowing, or stiffening of the jaw and neck; this is followed by painful convulsions of the jaw and whole body.

Rabies Rabies is found in many countries, including Thailand, and is caused by a bite or scratch by an infected animal. Dogs are noted carriers as are monkeys and cats. Any bite, scratch or even lick from a warmblooded, furry animal should be cleaned immediately and thoroughly. Scrub with soap and running water, and then clean with an alcohol solution. If there is any possibility that the animal is infected, medical help should be sought immediately. Even if the animal is not rabid, all bites should be treated seriously as they can become infected or can result in tetanus.

Tuberculosis (TB) TB is a bacterial infection which is usually transmitted by coughing but may be transmitted through drinking unpasteurised milk. Milk that has been boiled is safe to drink, and the souring of milk to make yoghurt or cheese also kills the bacilli. Typically many months of contact with the infected person are required before the disease is passed on.

Sexually Transmitted Diseases (STDs) Sexual contact with an infected sexual partner spreads these diseases. While abstinence is the only 100% preventative, using latex condoms is also effective. In Thailand, gonorrhoea, non-specific urethritis (NSU) and syphilis are the most common of these diseases; sores, blisters or rashes around the genitals, discharges or pain when urinating are common symptoms. In some STDs, such as wart virus and chlamydia, symptoms may be less marked or not observed at all in women. Syphilis symptoms eventually disappear completely but the disease continues and can cause severe problems in later years. The treatment of gonorrhoea and syphilis is with antibiotics.

There are numerous other STDs, for most of which effective treatment is available. However, there is no cure for herpes and there is also no cure for Acquired Immune Deficiency Syndrome (AIDS).

HIV/AIDS The Human Immunodeficiency Virus (HIV), could develop into AIDS. HIV is a major health problem in Thailand, although the overall incidence of infection has slowed over recent years. Any exposure to blood, blood products or bodily fluids may put the individual at risk. In Thailand transmission is predominantly through heterosexual sexual activity (40%); the second most common source of HIV infection is intravenous injection by drug addicts who share needles (33%). Apart from abstinence, the most effective preventative is always to practise safe sex using condoms. It is impossible to detect the HIV-positive status of an otherwise healthy-looking person without a blood test.

The Thai phrase for 'condom' is *thũng anaamai*. Latex condoms are more effective than animal-membrane condoms in preventing disease transmission; to specify latex condoms ask for *thũng yaang anaamai*. Good-quality latex condoms are distributed free by offices of the Ministry of Public Health throughout the country – they come in numbered sizes, like shoes! Condoms can also be purchased at any pharmacy, but those issued by the Ministry of Public Health are considered the most effective; a recent ministry survey found that around 11% of commercial Thai condoms were damaged, mostly due to improper storage.

It can also be spread by dirty needles – vaccinations, acupuncture, tattooing and body piercing can potentially be as dangerous as intravenous drug use if the equipment is not clean. If you do need an injection, ask to see the syringe unwrapped in front of you, or better still, take a needle and syringe pack with you overseas – it is a cheap insurance package against infection with HIV.

Fear of HIV infection should never preclude treatment for serious medical conditions. Although there may be a risk of infection, it is very small indeed.

Insect-Borne Diseases
Malaria This serious disease is spread by mosquito bites. If you are travelling in endemic areas it is extremely important to take malarial prophylactics. Symptoms include headaches, fever, chills and sweating which may subside and recur. Without treatment malaria can develop more serious, potentially fatal effects. Antimalarial drugs do not prevent you from being infected but kill the parasites during a stage in their development.

There are a number of different types of malaria. The one of most concern is falciparum malaria, which is responsible for the very serious cerebral malaria. Malaria risk exists throughout the year in rural Thailand, especially in forested and hilly areas. At the moment Thailand's high-risk areas include northern Kanchanaburi Province (especially Thung Yai Naresuan National Park) and parts of Trat Province along the Cambodian border (including Ko Chang). According to the CDC and Thailand's Ministry of Public Health, there is virtually no risk of malaria in urban areas or the main tourist areas (eg Bangkok, Phuket, Pattaya and Chiang Mai).

Expert advice should be sought, as there are many factors to consider when deciding on the type of antimalarial medication you should use, including the area to be visited, the risk of exposure to malaria-carrying mosquitoes, your current medical condition, and your age and pregnancy status. It is also important to discuss the side-effect profile of the medication, so you can work out some level of risk-versus-benefit ratio. It is also very important to be sure of the correct dosage of the medication prescribed to you. Some people have inadvertently taken weekly medication (chloroquine) on a daily basis, with disastrous effects. While discussing dosages for prevention of malaria, it is often advisable to include the dosages required for treatment, especially if your trip is through a high-risk area where you would be isolated from medical care.

All commonly prescribed malarial suppressants (eg chloroquine) have the potential to cause side effects. Mefloquine may affect motor skills and cause bad dreams. There is some resistance to mefloquine, but it is still a useful drug.

In Thailand, where malaria tends to be resistant to most if not all the previously mentioned prophylactics, the Chinese herb *qinghao* – or its chemical derivative artemether – has proven to be very effective. Its use in Thailand (and other mainland South-East Asian countries) has recently been endorsed by the UN Tropical Disease Programme as well as the WHO director-general. Many doctors in Thailand are now recommending halofantrine, marketed under the name Hal-Fan, as the latest and greatest cure.

The main messages are:

- Primary prevention must always be in the form of mosquito avoidance measures. The mosquitoes (Anopheles) that transmit malaria bite from dusk to dawn and during this period travellers are advised to: wear light-coloured clothing, long pants and long-sleeved shirts; use mosquito repellents containing the compound DEET on exposed areas (commercial repellents containing no more than 35% DEET can be purchased at well-stocked Thai pharmacies); avoid highly scented perfumes or aftershave; and use a mosquito net (it may be worth taking your own).
- While no antimalarial is 100% effective, taking the most appropriate drug significantly reduces the risk of contracting the disease.
- No-one should ever die from malaria. It can be diagnosed by a simple blood test. Symptoms range from fever, chills and sweating, headache and abdominal pains to a vague feeling of ill-health – so seek examination immediately if there is any suggestion of malaria.

- Contrary to popular belief, once a traveller contracts malaria they do not have it for life. One of the parasites may lie dormant in the liver but this can also be eradicated using a specific medication. Malaria is curable, as long as the traveller seeks medical help when symptoms occur.
- For those with an allergy or aversion to synthetic repellents, citronella makes a good substitute. Mosquito coils *(yaa kan yung bàep jùt)* do an excellent job of repelling mosquitoes in your room and are readily available in Thailand. Day mosquitoes do not carry malaria, so it is only at night that you have to worry – peak biting hours are a few hours after dusk and a few hours before dawn.
- Like many other tropical diseases, malaria is frequently mis-diagnosed in western countries. If you should develop the symptoms after a return to your home country, be sure to seek medical attention immediately and inform your doctor that you may have been exposed to malaria.

Dengue Fever In some areas of Thailand there is a risk, albeit low, of contracting dengue fever via mosquitoes. This time it's a day variety (Aedes) you have to worry about. Like malaria, dengue fever seems to be on the increase in tropical Asia in recent years. Dengue is found in urban as well as rural areas, especially in areas of human habitation (often indoors) where there is standing water.

Unlike malaria, dengue fever is caused by a virus and there is no chemical prophylactic or vaccination against it. The symptoms come on suddenly and include high fever, severe headache, and heavy joint and muscle pain (hence its older name of 'breakbone fever'), followed a few days later by a rash that spreads from the torso to the arms, legs and face. Various risk factors such as age, immunity and viral strain may mitigate these symptoms so that they are less severe or last only a few days. Even when the basic symptoms are short-lived, it can take several weeks to recover fully from the resultant fatigue.

In rare cases dengue fever may develop into a more severe condition known as dengue haemorrhagic fever (DHF), or dengue toxic shock syndrome, which is often fatal. DHF is most common among Asian children under 15 years who are undergoing a second dengue infection, so the risk of

DHF for most international travellers is very low.

Not all mosquito bites are infectious. The mosquito which carries the disease tends to bite during the day and lives around houses. The best way to prevent dengue, as with malaria, is to take care not to be bitten at all.

The only treatment for dengue is bed rest, constant rehydration and paracetamol acetaminophen (Tylenol, Panadol). Avoid aspirin, which increases the risk of haemorrhaging. Hospital supervision is necessary in severe cases.

Cuts, Bites & Stings

Cuts & Scratches Skin punctures can easily become infected in hot climates and may be difficult to heal. Treat any cut with an antiseptic such as Betadine. Where possible avoid bandages and Band-Aids, which can keep wounds wet. Coral cuts are notoriously slow to heal, as the coral injects a weak venom into the wound. Avoid touching and walking on fragile corals in the first place, but if you are near coral reefs, wear shoes and clean any cut thoroughly with hydrogen peroxide if available.

Bites & Stings Bee and wasp stings are usually painful rather than dangerous. Calamine lotion will give relief and ice packs will reduce the pain and swelling. There are some spiders with dangerous bites but antivenenes are usually available. Scorpion stings are notoriously painful. Scorpions often shelter in shoes or clothing.

There are various fish and other sea creatures which can sting or bite dangerously, or which are dangerous to eat. Local advice usually offers the best prevention.

Snakes To minimise your chances of being bitten always wear boots, socks and long trousers when walking through undergrowth where snakes may be present. Don't put your hands into holes and crevices, and be careful when collecting firewood.

Snake bites do not cause instant death and antivenenes are usually available. Keep the victim calm and still, wrap the bitten limb tightly, as you would for a sprained ankle, and then attach a splint to immobilise it. Then seek medical help, if possible taking along the dead snake for identification. Don't attempt to catch the snake if there is even a remote possibility of being bitten again. Tourniquets and sucking out the poison are now comprehensively discredited as first aid treatments.

Snakebite antivenene is available at Chulalongkorn Hospital (☎ (2) 252-8181/9), Rama IV Rd, Bangkok.

Jellyfish See the Hazardous Marine Life boxed aside on the following pages and the Dive Medicine section further on.

Bedbugs & Lice Bedbugs live in various places, but particularly in dirty mattresses and bedding. Spots of blood on bedclothes or on the wall around the bed can be read as a suggestion to find another hotel. Bedbugs leave itchy bites in neat rows. Calamine lotion may help.

All lice cause itching and discomfort. They make themselves at home in your hair, your clothing or your pubic hair. You catch lice through direct contact with infected people or by sharing combs, clothing and the like. Powder or shampoo treatment will kill the lice and infected clothing should then be washed in very hot water.

Leeches & Ticks Leeches may be present in damp rainforest conditions; they attach themselves to your skin to suck your blood. Trekkers often get them on their legs or in their boots. Salt or a lighted cigarette end will make them fall off. Do not pull them off, as the bite is then more likely to become infected. An insect repellent may keep them away.

You should always check your body if you have been walking through a potentially tick-infested area as ticks can cause skin infections and other more serious diseases. If a tick is found attached, press down around the tick's head with tweezers, grab the head and gently pull upwards. Avoid pulling the

Hazardous Marine Life

Several organisms living in the sea can cause physical pain and discomfort to humans who come into close contact with them. Although such occurrences are largely a matter of bad luck, it helps if you're familiar with the potential hazards and conversant in ways to avoid contact. As a general rule of thumb, never touch anything underwater except rocks or sand. Also, never reach beneath rocks or into holes, crevices or other places where marine life may be.

Jellyfish stings are the most common source of organic marine mishaps after sunburn. The presence of jellyfish at a beach is largely seasonal and/or storm related; one beach may be free of jellyfish one day, seemingly full of them the next. Small ones without dangling tentacles (some of which may be almost invisible to the eye) usually cause only a transitory itching or burning that disappears after a few minutes once contact ends. Larger jellyfish, especially those with long tentacles, can cause more severe and lasting pain.

For the latter, treat by removing any tentacles that may have detached themselves from the jellyfish. Don't use your hands to do this, but rather newspaper, leaves or some other object. Smaller, more clinging tentacles or tentacle particles may require removal with soap and razor. Once all the stinging bits have been removed, wash the affected area with salt water, then rinse thoroughly with vinegar to de-activate any stingers which have not 'fired'. When vinegar isn't available, urine reportedly produces the same de-activating effect. Calamine lotion, antihistamines and analgesics may reduce the reaction and relieve the pain.

Fire coral, found among reefs and other coral sites, is a branching hydroid (not actually a coral) that looks harmlessly fern-like but packs a distinctly uncomfortable – sometimes quite intense – prickle if exposed skin brushes against it. Treat as for jellyfish.

Coral cuts acquired by brushing against dead coral can easily become infected as tiny pieces of bacteria-infested coral can work themselves deep into the cuts. Wash thoroughly with soap and hot water, disinfect with alcohol or hydrogen peroxide, apply antibiotic ointment and bandage.

Sea urchins are found in sandy spots near rocks and coral, often in popular snorkelling areas. They are generally spotted easily – look for dark spheres radiating thin spines. In such environments, take care when wading or snorkelling not to be knocked over by waves or tidal surges. Contact with sea urchins may leave their spines imbedded in your skin. The larger spines can sometimes be removed with tweezers. When spines are too fine to be plucked out, the preferred local method is to break them up using a blunt instrument such as a smooth stone or knife handle. Once the spines have been dealt with, the painful venom can be neutralised by immersing the affected area in very hot water

---

rear of the body as this may squeeze the tick's gut contents through the attached mouth parts into the skin, increasing the risk of infection and disease. Smearing chemicals on the tick will not make it let go and is not recommended.

Women's Health

Gynaecological Problems Poor diet, lowered resistance due to the use of antibiotics for stomach upsets and even contraceptive pills can lead to vaginal infections when travelling in hot climates. Keeping the genital area clean, and wearing skirts or loose fitting trousers and cotton underwear, will help prevent infections.

Yeast infections, characterised by a rash, itch and discharge, can be treated with a vinegar or even lemon-juice douche or with yoghurt. Nystatin, miconazole or clotrimazole suppositories are the usual medical prescription. Trichomonas and gardnerella are more serious infections; symptoms are a smelly discharge and sometimes a burning sensation when urinating. Sexual partners must also be treated, and if a vinegar-water douche is not effective medical attention should be sought. Metronidazole (Flagyl) is the prescribed drug.

Pregnancy Most miscarriages occur during the first three months of pregnancy, so this is the most risky time to travel as far as your own health is concerned. Miscarriage is not uncommon, and can occasionally lead to severe bleeding. The last three months (recommended 43 to 45°C, or as hot as you can stand) for a half-hour to 90 minutes. Marine life venoms are protein based; intense heat breaks down the poison.

Scorpionfish, lionfish and **zebrafish** all look very colourful and interesting but their dorsal spines can pack a painful wallop – don't touch! It's very unlikely that you will be stung by one of these bizarre beauties, but if so use the hot water treatment described for sea urchins.

Cone shells are cone-shaped sea snails with a venomous proboscis that darts from the narrow end of the shell to ward off aggressors. The pain of their sting can be quite intense, and venom doses are sometimes fatal. Never touch or even get close to a cone-shaped shell in the sea. For emergency treatment, immobilise the affected limb if possible and keep it at a lower level than the victim's heart. Dress the wound with an elastic bandage to prevent the spread of venom, and seek medical help. If help is unavailable, apply the hot water treatment described for sea urchins.

Stonefish, which as their name suggests may resemble stones lying in the sand, also have a rather potent venom. Treat as for cone shell stings.

Sea snakes, all of which produce some venom, are common but tend to avoid humans. At any rate their mouths are so small that it's very difficult for them to bite humans except between the fingers and toes. In the highly unlikely event of a bite, wrap the bite with an elastic bandage, immobilise the affected limb and seek medical help for an injection of commonly available antivenin.

Sting rays have barbed tailspines that can inflict painful wounds. Experienced beachgoers perform the 'stingray shuffle' when walking on sandy bottoms. If you bump into a ray resting on the bottom, it will usually swim away; if you step on one, it's likely to give you a flick of the barb. Treat using very hot water as previously described but be sure to remove the barb sac, which continues to release venom, from the wound first. Remember that all protein-based venoms break down when heated.

Sharks have a bad rep worldwide but they are *not* a significant danger in Thailand. In fact, there has never been a single report of a shark attack on humans in Thai waters, which favours the propagation of smaller species such as the leopard shark, nurse shark, and whitetip or blacktip reef shark – all of which tend to be quite timid. One exception to the 'small sharks' rule is the Burma Banks area of the Andaman Sea (and possibly other as yet unexplored areas far west of the mainland), where there are some large hammerheads and tiger sharks with the potential to inflict serious bites on humans.

Nevertheless, handing food to sharks underwater – an activity practised and promoted by a few recreational dive operations in Thailand – is never a good idea. Besides the potential risk it poses (long-term studies suggest hand-feeding makes sharks more aggressive around humans), such practices habituate wildlife to getting human handouts. This interrupts the natural marine food chain and disrupts the undersea ecological balance. ■

---

should also be spent within reasonable distance of good medical care. A baby born as early as 24 weeks stands a chance of survival, but only in a good modern hospital. Pregnant women should avoid all unnecessary medication, but vaccinations and malarial prophylactics should still be taken where possible. Additional care should be taken to prevent illness and particular attention should be paid to diet and nutrition. Alcohol and nicotine, for example, should be avoided.

Women travellers often find that their periods become irregular or even cease while they're on the road. Remember that a missed period in these circumstances doesn't necessarily indicate pregnancy. There are health posts or family planning clinics in many small and large urban centres, where you can seek advice and have a urine test to determine whether you are pregnant or not.

Hospitals & Clinics

Thailand's most technically advanced hospitals are in Bangkok. In the south, Phuket and Hat Yai have the best medical care. Elsewhere in the country, every provincial capital has at least one hospital of varying quality as well as several public and private clinics. The best emergency health care, however, can usually be found in military hospitals (*rohng phayaabaan tha-hăan*); they will usually treat foreigners in an emergency. See the respective destination chapters for information on specific health-care facilities.

Should you need urgent dental care, suggested contacts in Bangkok include:

Bumrungrad Medical Centre – 33 Soi 3, Sukhumvit Rd (☎ (2) 253-0250)
Dental Polyclinic – 2111/3 New Phetburi Rd (☎ (2) 314-5070)
Ploenchit Clinic – Maneeya Bldg, Ploenchit Rd (☎ (2) 251-1567/8902)
Siam Dental Clinic – 412/11-2 Soi 6, Siam Square (☎ (2) 251-6315)

In Phuket try one of the following:

City Park Dental Clinic – 183/36 Phang-Nga Rd (☎ (76) 233-241)
Dental Care Clinic – 62/5 Rasada Rd (☎ (76) 215-025)

For urgent eye care, the best choices are in Bangkok. Try the Rutnin Eye Hospital (☎ (2) 258-0442) at 80/1 Soi Asoke or the Pirompesuy Eye Hospital (☎ (2) 252-4141) at 117/1 Phayathai Rd.

Counselling Services

Qualified professionals at Community Services of Bangkok (☎ (2) 258-4998), 15 Soi 33, Sukhumvit Rd, offer a range of counselling services to foreign residents and newcomers to Thailand.

Members of Alcoholics Anonymous who want to contact the Bangkok group or anyone needing help with a drinking problem can call AA at ☎ (2) 253-6305 from 6 am to 6 pm or ☎ (2) 256-6578 from 6 pm to 6 am for information. Meetings are held daily at Holy Redeemer Catholic Church, 123/19 Soi Ruamrudee. There are also regular meetings in Pattaya and Phuket.

TOILETS & SHOWERS

In Thailand, as in many other Asian countries, the 'squat toilet' is the norm except in hotels and guesthouses geared toward tourists and international business travellers. Instead of trying to approximate a chair or stool like a modern sit-down toilet, a traditional Asian toilet sits more or less flush with the surface of the floor, with two footpads on either side of the porcelain abyss. For people who have never used a squat toilet it takes a bit of getting used to. If you find yourself feeling awkward the first couple of times you use

one, you can console yourself with the knowledge that, according to those who study such matters, people who use squat toilets are much less likely to develop haemorrhoids than people who use the sit-down toilets.

Next to the typical squat toilet is a bucket or cement reservoir filled with water. A plastic bowl usually floats on the water's surface or sits nearby. This water supply has a two fold function; toilet-goers scoop water from the reservoir with the plastic bowl and use it to clean the nether regions while still squatting over the toilet. Since there is usually no mechanical flushing device attached to a squat toilet, a few extra scoops must be poured into the toilet basin to flush waste into the septic system. In larger towns, mechanical flushing systems are becoming increasingly common, even with squat toilets. More rustic toilets in rural areas may simply consist of a few planks over a hole in the ground.

Even in places where sit-down toilets are installed, the plumbing may not be designed to take toilet paper. In such cases the usual washing bucket will be standing nearby or there will be a waste basket where you're supposed to place used toilet paper.

Public toilets are common in cinemas, department stores, bus and train stations, larger hotel lobbies and airports. While on the road between towns and villages it is perfectly acceptable to go behind a tree or bush or even to use the roadside when nature calls.

Bathing

Some hotels and most guesthouses in the country do not have hot water, though places in the larger cities will usually offer small electric shower heaters in their more expensive rooms. Few boiler-style water heaters are available outside larger international-style hotels.

Many rural Thais bathe in rivers or streams. Those living in towns or cities may have washrooms where a large jar or cement trough is filled with water for bathing. A plastic or metal bowl is used to sluice water from the jar or trough over the body. Even in homes where showers are installed, heated water is uncommon. Most Thais bathe at least twice a day.

If ever you find yourself having to bathe in a public place you should wear a *phâa-khamāa* or *phâa sîn* (cotton wraparounds for men and women respectively); nude bathing is not the norm.

WOMEN TRAVELLERS
Attitudes toward Women
Chinese trader Ma Huan noted in 1433 that among the Thais 'All affairs are managed by their wives, all trading transactions large or small'. In rural areas females typically inherit land and throughout the country they tend to control family finances. The 1995 UNDP Human Development Report noted that on the Gender-Related Development Index (GDI) Thailand ranked 31st of 130 countries, thus falling into the 'progressive' category. The nation's GDI increase was greater than that of any country in the world over the past 20 years. According to the report, Thailand 'has succeeded in building the basic human capabilities of both women and men, without substantial gender imparity'. Thailand's work force is 44% female, ranking it 27th on a world scale, just ahead of China and the USA.

So much for the good news. The bad news is that although women generally fare well in the labour force and in rural land in heritance, their cultural standing is a bit further from parity. An oft-repeated Thai saying reminds us that men form the front legs of the elephant, women the hind legs (at least they're pulling equal weight). Thai Buddhism commonly holds that women must be reborn as men before they can attain nirvana, though many Thai *dharma* teachers point out that this presumption isn't supported by the *suttas* (discourses of the Buddha) or by the commentaries. But it is a common belief, supported by the availability of a fully ordained Buddhist monastic status for men and a less prestigious eight precept ordination for women. On a legal level, men enjoy more privilege. Men may divorce their wives for committing adultery, but not vice versa, for example. Men who take a foreign spouse continue to have the right to purchase and own land, while Thai women who marry foreign men lose this right.

Safety Precautions
Around 38% of foreign visitors to Thailand are women, a figure equal to the worldwide average as measured by the World Tourism Organisation, and on a par with Singapore and Hong Kong. For all other Asian countries the proportion of female visitors runs lower than 35%. The ratio of women travellers is growing year by year; the overall visitor increase between 1993 and 1994, for example, was 2.3%, while the number of women visitors jumped 13.8%.

Everyday incidents of sexual harassment are much less common in Thailand than in India, Indonesia or Malaysia, and this may lull women who have recently travelled in these countries into thinking that Thailand travel is safer than it is. Over the past seven years, several foreign women have been attacked while travelling alone in remote areas. If you're a woman travelling alone, try to pair up with other travellers when travelling at night or in remote areas. Urban areas seem relatively safe; the exceptions are Chiang Mai in the north and Ko Pha-Ngan, where there have been several reports of harassment (oddly, we've had no reports from Bangkok). Make sure hotel and guesthouse rooms are secure at night – if they're not, demand another room or move to another hotel/guesthouse.

In social situations, especially in bars or at beach resorts, it's also good to bear in mind that Thai women are very modest in their behaviour. This makes it that much easier for Thai men to misinterpret even platonic friendly gestures from western women. There are Thai males who already view western women as 'easy': exercising discreet behaviour is the best way not to encourage such attitudes.

Prostitution
As throughout most of south and South-East

Asia, men in Thailand have greater freedom in their sexual activities than women, who are expected to arrive at the marriage altar as virgins and to refrain from extramarital affairs. This attitude creates a sexual imbalance in which large numbers of males are seeking casual sexual contact, but few females are available. The resulting commercial sex industry, catering largely to indigenous demand, thus maintains an ongoing reservoir of sex workers and clients. In Bangkok (and to a much lesser degree in other large urban centres), the imbalance is righting itself as premarital/extramarital sex between non-paying consenting Thais becomes more common.

Among foreigners it's a common perception that Thai women become sex workers because they don't have recourse to similar or better-paying employment in other fields. But the employment statistics cited above don't seem to support this. On a purely economic level there is no compelling reason to choose prostitution over weaving, rice-milling or office work. Thai women who participate in prostitution either do so unwillingly – in the case of bonded or forced service – or willingly in hopes of obtaining luxuries in excess of mere livelihood. In either case it's the demand side of the equation – caused by the lack of available female sex partners – that appears to drive the industry.

GAY & LESBIAN TRAVELLERS

Thai culture is very tolerant of homosexuality, both male and female. The nation has no laws that discriminate against homosexuals and there is a fairly prominent gay/lesbian scene around the country. Since there's no anti-gay establishment to move against, there is no 'gay movement' in Thailand as such. Whether speaking of dress or mannerism, lesbians and gays are generally accepted without comment.

Public displays of affection – whether heterosexual or homosexual – are frowned upon. As the guide *Thai Scene* (Gay Men's Press, Box 247, London N6 4AT, England) has written, 'For many gay travellers, Thailand is a nirvana with a long-established gay

bar scene, which, whilst often very Thai in culture, is particularly welcoming to tourists. There is little, if any, social approbation toward gay people, providing Thai cultural mores are respected. What people do in bed, whether straight or gay, is not expected to be a topic of general conversation nor bragged about'.

Utopia (☎ (2) 259-1619; fax 258-3250), at 116/1 Soi 23, Sukhumvit Rd, is a gay and lesbian multi-purpose Bangkok centre consisting of a guesthouse, bar, cafe, gallery and gift shop. Utopia maintains an Internet site called the Southeast Asia Gay and Lesbian Resources ('Utopia Homo Page') at www.utopia-asia.com as well as an email address (utopia@ksc9.th.).

DISABLED TRAVELLERS

Thailand presents one large, ongoing obstacle course for the mobility-impaired. With its high curbs, uneven sidewalks and nonstop traffic, Bangkok can be particularly difficult – many streets must be crossed via pedestrian bridges flanked with steep stairways, while buses and boats don't stop long enough for even the mildly handicapped. Rarely are there any ramps or other access points for wheelchairs.

Hyatt International (Bangkok, Pattaya), Novotel (Bangkok, Phuket), Sheraton (Bangkok, Phuket) and Holiday Inn (Bangkok, Phuket) are the only hotel chains in coastal Thailand that make consistent design efforts to provide handicapped access for each of their properties. Because of their high employee-to-guest ratios, home-grown luxury hotel chains such as those managed by Dusit, Amari and Royal Garden Resorts are usually very good in accommodating the mobility-impaired by providing staff help where architecture fails. For the rest, you're pretty much left to your own resources.

For wheelchair travellers, any trip to Thailand will require a good deal of advance planning; fortunately a growing network of information sources can put you in touch with those who have wheeled through Thailand before. There is no better source of information than someone who's done it.

A reader recently wrote with the following tips:

- The difficulties you mention in your book are all there. However, travel in the streets is still possible, and enjoyable, providing you have a strong, ambulatory companion. Some obstacles may require two carriers; Thais are by nature helpful and could generally be counted on for assistance.
- Don't feel you have to rely on organised tours to see the sights – these often leave early in the morning at times inconvenient to disabled people. It is far more convenient (and often cheaper) to take a taxi or hired car. It's also far more enjoyable as there is no feeling of holding others up.
- Many taxis have an LPG tank in the boot (trunk) which may make it impossible to get a wheelchair in and close it. You might do better to hire a private car and driver (this usually costs no more and sometimes less – than a taxi).
- A tuk-tuk is far easier to get in and out of and to carry two people and a wheelchair than a taxi. Even the pedicabs can hang a wheelchair on the back of the carriage.
- Be ready to try anything – in spite of my worries, riding an elephant proved quite easy.

Three international organisations which act as clearing houses for information on world travel for the mobility-impaired are:

Access Foundation, PO Box 356, Malverne, NY 11565, USA (☎ (516) 887-5798)
Mobility International USA, PO Box 10767, Eugene, OR 97440, USA (☎ (541) 343-1284)
Society for the Advancement of Travel for the Handicapped (SATH), 26 Court St, Brooklyn, NY 11242, USA (☎ (718) 858-5483)

In Thailand you can also contact:

Association of the Physically Handicapped of Thailand – 73/7-8 Soi 8 (Soi Thepprasan), Tivanon Rd, Talaat Kawan, Nonthaburi 11000 (☎ (2) 951-0569; fax 580-1098 ext 7)
Disabled Peoples International (Thailand) – 78/2 Tivanon Rd, Pak Kret, Nonthaburi 11120 (☎ (2) 583-3021; fax 583-6518)
Handicapped International – 87/2 Soi 15, Sukhumvit Rd, Bangkok 10110
Thai Disability Organisations – David Lambertson, Ambassador (☎/fax (2) 254-2990)

SENIOR TRAVELLERS

Senior discounts aren't generally available in Thailand, but the Thais more than make up for this in the respect they typically show for the elderly. In traditional Thai culture status comes with age; there isn't as heavy an emphasis on youth as in the western world. Deference for age manifests itself in the way Thais go out of their way to help older persons in and out of taxis or with luggage, and – usually but not always – in waiting on them first in shops and post offices.

Nonetheless, some cultural spheres are reserved for youth. Cross-generational entertainment in particular is less common than in western countries. There is strict stratification among discos and nightclubs, for example, according to age group. One place will cater to teenagers, another to people in their early 20s, one for late 20s and 30s, yet another for those in their 40s and 50s, and once you've reached 60 you're considered to old to go clubbing! Exceptions to this rule include the more traditional entertainment venues, such as rural temple fairs and other wat-centred events, where young and old will dance and eat together. For men, massage parlours are another place where old and young clientele mix.

TRAVEL WITH CHILDREN

Like many places in South-East Asia, travelling with children in Thailand can be a lot of fun as long as you come well prepared with the right attitudes, physical requirements and the usual parental patience. Lonely Planet's *Travel with Children* by Maureen Wheeler and others contains useful advice on how to cope with kids on the road and what to bring along to make things go more smoothly, with special attention paid to travel in developing countries.

Thais love children and in many instances will shower attention on your offspring, who will find ready playmates among their Thai counterparts and a temporary nanny service at practically every stop.

For the most part parents needn't worry too much about health concerns, though it pays to lay down a few ground rules – such as regular hand-washing – to head off potential problems. All the usual health precautions apply (see the Health section earlier for details); children should especially be warned not to play with animals as rabies is relatively common in Thailand.

DANGERS & ANNOYANCES
Precautions
Although Thailand is in no way a dangerous country to visit, it's wise to be a little cautious, particularly if you're travelling alone. Solo women travellers should take special care on arrival at Bangkok international airport, particularly at night. Don't take one of Bangkok's very unofficial taxis (black and white licence tags) by yourself – better a licensed taxi (yellow and black tags) or even the public bus. Both men and women should ensure their rooms are securely locked and bolted at night. Inspect cheap rooms with thin walls for strategic peepholes. Take caution when leaving your valuables in hotel safes.

Many travellers have reported unpleasant experiences at Ko Samui guesthouses (particularly on Chaweng beach). Make sure you obtain an itemised receipt for property left with hotels or guesthouses – note the exact quantity of travellers cheques and all other valuables. On the road, keep zippered luggage secured with small locks, especially while travelling on buses and trains.

Credit Cards
After returning home, some visitors have received huge credit card bills for purchases (usually jewellery) charged to their cards while the cards had, supposedly, been secure in the hotel or guesthouse safe. It's said that over the two peak months that this was first noticed, credit card companies lost over US$20 million in Thailand – one major company had 40% of their worldwide losses here! You might consider taking your credit cards with you if you go trekking – if they're stolen on the trail at least the bandits won't be able to use them. Organised gangs in Bangkok specialise in arranging stolen credit card purchases – in some cases they pay 'down and out' foreigners to fake the signatures.

When making credit card purchases, don't let vendors take your credit card out of your sight to run it through the machine. Unscrupulous merchants have been known to rub off three or four or more receipts with one credit card purchase; after the customer leaves the shop, they use the one legitimate receipt as a model to forge your signature on the blanks, then fill in astronomical 'purchases'. Sometimes they wait several weeks – even months – between submitting each charge receipt to the bank, so that you can't remember whether you'd been billed at the same vendor more than once.

Druggings
On trains and buses, particularly in the south, beware of friendly strangers offering cigarettes, drinks or sweets (candy). Several travellers have reported waking up with a headache sometime later to find that their valuables have disappeared. One traveller was offered what looked like a machine-wrapped, made-in-England Cadbury's chocolate. His girlfriend spat it out immediately, while he woke up nine hours later in hospital having required emergency resuscitation after his breathing nearly stopped. This happened on the Surat Thani to Phuket bus.

Travellers have also encountered drugged food or drink from friendly strangers in bars and from prostitutes in their own hotel rooms. Thais are also occasional victims, especially at the Northern (Moh Chit) bus terminal and Chatuchak Park in Bangkok, where young girls are sometimes drugged and sold to brothels. Conclusion – don't accept gifts from strangers.

Assault
Robbery of travellers by force is very rare in Thailand, but it does happen. Statistics from 1991, the most recent year for which figures are available, show that Thailand claims only 15 violent crimes – including murder and armed robbery – per 100,000 population per year. This is some distance behind Malaysia (42), Australia (57.5), Britain (97), Hong Kong (208) and the USA (282). Isolated incidences of armed robbery have occurred along the Thai-Burmese and Thai-Cambodian

borders and on remote islands. The safest practice in remote areas is not to go out alone at night, and if trekking, go in a group.

Touts

Touting – grabbing newcomers in the street or in train stations, bus terminals or airports to sell them a service – is a long-time tradition in Asia, and while Thailand doesn't have as many touts as, say, India, it has its share. In the popular tourist spots it seems like everyone – young boys waving flyers, tuk-tuk drivers, samlor drivers, schoolgirls – is touting something, usually hotels or guest-houses.

For the most part they're completely harmless and sometimes they can be very informative. But take anything a tout says with two large grains of salt. Since touts work on commission and get paid just for delivering you to a guesthouse or hotel (whether you check in or not), they'll say anything to get you to the door. Often the best (most honest and reliable) hotels and guest-houses refuse to pay tout commissions – so the average tout will try to steer you away from such places. Hence don't believe them if they tell you the hotel or guesthouse you're looking for is 'closed', 'full', 'dirty' or 'bad'.

Sometimes (rarely) they're right but most times it's just a ruse to get you to a place that pays more commission. Always have a careful look yourself before checking into a place recommended by a tout. Tuk-tuk and samlor drivers often offer free or low-cost rides to the place they're touting; if you have another place you're interested in, you might agree to go with a driver only if he or she promises to deliver you to your first choice after you've had a look at the place being touted. If drivers refuse, chances are it's because they know your first choice is a better one.

This type of commission work isn't limited to low-budget guesthouses. Taxi drivers and even airline employees at Thailand's major airports – including Bangkok and Ko Samui – reap commissions from the big hotels as well. At either end of the budget spectrum, the customer ends up paying the commission indirectly through raised room rates. Bangkok international airport employees are notorious for talking newly arrived tourists into staying at badly located, overpriced hotels.

Insurgent Activity

Since the 1920s and 30s several insurgent groups have operated in Thailand: the Communist Party of Thailand (CPT), with its tactical force the People's Liberation Army of Thailand (PLAT) in rural areas throughout the country; Hmong guerrillas in the north hoping to overthrow the Communist regime in Laos; and Malay separatists and Muslim revolutionaries in the extreme south.

These groups have been mainly involved in propaganda activity, village infiltration and occasional clashes with Thai government troops. Very rarely have they had encounters with foreign travellers. Aside from sporadic terrorist bombings – mostly at train stations in the south and sometimes at up-country festivals – 'innocent' people have not been involved in the insurgent activity. In the south, traditionally a hot spot, Communist forces have been all but limited to Camp 508 in a relatively inaccessible area along the Surat Thani-Nakhon Si Thammarat provincial border.

The Betong area of Yala Province on the Thai-Malaysian border was until six years ago the tactical headquarters for the armed Communist Party of Malaya (CPM). Thai and Malaysian government troops occasionally clashed with the insurgents, who from time to time hijacked trucks along the Yala to Betong road. But in December 1989, in exchange for amnesty, the CPM agreed 'to terminate all armed activities' and to respect the laws of Thailand and Malaysia. It appears that this area is now safe for travel.

PULO One continuing thorn in the side of the Thai government is the small but militant Malay-Muslim movement in the south. The Pattani United Liberation Organisation (PULO), formed in 1957, trained in Libya and reached its peak in 1981 with a guerrilla strength of around 1800. The PULO refers to Thailand's three predominantly Muslim, Malay-speaking provinces of Pattani, Yala and Narathiwat collectively as 'Pattani'; their objective is to create a separate, sovereign state or, at the very least, to obtain annexation to Malaysia.

Intelligence sources claim the rebels are supported by PAS, Malaysia's main opposition party, which is dedicated to making Malaysia more fundamentally Islamic. A group of 111 Muslim separatists belonging to the PULO, Barisan Revolusi Nasional (BRN, or National Revolutionary Front) and Barisan Nasional Pembebasan Pattani (BNPP, or National Front for the Freedom of Pattani) surrendered in late 1991, but PULO remnants persist in southern Thailand villages and jungles. This was its fourth mass surrender in five years – only a few dozen guerrillas are still active, mainly involved in propaganda and extortion activities plus the occasional attack on Thai government vehicles.

PULO members collect regular 'protection' payments, eg from rubber plantations. In August 1992 a powerful bomb exploded in the Hat Yai train station, killing three and injuring 75; a PULO-signed letter was found in the station. This was the first bombing of this nature since the early 1980s. A second bombing occurred along the Bangkok to Sungai Kolok rail line in Songkhla Province on 30 March; there were no serious injuries this time. In August 1993 a coordinated terrorist effort set fire to 35 government schools in Pattani, Yala and Narathiwat. Since those fires, law enforcement in the south has been intensified and the area has stayed relatively quiet.

Drugs

Opium, heroin and marijuana are widely used in Thailand, but it is illegal to buy, sell or possess these drugs in any quantity. A lesser known narcotic, *kràtom* (a leaf of the *Mitragyna speciosa* tree), is used by workers and students as a stimulant – similar to Yemen's *qat*. A hundred kràtom leaves sell for around 50B, and are sold for 3 to 5B each; the leaf is illegal and is said to be addictive.

In the south, especially on the rainy gulf islands, mushrooms (*hèt khîi khwai*, 'buffalo-shit mushrooms', or *hèt mao*, 'drunk

Drug Penalties		
Drug	*Quantity*	*Penalty*
Marijuana		
Smuggling	any amount	2 to 15 years imprisonment
Possession	less than 10kg	up to 5 years imprisonment
Possession	10kg +	2 to 15 years imprisonment
Heroin		
Smuggling	any amount	life imprisonment
Smuggling	any amount with intent to sell	execution
Possession	10g +	imprisonment or execution

* Note: 'Smuggling' refers to any drug possession at a border or airport Customs check.

mushrooms') which contain the hallucinogen psilocybin are sometimes sold to or gathered by foreigners. The legal status of mushroom use or possession is questionable; police have been known to hassle Thais who sell them. Using such mushrooms is a risky proposition as the dosage is always uncertain; there is one confirmed story of a foreigner who swam to his death off Ko Pha-Ngan after a 'special' mushroom omelette.

Although in certain areas of the country drugs seem to be used with some impunity, enforcement is arbitrary – the only way not to risk getting caught is to avoid the scene entirely. Every year perhaps dozens of visiting foreigners are arrested in Thailand for drug use or trafficking and end up doing hard time. A smaller but significant number die of a heroin overdose. Penalties for drug offences are stiff: if you're caught using marijuana, you face a fine and/or up to one year in prison, while for heroin, the penalty for use can be anywhere from six months to

10 years imprisonment. In the table in this section, 'smuggling' refers to any drug possession at a border or airport Customs check.

Thai authorities kicked off 1997 with an anti-drug campaign aimed at Bangkok's nightlife sector, which forced many clubs to close earlier (around 3 am) or, in some cases, shut down altogether. Local wags note that such crackdowns often follow the election of a new government, which just happened to have taken place in November 1996.

Police in southern Thailand, particularly the islands of Ko Samui and Ko Pha-Ngan, have also been more alert than usual in prowling for pot-smoking foreigners and carting them off to the local jail, usually releasing them after a substantial 'fine' has been paid.

BUSINESS HOURS

Most government offices are open from 8.30 am to 4.30 pm Monday to Friday, but closed from noon to 1 pm for lunch. Banks are open from 9.30 am to 3.30 pm Monday to Friday, but in Bangkok in particular several banks have special foreign-exchange offices which are open longer hours (generally until 8 pm) and every day of the week.

Businesses usually operate between 8.30 am and 5 pm Monday to Friday, and sometimes Saturday morning as well. Larger shops usually open from 10 am to 6.30 or 7 pm but smaller shops may open earlier and close later.

PUBLIC HOLIDAYS & SPECIAL EVENTS

The number and frequency of festivals and fairs in Thailand is incredible – there always seems to be something going on, especially during the cool season between November and February. Exact dates for festivals vary from year to year, either because of the lunar calendar – which isn't quite in sync with our solar calendar – or because local authorities decide to change festival dates.

The TAT publishes an up-to-date *Major Events & Festivals* calendar each year. A major upcoming event not listed below, the 13th Asian Games, will be held at the National Stadium in Bangkok in 1998. For informa-

tion on either event contact a TAT office in Thailand or abroad.

1 January
  New Year's Day – a rather recent public holiday in deference to the western calendar.
February
  Magha Puja (Makkha Buchaa) – held on the full moon of the third lunar month to commemorate the preaching of the Buddha to 1250 enlightened monks who came to hear him 'without prior summons'. A public holiday throughout the country, it culminates in a candle-lit walk around the main chapel at every wat.
Late February to early March
  Chinese New Year – called *trùt jiin* in Thai, Chinese populations all over Thailand celebrate their lunar new year (the date shifts from year to year) with a week of house-cleaning, lion dances and fireworks. The most impressive festivities take place in the Chinese-dominated province capital of Nakhon Sawan.
March
  ASEAN Barred Ground Dove Fair – large dove-singing contest held in Yala that attracts dove-lovers from all over Thailand, Malaysia, Singapore and Indonesia.
3rd week of March
  Bangkok International Jewellery Fair – held in several large Bangkok hotels, this is Thailand's most important annual gem and jewellery trade show. Runs concurrently with the Department of Export Promotion's *Bangkok Gems & Jewellery Fair*.
6 April
  Chakri Day – a public holiday commemorating the founder of the Chakri dynasty, Rama I.
13 to 15 April
  Songkhran Festival – the New Year's celebration of the lunar year in Thailand. Buddha images are 'bathed', monks and elders receive the respect of younger Thais who sprinkle water over their hands, and a lot of water is tossed about for fun. Songkhran generally gives everyone a chance to release their frustrations and literally cool off during the peak of the hot season. Hide out in your room or expect to be soaked; the latter is a lot more fun.
May (Full Moon)
  Visakha Puja (Wisakha Buchaa) – a public holiday which falls on the 15th day of the waxing moon in the 6th lunar month. This is considered the date of the Buddha's birth, enlightenment and *parinibbana*, or passing away. Activities are centred around the wat, with candle-lit processions, much chanting and sermonising.
5 May
  Coronation Day – public holiday. The king and queen preside at a ceremony at Wat Phra Kaew in Bangkok, commemorating their 1946 coronation.

Mid-May to mid-June

Royal Ploughing Ceremony – to kick off the official rice-planting season, the king participates in this ancient Brahman ritual at Sanam Luang (the large field across from Wat Phra Kaew) in Bangkok in the second week of the month. Thousands of Thais gather to watch, and traffic in this part of the city comes to a standstill.

July

Asanha Puja – full moon is a must for this public holiday which commemorates the first sermon preached by the Buddha.

Mid to late July

Khao Phansaa – a public holiday and the beginning of Buddhist 'lent', this is the traditional time of year for young men to enter the monkhood for the rainy season and for all monks to station themselves in a single monastery for the three months. It's a good time to observe a Buddhist ordination.

12 August

Queen's Birthday – public holiday. In Bangkok, Ratchadamnoen Klang Rd and the Grand Palace are festooned with coloured lights.

Mid-September

Thailand International Swan-Boat Races – these take place on the Chao Phraya River in Bangkok near the Rama IX Bridge.

Last week of September

Narathiwat Fair – an annual festival celebrating local culture with boat races, dove-singing contests, handicraft displays, traditional southern Thai music and dance. The king and queen almost always attend.

Late September to early October

Vegetarian Festival – a nine day celebration in Trang and Phuket during which devout Chinese Buddhists eat only vegetarian food. There are also various ceremonies at Chinese temples and merit-making processions that bring to mind Hindu Thaipusam in its exhibition of self-mortification. Smaller towns in the south such as Krabi and Phang-Nga also celebrate the veggie fest on a smaller scale.

23 October

Chulalongkorn Day – a public holiday in commemoration of King Chulalongkorn (Rama V).

Mid-October to mid-November

Thawt Kathin – a one month period at the end of the Buddhist 'lent' *(phansāa)* during which new monastic robes and requisites are offered to the Sangha.

November

Loi Krathong – on the proper full-moon night, small lotus-shaped baskets or boats made of banana leaves containing flowers, incense, candles and a coin are floated on Thai rivers, lakes and canals. This is a peculiarly Thai festival that probably originated in Sukhothai and is best celebrated in the north.

5 December

King's Birthday – this is a public holiday which is celebrated with some fervour in Bangkok. As with the queen's birthday, it features lots of lights along Ratchadamnoen Klang Rd. Some people erect temporary shrines to the king outside their homes or businesses.

10 December

Constitution Day – public holiday.

ACCOMMODATION

Places to stay are abundant, varied and reasonably priced in coastal Thailand.

A word of warning though: don't believe touts who say a place is closed, full, dirty or crooked. Sometimes they're right but most times they just want to get you to a place that pays them more commission. (See the Touts entry in the earlier Dangers & Annoyances section for more information.)

National Park Accommodation/Camping

All but 10 of Thailand's national parks have bungalows for rent that sleep as many as 10 people for 500 to 1500B, depending on the park and the size of the bungalow. During the low season you can often get a room in one of these park bungalows for 100B per person. A few parks also have *reuan tháew* or long houses, where rooms are around 150 to 200B for two, or tents on platforms for 50 to 60B a night.

Camping is allowed in all but four of the national parks (Nam Tok Phliu in Chanthaburi Province, Doi Suthep-Pui in Chiang Mai Province, Hat Chao Mai in Trang Province and Thap Laan in Prachinburi Province) for only 5 to 10B per person per night. Some parks have tents for rent at 50 to 60B a night, but always check the condition of the tents before agreeing to rent one.

On weekends and holidays, reservations for bungalows are recommended. In Bangkok the reservations office is at the National Parks Division of the Forestry Department (☎ (2) 579-4842/0529), Phahonyothin Rd, Bangkhen (north Bangkok). Bookings from Bangkok must be paid in advance.

Temple Lodgings

If you are a Buddhist or can behave like one, you may be able to stay overnight in some temples for a small donation. Facilities are very basic, though, and early rising is expected. Temple lodgings are usually for men only, unless the wat has a place for lay women to stay. Neat, clean dress and a basic knowledge of Thai etiquette are mandatory.

Beach Huts

Simple palm-thatch and bamboo beach huts are generally the cheapest beach and island accommodation in Thailand. Often referred to as 'bungalows', beach huts vary quite a bit in facilities and are particularly popular in the Samui archipelago and on Ko Chang.

Nightly rates vary according to the popularity of the beach, from a low of 40B per night for a simple hut with shared toilet and shower on the north-western beaches of Ko Pha-Ngan to around 500B for a high-season beach hut with private facilities on Ko Samui's Hat Chaweng. Competition keeps rates low on Ko Pha-Ngan and Ko Chang, while Ko Tao seems to be in a transition phase much like Ko Samui, albeit on a smaller scale due to its relatively small size.

Some beach huts are especially good value, while others are mere flophouses. Many serve food, although there tends to be a bland sameness to meals at beach huts wherever you are in Thailand.

In Phuket – and on many parts of Ko Samui – beach huts have given way to more luxurious beach cottages made of wood, brick and tile costing 500 to 1500B a night. These same islands also now feature highrise hotels and international-quality beach resorts that offer much more in terms of amenities and recreational options – and charge accordingly.

Guesthouses

Cheap urban guesthouses so prevalent in Bangkok and Chiang Mai, as well as in a few other towns in northern and north-eastern Thailand, for the most part don't exist in the coastal areas. Beach huts replace guesthouses on the beaches, while cheap Chinese-Thai hotels for the most part fill the bill in the inland cities. Exceptions include the provincial capitals of Trat, where there are three or four guesthouses, and Krabi, which has over a dozen guesthouses, and the beach resorts of Hua Hin and Pattaya, which have guesthouses in neighbourhoods back from the beach.

The typical Thai guesthouse features simple rooms with very little furniture – at their most basic no more than a mattress on the floor. The cheaper places have shared toilet and shower facilities for 50 to 100B per night; some places have private facilities for 100 to 300B a night.

Chinese-Thai Hotels

In inland cities such as Hat Yai, Trat or Surat Thani, standard Thai hotels – often run by Chinese-Thai families – are the most economical accommodation and generally have very reasonable rates (average 80 to 100B for rooms without bath or air-con, 120 to 250B with fan and bath, 250 to 500B with air-con). They may be located on the main street of town and/or near bus and train stations.

The cheapest hotels are those without air-con; typical rooms are clean and include a double bed and a ceiling fan. Some have attached Thai-style bathrooms (this will cost a little more). Rates may or may not be posted; if not, they may be increased for foreigners, so it is worthwhile bargaining. It's best to have a look around before agreeing to check in, to make sure the room *is* clean, the fan and lights work and so on. If there is a problem, request another room or a good discount. If possible, always choose a room off the street and away from the front lounge to cut down on ambient noise.

For a room without air-con, ask for a *hâwng thammádaa* (ordinary room) or *hâwng phát lom* (room with fan). A room with air-con is *hâwng ae*. Sometimes travellers asking for air-con are automatically offered a 'VIP' room, which usually comes with air-con, hot water, fridge and TV and is about twice the price of a regular air-con room. The cheapest hotels may have their names posted in Thai and Chinese only, but you will learn how to find and identify them with experience. Many of these hotels have restaurants downstairs; if they don't, there are usually restaurants and noodle shops nearby.

Tourist-Class, Business & Luxury Hotels

These are found only in the main tourist and business destinations: Bangkok, Pattaya, Cha-am, Hua Hin, Ko Pha-Ngan, Ko Samui, Phuket, Songkhla, Hat Yai, and a sprinkling of large provincial capitals such as Chumphon and Surat Thani. Prices start at around 600B outside Bangkok and proceed to 2000B or more – genuine tourist-class hotels in Bangkok start at 1000B or so and go to 2500B for standard rooms, and up to 5000 or 8000B for a suite. These will all have air-con, TV, western-style toilets and restaurants.

Hotels in the provinces tend to cost around 30% less than Bangkok hotels, even in Pattaya and Phuket. Tariffs of around 800 to 1500B usually buys the above-mentioned amenities, plus a pool, while anything over 1500B might include additional restaurants and recreational facilities. The most exclusive places, such as Phuket's Amanpuri, charge as much as 15,000B for their more luxurious quarters. Virtually all beach and island destinations apply peak season surcharges – anywhere from 15 to 50% – from around mid-December to mid-March. Added to this is an 11% government tax on hotels, and most of establishments will include an extra service charge of 8 to 10%.

In addition to the reputable international hotel chains of Hyatt, Sheraton, Accor, Hilton and Westin, Thailand has several respectable home-grown chains, including Dusit, Amari and Royal Garden. Of the internationals, Accor is expanding the most rapidly, introducing moderately priced tourist/business hotels in provincial capitals under the Ibis and Mercure brands to complement their more upscale Sofitel/Novotel properties. Amari is the most active in terms of managing new or newly acquired hotels, while Royal Garden is for the moment focusing on further developing its existing properties.

Resorts

In most countries 'resort' refers to hotels which offer substantial recreational facilities (eg tennis, golf, swimming, sailing etc) in addition to high-class accommodation and dining. In Thai hotel lingo, however, the term simply refers to any hotel that isn't located in an urban area. Hence a few thatched beach huts or a cluster of bungalows in a forest may be called a 'resort'. Several places in Thailand fully deserve the name under any definition – but it pays to look into the facilities before making a reservation.

ENTERTAINMENT

Cinemas

Movie theatres are found across the country. Typical programs include US and European shoot-em-ups mixed with Thai comedies and romances. Violent action pictures are always a big draw; as a rule of thumb, the smaller the town, the more violent the film offerings. English-language films are only shown with their original soundtracks in a handful of theatres in Bangkok, Phuket and Hat Yai; elsewhere all foreign films are dubbed in Thai. Tickets cost 10 to 70B. Every film in Thailand begins with the playing of the royal anthem, accompanied by projected pictures of the royal family. Viewers are expected to stand during the anthem.

Bars & Member Clubs

Urban Thais are night people and every town of any size has a selection of nightspots. For the most part they are male-dominated, though the situation is changing rapidly in the larger cities, where young couples are increasingly seen in bars. Of the many types of bars, probably the most popular continues to be the 'old west' style, patterned after Thai fantasies of the 19th century American west – lots of wood and cowboy paraphernalia.

Another favoured style is the 'Thai classic' pub, which is typically decorated with old black & white photos of Thai kings Rama VI and Rama VII, along with Thai antiques from northern and central Thailand. The old west and Thai-classic nightspots are cosy, friendly and popular with couples as well as singles. In beach areas, 'reggae bars', with lots of recorded Marley and Tosh, are slowly multiplying.

The 'go-go' bars seen in lurid photos published by the western media are limited to a few areas in Bangkok, Pattaya and Phuket's Patong beach. These are bars in which girls typically wear swimsuits or other scant apparel. In some bars they dance to recorded music on a narrow raised stage. To some visitors it's pathetic, to others paradise. 'Member clubs,' similar to old-style Playboy clubs, provide a slinky, James Bond atmosphere of feigned elegance and savoir faire in which women clad in long gowns or tight skirts entertain suited men in softly lit sofa groups. Private rooms are also available. A couple of drinks and a chat with the hostesses typically costs around US$50, including membership. These clubs are thinly scattered across the Soi Lang Suan and Sukhumvit Rd areas in Bangkok.

Under a law passed in 1995, all bars and clubs which don't feature live music or dancing are required to close by 1 am. Many get around the law by bribing local police.

Coffee Houses

Aside from the western-style cafe, which is becoming increasingly popular in Bangkok, there are two other kinds of cafes or coffee shops in Thailand. One is the traditional Hokkien-style coffee shop (*ráan kaa-fae*), where thick, black, filtered coffee is served in simple, casual surroundings. These coffee shops are mostly found in the Chinese quarters of southern Thai provincial capitals. Frequented mostly by older Thai and Chinese men, they offer a place to read the newspaper, sip coffee and gossip about neighbours and politics. The other type, called *kaa-feh* (cafe) or 'coffee house', is more akin to a nightclub, where Thai men consort with a variety of Thai female hostesses. This is the Thai counterpart to farang go-go bars, except girls wear dresses instead of swimsuits.

A variation on this theme is the 'sing-song' cafe in which a succession of female singers front a live band. Small groups of men sit at tables ogling the girls while putting away prodigious amounts of Johnnie Walker, J&B or Mekong whisky. For the price of a few house drinks, the men can invite one of the singers to sit at their table for a while. Some of the singers work double shifts as part-time mistresses, others limit their services to singing and pouring drinks.

Cafes which feature live music are permitted to stay open till 2 am.

Discos & Beach Clubs

Discotheques are popular in larger cities; outside Bangkok they're mostly attached to tourist or luxury hotels. The main disco clientele is Thai, though foreigners are welcome. Some provincial discos retain female staff as professional dance partners for men, but for the most part discos are considered fairly respectable nightspots for couples.

Beach clubs on Ko Samui and Phuket – mostly open-air ones – take the place of discos. Here the ratio of foreigners to Thais is reversed, with the former usually outnumbering the latter. The most numerous and popular beach clubs nowadays are those found on Ko Samui's Chaweng beach.

Thai law permits discotheques and beach clubs to stay open till 2 am. But many beach clubs stay open till 3 or 4 am – something to be aware of if you're looking at a hotel or beach bungalow sitting next to one.

SPECTATOR SPORTS
Thai Boxing (Muay Thai)

Almost anything goes in this martial sport, both in the ring and in the stands. If you don't mind the violence (in the ring), a *muay thai* match is worth attending for the pure spectacle – the wild musical accompaniment, the ceremonial beginning of each match and the frenzied betting around the stadium. Thai boxing is also telecast on Thai TV every Sunday afternoon; if you're wondering where everyone is, they're probably inside watching the national sport.

History Most of what is known about the history of Thai boxing comes from Burmese accounts of warfare between Myanmar and Thailand during the 15th and 16th centuries.

The earliest reference (1411 AD) mentions a ferocious style of unarmed combat that decided the fate of Thai kings. A later description tells how Nai Khanom Tom, Thailand's first famous boxer and a prisoner of war in Myanmar, gained his freedom by roundly defeating a dozen Burmese warriors before the Burmese court. To this day, many martial art aficionados consider the Thai style the ultimate in hand-to-hand fighting. Hong Kong, China, Singapore, Taiwan, Korea, Japan, the USA, Netherlands, Germany and France have all sent their best challengers and none have been able to defeat top-ranked Thai boxers. On one famous occasion, Hong Kong's top five Kung Fu masters were all dispatched in less than 6½ minutes, all knock outs.

Modern Thai Boxing The high incidence of death and physical injury led the Thai government to institute a ban on muay thai in the 1920s, but in the 30s the sport was revived under a modern set of regulations based on the international Queensberry rules. Bouts were limited to five three-minute rounds separated by two-minute breaks. Contestants had to wear international-style gloves and trunks (always either red or blue), and their feet were taped – to this day no shoes are worn.

There are 16 weight divisions in Thai boxing, ranging from mini-flyweight to heavyweight, with the best fighters said to be in the welterweight division (67kg maximum). As in international-style boxing, matches take place on a 7.3 sq metre canvas-covered floor with rope retainers supported by four padded posts, rather than the traditional dirt circle. In spite of these concessions to safety, today all surfaces of the body are still considered fair targets and any part of the body except the head may be used to strike an opponent. Common blows include high kicks to the neck, elbow thrusts to the face and head, knee hooks to the ribs and low crescent kicks to the calf. A contestant may even grasp an opponent's head between his hands and pull it down to meet an upward knee thrust. Punching is considered the weakest of all

blows and kicking merely a way to 'soften up' one's opponent; knee and elbow strikes are decisive in most matches.

The woven headbands and armbands worn into the ring by fighters are sacred ornaments which bestow blessings and divine protection; the headband is removed but the armband, which actually contains a small Buddha image, is worn throughout the match. After the bout begins, the fighters continue to bob and weave in rhythm until the action begins to heat up.

Musicians play throughout the match and the volume and tempo of the music rises and falls with the events in the ring. As Thai boxing has become more popular among westerners (both spectators and participants), an increasing numbers of bouts are staged for tourists in places like Pattaya, Phuket and Ko Samui. In these matches, the action may be genuine but the judging below par. Nonetheless, dozens of authentic matches are held every day of the year at the major Bangkok stadiums and in the provinces (there are about 60,000 full-time boxers in Thailand), and these are easily found.

Tàkrâw

Sometimes called Siamese football in old English texts, *tàkrâw* refers to a game in which a woven rattan ball about 12cm in diameter is kicked around. The rattan (or sometimes plastic) ball itself is called a *lûuk tàkrâw*. Tàkrâw is also popular in several neighbouring countries; it was originally introduced to the SEA Games by Thailand, and international championships tend to alternate between the Thais and Malays. The traditional way to play tàkrâw in Thailand is for players to stand in a circle (the size of the circle depends on the number of players) and simply try to keep the ball airborne by kicking it soccer style. Points are scored for style, difficulty and variety of kicking manoeuvres.

A popular variation on tàkrâw – and the one used in intramural or international competitions – is played with a volleyball net, using all the same rules as volleyball except only the feet and head are permitted to touch the ball. It's amazing to see the players perform aerial pirouettes, spiking the ball over the net with their feet. Another variation has players kicking the ball into a hoop 4.5m above the ground – basketball with feet, but without a backboard!

THINGS TO BUY

Many bargains await you in Thailand if you can carry them home. Always haggle to get the best price, except in department stores. And don't go shopping in the company of touts, tour guides or friendly strangers as they will inevitably – no matter what they say – take a commission on anything you buy, thus driving prices up.

Textiles

Fabric is possibly the best all-round buy in Thailand. Thai silk is considered the best in the world – its coarse weave and soft texture means it is more easily dyed than harder, smoother silks, resulting in brighter colours and a unique lustre. Silk can be purchased in Bangkok and in provincial capitals throughout Thailand. Excellent and reasonably priced tailor shops can make your choice of fabric into almost any garment. A Thai silk suit should cost around 4000 to 6500B. Chinese silk is about half the price – 'washed' Chinese silk makes inexpensive, comfortable shirts or blouses. Cottons are also a good deal – common items like the phâakhamãa (short Thai-style sarong for men – reputed in Thailand to have over a hundred uses) and the phâasîn (the slightly larger female equivalent) make great tablecloths and curtains. Good ready-made cotton shirts are available, such as the mâw hâwm (Thai work shirt) and the kúay hâeng (Chinese-style shirt) – see Ko Yo in the South-Western Gulf Coast chapter for places to see cotton-weaving.

Hat Yai is a big centre for trade in Thai cotton fabrics. Fairly nice batik (pa-té) is available in the south in patterns that are similar to batik found in Malaysia and Indonesia. Textiles from northern and north-eastern Thailand, including mát-mìi cloth, a thick cotton or silk fabric woven from tie-dyed threads, can often be found in larger markets throughout Thailand, including the south.

Clothing

Tailor-made and ready-made clothes are relatively inexpensive. If you're not particular about style you could pick up an entire wardrobe of travelling clothes at one of Bangkok's many street markets (eg Pratunam) for what you'd pay for one designer shirt in New York or Paris. You're more likely to get a good fit if you resort to a tailor but be wary of the quickie 24 hour tailor shops; the clothing is often made of inferior fabric or the poor tailoring means the arms start falling off after three weeks wear. It's best to ask Thai or long-time foreign residents for a tailor recommendation and then go for two or three fittings.

Antiques

Real antiques cannot be taken out of Thailand without a permit from the Fine Arts Department. No Buddha image, new or old, may be exported without permission – again, refer to the Fine Arts Department, or, in some cases, the Department of Religious Affairs, under the Ministry of Education. Too many private collectors smuggling and hoarding Siamese art (Buddhas in particular) around the world have led to strict controls. See the Customs section earlier in this chapter for more information on the export of art objects and antiques.

Chinese and Thai antiques are sold in Bangkok's Chinatown in two areas: Wang Burapha (the streets which have Chinese 'gates' over their entrance) and Nakhon Kasem. Some antiques (and many fakes) are sold at Chatuchak (Weekend) Market in Chatuchak Park. At the tourist antique shops art objects are fantastically overpriced, as would be expected. In recent years northern Thailand has become a good source of Thai antiques – prices are about half what you'd typically pay in Bangkok.

Jewellery

Thailand is one of the world's largest exporters of gems and ornaments, rivalled only by India and Sri Lanka. The International Colorstones Association (ICA) relocated from Los Angeles to Bangkok's Chan Issara Tower a few years ago, and the World

Federation of Diamond Bourses (WFDB) has established a bourse in Bangkok – both events recognise that Thailand has become the world trade and production centre for precious stones. The biggest importers of Thai jewellery are the USA, Japan and Switzerland. Although rough stone sources in Thailand have decreased dramatically, stones are now imported from Australia, Sri Lanka and other countries to be cut, polished and traded here.

There are over 30 diamond-cutting houses in Bangkok alone. One of the results of this remarkable growth of the gem industry – in Thailand the gem trade has increased nearly 10% every year for the past 15 years – is that the prices are rising rapidly. If you know what you are doing you can make some really good buys in both unset gems and finished jewellery. Gold ornaments are sold at a good rate as labour costs are low. The best bargains in gems are jade, rubies and sapphires. Buy from reputable dealers only, unless you're a gemologist.

Warning Be wary of special 'deals' that are offered for one day only or which set you up as a 'courier' in which you're promised big money. Many travellers end up losing big. Shop around and *don't be hasty*. Remember: there's no such thing as a 'government sale' or a 'factory price' at a gem or jewellery shop; the Thai government does not own or manage any gem or jewellery shops.

Hill-Tribe Crafts
Interesting embroidery, clothing, bags and jewellery from the north can be bought in Bangkok at Narayan Phand, Lan Luang Rd, at branches of the Queen's Hillcrafts Foundation, at Chatuchak (Weekend) Market and at various tourist shops around town. See Things to Buy in the Bangkok chapter for details. Hill-tribe crafts are almost impossible to find in the south.

Lacquerware
Thailand produces some good lacquerware, much of it made and sold along the northern Burmese border. It's also available in Bang-

kok at the same sources named in the Hill-Tribe Crafts entry above and at some tourist shops in Phuket.

Styles available today originated in 11th century Chiang Mai; in 1558 Myanmar's King Bayinnaung captured a number of Chiang Mai lacquer artisans and brought them to Bago in central Myanmar to establish the incised lacquerware tradition. Lacquer comes from the *Melanorrhea usitata* tree (not to be confused with 'lac', which comes from an insect), and in its most basic form is mixed with paddy-husk ash to form a light, flexible, waterproof coating over bamboo frames.

From start to finish it can take five or six months to produce a high-quality piece of lacquerware, which may have as many as five colours. Flexibility is one characteristic of good lacquerware. A top-quality bowl can have its rim squeezed together until the sides meet without suffering damage. The quality and precision of the engraving is another thing to look for.

Nielloware
This art came from Europe via Nakhon Si Thammarat and has been cultivated in Thailand for more than 700 years. Engraved silver is inlaid with niello – an alloy of lead, silver, copper and sulphur – to form striking black-and-silver jewellery designs. Nielloware is one of Thailand's best buys.

Ceramics
Many kinds of hand-thrown pottery, old and new, are available throughout the kingdom. Most well known are the greenish Sangkhalok or Thai celadon products from the Sukhothai-Si Satchanalai area and central Thailand's *bencharong* or 'five-colour' style. The latter is based on Chinese patterns, while the former is a Thai original that has been imitated throughout China and South-East Asia. Rough, unglazed pottery from the north and north-east can also be very appealing.

Other Crafts
Under Queen Sirikit's Supplementary Occupations & Related Techniques (SUPPORT)

foundation, a number of regional crafts from around Thailand have been successfully revived. *Málaeng tháp* collages and sculptures are made by the artful cutting and assembling of the metallic, multicoloured wings and carapaces of female wood-boring beetles *(Sternocera aequisignata)*, harvested after they die at the end of their reproductive cycle between July and September each year. Hailing mostly from the north and northeast, they can nonetheless be found in craft shops all over Thailand. For 'Damascene ware' *(kràm)*, gold and silver wire is hammered into a cross-hatched steel surface to create exquisitely patterned bowls and boxes. Look for them in more upscale Bangkok department stores and craft shops.

Yaan lipao is a type of intricately woven basket made from a hardy grass in southern Thailand. Ever since the queen and other female members of the royal family began carrying delicate yaan lipao purses, they've been a Thai fashion staple. Basketry of this type is most easily found in the southern provincial capitals, or in Bangkok shops that specialise in regional handicrafts.

Fake or Pirated Goods

In Bangkok, Phuket and other tourist centres, there is black-market street trade in fake designer goods; particularly Benneton pants and sweaters, Lacoste (crocodile-logo) and Ralph Lauren polo shirts, Levi's jeans, and Rolex, Dunhill and Cartier watches. Tin-Tin T-shirts are also big. No-one pretends they're the real thing, at least not the vendors themselves. The European and American manufacturers are applying heavy pressure on the Asian governments involved to get this stuff off the street, so it may not be around for much longer.

In some cases foreign name brands are legally produced under licence in Thailand and are still good value. A pair of legally produced Levi's 501s, for example, typically costs US$10 from a Thai street vendor, and US$30 to US$40 in Levi's home town of San Francisco! Careful examination of the product usually reveals telltale characteristics that confirm or deny the item's legality.

Pre-recorded cassette tapes are another illegal bargain in Thailand. The tapes are 'pirated', that is, no royalties are paid to the copyright owners. Prices average 25 to 35B per cassette. These are becoming harder to find however, as the government has cracked down on pirating in response to pressure from the US music industry. At the time of writing it was becoming quite difficult to find pirated tapes anywhere in the country except on Bangkok's Khao San Rd. Licensed western-music tapes, when available, cost 70 to 110B each (average price 90B); Thai music tapes cost the same.

Getting There & Away

AIR

The expense of getting to Bangkok per air kilometre varies quite a bit depending on your point of departure. However, you can take heart in the fact that Bangkok is one of the cheapest cities in the world to fly out of, due to the Thai government's loose restrictions on airfares and the close competition between airlines and travel agencies. The result is that with a little shopping around you can come up with some real bargains. If you can find a cheap one way ticket to Bangkok, take it, because you are virtually guaranteed to find a return trip ticket of equal or lesser cost once you get there.

From most places around the world your best bet will be budget, excursion or promotional fares – when speaking to airlines ask for the various fares in that order. Each carries its own set of restrictions and it's up to you to decide which works best in your case. Fares fluctuate, but in general they are cheaper from September to April (northern hemisphere) and from March to November (southern hemisphere).

Fares listed in this section should serve as a guideline – don't count on them staying this way (they may go down!).

Airports & Airlines

Thailand has four international airports – in Bangkok, Chiang Mai, Phuket and Hat Yai. Chiang Rai and Sukhothai are both designated 'international', but at the time of writing they did not actually field any international flights.

Three domestic carriers, Thai Airways International (commonly known as THAI), Bangkok Airways and Orient Express Air, use international and domestic airports in 26 cities around the country.

See the Getting Around chapter for a list of the Thai offices of the domestic airlines and the Getting There & Away section of the Bangkok chapter for the Bangkok offices of all the international airlines.

For information on arrival and departure procedures in Bangkok, as well as details on getting to/from the international and domestic airports, see the Air section of the Getting Around chapter.

Buying Tickets

Although other Asian centres are now competitive with Bangkok for buying discounted airline tickets, Bangkok is still a good place for shopping around.

Travellers should note, however, that some Bangkok travel agencies have a shocking reputation. Taking money and then delaying or not coming through with the tickets, as well as providing tickets with limited validity periods or severe restrictions are all part of the racket. There are a large number of perfectly honest agents, but beware of the rogues.

Some typical discount fares being quoted from Bangkok include:

Around Asia	Fare (B)
Calcutta	3100 to 3500
Colombo	3100 to 4000
Delhi	4100
Hong Kong	3150
Jakarta	5800
Kathmandu	3900
Kuala Lumpur	2750
Penang	2500 to 3300
Singapore	1850 to 3000
Tokyo	4800
Yangon (Rangoon)	1900 to 3150

Australia & New Zealand	Fare (B)
Sydney, Brisbane, Melbourne	10,400
Darwin, Perth	7400
Auckland	12,000 to 13,200

Europe	Fare (B)
Athens, Amsterdam, Frankfurt, London, Paris, Rome or Zurich	9200 to 9700

USA	Fare (B)
San Francisco, Los Angeles	11,200
via Australia	25,000
New York	13,200

Booking Problems The booking of flights in and out of Bangkok during the high season (December to March) can be difficult. For air travel during these months you should book as far in advance as possible. THAI is finally loosening its stranglehold on air routes in and out of Thailand, so the situation has improved since the late 1980s. The addition of a second international terminal in Bangkok has also helped.

Also, for most airlines you'll need to confirm return or ongoing tickets when you arrive in Thailand. Failure to do so could mean losing your reservation. The exception is THAI, which no longer requires confirmation of either domestic or international tickets.

USA

If you fly from the West Coast, you can get some great deals through the many bucket shops (who discount tickets by taking a cut in commissions) and consolidators (agencies that buy airline seats in bulk) operating in Los Angeles and San Francisco. Through agencies such as these a return (round trip) airfare to Bangkok from any of 10 West Coast cities starts at around US$750.

One of the most reliable discounters is Avia Travel (☎ (800) 950-AVIA toll-free, (415) 668-0964; fax (415) 386-8519) at 5429 Geary Blvd, San Francisco, CA 94121. Avia specialises in custom-designed around-the-world fares, for example, San Francisco-London-Delhi-Bangkok-Seoul-San Francisco for US$1486 or San Francisco-Tokyo-Kuala Lumpur-Bangkok-Amsterdam/Rome/Madrid/Athens/Paris (choice of one)-London-San Francisco for US$1512, as well as 'Circle Pacific' fares such as San Francisco-Hong Kong-Bangkok-Singapore-Jakarta-Denpasar-Los Angeles for US$1230. The agency sets aside a portion of its profits for Volunteers in Asia, a nonprofit organisation that sends grassroots volunteers to work in South-East Asia.

Another agency that works hard to get the cheapest deals is Air Brokers International (☎ (800) 883-3273 toll-free, (415) 397-1383; fax (415) 397-4767) at Suite 411, 323 Geary St, San Francisco, CA 94102. One of its 'Circle Pacific' fares, for example, offers a Los Angeles-Hong Kong-Bangkok-Denpasar-Los Angeles ticket for US$975 plus tax during the low season. You can add Honolulu, Singapore, Jakarta or Yogyakarta to this route for US$50 each stop. San Francisco/Los Angeles-Hong Kong-Bangkok-Delhi-Bombay-Rome/London-San Francisco/Los Angeles costs US$1449, or you could go New York-Los Angeles-Bali-Singapore-Bangkok-Hong Kong-New York for US$1399.

While the airlines themselves can rarely match the prices of the discounters, they are worth checking if only to get benchmark prices for comparison. Tickets bought directly from the airlines may also have fewer restrictions and/or less strict cancellation policies than those bought from discounters (though this is not always true).

Cheapest from the West Coast are: THAI, China Airlines and Korean Air. Each of these has a budget and/or 'super Apex' fare that costs US$900 to US$1200 return from Los Angeles, San Francisco or Seattle. THAI is the most overbooked of these airlines from December to March and June to August, and hence its flight schedule during these months may suffer delays (if you're lucky enough to get a seat at all). Several of these airlines also fly out of New York, Dallas, Chicago and Atlanta – add another US$150 to US$250 to their lowest fares.

Tarom (Romanian Air Transport) offers one way excursion fares from New York to Bangkok for US$500.

Direct to Phuket If you want to fly straight through to Phuket without staying overnight in Bangkok, Avia Travel in San Francisco quotes fares of US$886 (China Airlines) and US$1050 (Singapore Airlines). Singapore Airlines requires a layover of a few hours in Singapore on the way; for China Airlines it's in Bangkok. If you don't mind overnighting in Bangkok, you have the option of many different daily connections the day after your international flight.

Canada

Canadian Airlines International flies from Vancouver to Bangkok at fares from around

Air Travel Glossary

Apex Apex ('advance purchase excursion') is a discounted ticket which must be paid for in advance. There are penalties if you wish to change it.

Baggage Allowance This will be written on your ticket: usually one 20kg item to go in the hold, plus one item of hand luggage.

Bucket Shop An 'unbonded' travel agency specialising in discounted airline tickets.

Bumped Just because you have a confirmed seat doesn't mean you're going to get on the plane (see Overbooking).

Cancellation Penalties If you have to cancel or change an Apex ticket there are often heavy penalties; insurance can sometimes be taken out against these penalties. Some airlines impose penalties on regular tickets as well, particularly against 'no-show' passengers.

Check In Airlines ask you to check in a certain time ahead of the flight departure (usually two hours on international flights). If you fail to check in on time and the flight is overbooked the airline can cancel your booking and give your seat to somebody else.

Confirmation Having a ticket written out with the flight and date you want doesn't mean you have a seat until the agent has checked with the airline that your status is 'OK' or confirmed. Meanwhile you could just be 'on request'.

Discounted Tickets There are two types of discounted fares – officially discounted (see Promotional Fares) and unofficially discounted. The lowest prices often impose drawbacks like flying with unpopular airlines, inconvenient schedules, or unpleasant routes and connections. A discounted ticket doesn't necessarily have to save you money – you may be able to pay Apex prices without the associated Apex advance booking and other requirements. Discounted tickets only exist where there is fierce competition.

Full Fares Airlines traditionally offer 1st class (coded F), business class (coded J) and economy class (coded Y) tickets. These days there are so many promotional and discounted fares available from the regular economy class that few passengers pay full economy fare.

Lost Tickets If you lose your airline ticket an airline will usually treat it like a travellers cheque and, after enquiries, issue you with another one. Legally, however, an airline is entitled to treat it like cash and if you lose it then it's gone forever. Take good care of your tickets.

No-Shows No-shows are passengers who fail to show up for their flight, sometimes due to unexpected delays or disasters, sometimes due to simply forgetting, sometimes because they made more than one booking and didn't bother to cancel the one they didn't want. Full-fare passengers who fail to turn up are sometimes entitled to travel on a later flight. The rest of us are penalised (see Cancellation Penalties).

C$850 return for advance purchase excursion fares. Travellers living in eastern Canada will usually find the best deals out of New York or San Francisco, adding fares from Toronto or Montreal (see the previous USA entry).

Australia

The full economy fare from Australia to Bangkok is around A$4000 from Sydney, Melbourne or Brisbane and A$3330 from Perth; however, tickets discounted either by travel agents or airlines are much cheaper. None of these are advance purchase nowadays, but they tend to sell out early – the airlines only allocate a limited number of these super-cheap seats to each flight. Prices start at about A$575 (one way) and A$799 (return) from Melbourne or Sydney on the cheaper carriers (eg Olympic and Alitalia), and get more expensive the better the airline's 'reputation'.

On Request An unconfirmed booking for a flight (see Confirmation).

Open Jaw A return ticket where you fly out to one place but return from another. If available, this can save you backtracking to your arrival point.

Overbooking Airlines hate to fly empty seats and since every flight has some passengers who fail to show up (see No-Shows), airlines often book more passengers than they have seats. Usually the excess passengers balance those who fail to show up, but occasionally somebody gets bumped. If this happens guess who it is most likely to be? The passengers who check in late.

Promotional Fares Officially discounted fares like Apex fares which are available from travel agents or direct from the airline.

Reconfirmation At least 72 hours prior to departure time of an onward or return flight you must contact the airline and 'reconfirm' that you intend to be on the flight. If you don't do this the airline can delete your name from the passenger list and you could lose your seat. You don't have to reconfirm the first flight on your itinerary or if your stopover is less than 72 hours. It doesn't hurt to reconfirm more than once.

Restrictions Discounted tickets often have various restrictions on them – advance purchase is the most usual one (see Apex). Others are restrictions on the minimum and maximum period you must be away, such as a minimum of 14 days or a maximum of one year (see Cancellation Penalties).

Standby A discounted ticket where you only fly if there is a seat free at the last moment. Standby fares are usually only available on domestic routes.

Tickets Out An entry requirement for many countries is that you have an onward or return ticket – in other words, a ticket out of the country. If you're not sure what you intend to do next, the easiest solution is to buy the cheapest onward ticket to a neighbouring country or a ticket from a reliable airline which can later be refunded if you do not use it.

Transferred Tickets Airline tickets cannot be transferred from one person to another. Travellers sometimes try to sell the return half of their ticket, but officials can ask you to prove that you are the person named on the ticket. This is unlikely to happen on domestic flights; on an international flight tickets may be compared with passports.

Travel Agencies Travel agencies vary widely and you should ensure you use one that suits your needs. Some simply handle tours, while full-service agencies handle everything from tours and tickets to car rental and hotel bookings. A good one will do all these things and can save you a lot of money, but if all you want is a ticket at the lowest possible price, then you really need an agency specialising in discounted tickets. A discounted ticket agency, however, may not be useful for other things, like hotel bookings.

Travel Periods Some officially discounted fares, Apex fares in particular, vary with the time of year. There is often a low (off-peak) season and a high (peak) season. Sometimes there's an intermediate or shoulder season as well. At peak times, when everyone wants to fly, not only will the officially discounted fares be higher but so will unofficially discounted fares, or there may simply be no discounted tickets available. Usually the fare depends on your outward flight – if you depart in the high season and return in the low season, you pay the high-season fare. ■

From Australia to most Asian destinations, including Bangkok, the airlines have recently introduced new seasons: the peak is December to 15 January; school holiday periods are 'shoulder' seasons; and the rest of the year is low season. Fares now also vary depending on how long you want to stay away – a fare valid for 35 days travel is about A$50 to A$60 cheaper than one valid for 90 days. This rule varies, so check with individual airlines for the best deal.

At the time of writing, fares available through agents specialising in discount fares on the better known airlines (eg THAI, Qantas and British Airways) are: A$1049/1129/1239 (low/shoulder/peak season) from Sydney, Melbourne or Brisbane and A$899/949/1089 from Perth. Garuda Indonesia has cheap fares to Bangkok via Bali (Denpasar) or Jakarta (these flights continue on to London) for around A$929 one way, A$1579 return.

New Zealand

THAI flies from Auckland to Bangkok daily. Fares start at NZ$1499 return for advance purchase and excursion fares.

UK & Continental Europe

London 'bucket shops' offer quite a range of cheap tickets to Bangkok: a student fare on Kuwait Airways is UK£215 one way and UK£355 return, and on THAI it's UK£275 and UK£459. KLM offers a fare for UK£350 one way and UK£580 return.

It's also easy to stop over in Bangkok between London and Australia, with return fares for around UK£689 on THAI to the Australian east coast, UK£550 on Royal Brunei to Brisbane or Perth, and UK£730 on KLM to Sydney. Good travel agencies to try for these sorts of fares are Trailfinders on Kensington High St (☎ (0171) 938-3939) and Earls Court Rd (☎ (0171) 938-3366), or STA Travel (☎ (0171) 937-9962) on Old Brompton Rd and at the universities of London, Kent, Birmingham and Loughborough. Or you can simply check the travel ads in *Time Out*, *Evening Standard* and *TNT*. For discounted flights out of Manchester or Gatwick, check with Airbreak Leisure (☎ (0171) 712-0303) at South Quay Plaza 2, 193 Marsh Wall, London E14 92H.

One of the cheapest deals going is on Tarom (the Romanian carrier), which has Brussels-Bangkok-Brussels fares valid for a year. Uzbekistan Airways does a London to Bangkok flight via Tashkent. Other cheapies are Lauda Air from London (via Vienna) and Czech Airlines from Prague (via London, Frankfurt and Zurich).

Asia

To Bangkok International Airport There are regular flights to Bangkok international airport from every major city in Asia and, conveniently, most airlines offer about the same fares. Here is a sample of current estimated one way fares:

From	Fare (US$)
Singapore	110-195
Hong Kong	140-200
Kuala Lumpur	110-195
Taipei	220-373
Calcutta	170
Kathmandu	210-276
Colombo	236
New Delhi	236
Manila	200-231
Kunming	250
Vientiane	100
Phnom Penh	150

The Association of South-East Asian Nations (ASEAN) promotional fares (return from any city, eg a Bangkok-Manila-Jakarta fare allows you to go between Manila, Jakarta, Bangkok and Manila; or Jakarta, Bangkok, Manila and Jakarta; or Bangkok, Manila, Jakarta and Bangkok) include:

Route	Fare (US$)
Bangkok-Manila-Jakarta	545
Bangkok-Singapore-Manila	440
Bangkok-Jakarta-Kuala Lumpur	410
Bangkok-Manila-Brunei-Jakarta-Singapore-Kuala Lumpur	580
Bangkok-Singapore-Jakarta-Yogyakarta-Denpasar	580

To Other Thai International Airports Travellers heading for southern Thailand can skip Bangkok altogether by flying directly to several cities. THAI has regular flights to Phuket and Hat Yai from Singapore, and to Phuket from Perth, Australia. During the winter, German carrier LTU offers direct flights to Phuket from Düsseldorf and Munich.

You can also arrange a same-day connection through Bangkok to Phuket from other departure points, depending on your Bangkok arrival time – only international flights arriving during the day will leave you enough time to make afternoon or evening connections to Phuket.

Bangkok Airways hopes to expand its Ko Samui service to Medan, Langkawi and Singapore someday.

Regional Services Thailand's Ministry of Transport allows several international air carriers to provide regional air services to Myanmar (Burma), Vietnam, Laos and Cambodia. Routes to/from Thailand include Yunnan

Airways and China Southwest flights from Kunming to Bangkok; Silk Air between Singapore and Phuket; Dragonair between Hong Kong and Phuket; Malaysia Airlines between Ipoh, Malaysia, and Hat Yai; Royal Air Cambodge between Bangkok and Phnom Penh; Lao Aviation between Bangkok and Vientiane; and Vietnam Airlines between Bangkok and Ho Chi Minh City.

LAND
Malaysia
Hat Yai is the major transport hub in southern Thailand. See the South-Western Gulf Coast chapter for more details on land transport to Malaysia.

You can cross the border's western end by taking a bus to one side and another bus from the other side, the most obvious direct route being between Hat Yai and Alor Setar. This route, used by taxis and buses, connects at Sadao (also known as Dan Nok) on the Thai side of the border, Changlun on the Malaysia side. There are also direct buses to Hat Yai from Alor Setar, Butterworth and Penang – no need to change at the border for these.

You can also cross via nearby Padang Besar, where the western train line crosses the border. As at Sadao/Changlun, here you can get a bus right up to the border, walk across and take another bus or taxi on the other side. On either side you'll most likely be mobbed by taxi and motorcycle drivers wanting to take you to immigration. It's better to walk over the railway by bridge into Thailand, and then ignore the touts until you get to 'official' Thai taxis who will take you all the way to Hat Yai, with a stop at the immigration office (2.5km from the border), for 30 to 40B. A new immigration/Customs office and bus/train station complex has been constructed on the Thai side, making the whole transition smoother.

There's also a border crossing at Keroh (Thai side – Betong), right in the middle of the east and west coasts of the Thai-Malay peninsula. This may be used more now that the Penang to Kota Baru road is open.

For more information on crossing the Thai-Malaysian border see individual town

entries in the South-Western Gulf Coast chapter.

Riding the rails from Singapore to Bangkok via Butterworth, Malaysia, is a great way to travel to Thailand – as long as you don't count on making a smooth change between the Kereta Api Tanah Melayu (KTM) and State Railway of Thailand (SRT) trains. The Thai train almost always leaves on time; the Malaysian train rarely arrives on time. Unfortunately, the Thai train leaves Padang Besar even if the Malaysian railway express from Kuala Lumpur (or the 2nd class connection from Butterworth) is late. To be on the safe side, purchase the Malaysian and Thai portions of your ticket with departures on consecutive days and plan a Butterworth/Penang stopover.

Bangkok to Butterworth/Penang The daily special express No 11 leaves from Bangkok's Hualamphong station at 3.15 pm, arriving in Hat Yai around 7 am the next day and terminating at Padang Besar at 8 am. Everyone disembarks at Padang Besar, proceeds through immigration, then boards 2nd class KTM train No 99 for a Butterworth arrival at 12.40 pm Malaysian time (one hour ahead of Thai time). The fare to Padang Besar is 767B for 1st class, 360B for 2nd, plus a 70B special express charge, and 120B for air-con. There is no 3rd class seating on this train.

For a sleeping berth in 2nd class add 100B for an upper berth, 150B for a lower. In 1st class it's 520B per person.

Bangkok to Kuala Lumpur & Singapore For Kuala Lumpur, make the Thai and Malaysian rail connections to Butterworth as described above, changing to an express or limited express from Butterworth. There are early morning, noon and evening services to Kuala Lumpur, and the trip takes from six to seven hours.

There are daily services running between Kuala Lumpur and Singapore – early morning, early afternoon and evening – which take from 6½ to 9 hours, depending on what type of train you take.

KTM fares from Butterworth to Kuala Lumpur on the air-con express trains (1st and 2nd class only; overnight sleepers also available) are M$34 for 2nd class and M$67 for 1st class. On the limited express trains (which don't always have 1st class) the fares are M$14.40 for 3rd class, M$25.40 for 2nd and M$58.50 for 1st. Butterworth to Singapore fares on the express are M$34, M$60 and M$127 respectively; M$29.90, M$51.40 and M$118.50 on the limited express.

The information offices at the train terminals in Butterworth (☎ (04) 334-7962) and Kuala Lumpur (☎ (03) 274-7435) can provide more information about schedules, fares and seat availability on the Malaysian and Singaporean services.

Laos

Lonely Planet's *Laos* and *Thailand* guides contain complete details on how and where to cross the border between these two countries by land or river. Below is a summary of the possibilities.

A new 1190m Australian-financed bridge across the Maekhong River near Nong Khai opened in April 1994. Called the Thai-Lao Friendship Bridge (Saphan Mittaphap Thai-Lao), it spans a section of the river between Hat Jommani on the Thai side to Tha Naleng on the Lao side – very near the old vehicle ferry.

The next stage in the plan is to construct a parallel rail bridge in order to extend the Bangkok-Nong Khai railway into Vientiane.

Construction began in early 1996 on a second Maekhong bridge to span the river between Thailand's Chiang Khong and Laos' Huay Xai. If all goes as planned, this bridge should be operational by early 1998 and will link Thailand with China by road via Laos' Bokeo and Luang Nam Thai provinces.

A third bridge is being planned for either Tha Khaek (opposite Thailand's Nakhon Phanom) or Savannakhet (opposite Mukdahan).

There is a land crossing from Champasak Province in Laos to Chong Mek in Thailand's Ubon Ratchathani Province that is open to foreign visitors. To use this crossing you'll need a visa valid for entry via Chong Mek and Pakse – this must usually be arranged in advance through a Lao consulate or sponsoring agency.

A new Laos tourist visa 'on arrival' policy was initiated in 1997. As far as we know you can only get the visa at the Nong Khai bridge crossing in far north-east Thailand and at Vientiane airport in Laos. You only need a valid passport and 1275B – no other documents or paperwork – to receive the visa, which is valid for two weeks and can be renewed for an additional two weeks in Laos.

Travellers planning to use any of the above land crossings should double-check with a Lao consulate about current visa requirements for the specific entry points before heading up to the border.

Myanmar (Burma)

Several border crossings between Thailand and Myanmar are open to day trippers or for short excursions in the vicinity, though most of these are in northern Thailand. As yet none of these link up with routes to Yangon or Mandalay or any other cities of size. Nor are you permitted to enter Thailand from Myanmar, at least not yet.

For more detail, see Lonely Planet's *Thailand* and *Myanmar* guides.

Cambodia

There is currently no legal land passage between Cambodia and Thailand, and the Cambodian border won't be safe for land crossings until mines and booby traps left over from the conflict between the Khmer Rouge and the Vietnamese are removed or detonated.

It is possible to travel by boat between Hat Lek in Thailand's Trat Province and the Cambodian coast. See the Hat Lek to Cambodia section in the Eastern Gulf Coast chapter for details.

China

The governments of Thailand, Laos, China and Myanmar recently agreed to the construction of a four nation ring road through all four countries. The western half of the loop will proceed from Mae Sai, Thailand, to Jinghong, China, via Myanmar's Tachilek (opposite Mae Sai) and Kengtung (near Dalau on the China-Myanmar border), while the eastern half will extend from Chiang Khong, Thailand, to Jinghong via Huay Xai, Laos (opposite Chiang Khong) and Boten, Laos (on the Yunnanese border south of Jinghong).

Once the roads are built and the visa formalities have been worked out, this loop will provide alternative travel connections between China and South-East Asia, in much the same way as the Karakoram Highway has forged new links between China and south Asia. It's difficult to predict when all the logistical variables will be settled, but progress so far points to a cleared path by the end of the decade.

Future Rail Possibilities
At a 1995 summit meeting in Bangkok, representatives of ASEAN proposed a regional rail network linking Singapore with China via Malaysia, Thailand, Laos and Vietnam. In all but Laos and Cambodia, railbeds for such a circuit already exist. Current plans call for the extension of a rail line across the Maekhong River from Thailand to Laos via the existing Thai-Lao Friendship Bridge. If completed, this line may someday connect with a proposed north-south line from Vientiane to Savannakhet in Laos and then with a west-east line from Savannakhet to Dong Ha, Vietnam.

SEA
Malaysia
There are several ways of travelling between Malaysia and southern Thailand by sea. Simplest is to take a long-tail boat between Satun, right down in the south-west corner of Thailand, and Kuala Perlis, Malaysia. The cost is about M$4, or 40B, and boats cross over fairly regularly. You can also take a ferry to the Malaysian island of Langkawi from Satun. There are immigration posts at both ports so you can make the crossing quite officially.

If you're coming from Malaysia, once in Satun you can take a bus to Hat Yai and then arrange transport to other points in the south or further north. It's possible to bypass Hat Yai altogether, by heading directly for Phuket or Krabi via Trang.

You can also take a ferry to Ban Taba on the South-Western Gulf of Thailand from near Kota Baru – see the Sungai Kolok and Ban Taba sections in the South-Western Gulf Coast chapter.

See the yachting entry under Phuket in the Northern Andaman Coast chapter for information on yachts to Penang and other places.

On-again, off-again passenger ferry services also run between Malaysia's Pulau Langkawi and either Satun or Phuket. None ever seems to last longer than nine months or so; your best bet is to make enquiries through local travel agents to find out the latest on sea transport to/from the island.

Laos
It is legal for non-Thai foreigners to cross the Maekhong River by ferry between Laos and Thailand at the following points: Nakhon Phanom (opposite Tha Khaek), Chiang Khong (opposite Huay Xai) and Mukdahan (opposite Savannakhet).

China
China's Yunnan Province can be reached from Thailand by boat along the Maekhong River. Several surveys of the waterway have been completed, and a specially constructed express boat made its inaugural run between Sop Ruak, Chiang Rai Province, and China's Yunnan Province in early 1994. For the moment, permission for such travel is restricted to private tour groups, but it's reasonable to assume that in the future – if demand is high enough – some sort of scheduled public service may become available. The boat trip takes six hours – considerably quicker than any now possible road route.

WARNING
The information in this chapter is particularly vulnerable to change: prices for international travel are volatile, routes are introduced

and cancelled, schedules change, special deals come and go, and rules and visa requirements are amended. Airlines and governments seem to take a perverse pleasure in making price structures and regulations as complicated as possible. You should check directly with the airline or a travel agent to make sure you understand how a fare (and ticket you may buy) works. In addition, the travel industry is highly competitive and there are many lurks and perks.

The upshot of this is that you should get opinions, quotes and advice from as many airlines and travel agents as possible before you part with your hard-earned cash. The details given in this chapter should be regarded as pointers and are not a substitute for your own careful, up-to-date research.

Getting Around

AIR

Thai Airways International

Most domestic air services in Thailand are operated by Thai Airways International (THAI), which covers 20 airports throughout the kingdom. On certain southern routes, domestic flights through Hat Yai continue on to Malaysia (Penang, Kuala Lumpur), Singapore and Brunei (Bandar Seri Begawan). THAI operates Boeing 737 or Airbus 300 series aircraft on its main domestic routes.

The accompanying Airfares & Railways map shows some of the fares on routes to coastal Thailand. Note that through fares generally cost less than combination fares. This does not always apply to international fares, however. It's much cheaper to fly from Bangkok to Penang via Phuket or Hat Yai than direct, for example.

Air Passes THAI offers special four-coupon passes – available only outside Thailand for foreign currency – in which you can book any four domestic flights for one fare of US$259 as long as you don't repeat the same leg. Unless you plan carefully this isn't much of a saving, since it's hard to avoid repeating the same leg in and out of Bangkok.

For information on the four coupon deal, known as the 'Discover Thailand fare', enquire at any THAI office outside Thailand.

THAI Offices Offices for THAI's domestic services can be found throughout coastal Thailand:

Bangkok – Head Office, 89 Vibhavadi Rangsit Rd (☎ (2) 513-0121, reservations: ☎ 280-0060); 485 Silom Rd (☎ (2) 234-3100/19); 6 Lan Luang Rd (☎ (2) 280-0060, 628-2000); Asia Hotel, 296 Phayathai Rd (☎ (2) 215-2020/1); Grand China Tower, 3rd floor, 215 Yaowarat Rd (☎ (2) 223-9746/50); Bangkok international airport, Don Muang (☎ (2) 535-2081/2, 523-6121)
Hat Yai – 166/4 Niphat Uthit 2 Rd (☎ (74) 245851, 246165, reservations: ☎ 233433)

Nakhon Si Thammarat – 1612 Ratchadamnoen Rd (☎ (75) 342491)
Narathiwat – 322-4 Phupa Phakdi Rd (☎ (73) 511161, 513090/2)
Pattani – 9 Prida Rd (☎ (73) 349149)
Pattaya – Royal Cliff Beach Resort, Cliff Rd (☎ (38) 250286/7, 250804)
Phuket – 78 Ranong Rd (☎ (76) 211195, 212499/946); 41/33 Montri Rd (☎ (76) 212400/644/880)
Songkhla – 2 Soi 4, Saiburi Rd (☎ (74) 311012)
Surat Thani – 3/27-8 Karunarat Rd (☎ (77) 273710/355)
Trang – 199/2 Visetkul Rd (☎ (75) 218066)

Bangkok Airways

Bangkok Airways, owned by Sahakol Air, flies five main routes: Bangkok-Hua Hin; Bangkok-Ranong; Bangkok-Ko Samui-Phuket; Bangkok-Sukhothai-Chiang Mai; and U Taphao (Pattaya)-Ko Samui. The mainstay of the Bangkok Airways fleet is the Franco-Italian ATR-72, and the most profitable route, by far, is the one between Bangkok and Ko Samui.

Bangkok Airways' fares are competitive with THAI's but the company is small and it remains to be seen whether or not it will grow to become a serious contender.

The airline's head office (☎ (2) 229-3434/56; fax 229-3450) is at Queen Sirikit National Convention Centre, New Ratchadaphisek Rd, Khlong Toey, Bangkok 10110. There are also offices in Hua Hin, Pattaya, Phuket and Ko Samui.

Orient Express Air

Formerly a carrier in Cambodia known as SK Air, relative newcomer Orient Express Air (OEA) operates charter tour package flights between Chiang Mai and Phuket, along with 20 scheduled domestic routes linking the north with the south and northeast without Bangkok stopovers. The company uses B727-200s for all flights. OEA (☎ (53) 818092, 201566) has headquarters at Chiang Mai international airport.

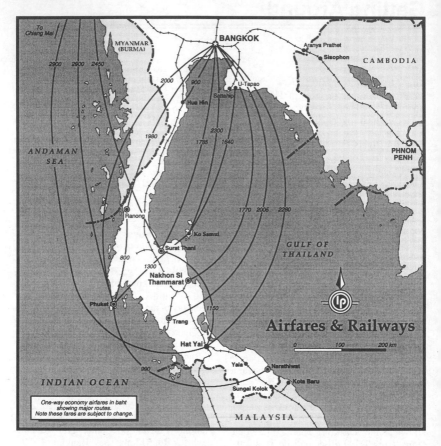

MYANMAR (BURMA)

To Chiang Mai

BANGKOK

Aranya Prathet

Sisophon

CAMBODIA

2900   2900   2450

2000   900

U-Tapao

Hua Hin   Sattahip

1980   2300

1785   1640

PHNOM PENH

ANDAMAN SEA

Ranong

Ko Samui   1770   2005   2280

Surat Thani   GULF OF THAILAND

800   1300

Nakhon Si Thammarat

Phuket   1150

Trang

Hat Yai

Yala   Narathiwat

990   Kota Baru

Sungai Kolok

INDIAN OCEAN

Airfares & Railways

0   100   200 km

MALAYSIA

One-way economy airfares in baht showing major routes.
Note these fares are subject to change.

Bangkok International Airport

Airport Facilities During the past decade, the airport facilities at Bangkok international airport have undergone a US$200 million redevelopment, including the construction of an international terminal that is one of the most modern and convenient in Asia. However, the very slow immigration lines in the upstairs arrival hall in Terminal 1 are still a problem. Despite a long row of impressive-looking immigration counters, there never seem to be enough clerks on duty, even at peak arrival times. Even when the booths are fully staffed, waits of 45 minutes to an hour are not unusual. On the other hand, baggage claim is usually quick and efficient (of course, they have lots of time to get it right while you're inching along through immigration).

The Customs area has a green lane for passengers with nothing to declare – just walk through if you're one of these and hand your Customs form to one of the clerks by the exit. Baggage trolleys are free for use inside the terminal.

The Thai government has planned for some time to open another international airport about 20km east of Bangkok at Nong

Ngu Hao. In theory, the new facility is supposed to be open by 2004, but the project's future is murky at best; it's already three years behind schedule, and some government officials have said construction will be suspended for 10 years. At the time of writing, local media reported that the government was instead planning to concentrate on further expansion at the existing international airport.

In the meantime Terminal 2, a second international terminal adjacent to Terminal 1, has opened to accommodate increasing air traffic. Terminal 2 has few facilities other than currency exchange booths, a public taxi desk and some restaurants on the 4th floor.

Currency Exchange The foreign currency booths (Thai Military Bank, Bangkok Bank, Krung Thai Bank) on the ground floor of the arrival hall and in the departure lounge of both terminals give a good rate of exchange, so there's no need to wait till you're in the city centre to change money if you need Thai currency. Each of these banks also operates ATMs in the arrival and departure halls.

Post & Telephone There is a 24 hour post/telephone office with a Home Direct phone service in the departure hall (3rd floor) of Terminal 1. Another 24 hour post office is located in the departure lounge; a third one in the arrival hall is open Monday to Friday from 9 am to 5 pm.

Left Luggage & Day Rooms Left-luggage facilities (20B per piece per day, three months maximum) are available in the departure hall in both terminals. In the transit lounge of Terminal 1, clean day rooms with washing and toilet facilities can be rented for 900B per six hours.

Food On the 4th floor of Terminal 1 is a small 24 hour cafeteria area where you can choose from Thai, Chinese and European dishes at fairly reasonable prices. Next door is the larger THAI restaurant with more expensive fare. On the 2nd level above the arrival area is a coffee shop which is open from 6 am to 11 pm, and there is also a small snack bar in the waiting area on the ground floor. The departure lounge has two snack bars which serve beer and liquor.

On the 4th floor of Terminal 2 is a cluster of new fast-food-style places, including Swenson's, John Bull Pub, Burger King and Pizza Hut. Opposite these is a posh Chinese restaurant. On the arrival floor of this terminal is a KFC.

The Airbridge Cafe, a European-style coffee shop on the enclosed bridge between Terminal 1 and the Amari Airport Hotel, provides a quiet alternative to the airport places.

Shopping There are several newsstands and souvenir shops in the arrival and departure areas of Terminal 1. Duty-free shopping is available in the departure lounge as well. The book and magazine selection at the airport newsstands is spotty; if you have enough time to walk across the enclosed footbridge from Terminal 1 to the Amari Airport Hotel, you'll find a much better bookshop in the hotel's shopping arcade (south of reception).

Near the Airport If you leave the airport building area and cross the expressway on the pedestrian bridge (just north of the passenger terminal), you'll find yourself in Don Muang town where there are all sorts of shops, a market, lots of small restaurants and food stalls, even a wat, all within 100m or so of the airport.

The modern and luxurious Amari Airport Hotel (☎ (2) 566-1020/1) has its own air-conditioned, enclosed footbridge from Terminal 1 and 'special mini-stay' daytime rates (8 am to 6 pm) for stays of up to a maximum of three hours for around 500B for singles/doubles, including tax and service. Longer daytime rates are available on request. For additional information on overnight accommodation in the Don Muang area, see Places to Stay in the Bangkok chapter.

The Amari also has a selection of decent restaurants serving Italian, Japanese and Thai food.

To/From the Airport Bangkok international airport (and the adjacent domestic terminal) is located in Don Muang district, approximately 25km north of Bangkok. You have a choice of transport modes from the airport to the city ranging from 3.50 to 300B.

To Pattaya THAI operates direct air-con buses to Pattaya from the airport thrice daily at 9 am, noon and 7 pm; the fare is 200B one way. Private sedans cost 1500B per trip.

Airport Bus In mid-1996 a new airport express bus service began operating from Bangkok international airport to three Bangkok districts for 70B per person. Buses run every 15 minutes from 5 am to 11 pm. A map showing the designated stops is available at the airport; each route makes approximately six stops in each direction. A great boon to travellers on a budget, these new buses mean you can avoid hassling with taxi drivers to get a reasonable fare as well as forgo the slow pace of the regular bus routes.

Since this service is quite new, the routes, fares and hours could change during the first year or two of operation. So far few airport arrivals seem to be using the service – one hopes it won't be cancelled as a result.

The airport bus counter is around 200m to the left (with your back to Terminal 1) of the city taxi counter. Three current routes are:

A-1 – to the Silom Rd business district via Pratunam and Ratchadamri Rd, stopping at big hotels like the Indra, Grand Hyatt Erawan, Regent Bangkok and Dusit Thani

A-2 – to Sanam Luang via Phayathai, Lan Luang, Ratchadamnoen Klang and Tanao Rds; this is the one you want if you're going to the Siam Square or Banglamphu areas

A-3 – to the Phrakhanong district via Sukhumvit Rd

Public Bus Cheapest of all are the public buses to Bangkok which stop on the highway in front of the airport. There are two non-air-con bus routes and four air-con routes that are particularly useful for getting into the city. The non-air-con buses, however, no longer accept passengers carrying luggage.

Air-con bus No 29 costs 16B and plies one of the most useful, all-purpose routes from the airport into the city as it goes to the Siam Square and Hualamphong areas. After entering the city limits via Phahonyothin Rd (which turns into Phayathai Rd), the bus passes Phetburi Rd (where you'll want to get off to change buses for Banglamphu), then Rama I Rd at the Siam Square/Mahboonkrong intersection (for buses out to Sukhumvit Rd, or to walk to Soi Kasem San 1 for various lodgings) and finally turns right on Rama IV Rd to go to the Hualamphong district (where the main train station is located). You'll want to go the opposite way on Rama IV Rd for the Soi Ngam Duphli area. Bus No 29 runs only from 5.45 am to 8 pm, so if you're arriving on a late-night flight you'll miss it.

Air-con bus No 13 (16B; 5.45 am to 8 pm) also goes to Bangkok from the airport, coming down Phahonyothin Rd (like No 29), turning left at the Victory Monument to Ratchaprarop Rd, then south to Ploenchit Rd, where it goes east on Sukhumvit Rd all the way to Bang Na. This is definitely the one to catch if you're heading for the Sukhumvit Rd area.

Air-con bus No 4 (16B; 5.45 am to 8 pm) begins with a route parallel to that of the No 29 bus – down Mitthaphap Rd to Ratchaprarop and Ratchadamri Rds (Pratunam district), crossing Phetburi, Rama I, Ploenchit and Rama IV Rds, then down Silom Rd, left on Charoen Krung Rd and across the river to Thonburi.

No backpacks or large luggage are allowed onto the non-air-con, ordinary buses. Ordinary bus No 59 costs only 3.50B (5B between 11 pm to 5 am) and operates 24 hours – it zigzags through the city to Banglamphu (the Democracy Monument area) from the airport, a trip that can take up to 1½ hours or more in traffic.

Ordinary bus No 29 (3.50B; or 5B from 11 pm to 5 am; 24 hours) plies much the same route as air-con bus No 29. Green bus No 2 (16B; 5.30 am to 10 pm) has a similar route to the air-con No 4; first it goes through Pratunam, then direct to Ratchadamri, Silom and Charoen Krung Rds.

Unless you're really strapped for baht, it's

worth the extra 12.50B for the air-con and almost guaranteed seating, especially in the hot season, since the trip to central Bangkok by bus usually takes an hour or more. Even better is the 70B Airport Bus, described in the previous Airport Bus entry.

Train You can also get into Bangkok from the airport by train. From Terminal 1, turn right (north), cross the highway via the covered pedestrian bridge, turn left and walk about 100m towards Bangkok. Opposite the big Amari Airport Hotel is the small Don Muang station – trains depart regularly to Bangkok from here. The 3rd class fare from Don Muang is only 10B on the ordinary and commuter trains if you buy your ticket on the platform, 20B if purchased on the train. Tickets for rapid or express trains cost 50B.

There are trains every 15 to 30 minutes between 5 am and 8 pm, and it takes about 45 minutes to reach Hualamphong, the main station in central Bangkok. In the opposite direction trains run frequently between 4.20 am and 8 pm. From Hualamphong station you can walk to the bus stop almost opposite Wat Traimit for bus No 23 to Banglamphu.

Taxi Hassles with airport taxi drivers continue to plague Bangkok international airport. The taxis that wait near the arrival area of the airport are supposed to be airport-regulated. Ignore all the touts waiting like sharks near the Customs area and buy a taxi ticket from the public taxi booth at the southern end of the arrival hall (to the far left as you leave Customs). Fares are set according to city destination and no haggling should be necessary; most destinations in central Bangkok are 200B (eg Siam Square) or 300B (eg Banglamphu). Taxis using this system are not required to use their meters. Two, three or even four passengers (if they don't have much luggage) can split the fare.

Sometimes unscrupulous drivers will approach you before you reach the desk and try to sell you a ticket for 350 or 400B – ignore them and head straight for the desk. A few touts from the old taxi mafia that used to prowl the arrival area are still around and

may approach you with fares of around 150B. Their taxis have white-and-black plates and are not licensed to carry passengers, hence you have less legal recourse in the event of an incident than if you take a licensed taxi (yellow-and-black plates).

The real hassle begins if you decide you'd prefer to take a metered taxi rather than pay the rather high 250B most drivers want. You're *supposed* to be able to take a metered taxi from the airport if you so choose, but the reality is that most drivers refuse to run the meters – in clear violation of the regulations printed on sheets given to all passengers in advance – and ask for 250B. Drivers complain that it really doesn't pay for them to queue up for passengers at the current metered rates. In mid-1996 the Ministry of Transport authorised drivers of metered taxis from the airport to collect a 100B surcharge over the meter reading. With surcharge included you shouldn't have to pay more than 210 to 240B for most destinations in Bangkok. One hopes the new surcharge – if actually followed – will result in fewer arguments between passenger and driver.

Going to the airport from the city, a metered taxi costs from 115B (eg from Siam Square) to 140B (from Banglamphu or the Silom Rd area). The occasional driver will refuse to use his meter and quote a flat rate of 150 to 200B.

On a metered taxi trip to/from the airport, passengers are responsible for the 20B or 30B (depending on which entrance the driver chooses) expressway tolls. If you take a flat-rate taxi, the driver should pay, though they may not always agree to this. During heavy traffic you can save money by staying on the surface (non-expressway) streets – which are just as speedy as (if not speedier than) the expressway during heavy commuter hours.

One way to get an unsurcharged metered taxi from the airport is to go upstairs to the departure area and get an incoming city taxi that has just dropped passengers off. These will usually take you to Bangkok on the meter. The downstairs taxi mafia frowns on this practice, however, and you may be hassled.

Metered taxis flagged down on the highway in front of the airport (turn left from the arrival hall) are even cheaper – 100 to 120B for central Bangkok. When the queue at the public taxi desk is particularly long, it's sometimes faster to go upstairs or walk out to the highway and flag one down.

THAI Limousine THAI offers an airport limousine, which is really just a glorified air-con taxi service, that will take you to your hotel for 500 to 650B.

Terminal Shuttle THAI operates a free shuttle bus between the international and domestic terminals every 15 minutes between 6 am and 11.20 pm.

Boat The Riverjet (☎ (2) 585-9120) is a fast hydrofoil that operates in conjunction with a bus service from the airport to a pier near the Rama VII Bridge in northern Bangkok to service the following hotels along the river: Oriental, Shangri-La, Royal Orchid Sheraton and the Marriott Royal Garden Riverside. Tickets are a steep 700B; although the Riverjet boat/bus service is quicker during peak traffic periods (6.30 to 9.30 am, 3.30 to 8 pm), the rest of the time it's faster to take a taxi. It runs from 7 am to 10 pm.

Helicopter The Shangri-La Hotel (☎ (2) 236-7777) has its own helicopter service – introduced for the World Bank/ IMF meeting in 1991 – from Bangkok international airport to the hotel rooftop for 3500B per person, minimum three passengers. The flight takes only 10 minutes but is reserved for Shangri-La guests only. If you can afford the copter flight you can certainly afford this hotel, which has one of Bangkok's best river locations.

Warning Beware of airport touts – this means anyone trying to steer you away from the city taxi counter or asking where you plan to stay while you're in Bangkok. A legion of touts – some in what appear to be airport or airline uniforms – are always waiting in the arrival area, and will begin their badgering as soon

as you clear Customs. Posing as helpful tourist information agents, their main objective is to get commissions from overpriced taxi rides or hotel rooms. If you're foolish enough to mention the hotel or guesthouse you plan to stay at, chances are they'll tell you it's full and that you must go to another hotel (which will pay them a commission, though they may deny it). Sometimes they'll show you a nice collection of photos; don't get sucked in, as these touted hotels are often substandard and badly located.

The hotel reservation desks operated by the Thai Hotels Association (THA) at the back of the arrival hall in both terminals also take a commission on every booking, but at least they have a wide selection of accommodation. There have been reports that the THA desks occasionally claim a hotel is full when it isn't, just to move you into a hotel that pays higher commissions. If you protest, the staff may ask you to speak to the 'reservations desk' on the phone – usually an accomplice who confirms the hotel is full. Dial the hotel yourself if you want to be certain.

Don Muang Domestic Airport
Bangkok's domestic airport stands a few hundred metres south of Bangkok international airport. Facilities at Don Muang include a post and telephone office on the ground floor, a snack bar in the departure lounge and a restaurant on the 2nd floor. THAI operates a free shuttle bus between the international and domestic terminals every 15 minutes between 6 am and 11.20 pm.

Departure Tax
Airport departure tax is 250B for international flights departing from Bangkok international airport, 200B for international departures from Phuket and Chiang Mai, and 30B for domestic flights. Children under two are exempt.

BUS
Government Bus
Several types of buses ply the roads of Thailand. The cheapest and slowest are the

ordinary government-run buses (rót thamá-daa) that stop in every little town and for every waving hand along the highway. For some destinations – smaller towns – these orange-painted buses are your only choice, but at least they leave frequently. The government also runs faster, more comfortable, but less frequent, air-conditioned buses called rót ae or rót pràp aakàat; these are painted with blue markings. If these are available to your destination, they are your best choice since they don't cost that much more than the ordinary stop-in-every-town buses. The government bus company is called Baw Khaw Saw, an abbreviation of Borisàt Khõn Sòng (literally, 'the transportation company'). Every city and town in Thailand linked by bus has a Baw Khaw Saw terminal, even if it's just a patch of dirt by the roadside.

The service on the government air-con buses is usually quite good, and includes drinks service and video. On longer routes (eg Bangkok to Ko Samui, Bangkok to Phuket), the air-con buses even distribute claim checks (receipt dockets) for your baggage. Longer routes may also offer two classes of air-con buses, regular and 1st class; the latter buses have toilets. 'VIP' buses have fewer seats (30 to 34 instead of 44; some routes have Super VIP, with only 24 seats) so that each seat reclines more. Sometimes these are called rót nawn or sleepers. For small-to-medium-sized people they are more comfortable, but if you're big in girth you may find yourself squashed on the 34-seaters when the person in front of you leans back.

Occasionally you'll get a government air-con bus in which the air-con is broken or the seats are not up to standard, but in general they are more reliable than the private tour buses.

Private Bus

Private buses are available between major tourist and business destinations: Surat, Ko Samui, Phuket, Hat Yai, Pattaya, Hua Hin and others. To Phuket, for example, several companies run daily buses out of Bangkok. These can be booked through most hotels or any travel agency, although it's best to book directly through a bus office to be sure you get what you pay for.

Fares may vary from company to company, but usually not by more than a few baht. However, fare differences between the government and private bus companies can be substantial. Using Surat Thani as an example, the state-run buses from the southern bus terminals are 158B for ordinary bus, 285B (1st class) air-con, while the private companies charge up to 385B. On the other hand, to Phuket the private buses often cost less than the government buses, although those that charge less offer inferior service. Departures from some private companies are more frequent than for the equivalent Baw Khaw Saw route.

There are also private buses running between major destinations within the various regions, eg Nakhon Si Thammarat to Hat Yai in the south. New companies are cropping up all the time. Their number seemed to reach a peak in the 1980s, but they have now stabilised because of a crackdown on licensing. Minibuses are used on some routes, eg Surat to Krabi and Ranong to Takua Pa.

The private air-con buses are usually no more comfortable than the government air-con buses and feature similarly narrow seats and a hair-raising ride. On overnight journeys the buses usually stop somewhere en route and passengers are woken to get off the bus for a free meal of fried rice or rice soup. A few companies even treat you to a meal before a long overnight trip.

Like their state-run equivalents, the private companies offer VIP (sleeper) buses on long hauls. In general, private bus companies that deal mostly with Thais are good, while tourist-oriented ones – especially those connected with Khao San Rd – are the worst as the agents know they don't need to deliver good service because very few customers will be returning. In recent years, the service on many private lines has in fact declined, especially on the Bangkok to Ko Samui, Surat to Phuket and Surat to Krabi routes.

Sometimes the cheaper lines – especially those booked on Khao San Rd in Bangkok

– will switch vehicles at the last moment so that instead of the roomy air-con bus advertised, you're stuck with a cramped van with broken air-con. Another problem with the private companies is that they generally spend more time cruising the city for passengers before getting under way, meaning that they rarely leave at the advertised departure time. To avoid situations like this, it's always better to book bus tickets directly at a bus office – or at the government Baw Khaw Saw station – rather than through a travel agency.

Out of Bangkok, the safest, most reliable private bus services are the ones which operate from the three official Baw Khaw Saw terminals rather than from hotels or guesthouses. Picking up passengers from any points except these official terminals is actually illegal, and services promised by companies who flout the law are often not delivered. Although it can be a hassle getting out to the Baw Khaw Saw terminals, you're generally rewarded with safer, more reliable and punctual service.

Safety

Statistically, private tour buses meet with more accidents than government air-con buses. Turnovers on tight corners and head-on collisions with trucks are probably due to the inexperience of the drivers on a particular route. This in turn is probably a result of companies opening and folding so frequently, and because of the high priority given to making good time – Thais buy tickets on a company's reputation for speed.

As private bus fares are typically higher than government bus fares, the private bus companies attract a better-heeled clientele among Thais, as well as among foreign tourists. One result of this is that a tour bus loaded with money or the promise of money is a temptation for upcountry bandits. Hence, private tour buses occasionally get robbed by bands of thieves, but these incidents are diminishing due to increased security under provincial administration.

In an effort to prevent druggings and robbery in southern Thailand, which peaked in the 1980s, Thai police now board tour buses plying the southern roads at unannounced intervals, taking photos and videotapes of the passengers and asking for IDs. Reported incidents are now on the decrease.

Keep an eye on your bags when riding buses – thievery by stealth is still the most popular form of robbery in Thailand (eminently preferable to the forceful variety in my opinion), though again the risks are not that great – just be aware. Most pilfering seems to take place on the private bus runs between Bangkok and Chiang Mai, especially on buses booked on Khao San Rd. Keep zippered bags locked and well secured.

TRAIN

The railway network in Thailand, run by the government-subsidised State Railway of Thailand (SRT), is surprisingly good. In fact, in many ways it's the best form of public transport in the kingdom. If you travel 3rd class, it is often the cheapest way to cover a long distance; by 2nd class it's about the same as a 'tour bus' but much safer and more comfortable. Trains take a bit longer than chartered buses on the same journey but, on overnight trips especially, are worth the extra travel time.

The trains have many advantages; there is more space and more room to breathe and stretch out (even in 3rd class) than there is on the best buses. The windows are big and usually open, so that there is no glass between you and the scenery (good for taking photos) and more to see. The scenery itself is always better along the train routes than the scenery along Thai highways – the trains regularly pass small villages, farmland, old temples etc. The pitch-and-roll of the railway cars is much easier on the bones, muscles and nervous system than the quick stops and starts, the harrowing turns and the pothole jolts endured on buses. The train is safer in terms of both accidents and robberies.

Rail Routes

Four main rail lines cover 4500km along the northern, southern, north-eastern and eastern routes. There are several side routes, notably between Nakhon Pathom and Nam Tok (stopping in Kanchanaburi) in the west central region, and between Tung Song and Kantang (stopping in Trang) in the south. The southern line splits at Hat Yai, one route going to Sungai Kolok on the Malaysian east coast border, via Yala, and the other route going to Padang Besar in the west, also on the Malaysian border.

A Bangkok to Pattaya spur has not been as popular as expected. Within the next few years, a southern spur may be extended from Khiriratnikhom to Phuket, establishing a rail link between Surat Thani and Phuket.

Bangkok Terminals Most long-distance trains originate from Bangkok's Hualamphong station. Before a railway bridge was constructed across the Chao Phraya River in 1932, all southbound trains left from Thonburi's Bangkok Noi station. Today Bangkok Noi station services commuter and shortline trains to Kanchanaburi/Nam Tok, Suphanburi, Ratchaburi and Nakhon Pathom (Ratchaburi and Nakhon Pathom can also be reached by train from Hualamphong). A slow night train to Chumphon and Lang Suan, both in southern Thailand, leaves nightly from the Bangkok Noi station but it's rarely used by long-distance travellers.

Classes

The SRT operates passenger trains in 1st, 2nd and 3rd class – but each varies considerably depending on whether you're on an ordinary, rapid or express train.

Third Class A typical 3rd class car consists of two rows of bench seats divided into facing pairs. Each bench seat is designed to seat two or three passengers, but on a crowded upcountry line nobody seems to care about design considerations. On a rapid train (which carries 2nd and 3rd class cars only), 3rd class seats are padded and reasonably comfortable for shorter trips. On ordinary, 3rd class-only trains in the east and north-east, seats are sometimes made of hard wooden slats, and are not recommended for more than a couple of hours. Express trains

do not carry 3rd class cars at all. Commuter trains in the Bangkok area are all 3rd class, and the cars resemble modern subway or rapid transit trains, with plastic seats and ceiling loops for standing passengers.

Second Class In a 2nd class car, seating is similar to those on a bus, with pairs of padded seats all facing the front of the train. Usually the seats can be adjusted to recline, and for some people this is good enough for overnight trips. In a 2nd class sleeper, you'll find rows of facing seat pairs; each pair is separated from the next by a dividing wall. A table folds down between each pair and at night the seats convert into two fold-down berths, one over the other. Curtains provide a modicum of privacy and the berths are fairly comfortable, with fresh linen for every trip. A toilet stall is located at one end of the car and washbasins at the other. Second class cars are found only on rapid and express trains; some routes offer air-con 2nd class as well as ordinary 2nd class.

First Class First class cars provide private cabins for singles or couples. Each private cabin has individually controlled air-con, an electric fan, a fold-down washbasin and mirror, a small table and a long bench seat (or two in a double cabin) that converts into a bed. Drinking water and towels are provided free. First class cars are available only on express and special express trains.

Reservations

The disadvantage of travelling by rail, in addition to the time factor mentioned earlier, is that trains can be difficult to book. This is especially true around holiday time, eg the middle of April approaching Songkhran Festival, since many Thais also prefer the train. Trains out of Bangkok should be booked as far in advance as possible – a minimum of a week for popular routes such as the northern line to Chiang Mai and southern line to Hat Yai, especially if you want a sleeper. For the north-eastern and eastern lines a few days will suffice.

Advance bookings may be made one to 90

days before your date of departure. If you want to book tickets, go to Hualamphong station in Bangkok, walk through the front of the station house and go straight to the back right-hand corner where a sign says 'Advance Booking' (open from 8.30 am to 4 pm daily). The other ticket windows, on the left-hand side of the station, are for same-day purchases, mostly 3rd class.

Reservations are now computerised in the Advance Booking office. Instead of having to stop at three different desks as in previous years, you simply take a queue number, wait until your number appears on one of the electronic marquees, report to the correct desk (one for the southern line, one for north and north-eastern) and make your ticket arrangements. Only cash baht is acceptable here.

Note that buying a return ticket does not necessarily guarantee you a seat on the way back, it only means you do not have to buy a ticket for the return. If you want a guaranteed seat reservation it's best to make that reservation for the return as soon as you arrive at your destination.

Booking seats back to Bangkok is generally not as difficult as booking them out of Bangkok; however, at some stations this can be quite difficult, eg buying a ticket from Surat Thani to Bangkok.

Tickets between any station in Thailand can be purchased at Hualamphong station (☎ (2) 223-7010, 223-7020). You can also make advance bookings at Don Muang station, across from Bangkok international airport. SRT ticket offices are open from 8.30 am to 6 pm Monday to Friday, and until noon on weekends and public holidays.

Train tickets can also be purchased at certain travel agencies in Bangkok (see the Travel Agencies section in the Bangkok chapter). It is much simpler to book trains through these agencies than to book them at the station; however, they usually add a surcharge of 50 to 100B to the ticket price.

Charges & Surcharges

There is a 50B surcharge for express trains (rót dùan) and 30B for rapid trains (rót raew). These trains are somewhat faster than

the ordinary trains, as they make fewer stops. For the special express trains (rót dùan phísèt) that run between Bangkok and Padang Besar there is a 70B surcharge.

The charge for 2nd class sleeping berths is 100B for an upper berth and 150B for a lower berth (or 130B and 200B respectively on a special express). The difference between upper and lower is that there is a window next to the lower berth and a little more headroom. The upper berth is still quite comfortable. For 2nd class sleepers with aircon add 220/270B per upper/lower ticket (or 250/320 for special express trains). No sleepers are available in 3rd class.

All 1st class cabins are air-con. A two-bed cabin costs 520B per person; single cabins are no longer available.

Eating Facilities

Meals are available in dining cars and at your seat in 2nd and 1st class cars. Menus change as frequently as the SRT changes catering services. The food is usually not all that great, especially considering the relatively high prices.

Train staff sometimes hand out face wipes, then come by later to collect 10B each for them – a racket since there's no indication to passengers that they're not complimentary. (On government buses they're free, and they're available in the station for 1B.) Drinking water is provided, albeit in plastic bottles; sometimes it's free, sometimes it costs 5 to 10B per bottle.

Several readers have written to complain about being overcharged by meal servers on trains. If you do purchase food on board, be sure to check prices on the menu rather than trusting server quotes. Also, check the bill carefully to make sure you haven't been overcharged.

Station Services

Accurate, up-to-date information on train travel is available at the Rail Travel Aids counter at Hualamphong station. You can pick up timetables or ask about fares and scheduling – one person behind the counter usually speaks a little English. There are two types of timetable available: two condensed English timetables (one for the south, another for the northern, north-eastern and eastern lines), with fares, schedules and routes for rapid, express and special express trains on the four trunk lines; and four complete, separate Thai timetables for each trunk line, with side lines as well. These latter timetables give fares and schedules for all trains – ordinary, rapid and express. The English timetables only display a couple of the ordinary routes.

All train stations in Thailand have baggage storage services (sometimes called the 'cloak room'). The rates and hours of operation vary from station to station. At Hualamphong station the hours are from 4 am to 10.30 pm, and left luggage costs 30B per piece per day. Hualamphong station also has a 5B shower service in the rest rooms.

All stations in provincial capitals have restaurants or cafeterias as well as various snack vendors. These stations also offer an advance-booking service for rail travel anywhere in Thailand. Hat Yai station is the only one with a hotel attached, but there are usually hotels within walking distance of other major stations.

Hualamphong station has a travel agency where other kinds of transport can be booked. It also has a post office that's open from 7.30 am to 5.30 pm Monday to Friday, from 9 am to noon Saturday and holidays, and closed Sunday.

CAR & MOTORCYCLE
Roadways
Thailand has more than 170,000km of roadways. Around 16,000km are classified 'national highways' (both two lane and four lane), which means they're generally well maintained. Route numbering is fairly consistent; some of the major highways have two numbers, one under the national system and another under the optimistic 'Asia Highway' system which indicates highway links with neighbouring countries. Route 105 to Mae Sot on the Burmese border, for example, is also called 'Asia 1', while Highway 2 from Bangkok to Nong Khai is 'Asia

12'. For the time being, the only border regularly crossed by noncommercial vehicles is the Thai-Malaysian border.

Kilometre stones are placed at regular intervals along most larger roadways, but place names are usually printed on them in Thai script only. Highway signs in both Thai and roman script showing destinations and distances are becoming increasingly common.

Road Rules
Thais drive on the left-hand side of the road – most of the time. Other than that just about anything goes, in spite of road signs and speed limits – Thais are notorious scofflaws when it comes to driving. Like many places in Asia, every two lane road has an invisible third lane in the middle that all drivers feel free to use at any time. Passing on hills and curves is common – as long as you've got the proper Buddhist altar on the dashboard, what could happen?

The main rule to be aware of is that the right of way belongs to the bigger vehicle; this is not what it says in the Thai traffic law, but it's the reality. Maximum speed limits are 60km/h within city limits, 80km/h on highways – but on any given stretch of highway you'll see vehicles travelling as slowly as 30km/h or as fast as 150km/h. Speed traps are becoming more common; they seem especially common along Highway 4 in the south and Highway 2 in the north-east.

Turn signals are often used to warn passing drivers about oncoming traffic. A left-turn signal means it's okay to pass, while a right-turn signal means someone's approaching from the other direction.

The principal hazard to driving in Thailand besides the general disregard for traffic laws is having to contend with so many different types of vehicles on the same road – bullock carts, 18-wheelers, bicycles, tuk-tuks and customised racing bikes. In village areas the vehicular traffic is lighter but you have to contend with stray chickens, dogs, water buffaloes, pigs, cats and goats. Once you get used to the challenge, driving in Thailand is very entertaining, but first-timers tend to get a bit unnerved.

Checkpoints Military checkpoints are common along highways throughout northern and north-eastern Thailand, especially in border areas. Always slow down for a checkpoint – often the sentries will wave you through without an inspection, but occasionally you'll be stopped and briefly questioned. Use common sense and don't be belligerent or you're likely to be detained longer than you'd like.

Rental

Cars, jeeps and vans can be easily rented in Bangkok, Pattaya, Phuket, Ko Samui and Hat Yai. A Japanese sedan (eg Toyota Corolla) typically costs 1000 to 1500B per day; minivans (eg Toyota Hi-Ace, Nissan Urvan) go for around 1800B a day. Hertz rents Mitsubishi 1.3L Champs for 800B a day plus 4B per kilometre or unlimited kilometres for 1200 to 1400B a day. Slightly larger Toyota Coronas or Mitsubishi Lancers are 1100 to 1500B a day plus 4 to 5B per kilometre, or 1500 to 1600B a day unlimited. The best deals are usually on 4WD Suzuki Caribians (sic) or Daihatsu Miras, which can be rented for as little as 700 to 800B per day with no per-kilometre fees for long-term rentals or during low seasons. Unless you absolutely need the cheapest vehicle, you might be better off with a larger vehicle (eg the Toyota 4WD Mighty X Cab, if you absolutely need 4WD); Caribians are notoriously hard to handle at speeds above 90km/h (if you can even get it to go that fast) and tend to crumple dangerously in crashes. Cars with automatic shift are uncommon. Drivers can usually be hired with a rental car for an additional 300 to 400B per day.

Check with travel agencies or large hotels for rental services. Always verify that a vehicle is insured for liability before signing a rental contract; you should also ask to see the dated insurance documents. If you have an accident while driving an uninsured vehicle you're in for some major hassles.

Motorcycles can be rented in major towns as well as many smaller tourist centres like Krabi, Ko Samui, Ko Pha-Ngan, Ko Chang etc (see Motorcycle Touring in this section).

Rental rates vary considerably from one agency to another and from city to city. Since there is a glut of motorcycles for rent on Ko Samui and Phuket these days, they can be rented on these islands for as little as 80B per day. A substantial deposit is usually required to rent a car; motorcycle rental usually requires that you leave your passport.

Driving Permits

Foreigners who wish to drive motor vehicles (including motorcycles) in Thailand need a valid international driving permit. If you don't have one, you can apply for a Thai driver's licence at the Police Registration Division (PRD; ☎ (2) 513-0051/5) on Phahonyothin Rd in Bangkok. Provincial capitals also have PRDs. If you present a valid foreign driver's licence at the PRD you'll probably only have to take a written test; other requirements include a medical certificate and three passport-sized colour photos. The forms are in Thai only, so you'll also need an interpreter.

Fuel & Oil

Modern petrol (gasoline) stations with electric pumps are plentiful in Thailand where there are paved roads. In more remote off-road areas, petrol *(ben-sin* or *náam-man rót yon)* is usually available at small roadside or village stands – typically just a couple of ancient hand-operated pumps fastened to petrol barrels. As this book went to press, regular *(thamádaa)* petrol cost about 10B per litre, super *(phísèt)* a bit more. Diesel *(dii-soen)* fuel is available at most pumps for around 8.50 to 9B.

The Thai phrase for 'motor oil' is *náam-man khrêuang*.

Motorcycle Touring

Motorcycle travel is becoming a popular way to get around Thailand, especially in the north. In the south there is less long-distance motorbiking and more round-island touring. Dozens of places in tourist areas, including many beach huts and guesthouses, have set up shop with no more than a couple of motorbikes for rent. It is also possible to buy a new or used motorbike and sell it before you leave the country – a good used 125cc bike costs around 20,000B.

Daily rental ranges from 80 to 100B a day for a 100cc step-through (eg Honda Dream, Suzuki Crystal) to 400B a day for a good 250cc dirt bike. The motorcycle industry in Thailand has stopped assembling dirt bikes, so many of those for rent are getting on in years – when they're well maintained they're fine. When they're not well maintained, they can leave you stranded if not worse. The latest trend in Thailand is for small, heavy racing bikes that couldn't be less suitable for the typical farang body.

The legal maximum size for motorcycle manufacture in Thailand is 150cc, though in reality few bikes on the road exceed 125cc. Anything over 150cc must be imported, which means an extra 600% in import duties. The odd rental shop specialises in bigger motorbikes (average 200 to 500cc) – some were imported by foreign residents and later sold on the local market but most came into the country as 'parts' and were discreetly assembled, and licensed under the table.

While motorcycle touring is undoubtedly one of the best ways to see Thailand, it is also undoubtedly one of the easiest ways to cut your travels short, permanently. You can also run up very large repair and/or hospital bills in the blink of an eye. However, with proper safety precautions and driving conduct adapted to local standards, you can see parts of Thailand inaccessible by other modes of transport and still make it home in one piece. Some guidelines to keep in mind:

- If you've never driven a motorcycle before, stick to the smaller 100cc step-through bikes with automatic clutches. If you're an experienced rider but have never done off-the-road driving, take it slowly the first few days.
- Always check a machine over thoroughly before you take it out. Look at the tyres to see if they still have tread, look for oil leaks, test the brakes. You may be held liable for any problems that weren't duly noted before your departure. Newer bikes cost more than clunkers, but are generally safer and more reliable. Street bikes are more comfortable and ride more smoothly on paved roads than dirt bikes; it's silly to rent an expensive dirt bike if most

of your riding is going to be along decent roads. A two stroke bike suitable for off-roading generally uses twice the fuel of a four stroke bike with the same size engine, thus lowering your cruising range in areas where roadside pumps are scarce (eg the 125cc Honda Wing gives you about 300km per tank, while a 125cc Honda MTX gets about half that).

- Wear protective clothing and a helmet (the latter is now legally required in Thailand, though enforcement varies from place to place). Without a helmet, a minor slide on gravel can leave you with concussion, cuts or bruises. Long pants, long-sleeved shirts and shoes are highly recommended as protection against sunburn and as a second skin if you fall. If your helmet doesn't have a visor, then wear goggles, glasses or sunglasses to keep bugs, dust and other debris out of your eyes. Gloves are also a good idea, to prevent blisters caused by holding on to the twist-grips for long periods of time. It is practically suicidal to ride on Thailand's highways without taking these minimum precautions.
- For distances of over 100km or so, take along an extra supply of motor oil, and if riding a two stroke machine carry two stroke engine oil. On long trips, oil burns fast.
- You should never ride alone in remote areas, especially at night. There have been incidents where farang bikers have been shot or harassed while riding alone, mostly in remote rural areas. When riding in pairs or groups, spread out so you'll have room to manoeuvre or brake suddenly if necessary.
- In Thailand, the de facto right of way is determined by the size of the vehicle, which puts the motorcycle pretty low in the pecking order. Don't fight it and keep clear of trucks and buses.
- Distribute whatever weight you're carrying on the bike as evenly as possible across the frame. Too much weight at the back of the bike makes the front end less easy to control and prone to rising up suddenly on bumps and inclines.
- Get insurance with the motorcycle if at all possible. The more reputable motorcycle rental places insure all their bikes; some will do it for an extra charge. Without insurance you're responsible for anything that happens to the bike. If an accident results in the bike being 'totalled', or if the bike is lost or stolen, you can be out 25,000B plus. To be absolutely clear about your liability, ask for a written estimate of the replacement cost for a similar bike – take photos as a guarantee. Some agencies will only accept the replacement cost of a new bike. Health insurance is also a good idea – get it before you leave home and check the conditions in regard to motorcycle riding.

BICYCLE

Bicycles can be hired in many locations; guesthouses often have a few for rent at only

20 to 30B per day. Just about anywhere outside Bangkok, bikes are the ideal form of local transport because they're cheap, non-polluting and keep you moving slowly enough to see everything. Carefully note the condition of the bike before hiring; if it breaks down you are responsible and parts can be very expensive.

Many visitors are bringing their own touring bikes to Thailand these days. Grades in most parts of the country are moderate; exceptions include the far north. There is plenty of opportunity for dirt-road and off-road pedalling, so a sturdy mountain bike would make a good alternative to a touring rig. Good potential touring routes include the back roads of Yala, Pattani and Narathiwat provinces in the deep south – the terrain is mostly flat and the village scenery is inspiring.

No special permits are needed for bringing a bicycle into the country, although bikes may be registered by Customs – which means if you don't leave the country with your bike you'll have to pay a huge Customs duty. Most larger cities have bike shops but they often stock only a few Japanese or locally made parts. All the usual bike trip precautions apply – bring a small repair kit with plenty of spare parts, a helmet, reflective clothing and plenty of insurance.

Thailand Cycling Club, established in 1959, serves as an information clearinghouse on biking tours and cycle clubs around the country; call ☎ (2) 243-5139 or ☎ (2) 241-2023 in Bangkok. One of the best shops for cycling gear in Thailand is the Bike Shop in Bangkok, which has branches on New Phetburi Rd opposite Wat Mai Chonglom (☎ (2) 314-6317), at Sukhumvit Rd Soi 62 (☎ (2) 332-3538) and on Si Ayuthaya Rd (☎ (2) 247-7220) near Phayathai Rd.

HITCHING

Hitching is never entirely safe in any country in the world, and we don't recommend it. Travellers who decide to hitch should understand that they are taking a small but serious risk. You may not be able to identify the local rapist/murderer before you get into his vehicle. However, many people do choose to hitch, and the advice that follows should help to make the journeys as fast and safe as possible.

People have mixed success with hitchhiking in Thailand; sometimes it's great and other times no-one will pick you up. It seems easiest in the more touristed areas of the north and south, most difficult in the central and north-eastern regions where foreigners are a relatively rare sight. To stand on a road and try to flag every vehicle that passes by is, to the Thais, something only an uneducated village dweller would do.

If you're prepared to face this perception, the first step is to use the correct gesture used for flagging a ride – the thumb-out gesture isn't recognised by the average Thai. When Thais want a ride they stretch one arm out with the hand open, palm facing down, and move the hand up and down. This is the same gesture used to flag a taxi or bus, which is why some drivers will stop and point to a bus stop if one is nearby.

In general, hitching isn't worth the hassle as ordinary non-air-con buses are frequent and fares are cheap. There's no need to stand at a bus terminal – all you have to do is stand on any road going in your direction and flag down a passing bus or songthaew (see the Songthaew entry later in this chapter).

The exception is in areas where there isn't any bus service, though in such places there's not likely to be very much private vehicle traffic either. If you do manage to get a ride it's customary to offer food or cigarettes to the driver if you have any.

BOAT

As any flight over Thailand will reveal, there is plenty of water to get out on during your trip. The true Thai river and marine bay transport is the 'long-tail boat' *(reua hang yao)*, so called because the propeller is mounted at the end of a long drive shaft extending from the engine. The engine, which varies from a small marine engine to a large car engine, is mounted on gimbals and the whole unit is swivelled to steer the boat. Long-tail boats can travel at a phenomenal speed.

Between the mainland and islands in the

Gulf of Thailand or Andaman Sea, all sorts of larger ocean-going craft are used. The standard is an all-purpose wooden boat 8 to 10m long with a large inboard engine, a wheelhouse, and a simple roof to shelter passengers and cargo. Faster, more expensive hovercraft or jetfoils are sometimes available in tourist areas.

LOCAL TRANSPORT
The Getting Around section in the Bangkok chapter has more information on various forms of local transport.

Bus
In most larger provincial capitals, there are extensive local bus services, generally operating with very low fares (2 to 6B).

Taxi
Many regional centres have taxi services, but while there may well be meters, they're never used. Establishing the fare before departure is essential. Try to get an idea of the fare from a third party and be prepared to bargain. In general, fares are reasonably low.

Samlor/Tuk-Tuk
Samlor means 'three' *(sǎam)* 'wheels' *(láw)*, and that's just what they are – three wheeled vehicles. There are two types of samlor, motorised and non-motorised. You'll find motorised samlors throughout the country. They're small utility vehicles, powered by a horrendously noisy two stroke engine – if the noise and vibration doesn't get you, the fumes will. These samlors are more commonly known as *túk-túks* from the noise they make. The non-motorised version, on the other hand, are bicycle rickshaws, similar to those seen all over Asia. There are no bicycle samlors in Bangkok but you will find them elsewhere in the country. For both types of samlor the fare must be established, by bargaining if necessary, before departure.

Songthaew
A *songthaew (sǎwng tháew*, literally 'two rows') is a small pick-up truck with two rows

Small three wheeled taxicabs known as tuk-tuks sound like power saws gone beserk, commonly leaving trails of blue smoke whenever they rev up.

of bench seats down the sides, very similar to an Indonesian *bemo* or a Filipino *jeepney*. Songthaews sometimes operate fixed routes, just like buses, but they may also run a share-taxi type of service or even be booked individually like a regular taxi.

ORGANISED TOURS
Many tour operators around the world can arrange guided tours of Thailand. Most of them simply serve as brokers for tour companies based in Thailand; they buy their trips from a wholesaler and resell them under various names in travel markets overseas. Hence, one is much like another and you might as well arrange a tour in Thailand at a lower cost. Two of Thailand's largest tour wholesalers in Bangkok are: World Travel Service (☎ (2) 233-5900; fax 236-7169) at 1053 Charoen Krung Rd; and Deithelm Travel (☎ (2) 255-9150; fax 256-0248) at Kian Gwan Building II, 140/1 Withayu Rd.

Several Bangkok-based companies specialise in ecologically oriented tours, including: Friends of Nature Eco-Tours (☎ (2) 642-4426; fax 642-4428), 133/21 Ratchaprarop Rd, Ratthewi; and Khiri Travel (☎ (2) 629-0491; fax 629-0493), Viengtai Hotel, 42 Thani Rd, Banglamphu.

The better overseas tour companies build their own Thailand itineraries from scratch and choose their local suppliers based on which ones best serve these itineraries. Of these, several specialise in adventure and/or ecological tours, including those listed below. Bolder Adventures, for example, offers trips across a broad spectrum of Thai destinations and activities, from northern Thailand trekking to sea canoeing in the Phuket Sea, plus tour options that focus exclusively on northeast Thailand. The average trip runs 14 to 17 days.

Backroads – 801 Cedar St, Berkeley, CA 94710, USA (☎ (800) 462-2848, (510) 527-1555; fax (510) 527-1444)

Bolder Adventures – PO Box 1279, Boulder, CO 80306, USA (☎ (800) 642-2742, (303) 443-6789; fax (303) 443-7078)

Exodus – 9 Weir Rd, London SW12 0LT, UK (☎ (0181) 673-5550; fax 673-0779)

Intrepid Travel – 246 Brunswick St, Fitzroy, Victoria 3065, Australia (☎ (03) 9416-2655; fax 9419-4426)

Mountain Travel-Sobek – 6420 Fairmount Ave, CA 94530, USA (☎ (800) 227-2384, (510) 527-8100; fax (510) 525-7710)

Bangkok

Bangkok Highlights

○ BANGKOK

- ☎ (2) • pop 10 million
- Wat Phra Kaew – the home of the diminutive but mysterious Emerald Buddha glistens with its colourful mosaics, gold leaf and breathtaking spires
- Jim Thompson's House – the American silk entrepreneur's house is a beautifully maintained example of authentic Thai residential architecture, displaying Thompson's extensive Asian art collection
- Vimanmek Teak Mansion – one of the world's largest golden teak buildings
- River or Canal trips – observe Thai river life from a Chao Phraya River Express boat, go for a dinner cruise or see the bustling floating markets
- Eating – evenings can be devoted to sampling Bangkok's incredible Thai restaurants. Try at least one riverside place to soak up the languid ambience of old Bangkok
- Wat Pho – Bangkok's oldest and largest temple contains the country's largest reclining Buddha and the largest collection of Buddha images
- Traditional Dance-Drama – catch a khŏn performance at the Thai Deco Chalermkrung Royal Theatre or shrine dancing at various wats

The epitome of the modern, steamy Asian metropolis, Bangkok (560 sq km) has a surplus of attractions if you can tolerate the traffic, noise, heat (in the hot season), floods (in the rainy season) and heavily polluted air. The city is incredibly urbanised, but beneath its modern veneer lies an unmistakable Thainess.

Those anxious to get to Thailand's sand and surf may just want to skip this massive urban sprawl and head directly south or east. But there is plenty to see in Bangkok, should you decide to stop over for a few days. Even if you're just in town for the afternoon, say waiting for the overnight train to Surat Thani, it's worth taking in a few sights and absorbing the frenetic energy that makes this one of Asia's most fascinating cities.

Bangkok caters to diverse interests: there are temples, museums and other historic sites for those interested in traditional Thai culture; an impressive variety of good restaurants, clubs, international cultural and social events, movies in several languages, discos, heavy metal pubs and folk cafes; and modern art galleries. As the dean of expat authors in Thailand, William Warren, has said, 'The gift Bangkok offers me is the assurance I will never be bored'.

The capital of Thailand was established at Bangkok in 1782 by the first king of the Chakri Dynasty, Rama I. The name Bangkok comes from *bang makok*, meaning 'place of olive plums' and refers to the original site, which is only a very small part of what is today called Bangkok by foreigners. The official Thai name is quite a tongue twister: Krungthep mahanakhon bowon rattanakosin mahintara ayuthaya mahadilok popnopparat ratchathani burirom udomratchaniwet - mahasathan amonpiman avatansathir sakkathatitya visnukamprasit.

Fortunately, this is shortened to Krung Thep (City of Angels) in everyday usage. Metropolitan Krung Thep includes Thonburi, the older part of the city (and predecessor to Bangkok as the capital), which is across the Chao Phraya River to the west.

Following is a fairly selective guide to Bangkok's sights, accommodation, eateries and entertainment. For a more detailed look at the city, see Lonely Planet's *Bangkok city guide* and *Thailand* country guide.

Orientation

The east side of the Chao Phraya River, Bangkok proper, can be divided in two by the main north-south train line. The portion between the river and the railway is old Bangkok (often called Ko Ratanakosin), where most of the older temples and the original palace are located, as well as the Chinese and Indian districts. The part of the city east of the railway, which covers many times more area than the old districts, is 'new' Bangkok. It can be divided again into the business/tourist district wedged between Charoen Krung (New) and Rama IV Rds, and the sprawling business/residential/tourist district stretching along Sukhumvit and New Phetburi Rds.

This leaves the hard-to-classify areas below Sathon Tai Rd (which includes Khlong Toey, Bangkok's main port), and the area above Rama IV Rd between the railway and Withayu (Wireless) Rd – where there are scores of office blocks, several movie theatres, civil service buildings, the shopping area of Siam Square, Chulalongkorn University and the National Stadium). The areas along the east bank of the Chao Phraya River are undergoing a surge of redevelopment and many new buildings, particularly condos, are going up.

On the opposite (west) side of the Chao Phraya River is Thonburi, which was Thailand's capital for 15 years before Bangkok was founded. Few tourists ever set foot on the Thonburi side except to visit Wat Arun, the Temple of Dawn. Fang Thon (Thon Bank), as it's often called by Thais, seems an age away from the glittering high-rises on the river's east bank, although it is an up-and-coming area for condo development.

Maps A map is essential for finding your way around Bangkok, and the best one, be-

cause it clearly shows all the bus routes, is the *Bangkok Bus Map (Walking Tours)* published by Bangkok Guide. The map costs 35 to 40B and, although it's regularly updated, some bus routes will inevitably be wrong, so take care. Other companies put out similar maps such as *Tour'n Guide Map to Bangkok Thailand* and *Latest Tour's Map to Bangkok & Thailand*, that will also do the job. *Nancy Chandler's Map of Bangkok* (80B) has good tips on out-of-the-way places and where to buy unusual items around the city.

Information

Tourist Offices The Tourism Authority of Thailand (TAT) has a desk in the arrivals area at Bangkok international airport that's open from 8 am to midnight. The TAT's head office (☎ 281-0422) is at 4 Ratchadamnoen Nok Rd, near the Ratchadamnoen Boxing Stadium. Somewhat more conveniently located is the TAT's 'temporary' office (☎ 226-0060, 226-0072/6, ext 101-103), housed in a small round building at the centre of a government compound on the corner of Bamrung Meuang and Worachak Rds. Both offices have English-speaking staff and some fairly helpful information, including transport schedules, maps, accommodation lists and regional leaflets. Both offices are open daily from 8.30 am to 4.30 pm.

The TAT also maintains a Tourist Assistance Centre (TAC; ☎ 282-8129, 281-5051) at its head office for matters relating to theft and other mishaps; it's open from 8 am to 4.30 pm. The paramilitary arm of the TAT, the tourist police, can be quite effective in dealing with such matters, particularly 'unethical' business practices – which sometimes turn out to be cultural misunderstandings. But be aware that if you think you've been overcharged for gems (or any other purchase), there's very little the TAC can do.

Foreign Embassies See the Facts for the Visitor chapter for a list of embassies in Bangkok.

Immigration Department For visa extensions or applications, you'll need to visit the

Immigration Department office (☎ 287-1774) on Soi Suan Phlu, off Sathon Tai Rd. It's open Monday to Friday from 8.30 am to 4.30 pm (with limited staff from noon to 1 pm), and Saturday until noon. Most applications/extensions require two photos and a photocopy of the photo page of your passport.

Money Regular bank hours in Bangkok are Monday to Friday from 9.30 am to 3.30 pm. ATMs are common in all areas of the city. Many Thai banks also have currency exchange offices in tourist-oriented areas of Bangkok which are open from 8.30 am to 8 pm (some even later) every day of the year. You'll find them in several places along Sukhumvit, Nana Neua, Khao San, Patpong, Surawong, Ratchadamri, Rama IV, Rama I, Silom and Charoen Krung Rds. If you're after currency for other countries in Asia, check with the moneychangers along Charoen Krung (New) Rd near the GPO.

Post & Communications The GPO is on Charoen Krung Rd. The easiest way to get there is via the Chao Phraya River Express, which stops at Tha Meuang Khae at the river end of Soi Charoen Krung 34, next to Wat Meuang Khae, just south of the GPO. The poste-restante counter is open Monday to Friday from 8 am to 8 pm, and on weekends until 1 pm. Each letter you collect costs 1B, parcels 2B. The staff are very efficient.

There's also a packaging service at the GPO where parcels can be wrapped for 4 to 10B plus the cost of materials (up to 35B). Or you can simply buy the materials at the counter and do it yourself. The packaging counter is open Monday to Friday from 8 am to 4.30 pm, and Saturday from 9 am to noon.

Branch post offices throughout the city also offer poste restante and parcel services.

The Communications Authority of Thailand (CAT) international telephone office, around the corner from the main GPO building, is open 24 hours. At the time of writing, the GPO was being renovated to allow for more telecommunications facilities in the main building, so by the time you have this book in your hands the layout may have changed slightly.

At last count, 16 countries had Home Direct service, which means you can get one button connection to an international operator in any of these countries from a Home Direct booth (see the Telephone section in the Facts for the Visitor chapter for a country list). Other countries (except Laos and Malaysia) can be reached via IDD phones. Faxes can also be sent from the CAT office.

Home Direct phones can be found at Queen Sirikit National Convention Centre, World Trade Centre, Sogo Department Store and at the Banglamphu and Hualamphong post offices.

Calls to Laos and Malaysia can only be made from the TOT office on Ploenchit Rd – but this office accepts cash only, no reverse-charge or credit-card calls – or from private phones.

Travel Agencies Bangkok is packed with travel agencies of every manner and description, but if you're looking for cheap airline tickets it's wise to be cautious. In the past three or four years, at least two agencies on Khao San Rd have closed up shop and absconded with the full airfare payments of more than 30 tourists who, of course, never received their tickets. The really bad agencies change their names frequently, so ask other travellers for advice. Wherever possible, try to see the tickets before you hand over the money.

STA Travel maintains reliable offices specialising in discounted yet flexible air tickets at Wall Street Tower (☎ 233-2582), Room 1405, 33 Surawong Rd, and in the Thai Hotel (☎ 281-5314), 78 Prachatipatai Rd, Banglamphu. Another reliable, long-running agency is Vieng Travel (☎ 280-3537), Trang Hotel, 99/8 Wisut Kasat Rd, Banglamphu.

Some agencies will book train tickets and pick them up by courier – a service for which there's usually a 100B surcharge. Four agencies permitted to arrange direct train bookings (without surcharge) are:

BANGKOK

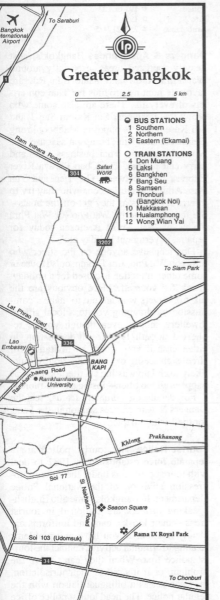

Greater Bangkok

0   2.5   5 km

BUS STATIONS
1 Southern
2 Northern
3 Eastern (Ekamai)

TRAIN STATIONS
4 Don Muang
5 Laksi
6 Bangkhen
7 Bang Seu
8 Samsen
9 Thonburi
  (Bangkok Noi)
10 Makkasan
11 Hualamphong
12 Wong Wian Yai

Airland – 866 Ploenchit Rd (☎ 255-5432)

Songserm Travel Center – 121/7 Soi Chalermla, Phayathai Rd (☎ 255-8790); 172 Khao San Rd (☎ 282-8080)

SEA Tours – Suite 414, 4th floor, Siam Center, Rama I Rd (☎ 251-4862, 255-2080)

Thai Overland Travel & Tour – 407 Sukhumvit Rd, between Sois 21 and 23 (☎ 635-0500; fax 635-0504)

Magazines & Newspapers Several ad-laden free magazines and papers contain tourist information, but the best all-around source for straight info is the *Bangkok Metro* magazine. A lifestyle monthly, it is packed with listings on health, entertainment, events, social services, travel tips and consumer-oriented articles. The *Nation* and the *Bangkok Post* also contain useful articles and event listings.

Bookshops Bangkok has many good book-shops, possibly the best selection in South-East Asia.

For new books and magazines the two best chains are Asia Books and Duang Kamol (DK) Book House. Asia Books lives up to its name by having one of the largest selections of English-language titles on Asia in Bangkok. Its main branch is at 221 Sukhumvit Rd at Soi 15 (☎ 252-7277). Other large branches are at: Landmark Plaza, Sois 3 and 4, Sukhumvit Rd (☎ 253-5839); 2nd floor, Peninsula Plaza, next to the Regent Bangkok on Ratchadamri Rd (☎ 253-9786); 3rd floor, World Trade Centre (☎ 255-6209); 3rd floor, Thaniya Plaza, Silom Rd (☎ 250-0162); and Seacon Square, Si Nakharin Rd (☎ 721-8867). Smaller Asia Books stalls can be found in several of the larger hotels and at Thai airports.

DK Book House (☎ 251-6335, 251-1467) has headquarters at Siam Square, off Rama I Rd, with additional branches on Surawong Rd near Patpong Rd and on Sukhumvit Rd across from the Ambassador City complex (the latter branches are excellent for fiction titles – the Siam Square branch is better for textbooks). DK also has a branch in the Mahboonkrong shopping centre opposite Siam Square.

On Khao San Rd in Banglamphu, at least three streetside vendors specialise in used paperback novels and guidebooks, including numerous Lonely Planet titles. Shaman Books (☎ 629-0418) at 71 Khao San Rd carries a good selection of guidebooks, maps and books on spirituality in several languages.

Medical Services Bangkok is Thailand's leading health care centre, with three university research hospitals, 12 public and private hospitals, and hundreds of medical clinics. Australian, US and UK embassies usually keep up-to-date lists of doctors who speak English; for doctors who speak other languages, contact the relevant embassy or consulate. Bangkok's better hospitals include:

Bangkok Adventist (Mission) Hospital – 430 Phitsanulok Rd (☎ 281-1422, 282-1100)
Bangkok Christian Hospital – 124 Silom Rd (☎ 233-6981/9, 235-1000)
Bangkok General Hospital – Soi 47, New Phetburi Rd (☎ 318-0066)
Bangkok Nursing Home – 9 Convent Rd (☎ 233-2610/9)
Bumrumgrad Hospital – 33 Soi 3, Sukhumvit Rd (☎ 253-0250)
Chao Phraya Hospital – 113/44 Pinklao Nakhon-Chaisi Rd, Bangkok Noi (☎ 434-6900)
Phayathai Hospital – 364/1 Si Ayuthaya Rd (☎ 245-2620); 943 Phahonyothin Rd (☎ 270-0780)
Samitivej Hospital – 133 Soi 49, Sukhumvit Rd (☎ 392-0010/9)
Samrong General Hospital – Soi 78, Sukhumvit Rd (☎ 393-2131/5)
St Louis Hospital – 215 Sathon Tai Rd (☎ 212-0033/48)

Emergency All of the hospitals listed above offer 24 hour service. Bangkok does not have an emergency phone system staffed by English-speaking operators. Between 8 am and midnight, your best bet for English-speaking assistance is the Tourist Assistance Centre (☎ 281-5051, 282-8129). After midnight, you'll have to rely on your own resources or on English-speaking hotel staff.

If you can find a Thai to call on your behalf, here are the city's main emergency numbers:

Police	☎ 191 or 123
Fire	☎ 199
Ambulance	☎ 252-2171/5

Dangers & Annoyances Bangkok's most heavily touristed areas, especially around Wat Phra Kaew and Khao San Rd, are favourite hunting grounds for Thai con artists of every ilk. There are also some who prowl the areas near Soi Kasem San 1 and Soi Kasem San 2, opposite Mahboonkrong Centre and near Jim Thompson's House, and typically dress in Thai business suits and carry cell phones. The Chao Phraya River Express piers between Tha Tien and Tha Phra Athit also attract cons who may try to intercept tourists as they get off the boats – the favourite line is 'Wat Pho (or Wat Phra Kaew, or Wat Arun) is closed today for repairs, government holiday etc'.

Don't believe anyone on the street who tells you Wat Pho, Jim Thompson's House or some other attraction is closed for a holiday; check for yourself. More obvious are the tuk-tuk drivers who are out to make a commission by dragging you to a local silk or jewellery shop – even though you've requested an entirely different destination. In either case if you accept an invitation for 'free' sightseeing or shopping, you're quite likely to end up wasting an afternoon or – as happens all too often – losing a lot of money.

For details on common scams, see the Dangers & Annoyances section in the Facts for the Visitor chapter.

Tourist Police The tourist police are a separate force established in 1982 to deal with tourist problems under the Crime Suppression Division of the National Police Department. In Bangkok, some 500 English-speaking officers are stationed in tourist areas – their kiosks, cars and uniforms are clearly marked. If you have any problems relating to criminal activity, contact the tourist police first. When they can't solve the problem, or if it's out of their jurisdiction, they can act as a bilingual liaison with the regular police. The head tourist police office (☎ 652-1721/6) at 29/1 Soi Lang Suan,

Ploenchit Rd, deals with tourism-related crime, particularly gem fraud; they can be reached by dialling ☎ 1699. The tourist police also have a branch at the TAT compound on Bamrung Meuang Rd (see the earlier Tourist Offices entry for details).

Wat Phra Kaew & Grand Palace

Also called the Temple of the Emerald Buddha (official name: Wat Phra Si Ratana Satsadaram), this wat adjoins the Grand Palace (Phra Borom Maharatchawong in Thai) on common ground which was consecrated in 1782, the first year of Bangkok rule. In aggregate, the 945,000 sq metre grounds encompass over a hundred buildings that represent 200 years of royal history and architectural experimentation. Most of the architecture, royal or sacred, can be classified Bangkok or Ratanakosin style, with lots of minor variation.

The wat structures are extremely colourful, being comprised of gleaming, gilded *chedis* (stupas), polished orange and green roof tiles, mosaic-encrusted pillars and rich marble pediments. Extensive murals depicting scenes from the *Ramakian* (the Thai version of the Indian epic the *Ramayana)* line the inside walls of the compound. Originally painted during Rama I's reign (1782-1809), the murals have undergone several restorations, including a major one finished in time for the 1982 Bangkok/Chakri Dynasty bicentennial. Divided into 178 sections, the murals illustrate the epic in its entirety, beginning at the north gate and moving clockwise around the compound.

Except for an anteroom here and there, the interiors of the Grand Palace are used by the king only for certain ceremonial occasions, such as Coronation Day (his current residence is Chitlada Palace in the north of the city), and are closed to the public. The exteriors of the four buildings are worth a swift perusal, however, for their royal bombast.

Admission to the Wat Phra Kaew/Grand Palace compound is 125B, and opening hours are from 8.30 am to 3.30 pm. The admission fee includes entry to the Royal Thai Decorations & Coins Pavilion (on the same grounds) and to both Vimanmek ('the world's largest golden teak-wood mansion')

Emerald Buddha

The so-called Emerald Buddha or Phra Kaew, 60 to 75cm high (depending on how it is measured), is actually made of a type of jasper or perhaps nephrite (a type of jade), depending on who you believe. An aura of mystery surrounds the image, enhanced by the fact that it cannot be examined closely (it sits in a glass case, on a pedestal high above the heads of worshippers) and photography within the bòt is forbidden. Its mystery further adds to the occult significance of the image, which is considered the 'talisman' of the Thai kingdom, the legitimator of Thai sovereignty.

It is not known for certain where the image originated or who sculpted it, but it first appeared on record in 15th century Chiang Rai. Legend says it was sculpted in India and brought to Siam by way of Ceylon, but stylistically it seems to belong to the Chiang Saen or Lanna period (13th to 14th centuries). Sometime in the 15th century, the image is said to have been covered with plaster and gold leaf and placed in Chiang Rai's own Wat Phra Kaew (literally, 'Temple of the Jewel Holy Image'). While being transported elsewhere after a storm had damaged the chedi in which it was kept, the image supposedly lost its plaster covering in a fall. It next appeared in Lampang, where it enjoyed a 32 year stay (again at a Wat Phra Kaew) until it was brought to Wat Chedi Luang in Chiang Mai.

Laotian invaders took the image from Chiang Mai in the mid-16th century and brought it to Luang Prabang in Laos. Later it was moved to Wiang Chan (Vientiane). When Thailand's King Taksin waged war against Laos 200 years later, the image was taken back to the Thai capital of Thonburi by General Chakri, who later succeeded Taksin as Rama I, the founder of the Chakri Dynasty. Rama I had the Emerald Buddha moved to the new Thai capital in Bangkok and had two royal robes made for it, one to be worn in the hot season and one for the rainy season. Rama III added another to the wardrobe to be worn in the cool season. The three robes are still solemnly changed at the beginning of each season by the king himself. Wat Phra Kaew's huge bòt, in which the Emerald Buddha is displayed, was built expressly for the purpose of housing the diminutive image. ∎

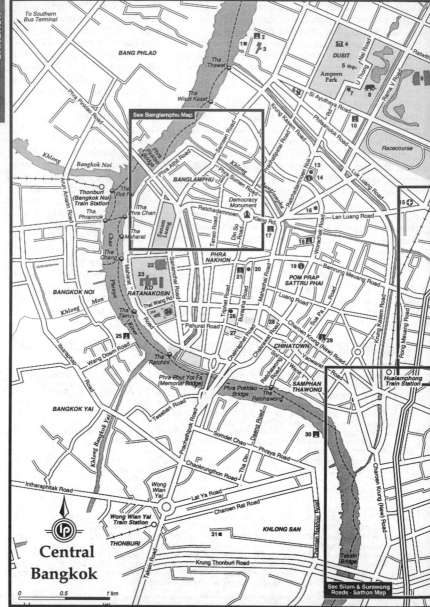

Central Bangkok

0   0.5   1 km

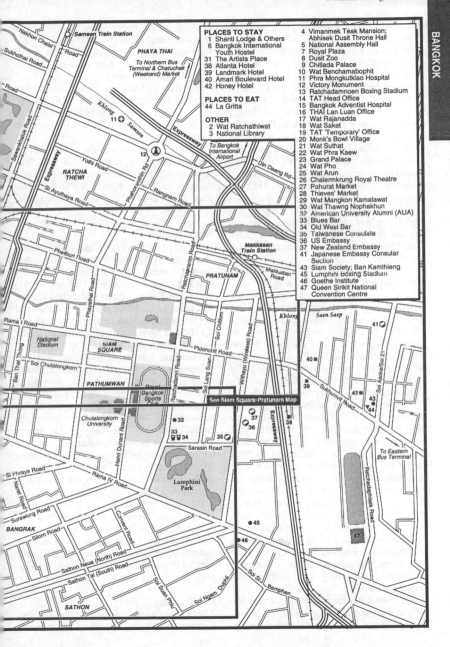

PLACES TO STAY
1 Shanti Lodge & Others
6 Bangkok International Youth Hostel
31 The Artists Place
38 Atlanta Hotel
39 Landmark Hotel
40 Amari Boulevard Hotel
42 Honey Hotel

PLACES TO EAT
44 La Gritta

OTHER
2 Wat Ratchathiwat
3 National Library
4 Vimanmek Teak Mansion; Abhisek Dusit Throne Hall
5 National Assembly Hall
7 Royal Plaza
8 Dusit Zoo
9 Chitlada Palace
10 Wat Benchamabophit
11 Phra Mongkutklao Hospital
12 Victory Monument
13 Ratchadamnoen Boxing Stadium
14 TAT Head Office
15 Bangkok Adventist Hospital
16 THAI Lan Luan Office
17 Wat Rajanadda
18 Wat Saket
19 TAT 'Temporary' Office
20 Monk's Bowl Village
21 Wat Suthat
22 Wat Phra Kaew
23 Grand Palace
24 Wat Pho
25 Wat Arun
26 Chalermkrung Royal Theatre
27 Pahurat Market
28 Thieves' Market
29 Wat Mangkon Kamalawat
30 Wat Thawng Nophakhun
32 American University Alumni (AUA)
33 Blues Bar
34 Old West Bar
35 Taiwanese Consulate
36 US Embassy
37 New Zealand Embassy
41 Japanese Embassy Consular Section
43 Siam Society; Ban Kamthieng
45 Lumphini Boxing Stadium
46 Goethe Institute
47 Queen Sirikit National Convention Centre

and Abhisek Dusit Throne Hall, near the Dusit Zoo.

Since wats are a sacred place to Thai Buddhists – this one particularly so because of its monarchical associations – visitors should dress and behave decently for their visit. If you wear shorts or a sleeveless shirt you may be refused admission; a sarong or baggy pants are sometimes available on loan at the entry area. For walking in the courtyard areas you must wear shoes with closed heels and toes – 'thongs' aren't permitted. As in any temple compound, shoes should be removed before entering the main chapel (bòt) or sanctuaries (wihãan) of Wat Phra Kaew.

The most economical way of reaching Wat Phra Kaew and the Grand Palace is by aircon bus No 8 or 12. You can also take the Chao Phraya River Express, disembarking at Tha Chang.

Wat Pho (Wat Phra Chetuphon)

A long list of superlatives for this one: the oldest and largest wat in Bangkok, it features the largest reclining Buddha and the largest collection of Buddha images in Thailand, and was the earliest centre for public education. As a temple site Wat Pho dates back to the 16th century, but its current history really begins in 1781 with the complete rebuilding of the original monastery.

Narrow Chetuphon Rd divides the grounds in two, with each section surrounded by huge whitewashed walls. The most interesting part is the northern compound. It includes a very large bòt enclosed by a gallery of Buddha images and four wihãan (the counterpart to the bòt), four large chedis commemorating the first three Chakri kings (Rama III has two chedis), 91 smaller chedis, an old tripitaka (Buddhist scriptures) library, a sermon hall, the large wihãan which houses the reclining Buddha, and a school building for classes in Abhidhamma (Buddhist philosophy), plus several less important structures. The temple is currently undergoing a 53 million baht renovation.

Wat Pho is the national headquarters for the teaching and preservation of traditional Thai medicine, including Thai massage. A massage school convenes in the afternoons at the eastern end of the compound; a massage costs 180B per hour, 100B for a half hour. You can also study massage here in seven to 10 day courses.

You may hire English, French, German or Japanese-speaking guides for 150B for one visitor, 200B for two, 300B for three. Also on the premises are a few astrologers and palm readers.

The temple is open to the public from 9 am to 5 pm daily; admission is 20B. The ticket booth is closed from noon to 1 pm. Air-con bus Nos 6, 8 and 12 stop near Wat Pho. The nearest Chao Phraya Express pier is Tha Tien.

Wat Mahathat

Founded in the late 18th century, Wat Mahathat is a national centre for the Mahanikai monastic sect and houses one of Bangkok's two Buddhist universities, Mahathat Rajavidyalaya. The university is the most important place of Buddhist learning in mainland South-East Asia; the Lao, Vietnamese and Cambodian governments send selected monks to further their studies here.

Mahathat and its surrounding area developed into an informal Thai cultural centre of sorts, though this may not be obvious at first glance. A daily open-air market features traditional Thai herbal medicine, and out on the street you'll find a string of shops selling herbal cures and Thai massage. On weekends, a large produce market held on the temple grounds attracts people from all over Bangkok and beyond.

The temple complex is open to visitors from 9 am to 5 pm every day and on wan phrá – Buddhist holy days (the full and new moons every fortnight). Admission is free.

Wat Mahathat is right across the street from Wat Phra Kaew, on the west side of Sanam Luang. Air-con bus Nos 8 and 12 both pass by it, and the nearest Chao Phraya Express pier is Tha Maharat.

Wat Traimit

Also known as the Temple of the Golden Buddha, the main attraction here is, of course, the impressive 3m-tall, 5½ tonne, solid-gold Buddha image. Sculpted in the graceful Sukhothai style, the image was 'rediscovered' some 40 years ago beneath a stucco or plaster exterior when it fell from a crane or plaster exterior while being moved to a new building within the temple compound. It has been theorised that the covering was added to protect it from 'marauding hordes', either during the late Sukhothai period or later in Ayuthaya when the city was under siege by the Burmese. The temple itself is said to date from the early 13th century.

The golden image can be seen every day from 9 am to 5 pm, and admission is 10B. Wat Traimit is near the intersection of Yaowarat and Charoen Krung Rds, near Hualamphong station.

Wat Arun

The striking 'Temple of Dawn', named after the Indian god of dawn, Aruna, appears in all the tourist brochures and is on the Thonburi side of the Chao Phraya River. The present wat was built on the site of 17th century Wat Jang, which served as the palace and royal temple of King Taksin when Thonburi was the Thai capital; hence, it was the last home of the Emerald Buddha before Rama I brought it across the river to Bangkok.

The tall, 82m *prang* (Khmer-style tower) was constructed during the first half of the 19th century by Rama II and Rama III. Its brick core has a plaster covering embedded with a mosaic of broken, multi-hued Chinese porcelain. Steep stairs reach a lookout point about halfway up the prang from where there are fine views of Thonburi and the river. During certain festivals, hundreds of lights illuminate the outline of the prang at night.

Wat Arun is open daily from 7 am to 5 pm; admission is 10B. To reach Wat Arun from the Bangkok side, catch a cross-river ferry from Tha Tien at Thai Wang Rd, Ratanakosin. Crossings are frequent and cost only 1B.

Wat Benchamabophit

This wat of white Carrara marble (hence its tourist name, 'Marble Temple') was built at the turn of the century under King Chulalongkorn (Rama V). The large cruciform bòt is a prime example of modern Thai wat architecture. The base of the central Buddha image, a copy of Phitsanulok's Phra Phuttha Chinnarat, contains the ashes of Rama V. The courtyard behind the bòt exhibits 53 Buddha images (33 originals and 20 copies) representing famous figures and styles from all over Thailand and other Buddhist countries – an education in itself if you're interested in Buddhist iconography.

Wat Ben is on the corner of Si Ayuthaya and Rama V Rds, diagonally opposite the south-west corner of Chitlada Palace. It's open daily from 9 am to 5 pm, and admission is 10B. Bus Nos 2 (air-con) and 72 (non air-con) stop nearby.

Wat Saket

Wat Saket is an undistinguished temple except for the Golden Mount (Phu Khao Thong) on the western side of the grounds which provides a good view over Bangkok rooftops. The artificial hill was created when a large chedi being built by Rama III collapsed because the soft soil beneath would not support it. The resulting mud-and-brick hill was left to sprout weeds until Rama IV built a small chedi on its crest.

Rama V later added to the structure and housed a Buddha relic from India (given to him by the British government) in the chedi. The concrete walls were added during WWII to prevent the hill from eroding. Every November there is a big festival on the grounds of Wat Saket, which includes a candle-lit procession up the Golden Mount.

Admission to Wat Saket is free except for the final approach to the summit of the Golden Mount, which costs 5B. The temple is within walking distance of the Democracy Monument; air-con bus Nos 11 and 12 pass nearby.

Wat Bovornives (Bowonniwet)

Wat Bowon, on Phra Sumen Rd in Banglamphu, is the national headquarters for the Thammayut monastic sect, a minority in

Thai Buddhism. There is approximately one Thammayut monk for every 35 Mahanikai monks. King Mongkut, founder of the Thammayuts, began a royal tradition by residing here as a monk – in fact, he was the abbot of Wat Bowon for several years. King Bhumibol and Crown Prince Vajiralongkorn, as well as several other males in the royal family, have been temporarily ordained here as monks. The temple was founded in 1826, when it was known as Wat Mai.

Bangkok's second Buddhist university, Mahamakut University, is housed at Wat Bowon. India, Nepal and Sri Lanka all send monks to study here. Across the street from the main entrance to the wat are an English-language Buddhist bookshop and a Thai herbal clinic.

Because of its royal status, be particularly careful to dress properly when visiting this wat – no shorts or sleeveless shirts.

National Museum

On Na Phra That Rd, west of Sanam Luang, the National Museum is the largest museum in South-East Asia and an excellent place to learn something about Thai art. All periods and styles are represented from Dvaravati to Ratanakosin, and English-language literature is available. Room 23 contains a well-maintained collection of traditional musical instruments from Thailand, Laos, Cambodia and Indonesia. Other permanent exhibits include ceramics, clothing and textiles, woodcarving, royal regalia, Chinese art and weaponry.

The museum buildings themselves were built in 1782 as the palace of Rama I's viceroy, Prince Wang Na. Rama V (Chulalongkorn) turned it into a museum in 1884.

In addition to the exhibition halls, the museum grounds contain the restored **Buddhaisawan (Phutthaisawan) Chapel**. Inside the chapel (built in 1795) are some well-preserved murals and one of the country's most revered Buddha images, Phra Phut Sihing. Legend has it that the image came from Ceylon, but art historians attribute it to 13th century Sukhothai.

Free English-language tours of the museum are given by volunteers on Wednesday (Buddhism) and Thursday (Thai art, religion and culture), starting from the ticket pavilion at 9.30 am. These guided tours are excellent and many people have written to recommend them. The tours are also conducted in French (Wednesday), German (Thursday) and Japanese (Wednesday). For more information on the tours, contact the museum on ☎ 224-1333. The museum is open from 9 am to 4 pm Wednesday to Sunday; admission is 20B.

Jim Thompson's House

This is a great spot to see authentic Thai residential architecture and South-East Asian art. Located at the end of an undistinguished soi next to Khlong Saen Saep, the premises once belonged to American silk entrepreneur Jim Thompson, who deserves most of the credit for the current worldwide popularity of Thai silk.

Born in Delaware in 1906, Thompson was a New York architect who briefly served in the Office of Strategic Services (OSS, forerunner of the CIA) in Thailand during WWII. After the war he found New York too tame and moved to Bangkok. Thai silk caught his connoisseur's eye; he sent samples to fashion houses in Milan, London and Paris, gradually building a worldwide clientele for a craft that had been in danger of dying out.

A tireless promoter of traditional Thai arts and culture, Thompson collected parts of various derelict Thai homes in central Thailand and reassembled them in the current location in 1959.

Thompson disappeared under quite mysterious circumstances while out for an afternoon walk in the Cameron Highlands of west Malaysia in 1967. He has never been heard from since. That same year his sister was murdered in the USA, fuelling various conspiracy theories about the disappearance. Was it a man-eating tiger? Communist spies? Business rivals? The most recent theory – for which there is apparently some hard evidence – is that the silk magnate was accidentally run over by a Malaysian truck driver who hid his remains.

On display in the main house is his small but splendid Asian art collection as well as his personal belongings. The Jim Thompson Foundation has a table at the front where you can buy prints of old Siam maps and Siamese horoscopes in postcard and poster form.

The house, on Soi Kasem San 2, off Rama I Rd, is open from 9 am to 4.30 pm Monday to Saturday. Admission is 100B (proceeds go to Bangkok's School for the Blind) but you can wander around the grounds for free. Students under 25 years get in for 40B.

Vimanmek Teak Mansion
(Phra Thii Nang Wimanmek)

First built on Ko Si Chang in 1868 and moved to the present site in 1910, this beautiful L-shaped, three storey mansion contains 81 rooms, halls and anterooms, and is said to be the world's largest golden teak building. Teak was once one of Thailand's greatest natural resources (it has since all but disappeared) and makes an especially good wood for building houses because it's so durable.

Vimanmek was the first permanent building on the Dusit Palace grounds. It served as King Rama V's residence in the early 1900s, was closed in 1935 and reopened in 1982 for the Ratanakosin bicentennial. The mansion contains various personal effects of the king, and a treasure trove of early Ratanakosin art objects and antiques.

English-language tours leave every half hour from 9.45 am, with the last one at 3.15 pm. The tour covers around 30 rooms and lasts an hour. Smaller adjacent buildings display historic photography documenting the Chakri Dynasty. Thai classical and folk dances are performed in the late morning and early afternoon in a pavilion on the canal side of the mansion.

Vimanmek is open from 9 am to 4 pm daily; admission is 50B for adults, 20B for children. It's free if you've already been to the Grand Palace/Wat Phra Kaew and kept the entry ticket for Vimanmek/Abhisek. As this is royal property, visitors wearing shorts or sleeveless shirts will be refused entry.

Abhisek Dusit Throne Hall
(Phra Thii Nang Aphisek Dusit)

This hall is a smaller wood, brick and stucco structure completed in 1904 for Rama V. Typical of the finer architecture of this era, the Victorian-influenced gingerbread and Moorish porticoes blend to create a striking and distinctly Thai exterior. The hall houses an excellent display of regional handiwork crafted by members of the Promotion of Supplementary Occupations & Related Techniques (SUPPORT) foundation, an organisation sponsored by the queen. Among the exhibits are *mát-mìi* cotton and silk, *málaeng tháp* collages (made from metallic, multi-coloured beetle wings), Damascene ware, neilloware and *yaan lipao* basketry.

Abhisek is open from 10 am to 4 pm daily, and admission is 50B (or free with a Wat Phra Kaew/Grand Palace/Vimanmek ticket). There is souvenir shop on the premises. As at Wat Phra Kaew and Vimanmek, visitors must be properly dressed – no sleeveless shirts or shorts.

Vimanmek and Abhisek lie towards the northern end of the Dusit Palace grounds, off U Thong Nai Rd (between Si Ayuthaya and Ratwithi Rds), across from the western side of the Dusit Zoo. An air-con No 3 (Si Ayuthaya Rd), air-con No 10 (Ratwithi Rd) or red microbus No 4 (Ratwithi Rd) will drop you nearby.

Art Galleries

Opposite the National Theatre, on Ratchini Rd, the **National Gallery** (☎ 281-2224) displays traditional and contemporary art. Most of the art here is by artists who receive government support; the general consensus is that it's not Thailand's best, but the gallery is worth a visit for die-hard art fans or if you're in the vicinity. The gallery is closed Monday and Tuesday, and open from 9 am to 4 pm on other days. Admission is 10B.

At the forefront of the contemporary Buddhist art movement is the **Visual Dhamma Art Gallery** (☎ 258-5879) at 44/28 Soi Asoke (Soi 21), Sukhumvit Rd. Work by some of Thailand's most prominent muralists are sometimes displayed here, along with the occasional foreign exhibition. The gallery is open Monday to Friday from 1 to 6 pm, Saturday from 10 am to 5 pm, or by appointment. Although the address is Soi Asoke, the gallery is actually off Asoke – coming from Sukhumvit Rd, take the second right into a small lane opposite Singha Bier Haus.

Bangkok's latest trend in public art consumption is the 'gallery pub', an effort to place art in a social context rather than leaving it to sterile galleries and museums. **Why Art? Pub & Gallery**, behind Cool Tango in the Royal City Avenue complex (Soi Sunwichai, Rama IX Rd), has a pub on the first two floors with copies of Michaelangelo and Botticelli murals done by Silpakorn University art students, and an art display space on the third floor. **Seri Art Gallery**, at Premier entertainment complex, is similar in concept. The place that initiated this trend, **Ruang Pung Art Community**, opposite section 13 in Chatuchak Market, has been in business for around 12 years. It's open weekends from 11 am to 6 pm and features rotating exhibits.

Utopia Gallery, a gallery-pub-social centre opposite Tia Maria Restaurant at 116/1 Soi 23, Sukhumvit Rd, specialises in gay and lesbian art, and is open daily from noon to 10 pm.

Chinatown (Sampeng)
Bangkok's Chinatown, off Yaowarat and Ratchawong Rds, comprises a confusing and crowded array of jewellery, hardware, wholesale food, automotive and fabric shops, as well as dozens of other small businesses. It's a good place to shop since goods here are cheaper than almost anywhere else in Bangkok and the Chinese proprietors like to bargain, especially along Soi Wanit 1 (also known as Sampeng Lane). Chinese and Thai antiques in various grades of age and authenticity are available in the so-called Thieves' Market (Nakhon Kasem), but it's better for browsing than buying these days.

During the annual Vegetarian Festival, celebrated fervently by Thai Chinese for the first nine days of the ninth lunar month (September-October), Bangkok's Chinatown becomes a virtual orgy of vegetarian Thai and Chinese food. The festivities are centred on **Wat Mangkon Kamalawat** (Neng Noi Yee), one of Chinatown's largest temples, on Charoen Krung Rd. All along Charoen Krung Rd in this vicinity, as well as on Yaowarat Rd to the south, restaurants and noodle shops offer hundreds of vegetarian dishes.

Pahurat
At the edge of Chinatown, around the intersection of Pahurat (Phahurat) and Chakraphet (Chakkaphet) Rds, is a small but thriving Indian district, generally called Pahurat. Here dozens of Indian vendors sell all kinds of fabric and clothes. This is the best place in the city to bargain for such items, especially silk. The selection is unbelievable, and Thai shoulder bags (*yaams*) sold here are the cheapest in Bangkok, perhaps in Thailand.

Behind the more obvious storefronts along these streets, in the 'bowels' of the blocks, is a seemingly endless Indian bazaar selling not only fabric but household items, food and other necessities. There are also some good, reasonably priced Indian restaurants in this area, and a Sikh temple off Chakraphet Rd.

Dusit Zoo (Suan Sat Dusit)
The collection of animals at Bangkok's 19 hectare zoo comprises more than 300 mammals, 200 reptiles and 800 birds, including relatively rare indigenous species such as banteng, gaur, serow and rhinoceros. Originally a private botanical garden for King Rama V, it was converted into a zoo in 1938 and is now one of the best zoological facilities in South-East Asia. The shady grounds feature trees labelled in English, Thai and Latin – plus a lake in the centre with paddle boats for rent. There's also a small children's playground.

If nothing else, the zoo is a nice place to get away from the noise of the city and observe how the Thais amuse themselves – mainly by eating. A couple of lakeside restaurants serve good, inexpensive Thai food. Entry to the zoo is 20B for adults, 5B for children, 10B for those over 60; it's open from 8 am to 6 pm daily. Sunday can be a bit crowded – if you want the zoo mostly to yourself, go on a weekday.

The zoo is in the Dusit district between Chitlada Palace and the National Assembly Hall; the main entrance is off Ratwithi Rd. Buses that pass the entrance include the ordinary Nos 18 and 28 and the air-con No 10.

Queen Saovabha Memorial Institute (Snake Farm)

At this research institute (☎ 252-0161), formerly known as the Pasteur Institute, on Rama IV Rd (near Henri Dunant Rd), venomous snakes are milked daily to make snake-bite antidotes, which are distributed throughout the country. The milking sessions – at 10.30 am and 2 pm Monday to Friday, 10.30 am only on weekends and holidays – have become a major Bangkok tourist attraction. Unlike other 'snake farms' in Bangkok, this is a serious herpetological research facility; a very informative half hour slide show on snakes is presented before the milking sessions. This will be boring to some, fascinating to others. Feeding time is 3 pm. Admission is 70B.

A booklet entitled *Guide to Healthy Living in Thailand*, published jointly by the Thai Red Cross and US embassy, is available here for 100B. You can also get vaccinations against such diseases as cholera, typhoid, hepatitis A and smallpox.

Lumphini Park

Named after Buddha's birthplace in Nepal, this is Bangkok's largest and most popular park (not that there's much in the way of competition). The park is bordered by Rama IV Rd to the south, Sarasin Rd to the north, Withayu Rd to the east and Ratchadamri Rd to the west, with entrance gates on all sides. A large artificial lake in the centre is surrounded by broad, well-tended lawns, wooded areas and walking paths.

One of the best times to visit the park is in the early morning before 7 am when the air is fresh (well, relatively so for Bangkok) and legions of Chinese are practising t'ai chi.

Also in the morning, vendors set up tables to dispense fresh snake blood and bile, considered health tonics by many Thais and Chinese. Rowboats and paddle boats can be rented at the lake for 20B per half hour. A weight-lifting area in one section becomes a miniature 'muscle beach' on weekends.

During the kite-flying season (in mid-February to April), Lumphini is a favoured flight zone; kites *(wâo)* can be purchased in the park during these months.

River & Canal Trips

In 1855 British envoy Sir John Bowring wrote, 'The highways of Bangkok are not streets or roads but the river and the canals'. The wheeled motor vehicle has long since become Bangkok's conveyance of choice, but fortunately it hasn't yet become universal. A vast network of canals and river tributaries surrounding Bangkok still carry a motley fleet of watercraft, from canoes to rice barges. In these areas many homes, trading houses and temples remain oriented towards water life and provide a fascinating glimpse into the past, when Thais still considered themselves *jâo nâam* or 'water lords'.

Chao Phraya River Express You can observe urban river life for 1½ hours for only 16B by climbing aboard a Chao Phraya River Express boat at Tha Wat Ratchasingkhon, just north of Krungthep Bridge. If you want to ride the entire length of the express route all the way to Nonthaburi, this is where you must begin. Ordinary bus Nos 1, 17 and 75, air-con bus No 4 and red microbus No 2 Kaw (2A) pass Tha Ratchasingkhon. Or you could board at any other express boat pier in Bangkok for a shorter ride to Nonthaburi; for example, 20 minutes from Tha Phayap (the first stop north of Krungthon Bridge), or 30 minutes from Tha Phra Athit (near the Phra Pinklao Bridge). Express boats run about every 15 minutes from 6 am to 6 pm daily. See the Know Your Boats boxed aside in the Getting Around section later in this chapter for more information on the Chao Phraya River Express service.

Khlong Bangkok Noi Taxi Another good boat trip is the Bangkok Noi canal taxi route which leaves from Tha Maharat next to Silpakorn University. You can sometimes also catch taxis from nearby Tha Chang. The fare is only a few baht and the further up Khlong Bangkok Noi you go, the better the scenery becomes, with teak houses on stilts, old wats and plenty of greenery.

Stop off at Wat Suwannaram to view 19th century *jataka* (life stories of the Buddha) murals painted by two of early Bangkok's foremost religious muralists. Art historians consider these the best surviving temple paintings in Bangkok. A one way fare anywhere is 10B.

Other Canal Taxis From Tha Tien pier near Wat Pho, get a canal taxi along **Khlong Mon** (leaving every half hour from 6.30 am to 6 pm, 4B) for more typical canal scenery, including orchid farms. A longer excursion could be made by making a loop along khlongs Bangkok Noi, Chak Phra and Mon, an all day trip. An outfit called Chao Phraya Charters (☎ 433-5453) runs a tour boat to Khlong Mon from Tha Tien each afternoon from 3 to 5 pm for 360B per person, including refreshments.

Boats from Tha Chang to **Khlong Bang Yai** (10B) leave every half hour from 6.15 am to 10 pm – this is the same trip that passes the Bang Khu Wiang Floating Market (see Floating Markets following this section). Though the market itself is over by 7 am, this trip is worthwhile later in the day as it passes a number of interesting wats, traditional wooden homes and the Royal Barges, ornate long former war vessels now only used for high royal occasions.

From the Tha Phibun Songkram pier in Nonthaburi, you can board a boat taxi up picturesque **Khlong Om** and see durian plantations. Boats leave every 15 minutes from 4 am to 9 pm.

For details on boat transport on the Bangkok side of the river, where four lengthy canal routes have been revived, see the Getting Around section at the end of this chapter. Although they provide quick transport, none

of the four right-bank canal routes can be recommended for sightseeing.

Boat Charters If you want to see the Thonburi canals at your own pace, the best thing to do is charter a long-tail boat – it needn't be expensive if you can get a small group together to share the costs. The usual price is 300B per hour and you can choose from among eight canals in Thonburi alone. Beware of 'agents' who try to put you on the boat and rake off an extra commission. Before travelling by boat, establish the price – you can't bargain when you're in the middle of the river!

The best piers for hiring a boat are **Tha Chang, Tha Saphaan Phut** and **Tha Si Phraya**. Close to the latter, to the rear of the River City Shopping Complex, the **Boat Tour Centre** charges the same basic hourly price (300B) and there are no hassles with touts. Of these four piers, Tha Chang usually has the largest selection of boats.

Dinner Cruises A dozen or more companies run regular cruises along the Chao Phraya River for rates ranging from 50 to 700B per person, depending on how far they go and whether dinner is included. Most require advance bookings.

The less expensive, more casual cruise operators allow you to order as little or as much as you want from moderately priced menus; a modest charge of 40 to 70B per person is added to the bill for the cruise. It's a fine way to dine outdoors when the weather is hot, away from city traffic and cooled by a river breeze. Those dinner cruises offering the à-la-carte menu plus surcharge include:

Khanap Nam Restaurant – Krungthon Bridge to Sathon Bridge; twice daily (☎ 433-6611)
Riverside Company – Krungthon Bridge to Rama IX Bridge; daily (☎ 434-0090)
Yok Yor Restaurant – Yok Yor Restaurant (Tha Wisut Kasat) to Rama IX Bridge; daily (☎ 281-1829, 282-7385)

More swanky dinner cruises charge a set price of 700 to 900B per person for the cruise and dinner; beer and liquor cost extra.

Loy Nava Co – Tha Si Phraya to Tha Wasukri; twice daily (☎ 437-4932/7329)

Manohra Cruises – Marriott Royal Garden Riverside Hotel to Krungthep Bridge; nightly (☎ 476-0021)

Wanfah Cruise – River City to Krungthon Bridge; twice daily (☎ 433-5453, 424-6218)

Sunset Cruise Two hours before its regular 2½ hour 7.30 pm dinner cruise, the *Manohra* sails from the Marriott Royal Garden Riverside Hotel for an hour-long sunset cocktail cruise. Boarding is free; passengers are only charged for drinks purchased from the well-stocked on-board bar. A free river taxi operates between the River City Pier and the Royal Garden Pier at 5 pm, just in time for the 5.30 pm cruise departure. Call ☎ 476-0021 for more information.

Floating Markets
Among the most heavily published photo images of Thailand are those of wooden canoes laden with multicoloured fruits and vegetables, paddled by Thai women wearing indigo-hued clothes and wide-brimmed straw hats. Such floating markets *(talàat náam)* do exist in various locations throughout the huge canal system that surrounds Bangkok – but if you don't know where to go you may end up at a very unauthentic tourist-show scene.

Bang Khu Wiang Floating Market At Khlong Bang Khu Wiang in Thonburi a small floating market operates between 4 and 7 am. Boats to the Khu Wiang Market (Talaat Naam Khuu Wiang) leave from Tha Chang near Wat Phra Kaew every morning between 6.15 and 8 am; take the earliest one to catch the market before it's over, or arrange to charter a long-tail boat at an earlier hour.

Damnoen Saduak Floating Market There is a larger, if somewhat more commercial, floating market on Khlong Damnoen Saduak in Ratchaburi Province, 104km south-west of Bangkok, between Nakhon Pathom and Samut Songkhram. You can catch a bus from the Southern bus terminal at the intersection of Hwy 338 (Nakhon Chaisi Rd) and Phra Pinklao Rd to Damnoen Saduak starting at 6 am. Get there as early in the morning as possible to escape the hordes.

Wat Sai Floating Market In recent years, visitors to the floating market near Wat Sai on Khlong Sanam Chai (off Khlong Dao Khanong) have outnumbered vendors to the point that opinion is now virtually unanimous – don't waste your time at this so-called market. Go to Bang Khu Wiang or Damnoen Saduak instead – or find your own.

If you're set on doing the Wat Sai trip, take one of the floating-market tours that leave from Tha Oriental (Soi Oriental) or Tha Maharat near Silpakorn University – your only alternative is to charter a boat (at Tha Oriental), which can be quite expensive, around 800B. Floating-market tours cost from 50B, and give you only 20 minutes or so at the market (probably more than enough for this non-event). Most tours charge 300 to 400B for 1½ hours. Be prepared for a very touristy experience.

Places to Stay – bottom end
Bangkok has perhaps the best variety and quality of budget places to stay of any Asian capital – which is one of the reasons it's such a popular destination for roving world travellers. Because of the wide distribution of places, your choice actually depends on what part of the city you want to be in – the tourist ghettos of Sukhumvit Rd and Silom-Surawong Rds, the backpacker ghetto of Banglamphu (north of Ratchadamnoen Klang Rd), the centrally located Siam Square area, or the narrow streets of Chinatown.

In this chapter, bottom-end accommodation covers places costing 60 to 500B per night; mid-range roughly 500 to 2000B per night and top end 2000B up.

Banglamphu If you're on a really tight budget head for the Khao San Rd area, near the Democracy Monument, parallel to Ratchadamnoen Klang Rd – ordinary bus Nos 2, 15, 17, 44, 56 and 59 will get you there, as well as air-con bus Nos 11 and 12.

BANGKOK

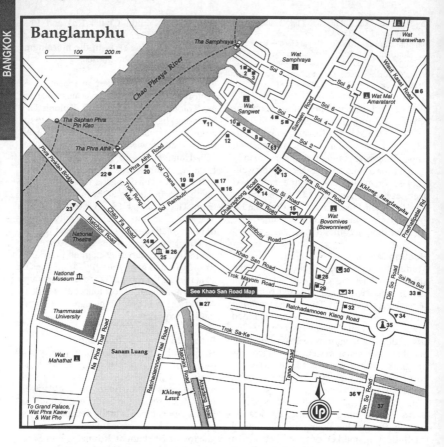

This is the main travellers' centre these days and new guesthouses are continually springing up.

The least expensive rooms are 80/120B (60/100B with haggling in the low season) for singles/doubles, though these are hard to come by due to the hordes of people seeking them out. More common are the 100/140B rooms. Occasionally, triple rooms are available for as low as 160B and dorm beds for 50B. Most of the year, it pays to visit several guesthouses before making a decision, but in the high season (December to February), you'd better take the first vacant bed you

come across. The best time of day to find a vacancy is around 9 or 10 am. At night during the peak months (December to March), Khao San Rd is bursting with life.

A tip: the guesthouses along Khao San Rd tend to be cubicles in modern shophouses, while those in Banglamphu's quieter lanes and alleys are often housed in old homes, some of them with a lot of character.

At the cheaper places it's not worth calling ahead, since the staff usually won't hold a room for you unless you pay in advance. Telephone numbers have been included for the places that *may* take reservations.

PLACES TO STAY	18	Merry V Guest	23	Wang Ngar
1 Home & Garden		House		Restaurant
Guest House	19	Green Guest House	34	Vijit Restaurant
2 Clean & Calm Guest	20	New Merry V Guest	36	Arawy Restaurant
House		House		
3 River House	21	Phra Athit Mansion	**OTHER**	
4 Villa Guest House	24	Chai's House	7	Siam Commercial
5 Truly Yours Guest	26	Charlie's House		Bank
House	27	Royal Hotel	13	New World
6 Trang Hotel;	28	Central Guest		Shopping Centre
Vieng Travel		House	14	Banglamphu
8 Banglamphu Square	29	Srinthip Guest		Department Store
Guest House		House	15	Post Office
9 Gipsy Guest House	32	Sweety Guest	22	UNICEF
10 PS Guest House		House	25	National Gallery
12 KC Guest House	33	Prasuri Guest	30	Mosque
16 Sawasdee House;		House	31	Post Office
Terrace Guest			35	Democracy
House	**PLACES TO EAT**			Monument
17 Chusri Guest House	11	Roti-Mataba	37	City Hall

Khao San Rd The hub of Bangkok's swirling backpacker universe. Here you'll find dozens of simple, adequate places with rooms for 60 to 100B a single, 80 to 120B a double, including the following:

Chada Guest House (plus air-con for 250B); *VIP Guest House* (all rooms 80B); *Bonny Guest House* (dorm beds for 60B); *Khao San Guest House*; *Buddy Guest House*; *Lek Guest House*; *Hello Guest House* (complaints in the past for rudeness); *Prakorp's House & Restaurant* (highly recommended); *Chart Guest House* (plus air-con for 450B); *NS Guest House*; *Thai Guest House*; and *Sitdhi Guest House & Restaurant*.

The *Khaosan Palace Hotel* (☎ 282-0578), set off down an alley at 139 Khao San Rd, has seen a facelift; rooms cost 250/350B a single/double with ceiling fan and private bath, 450/500B with air-con and hot water. Down a parallel alley, the *New Nith Jaroen Hotel* (☎ 281-9872) has similar rates and rooms to the Khaosan Palace, but slightly better service. The new *Nana Plaza Inn* (☎ 281-6402), near the Siri Guest House towards Khao San's east end, is a large, hotel-like enterprise built around a restaurant; air-con/hot-water rooms go for 400/500B a single/double.

Two narrow alleys between Khao San and Rambutri Rds feature a string of cramped places that nonetheless manage to fill up. The alley furthest west off Khao San sports *Doll, Suneeporn, Leed, Jim's, AT* and *Green House* (☎ 281-0323). Except for the Green House, all feature small, luggage-crammed lobbies with staircases leading to rooms layered on several floors, which cost around 60 to 100B. Green House is a bit more expansive, with rooms with fan and private bath for 150 to 200B, and a pleasant restaurant downstairs.

East down Khao San is a wider alley that's a bit more open, with the small, Indian-run *Best Aladdin Guest House & Restaurant*, which has rooms for 90/160B, and the hotel-like *Marco Polo Hostel*, which has rooms from 120 to 250B (most rooms with private bath).

Parallel to Khao San Rd to the south, but much quieter, is Trok Mayom, an alley reserved mostly for pedestrian traffic. *J & Joe* (☎ 281-2949; fax 281-1198) is an old teak home with pleasant rooms for 90 to 160B; not surprisingly, it's almost consistently full. There's also *New Joe* (☎ 281-2948) on Trok Mayom, a new rather modern-looking place set off the alley a bit with an outdoor cafe downstairs. Rooms cost 170/250B a single/double with private bath, 350B with air-con; email and fax services are available. Further east, towards Tanao Rd, *Ranee Guest*

BANGKOK

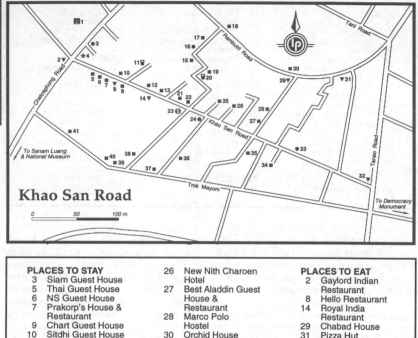

Khao San Road

0   50   100 m

PLACES TO STAY		26	New Nith Charoen Hotel	PLACES TO EAT	
3	Siam Guest House	27	Best Aladdin Guest House & Restaurant	2	Gaylord Indian Restaurant
5	Thai Guest House			8	Hello Restaurant
6	NS Guest House	28	Marco Polo Hostel	14	Royal India Restaurant
7	Prakorp's House & Restaurant	30	Orchid House	29	Chabad House
9	Chart Guest House	34	Nana Plaza Inn	31	Pizza Hut
10	Sitdhi Guest House	35	VIP Guest House	32	Arawy Det
12	Hello Guest House	36	Bonny Guest House		
13	Mam's Guest House	37	Thai Massage Guest House	**OTHER**	
15	Suneeporn Guest House	38	Kaosarn Privacy Guest House	1	Wat Chana Songkhram
16	AT; Leed & Jim's Guesthouses	39	Ranee Guest House	4	Chana Songkhram Police Station
17	Green House	40	New Joe Guest House	11	Paradise; No-Name; Hole in the Wall
18	Viengtai Hotel	41	J & Joe Guest House	20	Artsy Fartsy Bar & Art Gallery
19	Doll Guest House & Others			23	Krung Thai Bank
21	Lek Guest House			24	Shops
22	Buddy Guest House			33	Central Minimart
25	Khaosan Palace Hotel				

House charges 90/160B for rooms with shared bath.

West Banglamphu Several long-running guesthouses are on sois between Chakraphong Rd and the Chao Phraya River, putting them within walking distance of the Phra Athit pier, where you can catch express boats.

West of Chakraphong on Soi Rambutri, *Sawasdee House* (☎ 281-8138) follows the trend towards hotel-style accommodation in the Khao San Rd area. With a large restaurant downstairs, its small to medium-sized rooms on several floors upstairs, all with private bath, are in the 120 to 300B range. Next along Soi Rambutri are the *Chusri* and *Terrace* guesthouses, which have adequate rooms for 50 to 60B per person but are nothing special.

Right around the bend along Soi Rambutri is the popular *Merry V Guest House* (☎ 282-9267), with rooms from 100 to 160B; the cosy, similarly priced *Green* is next door.

Also in this vicinity, off the southern end of Soi Rambutri, the family-run *Chai's House* offers clean rooms for 100/200/300B a single/double/triple, or 300B a single/double with air-con, all with shared bath. It's a quiet, security-conscious place with a sitting area at the front. The food must be cheap and good, as it's a favourite gathering spot for local Thai college students on weekends.

East Banglamphu There are several guest-houses clustered in the alleys east of Tanao Rd. In general, rooms are bigger and quieter here than at places on or just off Khao San Rd. *Central Guest House* (☎ 282-0667) is just off Tanao Rd on Trok Bowonrangsi (trawk or trok means 'alley') – look for the rather inconspicuous signs. This is a very pleasant guesthouse, with clean, quiet rooms for 60B per person. There are some more spacious doubles for 120B.

Further south, off Trok Bowonrangsi, the *Srinthip* has dorm beds at 50B, and singles/doubles from 70/100B. Around the corner on a small road parallel to Ratchadamnoen Klang is *Sweety Guest House*, with decent rooms for 70 to 80B a single, 100 to 150B a double. Sweety has a roof terrace for lounging and for hanging clothes.

If you follow Trok Mayom Rd east, away from Tanao Rd, you'll reach Din So Rd. Cross Din So, walk away from the round-about and you'll see a sign for *Prasuri Guest House* (☎ 280-1428), down Soi Phra Suri on the right; clean singles/doubles/triples cost 190/220/300B with fan or 330/360/390B with air-con – all rooms come with private bath.

North Banglamphu At 11/1 Soi Surao, off Chakraphong Rd towards the Banglamphu Department Store and market, the friendly *BK Guest House* (☎ 281-3048) offers clean singles/doubles with shared bath for 120/150B with fan, 300/350B with air-con. *PS*

Guest House (☎ 282-3932), a Peace Corps favourite, is all the way at the western end of Phra Sumen Rd towards the river, on the south bank of Khlong Banglamphu; its well-kept rooms go for 110 to 160B. Next door is the similar *Gipsy Guest House*, and further south-east the more modern-looking *Banglamphu Square Guest House*, which has a coffee shop downstairs.

Off Samsen Rd, north of Khlong Bang-lamphu, is a small cluster of guesthouses conveniently close to the Tha Samphraya river express stop. On Soi 1 Samsen, just off Samsen Rd, the Khao San Rd-style *Truly Yours* (☎ 282-0371) offers 100/160B rooms over a large downstairs restaurant. A bit further along Soi 1, *Villa Guest House* offers a quiet, leafy, private home with 10 rooms from 200 to 450B; it's often full. Up on Soi 3 Samsen (also known as Soi Wat Sam-phraya), are the *River House* (☎ 280-0876), *Home & Garden* (☎ 280-1475) and *Clean & Calm*, each with small but clean rooms with shared bath for 60 to 120B. Note that Soi 3 zigs left, then zags right before reaching these three guesthouses – a good 10 minute walk from Samsen Rd. River House is the best of the three; there have been complaints of an attempted sexual assault on a guest at the Clean & Calm.

Thewet & National Library Area The next district north of Banglamphu near the National Library is another little travellers' enclave, though considerably quieter and less crowded than it's neighbour to the south.

Heading north up Samsen Rd from Wisut Kasat Rd, you'll come to *TV Guest House* (☎ 282-7451) at 7 Soi Phra Sawat, just off Samsen Rd to the east. It's clean, modern and good value at 40B for a dorm bed, 80B a double.

Continue for another half a kilometre or so and cross the canal to the intersection of Phitsanulok, Samsen and Si Ayuthaya Rds. Just beyond this junction is the National Library. On two parallel sois off Si Ayuthaya Rd towards the river (west from Samsen Rd) are five guesthouses run by various members of the same extended family: *Tavee Guest House* (☎ 282-5983); *Sawatdee Guest House*

(☎ 282-5349); *Backpacker's Lodge* (☎ 282-3231); *Shanti Lodge* (☎ 281-2497); and *Original Paradise Guest House* ◦(☎ 282-8673). All are clean, well kept and fairly quiet, and cost 50B for a dorm bed and from 100/150B for singles/doubles. There's a good market across the road from both sois, and a few small noodle and rice shops along Krung Kasem Rd, the next parallel street south of Si Ayuthaya (and west of Samsen Rd), which leads to Tha Thewet.

Another way to get to/from the National Library area is by taking advantage of Tha Thewet, a Chao Phraya River Express pier; from the pier you walk east along Krung Kasem Rd to Samsen Rd, turn left, cross the canal and then take another left onto Si Ayuthaya Rd. Ordinary bus Nos 16, 30 and 53, and air-con bus Nos 56 and 6 pass Si Ayuthaya Rd while going up and down Samsen Rd; ordinary bus No 72 terminates on the corner of Phitsanulok and Samsen Rds, a short walk from Si Ayuthaya. Air-con bus No 10 from the airport also passes close to this area along Ratwithi Rd to the north, before crossing Krungthon Bridge.

East of Samsen Rd, the *Bangkok International Youth Hostel* (☎ 282-0950, 281-0361) is in the same neighbourhood at 25/2 Phitsanulok Rd. A bed in the fan dorm costs 70B a night, while in the air-con dorm it's 80B. Rooms with fan and bath are 200B, while air-con singles/doubles with hot water are 250/300B. The rooms with fan are larger than the air-con rooms, and there's a cafeteria downstairs. Annual Hostelling International (formerly IYHF) membership costs 300B, or you can purchase a temporary membership for 50B. The Bangkok hostel gets mixed reports – the rooms seem nice enough but the staff can be quite rude.

Chinatown & Hualamphong Station This area is central and colourful, although rather noisy. There are numerous cheap hotels but it's not a travellers' centre like Banglamphu. Watch your pockets and bag around Hualamphong, both on the street and on the bus. The cream of the razor artists operate here as train passengers make good pickings.

The *New Empire Hotel* (☎ 234-6990/6) is at 572 Yaowarat Rd, near the Charoen Krung Rd intersection, a short walk from Wat Traimit. Air-con singles/doubles with hot water are 450B, with a few more expensive rooms for up to 800B – a bit noisy but a great location if you like Chinatown. The New Empire is a favourite among Chinese Thais from the southern region.

Other Chinatown hotels of this calibre, most without English signs out the front, can be found along Yaowarat, Chakraphet and Ratchawong Rds. The *Burapha Hotel* (☎ 221-3545/9) at the intersection of Mahachai and Charoen Krung Rds, on the edge of Chinatown, is a notch better than the Empire and costs 500B a single/double, up to 1000B for a deluxe room.

Straddling the bottom and mid-range is the *River View Guest House* (☎ 234-5429, 235-8501) at 768 Soi Phanurangsi, Songwat Rd, in the Talaat Noi area – wedged between Bangrak (Silom) and Chinatown. The building is behind the Jao Seu Kong Chinese Shrine, about 400m from the Royal Orchid Sheraton, in a neighbourhood filled with small machine shops. To get there, turn right from the corner of Si Phraya Rd (facing the River City shopping complex), take the fourth left, then the first right. Large rooms are 450B with fan and private bath, 700 to 800B with air-con and hot water. If you call from the River City complex, someone from the guesthouse will pick you up.

Siam Square Several good places can be found in this centrally located area, which has the additional advantage of being located on the Khlong Saen Saep canal taxi route.

There are several low to mid-range places on or near Soi Kasem San 1, off Rama I Rd near Jim Thompson's House and the National Stadium. The eight storey *Muangphol (Muangphon) Mansion* (☎ 215-0033) on the corner of Soi Kasem San 1 and Rama I Rd (931/8 Rama I Rd) has singles/doubles for 450/550B. It's good value – with air-con, hot water, a 24 hour restaurant and good service.

White Lodge (☎ 216-8867, 216-8228) at

36/8 Soi Kasem San 1, on the left past the more expensive Reno Hotel, offers clean if somewhat small rooms for 400B for singles/doubles. There's a pleasant terrace cafe at the front. The next one down on Soi Kasem San 1 is the three storey *Wendy House* (☎ 216-2436), where small but clean rooms with air-con, hot shower and TV go for 400/450B. If you're carrying unusually heavy bags, note there's no lift. A small restaurant is on the ground floor.

The *A-One Inn* (☎ 215-3029; fax 216-4771) at No 25/12-15 is a friendly and pleasant place that gets a lot of return business. Fair-sized air-con doubles with bath and hot water are 400B; spacious triples are 500B (rates may drop 100B in the low season). The similar *Bed & Breakfast Inn* diagonally opposite the A-One has room rates that fluctuate from 350 to 500B depending on demand; air-con rooms are substantially smaller than the A-One's, but the price includes continental breakfast.

Sukhumvit Rd Staying in this area puts you in the newest part of Bangkok and the furthest from old Bangkok near the river. Taxis take longer to get here because of the one way street system. The majority of the hotels in this area are in the middle-price range but you can find some lower end places.

The oldest hostelry in the Sukhumvit area is the historic *Atlanta Hotel* (☎ 252-1650, 252-6069) at 78 Soi 2 (Soi Phasak), Sukhumvit Rd. Owned since its 1950s construction by Dr Max Henn, a former secretary to the maharajah of Bikaner and owner of Bangkok's first international pharmacy, the Atlanta is a simple but reliable stand-by with clean, comfortable rooms in several price categories. Rooms with private shower, fan, balcony and one large double bed cost 300/400B a single/double, while similar rooms with twin beds (no balcony) go for 300/400/500B a single/double/triple. Air-con rooms with hot showers and built-in safe boxes go for 450/550/605B on the 3rd floor, 50B extra for lower floors.

Best Inn (☎ 253-0573) at 75/5-6 Soi 3, Sukhumvit Rd, provides smallish rooms

with fan for 350B and air-con rooms for 450B. Also in the inner Sukhumvit area is *Thai House Inn* (☎ 255-4698; fax 253-1780), between Sois 5 and 7. Rooms with air-con and hot water are 500B a single or double; facilities include a safety-deposit service and a coffee shop. On the other side of Sukhumvit Rd, the newish *Uncle Rey* (☎ 252-5565) at 7/10 Soi 4 offers simple air-con lodging for 400B.

Moving further out on Sukhumvit Rd, the *Miami Hotel* (☎ 252-5140/4759/5036) at Soi 13, Sukhumvit Rd, dates back to the 1960s and 70s R&R peak. The room and service quality seems to seesaw every three years or so but recent reports reckon it's decent value at 500/550B a single/double for air-con rooms and a swimming pool.

Places to Stay – middle
Bangkok is saturated with small and medium-sized hotels in this category. In the low season (March to November) you may be able to get a low-occupancy discount off the rates listed below.

Banglamphu Before Khao San Rd was 'discovered', the most popular Banglamphu hotel was the *Viengtai Hotel* (☎ 280-5434; fax 281-8153) at 42 Rambutri Rd. Over the past decade or so the Viengtai has steadily raised its prices until it now sits solidly in the middle-price range of Bangkok hotels; singles/doubles with TV, phone, hot water and air-con are 1400B.

On Phra Athit Rd, close to the Tha Phra Athit riverboat stop, the apartment-style *Phra Athit Mansion* offers rooms with air-con, TV, hot water shower and fridge for 650B a single/double, 850B a triple.

Besides the Oriental and the Atlanta, the oldest continually operating hotel in the city is the *Royal Hotel* (☎ 222-9111/20), still going strong on the corner of Ratchadamnoen Klang and Atsadang Rds near the Democracy Monument. The Royal's 24 hour coffee shop is a favourite local rendezvous; this is one of the few upper mid-range places where there are as many Asian as non-Asian guests. Singles/doubles start at 960B; during the low season this can sometimes be negotiated down to around 700B. A place of similar vintage and atmosphere, the *Majestic Hotel* (☎ 281-5000; fax 280-0965) is right around the corner at 97 Ratchadamnoen Klang Rd near the Democracy Monument. Rooms here start at 1200B.

Another mid-range place in this area is the *Thai Hotel* (☎ 282-2833) at 78 Prachatipatai Rd, which has singles/doubles at 1100/1250B.

Chinatown Mid-range hotels in the Chinatown area are tough to find. Best bets are the 80 room *Chinatown* (☎ 226-1267) at 526 Yaowarat Rd, which has rooms for 700 to 1200B, and the *Miramar Hotel* (☎ 222-4191) at 777 Mahachai Rd, where standard singles/doubles cost 780 to 1800B.

Silom & Surawong Rds This area is packed with upper mid-range places; discounts are often dispensed from April to October. Bangkok has a YMCA and YWCA, both in the Silom and Surawong Rds area. The *YMCA Collins International House* (☎ 287-1900/2727; fax 287-1996) at 27 Sathon Tai (South) Rd has air-con rooms with TV, telephone and private bath from 1377B. Guests may use the Y's massage room, gym, track and swimming pool. The *YWCA* (☎ 286-1936) at 13 Sathon Tai Rd has cheaper air-con rooms starting at 567B.

On the south side of Silom Rd is Soi Suksavitthaya (Seuksa Withaya), where the *Niagara Hotel* (☎ 233-5783/4) is located. Clean air-con rooms with hot water and telephone are a bargain 550 to 600B. Nearby, but on Silom Rd itself, the *Tower Inn* (237-8300) is at the top of the mid-range at 1500B for a double, but you get huge rooms (the place used to be all serviced apartments), free breakfast buffet and a rooftop swimming pool for the money.

Another decent upper mid-range choice in the Silom-Surawong area is the *Newrotel* (☎ 237-1094; fax 237-1102) at 1216/1 Charoen Krung Rd, near the GPO and the river. Air-con singles/doubles cost 1200B.

Classic mid-range hotels along Surawong

Rd include the *New Fuji* (☎ 234-5364) at No 299-310, with rooms from 1124 to 1338B, and the *New Trocadero Hotel* (☎ 234-8920/9) at No 34, where singles or doubles are 770 to 1400B. Because they both offer good service and amenities for under 1500B, these two have been favourites among journalists. A fair number of package tours stop here as well.

Siam Square/Hualamphong Station This area tends to offer either upper-end budget or top-end luxury hotels, with little in the middle. *Krit Thai Mansion* (☎ 215-3042), out on busy Rama I Rd opposite the National Stadium, costs 700 to 800B for rooms with air-con, hot water, private bath, telephone, colour TV/video, fridge and security parking. The coffee shop downstairs is open 24 hours. Reports are mixed on this one – some seem to like it, some don't.

An old Siam Square stand-by, the *Reno Hotel* (☎ 215-0026) on Soi Kasem San 1 is a veteran from the Vietnam War days when a spate of hotels opened in Bangkok with names of US cities. Singles/doubles/triples with air-con and hot water cost 550 to 990B; there's a pool on the premises.

On Soi Kasem San 1 is the ancient *Star Hotel* (☎ 215-3381) at 36/1 Soi Kasem San 1, a classic sort of mid-1960s Thai no-tell motel, with fairly clean, comfortable, air-con rooms with bath and TV for 550 to 650B a double, depending on the room – a bit steep for this area. Perhaps the high room rate is due to the curtained parking slots next to ground floor rooms, which hide cars belonging to guests from casual passers-by.

The *Siam Orchid Inn* (☎ 255-2119; fax 255-3144), off Soi Gaysorn close to Le Meridien President Hotel, offers well-appointed rooms with all the amenities for around 1500B.

For anyone who wants to be near the Royal Orchid Sheraton, River City complex and the river (Tha Si Phraya landing), the *Orchid Inn* (☎ 234-8934; fax 234-4159) at 719/1 Si Phraya Rd provides decent mid-range value at 750/900B (discounts of 100 to 150B often available) for tidy air-con rooms

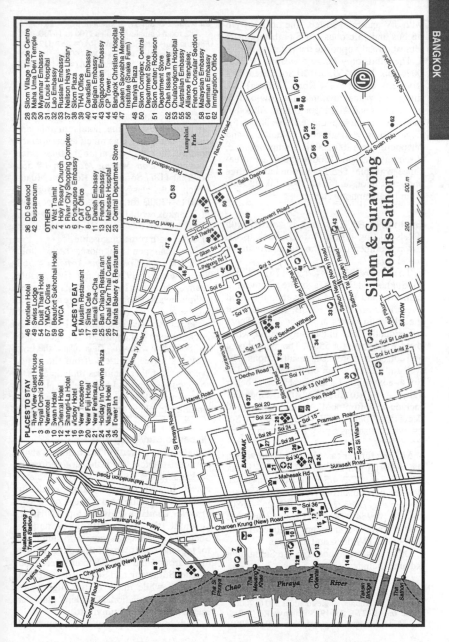

PLACES TO STAY
1 River View Guest House
3 Royal Orchid Sheraton
9 Newrotel
10 Swan Hotel
12 Oriental Hotel
14 Shangri-La Hotel
16 Victory Hotel
19 New Trocadero
20 New Fuji Hotel
21 New Peninsula
24 Holiday Inn Crowne Plaza
34 Niagara Hotel
35 Tower Inn
46 Montien Hotel
49 Swiss Lodge
54 Dusit Thani Hotel
57 YMCA Collins
59 Beaufort Sukhothai Hotel
60 YWCA

PLACES TO EAT
15 Muslim Restaurant
17 Simla Cafe
18 Himali Cha-Cha
25 Ban Chiang Restaurant
26 Chaai Karr Thai Cuisine
27 Maria Bakery & Restaurant
36 DC Seafood
42 Bussaracum

OTHER
2 Wat Traimit
4 Holy Rosary Church
5 River City Shopping Complex
6 Portuguese Embassy
7 CAT Office
8 GPO
11 Danish Embassy
13 French Embassy
22 Mahesak Hospital
23 Central Department Store
28 Silom Village Trade Centre
29 Maha Uma Devi Temple
30 Myanmar Embassy
31 St Louis Hospital
32 Lao Embassy
33 Russian Embassy
37 Neilson Hays Library
38 Silom Plaza
39 THAI Office
40 Canadian Embassy
41 Belgian Embassy
43 Singaporean Embassy
44 CP Tower
45 Bangkok Christian Hospital
47 Queen Saovabha Memorial Institute (Snake Farm)
48 Thaniya Plaza
50 Silom Complex; Central Department Store
51 Silom Center; Robinson Department Store
52 Chan Issara Tower
53 Chulalongkorn Hospital
55 Australian Embassy
56 Alliance Française;
French Consular Section
58 Malaysian Embassy
61 German Embassy
62 Immigration Office

Silom & Surawong Roads-Sathon

with TV and mini-fridge. The ordinary No 36 bus and Microbus No 6 both terminate almost directly opposite the hotel.

The multistorey *Tong Poon Hotel* (☎ 216-0020; fax 215-0450) at 130 Soi 8 Rama VI (formerly called Soi 4 Rong Meuang) is a mid-price place favoured for low-budget conventions and Asian tour groups. Although rack rates (room rates quoted to walk-ins) for large rooms with air-con, colour TV and telephone are 1800/2000B a single/double, discounts to around 1000 to 1500B are sometimes available. The Tong Poon has a coffee shop and pool, and it's a short tuk-tuk ride from Hualamphong station.

Sukhumvit Rd This area is choked with hotels costing 800 to 1500B. Stick to the lower numbered sois to save crosstown travel time.

The *Federal Hotel* (☎ 253-0175) at 27 Soi 11, Sukhumvit Rd, is a favourite among Vietnam War and Peace Corps vets but is a bit overpriced at 700 to 1050B, especially for the added-on rooms at ground level. These occasionally flood in the rainy season, when they're available for 550B. The modest pool and coffee shop are the main attractions. The well-run *Parkway Inn* on Sukhumvit Rd at Soi 4, next to the Landmark Hotel, is better value at 800 to 1000B a night; amenities include a rooftop pool. Another fairly good deal is the *Honey Hotel* (☎ 253-0646) on Soi 19, which also has a pool and air-con rooms from 650B.

Moving further east along Sukhumvit Rd, the well-run *Carlton Inn* (☎ 258-0471; fax 258-3717) at 22/2-4 Soi 21, Sukhumvit Rd, has decent rooms from 750B. A bit nicer are the two *City Lodges* on Sois 9 (☎ 253-7680) and 19 (☎ 254-4783). Rooms at either are 1016B a single/double, and include air-con, telephone, TV/video and mini-bar.

Other mid-range hotels in the Sukhumvit Rd area include:

Business Inn, 155/4-5 Soi 11, Sukhumvit Rd (☎ 254-7981); 70 rooms, singles/doubles 500 to 700B
China Inn, 19/27-8 Soi 19, Sukhumvit Rd (☎ 255-7571); 27 rooms, singles/doubles 650 to 750B

Euro Inn, 249 Soi 31, Sukhumvit Rd (☎ 259-9480); 82 rooms, singles/doubles 1100 to 1570B
Fortuna Hotel, 19 Sukhumvit Rd (☎ 251-5121); 110 rooms, singles/doubles 900/1100B
White Inn, 41 Soi 4, Sukhumvit Rd (☎ 251-1662); 11 rooms, singles/doubles 750B

Airport Area Finding decent, moderately priced accommodation in the airport area is difficult. Most of the hotels in this area charge nearly twice as much as comparable hotels in the city. Typical among these price-gougers is *Don Muang Mansion* (☎ 566-3095) at 118/7 Soranakom Rd, Don Muang, which looks classy on the outside but asks 1000 to 1200B for a small, stuffy room that in Bangkok would cost 500 to 750B at the most. It's possible to negotiate a lower rate of 800B with some discussion.

If you can spend a bit more, a better choice is the 150 room *Comfort Inn Airport* (☎ 552-8929; fax 552-8920), about five minutes south of the airport by car at 88/117 Vibhavadi (Wiphaawadi) Rangsit Rd. Large rooms with all the amenities (satellite TV, air-con, hot water bath/shower) cost 1500 to 1800B if you book through a Bangkok travel agent, 2500 to 2800B for walk-ins. Best of all, the hotel provides a free shuttle to/from the airport every hour. Other facilities include a coffee shop, pool, sauna and health club; about the only drawback is that you can hear planes landing and taking off until around midnight.

Places to Stay – top end
Bangkok has all sorts of international standard tourist hotels, from the straightforward package places to some of Asia's classic hotels. In fact, three of Bangkok's luxury hotels consistently make the Condé Nast *Traveler* annual worldwide top 25 list: the Oriental, the Regent Bangkok and the Shangri-La. Although there's no single area for top-end hotels, you'll find quite a few of them around the Siam Square area, along parallel Surawong and Silom Rds, and along the river, while many of the slightly less expensive 'international standard' places are scattered along Sukhumvit Rd.

With lower occupancy rates, you should

still be able to negotiate discounts of up to 40% on the rates listed. Booking through a travel agency almost always means lower rates – also try asking for a hotel's 'corporate' discount. Several luxury hotels have even lowered their rack rates from two years ago.

A welcome trend in Bangkok hotels in the past few years has been the appearance of several European-style 'boutique' hotels – small, business-oriented places of around 100 rooms or less with rates in the 2000 to 3000B range – like the *Mansion Kempinski* (☎ 255-7200; fax 253-2329), 75/23 Soi 11, Sukhumvit Rd, and the *Swiss Lodge* (☎ 233-5345; fax 236-9425), 3 Convent Rd. Many experienced Bangkok business travellers prefer this type of hotel because they get personal service for about 1000B less than the bigger hotels; also these smaller hotels don't accept tour groups, so regular guests don't have to wade through crowds in the lobby.

Newer hotel standouts include the *Chateau de Bangkok* (☎ 290-0125; fax 290-0167) at 25 Soi Ruam Rudi, Ploenchit Rd, opposite the US embassy. Owned by the French hotel group Accor, it offers 139 service studios – one and two-bedroom apartments, each with walk-in closet, IDD phone and fax – for 2500B a night.

The less expensive, tastefully decorated *Hotel Rembrandt* (☎ 261-7100; fax 261-7107) at Soi 18, Sukhumvit Rd, has 406 large rooms that were going for 2700B at the time of writing, though rack rates were listed at 3000B and over. Facilities include a swimming pool and the best Mexican restaurant in Bangkok, Señor Pico's of Los Angeles. Another advantage is the Rembrandt's proximity to Queen Sirikit National Convention Centre, off Soi 16.

All of the hotels in this category add a 10% service charge plus 7% tax to hotel bills.

On the River The 120-year-old *Oriental Hotel* (☎ 236-0400/39) at 48 Oriental Ave, on the Chao Phraya River, is one of the most famous hotels in Asia, right up there with the Raffles in Singapore or the Peninsula in Hong Kong. What's more it's also rated as one of the very best hotels in the world, as well as being just about the most expensive in Bangkok. The hotel management prides itself on providing highly personalised service through a staff of 1200 (for 398 rooms) – once you've stayed here they'll remember your name, what you like to eat for breakfast, even what type of flowers you prefer in your room.

Nowadays the Oriental is looking more modern and less classic – the original Author's Wing is dwarfed by the Tower (built in 1958) and River (1976) wings. Authors who have stayed at the Oriental and had suites named after them include Joseph Conrad, Somerset Maugham, Noel Coward, Graham Greene, John Le Carré, James Michener, Gore Vidal and Barbara Cartland. Room rates start at 6500B, suites as much as 10 times that. It's worth wandering in if only to see the lobby (no shorts, sleeveless shirts or thongs allowed – dress politely or you'll be refused entry).

On the Thonburi bank of the Chao Phraya River, a bit south of central Bangkok, the tastefully appointed, 420 room *Marriott Royal Garden Riverside Hotel* (☎ 476-0021; fax 460-1805), 257/1-3 Charoen Nakhon Rd, near Krungthep Bridge, is highly valued for its serene atmosphere and expansive, airy public areas. The grounds feature a large swimming pool, lush gardens, two lighted tennis courts and a world-class health club. Rack rates for very spacious rooms are 4200B, or 4800B with a river view. A free water taxi service shuttles guests back and forth to the Oriental and River City piers every hour from 7 am to 11 pm.

Two other luxury gems along the river are the *Shangri-La* (☎ 236-7777; fax 236-8570) at 89 Soi Wat Suan Phlu, Charoen Krung Rd, and the *Royal Orchid Sheraton* (☎ 266-0123; fax 236-8320), 2 Captain Bush Lane, Si Phraya Rd. The Shangri-La has 694 rooms starting from 5265B, and its own helicopter transport from the airport, while the Sheraton (776 rooms, from 5649B) is known for crisp, efficient service (the business centre is open 24 hours).

Siam Square/Pratunam People accustomed to heady hotels claim the plush *Regent*

Bangkok (☎ 251-6127; fax 253-9195) at 155 Ratchadamri Rd tops the Oriental for overall quality for money (local calls are free at the Regent – probably the only luxury hotel in the city to offer this courtesy). It's also one of the city's top choices for visiting business travellers because of its efficient business centre and central location. The hotel also offers (for 1650B an hour) an 'office on wheels', a high-tech, multi-passenger van equipped with computers, cell phones, fax machines, TVs/VCRs and swivelling leather seats so that small business conferences can be held while crossing town in Bangkok's turgid traffic. The Regent's 415 rooms start at 5885B.

Another top executive choice is the *Hilton International Bangkok* (☎ 253-0123; fax 253-6509) on Withayu Rd, where you won't find tour groups milling around in the lobby; its 343 rooms start at 4400B. The expansive grounds are a major plus; only Bangkok's older hotel properties are so fortunate.

Another of this generation, the 400 room *Siam Intercontinental* (☎ 253-0355; fax 253-0355), ensconced on spacious grounds at 967 Rama I Rd (near Siam Square), takes in a mix of well-heeled pleasure and business travellers. Standard rooms start at 5179B.

The *Grand Hyatt Erawan* (☎ 254-1234; fax 2253-5856), at the intersection of Ratchadamri and Ploenchit Rds, was built on the site of the original Erawan Hotel (which came up at the same time as the Royal but was torn down some years ago) in 1991 and has obvious ambitions to become the city's No 1 hotel. The neo-Thai architecture has been well executed; inside is the largest collection of contemporary Thai art in the world. Adding to the elite atmosphere, rooms at the rear of the hotel overlook the Bangkok Royal Sports Club racetrack. For most visitors – whether for business or leisure – it vies with the Novotel Bangkok on Siam Square for having the best location of all the city's luxury hotels vis-à-vis transport and proximity to shopping. Huge rooms start at 5000B.

Thailand's own Amari Hotels & Resorts opened the 34 storey *Amari Watergate* (☎ 267-653-9000; fax 653-9045) at the end of 1994 right in the centre of Bangkok's busiest district, Pratunam. The neo-classic interior blends Thai and European motifs, guest rooms are large and facilities include the 900 sq metre Clark Hatch fitness centre, free-form pool, two squash courts, Thai massage, a 24 hour business centre, an American-style pub, and very highly rated Cantonese and Italian restaurants. The hotel is on Phetburi Rd near the Ratchaprarop Rd intersection. Tour groups check in via a separate floor and lobby while other guests use the main lobby, a boon to business travellers. Spacious rooms cost 4200/4600B a single/double; the three top floors contain more luxuriously appointed executive rooms at 5200/5800B.

Another well-located hotel for business or leisure is the 429 room *Novotel Bangkok* (☎ 366-8666; fax 366-8699). Just steps away from the vibrant shopping and entertainment district of Siam Square, the Novotel boasts a full business centre, bakery, pool and various restaurants. Rooms cost 4100/4500B.

Silom & Surawong Rds/Sathon This area has many hotels with similar amenities to the Regent, Hilton and Sheraton, but are a step down in price because of their location or smaller staff-to-guest ratios. In the Silom and Surawong Rds areas these include the *Montien* (☎ 234-8060; fax 234-8060) at 54 Surawong Rd (500 rooms, from 4680B), a very Thai hotel; the *Dusit Thani* (☎ 233-1130; fax 2366400) on Rama IV Rd (520 rooms, from 6120B), a great hotel in a busy location; and the *Holiday Inn Crowne Plaza* (☎ 238-4300/34; fax 238-5289) at 981 Silom Rd (662 rooms, from 3200B).

Another entry in the luxury/executive market is the 190 room *Beaufort Sukhothai* (☎ 287-0222; fax 287-4980) at 13/3 Sathon Tai Rd. The Sukhothai features Asian minimalist decor, including an inner courtyard with lily ponds; the same architect and interior designer created Phuket's landmark Amanpuri. Standard rooms start at 5297B.

Also new to the scene is the ultra-modern

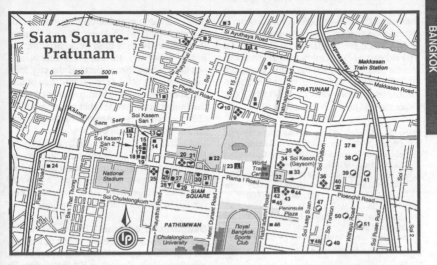

Siam Square-Pratunam

0   250   500 m

PLACES TO STAY
- 2 Florida Hotel
- 3 Siam City Hotel
- 8 Amari Watergate Hotel
- 11 Asia Hotel
- 14 A-One Inn
- 15 Star Hotel; Bed & Breakfast Inn
- 16 White Lodge; Wendy House
- 17 Reno Hotel
- 18 Krit Thai Mansion
- 19 Muangphol Mansion
- 22 Siam Intercontinental Hotel
- 24 Tong Poon Hotel
- 31 Novotel Bangkok
- 33 Siam Orchid Inn
- 37 Hilton International Bangkok
- 45 Grand Hyatt Erawan
- 46 Regent Bangkok

PLACES TO EAT
- 28 Hard Rock Cafe
- 48 Whole Earth Restaurant

OTHER
- 1 Payathai Plaza
- 4 Wang Suan Phakkard
- 5 Baiyoke Tower
- 6 Post Office
- 7 Pratunam Market
- 9 Phanthip Plaza
- 10 Indonesian Embassy
- 12 Jim Thompson's House
- 13 Tha Ratchathewi (Canal Taxis)
- 20 Siam Center
- 21 Post Office
- 23 Wat Patum
- 25 Mahboonkrong Shopping Centre
- 26 Scala Cinema
- 27 DK Book House
- 29 British Council
- 30 Siam Square Multiplex 5 (Cinema)
- 32 Gaysorn Plaza
- 34 Narayana Phand
- 35 Robinson Department Store
- 36 Central Department Store
- 38 Norwegian Embassy
- 39 UK Embassy
- 40 TOT Office
- 41 Swiss Embassy
- 42 Erawan Shrine (Saan Phra Phrom)
- 43 Sogo Department Store
- 44 Maneeya Building
- 47 Israeli Embassy
- 49 Dutch Embassy
- 50 Spanish Embassy
- 51 Vietnamese Embassy

Westin Banyan Tree (☎ 679-1200; fax 679-1199), which towers over Sathon Tai Rd with 216 business suites. The hotel is ensconced on the lower two and top 28 floors of the 60 storey Thai Wah Tower II, the tallest building in Thailand. The Banyan Tree's huge rooms feature separate work and sleep areas, two line speaker phones, data ports and two TV sets along with all the other amenities expected of lodgings that cost over 6000B a night. The spa-fitness centre spans four floors.

Sukhumvit Rd Two new Amari hotels in central Bangkok include the *Amari Atrium* (☎ 318-5295; fax 319-0789) on Phetburi Tat Mai Rd east of Soi Asoke, with singles/doubles for 3000/3200B, and the *Amari Boulevard* (☎ 255-2930; fax 255-2950) at Soi 5, Sukhumvit Rd, which has rooms for 3000 to 4200B. Other top-end hotels in this area include:

Delta Grand Pacific Hotel, Soi 17-9, Sukhumvit Rd (☎ 233-2922/7; fax 237-5740); 400 rooms, easy access to Queen Sirikit National Convention Centre, from 4914B
Landmark, 138 Sukhumvit Rd (☎ 254-0404; fax 255-8419); 415 rooms, has a Videotex in every room, very good business centre, 4826 to 9416B
Novotel Lotus Bangkok, 1 Soi Daeng Udom, Soi 33, Sukhumvit Rd (☎ 261-0111; fax 262-1700); 219 rooms, 4826B
Park Hotel, 6 Soi 7, Sukhumvit Rd (☎ 255-4300; fax 255-4309); 128 rooms, 2000 to 6000B

Airport Area The 434 room *Amari Airport Hotel* (☎ 566-1020; fax 566-1941), directly across from the airport, has recently been renovated and is quite well appointed. The executive floor has huge suites and 24 hour butler service. Rates start at 4200B for a standard double. Another luxury-class hotel near the airport is the *Central Plaza Bangkok* (☎ 541-1234; fax 541-1087) at 1695 Phahonyothin Rd, overlooking the Railway Golf Course and Chatuchak Park. There are 600 rooms, starting at 3955B for a standard room. Or stay five minutes from the airport at the less expensive *Comfort Inn Airport* (see Places to Stay – Middle).

A new top-end project, the *Asia Airport Hotel*, is due to open nearby soon after this book's publication.

Places to Eat

No matter where you go in Bangkok, you're almost never more than 50m away from a restaurant or sidewalk food vendor. The variety of places to eat is simply astounding and defeats all but the most tireless food samplers in their quests to say they've tried everything. As with seeking a place to stay, you can find something in every price range in most districts – with a few obvious excep-

tions. Chinatown is naturally a good area for Chinese food, while Bangrak and Pahurat (both districts with high concentrations of Indian residents) are good for Indian and Muslim cuisine. Some parts of the city tend to have higher priced restaurants than others (eg Siam Square, and Silom, Surawong and Sukhumvit Rds), while other areas are full of cheap eats (eg Banglamphu and the river area around Tha Maharat).

As transport can be such a hassle in Bangkok, most visitors choose a place to eat according to which district is most convenient to reach (rather than seeking out a specific restaurant). This section has therefore been organised by area, rather than cuisine.

Banglamphu & Thewet This area near the river and old part of the city is one of the best for cheap eating establishments. Many of the guesthouses on Khao San Rd have open-air cafes, which are packed with travellers from November to March and July to August. The typical cafe menu here has a few Thai and Chinese standards, plus a variety of traveller favourites like fruit salad, muesli and yoghurt. None of them particularly stand out, though the side-by-side *Orm* and *Wally House* produce fair Thai, farang and vegetarian meals, while *Prakorp's House* makes good coffee. *Arawy Det*, an old Hokkien-style noodle shop on the corner of Khao San and Tanao Rds, has somehow managed to stay authentic amid the cosmic swirl.

Gaylord Indian Restaurant, hidden away in the rear upstairs of a building on Chakraphong Rd opposite the west entrance to Khao San Rd, has decent Indian food. *Royal India* on the south side of Khao San Rd used to be good but has slid downhill since it moved across the street (the original Royal India in Pahurat district is still worth trying). *Chabad House*, a Jewish place of worship on Rambutri Rd, serves Israeli-style kosher food downstairs.

Rambutri Rd, the next street north of Khao San, is also good for more authentic (and cheaper) Thai food. At the western end of the street are several open-air restaurants serving excellent Thai food at low prices.

On the corner of Phra Athit and Phra Sumen Rds near the river, a small shop called *Roti-Mataba* (no English sign) offers delicious kaeng mátsaman (Thai Muslim curry), chicken kurma, chicken or vegetable mátàbà (a sort of stuffed crepe) and a bilingual menu; look for a white sign with red letters. There are several unassuming Chinese dim sum and noodle places along Phra Athit Rd north of the New Merry V Guest House, plus a couple of Thai curry shops. The *Raan Kin Deum* (no English sign), a few doors down from New Merry V, is a nice two storey cafe with wooden tables and chairs, traditional Thai food and live folk music nightly. The laid-back atmosphere reaches its acme in the evenings when Thais and farangs crowd the place.

At Tha Wisut Kasat in north-western Banglamphu, there's a very good floating seafood restaurant called *Yok Yor*. Especially good is its hàw mòk (fish curry). Yok Yor also offers inexpensive evening dining cruises – you order from the regular menu and pay a nominal 50B charge for the boat service. Nearby is the similar *Chawn Ngoen*; it has no English sign, but there is an English menu. *Wang Ngar*, in West Banglamphu next to the Phra Pinklao Bridge, is another decent waterfront place.

Silom & Surawong Rds This area is the heart of the financial district so it has a lot of pricey restaurants, along with cheaper ones that attract office workers as well as the more flush. Many restaurants are found along the main avenues but there's an even greater number tucked away in sois and alleys. *DD Seafood*, a parking lot next to the Tower Inn that turns into an outdoor restaurant in the evenings, is praised by locals for its excellent (and affordable) seafood dinners.

The river end of Silom and Surawong Rds towards Charoen Krung Rd (the Bangrak district) is a good hunting ground for Indian food.

Thai & Other Asian The *Soi Pracheun (Soi 20) Night Market*, which assembles each evening off Silom Rd in front of the municipal market pavilion, is good for cheap eats.

During the day there are also a few food vendors on this soi. At lunch and early evening a batch of food vendors – selling everything from noodles to raw oysters – set up on Soi 5 next to Bangkok Bank's main branch.

The area to the east of Silom Rd off Convent and Sala Daeng Rds is a Thai gourmets' enclave. Most of the restaurants tucked away here are very good, but a meal for two will cost 600 to 800B. One such up-market spot is *Bussaracum* (☎ 235-8915), pronounced 'boot-sa-ra-kam', at 35 Soi Phipat, off Convent Rd. Bussaracum specialises in 'royal Thai' cuisine, that is, recipes that were created for the royal court in days past (these recipes were kept secret from 'commoners' until late this century). Every dish is supposedly prepared only when ordered, from fresh ingredients and freshly ground spices. Live classical Thai music, played at a subdued volume, is also provided. This is a fancy place, recommended for a splurge. Two can eat for around 650 to 850B; call ahead to be sure of a table.

Another great place for traditional Thai – at moderate prices – is *Ban Chiang* (☎ 236-7045), a restored wooden house in a verdant setting at 14 Soi Si Wiang, Pramuan Rd (off Silom Rd west of Maha Uma Devi Temple). Owned by a Thai movie star, *Thanying* (☎ 236-4361) at 10 Soi Pramuan, off Silom Rd, features an elegant decor and very good, moderately expensive royal Thai cuisine. It's open daily from 11 am to 10.30 pm; there's another branch at the World Trade Centre on Ploenchit Rd.

Towards the eastern end of Surawong Rd, about a 10 minute walk west of Montien Hotel, is the famous *Somboon Seafood* (open from 4 pm to midnight), a good, reasonably priced seafood restaurant known for having the best crab curry in town. Soy-steamed seabass (plaa kràphong nêung sii-yíu) is also a speciality. Somboon has a second branch called *Somboon Chinese* further north, across Rama IV Rd near Chulalongkorn University at Soi Chulalongkorn 8 (711-7 Chula Soi 8, Ban That Thong Rd).

Towards the other end of Surawong Rd at No 311/2-4 (on the corner of Soi Pramot), the economical *Maria Bakery & Restaurant* is well known for its fresh Vietnamese and Thai food as well as French pastries, pizza and vegetarian dishes. A newer Maria branch can be found at 909-11 Silom Rd, opposite Central Department Store. Both are clean and air-conditioned, and have reasonable prices.

Indian & Muslim Further towards the western end of Silom and Surawong Rds – an area known as Bangrak – Indian eateries begin to appear. Unlike at Indian restaurants elsewhere in Bangkok, the menus in Bangrak don't necessarily exhibit the usual, boring predilection toward north Indian Moghul-style cuisine. For authentic south Indian food (dosa, idli, vada etc), try the *Madras Cafe* (☎ 235-6761) in the Madras Lodge at 31/10-1 Vaithi Lane (Trok 13), off Silom Rd near the Narai Hotel. It's open daily from 9 am to 10 pm. Another place serving south Indian (in addition to north Indian) food is the very basic *Simla Cafe* at 382 Soi Tat Mai (opposite Borneo & Co) off Silom Rd, in an alley behind the Victory Hotel. Across from the Narai Hotel, near the Maha Uma Devi temple, street vendors sometimes sell various Indian snacks.

India Hut (☎ 237-8812), a new place on Surawong Rd opposite the Manohra Hotel, specialises in Nawabi (Lucknow) cuisine; it's quite good and friendly, with moderate to medium-high prices (45 to 100B per dish). The vegetarian samosas and fresh prawns cooked with ginger are particularly good. It's three flights of steps off the street, with a modern Indian decor.

Himali Cha-Cha (☎ 235-1569) at 1229/11 Charoen Krung Rd features good north Indian cuisine at slightly higher prices. Founder Cha-Cha reportedly worked as a chef for India's last viceroy; his son has taken over the kitchen here. It's open daily for lunch and dinner.

Other Cuisines If you crave western food, there are plenty of places serving a variety of cuisines on and around Patpong Rd. *Bobby's Arms*, an Aussie-Brit pub on Patpong 2

(through a garage), has good fish & chips. The *Brown Derby* on Patpong 1 is recommended for American-style deli sandwiches. Authentically decorated *Delaney's Irish Pub* (☎ 266-7160) at 1-4 Sivadon Building, Convent Rd in the Silom Rd, district serves a set lunch menu for 130 to 160B from Monday to Friday, plus other pub grub daily. Irish bands play nightly.

Probably the best Patpong find of all is the *Cafe de Paris* (☎ 237-2776) on Patpong 2, an air-con spot popular with French expats for its decent approximations of Parisian-style bistro fare; it's open daily from 11 am to 1 am.

The tiny *Harmonique* (☎ 237-8175) on Soi Charoen Krung 34, around the corner from the GPO, is a refreshing oasis in this extremely busy, smog-filled section of Charoen Krung. European-managed and unobtrusive, the little shop serves a variety of teas, fruit shakes and coffee on Hokkien-style marble-topped tables – a pleasant spot to read poste-restante mail while quenching a thirst. Well prepared if pricey (60 to 150B per dish) Thai food is also available. The shop discreetly sells silk, silverwork and antiques. It's open daily from 10 am to 10 pm.

Siam Square This shopping area is interspersed with several low and medium-priced restaurants as well as American fast-food franchises. Chinese food seems to dominate, probably because it's the well-off Chinese Thais that most frequent Siam Square. Soi 1 has three shark-fin places: *Scala*, *Penang* and *Bangkok*. At the other end of Siam Square, on Henri Dunant Rd, the big noodle restaurant called *Coca Garden* (open from 10.30 am to 10.30 pm) is good for Chinese-style sukiyaki.

Can't decide what kind of Asian or farang food you're in the mood for? Then head for *S&P Restaurant & Bakery* on Soi 12. The extensive menu features Thai, Chinese, Japanese, European and vegetarian specialities, plus a bakery with pies, cakes and pastries – all high-quality fare at low to moderate prices.

On Soi 11, the Bangkok branch of the *Hard Rock Cafe* serves good American and Thai food; prices are about the same as at other Hard Rocks around the world. Look for the tuk-tuk captioned 'God is my co-pilot' coming out of the building's facade. The Hard Rock stays open till 2 am, a bit later than many Siam Square eateries.

Sukhumvit Rd This avenue stretching east all the way to the city limits has hundreds of Thai, Chinese and farang restaurants to choose from.

Thai & Other Asian The ground floor of the *Ambassador Hotel* between Sois 11 and 13 has a good food centre. It offers several varieties of Thai, Chinese, Vietnamese, Japanese, Muslim and vegetarian food at 20 to 40B per dish – you must buy coupons first and exchange them for dishes you order.

Cabbages & Condoms at No 10, Soi 12, is run by the Population & Community Development Association (PDA), the brainchild of Mechai Viravaidya who popularised condoms in Thailand – first for birth-control purposes and now as STD prevention. The restaurant offers not only a great selection of condoms, but great Thai food at reasonable prices as well. The tôm khàa kài (chicken-coconut soup) is particularly tasty. The restaurant is open from 11 am to 10 pm.

The *Mandalay* (☎ 255-2893) at 23/7 Soi Ruam Rudi is supposedly the only Burmese restaurant in town; it's good but not cheap.

The famous *Djit Pochana* (☎ 258-1578) has a branch on Soi 20 and is one of the best value restaurants in town for traditional Thai dishes. The all-you-can-eat lunch buffet is 90B. This central section of Sukhumvit Rd is loaded with medium-priced Thai restaurants with modern decors but real Thai food. *Baan Kanitha* (☎ 258-4181), 36/1 Soi 23, Sukhumvit Rd, offers traditional decor and authentic Thai food; the plaa kràphong nêung mánao (seabass in lime sauce) and tôm hhàa kài (chicken in coconut-galangal broth) are tops.

For nouvelle Thai cuisine, try the *Lemon-grass* (☎ 258-8637) at 5/21 Soi 24, which is atmospherically set in an old Thai house decorated with antiques. The food is exceptional; try the yam pèt (Thai-style duck salad). It is open from 11 am to 2 pm and 6 to 11 pm.

The upscale *Le Dalat* (☎ 258-0290) at 47/1 Soi 23, Sukhumvit Rd, has the most celebrated Vietnamese cuisine in the city. A house speciality is năem meuang, grilled meatballs which you place on steamed rice-flour wrappers, then add chunks of garlic, chilli, ginger, starfruit and mango along with a tamarind sauce, and finally wrap the whole thing into a lettuce bundle before popping it in your mouth. There are two other branches: Patpong Business Centre, 2nd floor, Surawong Rd (☎ 234-0290); and Premier Shopping Village, Chaeng Wattana Rd (☎ 573-7017). Also good for a stylish Vietnamese meal is *Pho* (☎ 252-5601) on the 3rd floor of Sukhumvit Plaza, Soi 12, Sukhumvit Rd. A second branch can be found in the Alma Link Building, 25 Soi Chitlom, Ploenchit Rd; both are open daily for lunch and dinner.

Indian & Muslim *Mrs Balbir's* (☎ 253-2281) at 155/18 Soi 11 (behind the Siam Commercial Bank) has a good variety of moderately priced vegetarian and non-vegetarian Indian food (mostly northern Indian). Mrs Balbir has been teaching Indian cooking for many years and has her own Indian grocery store as well.

The splurge-worthy *Rang Mahal* (☎ 261-7100), a rooftop restaurant in the Rembrandt Hotel on Soi 18, offers very good north and south Indian 'royal cuisine' with cityscape views. On Sunday the restaurant puts on a sumptuous Indian buffet from 11.30 am to 3 pm. Another decent Indian place is *Bangkok Brindawan* (☎ 258-8793) at 15 Soi 35 near the Fuji supermarket. This one specialises in south Indian food; an all-you-can-eat 120B lunch buffet is offered Monday to Friday from 11 am to 3 pm.

A few medium to expensive restaurants serving Pakistani and Middle Eastern food can be found in the 'Little Arabia' area of Soi 3 (Soi Nana Neua). The best value in the whole area is *Al Hossain*, a roofed outdoor cafe on the corner of a lane (Soi 3/5) off the east side of Soi Nana Neua. A steam table holds a range of vegetarian, chicken, mutton and fish curries, along with dal (curried lentils), aloo gobi (spicy potatoes and cauliflower), nan (flat bread) and rice. Dishes costs 20 to 40B each. *Shiraz* on the same soi is a slightly pricier indoor place that provides hookahs for Middle Eastern gentlemen wanting to while away the afternoon smoking out the front. Similar places in the vicinity include *Mehmaan, Akbar's, Al Hamra* and *Shaharazad.*

Western Cuisines Homesick Brits need look no further than *Jool's Bar & Restaurant* at Soi 4 (Soi Nana Tai), past Nana Plaza on the left walking from Sukhumvit Rd. The British-style bar downstairs is a favourite expat hang-out, while the dining room upstairs serves decent English food.

Several rather expensive west European restaurants (Swiss, French, German etc) are also found on touristy Sukhumvit Rd. *Bei Otto*, between Sois 12 and 14, is one of the most popular German restaurants in town and has a comfortable bar. *Haus München* (☎ 252-57776), 4 Soi 15, Sukhumvit Rd, serves large portions of good German and Austrian food; prices are reasonable and there are recent German-language newspapers on hand. It's open daily for breakfast, lunch and dinner

Nostalgic visitors from the USA, especially those from southern USA, will appreciate the well-run *Bourbon St Bar & Restaurant* on Soi 22 (behind the Washington Theatre). The menu here emphasises Cajun and Creole cooking; some nights there is also free live music.

One of the top French restaurants in the city, and probably the best not associated with a luxury hotel, is *Le Banyan* (☎ 253-5556) at 59 Soi 8 in a charming early Bangkok-style house. The kitchen is French-managed, and the menu covers the territory from ragout d'escargot to canard maigret avec foie gras. It has a superb wine list. This is definitely a splurge experience – although the prices are moderate when compared with other elegant French restaurants in the city.

Pomodoro (☎ 252-9090), a place with floor-to-ceiling windows on the ground floor of the Nai Lert Building on Sukhumvit Rd (between Sois 3 and 5), specialises in Sardinian cuisine. It is open daily from 10 am to 11 pm. *La Gritta* (☎ 255-7350) serves tasty and authentic Italian dishes, though portions can be a bit small.

If you're looking for Mexican food, the city's best can be found at *Señor Pico's of Los Angeles* (☎ 261-7100), on the 2nd floor of the Rembrandt Hotel, Soi 18, Sukhumvit Road. This brightly decorated, festive restaurant offers reasonably authentic Tex-Mex cuisine, including fajitas, carnitas, nachos and combination platters. Expect to spend around 400 to 600B for two.

Chinatown, Hualamphong & Pahurat Some of Bangkok's best Chinese and Indian food is found in these adjacent districts, but because few tourists stay in this part of town (for good reason – it's simply too congested) they rarely make any eating forays into the area.

The large, banquet-style Chinese places are mostly found along Yaowarat and Charoen Krung Rds, and include *Lie Kee* (on the corner of Charoen Krung and Bamrungrat Rds, a block west of Ratchawong Rd), *Laem Thong* (on Soi Bamrungrat just off Charoen Krung Rd) and *Yau Wah Yuen* (near the Yaowarat and Ratchawong Rds intersection). Each of these has an extensive menu, including dim sum before lunch time.

All-night *food hawkers* are set up along Yaowarat Rd at the Ratchawong Rd intersection, opposite Yaowarat Market and near the Cathay Department Store; this is the least expensive place to eat in Chinatown. The city reportedly has plans to relocate all the vendors from this area to a new 'Chinatown Night Plaza' around the corner on Ratchawong Rd to reduce traffic on Yaowarat Rd.

Suki Jeh Yuu Seu (the English sign reads 'Health Food'), a Chinese vegetarian restaurant just 70m down Rama IV Rd from Hualamphong station, serves excellent but a bit pricey vegetarian food in a clean, air-con atmosphere. The fruit shakes are particularly good; this is a great place to fortify oneself with food and drink while waiting for a train at Hualamphong.

Over in Pahurat, the Indian fabric district, most places serve north Indian cuisine, heavily influenced by Moghul or Persian flavours and spices. Many people think the best north Indian restaurant in town is the *Royal India* at 392/1 Chakraphet Rd. It can be very crowded at lunch – almost exclusively with Indian residents – so it might be better to go there after the standard lunch hour or at night. The place has very good curries (vegetarian and non-vegetarian), dal, Indian breads (including six kinds of paratha), raita, lassi etc – all at quite reasonable prices. Royal India also has a branch on Khao San Rd in Banglamphu but it's not as good.

Vegetarian Many of the Khao San Rd guesthouse cafes offer vegetarian dishes. For an all-vegie menu at low prices, seek out the *Vegetarian Restaurant* at 117/1 Soi Wat Bowon, near Srinthip Guest House. To find this out-of-the-way spot, turn left on Tanao Rd at the eastern end of Khao San Rd, cross the street and turn right down the first narrow alley, then left at Soi Wat Bowon – an English sign reads 'Vegetarian'. The fare is basically western vegetarian, with wholemeal breads, salads and sandwiches. It's open from 8 am until around 10 pm.

During the annual Vegetarian Festival (centred on Wat Mangkon Kamalawat on Charoen Krung Rd in September-October), Bangkok's Chinatown becomes a virtual orgy of Thai and Chinese food. Restaurants and noodle shops in the area offer hundreds of different vegetarian dishes. One of the best spreads is at *Hua Seng Restaurant*, a few doors west of Wat Mangkon on Charoen Krung Rd.

Mega-Restaurants *Tum-Nak-Thai (Tamnak Thai*; ☎ 276-7810), 131 Ratchadaphisek Rd, is one of several large outdoor restaurants built over boggy areas of Bangkok's Din Daeng district north of Phetburi Rd.

Built on four hectares of land and water, it can serve up to 3000 diners at once. The menu has more than 250 items, and includes Thai, Chinese, Japanese and European food. Orders are computer processed and some of the waiters glide by on roller skates. One section of the restaurant offers while-you-dine Thai classical dance performances. Two can eat here for under 400B, including beer.

Tum-Nak-Thai was billed as the largest outdoor restaurant in the world – as verified by the *Guinness Book of Records* – until *Mang Gorn Luang (Royal Dragon) Seafood Restaurant* (☎ 398-0037) opened recently at Km 1 on the Bangna-Trat expressway. Around 1200 roller-skating servers in traditional Thai costumes, along with waitresses paddling along artificial canals in 'happy boats', serve up to 10,000 diners per day. Other loony touches include soundproof karaoke pavilions and a dining area housed in a seven storey pagoda. House specialities on the 440 item menu (not including drinks or desserts) include hàw mòk (thick seafood curry steamed in banana leaves) and yam yong (sweet and salty banana shoot salad). Figure on spending 300 to 500B for two diners.

Dinner Cruises There are a number of companies that run cruises during which you eat dinner. Prices range from 40 to 700B per person depending on how far they go and whether dinner is included in the fare. For more information, see Dinner Cruises under River & Canal Trips earlier in this chapter.

Entertainment

In their round-the-clock search for *khwaam sanùk* (fun), Bangkokians have made their metropolis one that literally never sleeps. To get an idea of what's available, check the entertainment listings in the daily *Bangkok Post* and the *Nation*, the free tourist-oriented weeklies *This Week* and *Angel City*, or the relatively new monthly *Bangkok Metro*.

Possibilities include classical music, rock concerts, videotheque dancing, touring Asian music/theatre ensembles, art shows, international buffets etc. Boredom should not be a problem in Bangkok, at least not for a short-term visit; however, save some energy and money for your islands and beaches trip!

Cinemas Dozens of movie theatres around town show Thai, Chinese, Indian and western movies. The main ones showing commercial English-language films are: *Scala, Lido 1, 2 & 3* and *Siam Square Multiplex 5* at Siam Square; *Major 1 & 2* at Mahboonkrong; *Hollywood* at Hollywood Street Center, Phetburi Rd; *Metro*, Phetburi Rd; *World Trade Center 1, 2 & 3*, Ratchadamri Rd; *Century 1 & 2* and *Mackenna* on Phayathai Rd; and the *Washington 1 & 2* at Soi 24, Sukhumvit Rd. Movie ads appear daily in the *Nation* and the *Bangkok Post*; listings in the *Nation* include addresses and program times.

The majority of films shown are comedies and shoot-em-ups, with the occasional drama slipping through. Foreign films are often altered by Thailand's board of censors before distribution; usually this involves obscuring nude sequences with Vaseline 'screens'.

These cinemas are air-con and quite comfortable, with reasonable ticket prices (40 to 80B). All movies are preceded by the Thai royal anthem along with projected pictures of King Bhumibol and other members of the royal family. Everyone in the cinema stands quietly and respectfully for the duration of the anthem (which was written by the king).

Night life Bangkok's over-publicised naughty night life image is linked to the bars, coffee houses, nightclubs and massage parlours left over from the days when the City of Angels was an R&R stop for GIs serving in Vietnam. By and large these throwbacks are seedy, expensive and cater only to men – Thai men nowadays. Then there is the new breed of Sex & Sin (S&S) bar, some merely refurbished R&R digs, that are more modest, classy, and welcome females and couples. Not everybody's cup of tea, but they do good business. More recently, other places have appeared which are quite chic and suitable for either sex.

All the major hotels have flashy nightclubs. Many feature live music – rock, country & western, Thai pop and jazz. Hotels catering to tourists and business-people often have trendy discos. You'll find the latest recorded music hits being played in the smaller neighbourhood bars as well as the mega-discos.

All bars and clubs are supposed to close at 1 or 2 am (the latter closing time is for places with dance floors and/or live music), but in reality only a few obey the law.

Live Music Bangkok's live music scene has expanded rapidly over the past five years or so, with a multiplicity of new, extremely competent bands and new clubs. The three storey *Saxophone Pub Restaurant* (☎ 246-5472), south-east of the Victory Monument circle at 3/8 Soi Victory Monument, Phayathai Rd, has become a Bangkok institution for musicians of several genres. On the ground floor is a bar/restaurant featuring jazz from 9 pm to 1.30 am; the next floor has a billiards hall with recorded music; and the top floor has live reggae, R&B, jazz or blues bands from 10.30 pm to 4 am, and on Sunday there's an open jam session. There's never a cover charge at Saxophone and you don't need to dress up.

Another very casual spot to listen to music is the open-air bar operated by *Ruang Pung Art Community* next to Chatuchak Market. Thai rock, folk, blues and jam sessions attract an artsy Thai crowd.

Bars with regular live jazz include *Why Art?* in the Royal City Avenue complex, off New Phetburi Rd (nightly from 10 pm to 2 am), *Imageries by the Glass* on Soi 24, Sukhumvit Rd (Monday and Tuesday nights only), and *Blues/Jazz* (☎ 258-7747) at Soi 53, Sukhumvit Rd. The Oriental's famous *Bamboo Bar* has live jazz nightly from 5 to 8.30 pm in an elegant but relaxed atmosphere; other hotel jazz bars include *Entrepreneur* at the Asia Hotel (Saturday night only), the Grand Hyatt's *Garden Lounge* (Tuesday to Sunday), the Beaufort Sukhothai Hotel's *Colonnade* (Tuesday to Sunday) and the Hilton's *The Lounge* (Friday night only).

The imaginatively named *Rock Pub*, opposite the Asia Hotel on Phayathai Rd, offers Thai heavy metal – with plenty of hair-throwing and lip-jutting – nightly. Regular performers include Kaleidoscope, Wizard, Uranium and the Olarn Project. The *Hollywood Rock Place* on Phayathai Rd near the Mackenna cinema is similar.

Not to be overlooked, the *Old West* on Sarasin Rd (Thailand's original old west-style pub) books good Thai folk and blues groups – look for a rockin' outfit called D-Train here. Down the road a bit, *Blues Bar* is similar.

The *Magic Mushroom* at 212/33 Sukhumvit Road (next to Soi 12) hires a variety of rock and blues acts nightly, including some of Bangkok's biggest names. The *Front Page* (Soi Sala Daeng, off Rama IV Rd) hosts journeyman folk and blues groups on Monday, Tuesday and Saturday nights.

Bars Bangkok has definitely outgrown the days when the only bars around catered to male go-go oglers. Trendy among locals these days are bars which strive for a more sophisticated atmosphere, with good service and choice music. The Thais call them pubs but they bear little resemblance to the traditional English pub. Some are 'theme' bars, conceived around a particular aesthetic. All the city's major hotels feature western-style bars as well.

One of the main hotspots in town for young Thais is a huge bar and dance club complex called *Royal City Avenue* (Soi Sunwichai, north off New Phetburi Rd). Originally designed a few years ago as a shopping centre, RCA has been taken over by a 2.5km strip of high-tech bars with names like *Absolute Zero, Baby Hand Pub, Bar Code, Chit, Cool Tango, Exit, Fahrenheit, Jigsaw, Radio Underground, Relax, Route 66, Shit Happens, Why Art?* and *X Symbol*. Most have recorded music – everything from soul to techno to Thai pop – but a few also feature local bands. *Cool Tango* has the best live music and most international ambience; bands from overseas play there regularly.

RCA was immensely popular in 1995 and early 1996 until a police crackdown on under-18 drinkers stifled things a bit. Such enforcement is a first for Thailand, a country where any six-year-old child can walk into a market and buy a beer. Most of the RCA clientele are in their teens and early 20s; some bars are owned by loose collectives of 20 or more university students who just want a place to hang out with their friends and make a little extra money while others are serious high-roller clubs. Bar names change frequently.

A similarly youthful scene can be found at another new complex called *Premier*. Aesthetically this one has a more interesting layout, as the bars and restaurants are centred around a fountain pool. Modernist pubs here include *Pool Side, Talk of the Town, Zeal, Tied Up, Vintage Special, Sanggasi, Le Mans* and *La Dee Da*, each with an artsy decor. The *Nude Bar* sports Robert Mapplethorpe prints, while the *Seri Art Gallery* doubles as a pub and Thai art gallery. There's also a *beer garden* open during the cool season only, and nearly a dozen restaurants serving Thai, American and French food. Premier is on New Rama IX Rd, past Ramkhamhaeng Rd, near Soi 24 (Soi Seri) just before New Rama IX Rd intersects Si Nakarin Rd.

Bangkok is a little short on plain neighbourhood bars without up-market pretensions or down-market sleaze. One that's close to fitting the bill is the *Front Page*, a one-time journalists' hang-out (before the nearby *Bangkok Post* offices moved to Khlong Toey) on Soi 1, Sala Daeng (off Silom and Rama IV Rds). Two low-key, Brit-style taverns include *Jool's* on Soi 4 near Nana Plaza, *Bull's Head* on the ground floor of Angus Steak House, Soi 33/1, Sukhumvit Rd, and the *Witch's Tavern* at 306/1 Soi 55, Sukhumvit Rd. The latter features live music on weekends.

Delaney's Irish Pub (☎ 266-7160), a new place at 1-4 Sivadon Building, Convent Rd, in the Silom Rd district, is so far the only place in Bangkok that serves Guinness on tap (at a painful 175B per pint!). The interior wood panels, glass mirrors and bench seats were all custom-made and imported from Ireland. Delaney's has a daily happy hour and live Irish music Tuesday to Saturday.

Henry J Bean's Bar & Grill, in the basement of the Amari Watergate Hotel on Phetburi Rd in Pratunam, is a relaxed spot with an American-style 1950s and 60s decor. Performing bartenders flip bottles and glasses while serving, and there's an early evening happy hour daily. A house band called the Nighthawks plays roots rock and reggae most nights; other live bands occasionally perform. There's a separate street entrance for the bar so you don't have to walk through the hotel.

Wong's Place at 27/3 Si Bamphen is a low-key hang-out for locals and visitors staying in the Soi Ngam Duphli area. It sports a good collection of music videos.

The guitar-shaped bar at Bangkok's *Hard Rock Cafe* (☎ 251-0792), Siam Square, Soi 11, serves a full line of cocktails and a small assortment of local and imported beers. The crowd is an ever-changing assortment of Thais, expats and tourists. From 10 pm on there's also live music.

For slick aerial city views, the place to go is the *Sky Lounge* in the Baiyoke Tower on Ratchaprarop Rd, Pratunam. It's 43 floors above the city and open 24 hours. The *Compass Rose*, a new bar on the 59th floor of the Westin Banyan Tree on Sathon Tai Rd, is even higher, but is only open from 10 am to 1 am.

Wireheads can check their email or surf the Net at the new *CyberPub* (☎ 236-0450, ext 2971) in the Dusit Thani Hotel on the corner of Silom and Rama IV Rds. Booze and food are available, along with a bank of 10 up-to-date computer stations. It costs 5B per online minute; you pay for food, beverages and online time using a 'smart card' issued by CyberPub.

Discos & Dance Clubs All the major hotels in the city have international-style discotheques but only a small number of them – those at the Dusit Thani, the Shangri-La, the Grand Hyatt and The Regent – can really be recommended as attractions. Cover charges are pretty uniform: around 150 to 200B on weeknights, including one drink, and around 300 to 350B on weekends, including two

drinks. Most places don't begin filling up till after 11 pm.

Bangkok is famous for its huge high-tech discos that hold up to 5000 people and feature mega-watt sound systems, giant-screen video and the latest in light-show technology. The most 'in' disco at the moment is *Phoebus Amphitheatre Complex* on Ratchadapisek Rd. Other biggies include *Paradise* on Arun Amarin Rd in Thonburi and the *Palace* on Vibhavadi Rangsit Hwy, towards the airport. A mega-disco that gets older as well as younger Thais is the *Galaxy* on Rama IV Rd, from which WBA world boxing champions Khaosai Galaxy and his brother Khaokor have taken their surname.

Well-heeled Thais and Thai celebrities frequent the more exclusive, high-tech *Narcissus* (☎ 258-2549) at 112 Soi 23, Sukhumvit Rd. *FM 228* (☎ 231-1228), in the United Center Building, 323 Silom Rd, tries to cover all the bases with separate rooms featuring videotheque dancing, live music, and karaoke, plus an American restaurant and bar.

Dance clubs sprinkled throughout the Royal City Avenue and Premier entertainment complexes have become very popular very quickly, especially among young (late teens and early 20s) Thais – see the previous Bars entry for details.

A string of small dance clubs on Soi 2 and Soi 4 (Soi Jaruwan), both parallel to Patpong 1 and 2, off Silom Rd, attracts a more mixed crowd in terms of age, gender, nationality and sexual orientation than either the hotel discos or the RCA/Premier entertainment complexes. The norm for recorded music here includes techno, trance, hip-hop and other current dance trends. Main venues – some of which are small and narrow – include *Disco Disco (DD)* and *DJ Station* on Soi 2, and *Hyper, Divine, Deeper, Rome Club* and *Sphinx* on Soi 4. The larger places collect cover charges of 100 to 300B depending on the night of the week; the smaller ones are free. The clientele at these clubs was once predominantly gay but has become more mixed as word spread about the great dance scene. Things don't get started here till relatively late – around midnight; in fact, on most nights the Soi 2/Soi 4 dance clubs serve more as 'after hours' hang-outs since they usually stay open past the official 2 am closing time.

Temptations, at the Novotel Bangkok in Siam Square, provides big band music for *lii-lâat*, or ballroom dancing. Every night of the week a dressed-to-the-nines crowd of Bangkok Thais cha-cha, foxtrot, tango and rumba across the glazed dance floor. In addition to serving drinks, waiters and waitresses lead novices through the steps. The cover charge of 400B includes one drink and all the instruction necessary to turn you into a *nák lii-lâat*.

Go-Go Bars These are concentrated along Sukhumvit Rd (between Sois 21 and 23), off Sukhumvit Rd on Soi Nana Tai and in the world-famous Patpong Rd area, between Silom and Surawong Rds.

Patpong's neon-lit buildings cover roughly 4 acres standing on what was once a banana plantation owned by the Bank of Indochina, which sold the land to the Hainanese-Thai Patpongphanit family for 60,000B (US$2400) just before WWII. By the 1960s Patpong had a flourishing local nightclub scene that was further boosted by the arrival of American GIs in the early 1970s.

Patpong has calmed down a bit over the years. These days it has more of an open-air market feel as several of the newer bars are literally on the street, and vendors set up shop in the evening hawking everything from roast squid to fake designer watches. On Patpong's two parallel lanes there are around 38 go-go bars, plus a sprinkling of restaurants and cocktail bars. The typical bar measures 4m wide by 12m deep.

The downstairs clubs with names like *King's Castle* and *Pussy Galore* have go-go dancing, while upstairs the real raunch is kept behind closed doors. Don't believe the touts on the street who say the upstairs shows – featuring amazing anatomical feats – are free; after the show, a huge bill usually arrives. The 1 am closing law is strictly enforced on Patpong 1 and 2.

Another holdover from the R&R days is *Soi Cowboy*, a single-lane strip of 25 to 30 bars off Sukhumvit Rd between Sois 21 and 23. *Nana Entertainment Plaza*, off Soi 4 (Soi Nana Tai), Sukhumvit Rd, is a newer three storey complex which has surged in popularity among resident and visiting oglers. Nana Plaza has its own guesthouses – used almost exclusively by Nana Plaza's female bar workers for illicit assignations. There are only 18 bars in the whole complex.

Soi Tantawan and Thaniya Rd, on either side of and parallel to Patpong Rds 1 and 2, feature expensive Japanese-style hostess bars (from which non-Japanese are usually barred) as well as a handful of gay bars with male go-go dancers and 'bar boys'.

Transvestite Cabaret Transvestite revues are big in Bangkok and several are found in the Patpong area. *Calypso Cabaret* (☎ 261-6355), in the Ambassador Hotel at Soi 11, has the largest regularly performing transvestite troupe in town, with nightly shows at 8.30 and 10 pm. Some of the gay bars on Sois 2 and 4 off Silom Rd also feature short drag shows during intermissions between dance sets.

Gay/Lesbian Scene For places that attract a mixed gay/straight/bi clientele, see the comments on the Soi 2 and Soi 4 Silom Rd dance club scene under Discos & Dance Clubs. In general, the Soi 2 clubs are more gay than the Soi 4 bars, though Soi 4's *Telephone* is more exclusively gay than other bars on this street. The hottest gay dance scene on Soi 2 is currently *DJ Station*. *Khrua Silom*, in Trok Silom off Soi 2, attracts a young Thai gay and lesbian crowd. There's a cluster of seedier gay bars off Soi Anuman Ratchathon, off Silom Rd opposite the Tawana Ramada Hotel – more or less the gay equivalent of Patpong.

Utopia (☎ 259-9619) at 116/1 Soi 23, Sukhumvit Rd, is a combination bar, gallery, cafe and information clearing house for the local gay and lesbian community – the only such facility in South-East Asia. Friday night is designated women's night, and there are regular film nights as well as Thai lessons. Special events – such as Valentine's Day candlelight dinners – are held from time to time. Utopia is open daily from noon to 2 am.

Other lesbian venues include: *By Heart Pub* (☎ 570-1841) at 117/697, Soi Sainanikhom 1, Bang Kapi; *Be My Guest*, around the corner from Utopia on Soi 31; and *Obsession* in the Royal City Avenue Complex.

Babylon Bangkok (☎ 213-2108) at 50 Soi Atakanprasit, off Sathon Tai Rd, is a four storey gay sauna which the guide *Thai Scene* called one of the top ten gay saunas in the world. Facilities include a bar, roof garden, gym, massage room, steam and dry saunas, and jacuzzi baths. It's open from 5 to 11 pm daily.

Thai Dance-Drama Thailand's most traditional lákhon and khŏn performances are held at the *National Theatre* (☎ 224-1342) on Ratchini Rd near Phra Pinklao Bridge. The theatre's regular public roster schedules six or seven performances per month, usually on weekends. Admission fees are very reasonable – around 20 to 200B depending on the seating. Attendance at a khŏn performance (masked dance-drama based on stories from the *Ramakian*) is highly recommended.

Chalermkrung Royal Theatre The 1993 renovation of this Thai Deco building at the edge of the city's Chinatown-Pahurat district provides a striking new venue for khŏn performance in Thailand. When originally opened in 1933, the royally funded Chalermkrung was the largest and most modern theatre in Asia, with state-of-the-art motion picture projection technology and the first chilled-water air-con system in the region. Prince Samaichaloem, a former student of the École des Beaux-Arts in Paris, designed the hexagonal building.

The reborn theatre's 80,000 watt audio system, combined with computer-generated laser graphics, enable the 170 member dance troupe to present a technologically enhanced version of traditional khŏn. Although the special effects are reasonably impressive, the excellent costuming, set design, dancing and music are reason enough to attend.

The khŏn performance lasts about two hours with intermission; performances are generally held twice a week (usually Tuesday and Thursday at 8 pm), but this changes from time to time as the theatre feels its way through the Bangkok cultural market. Other Thai performing arts are also scheduled at the theatre.

Khŏn tickets cost a steep 500, 700, 800 and 1000B. For reservations call ☎ 222-0434 or visit the box office. The theatre requests that patrons dress respectfully, which means no shorts or thongs. Bring a wrap or long-sleeved shirt in case the air-con is running full blast.

The Chalermkrung Royal Theatre is on the corner of Charoen Krung and Triphet Rds, adjacent to the Old Siam Plaza complex and a block from the Pahurat fabric market. Air-con bus Nos 8, 48 and 73 pass the theatre (going west on Charoen Krung Rd). You can also walk to the theatre from the western terminus of the Khlong Saen Saep canal ferry. Taxi drivers may know the theatre by its original name, Sala Chalerm Krung, which is spelt out in Thai in the lighted sign surmounting the front of the building.

Dinner Theatres Most tourists see performances put on solely for their benefit at one of the several Thai classical dance/dinner theatres in the city (see following list). Admission prices at these evening venues average 200 to 500B per person and include a 'typical' Thai dinner (often toned down for farang palates), a couple of dance performances and a martial arts display.

The historic Oriental Hotel has its own dinner theatre (the *Sala Rim Nam*) on the Thonburi side of the Chao Phraya River, opposite the hotel. The admission price is well above average but so is the food and the performance; the river ferry between the hotel and restaurant is free. The much less expensive dinner performance at Silom Village's *Ruen Thep* restaurant on Silom Rd is recommended because of the relaxed, semi-outdoor setting.

Baan Thai Restaurant – 7 Soi 32, Sukhumvit Rd (☎ 258-5403)

Maneeya Lotus Room – 518/5 Ploenchit Rd (☎ 251-0382)

Phiman Restaurant – 46 Soi 49, Sukhumvit Rd (☎ 258-7866)

Ruen Thep – Silom Village, Silom Rd (☎ 233-9447)

Sala Norasing – Soi 4, Sukhumvit Rd (☎ 251-5797)

Sala Rim Nam – opposite Oriental Hotel, Charoen Nakhon Rd, Thonburi (☎ 437-6221/3080)

Suwannahong Restaurant – Si Ayuthaya Rd (☎ 245-4448/3747)

Tum-Nak-Thai Restaurant – 131 Ratchadaphisek Rd (☎ 277-3828)

Muay Thai Thai boxing *(muay thai)* can be seen at two boxing stadiums, *Lumphini* (on Rama IV Rd near Sathon Tai (South) Rd) and *Ratchadamnoen* (on Ratchadamnoen Nok Rd, next to the TAT office). Admission fees vary according to seating; the cheapest seats are now around 170B and ringside seats cost 500B or more. On Monday, Wednesday, Thursday and Sunday, the matches are at Ratchadamnoen, while on Tuesday, Friday and Saturday they're at Lumphini. The Ratchadamnoen matches begin at 6 pm (except for the Sunday shows which start at 5 pm) and the Lumphini matches all begin at 6.20 pm. Aficionados say the best-matched bouts are reserved for Tuesday night at Lumphini and Thursday night at Ratchadamnoen.

Things to Buy

Regular visitors to Asia know that, in many ways, Bangkok beats Hong Kong and Singapore for deals on handicrafts, textiles, gems, jewellery, art and antiques – nowhere else will you find the same selection, quality and prices. The trouble is finding the good spots, as the city's intense urban tangle makes orientation sometimes difficult.

Be sure to re-read the introductory Things to Buy section in the Facts for the Visitor chapter before setting out on a buying spree. Amid all the bargains are a number of cleverly disguised rip-off schemes – *caveat emptor!*

The Thai word for 'market' is *tàlàat*.

Chatuchak (Weekend) Market Chatuchak Market is the Disneyland of Thai markets; on weekends 8672 vendor stalls cater to an estimated 200,000 visitors a day. Everything is sold here, from live chickens and snakes to opium pipes and herbal remedies. Thai clothing such as the *phâakhamáa* (sarong for men) and the *phâasîn* (sarong for women), *kaang keng jiin* (Chinese pants) and *sêua mâw hâwm* (blue cotton farmer's shirt) are good buys. You'll also find musical instruments, hill-tribe crafts, religious amulets, antiques, flowers, clothes imported from India and Nepal, camping gear and military surplus. The best bargains of all are household goods like pots and pans, dishes, drinking glasses etc. Don't forget to bargain. There is plenty of interesting and tasty food, and live music in the early evening in Thai folk music cafes. If you need some cash, a couple of banks have ATMs and foreign-exchange booths at the Chatuchak Park offices, near the north end of the market's Sois 1, 2 and 3. Plan to spend a full day, as there's plenty to see, eat and listen to. And leave time for getting lost!

An unfortunate footnote is that Chatuchak Park remains an important hub of Thailand's illegal exotic wildlife trade – in spite of occasional police raids – as well as a conduit for endangered species from surrounding countries. Some species are sold for their exotic food value, eg barking deer, wild boar, crocodiles and pangolins, while some are sold for their supposed medicinal value, eg rare leaf-monkeys. Thai laws protect most of these species, but Thais are notorious scofflaws. Not all wildlife trade here is illicit though; many of the birds sold, including the hill mynah and zebra dove, have been legally raised for sale as pets.

The main part of Chatuchak Market is open on weekends from around 8 am to 8 pm. There are a few vendors out on weekday mornings and a daily vegetable/plant/flower market opposite the market's south side. One section of the latter, known as the Aw Taw Kaw Market, sells organically grown (no chemical sprays or fertilisers) fruits and vegetables.

Chatuchak Market lies at the southern end of Chatuchak Park, off Phahonyothin Rd and across from the Northern (Maw Chit) bus terminal. Air-con bus Nos 2, 3, 9, 10 and 13, and a dozen other ordinary city buses (No 3 from Phra Athit Rd in Banglamphu), all pass the market – just get off before the Northern bus terminal. The air-con bus No 12 and ordinary bus No 77 conveniently terminate right next to the market.

Shopping Centres & Department Stores

The development of large and small shopping centres has accelerated over the past few years into a virtual boom. Central and Robinson department stores, the original stand-bys, have branches in the Sukhumvit and Silom Rds areas with all the usual stuff – designer clothes, western cosmetics, cassette tapes, fabrics and other local products that might be of interest to some travellers – plus supermarkets and Thai delis. Typical opening hours are from 10 am to 8 pm.

Oriental Plaza (Soi Oriental, Charoen Krung Rd) and River City shopping complex (near the Royal Orchid Sheraton, off Charoen Krung and Si Phraya Rds) are centres for high-end consumer goods. They're expensive but do have some unique merchandise; River City has two floors specialising in art and antiques.

The much smaller Silom Village Trade Centre on Silom Rd has a few antique and handicraft shops with merchandise several rungs lower in price. Anchored by Central Department Store, the six storey Silom Complex remains one of the city's busiest shopping centres. Also on Silom Rd is the posh Thaniya Plaza, a newer arcade housing clothing boutiques, bookshops, jewellery shops and more.

The eight floors of the relatively new World Trade Center (WTC) near the intersection of Rama I and Ratchadamri Rds seem to go on, wing after wing, with no end in sight. The main focus is the Zen Department Store, which has clothing shops reminiscent of Hong Kong's high-end boutiques. If you're looking for clothing or toys for kids, ABC Babyland on WTC's 2nd floor has just about everything. Asia Books has a branch in the WTC and more shops are opening as a new wing is being added, including a new

Thailand Duty Free Shop on the 7th floor (passport and airline ticket are required for purchases).

Siam Square, on Rama I Rd near Phayathai Rd, is a network of some 12 sois lined with shops selling mid-priced designer clothes, books, sporting goods and antiques. One of the most varied shopping centres is the Mahboonkrong (MBK) shopping centre near Siam Square. It's all air-con, but there are many small, inexpensive vendors and shops in addition to the flashy Tokyu Department Store. Bargains can be found here if you look. The Travel Mart on MBK's 3rd floor stocks a reasonable supply of travel gear and camping equipment – not the highest quality but useful in a pinch.

Antiques & Decorative Items Real Thai antiques are rare and costly. Most Bangkok antique shops keep a few antiques around for collectors, along with lots of pseudo-antiques or traditionally crafted items that look like antiques. The majority of shop owners are quite candid about what's really old and what isn't. As Thai design becomes more popular abroad, many shops are now specialising in Thai home decorative items.

Reliable antique shops (using the word 'antiques' loosely) include Elephant House (☎ 286-2780) at 67/12 Soi Phra Phinit, Soi Suan Phlu; Peng Seng on the corner of Rama IV and Surawong Rds; Asian Heritage (☎ 258-4157) at 57 Soi 23, Sukhumvit Rd; Thai House (☎ 258-6287), 720/6 Sukhumvit Rd, near Soi 28; and Artisan's in the Silom Village Trade Centre, Silom Rd. The River City and Oriental Plaza shopping complexes have several good, if pricey, antique shops.

Camera Supplies, Film & Processing For a wide range of camera models and brands, two of the best shops are Sunny Camera at 1267/1 Charoen Krung Rd (☎ 233-8378), at 134/5-6 Soi 8, Silom Rd (☎ 237-2054) and on the 3rd floor of the Mahboonkrong shopping centre (☎ 217-9293), and Niks (☎ 235-2929) at 166 Silom Rd.

Film prices in Bangkok are generally lower than anywhere else in Asia, including

Hong Kong. Both slide and print film is widely available, although the highest concentration of photo shops can be found along Silom and Surawong Rds. In Mahboonkrong shopping centre, FotoFile on the ground floor has the best selection of slide film, including refrigerated pro film.

Quick, professional-quality processing of most film types is available at E6 Processing Centre (☎ 259-9573) at 59/10 Soi 31, Sukhumvit Rd; IQ Lab at 60 Silom Rd (☎ 238-4001) or at 9/34 Thana Arcade, Soi 63, Sukhumvit Rd (☎ 391-4163); Eastbourne Professional Color Laboratories (☎ 236-1156) at 173/4-5 Surawong Rd; and Supertouch (☎ 235-4711, 235-6415) at 35/12 Soi Yommarat, Sala Daeng Rd.

Gems & Jewellery Recommending specific shops is tricky, since to the average eye one coloured stone looks as good as another, so the risk of a rip-off is much greater than for most other popular shopping items. One shop that's been a long-time favourite with Bangkok expats for service and value in set jewellery is Johnny's Gems (☎ 222-1756) at 199 Fuang Nakhon Rd (off Charoen Krung Rd). Another reputable jewellery place is Merlin et Delauney (☎ 234-3884), with a large showroom and lapidary at 1 Soi Pradit, Surawong Rd, and a smaller shop at the Novotel Bangkok, Soi 6, Siam Square. Both of the aforementioned places also have unset stones as well as jewellery; three dependable places that specialise in unset stones are Lambert International (☎ 236-4343) at 807 Silom Rd, Gemexpert (☎ 236-2638) at 50/29 Pan Rd and Thai Lapidary (☎ 214-2641) at 277/122 Rama I Rd.

Handicrafts Bangkok has some excellent buys in Thai handicrafts. Narayana Phand (☎ 252-4670) on Ratchadamri Rd is a bit on the touristy side but has a large selection and good marked prices – no haggling is necessary. Central Department Store on Ploenchit Rd has a Thai handicrafts section with marked prices.

Perhaps the most interesting places to shop for handicrafts are the smaller, independent handicraft shops – each of which has its own style and character. Quality is high at Rasi Sayam (☎ 258-4195), 32 Soi 23, Sukhumvit Rd; many of the items it carries – including wall-hangings and pottery – are made specifically for this shop. Another good one for pottery as well as lacquerware and fabrics (especially the latter) is Vilai's (☎ 391-6106) at 731/1 Soi 55 (Thong Lor), Sukhumvit Rd.

Nandakwang (☎ 258-1962), 108/3 Soi 23 (Soi Prasanmit), Sukhumvit Rd, is a branch of a factory shop of the same name in Pasang, northern Thailand. High-quality woven cotton clothing and household wares (tablecloths, napkins etc) are its speciality. Prayer Textile Gallery (☎ 251-7549), a small shop on the edge of Siam Square facing Phayathai Rd, stocks a nice selection of new and antique textiles – in both ready-to-wear original fashions or in traditional rectangular lengths – from Thailand, Laos and Cambodia.

Tailor-Made Clothing Bangkok abounds in places where you can have shirts, trousers, suits and just about any other article of clothing designed, cut and sewn by hand. Workmanship ranges from shoddy to excellent, so it pays to ask around before committing yourself. Shirts and trousers can be turned around in 48 hours or less with only one fitting. But no matter what a tailor may tell you, it takes more than one or two fittings to create a good suit – most reputable tailors will ask for three to five sittings. A custom-made suit, no matter what the material, should cost less than US$200.

The one area where you need to be most careful is fabric selection. If possible, bring your own fabric from home, especially if you want 100% cotton. Most of the so-called 'cotton' offered by Bangkok tailors is actually a blend of cotton and a synthetic; more than a few tailors will actually try to pass off full polyester or dacron as cotton. Good-quality silk, on the other hand, is plentiful. Tailor-made silk shirts should cost no more than US$12 to US$20, depending on the type of silk (Chinese silk is cheaper than Thai).

Virtually every other tailor working in

Bangkok is of either Indian or Chinese descent. Generally speaking the best shops are those found along the outer reaches of Sukhumvit Rd (out beyond Soi 20 or so) and on or off Charoen Krung (New) Rd. Silom Rd also has some good tailors. The worst tailor shops tend to be those in tourist-oriented shopping areas in inner Sukhumvit Rd, Khao San Rd, the River City shopping complex and other shopping malls. 'Great deals' like four shirts, two suits, a kimono and a safari suit all in one package almost always turn out to be of inferior materials and workmanship.

Recommended tailor shops include Marzotto at 3 Soi Wat Suan Phlu, off Charoen Krung Rd; Julie at 1279 Charoen Rd, near Silom Center; Marco Tailor at Amarin Plaza, Silom Complex and Siam Square; and Macway's Exporters at 248/3-4 Silom Rd, near the Narai Hotel. If Siam Center ever re-opens, Siam Emporium (3rd floor) can also be recommended.

Getting There & Away

Air Bangkok is a major centre for international flights throughout Asia, and Bangkok's international airport is a busy one. Bangkok is also a major centre for buying discounted airline tickets (see the Getting There & Away chapter for details). Domestic flights operated by THAI and Bangkok Airways also fan out from Bangkok all over the country. Addresses of airline offices in Bangkok are:

Aeroflot – 7 Silom Rd (☎ 233-6965)
Air China – 20th floor, CP Tower, 313 Silom Rd (☎ 631-0731)
Air France – Ground floor, Chan Issara Tower, 942 Rama IV Rd (☎ 234-1330/9; reservations ☎ 233-9477)
Air India – 16th floor, Amarin Tower, Ploenchit Rd (☎ 256-9620; reservations ☎ 256-9614/8)
Air Lanka – Chan Issara Tower, 942 Rama IV Rd (☎ 236-4981)
Air New Zealand – 1053 Charoen Krung Rd (☎ 233-5900/9, 237-1560/2)
Alitalia – 8th floor, Boonmitr Bldg, 138 Silom Rd (☎ 233-4000/4)
All Nippon Airways (ANA) – 2nd floor, CP Tower, 313 Silom Rd (☎ 238-5121)
American Airlines – 6th floor, Maneeya Bldg, 518/5 Ploenchit Rd (☎ 254-1270)

Asiana Airlines – 14th floor, BB Bldg, 54 Soi Asoke, Sukhumvit Rd (☎ 260-7700/4)
Bangkok Airways – Queen Sirikit National Convention Centre, New Ratchadaphisek Rd, Khlong Toey (☎ 229-3434/56, 253-4014); 1111 Ploenchit Rd (☎ 254-2903)
British Airways – Chan Issara Tower, 942 Rama IV Rd (☎ 236-0038)
Canadian Airlines International – 6th floor, Maneeya Bldg, 518/5 Ploenchit Rd (☎ 251-4521)
Cathay Pacific Airways – 11th floor, Ploenchit Tower, 898 Ploenchit Rd (☎ 263-0606)
China Airlines – Peninsula Plaza, 153 Ratchadamri Rd (☎ 253-5733; 253-4242)
China Southern Airlines – 1st floor, Silom Plaza Bldg, Silom Rd (☎ 266-5699)
Delta Air Lines – 6th floor, Panjaphat Bldg, 1 Surawong Rd (☎ 237-6855; 237-6838)
Egyptair – 3rd floor, CP Tower, 313 Silom Rd (☎ 231-0505/8)
EVA Airways – 2nd floor, Green Tower, 3656/4-5 Rama IV Rd (☎ 367-3388; 240-0890)
El Al Israel Airlines – 14th floor, Manorom Bldg, 3354/47 Rama IV Rd (☎ 671-6145, 249-8818)
Finnair – 175 Sathorn City Tower, Sathon Rd (☎ 679-6671)
Garuda Indonesia – 27th floor, Lumphini Tower, 1168 Rama IV Rd (☎ 285-6010)
Gulf Air – 15th floor, Maneeya Bldg, 518/5 Ploenchit Rd (☎ 254-7931/4)
Japan Airlines – 254/1 Ratchadaphisek Rd (☎ 692-5151)
KLM-Royal Dutch Airlines – 10th floor, Thai Wah Tower II, Sathon Tai Rd (☎ 679-1100, ext 11)
Korean Air – Kongboonma Bldg, 699 Silom Rd (☎ 635-0465/72)
Kuwait Airways – 12th floor, RS Tower, 121/50 Ratchadaphisek Rd (☎ 641-2864)
Lao Aviation – Ground floor, Silom Plaza, 491/17 Silom Rd (☎ 236-9821/3)
Lauda Air – 18th floor, Wall Street Tower, 33/90 Surawong Rd (☎ 233-2565)
LOT Polish Airlines – 485/11-2 Silom Rd (☎ 235-2223)
LTU International Airways – 11th floor, Bangkok Gem and Jewelry Tower, 322 Surawong Rd (☎ 267-1143)
Lufthansa Airlines – 18th floor, Asoke Bldg, Soi 21, Sukhumvit Rd (☎ 264-2400)
Malaysia Airlines – 20th floor, Ploenchit Tower, Ploenchit Rd (☎ 263-0565)
Myanmar Airways International – 23rd floor, Jewelry Trade Center Bldg, 919 Silom Rd (☎ 630-0338)
Northwest Airlines – 4th floor, Peninsula Plaza, 153 Ratchadamri Rd (☎ 254-0789)
Pakistan International Airlines – 2nd floor, 56 Surawong Rd (☎ 234-2961)
Philippine Airlines – 56 Surawong Rd (☎ 234-2483, 233-2350/2)

Qantas Airways – 14th floor, Abdulrahim Place, 990 Rama IV Rd (☎ 636-1747)

Romanian Air Transport (TAROM) – 89/12 Bangkok Bazaar, Ratchadamri Rd (☎ 253-1681)

Royal Air Cambodge – 17th floor, Two Pacific Place Bldg, 142 Rama IV Rd (☎ 653-2261)

Royal Brunei Airlines – 4th floor, Chan Issara Tower, 942 Rama IV Rd (☎ 233-0506, 235-4764)

Royal Jordanian – Yada Bldg, 56 Silom Rd (☎ 236-0030)

Royal Nepal Airlines Corporation – 9th floor, Phayathai Plaza Bldg, 128 Phayathai Rd (☎ 216-5691)

Sabena – 12th floor, Chan Issara Tower, 942 Rama IV Rd; CP Tower, 313 Silom Rd (☎ 233-7290)

Saudia – 19th floor, United Center Bldg, 323 Silom Rd (☎ 266-7392)

Scandinavian Airlines – 8th floor, Glas Haus Bldg, Soi 25, Sukhumvit Rd (☎ 260-0444)

Silk Air – see Singapore Airlines

Singapore Airlines – 12th floor, Silom Centre Bldg, 2 Silom Rd (☎ 236-0303; reservations ☎ 236-0440)

South African Airways – 6th floor, Maneeya Bldg, 518/5 Ploenchit Rd (☎ 254-8206)

Swissair – 1 Silom Rd (☎ 233-2930/4; 233-2935/8)

Thai Airways International (THAI) Head Office, 89 Vibhavadi Rangsit Rd (☎ 513-0121; reservations ☎ 280-0060); 485 Silom Rd (☎ 234-3100/19); 6 Lan Luang Rd (☎ 628-2000); Asia Hotel, 296 Phayathai Rd (☎ 215-2020/1); Bangkok international airport, Don Muang (☎ 535-2081/2, 523-6121)

United Airlines – 19th floor, Regent House, 183 Ratchadamri Rd (☎ 253-0558)

Vietnam Airlines (Hang Khong Vietnam) – 7th floor, Ploenchit Center Bldg, 2/4 Soi 2, Sukhumvit Rd (☎ 656-9056)

Bus Bangkok is the centre for bus services that fan out all over the kingdom. There are basically three types of long-distance buses: ordinary public buses; air-con public buses; and private air-con services which leave from various offices and hotels all over the city and provide a deluxe service for those people for whom simple air-con isn't enough!

Public Bus There are three main public bus stations. The Northern bus terminal (☎ 279-4484/7, 271-2961) is on Phahonyothin Rd on the way to the airport. It's also commonly called the Moh Chit station *(sathāanii māw chít)*. Buses depart here for north and northeastern destinations like Chiang Mai and Khorat, as well as places closer to Bangkok such as Ayuthaya and Lopburi. Buses to Aranya Prathet also go from here, not from

the Eastern bus terminal as you might expect. Air-con city buses Nos 2, 3, 9, 10, 12, 29 and 39, along with a dozen or more ordinary city buses and red microbus Nos 2 and 8 , all pass the terminal.

The Eastern bus terminal (☎ 391-2504 ordinary; ☎ 391-9829 air-con), the departure point for buses to Pattaya, Rayong, Chanthaburi and other eastern destinations, is a long way out along Sukhumvit Rd, at Soi 40 (Soi Ekamai) opposite Soi 63. Most folks call it Ekamai station *(sathāanii èk-amai)*. Air-con bus Nos 1, 8, 11 and 13 all pass this station, along with red microbus No 6.

The Southern bus terminal (☎ 434-5558 ordinary; ☎ 391-9829 air-con) for buses to Phuket, Surat Thani and closer centres to the west like Nakhon Pathom and Kanchanaburi, now has one Thonburi location for both ordinary and air-con buses at the intersection of Hwy 338 (Nakhon Chaisi Rd) and Phra Pinklao Rd. A convenient way to reach the terminal is by air-con city bus No 7, which terminates here; red microbus Nos 4 and 8 also pass the terminal.

When travelling on night buses take care of your belongings. Some of the long-distance buses leaving from Bangkok now issue claim checks for luggage stored under the bus, but valuables are still best kept on your person or within reach.

Allow an hour to reach the Northern bus terminal from Banglamphu or anywhere along the river, and more than an hour to reach the Southern bus terminal. The Eastern bus terminal is half an hour to 45 minutes away under most traffic conditions. During the occasional gridlock, eg Friday afternoons before a holiday, it can take up to three hours to get across town to one of the terminals by public transport.

Private Bus The more reputable and licenced private tour buses leave from the public (Baw Khaw Saw) terminals listed above. Some private bus companies arrange pick-ups at Khao San Rd and other guesthouse areas – these pick-ups are illegal since it's against municipal law to carry passengers within the city limits except en route to or from an official terminal. This is why the curtains on these buses are sometimes closed when picking up passengers.

Although fares tend to be lower on private buses, the incidence of reported theft is far greater than on the Baw Khaw Saw buses. They are also generally – but not always – less reliable and promise services (such as air-con or VIP seats) that they don't deliver. For safer, more reliable and more punctual service, stick to buses which leave from the official Baw Khaw Saw terminals.

See the Getting Around chapter for more information about bus travel to other parts of Thailand. Also, for details on bus fares to/from other towns and cities in Thailand, see the Getting There & Away sections under each destination.

Train Bangkok is the terminus for rail services to the south, north, north-east and east. There are two main train stations. The big Hualamphong station on Rama IV Rd handles services to the north, north-east and some of the southern services. The Thonburi (Bangkok Noi) station handles a few services to the south. If you're heading south, make sure you know which station your train departs from. See the Train section in the Getting Around chapter for further details on which southern lines correspond to which stations.

Getting Around
Getting around in Bangkok may be difficult for the uninitiated but once you're familiar with the bus system the whole city is accessible. The main obstacle is traffic, which moves at a snail's pace during much of the day. This means advance planning is a must when you are attending scheduled events or making appointments.

If you can travel by river or canal from one point to another, it's always the best choice.

Bus You can save a lot of money in Bangkok by sticking to the public buses, which are 2.50B for any journey under 10km on the ordinary blue or smaller green buses, 3.50B on the red buses or 6B for the first 8km on

the air-con lines. Longer trips cost more, up to 4B on ordinary buses or as high as 16B for air-con buses (eg from Silom Rd to Bangkok airport on air-con bus No 4). The air-con buses are not only cooler, but are usually less crowded (all bets are off during rush hours).

One air-con bus service that's never overcrowded is the new red microbus, which stops taking passengers once every seat is filled. You deposit the 30B flat fare in a box at the front of the bus rather than wait for an attendant to come around and collect it. A couple of useful microbus lines include the No 6, which starts on Si Phraya Rd (near the River City complex) and proceeds to the Mahboonkrong-Siam Square area, then out to Sukhumvit Rd (and vice versa), and the No 1, which runs between the Victory Monument area and Banglamphu district. TAT offices have English language lists of Bangkok bus and microbus routes.

Maps To do any serious bus riding you'll need a Bangkok bus map – the easiest to read is the *Bangkok Bus Map (Walking Tours)* published by Bangkok Guide, or Thaveepholcharoen's *Tour'n Guide Map to Bangkok Thailand*. The bus numbers are clearly marked in red, with air-con buses in larger type. Don't expect the routes to be 100% correct as a few will have changed since the maps last came out, but they'll get you where you're going most of the time. These maps usually sell for 35 or 40B.

Safety Be careful with your belongings while riding Bangkok buses. The place you are most likely to be 'touched' is on the crowded ordinary buses. Razor artists are common, particularly on buses in the Hualamphong train station area. These dextrous thieves specialise in slashing your backpack, shoulder bag or even your trouser pockets with a sharp razor and slipping your valuables out unnoticed. Hold your bag in front of you, under close attention, and carry money in a front shirt pocket, preferably (as the Thais do) maintaining a tactile and visual sensitivity to these areas if the bus is packed shoulder to shoulder.

Bangkok Traffic Alternatives

At times, Bangkok's traffic situation seems quite hopeless. An estimated three million vehicles (a figure rising by 1000 per day) crawl through the streets at an average of 13km/h during commuter hours, and nearly half the municipal traffic police are undergoing treatment for respiratory ailments! It's estimated that the typical Bangkok motorist spends a cumulative 44 days per year in traffic; petrol stations in the capital sell the Comfort 100, a portable potty that allows motorists to relieve themselves in their own vehicles during traffic jams. Cellular phones, TVs and food warmers are other commonplace auto accessories among wealthier drivers.

The main culprit, in addition to the influx of motor vehicles, is the lack of road surface, which represents only 8.5% of Bangkok's mass; to reach international standards the road surface needs to be increased to at least 20%. Privately owned automobiles aren't the gridlock's mainstay; only 25% of the city's population use personal cars. Motorcycles, buses, trucks and taxis make up the bulk of Bangkok traffic. In 1996 the government established an excise tax on products and services that harm the environment, beginning with two-stroke motorcycles, a major polluter. Buses are in dire need of attention, as they make up less than 1% of the vehicles on city roads but account for as much as half the pollutants found in the air.

Several mass transit systems (which are either in the planning or very early construction phases) promise much needed 'decongestion'. The one most likely to be completed first is the Bangkok Metropolitan Authority's (BMA) light rail system, about two-thirds of which will be elevated (Khlong Toey to Lat Phrao via Ratchadaphisek Rd) and one third will be underground (Hualamphong to Khlong Toey). This project has undergone so many reroutings (initially the north-south leg was to run parallel to Ratchaprarop, Ratchadamri and Sathon Tai Rds) that it's difficult to say with any certainty whether it will ever actually get off the ground. The BMA also plans to add several more elevated expressways; sceptics say building more roadways will simply encourage Bangkokians to buy more cars.

The much ballyhooed Skytrain network, a more extensive elevated rail project that was proposed in 1986, has gone from contractor to contractor and finally began construction in 1994. The US$1.3 billion project will initially consist of two lines, the Phrakhanong-Bang Seu (23km) and Sathon-Lat Phrao (11km) routes, plus two more lines in each direction to follow later. If all goes as planned, this one should be operating by 1999. A second project, the US$3.2 billion Hopewell Bangkok Elevated Road and Train System (BERTS), is supposed to offer 60km of light rail and 48km of expressways; the project is designed so that the railways will be stacked on top of the expressways, both of which are in turn stacked atop existing roadways. Five thousand piles for BERTS have already been driven throughout Bangkok, but this plan, too, has fallen victim to interdepartmental squabbles and problems with the Hong Kong contractor. BERTS may be taken over by the optimistically named Metropolitan Rapid Transit Authority (MRTA). Finally there's the MRTA's own US$3.2 billion underground rail, to consist of one 42km north-east to south-west main line, with a separate loop around central Bangkok. This one hasn't begun construction yet, though a 2003 completion is projected. As if all these plans weren't enough, there has also been serious talk of a monorail loop around outer Bangkok, with a feeder line for the Skytrain.

The problem with every one of these projects is the lack of coherent coordination. With separate contracts and separate supervision, it's doubtful any can remain on schedule. The main villains in all this appear to be BMA principals, who want inflexible control over every project brought to the table even where there are clear conflicts of interest. In 1993 the BMA shot down a reasonable proposal put before the Interior Ministry to split the 560 sq km city into five to eight separate townships to ease traffic administration.

The investments involved in these rail and road projects are enormous, but as current traffic congestion costs the nation over 14 billion baht per year in fuel costs, the potential savings far exceed the outlay. Bangkok lost to Singapore in a recent bid to be named the site of the new Asia-Pacific Economic Cooperation (APEC) secretariat largely because of the city's appalling traffic congestion.

One cheaper alternative which the government is seriously considering is a toll zone or traffic control zone within the central business district. City planners from the Massachusetts Institute of Technology, hired as consultants by BMA, concur that this would be the best approach for quick and lasting traffic congestion relief. This sort of plan has worked very well in nearby Singapore but it remains to be seen whether such a system would work in Bangkok, where even enforcement of traffic lights, parking and one way streets is shaky.

While you're stuck in a Bangkok traffic jam you can take comfort in knowing that average rush hour traffic flows are worse in Hong Kong (12.2km/h), Taipei (11.5km/h), Bombay (10.4km/h) and Manila (7.2km/h). Dirty air? Bangkok didn't even make UNEP/WHO's list of Asia's five worst cities for air pollution – the honours went to Delhi, Xian, Beijing, Calcutta and Shenyang. Ambient noise ratios are equal to those measured in Seoul, Chongqing and Saigon. ∎

BANGKOK

Car & Motorcycle Cars and motorbikes are easily rented in Bangkok, if you can afford it and have steel nerves. Rates start at around 1200B per day for a small car, much less for a motorbike, excluding insurance. For long-term rentals you can usually arrange a discount of up to 35% off the daily rate. An international driving permit and passport are required for all rentals.

For long, cross-country trips, you might consider buying a new or used motorcycle and reselling it when you leave – this can end up being cheaper than renting, especially if you buy a good used bike. See the Getting Around chapter for more details.

A few car-rental companies are:

Avis Rent-a-Car – 2/12 Withayu (Wireless) Rd (☎ 255-5300/4; fax 253-3734); branch offices at the Amari airport, Dusit Thani and Grand Hyatt Erawan hotels

Central Car Rent – 24 Soi Tonson, Ploenchit Rd (☎ 251-2778)

Hertz – Don Muang airport (☎ 535-3004); 1620 New Phetburi Rd (☎ 251-7575)

Highway Car Rent – 1018/5 Rama IV Rd (☎ 266-9393)

Krung Thai Car Rent – 233-5 Asoke-Din Daeng Rd (☎ 246-0089/1525)

Lumpinee Car Rent – 167/4 Withayu Rd (☎ 255-1966/3482)

Petchburee Car Rent – 23171 New Phetburi Rd (☎ 319-1393)

Sathorn Car Rent – 6/8-9 Sathon Neua Rd (☎ 633-8888)

SMT Rent-a-Car – 931/11 Rama I Rd (☎ 216-8020)

Thongchai Car Rent – 58/117 Si Nakharin Rd (☎ 322-3313)

Toyota Metro Rent-A-Car – 7th floor, Koolhiran Bldg, 1/1 Vibhavadi Rangsit Rd, Chatuchak (☎ 216-2181)

There are more car-rental agencies along Withayu and New Phetburi Rds. Some also rent motorcycles, but you're better off renting or leasing a bike at a place that specialises in motorcycles, such as:

Big Bike Rentals – Soi 55, Sukhumvit Rd (☎ 391-5670); hires 250 to 750cc bikes

Chusak Yont Shop – 1400 New Phetburi Rd (☎ 251-9225)

Visit Laochaiwat – 1 Soi Prommit, Suthisan Rd (☎ 278-1348)

Taxi Metered taxis *(tháeksii miitôe)* were finally introduced in Bangkok in 1993, and nowadays they outnumber the old no-meter taxis. The ones with meters have signs on top reading 'Taxi Meter', the others 'Taxi Thai' or just 'Taxi'. Fares for metered taxis are always lower than for non-metered, the only problem being that they can be a little harder to flag down during peak commuter hours. Demand often outstrips supply from 8 to 9 am and 6 to 7 pm, also late at night when the bars are closing (1 to 2 am). Because metered-taxi drivers use rented vehicles and must return them at the end of their shifts, they sometimes won't take longer fares as quitting time nears.

Metered taxis charge 35B at flagfall for the first 2km, then 2B for each half-kilometre increment thereafter when the cab travels at 6km/h or more; at speeds under 5km/h, a surcharge of 1B per minute kicks in. Freeway tolls – 10 to 30B depending on where you start – must be paid by the passenger. Since the introduction of metered taxis, the average passenger fare has dropped considerably. An airport trip from Siam Square, for example, once cost 150 to 250B (depending on your negotiation skills) in a non-metered cab; the typical meter fare for the same trip is now around 115 to 120B (excluding tolls). A jaunt to Silom Rd from the same area that previously cost 50 or 60B is now around 40B.

A 24 hour 'phone-a-cab' service (☎ 319-9911) is available for an extra 20B over the regular metered fare. This is only really necessary if you're in an area where there aren't a lot of taxis; residents who live down long sois are the main clientele. Previously such residents had to catch a motorcycle taxi or 'baht bus' to the *pàak soi* ('soi mouth', where a soi meets a larger street) to hail a taxi.

For certain routes it can be very difficult to find a taxi driver who's willing to use the meter. One such instance is going from the Southern bus terminal across the river to Bangkok proper – most drivers will ask for a flat 300B but settle for 200B. In the reverse direction you can usually get them to use the meter. Another route is from Bangkok

Know Your Boats

Chao Phraya River Express The main boats that you'll want to use are the rapid Chao Phraya River Express boats *(reua dùan)*, a sort of river bus service. These cost 5 to 10B (depending on the distance) and follow a regular route up and down the river; a trip from Banglamphu to the GPO, for example, costs 6B. They may not necessarily stop at each pier if there are no people waiting, or if no-one wants to get off. You buy your ticket on the boat. Chao Phraya River Express boats are big, long boats with numbers on their roofs; the last boat from either end of the route departs at 6 pm.

Chao Phraya River Express

This company has a new competitor called Laemthong Express which for the most part serves outlying areas to the north and south of central Bangkok. Hence it stops at some of the same piers but not necessarily at all of them. It also runs less frequently than the Chao Phraya River Express. The latter boats usually feature white bodies with red stripes, while Laemthong have blue or red bodies; if you're heading for one of the Chao Phraya River Express piers, be sure not to get on the wrong boat.

Cross-River Ferry From the main Chao Phraya stops and also from almost every other jetty, there are slower cross-river ferries *(reua khâam*

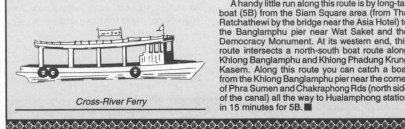

Cross-River Ferry

fâak) which simply shuttle back and forth across the river. The standard fares are 1B and you usually pay this at the entrance to the jetty. Be careful – there will probably be a pay window at the jetty and also a straight-through aisle for people taking other boats.

Long-Tail Taxi Finally there are the long-tail boats *(reua hang yao)* which operate a share taxi system off the main river and up the smaller khlongs. Fares usually start from 5B – you've really got to know where you're going on these. There are also river charter taxis where you take the whole boat – you'll find them at certain jetties (primarily Tha Chang, Tha Si Phraya), and you can charter them for trips around the river-canal system for a standard 300B per hour.

One of the most useful canal services for most visitors runs along Khlong Saen Saep. This one provides a quicker alternative to road transport between the river and eastern Bangkok (ie outer Sukhumvit and Bang Kapi). The boat from Banglamphu to the Ramkhamhaeng University area, for example, costs 10B and takes only 40 minutes. A bus would take at least an hour under normal traffic conditions. The main detraction of this route is the seriously polluted canal – passengers typically hold newspapers over their clothes and faces to prevent being splashed by the stinking black water. Not the best choice of transport if you're dressed for a formal occasion.

Long-Tail Taxi

A handy little run along this route is by long-tail boat (5B) from the Siam Square area (from Tha Ratchathewi by the bridge near the Asia Hotel) to the Banglamphu pier near Wat Saket and the Democracy Monument. At its western end, this route intersects a north-south boat route along Khlong Banglamphu and Khlong Phadung Krung Kasem. Along this route you can catch a boat from the Khlong Banglamphu pier near the corner of Phra Sumen and Chakraphong Rds (north side of the canal) all the way to Hualamphong station in 15 minutes for 5B. ■

international airport into town; in this case drivers want a flat 200 or 250B, even if you hired them through the airport taxi desk. Of course in either case it's illegal, but it can be very difficult to persuade them to take you otherwise.

You can hire a taxi all day for 1000 to 1500B depending on how much driving is involved. A better option – in terms of the quality of both car and driver – would be to hire through J&J Car Rent (☎ 531-2262), an agency that specialises in car/driver combos at competitive rates.

Tuk-Tuk In heavy traffic, tuk-tuks are usually faster than taxis since they're able to weave in and out between cars and trucks. Conversely, tuk-tuks are not air-conditioned, so you have to breathe in all that lead-soaked air (at its thickest in the middle of Bangkok's wide avenues), and they're also more dangerous since they easily flip when braking into a fast curve. The typical tuk-tuk fare nowadays offers no savings over a metered taxi – around 40B for a short hop (eg Siam Square to Soi 2, Sukhumvit Rd).

Tuk-tuk drivers tend to speak less English than taxi drivers, so many new arrivals have a hard time communicating their destination. Although some travellers have complained about tuk-tuk drivers deliberately taking them to the wrong destination (to collect commissions from certain restaurants, gem or silk shops), others never seem to have a problem with tuk-tuks, and swear by them. Beware tuk-tuk drivers who offer to take you on a sightseeing or factory tour for 10 or 20B – it's a touting scheme designed to pressure you into purchasing overpriced goods.

Motorcycle Taxi As passengers become more desperate in their attempts to beat rush-hour gridlocks, motorcycle taxis have moved from the sois to the main avenues. Fares for a motorcycle taxi are about the same as tuk-tuks except during heavy traffic, when they may cost a bit more.

Riding on the back of a speeding motorcycle taxi is even more of a kamikaze experience than riding in a tuk-tuk. Keep your legs tucked in – the drivers are used to carrying passengers with shorter legs than those of the average farang and they pass perilously close to other vehicles while weaving in and out of traffic.

Boat Although many of Bangkok's canals (khlongs) have been paved over, there is still plenty of transport along and across the Chao Phraya River and up adjoining canals. River transport is one of the best ways of getting around Bangkok as well as, quite often, being much faster than any road-based alternatives. For a start you get quite a different view of the city; also, it's much less of a hassle than tangling with the polluted, noisy, traffic-crowded streets. (Just try getting from Banglamphu to the GPO as quickly by road.) Over the past five years the Bangkok Metropolitan Authority (BMA) has revived four lengthy and very useful canal routes: Khlong Saen Saep (Banglamphu to Bang Kapi); Khlong Phrakhanong (Sukhumvit Rd to Sinakarin campus); Khlong Bang Luang/Khlong Lat Phrao (New Phetburi Rd to Phahonyothin Bridge); and Khlong Phasi Charoen in Thonburi (Kaset Bang Khae port to Rama I Bridge). Although the canal boats can be crowded, the service is generally much faster than either an auto taxi or bus. See the long-tail taxi entry in the Know Your Boats boxed aside for more details.

Eastern Gulf Coast

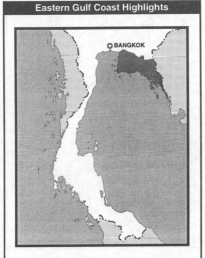

Eastern Gulf Coast Highlights

- Ko Chang archipelago – this remote national marine park has forest tracts, waterfalls, coastal walks, diving and coral reefs

- Ko Samet – this island boasts some of the whitest, squeakiest sand in the kingdom, delectable seafood and boat trips to uninhabited islands

- Popular Pattaya – Thailand's busiest beach resort, with palm-fringed beaches, diving at nearby islets, water-skiing, go-karting and exciting nightlife

- Gem trading – watch the money change hands at markets in Trat and Hat Lek on the Cambodian border

To the south-east of Bangkok, along the fast-developing east coast of the Gulf of Thailand, is a broken string of beach and island destinations that range from the country's most heavily touristed to some of its quietest. A major plus for this section of the gulf is that the waters tend to be calmer – during both monsoon seasons – than anywhere else in coastal Thailand, hence most of it can be considered a year-round destination. Another is that scuba divers and would-be divers will find in Pattaya some of Thailand's highest quality dive operations. And despite the negative aspects of Ao Pattaya (Pattaya Bay) itself, there are some decent dive sites nearby. The Eastern Gulf Coast's third asset is its proximity to Bangkok – the farthest coastal capital, Trat (the jumping-off point for Ko Chang National Marine Park), is only five to six hours away by bus. Ban Phe, where boats depart for the beautiful island of Ko Samet, is only a three hour ride away.

The downside is that this section of coastline – often termed the 'eastern seaboard' by the English-language press – is the country's most industrialised and developed. Some stretches of the coast, especially in Chonburi and Rayong provinces, are lined with factories, condo developments and fishing or shipping ports. But it's also a region of fruit plantations, saltwater estuaries, and beaches hardly anyone outside Thailand has heard of.

SI RACHA
- ☎ (38) • pop 23,000

About 105km from Bangkok on the east coast of the Gulf of Thailand is the small town of Si Racha, home of the famous spicy sauce *náam phrík sïi raachaa*. Some of Thailand's best seafood, especially the local oysters, is served here accompanied by this sauce.

Si Racha itself is not that interesting, but it's the departure point for boats to nearby Ko Si Chang, a small island flanked by two smaller islands – Kham Yai to the north and Khang Kao to the south. As this provides a natural shelter from the wind and sea, the lee of the island is used as a harbour by large incoming freighters. Smaller boats transport goods to the Chao Phraya delta some 50km away.

On **Ko Loi**, a small rocky island which is

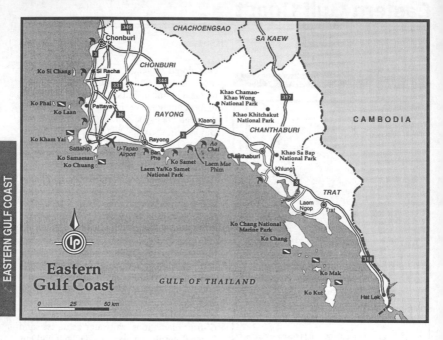

Eastern
Gulf Coast

GULF OF THAILAND

0   25   50 km

connected to the mainland by a long jetty, there is a Thai-Chinese Buddhist temple.

Places to Stay

For most people Si Racha is more of a transit point than an overnight stop. The best places to stay in Si Racha are the rambling wooden hotels built on piers over the waterfront – this is the part of town with the most character. The *Siriwatana Hotel*, across from Tessaban 1 Rd and the Bangkok Bank, is the cleanest of the lot and has the best service. There are rustic sitting areas with tables outside the rooms along the piers. Their basic fan-cooled rooms with attached shower cost 140B, while rooms with shared shower are 120B. Simple, inexpensive meals can be prepared on request or you're free to bring your own food and use the tables provided.

The *Siwichai*, next to the Siriwatana, has similar rooms for 200B, plus its own pier restaurant. The *Samchai*, on Soi 10, across from Surasakdi 1 Rd, has reasonable rooms

for 170B and some air-con rooms (350B) as well. All three are open and breezy, with outdoor tables where you can bring food in the evening from nearby markets.

On Soi 18, the *Grand Bungalows* rent bungalows of various sizes, built off the pier, for 400 to 1100B. Each one sleeps several people and they are very popular among holidaying Thais and Chinese.

There are several new top-end hotels in town, including the 20 storey *Laemthong Residence Hotel* (☎/fax 322888) in the centre of town, just off Sukhumvit Rd (Hwy 3). Comfortable rooms with all the amenities start at 900B; there's also a swimming pool and tennis courts.

The City Hotel (☎ 322700; fax 322739), a classy place at 6/126 Sukhumvit Rd, offers capacious rooms for 2293 to 3440B. An escalator leads from the pavement to 2nd floor reception; facilities include a pub, coffee shop, fitness centre and business centre.

Places to Eat

There is plenty of good seafood in Si Racha, but you have to watch the prices. Best known is the Chinese-owned *Chua Lee* on Jermjompol (Choemchomphon) Rd next to Soi 10, across from the Krung Thai Bank. The seafood is great but probably the most expensive in town. Next door and across the street are several seafood places with similar fare at much more reasonable prices, such as the *Fast Food Seafood Restaurant* opposite at 81/26-27.

Jarin, on the Soi 14 pier (the pier with boats to Ko Si Chang), has very good one-plate seafood dishes, especially seafood curry steamed with rice (khâo hàw mòk thaleh) and Thai-style rice noodles with fresh shrimp (kũaytǐaw phàt thai kûng sòt). It's a great place to kill time while waiting for the next boat to Ko Si Chang; prices are low to moderate.

At the end of the pier at Soi 18 is the large *Seaside Restaurant* – now just about the best all-round seafood place in town for atmosphere, service and value. The full-colour bilingual menu includes a tasty grilled seafood platter stacked with squid, mussels, shrimp and cockles. At last visit they even had Häagen-Dazs ice cream.

The most economical place to eat is in the *market* near the clock tower at the southern end of town. In the evening the market offers everything from noodles to fresh seafood, while in the daytime it's mostly an ordinary food and clothing market with some noodle and snack stands.

Outside town, off Sukhumvit Rd (Highway 3) on the way to Pattaya, there are a couple of cheap, but good, fresh seafood places. Locals favour a place near Laem Chabang, about 10km south of Si Racha, called *Sut Thang Rak* or 'End of Love's Way'. Closer to town is Ao Udom, a small fishing bay where there are several open-air seafood places.

Getting There & Away

Buses to Si Racha leave the Eastern bus terminal in Bangkok every 30 minutes or so from 5 am to 7 pm. The ordinary bus is 29B, the

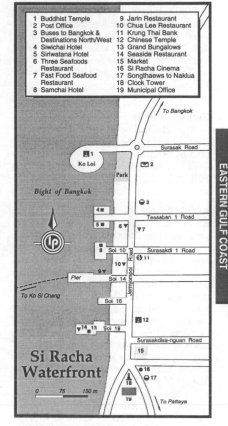

1	Buddhist Temple	9	Jarin Restaurant
2	Post Office	10	Chua Lee Restaurant
3	Buses to Bangkok & Destinations North/West	11	Krung Thai Bank
		12	Chinese Temple
4	Siwichai Hotel	13	Grand Bungalows
5	Siriwatana Hotel	14	Seaside Restaurant
6	Three Seafoods Restaurant	15	Market
		16	Si Racha Cinema
7	Fast Food Seafood Restaurant	17	Songthaews to Naklua
		18	Clock Tower
8	Samchai Hotel	19	Municipal Office

EASTERN GULF COAST

Si Racha Waterfront

air-con is 52B; it takes around 1¾ hours. From Pattaya, buses are 10B and take about 30 minutes. Ordinary direct buses stop near the pier for Ko Si Chang, but through and air-con buses stop on Sukhumvit Rd (Hwy 3), near the Laemthong Department Store, from where you can catch a tuk-tuk to the pier.

You can also reach Si Racha by 3rd class train, though not many people do this. Train No 151/239 leaves Hualamphong station at 7 am and arrives at Si Racha at 10.15 am (about an hour slower but far more scenic than the bus). The fare is 28B.

White songthaews bound for Naklua (North Pattaya) leave frequently from near the clock tower in Si Racha throughout the day. The fare is 10B and the ride takes about half an hour. Once you're in Naklua you can easily catch another songthaew on to Central Pattaya.

Getting Around

In Si Racha and on Ko Si Chang there are fleets of huge motorcycle taxis, many powered by Nissan engines, that will take you anywhere in town or on the island for 10 to 20B.

KO SI CHANG

Ko Si Chang makes a nifty one or two-day getaway from Bangkok. There is only one town on the island, facing the mainland; the rest of the island is practically deserted and fun to explore. Don't come here looking for perfect white sand and turquoise waters though, as the island's proximity to shipping lanes and fishing grounds means its shores are less than tidy. Depending on sea currents and time of year, the shoreline can be relatively clean or cluttered with flotsam. If you're going mainly for beaches, you're better off heading further south-east to Ko Samet.

Ko Si Chang's small population is made up of fisherfolk, retired and working mariners and government workers stationed with the Customs office or with one of the aquaculture projects on the island. Although there has been talk of building a deep-water port, so far Ko Si Chang has remained free of industry.

Information

Like most islands along Thailand's eastern seaboard, Ko Si Chang is best visited on weekdays; on weekends and holidays the island can get crowded.

A branch of Thai Farmer's Bank in town – on the main road to the right as you walk up from the pier – does foreign exchange on weekdays.

Things to See & Do

The main points of interest on the island are the ruins of a royal palace, a splendid Chinese temple, a Buddhist cave hermitage and a couple of so-so beaches.

On the opposite side of the island, facing out to sea, are some sandy areas with decent swimming – take care with the tide and the sea urchins, though.

Secluded **Hat Tham** (also called Hat Sai), can be reached by following a branch of the ring road on foot to the back of the island. During low tide there's a strip of sand here; when the tide comes in it disappears. A partially submerged cave can be visited at the east end of the little bay. There is also a more public – and generally less clean – beach at the western end of the island (about 2km from the pier) near the old palace grounds, called **Hat Tha Wang**. Thai locals and visitors from the mainland come here for picnics.

The palace was once used by King Chulalongkorn (Rama V) in the summer, but was abandoned when the French briefly occupied the island in 1893. Little remains of the various palace buildings, but there are a few ruins to see. The main throne hall – a magnificent golden teak structure called Vimanmek – was moved to Bangkok in 1910, but the stairs leading up to it are still there. If you follow these stairs to the crest of the hill overlooking Tha Wang, you'll come to a stone outcropping wrapped in holy cloth. The locals call it 'Bell Rock' because if struck with a rock or heavy stick it rings like a bell. Flanking the rock are what appear to be two ruined *chedi*. The large chedi on the left actually contains **Wat Atsadangnimit**, a small consecrated chamber where King Chulalongkorn used to meditate. The unique Buddha image inside was fashioned 50 years ago by a local monk who now lives in the cave hermitage. Attempts are being made to rebuild this palace and some work was underway at the time of writing.

Not far from Wat Atsadangnimit is a large limestone cave called **Tham Saowapha**, which appears to plunge deep into the island – over a kilometre according to the locals. If you have a torch, the cave might be worth exploring.

To the east of town, high on a hill overlooking the sea, is a large Chinese temple/shrine called **San Jao Phaw Khao Yai**. During Chinese New Year in February, the island is overrun with Chinese visitors from the mainland. This is one of Thailand's most interesting Chinese temples, with shrine-caves, several different temple levels and a good view of Si Chang and the ocean. It's a long and steep climb from the road below.

Yai Phrik Vipassana Centre, a meditation hermitage, is ensconced in limestone caves and palm huts along the island's centre ridge. The hermit caves make an interesting visit but should be approached with respect – monks and *mâe chii* from all over Thailand come here to take advantage of the peaceful environment for meditation. Be careful that you don't fall down a limestone shaft; some are nearly covered with vines.

Places to Stay

The cheapest place to stay is the rather bland *Tiewpai Guest House* (☎ 216084) in town, not far from the main piers. They have one basic room that costs 100B; the remaining nine rooms, arranged around a courtyard behind the restaurant and reception area, range from 160B for a simple double with shared facilities to nicer rooms with private shower for 250B and air-con rooms for 500B. Perhaps because they have the lowest prices on the island and send touts to the pier to meet arrivals, the place is often full and the staff can be rather cold.

Out near the gate to Hat Tha Wang, *Benz Bungalow* (☎ 216091) offers clean rooms facing the sea in a basic hotel-style building or in one of its unique stone bungalows for 300 to 500B with fan and bath, 600B with air-con.

Near Hat Tham toward the south side of the island is the *Si Phitsanu Bungalow* (☎ 216024). Rooms in a row house cost 300 to 500B per night, or you can get a one bedroom bungalow overlooking the small bay for 700B, or a two bedroom for 1000B.

Top Bungalow (☎ 216001), off the road on the way to Si Phitsanu, is similar in price but has no sea view; the buildings are decaying badly. To reach this area from town, take the first right past the Tiewpai Guest House, then follow the road straight past the Yai Phrik Vipassana Centre. Or take a motorcycle samlor for 20B one way.

The *Green House 84* (☎ 216024), off the ring road towards the Chinese temple, costs 150/300B for somewhat dark and dingy singles/doubles in a 10 room row house. Also in the vicinity of the Chinese temple is the rather new *Sichang View Resort* (☎ 216210), with 10 tidy apartment-style bungalows on nicely landscaped grounds for 800 to 1100B.

Sichang Palace (☎ 216276; fax 21630) is a new three storey, 62 room hotel in the middle of town on Atsadang Rd. Clean, comfortable rooms facing the swimming pool cost 1000/1200B single/double, while those with sea views are 1400/1600B. During the week the staff may knock 100 to 200B off these prices.

You can camp anywhere on the island without any hassle, including in Rama V's abandoned palace at Hat Tha Wang.

Places to Eat

The town has several small restaurants, but nothing special, with all the Thai and Chinese standard dishes. Along the road that leads to the public beach are a couple of rustic seafood places.

Sichang Palace and *Sichang View Resort* each have their own restaurants serving good seafood at medium-high prices. *Tiewpai Guest House* offers reasonably priced Thai and western food.

Getting There & Away

Boats to Ko Si Chang leave hourly from a pier in Si Racha at the end of Soi 14, Jermjompol Rd. The fare is 20B one way; the first boat leaves at about 5 am and the last at 7 pm. The last boat back to Si Racha from Si Chang is at 5 pm.

As you approach Ko Si Chang by boat,

check out the dozens of barges anchored in the island's lee. Their numbers have multiplied from year to year as shipping demand from Thailand's booming import and export business have increased.

Getting Around

There are fleets of motorcycle taxis that will take you anywhere in town for 10 to 20B. You can also get a complete tour of the island for 100 to 150B per hour. Asking prices for any ride tend to be outrageous; the supply of taxis is plentiful, however, and you can usually get the local price after talking to several drivers.

PATTAYA
• ☎ (38) • pop 55,000

Pattaya, 147km south-east of Bangkok, is Thailand's busiest beach resort with over 12,000 rooms available in hotels, bungalows and guesthouses spread along Pattaya Beach and adjoining Naklua and Jomtien beaches. Pattaya is the most active of the three, a crowded crescent of sand where jet-skis and powerboats slice the surf and parasails billow over the palms all day long. Sunburned Europeans jam the beachfront road in rented jeeps and motorbikes.

According to recent TAT statistics, an average one-third of foreign tourists in Thailand visit Pattaya; in a typical November to March season Pattaya receives around a million visitors. Depending on their tastes, some visitors may find Pattaya lacking in culture, since much of the place seems designed to attract tourists interested in a pre-fabricated, western-style beach vacation with almost no 'Thai' ingredients. Pattaya Beach is also not that great (although it must have been at one time) and the town's biggest businesses – water sports and street sex – have driven prices for food and accommodation beyond Bangkok levels. Still, it continues to attract a loyal following of Bangkok oil company expats, conventioneers and package tourists. Lately it has begun attracting families again, as the South Pattaya sex scene has diminished slightly.

Pattaya got its start as a resort when American GIs from a base in Nakhon Ratchasima began visiting the one-time fishing village on a regular basis in 1959. US navy men from nearby Sattahip added to the military influx during the Indochina War years. There are still plenty of sailors around, but of many nationalities. National and international convention-goers make up another large segment of the current market, along with Asian golfers seeking out the 12 local golf courses, including courses designed by Robert Trent Jones and Jack Nicklaus.

Pattaya is acclaimed for its seafood, though it's generally overpriced by national (but not international) standards. Pattaya's lingering notoriety for sex tourism revolves around a collection of discos, outdoor bars and transvestite cabarets comprising Pattaya's red-light district at the south end of the beach.

One of the best things the Pattaya area has going for it is diving centres (see further in this section and under Diving & Snorkelling in the Highlights & Activities of Coastal Thailand section). There are over a dozen nice islands off Pattaya's shore, although they can be expensive to reach. If you're a snorkelling or scuba enthusiast, equipment can be booked at any of the several diving shops/schools at Pattaya Beach. Ko Laan, the most popular of the offshore islands, even has places to stay.

Information
Tourist Office The Pattaya TAT office, at the midpoint of Pattaya Beach Rd, keeps an up-to-date list of accommodation in the Pattaya area, and is very helpful. The tourist police office (☎ 429371) has moved to a new location on Pattaya 2 Rd.

Post & Communications The GPO and international telephone office are in South Pattaya on Soi 15 (Soi Post Office). There are also several private long-distance phone offices in town: the best one is the Overseas Cafe, near the intersection of Pattaya Beach Rd and South Pattaya Rd. Rates are among the lowest in town, and it's open from 9 am to 4 am, allowing you to take advantage of night-time discounts.

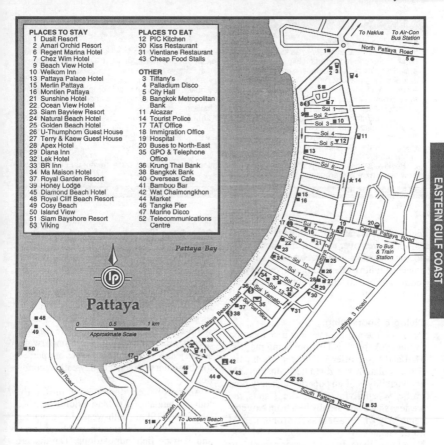

PLACES TO STAY
1 Dusit Resort
2 Amari Orchid Resort
6 Regent Marina Hotel
7 Chez Wim Hotel
9 Beach View Hotel
10 Welkom Inn
13 Pattaya Palace Hotel
15 Merlin Pattaya
16 Montien Pattaya
21 Sunshine Hotel
22 Ocean View Hotel
23 Siam Bayview Resort
24 Natural Beach Hotel
25 Golden Beach Hotel
26 U-Thumphom Guest House
27 Terry & Kaew Guest House
28 Apex Hotel
29 Diana Inn
32 Lek Hotel
33 BR Inn
34 Ma Maison Hotel
37 Royal Garden Resort
39 Honey Lodge
45 Diamond Beach Hotel
48 Royal Cliff Beach Resort
49 Cosy Beach
50 Island View
51 Siam Bayshore Resort
53 Viking

PLACES TO EAT
12 PIC Kitchen
30 Kiss Restaurant
31 Vientiane Restaurant
43 Cheap Food Stalls

OTHER
3 Tiffany's
4 Palladium Disco
5 City Hall
8 Bangkok Metropolitan Bank
11 Alcazar
14 Tourist Police
17 TAT Office
18 Immigration Office
19 Hospital
20 Buses to North-East
35 GPO & Telephone Office
36 Krung Thai Bank
38 Bangkok Bank
40 Overseas Cafe
41 Bamboo Bar
42 Wat Chaimongkhon
44 Market
46 Tangke Pier
47 Marine Disco
52 Telecommunications Centre

Pattaya

EASTERN GULF COAST

Newspapers & Magazines *Explore Pattaya*, a free monthly magazine distributed around town, contains information on current events, sightseeing suggestions and advertisements for hotel and restaurant specials. *Pattaya Mail*, a weekly newspaper, publishes articles on political, economic and environmental developments in the area as well as the usual ads.

Beaches

Curving around Ao Pattaya (Pattaya Bay), **Pattaya Beach** is a relatively scenic crescent of sand backed by a narrow layer of palms and a very dense layer of hotels, restaurants, dive shops, car and motorbike rental agencies and other commercial establishments.

A better beach in the immediate Pattaya area is 6km-long **Hat Jomtien** (Jawmthian), a couple of kilometres south of Pattaya. Here the water is cleaner and you're well away from the noisy Pattaya bar scene. The hotels and restaurants are more spread out here as well, so there's a better sense of space and relaxation.

Hat Naklua, a smaller bay north of Pattaya, is also quiet and fairly tastefully developed. Jomtien and Naklua are where families

EASTERN GULF COAST

Changing the Image

In many ways Pattaya serves as the prime example of what can happen to a beach resort area if no controls are applied to the quality and quantity of tourism development. After garnering a long streak of bad press in both the domestic and international media, Pattaya began experiencing a steady decline in tourism in the early 1990s. In 1992 Pattaya lost the privilege of hosting the annual Siam World Cup – one of Asia's biggest windsurfing competitions – to Phuket. The two principal complaints have been the sidewalk sex scene and Pattaya Bay's water quality. Powerboats zooming in and out of the beach swimming areas have been a nuisance as well as a hazard.

Local authorities and travel suppliers continue to struggle to upgrade Pattaya's image as well as clean the place up. You can actually begin to feel sorry for Pattaya in spite of the fact that local developers have dug their own graves, so to speak. It's too late to turn Pattaya back into the fishing village it once was, but it's not too late to re-create a clean, safe tourist destination if all concerned cooperate.

Positive signs that things are changing for the better include a waste water treatment plant and a new pier where powerboats must moor. ■

---

tend to stay, as Pattaya/South Pattaya is pretty much given over to single male tourists or couples on package tours. **Hat Cliff** is a small cove just south of Pattaya Beach, over which looms a set of cliffs that are home to Pattaya's glitziest hotels.

Diving & Snorkelling

Pattaya is the most convenient dive location to Bangkok, but it is far from being the best Thailand has to offer. Recent reports say the fish population has dwindled considerably and visibility is often poor due to heavy boat traffic. When diving at offshore islands, the western shores are usually best from November to May while eastern shores (or protected north-facing coves) are suitable for May to November dives. In most places expect 3 to 9m of visibility under good conditions, or in more remote sites 5 to 12m.

Equipment Seafari has the best selection of dive gear for sale and is a certified service centre for many brands of equipment. Scuba Professionals can sew custom-made wetsuits in 24 hours.

Dive Medicine Apakorn Kiatiwong Naval Hospital (☎ 601185), 26km south-east of Pattaya in Sattahip, has a fully operative recompression chamber; urgent care is available 24 hours.

Dive Sites The island of **Ko Laan**, about 9km west of Pattaya Beach (45 minutes by boat), has decent diving and snorkelling off a headland about midway down its western shore, where there is coral at depths of 5 to 25m. The nearby islet of **Ko Sak**, off Ko Laan's north-eastern tip, has hard corals on its north and west flanks. **Ko Krok** is to the south-west; both islets are suitable for both diving and snorkelling, with underwater scenery at 5 to 20m. These areas are perfect for beginners, given good weather conditions.

Accomplished divers may prefer the 'outer islands' of **Ko Man Wichai** and **Ko Rin**, about 19km south-west of Pattaya, for increased visibility, greater variety of corals and denser fish populations. Depths are suitable for both snorkelling and scuba diving.

South-east of Pattaya near the Thai naval base at Sattahip (two hours by boat), **shipwrecks** have created artificial reefs which remain the most interesting dive sites in the area. The *Petchburi Bremen* is a 110m freighter that foundered in the 1930s, the *Hardeep* a 65m Thai warship that was bombed during WWII. Expect depths of 25 to 28m at both sites; visibility isn't great but the variety of marine life is the best anywhere along the Eastern Gulf Coast west of the Ko Chang archipelago. Needless to say, these wrecks shouldn't be dived without a guide due to the difficulty of finding them and the extra caution and experience needed to explore them.

Dive Services Diving costs are reasonable: a two-dive shipwreck excursion averages 1250 to 1750B for the boat, equipment, underwater guide and lunch. Full NAUI or PADI certification, which takes three to four days, costs 7500 to 10,000B for all instruction and equipment. Some shops do snorkelling trips to nearby islands for as low as 500B, to islands a bit farther out for 650B; this includes lunch, beverages, transport and dive-master but not equipment hire. Average rental rates are: mask, fins and snorkel 125B; regulator w/SPG 250B; buoyancy compensation device 200 to 250B; weightbelt 100B; tank 125B and wetsuit 200B. Airfills typically cost 80B.

Shops along Pattaya Beach Rd advertise dive trips, and several Pattaya hotels arrange excursions and equipment.

Dave's Diver Den – Central Pattaya Rd (☎ 420411)
Diver's World – Soi Yamato, South Pattaya (☎ 426-517)
Mermaid's Dive School – Mermaid Beach Resort Hotel, Jomtien beach (☎ 232219; fax 232221)
Paradise Scuba Divers – Siam Bayview Resort (☎ 710587)
Scuba Professionals – 3 Pattaya-Naklua Rd (☎ 221-860; fax 221618)
Scuba Tek Dive Center – Weekender Hotel, Pattaya 2 Rd (☎ 361616)

Seafari Sports Center – Soi 5, North Pattaya (☎ 429253; fax 424708)
Steve's Dive Shop – Soi 4, North Pattaya (☎ 428392)

Places to Stay At the time of writing there was only one place to stay on Ko Laan. The *Ko Laan Resort* (☎ 428422) was being rebuilt and the mid-range rooms are expected to cost around 600 to 800B.

Water Sports

Pattaya and Jomtien have some of the best water sports facilities in Thailand. Water-skiing costs 800 to 1000B per hour including equipment, a boat and driver. Parasailing is 200 to 300B a shot (about 10 to 15 minutes) and windsurfing costs 500B an hour. Game-fishing is also a possibility; rental rates for boats, fishing guides and tackle are quite reasonable.

Jomtien beach is the best spot for windsurfing, not least because you're a little less likely to run into parasailors or jet-skiers. Surf House on Jomtien Beach Rd rents equipment and offers instruction.

Karting

One of the legacies left behind by American GIs in Pattaya is karting, the racing of miniature autos ('go-karts') powered by 5 to 15hp engines. Karting has since turned into an international sport often described as the closest thing to Formula One racing available to the regular driver.

EASTERN GULF COAST

The Problem of Pollution

One of Pattaya's main problems during recent years has been the emptying of raw sewage into the bay, a practice that has posed serious health risks for swimmers. Local officials have finally begun to take notice and are now taking regular bacteria counts along the shoreline and fining hotels or other businesses who release untreated sewage.

The Thai government recently allocated US$60 million to Pattaya for pollution cleanup and prevention. By the end of 1995, water treatment plants in Pattaya, Naklua and Jomtien were in full operation; authorities claimed the coastal waters would be pollution-free by 1997.

In the meantime, according to a TAT pamphlet entitled *Striving to Resolve Pattaya's Problems*, beach areas considered safe for swimming (with a coliform count of less than 1000 MPN per 100ml) include those facing Wong Amat Hotel, Dusit Resort Hotel, Yot Sak shopping centre and the Royal Cliff Hotel. Shoreline areas which exceed the coliform standard extend from Siam Commercial Bank in South Pattaya to where Khlong Pattaya empties into the sea. Coliform counts here exceeded 1700 MPN per 100ml. ■

Pattaya Kart Speedway (☎ 423062), at 248/2 Thepprasit Rd, boasts Asia's only track sanctioned by the Commission Internationale de Karting (CIK). It's a 1080m loop that meets all CIK safety and sporting standards, plus a beginners track and an 'off-road' (unpaved) track. It's open daily 9.30 am to 9.30 pm (except when international kart races are hosted). Prices range from 150B for 10 minutes of racing in a 5hp kart (oriented toward children) to 250B for a 10 to 15hp kart.

Other Sports

Out of the water, other recreational activities available in the Pattaya area include golf, bowling, snooker, archery, target-shooting, horseback riding and tennis. Among the several gyms and fitness centres is Gold's Gym in South Pattaya's Julie Complex. Gold's has a second branch in North Pattaya just past Soi 1 on Naklua-Pattaya Rd.

The Pattaya branch of the Hash House Harriers meets for their weekly hash run every Monday at 4 pm at the Wild Chicken Bar, Soi Post Office.

Places to Stay – bottom end

The number of places to stay in Naklua, Pattaya and Jomtien is mind-boggling, with close to 200 hotels, guesthouses and bungalows housing more than 13,000 rooms. Because of low occupancy rates, some hotels offer special deals, especially mid-week; bargaining for a room may also get a lower rate. On weekends and holidays the cheaper rooms tend to book out.

In Pattaya itself, North Pattaya and Naklua are quieter and better places to stay if you want to avoid the full-on night life of South Pattaya. Overall Jomtien beach is a much better place to stay, with clean water and beach, and no obvious sex scene. No place in the area is entirely immune from sex tourism, however; almost every place from Naklua to Jomtien comes with a significant clientele of fat European men and their tiny rent-by-the-day-or-week Thai girlfriends.

The average hotel price ranges from 350 to 2000B, and for guesthouses the range is 200 to 450B.

Central & South Pattaya The cheapest places in town are the guesthouses in South Pattaya along Pattaya 2 Rd, the street parallel to Pattaya Beach Rd. Most are clustered near Sois 6, 10, 11 and 12. One of the lowest-priced places in town last time we checked was *Lucky House* (☎ 428955) at 397/20 Pattaya 2 Rd between Sois 8 and 10. A simple but clean room costs just 100B – you may have to bargain to get this price – with fan and private bath. The *Honey Lodge* (☎ 429133) on 597/8 Muu 10, South Pattaya Rd, has rooms in the 300 to 400B range. The *U-Thumphorn* (☎ 421350), opposite Soi 10 on Pattaya 2 Rd, has OK fan rooms for 150 to 250B.

Also on Pattaya 2 Rd, the modern *Apex Hotel* (☎ 429233) at No 216/2 near Soi 11 has older rooms with air-con, TV and fridge for 250B and newer ones for 300B – great value. There's also a pool on the premises. Almost next door, the *Diana Inn* (☎ 429675; fax 424566) has large rooms with air-con and hot-water bath for 450 to 700B, plus a pool with bar service. Spacious but shabby fan rooms are available for 250B, not great value unless you figure in the pool.

Right around the corner from the Apex, at 528/29 Soi Sahasak, *Terry & Kaew Guesthouse* (☎ 720155) has nice rooms for 250B with fan and 300B for air-con. A good deal, the place has a comfortable, home-style atmosphere.

There are also a few cheap places along Soi Yamato which have fan rooms from 150 to 250B, like *Nipa House* (☎ 425851). The *Meridian Pattaya Hotel* (☎ 429008) on the same soi charges 300 to 350B for air-con rooms – check first if you want a room with a window.

In a lane south of Soi 12 the *BR Inn* (☎ 426449) offers 35 reasonably clean rooms for 200B with fan, 300B air-con. On Soi 13, the *Malibu Guest House* (☎ 423180) has 250B air-con rooms that include breakfast. The rest of the many guesthouses on Soi 13 are in the 200 to 350B range, but rooms are usually cramped and without windows. An exception is *Ma Maison* (☎ 429318), which offers chalet-style air-con rooms around a swimming pool for 600B; as the name suggests, it's French-managed and there's a French restaurant on the premises.

Down in South Pattaya on Soi Viking, the *Viking* (☎ 423164; fax 425964) has been a long-time favourite for its quiet 250 to 350B rooms and pool.

North Pattaya/Naklua Quiet Soi 1 in North Pattaya features the charming *Chez Wim* (☎ 429044), where bargain rooms cost 250B with fan or 350B with air-con. Wedged between North and Central Pattaya on North Pattaya Beach Rd, *BJ Guest House* (☎ 421-147) sits right across from the beach and rents air-con rooms for 350B, fan rooms from 200B.

In Naklua the *German Garden Hotel* (☎ 225612; fax 225932) on Soi 12, Naklua Rd, is a bit far from the beach but it's quiet and rooms cost from 400B. Another German-oriented place that has been recommended is *Welkom Inn* (☎ 422589; fax 361193), Beach Rd Soi 3, North Pattaya, where air-con doubles cost 350 to 500B; a large pool, Thai garden restaurant and Franco-Belgian restaurant are pluses.

Jomtien At Jomtien beach, the bottom end consists of several places around the mid-range Surf House International Hotel to the north of the beach. The *AA Guest House* (☎ 231183) has 350B rooms with air-con and TV. Right behind AA is the flashier *Moonshine Place* (☎ 231956) at 380B; though the popular bar-restaurant downstairs could make it noisy at night. Next to Surf House is *Sunlight* (☎ 429108) with similar 350 to 400B air-con rooms.

One of the cheapest places to stay is tidy *RS Guest House* (☎ 231867/8), which sits at the southern end of the beach, near Chalapruk Rd. Reasonable smallish rooms cost 250B with fan or 350B with air-con. The similarly priced *DD Inn* (☎ 232995) is at the north end of the beach, where the road turns towards Pattaya; very clean rooms cost 300B

with fan, 400B air-con; showers for beach-going non-guests cost 10B.

Nearby *JB Guest House* (☎ 231581) takes the prize with very decent fan rooms for 200/250B single/double, simple air-con rooms for 300B, air-con rooms with sea view for 400B, and larger rooms for 500B. *Seaview Villa* (☎ 422766) in the middle of the beach has seven fan-cooled bungalows for 300 to 400B. *Maisonette Guest House* (☎ 231-835; fax 232676) has the usual 400B rooms attached to a French restaurant.

You can also find unnamed *rooms* for rent in condotels along Jomtien beach for about 200 to 400B a night with fan, 400 to 600 with air-con.

Places to Stay – middle
In Pattaya the *Sunshine Hotel* (☎ 429247; fax 421302) is tucked away at 217/1 Soi 8, and all their fine rooms cost 550B. The hotel also has a pool. On Soi 11 in Pattaya the 70-room *Natural Beach Hotel* (☎ 429239; fax 429650) overlooks the beach with good air-con rooms from 400 to 700B, plus a seedier section of 180B fan rooms at the back. Farther south on the corner of Pattaya 2 Rd and Soi 13 is the high-rise *Lek Hotel* (☎ 425550/2; fax 426629) with decent air-con/TV rooms for 640B.

Lots of good middle-range places can be found in Naklua, North Pattaya and Jomtien. The *Garden Lodge* (☎ 429109), just off Naklua Rd, has air-con rooms for 650B, a clean pool, good service, and an open-air breakfast buffet. Small groups may like *Pattaya Lodge* (☎ 225464, Bangkok ☎ (2) 238-0230), which is farther off Naklua Rd, right on the beach. Two storey, air-con bungalows cost 2700B (two bedrooms, sleeps six), 3500B (three bedrooms, sleeps nine) and 3800B (four bedrooms, sleeps 12). The *Riviera Hotel Pattaya* (☎ 225230; fax 225764, Bangkok ☎ (2) 252-5068) stands between the road and the beach and has cosy, quiet air-con bungalows from 380 to 2000B.

Peaceful Jomtien beach has mostly middle-range 'condotel' places from 500 to 700B. The *Jomtien Bayview* (☎ 251889) and *Visit House* (☎ 426331) have air-con rooms

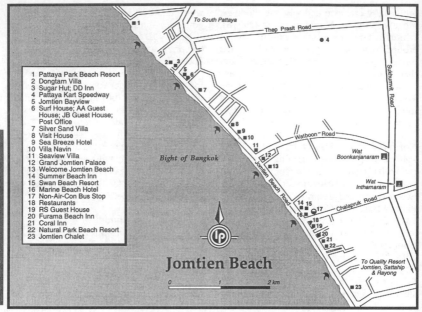

1 Pattaya Park Beach Resort
2 Dongtam Villa
3 Sugar Hut; DD Inn
4 Pattaya Kart Speedway
5 Jomtien Bayview
6 Surf House; AA Guest House; JB Guest House; Post Office
7 Silver Sand Villa
8 Visit House
9 Sea Breeze Hotel
10 Villa Navin
11 Seaview Villa
12 Grand Jomtien Palace
13 Welcome Jomtien Beach
14 Summer Beach Inn
15 Swan Beach Resort
16 Marine Beach Hotel
17 Non-Air-Con Bus Stop
18 Restaurants
19 RS Guest House
20 Furama Beach Inn
21 Coral Inn
22 Natural Park Beach Resort
23 Jomtien Chalet

Jomtien Beach

for 350 to 650B. The *Silver Sand Villa* (☎ 231-288/9; fax 231030) has spacious double air-con rooms costing 800B, which include an American-style breakfast, plus a swimming pool.

The friendly *Surf House International Hotel* (☎ 231025/6) has air-con rooms for 400B, or 500B with sea view; all rooms come with TV and fridge. The *Marine Beach Hotel* (☎ 231031) and the well-run *Sea Breeze* (☎ 231057; fax 231059) are just a bit more expensive at 500 to 700B per air-con room but the latter is very good value at this rate. Another good-value place is the friendly *Summer Beach Inn* (☎/fax 231777), where new rooms cost 650B, including satellite TV and mini-bar in all rooms. Another good deal is the new *Furama Beach Inn* (☎ 231545) near the beach mid-point, where standard rooms cost 655 to 700B, deluxe rooms 1200B.

Jomtien also has several more expensive places that rent bungalows in the 1000 to 2000B range (see top end – Jomtien beach). The high-rise development of Pattaya and Cliff beach is spreading fast to Jomtien.

Some other mid-range places include:

Ban Suan – (☎ 231072); 36 rooms, 800 to 1500B
Beach View – 389 Soi 2, Beach Rd (☎ 422660; fax 422664); 104 rooms, 590 to 850B (discounted from 850 to 1290B)
Coral Inn – (☎ 231283/7); 36 rooms, 850B
Grand Jomtien Palace – 356 Jomtien Beach Rd (☎ 231405/8; fax 231404, Bangkok ☎ (2) 271-3613); 252 rooms, 1300 to 1500B
Island View – Cliff Rd (☎ 250813; fax 250818, Bangkok ☎ (2) 249-8941); 150 rooms, 1200 to 1452B
Swan Beach Resort – (☎ 231464; fax 231266); 126 rooms, 1350 to 1584B

Places to Stay – top end

Pattaya is really a resort for package tourists and conventioneers so the vast majority of its accommodation is in this bracket. The two reigning monarchs of Pattaya luxury hotels are the *Dusit Resort*, at the northern end of

Pattaya Beach, with two pools, tennis courts, a health centre and exceptional dim sum in the rooftop restaurant, and the *Royal Cliff Beach Resort* (at the southern end of Pattaya), which is really three hotels in one: a central section for package tours and conventions, a family wing and the very up-market Royal Wing.

Another excellent choice in this category is the *Amari Orchid Resort*, set on 10 lush acres in North Pattaya, with an Olympic-size swimming pool, two lit tennis courts, a children's playground, garden chess and one of the best Italian restaurants in Pattaya. *Royal Garden Resort*, one of Pattaya's most well-established resorts, sits on 8 acres with palms, lotus ponds and Thai-style pavilions in Central Pattaya. It's attached to a new four storey shopping centre as well as a Ripley's Believe It or Not Museum; also on the premises are a fitness centre, two tennis courts, two cinemas and a pool.

All of the hotels listed below have air-con rooms and swimming pools (unless otherwise noted). In most cases the upper end of the price range represents suites, while the lower end are standard doubles. Many of the top-end hotels have lowered rates on standard singles and doubles so it's worth asking if anything cheaper is available. Rooms are also often cheaper when booked through a Bangkok travel agency.

Naklua Beach

Central Wong Amat Hotel – Naklua Rd (☎ 426990/9; fax 428599, Bangkok ☎ (2) 547-1234); 207 rooms, from 1600B

Garden Beach Resort – Mu 5, Soi Wong Amat, Pattaya-Naklua Rd (☎ 411940; fax 411949, Bangkok ☎ (2) 254-5220); 419 rooms, 2100 to 5800B

Loma Hotel – 193 Mu 5, Naklua Rd (☎ 426027; fax 421501); 120 rooms, 850 to 2100B

Woodlands Resort – Naklua Rd (☎ 421707; fax 425663); 80 rooms, 1600 and 2000B

North Pattaya

Amari Orchid Resort – North Pattaya (☎ 428161; fax 428165, Bangkok ☎ (2) 267-9708); 234 rooms, 1800 to 4400B

Dusit Resort – Mu 5, Pattaya-Naklua Rd (☎ 428541; fax 428239, Bangkok ☎ (2) 236-0450); 408 rooms, from 3500B

Merlin Pattaya – Beach Rd (☎ 428755/9; fax 421673, Bangkok ☎ (2) 253-2140); 360 rooms, 1800B

Montien Pattaya – Beach Rd (☎ 428155/6; fax 423155, Bangkok ☎ (2) 233-7000); 320 rooms, singles/doubles 2500 to 3000B

Pattaya Palace Hotel – Beach Rd (☎ 428319; 428026, Bangkok ☎ (2) 252-4926); 261 rooms, 1600 to 3600B

Regent Marina Hotel – North Pattaya Rd (☎ 429298; fax 423296, Bangkok ☎ (2) 390-2511); 208 rooms, from 1800B

Thai Garden Resort – North Pattaya Rd (☎ 424356; fax 426198); 170 rooms, 1200 to 2300B

Central & South Pattaya

Baiyoke Pattaya – Pratamnak Rd (☎ 423300; fax 426124, Bangkok ☎ (2) 255-0155); 136 rooms, 1521 to 1755B

Beverly Plaza – Pratamnak Rd (☎ 421278; fax 429718, Bangkok ☎ (2) 254-4221); 200 rooms, 1200 to 1800B

Golden Beach Hotel – 519/29 Pattaya 2 Rd (☎ 428891; fax 425935); 1700 and 2000B

Royal Century – Central Pattaya Rd (☎ 427800; fax 428069, Bangkok ☎ (2) 254-5220); 272 rooms, 1200 to 2000B

Royal Garden Resort – Beach Rd (☎ 428122/6/7; fax 429926, Bangkok ☎ (2) 476-0021); 300 rooms, from 2600B

Siam Bayshore Resort – South Pattaya Rd (☎ 428678/81; fax 428730, Bangkok ☎ (2) 221-1004); 270 rooms, 1600B

Siam Bayview Resort – Beach Rd (☎ 423871/7; fax 423879, Bangkok ☎ (2) 221-1004); 370 rooms, from 2236B up

Town in Town – Central Pattaya Rd (☎ 426350; fax 426351, Bangkok ☎ (2) 529-8358); 360 rooms, 1600 to 2000B

Cliff Beach

Asia Pattaya Beach Hotel – Cliff Rd (☎ 250602; fax 259496, Bangkok ☎ (2) 215-0808); 314 rooms, from 2119B

Cosy Beach – Cliff Rd (☎ 428818; fax 422818); 160 rooms, 1600 to 1800B

Golden Cliff House – Cliff Rd (☎ 231590; fax 231259, Bangkok ☎ (2) 258-8452); 50 rooms, 1000 to 3500B

Royal Cliff Beach Resort – Cliff Rd (☎ 250421/30; fax 250522, Bangkok ☎ (2) 282-0999); 650 rooms, from 3600B

Jomtien Beach

Dongtarn Villa – (☎ 231049); 23 bungalows, 1500 to 3000B

Natural Park Beach Resort – 412 Jomtien Beach Rd (☎ 231561; fax 231567, Bangkok ☎ (2) 247-2825); 122 rooms, from 1500B

Pattaya Park Beach Resort – 345 Jomtien Beach Rd (☎ 251201; fax 251209, Bangkok ☎ (2) 511-0717); 270 rooms, 1800 to 3600B

Quality Resort Jomtien – (☎ 231490; fax 231495, Bangkok ☎ (2) 254-8753); 137 rooms, 1500 to 2000B

Welcome Jomtien Beach – (☎ 231701/16; fax 232716, Bangkok ☎ (2) 252-0594); 382 rooms, from 1900B

Places to Eat

Most food in Pattaya is expensive by national standards, but good quality Thai food is available in shops along Pattaya's back street (Pattaya 2 Rd), away from the beach. The signs in front of the many snack bars reveal that bratwurst mit brot is far more readily available than khâo phàt.

Arabs and south Asians have been coming to Pattaya for many years now, so there are plenty of Indian/Pakistani/Middle Eastern restaurants in town, some with fairly moderate prices.

The best seafood restaurants are in South Pattaya, where you pick out the sea creatures yourself and are charged by weight. Prices are sky-high.

One moderately priced yet well-appointed Pattaya restaurant is the *PIC Kitchen* on Soi 5 (second entrance on Soi 4). The Thai-style *salas* have low wooden tables and cushions for dining and the emphasis is on Thai cuisine with a limited selection of western dishes. The upstairs bar area occasionally has live jazz. Another interesting place to eat is *Vientiane Restaurant* (☎ 411298) at 485/18 Pattaya 2 Rd, opposite Soi Yamato. The 503-item menu includes mostly Thai and Lao dishes ranging from 60 to 120B, plus lunch specials for 30 to 50B. The 24 hour *Kiss* on Pattaya 2 Rd, near the Diana Inn, has reasonably priced American and European breakfasts, Thai dishes, as well as snacks and drinks.

Opposite the bus station on the corner of Jomtien Beach and Chalapruk Rds are a few basic and cheap restaurants serving the usual Thai/Chinese dishes.

San Domenico's (☎ 426871), on Jomtien Beach Rd between South Pattaya and Jomtien beach, is operated by the same Italian family that started Pan Pan in Bangkok. The Italian menu is superb and though regular meals are pricey there is also an excellent buffet for just under 200B stocked with antipasto, pasta, seafood and Luciano Pantieri's famous desserts. *Moonshine Place* on Jomtien beach specialises in Mexican and southern Thai food; you can also buy a picnic lunch for the beach here. *Alt Heidelberg*, at 273 Beach Rd, South Pattaya, is one of the more established German restaurants (there are dozens of them). It opens at 9 am for breakfast and closes at 2 am.

Entertainment

Eating, drinking and making merry are the big pastimes once the sun goes down. Making merry in Pattaya, aside from the professional sex scene, means everything from hanging out in a video bar to dancing all night at one of the discos in South Pattaya. Two transvestite revues – *Alcazar* and *Tiffany's* – offer authentic drag-queen shows; Alcazar (☎ 428746), 78/14 Pattaya 2 Rd, is best and puts on three shows nightly – at 6.30, 8 and 9.30 pm.

Among the several discos in town, the very glitzy *Palladium* has a crowd capacity of 6000, reportedly the largest disco in Thailand. It's close to the Alcazar at 78/33-35 Pattaya 2 Rd. 'Pattaya Land', encompassing Sois 1, 2 and 3 in South Pattaya, is one of the most concentrated bar areas. The many gay bars on Soi 3 are announced by a sign over the soi reading 'Boys Town'.

Actually, one of the best things to do in the evening is just to stroll down Beach Rd and check out the amazing variety of bars – there's one for every proclivity, including a couple of outdoor Thai boxing bars featuring local talent. Truly the Garden of Earthly Delights, in the most Boschean sense.

With all the emphasis on girlie bars, there's precious little in the way of live music in Pattaya. One of the few places you can find it is at one of the town's original nightspots, the *Bamboo Bar*, on South Pattaya Rd near the intersection with Pattaya Beach Rd. There are two bands each night (the second act, starting around midnight, is usually better). There are of course plenty of hostesses happy to keep you company, but no-one minds if you just want to knock back a few drinks and take in the music. A smaller place with live tunes is *Orn's Beer Bar*, next to the Apex Hotel. The quality of the musicians varies, but the place has a good feel to it, and if you feel you can do justice to a song, you might be able to take to the stage yourself.

Pattaya's civic leaders are now attempting to clean up the town's seamy night life image. Though the bars and discos are still tolerated, public soliciting is discouraged outside that part of South Pattaya known as 'the village'. This area attracts a large number of Thai prostitutes as well as *ka-toeys* (Thai transvestites), who pose as hookers and ply their trade among the droves of well-heeled European tourists. There is also a prominent gay scene. Incidentally, the easiest way to tell a ka-toey is by the Adam's apple – a scarf covering the neck is a dead give-away. Nowadays, though, some ka-toeys have their Adam's apples surgically removed.

Getting There & Away

Air Bangkok Airways flies daily between U-Taphao airfield (about 30km south of Pattaya) and Ko Samui for 1640B each way.

At the moment there is no regularly scheduled air service to Pattaya from Bangkok. Two airlines, Tropical Sea Air and Bangkok Airways, have each tried this route but failed to make enough money to continue the service.

Direct road transport from Bangkok international airport to Pattaya is available; see under Bus below.

Bus Ordinary buses from Bangkok's Eastern bus terminal cost 37B one way and leave at 30 minute intervals from 5.20 am to 9 pm daily. In Pattaya they leave from the depot on Sukhumvit Rd, where it meets Central Pattaya Rd. Count on around three hours for this trip.

Air-con buses from the same station in Bangkok leave at similar intervals for 66B

(or 126B return) between 6.30 am and 8 pm. Air-con buses to Pattaya are also available from Bangkok's Northern bus terminal for 67B. In Pattaya the air-con bus stop is on North Pattaya Rd, near the intersection with Sukhumvit Rd. The air-con route takes around 2½ hours. Several hotels and travel agencies in Bangkok also run thrice-daily air-con tour buses to Pattaya for around 100 to 150B. Cramped mini-vans from Khao San Rd typically cost 170B per person. These buses take around two hours in either direction.

From Si Racha you can grab a public bus on Sukhumvit Rd to Pattaya for 10B.

There are also buses between Pattaya and several north-eastern towns, including Khon Kaen (225B air-con), Nong Khai (165B ordinary, 297B air-con) and Ubon Ratchathani (160B ordinary, 290B air-con). Pattaya has a separate bus stop for buses to the north-east on Central Pattaya Rd, a couple of blocks east of Pattaya 2 Rd.

Bangkok International Airport If you've just flown into Bangkok and need to get to Pattaya right away, there are airport minibuses that go directly to Pattaya at 9 am, noon and 7 pm daily for 200B one way. In the reverse direction, the THAI minibus leaves from the Royal Cliff Resort in Pattaya at 6 am, 12.30 pm and 6 pm; it takes around 2½ hours to reach Bangkok international airport. Some hotels in Pattaya also run their own buses to Bangkok for fares ranging from 160 to 300B one way.

Train A No 151/239 train goes from Hualamphong station to Pattaya via Chachoengsao daily at 7 am, arriving at 10.45 am. In the opposite direction train No 240 departs Pattaya at 1.47 pm and arrives at Hualamphong at 5.15 pm. The trip costs 31B one way. Although this is an hour longer than the typical bus ride from Bangkok, it beats biting your nails in traffic jams along the highway. The Pattaya train station is just north of the T-intersection of Central Pattaya Rd and Sukhumvit Rd.

Getting Around

Songthaew Songthaews cruise up and down Pattaya Beach and Pattaya 2 Rds frequently – just hop on and when you get out pay 5B anywhere between Naklua and South Pattaya, 10B as far as Jomtien. Don't ask the fare first as the driver may interpret this to mean you want to charter the vehicle. A chartered songthaew to Jomtien should be 30B. It's usually easier to get a share songthaew from Jomtien to Central Pattaya rather than vice versa.

Many readers have complained about riding the 5B songthaews with local passengers and then being charged a high charter price of 50B or more when they get off. In some instances drivers have threatened to beat farang passengers when they wouldn't pay the exorbitant fare. It's little use complaining to the tourist police unless you can give them the licence plate number of the offending driver's vehicle. A refund is highly unlikely but perhaps if the tourist police receive enough complaints, they'll take some action to reduce or eliminate the rip-offs. At the time of writing this seems to have been less of a problem than previously.

Car & Jeep Jeeps can be hired for around 700 to 900B per day, and cars start at 1200B depending on size and model; insurance and tax cost up to 160B more. All rentals in Pattaya are on a 24 hour basis.

Avis (☎ 428122) has offices at the Dusit Resort, and is by far the most expensive option. Budget (☎ 726185) has better rates, and has the same advantage as Avis: if something goes wrong you don't have to worry about any hassles (like a formerly unseen disclaimer popping up in your insurance policy). Both companies also offer pickup and drop off service at your hotel.

SIE (☎ 410629) located near the Diana Inn on Pattaya 2 Rd is pretty good, and has competitive rates. Although SIE has signs claiming it's 'European managed' don't expect smooth sailing if anything goes wrong with the car, or you decide to return it early. There's no refunds, no matter what.

Motorcycle Motorbikes cost 150 to 200B per

day for an 80 or 100cc; a 125cc will cost 250B and you'll even see a few 750 to 1000cc machines for 500 to 700B. There are several motorcycle hire places along Pattaya Beach Rd and a couple on Pattaya 2 Rd. Pattaya is a good place to purchase a used motorcycle – check the rental shops.

Boat The ferry to Ko Laan leaves from Tha Tangke in South Pattaya, takes 40 minutes and costs 100B. For 250B the ferry company will throw in lunch. The boat departs in the morning around 9 am and returns at 4 pm. Boat charters cost around 1000 to 1500B per day depending on the size of the boat.

AROUND PATTAYA

Farther south and then east from Pattaya are more beaches and more resorts. In fact, the more posh places may, in the future, be restructuring themselves towards the more middle-class tourists and conventioneers.

Bang Saray Villa (☎ 436070), in Bang Saray, has 24 air-con bungalows for a reasonable 300B, while the *Bang Saray Fishing Inn* (☎ 436095) and *Ban Saray Fishing Lodge* (☎ 436757) are small hotels with air-con rooms for 550 to 850B. *Nong Nooch Village* (☎ 429342) has a choice of rooms from 300B or bungalows from 1600B. *Sea Sand Club* (☎ 435163; fax 435166) has 46 air-con bungalows that cost 749B from Sunday to Thursday, and 856B on Friday and Saturday.

There are still some good seafood restaurants in Bang Saray – something Pattaya hasn't seen for years.

Still farther south is Sattahip, a vacation spot for the Thai military – some of the best beaches in the area are reserved for their use. There are several Thai navy and air-force bases in the vicinity.

RAYONG

• ☎ (38) • *pop 45,000*

Rayong municipality lies on the gulf coast 220km from Bangkok by the old highway (Hwy 3) or 185km on Hwy 36. Surrounding Rayong Province produces fine fruit (especially durian and pineapple) and *náam plaa* (fish sauce). The town of Rayong itself is not really worth visiting, but it is a transport hub for getting to some of the nearby beaches (see the following Coastal Rayong section). You can also get a songthaew from Rayong bus station to Ban Phe, the jumping-off point for Ko Samet, the province's premier tourist destination. However, if you're heading to Ko Samet you may as well catch one of the direct buses there from Bangkok.

Information

Tourist Office The TAT (☎ 655420) has a rather inconveniently located office 7km west of Rayong town on Route 3. They can provide maps and fairly up-to-date lists of accommodation and sights in Rayong and Chanthaburi provinces, but unless you're in dire need of this info, it's probably not worth the trip. Nice office though.

Money Several banks along Rayong's main drag, Sukhumvit Rd, have exchange services, including Bangkok Bank, Thai Farmers Bank and Bank of Ayudhya. Opening hours are 8.30 to 3.30 pm weekdays, 8.30 to noon on Saturday.

Places to Stay & Eat

Should you somehow get caught overnight in Rayong, there are a few inexpensive hotels near the bus station off Sukhumvit Rd. The *Rayong Otani*, at 69 Sukhumvit Rd, has fan rooms for 230B, air-con from 400B. Across the street and tucked down a small alley, the *Asia Hotel* looks a bit dubious, but has fan rooms from 120 to 180B and air-con for 280B. To get to either place, walk south from the bus station out to Sukhumvit Rd, turn left and proceed past Rayong hospital, soon after which you'll see signs for both places.

If you're looking for a more up-market stay, try the *Rayong President Hotel* (☎ 611-307), which has new air-con rooms from 550B. The hotel is located down a small side street, so it's probably quiet at night. From the bus station, cross to the other side of Sukhumvit Rd, turn right and after about three minutes you'll see a sign pointing down the side street to the hotel.

For cheap food, check the stalls near the bus station and along the sidewalk in front of Rayong hospital. If you have plenty of time to kill, head down to the mouth of the Rayong River at Laem Charoen, where the well-established *Laem Charoen* and the *Ocharos* serve moderately priced seafood. Songthaews (5B) from the bus station take you to a small wooden bridge that crosses the Rayong River onto a long spit of land. After crossing the bridge you can catch a motor-cycle taxi (10B) to the restaurants.

Getting There & Away

Regular buses to Rayong leave about every 15 minutes between 4.30 am and 10 pm from Bangkok's Eastern (Ekamai) bus terminal. The trip usually takes more than four hours. Air-con buses leave hourly from 5 am to 10 pm, cost 85B and take about three hours. Songthaews from Rayong bus station to Ban Phe cost 10B.

Ordinary buses to Chanthaburi or Pattaya from Rayong cost 20B and take about 1½ hours in either direction.

COASTAL RAYONG

• ☎ (38)

Though none can rival the beauty of Ko Samet, there are numerous beaches and islands along Rayong's coast. The tourists here are almost all Thai. Even the stretches of beach with strips of hotels have a sleepy feel that, for some, may make a nice change from doing the standard Thailand foreign tourist circuit. The few foreigners here are likely to be local residents, mostly employees from one of Rayong's major joint-venture industrial operations, like the enormous petro-chemical-refinery complex east of Rayong town.

Though not outstanding, some of the beaches, such as Mae Ramphung and Laem Mae Phim, are quite nice. One downside to this area for budget travellers is that it's often difficult to find accommodation for under 500B per night. Unlike foreign travellers, vacationing Thais are usually out to spend cash, and want air-con, a swimming pool and

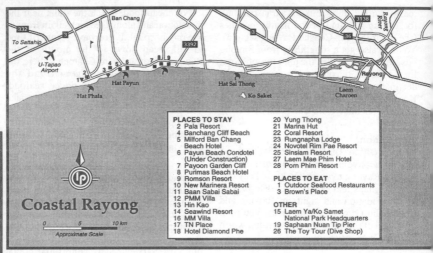

EASTERN GULF COAST

Coastal Rayong

0   5   10 km
Approximate Scale

PLACES TO STAY
2 Pala Resort
4 Banchang Cliff Beach
5 Milford Ban Chang
   Beach Hotel
6 Payun Beach Condotel
   (Under Construction)
7 Payoon Garden Cliff
8 Purimas Beach Hotel
9 Romson Resort
10 New Marinera Resort
11 Baan Sabai Sabai
12 PMM Villa
13 Hin Kao
14 Seawind Resort
16 MM Villa
17 TN Place
18 Hotel Diamond Phe

20 Yung Thong
21 Marina Hut
22 Coral Resort
23 Rungnapha Lodge
24 Novotel Rim Pae Resort
25 Sinsiam Resort
27 Laem Mae Phim Hotel
28 Porn Phim Resort

PLACES TO EAT
1 Outdoor Seafood Restaurants
3 Brown's Place

OTHER
15 Laem Ya/Ko Samet
   National Park Headquarters
19 Saphaan Nuan Tip Pier
26 The Toy Tour (Dive Shop)

TV, not simple thatched bungalows with bugs and no bath.

The best way to visit most of these places is to rent a car from Pattaya, and then go exploring. Nearly all the Thai tourists drive here themselves, so public transport is spotty.

Hat Phala & Hat Payun
These two beaches actually link together, making a 5km strip of yellow sand, casuarina trees and slightly cloudy surf. There's not a lot going on around here, even in the heat of high season. A lot of the accommodation is aimed at long-term visitors, with numerous apartment buildings and homes going for 15,000 to 25,000B per month.

Of the shorter term options, none are cheap. Starting at the bottom, the *Pala Resort* (☎ 630358) is about five minutes walk from Hat Phala, and has a small complex of air-con bungalows for 700B. Moving toward Hat Payun is the *Banchang Cliff Beach* (☎ 630316), a towering hotel with swimming pool, tennis courts and air-con rooms from 800B. However, it's not on the beach. Another kilometre east, and on the beach side of the road, the *Milford Ban Chang Beach Hotel* (☎ 630019, Bangkok (2) 261-

4271) is a palatial resort hotel where rates start at 2000B, excluding tax and service charges. It has a nice stretch of beach in front of it and it's quiet: the only sound you're likely to hear will be your own steps echoing down the vast hallways.

Towards the end of Hat Payun are two more luxury spots, the *Payun Garden Cliff* (☎ 630361) a soaring hotel/serviced apartment tower, and the *Purimas Beach Hotel* (☎ 630382), an elegantly designed resort complex. Both have pools, health clubs and business centres, and rooms start at around 3000B per night. Just a bit further east, *Romson Resort* has a nice restaurant and luxury bungalows for long-term rent, starting at 16,000B per month.

Aside from the hotels, there are numerous open-air seafood restaurants along the beaches, particularly at Hat Phala and at Hat Payun where the road from Ban Chang ends. *Brown's Place*, near the Banchang Cliff Beach, is a sleepy little place that has OK western and Thai food.

Getting There & Away To get there by public transport, take a bus to Rayong and get off at the town of Ban Chang. From there

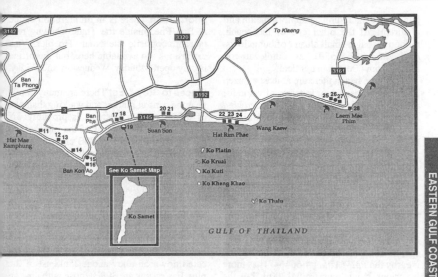

you can catch a songthaew to Payun (5B). Most of them stop where the road from Ban Chang meets the beach, so you may have to pay a bit extra if you want them to take you to your hotel, (although the more expensive places should have pickup service). There is no regular songthaew service to Hat Phala: a charter should cost around 20B.

If you're driving, just after entering Ban Chang, look for a sign indicating the turn-off for Hat Phala, soon after km marker 194 and opposite Route 3376. The beach is 6km south along this road. When you get to the intersection before the beach, turn right for Hat Phala, and left for Hat Payun.

Hat Sai Thong & Ko Saket

Forget what the TAT brochures tell you, there's no reason to come to these places. The beach of Hat Sai Thong has been replaced with a concrete breakwater, and the entire area is in spitting distance of the Maptaphut industrial park, home to massive petrochemical plants. Tiny Ko Saket, a 15 minute boat ride from Hat Sai Thong, used to have accommodation, but it has been razed as the island is now being adapted for industrial purposes.

Hat Mae Ramphung

This 10km stretch of beach is part of the Khao Laem Ya/Ko Samet National Park, though you'd never know it by the dozens of resort hotels and bungalows lining the road. Still it's one of the nicest of Rayong's mainland beaches: it has fairly soft, whitish sand, not much litter, and plenty of space for those long morning or evening walks. The western and middle sections of the beach are the best. The eastern part is a bit more cluttered as the fishing village of Ban Kon Ao is at this end.

The headquarters of Khao Laem Ya/Ko Samet National Park is on the headland behind the eastern end of Mae Ramphung. The office has very basic English info and maps of the park, and there are some trails to hike around the headland. However, the military occupies the very top portion and thus has kept the best views for itself. Entry to the park is 50B.

Again, most accommodation in this area is up-market. Budget travellers could try the *New Marinera Resort* (☎ 655101) which has somewhat mouldy bungalows from 450B. The place is a bit run-down, and is off the beach, but does have the unique feature of having several fruit-shaped concrete bungalows, including an apple, a melon and a durian! At the other end of the beach, hidden among a small cluster of bungalows, *MM Villa* (☎ 651559) has simple air-con rooms from 500B, a better deal.

Along the beach there are at least a dozen places to choose from. In terms of value for money, one of the better places is *Seawind Resort* (☎ 651562), where well-furnished air-con rooms go for 750B, though you may be able to bargain this down a bit if it's not full. The hotel has a pleasant courtyard around a large swimming pool (even though the beach is just across the road).

Hin Kao (☎ 664471) has small but pleasant fan and air-con bungalows from 600 and 800B respectively, though the price goes up by 200B on weekends. The grounds are well kept and there is a friendly manager who speaks English, a bit of a rarity in these parts. Nearby the *PMM Villa* (☎ 664647) has more luxurious bungalows from 1200B, but the manager here seems willing to drop the price to 800B.

Higher end travellers should skip all the high-rise hotels and head straight for *Baan Sabai Sabai* (☎ 898911, (01) 9823163), an immaculate, tastefully landscaped warren of cottages and small homes. Nightly rates range from 2850B for a double to 6500B for a suite, and luxury apartments are available for monthly rental from 25,000B.

Getting There & Away The easiest way to get here by public transport is to get a bus to Rayong, and then from the bus station catch a songthaew (12B) to Mae Ramphung. The latter run erratically, and you may have to wait for a while if you're going later in the afternoon. If you're driving, take Route 3 about 5km west past Rayong to the small town of Ban Ta Phong where you'll see a sign indicating the turn-off for the road to Mae Ramphung.

Ban Phe

After Hat Mae Ramphung, the coastal road passes through Ban Phe, the jumping-off point for Ko Samet. If you miss the last boat to Ko Samet, there are several hotels near the pier.

Information There is an immigration office at Ban Phe, inside the Thale Thawng restaurant, opposite the Nuan Tip pier. Visa extensions are available here, but the office is only open Monday, Wednesday and Friday.

Places to Stay & Eat There are many hotels near the central market and walking distance of the pier. Your best bet is probably *TN Place*, about 200m west of the pier, which has rooms with fan for 200B or with air-con for 300B. The owners are friendly and provide plenty of information, though the hotel can get a bit noisy.

Nearby is the mid-range, six storey *Hotel Diamond Phe* (☎ 651826; fax 424888), with air-con rooms for 700B, though the price can easily be talked down to 500B. The closest place to the pier is the newly built, but still rather dubious-looking *Kinghouse Hotel*, located down an alley about 25m east of the pier. Fan rooms are 300B, those with air-con 500B. Hourly rates are no doubt also available, though we didn't bother to get the specifics.

For places to eat, the *Thale Thawng* restaurant, where buses from Bangkok stop, has good Thai seafood dishes – especially recommended is the kũaytĩaw tha-leh, a seafood noodle soup. The shop across the street is a good place to stock up on food, mosquito coils, etc to take to Ko Samet. This is also a good spot to wait either for the boat to leave the nearby pier for Ko Samet or for the bus to arrive from Bangkok.

Getting There & Away Air-con buses to Ban Phe leave Bangkok's Eastern bus terminal every one to two hours between 8 am and 8 pm. The fare is 90B and the trip takes 3½ to four hours, more if traffic between Si Racha and Bangkok is bad. Ordinary buses cost only 50B, but leave less frequently and take quite a bit longer. Buses stop just in front of the restaurant opposite Tha Saphaan Nuan Tip. Bus tickets to Bangkok can be bought at a ticket window in the restaurant.

For information on boat travel between Ban Phe and Ko Samet, see the Ko Samet section later in this chapter.

Suan Son & Hat Rim Phae

East of Ban Phe the road is enveloped by a grove of casuarina pine trees that stretches along the beach for 4km. This area is known as Suan Son, and while the beach is no great shakes, the overall atmosphere is pleasant. It's also a popular spot for Thai picnickers.

Suan Son is also one of the few places where you can find more reasonably priced accommodation. As the trees thin out, one of the first places you'll come to is *Yung Thong* (☎ 648463), which has decent fan-cooled bungalows for 300 to 400B and air-con ones for 500B. There's no English sign: the resort is opposite a beachfront cafe with tables shaded by thatched umbrella 'roofs'.

A few hundred metres down the road, *Marina Hut* (☎ 648468) has good bungalows with fan and attached bath for 300B. It's conveniently near a row of beachfront restaurants and Thai-style beach bars.

After turning inland and crossing a small river, the road leads back toward the seashore and Hat Rim Phae. The beach gets quite nice around here, and although there are plenty of hotels and bungalows, there's more than enough room for everyone.

One of the best value accommodation places is the *Coral Resort* (☎ 648412, (01) 213-3174). It looks over a beautiful stretch of clean beach, has plenty of casuarina trees for shade, and has brick and concrete bungalows for 500B with fan, 600B with air-con. Next door, the *Rungnapha Lodge* (☎ 648292) enjoys the same fine beach, but is a bit more upscale, at least in price, with rooms/bungalows ranging from 1000 to 1500B.

For top-of-the-line luxury, you probably won't do better than the *Novotel Rim Pae Resort* (☎ 648008). This place is sheer elegance, with graceful architecture, five-star facilities including double swimming pool, a fitness centre, and sailing and canoeing. Rooms range from 2900B for a standard double to 6400B for a family villa.

Beyond Rim Pae lies the headland of **Wang Kaew**. Though trumpeted in tourist literature as one of coastal Rayong's most scenic spots, this place is actually fairly run-down, and the beach is definitely shabbier than others in the area. **Ko Thalu**, across from Wang Kaew, is said to be a good diving and snorkelling area, with beautiful, relatively intact coral. You can arrange trips there at The Toy Tour, in Laem Mae Phim (see below).

Getting There & Away Songthaews from Rayong and Ban Phe run past Suan Son and Rim Phae on their way to Laem Mae Phim. The fare should range from 10 to 15B depending on how far you're going.

Laem Mae Phim

This long stretch of beach rivals Mae Ramphung for beauty and cleanliness, and also benefits from shade trees along the entire beachfront. Unfortunately, this idyllic scene evaporates at the eastern end of the beach, where all the accommodation is concentrated. Of course this may explain why the rest of Laem Mae Phim is so pleasant, and in any event you need only walk west about 10 minutes to get away from the ugly buildings, jet-skis and speedboats.

Laem Mae Phim village has the area's only dive operation, The Toy Tour (☎ 638146). The shop has a fleet of speedboats, and rents snorkelling gear for 50B and full scuba sets for 950B. Boat charters range from 2500 to 6000B per day. The Toy Tour also operates daily trips out to **Ko Man Nai** and **Ko Thalu** for 300 and 400B per person respectively. The trips last about two hours and include snorkelling and the chance to see sea turtles. All-day fishing charters are 4000B.

One of the few places to stay actually on the beach is, sadly, the *Porn Phim Resort*, a dump of a place with tiny rooms in bungalows for 300B (fan) and 500 (air-con). This place also doubles as a karaoke parlour at night. You've been warned ...

Options in the village include the *Laem Mae Phim Hotel*, a white hulk with pseudo Greco-Italian columns and balconies. Air-con rooms are 400B. Nearby, the *Sinsiam Resort* (☎ 638114) is considerably more tastefully designed, but a bit pricey at 850B for an air-con room.

Getting There & Away Songthaews from Rayong and Ban Phe occasionally make their way down to Laem Mae Phim. Expect to pay around 15B to Ban Phe and up to 30B to get to Rayong. By car, you can either drive to Ban Phe and then follow the pleasant route along the coast east for about 15km, or take Route 3 to the intersection with Route 3192, which heads south to intersect with the coastal road.

Ko Man Klang & Ko Man Nok

Ko Man Klang and Ko Man Nok, along with Ko Man Nai to their immediate west, are part of Khao Laem Ya/Ko Samet National Park. As with Ko Samet, this official designation has not kept away development, only moderated it. The islands are in fair ecological condition, the main threat to the surrounding corals being the arrival of jet-skis.

Resorts on Ko Man Klang and Ko Man Nok, lying 7 to 10km off of Laem Mae Phim, offer accommodation packages that include boat transport from the nearest pier as well as three meals a day. These are best arranged by phone in advance through Bangkok reservation numbers. Just showing up isn't really practical: chartering a boat could easily cost several thousand baht, and the resorts may not have the food and other supplies needed to accommodate you. But book, and the resort operators should help arrange transport to the pier departure points, which can change depending on the season.

Ko Nok Resort (Bangkok ☎ (2) 255-0836) is located on Ko Man Nok and charges 1700 to 3500B per person for a one night, two day package. On Ko Man Klang, the *Raya Island Resort* (Bangkok ☎ (2) 316-6717) offers the same for 1100B; two nights and three days costs 2000B per person.

KO SAMET

Though relatively close to Bangkok and quite developed, this island still boasts some of Thailand's nicest beaches featuring the whitest, squeakiest sand in the kingdom. It is equally popular with Thais and foreigners, giving it a different feel than other established spots like Ko Samui or Ko Phi Phi,

which currently cater almost exclusively to farang tastes.

The northern end of the island is where most of the development is. Though there's nowhere near the kind of bar and entertainment scene you'd find on Ko Samui, there are some opportunities for more social travellers with a few late night bars and restaurants. As you move south things get progressively quieter, with the exception of the heavily built-up Ao Wong Deuan. Below there it really tones down: those seeking solitude will find several beaches and bungalows that should fit the bill.

The T-shaped island earned a permanent place in Thai literature when classical Thai poet Sunthorn Phu set part of his epic *Phra Aphaimani* on its shores. The story follows the travails of a prince exiled to an undersea kingdom ruled by a lovesick female giant. A mermaid aids the prince in his escape to Samet where he defeats the giant by playing a magic flute. Formerly called Ko Kaew Phitsadan or 'Vast Jewel Isle', a reference to the abundant white sand, this island became known as Ko Samet or 'Cajeput Isle' after the cajeput tree which grows in abundance here and which is very highly valued as firewood throughout South-East Asia. Locally, the *samet* tree has also been used in boat-building.

Ko Samet can be very crowded during Thai public holidays: 31 December to 1 January (New Year); mid-to-late February (Chinese New Year); mid-April (Songkran Festival); early November (Loi Krathong Festival); 5 December (King's Birthday). During these times there may be people sleeping on the floors of beach restaurants, on the beach, everywhere. September gets the lowest number of visitors (average 2500), March the most (around 40,000 – approximately 36,000 of them Thai). Thais in any month are more prevalent than foreigners but many are day visitors; most stay at Hat Sai Kaew or Ao Wong Deuan in the more up-market accommodation.

Ko Samet is a very dry island. While this makes it a good place to visit during the rainy season, it also means that fresh water can

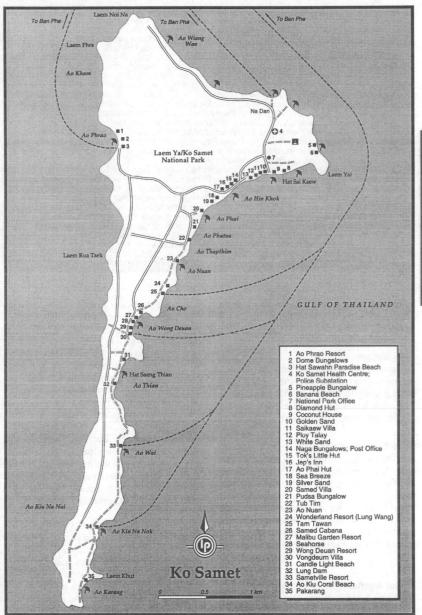

EASTERN GULF COAST

Ko Samet

1   Ao Phrao Resort
2   Dome Bungalows
3   Hat Sawahn Paradise Beach
4   Ko Samet Health Centre;
     Police Substation
5   Pineapple Bungalow
6   Banana Beach
7   National Park Office
8   Diamond Hut
9   Coconut House
10 Golden Sand
11 Saikaew Villa
12 Ploy Talay
13 White Sand
14 Naga Bungalows; Post Office
15 Tok's Little Hut
16 Jep's Inn
17 Ao Phai Hut
18 Sea Breeze
19 Silver Sand
20 Samed Villa
21 Pudsa Bungalow
22 Tub Tim
23 Ao Nuan
24 Wonderland Resort (Lung Wang)
25 Tam Tawan
26 Samed Cabana
27 Malibu Garden Resort
28 Seahorse
29 Wong Deuan Resort
30 Vongdeurn Villa
31 Candle Light Beach
32 Lung Dam
33 Sametville Resort
34 Ao Kiu Coral Beach
35 Pakarang

0   0.5   1 km

Ko Samet: Environment or Economics?

Beneath all the resorts, restaurants and jet-skis, Ko Samet is actually part of Khao Laem Ya/Mu Ko Samet Marine National Park. For years the National Parks Division of the Royal Forest Department has been trying to keep developers at bay, obviously with little success. But now there is a chance the tourist industry may be booted off the island in favour of the flora and fauna.

The park was established in 1981, around the same time that the 13.1 sq km island began receiving its first tourists – young Thais in search of a retreat from city life. They arrived to find only about 40 houses on the island, built by fisherfolk and Ban Phe locals. But Rayong and Bangkok speculators saw the sudden interest in Ko Samet as a chance to cash in on an 'up-and-coming Phuket' and began buying land along the beaches. No-one bothered about Ko Samet's national park status. When the flow of tourists started picking up, the National Parks Division stepped in and built a visitor office on the island, ordered that all bungalows be moved back behind the tree line and started charging a 5B admission to the park. In later years, the Royal Forest Department temporarily closed the park to all visitors a couple of times in an effort to halt encroachment, but always reopened the island within a month or less in response to protests by resort operators.

However, in late 1996 the Thai courts sided with the Forestry Department and, on a case-by-case basis, began ordering bungalow operations on Ko Samet to shut down. Resort owners say that no-one will have to do anything until the court wades its way through all the bungalow outfits, which should take at least until early 1998. Even then they should have one year to pack up and move out. And of course there's always the chance of a 'political solution'. So although the judicial die has been cast, resort owners are still confident they'll be on Ko Samet through 1999, and perhaps far longer. At the same time, some are looking into business opportunities on the mainland or other islands. 'The closure may not happen, but I'm not investing any more money here. This time there's really a chance we'll all have to leave'. said one Ko Samet bungalow operator. ∎

sometimes be scarce. Please try to conserve water and help ease the strain on an already overtaxed ecosystem.

Information

National Park Office Ko Samet is part of a marine national park, and there is a foreigner entry fee of 50B for adults, 35B for children. The park has a main office near Hat Sai Kaew, and a smaller one at Ao Wong Deuan.

Post & Communications A small post office next to Naga Bungalows has poste restante. It's open weekdays from 9 am to noon and from 1 to 4 pm, Saturday from 9 am to noon.

Ko Samet phone numbers are on the cellular system so dial (01) before dialling the number. Some places maintain telephone numbers in Rayong, where the area code is (38).

Travel Agencies Near Na Dan and on Hat Sai Kaew and Ao Wong Deuan are several small travel agencies that can arrange long-distance phone calls as well as bus and train reservations – they even do air ticketing.

Books An excellent guide to the history, flora and fauna of Ko Samet is Alan A Alan's 94-page *Samet*, published by Asia Books. Not just a straight-forward guidebook, Alan has woven the information into an amusing fictional travelogue involving a pair of Swedish twins on their first trip to the island.

Medical Services The Ko Samet Health Centre, a small public clinic, is located midway between the village harbour and Hat Sai Kaew. English-speaking doctors are on hand to help with problems like heat rash, or bites from poisonous sea creatures or snakes.

Malaria A few years ago, if you entered the park from the northern end of the island near the village, you'd see a large English-language sign warning visitors that Ko Samet was highly malarial. The sign is gone now and doctors at the Ko Samet Health Centre say they haven't seen a case of malaria in six years. Even so, some visitors still take anti-malarial drugs such as doxycycline or larium, and it's always a good idea to use insect repellent and mosquito nets at night. Malarial or not, Ko Samet has plenty of mosquitos. If you do develop a high fever while on Ko Samet, you can go to the health centre for a blood test.

Activities
Several bungalows on the island arrange boat trips to nearby reefs and uninhabited islands. Ao Phutsa, Naga beach (Ao Hin Khok), Hat Sai Kaew and Ao Wong Deuan each have windsurfing equipment rental places that do boat trips as well. Typical day trips to Ko Thalu, Ko Kuti etc cost 200 to 300B per person, including food and beverages (minimum of 10 people). Sailboards rent for around 150B per hour or 600 to 700B per day. Jaray Windsurfing School on Hat Sai Kaew gives one hour lessons for 80B.

Dutch-run Hat Sawahn Divers on the west side of the island offers dive trips for 500B and full open-water certification for 6250B.

Places to Stay
The two most developed beaches are Hat Sai Kaew and Ao Wong Deuan. All of the other spots are still quite peaceful. Every bungalow operation on the island has at least one restaurant and most now have running water and electricity. Most places have electric power from 5 or 6 pm till 6 am; the more up-market places have 24 hour power.

On less popular beaches you may come across abandoned bungalow sites, and even during the high season some of the most expensive places offer discounts for accommodation to attract customers. Very basic small huts with a hard mattress on the floor cost in the 50 to 80B range, similar huts with bath start from 80 to 120B, and those including a bed and a fan average 150 to 200B. Bungalows with furniture and air-con start at 600B. Most places offer discounts for stays of four or more days.

On weekends and public holidays most places raise their rates, sometimes quite dramatically. They can get away with this because the island can get absolutely packed

> ### Jet-ski Request
> The Rayong tourist police request that visitors refrain from hiring jet-skis on Samet beaches as they are harmful to coral and dangerous to swimmers. They're hard on the aural environment, too. The local police won't do anything about them even though they're illegal – either because they're afraid of beach developers or are in their pockets. You'll be doing Ko Samet (and your fellow visitors trying to relax on a quiet beach) a big favour by avoiding using these polluters. ■

out. Some resorts, mostly around the Hat Sai Kaew area, have also been known to boot out foreigners without warning to make room for free-spending Thai tour groups. You won't need to worry about this at the more reputable spots, like Naga and Samed Villa. But even so, if possible avoid Ko Samet during the peak times, especially public holidays.

Though not nearly as big a problem as on Ko Samui, bungalow thefts do occur on Ko Samet, especially at the cheaper huts. Nearly all places have safe-keeping boxes for guests' valuables: it's best to make use of them.

Since this is a national park, camping is allowed on any of the beaches. In fact, this is a great island to camp on because it rains very little – even during the south-west monsoon season. There is plenty of room; most of the island is uninhabited and, so far, tourism is pretty much restricted to the north-eastern and north-western beaches.

Places to Stay – East Coast
Hat Sai Kaew One of Samet's prettiest beaches, 'Diamond Sand', is a kilometre or so long and 25 to 30m wide. The bungalows here are the most commercial on the island, with video in the restaurants at night and lots of lights. They are fairly similar and most offer a range of accommodation from 80B (in the low season) for simple huts without fan or bath, 200 to 600B for one with fan, mosquito net and private bath, or as high as

2500B with air-con. In many cases huts don't have beach views, which are mostly given over to the resort seafood restaurants.

Coconut House – (☎ (01) 943-2134), 250 to 600B fan, 800 to 1500B air-con
Diamond Hut – (☎ (01) 321-0814), 350B fan, 700B air-con, 1200B air-con & three beds
Golden Sand – 200 to 350B
Ploy Talay – (☎ (01) 321-1109), 200B to 600B
Saikaew Villa – 500-700B fan, 1200B and up for air-con
White Sand – (☎ (01) 321-1734), 200 to 400B

Ao Hin Khok The beach here is about half the size of Sai Kaew but just as pretty – the rocks that give the beach its name add a certain character. Hin Khok is separated from Sai Kaew by a rocky point surmounted by a mermaid statue, a representation of the mermaid that carried the mythical Phra Aphaimani to Ko Samet in the Thai epic of the same name. Ao Hin Khok and Ao Phai, the next inlet south, offer the advantage of having among the least expensive huts on the island along with reasonably priced restaurants serving good food.

Two of Samet's original bungalow operations still reign here – *Naga* (☎ (01) 353-2575) and *Tok's Little Hut* (☎ (01) 323-0264). Naga offers simple bungalows set on a hill overlooking the sea for 100B and decent ones with a good mattress from 120B. The restaurant at Naga sells great bread (it is distributed to several other bungalows on the island), cookies, cakes, pizzas and other pastries. While Naga's owners are dead-set against video entertainment, there are billiards, darts, various board games and some interesting drinking bargains to keep guests amused. However, these can make for some noisy evenings: light sleepers beware. The bungalows at Tok's Little Hut are a little more solid and go for 100 to 200B.

A bit further down the road is *Jep's Inn*, with nicely designed, clean bungalows with bath and fan for 350B. The restaurant here is also quite good, and there's a nice shaded dining area right at the edge of the beach.

Farther down the beach you may see what looks like a Thai 'gathering of the tribes' – a colourful outpost presided over by Chawalee, a free-spirited Thai woman, who has lived on this beach since long before the bungalows came.

Ao Phai Around the next headland is another shallow bay with a nice wide beach, though it can get fairly crowded. At the north end is the friendly *Ao Phai Hut* (☎ (01) 211-2967), which has bungalows with bath and fan from 150/200B single/double and air-con ones for 600B; on weekends and holidays add 200B. They organise tours around the island and have an international telephone service, as well as basic postal services. The next place is *Sea Breeze* (☎ (01) 321-1397), with a variety of rather closely spaced bungalows from 100 to 500B. Adjacent is a small shop and a bookshop/library (no exchanges) that also has international phone and fax service. Next is *Silver Sand* (☎ (01) 211-0974), with good bungalows for 150 to 250B; there's a disco on Saturdays.

Swiss-run *Samed Villa* (☎ (01) 494-8090) has very clean, well-maintained bungalows from 400B for small huts with private bath and up to 700B for family accommodation. The food here is quite good, and some of the bungalows have great sea views. This is also one of the few places in the area that doesn't screen videos at night.

Near Sea Breeze the main road south to Ao Wong Deuan turns inland and heads down the middle of the island. A little further along the road from here is where the cross-island road to Ao Phrao on the west coast starts.

Ao Phutsa On Ao Phutsa, also known as Ao Thap Thim, the beach is smaller but a bit less trafficked. Here you'll find *Pudsa Bungalow*, where basic huts cost 200B to 300B and newer ones 500B. Some of the smaller huts are quite close to the water, making them pretty good value for money. At the south end of the beach *Tub Tim* (☎ (01) 321-1425) has older, smaller huts on a hillside for 200 to 300B, while newer more spacious bungalows with sea views cost 500B.

After Ao Phutsa, the remaining beaches south are separated from one another by fairly steep headlands. To get from one to the next, you have a choice of negotiating rocky paths over the hilly points or walking west to the main road that goes along the centre of the island, then cutting back on side roads to each beach.

Ao Nuan If you blink, you'll miss this beach, which is one of the more secluded places to stay without having to go to the far south of the island. The six huts at *Ao Nuan* have neither running water nor electricity. This certainly adds to the *thammachâat* (natural) ambience, but the rent's a bit steep at 300B. The food is said to be quite good here. It's a five minute walk over the headland from Ao Phutsa.

Ao Cho (Chaw) A five minute walk across the next headland from Ao Nuan, this bay has its own pier and can be reached directly from Ban Phe on the boat *White Shark* or aboard the supply boat. Though just north of crowded Ao Wong Deuan, it's fairly quiet here, though the beach is not among Samet's best.

At the north end of the beach *Wonderland Resort (Lung Wang;* ☎ (01) 321-0682) has basic, sometimes unkempt bungalows with attached shower and toilet for 100 to 350B. Huts at *Tarn Tawan* are fairly well kept but a bit pricey for what you get at 300B.

Ao Wong Deuan This once gorgeous bay is now filled with speedboats and jet-skis, and there's a lot of accommodation packed into a small area, making things a bit cramped. The crescent shaped beach is still nice, but it is noisy and often crowded.

Ao Wong Deuan mainly has expensive resort-type bungalows. The best of the lot is *Wong Deuan Resort* (☎ (01) 321-0731) with bungalows for 600 to 900B, complete with running water, flush toilet and fan. The air-con ones cost 1100 to 1200B. *Vongduern Villa* (☎ (01) 321-0789) has similar standards and prices, but also offers family-size VIP huts for 2500B.

The *Malibu Garden Resort* (☎ (01) 321-0345) has well-built brick or wood bungalows with fan for 500 to 700B, air-con for 1100 to 1200B; the more expensive rooms have TVs. The *Seahorse* (☎ (01) 323-0049, 353-3072) has carved a good swath of beachfront with two restaurants, a travel agency and fan rooms in a longhouse for 100B, or 300 to 400B for fan-equipped bungalows.

The one budget choice on this beach is *Samed Cabana*, which has quite simple bungalows with bath and fan for 200 and 300B.

Three boats go back and forth between Ao Wong Deuan and Ban Phe – the *Malibu, Seahorse* and *Vongduern Villa*.

Ao Thian Also known as Candlelight beach, from this point south things start to get much quieter. The bay is quite scenic, and rocky outcroppings break up the beach, though there's plenty of sand to stretch out upon.

Candle Light Beach has two clusters of huts that include some basic mattress-with-a-roof versions for 100 to 150B and larger bungalows with fan and bath for 350B. Some of the cheaper huts were tilting at pretty precarious angles when we last visited. At the southern end of the beach *Lung Dam* (☎ (38) 651810) charges 150B for quite roughly built huts with shared bath and 200 to 250B for ones with bath attached. There is also an interesting treehouse you can rent for 100B per night. The beach in front is a bit rocky.

Other Bays You really have to be determined to get away from it all to go farther south on the east coast of Ko Samet, but it can be well worth the effort. Lovely **Ao Wai** is about a kilometre from Ao Thian but can be reached by the boat *Phra Aphai* from Ban Phe, which sails once a day and charges 50B per person. There's only one bungalow operation here, the very private *Sametville Resort* (☎ (01) 321-1284, Bangkok ☎ (2) 246-3196) which offers a fine combination of upscale accommodation and isolation. Two-bed bungalows with attached bath cost 800 to 900B with fan, or 1300B with air-con. Most bookings are done in Bangkok, but you can try your luck by contacting someone on the *Phra Aphai* at the Ban Phe pier.

A 20 minute walk over the rocky shore from Ao Wai, **Ao Kiu Na Nok** also had only one place to stay at the time of writing – the friendly and clean *Ao Kiu Coral Beach* (☎ (01) 321-1231, (38) 652561). Bamboo huts are 300B while unattractive but better equipped cement huts cost 600 to 800B. Though short, the beach here is gorgeous, one of the nicest on the island. Another plus is that it's a mere five minute walk to the western side of the island and a view of the sunset.

About 20 minutes hike over the headlands is rocky **Ao Karang**. The very rustic *Pakarang* used to offer wooden huts (no electricity, no running water – just rainwater from ceramic jars) for 100B, but last time we checked some park officials were living there and the place was not taking guests.

Places to Stay – West Coast

Hat Ao Phrao This is the only beach on the west side of the island, and it has nice sunset views. In Thai the name means 'Coconut Bay beach' but for incomprehensible marketing reasons bungalow operators tend to use the cliched 'Paradise beach' moniker. So far there are no jet-skis on this side of the island, so it tends to be quieter than the island's east coast. Local bungalow operators also do a good job of keeping the beach clean.

At the northern end of the beach is *Ao Phrao Resort* (☎ (38) 651814, Bangkok ☎ (2) 438-9771), where well-designed, screened bungalows with fan and attached bath cost 850B during the week, 1100B on weekends and holidays; similar air-con bungalows cost from 1800 to 2500B, depending on the size and whether it's a weekday or weekend/ holiday.

In the middle of the beach is *Dome Bungalows* (Bangkok ☎ (2) 713-0046), which has small huts for 150/200B, nice huts built with private facilities on the hillside for 300 to 600B, or 1000B for four in a 'VIP' bungalow; the more expensive huts have screened windows. At the southern end near the cross-island trail is the very tidy *Hat Sawahn Paradise Beach* (☎ (01) 438-4916),

where bamboo huts with fan and bath cost 350B (up to 500B weekends and holidays). There's also a large 15-bed bungalow that goes for 1500B.

There is a daily boat between Ban Phe and Ao Phrao for 50B per person.

Places to Stay – Na Dan Area

To the north-west of Ko Samet's main pier is a long beach called Ao Wiang Wan, where several rather characterless bungalows are set up in straight lines facing the mainland. Here you get neither sunrise (maybe a little) nor sunset. The cheapest place here is *SK Bungalows* at 80 to 350B. There are several other places with rates in the 200 to 600B range.

Between Na Dan and Hat Sai Kaew, along the north-east corner of the island, are a couple of small beach bays with bungalow operations. Hardly anyone seems to stay here, and only *Pineapple Bungalow* at Laem Yai beach seemed to be showing any sign of life recently. The asking rate of 400B per bungalow is definitely not worth it.

Places to Eat

All bungalows except Pakarang at Ao Karang have restaurants offering mixed menus of Thai and traveller food; prices are typically 30 to 40B per dish. Fresh seafood is almost always available and costs around 60 to 100B per dish. The pleasant *Bamboo Restaurant* at Ao Cho, behind Tarn Tawan, offers inexpensive but tasty food and good service. It's open for breakfast, lunch and dinner. *Naga* on Ao Hin Khok has a very good bakery with all kinds of breads and cakes. Ao Wong Deuan has a cluster of restaurants serving western and Thai food: *Oasis*, *Nice & Easy* and *Ton's Restaurant*. At the southern tip of the beach the *Vongduern Villa* restaurant is a bit more expensive, but both the food and the location are quite nice.

On Hat Sai Kaew, the *White Sands Restaurant* has good seafood in the 100B range. For cheaper fare on this beach, try the popular *Toy Restaurant*, next to Saikaew Villa.

Getting There & Away
Bus Many Khao San Rd agencies in Bangkok do return transport to Ko Samet, including the boat trip, for 150 to 160B (250B return). This is more expensive than doing it on your own, but for travellers who don't plan to go anywhere else on the east coast it's convenient. For information on getting to Ban Phe by bus, see the Ban Phe section.

Boat There are various ways to get to and from the island by boat.

To Ko Samet There are three piers: Saphaan Nuan Tip for the regularly scheduled passenger boats, Saphaan Mai for supply boats and Saphaan Sri Ban Phe for tour groups. Nuan Tip is usually the only one you'll need, but if you arrive between passenger boat departure times you can try for a ride aboard one of the cargo boats from Saphaan Mai (you must still pay the regular passenger fare). Nuan Tip is also where buses from Bangkok arrive and depart. It's best to avoid the Saphaan Sri Ban Phe pier: without a doubt there are more sharks at the ticket booths here than in the surrounding waters.

Passenger boats to Ko Samet leave at regular intervals throughout the day starting at around 8 am and ending around 5 pm. How frequently they depart mostly depends on whether they have enough passengers and/or cargo to make the trip profitable, so there are more frequent boats in the high season (December to March). Still, there are always at least three or four boats a day going to Na Dan and Ao Wong Deuan.

It can be difficult to find the boat you need, as agents and boat owners want you to go with them rather than with their competitors. In most cases they'll be reluctant to tell you about another boat if they will not be making any money from you. Some travellers have reported being hassled by 'agents' who present photo albums of bungalows on Samet, claiming that they must book a bungalow for several days in order to get onto the island. This is false; ignore these touts and head straight for the boats. Report any problems to the TAT office in Rayong.

Probably the best place to head is the Nuan Tip pier ticket office, behind all the food and souvenir stalls. They sell tickets for a number of different boat operators, and also are willing to tell you about private resort boats.

For Hat Sai Kaew, Ao Hin Khok, Ao Phai and Ao Phutsa, catch a boat to Na Dan. These generally leave as soon as there are at least 20 passengers: the round trip fare is 60B. Ignore touts or ticket agents who claim the fare is 100B. From Na Dan you can either walk to these beaches (10 to 15 minutes) or take one of the trucks that go round the island. See the Getting Around section for standard fares.

The Nuan Tip pier ticket office also has boats to Ao Wong Deuan (50B one way), Ao Phrao (40B) and Ao Wai (100B). All boats need at least seven people before they'll depart.

The boat *White Shark* also goes directly to Ao Cho from Ban Phe for 30B – have a look around the Ban Phe pier to see if it's available, or ask the staff at the Nuan Tip pier ticket office.

The *Seahorse*, *Malibu* and *Vongduern* all go to Ao Wong Deuan for 30B. There's no jetty here, so passengers are pulled to shore on a raft or in long-tail boats. You can also get a truck-taxi here from Na Dan, but the fare could be as high as 200B if you're alone. For Ao Thian, you should get either the *White Shark* to Ao Cho or one of the Ao Wong Deuan boats.

The *Phra Aphai* makes direct trips to Ao Wai for 50B. For Ao Kiu Na Nok or Ao Karang, get the *Thep Chonthaleh* (50B).

For Ao Phrao, you can taxi from Na Dan or possibly get a direct boat from Ban Phe for 30B. The boat generally operates from December to May, but with the increase in passengers this service may soon go all year.

If you arrive in Ban Phe at night and need a boat to Samet, you can usually charter a one way trip at the Ban Phe pier for 250 to 300B (to Na Dan).

From Ko Samet Samet Tour seems to have the monopoly on return trips from Na Dan and they leave only when they're full – a minimum of 18 people for some boats, 25 for others – unless someone contributes more to the passage. The usual fare is 30B.

These days it is so easy to get boats back from the main beaches to Ban Phe that few tourists go to Na Dan to get a boat. There are four daily boats from Ao Wong Deuan, and at least one daily boat from Ao Wai, Ao Kiu Na Nok and Ao Phrao.

While waiting for a boat back to the mainland from Na Dan, you may notice a shrine not far from the pier. This *sāan jâo phâw* is a spirit shrine to Puu Dam (Grandfather Black), a sage who once lived on the island. Worshippers offer statues of *reusǐi* (hermit sages), flowers, incense and fruit.

Getting Around

If you take the boat from Ban Phe to Na Dan, you can walk to Hat Sai Kaew, Ao Phai or Ao Phutsa: to the latter it's about 1.5km. Don't believe the taxi operators who say these beaches are a long distance away. If you're going farther down the island, or have a lot of luggage, you can take the taxi (a truck or a three-wheeled affair with a trailer) as far as Ao Wong Deuan.

Set fares for transport around the island from Na Dan are posted on a tree in the middle of a square in front of the Na Dan harbour: 10B per person to Hat Sai Kaew (or 100B charter); 20B to Ao Phai or Ao Phutsa (150B to charter); 30B to Ao Wong Deuan or Ao Phrao (200B to charter); 40B to Ao Thian or Ao Wai (300B and 400B charter); 50B to Ao Kiu Na Nok (500B charter). Exactly how many people it takes to constitute 'public service' rather than a 'charter' is not a hard and fast number. Figure on 20B per person for six to eight people to anywhere between Na Dan and Ao Cho. If they don't have enough people to fill the vehicle, they either won't go, or passengers will have to pay up to 200B to charter the vehicle.

There are trails from Ao Wong Deuan all the way to the southern tip of the island, and a few cross-island trails as well. Taxis will make trips to Ao Phrao when the road isn't too muddy.

COASTAL CHANTHABURI
• ☎ *(39)*

Pickings are a bit more sparse here than in Rayong, with the nicest beaches pretty much confined to the western section of the province. While not spectacular, they feel even more remote than the beach areas of coastal Rayong. Adding to the sense of isolation is the fact that getting to these places can be quite difficult and time consuming unless you have your own vehicle. Even then, unless you speak Thai, finding your destination could still prove to be a bit of an adventure.

Chanthaburi's most promising beaches are all located around 25km south of Route 3, and about 14km west of the border with Rayong Province. Probably the quietest spot around the area is **Hat Khung Wiman**, a 500m strip of golden sand interspersed with rocky outcroppings. There is one bungalow operation here, *Khung Wiman Resort* (☎ (01) 213-0406), that has well-constructed slate

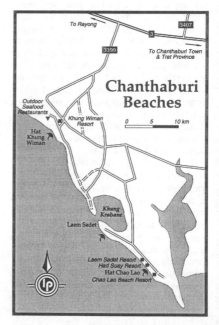

Chanthaburi Beaches

and plaster bungalows ranging from 1200B (two-person units) to 1500B (four-person). Discounts should be no problem for longer-term stays and during the off-season. Along the beach are about a dozen small thatched-roof open-air restaurant/bars. If you walk along the road leading south-east along the shore you'll come to a scenic, undeveloped bay.

A bit further east along the coast are the beaches of **Laem Sadet** and **Hat Chao Lao**. Together they form an 8km stretch of uninterrupted sand and surf. As with many other Thai resorts, litter is allowed to pile up on some parts of the beach, but it's not enough to ruin the scenery.

Laem Sadet ends in a small peninsula. There's no accommodation at this end, aside from some corporate and long-term facilities. But there are plenty of open-air restaurants and scores of casuarina pines provide good shade for picnicking.

Hat Chao Lao is a bit more developed, with several bungalow outfits and a few faded resort hotels. The beach seems to get a bit whiter as you move south, and even with the hotels nearby, a short walk either north or south will soon reward you with your own private patch of sand.

Despite it's name, *Laem Sadet Resort* (☎ 369194) actually overlooks Hat Chao Lao. It's one of the nicest bungalow outfits in the area, with spacious cottages, a grassy yard and scattered palm trees. But it's not cheap; rates range from 1200 to 1500B, depending on the size of the bungalow, though discounts are probably available here. A few hundred metres east, *Hud Suay Resort* (☎ 351078) is a bit more of a haphazard an operation, and has fan/air-con rooms for 600/1000B, and bungalows from 1500B.

Down near the end of Hat Chao Lao is the *Chao Lao Beach Resort* (☎ 321630). Though still the fanciest spot in the area, it looks a bit like its glory days have passed. You wouldn't know it from the rates, though: rooms in the multistorey hotel block are 1100B per night, and family-size two-tier bungalows are 3500B.

Getting There & Away

Hat Khung Wiman, Laem Sadet and Hat Chao Lao are all accessed via Route 3399, which heads south from Route 3 at km marker 302. If you're taking public transport, hop on a bus to Chanthaburi or Trat: you'll have to somehow let the driver know you want to get off at the intersection with Route 3399. There is no regular songthaew service to any of the beaches, so you'll probably have to charter one: there are usually a few hanging around the area where the buses stop. A charter to Khung Wiman should cost 120B (that's what the locals say), one to Laem Sadet or Hat Chao Lao around 150B.

If you're driving, about 12km south along Route 3399 you'll reach a sharp curve, with a road leading off it to the left. (The road is between the third and fourth black and yellow curve sign, and is also bracketed by a few small Thai billboards). Taking this road to the left is the quickest way to the beaches, and as you follow it you'll see signs for Khung Wiman and Laem Sadet. If you miss the left turn, you'll almost immediately see a sign saying 'Laem Sadet 15km': ignore this sign, look behind you and you'll see the road leading off to the left.

Heading to Laem Sadet you'll eventually reach a T-intersection near the beach; turning right takes you to Laem Sadet, left to Hat Chao Lao and accommodation. Laem Sadet Resort is 1.4km from the intersection, Had Suay 1.7km and Chao Lao Beach Resort 4.5km.

TRAT

• ☎ (39) • *pop 14,000*

About 400km from Bangkok, the provincial capital of Trat has little to offer except that it's a jumping-off point for the Ko Chang island group or for forays into outlying gem and Cambodian markets. The locals are friendly, however, and there are certainly worse places to spend a few days. Market fans will note Trat seems to have more markets for its size than almost any other town in Thailand – probably because it's the closest Thai provincial capital for Cambodian coastal trade.

Trat Province borders Cambodia and, as in Chanthaburi, gem mining and trading are important occupations. Gem markets *(talàat phloi)* are open intermittently at the **Hua Thung Market** in Bo Rai district and at the **Khlong Yaw Market** in the same district. Bo Rai is about 40km north of Trat on Route 3389. A smaller market is sometimes open all day in **Khao Saming** district, only 20km north-west of Trat.

Recently, there have been reports of a drop in activity in the gem markets due to the dwindling supply of local gem stock. Ask at the guesthouses in Trat for the latest. A sad by-product of the gem mining has been the destruction of vast tracts of land – the topsoil is stripped away, leaving acres of red-orange mud.

The other big industry in Trat is the smuggling of consumer goods between Cambodia and Trat. For this reason, travelling alone along the border, or between the offshore islands which serve as conduits for sea smuggling, requires caution. More and more people have discovered the beaches and islands of Trat, however, and as the locals and the police have begun to see the benefits of hospitality to outsiders, security has apparently improved.

One relatively safe spot for observing the border trade is at the Thai-Cambodian market in **Khlong Yai**, near the end of Route 318 south of Trat. As much as 10 million baht changes hands in the markets of Khlong Yai daily.

As Route 318 goes east and then south from Trat on the way to Khlong Yai district, the province thins to a narrow sliver between the Gulf of Thailand and Cambodia. Along this sliver are a number of little-known beaches, including **Hat Sai Ngoen, Hat Sai Kaew, Hat Thap Thim** and **Hat Ban Cheun**. Ban Cheun has a few bungalows, but there was no accommodation at the other beaches at the time of writing.

At Km 70, off Route 318, is **Jut Chom Wiw** (View-Admiring Point), where you can get a panorama of the surrounding area – including Cambodia. Trat Province's south-easternmost point is reached at **Hat Lek**, which is also a semi-legal jumping-off point for boat trips to the Cambodian coast. Although there are Thai military checkpoints between Trat and Hat Lek (two at last count), they seem to be getting less strict about allowing foreigners through. From time to time the Trat provincial government and their counterpart on the Cambodian side allow foreigners to cross by boat to Cambodia's Ko Kong.

Information

Ko Chang National Marine Park Information on Ko Chang National Marine Park is available at the park headquarters in Laem Ngop, a small town 20km south-west of Trat town. This is also where you get boats to Ko Chang.

Immigration There is no immigration office in Trat – you must go to the provincial offices in Khlong Yai or Laem Ngop for visa extensions or other immigration matters. If Cambodian border crossings from Trat by land or sea are permitted in the future, Khlong Yai is where you'll have to come to have your passport stamped upon return from Cambodia.

Money Bangkok Bank on Sukhumvit Rd has a foreign exchange window open daily from 8.30 am to 5 pm.

In Laem Ngop, the jumping-off point for boat trips to Ko Chang, a Thai Farmers Bank (near Chut Kaew Guest House) has an exchange counter open Monday to Friday from 8.30 am to 3.30 pm.

Post & Communications The main post office is a long walk from the city centre on Tha Reua Jang Rd. It's open from 8.30 am to 4.30 pm weekdays, 9 am to noon Saturday. The attached international phone office is open daily from 7 am till 10 pm.

Malaria Rates of infection for malaria are significantly higher for rural Trat (including Ko Chang) than for much of the rest of Thailand, so take the usual precautions. There is a malaria centre on the main road through Laem Ngop (20km south-west of

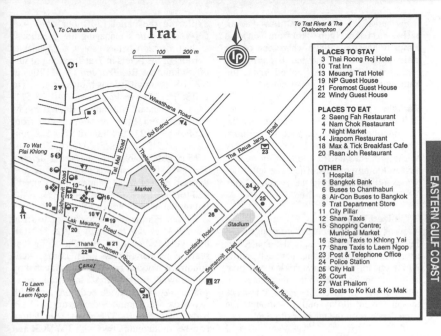

Trat

PLACES TO STAY
3 Thai Roong Roj Hotel
10 Trat Inn
13 Meuang Trat Hotel
19 NP Guest House
21 Foremost Guest House
22 Windy Guest House

PLACES TO EAT
2 Saeng Fah Restaurant
4 Nam Chok Restaurant
7 Night Market
14 Jiraporn Restaurant
18 Max & Tick Breakfast Cafe
20 Raan Joh Restaurant

OTHER
1 Hospital
5 Bangkok Bank
6 Buses to Chanthaburi
8 Air-Con Buses to Bangkok
9 Trat Department Store
11 City Pillar
12 Share Taxis
15 Shopping Centre;
    Municipal Market
16 Share Taxis to Khlong Yai
17 Share Taxis to Laem Ngop
23 Post & Telephone Office
24 Police Station
25 City Hall
26 Court
27 Wat Phailom
28 Boats to Ko Kut & Ko Mak

Trat); here you can get the latest information on the disease. This office can also assist with testing and/or treatment for malaria. Malaria is not that easy to contract, even in malarial areas, unless you allow the mosquitos open season on your flesh. That said, there are travellers who have contracted the disease while on Ko Chang, so malarial prophalactics are probably worth taking. And make sure you use repellent and mosquito nets at night.

Things to See & Do

Trat town's older homes and shophouses are along the canal – you may be able to rent a canoe from one of the guesthouses for a water-level look. During high tide it's possible to boat from the canal to the Trat estuary on the gulf. This can also be done from the Trat River, north of the city; enquire at Tha Chaloemphon (also known simply as *thâa reua* or 'boat pier').

Wat Plai Khlong (Wat Bupharam), 2km west of the city centre, is over 200 years old and worth a visit if you want to kill an hour or so. Several of the wooden buildings date to the late Ayuthaya period, including the *wihãan*, bell tower and *kutis* (monk quarters). The wihãan contains a variety of sacred relics and Buddha images dating from the Ayuthaya period and earlier.

Trat is famous for 'yellow oil' (*náam-man lẽuang*), an herb-infused liquid touted as a remedy for everything from arthritis to stomach upsets. It's produced by a local resident, **Mae Ang-kii** (Somthawin Pasananon), using a secret pharmaceutical recipe that has been handed down through her Chinese-Thai family for generations. Among Thais it is said that if you visit Trat and don't leave with a couple bottles of Mae Ang-kii's yellow oil, then you really haven't been to Trat. The stuff is available direct from her house at No 5 Rat Uthit Rd (☎ 511935) or from the Max & Tick Breakfast Cafe (see Places to Eat); Tick is Mae Ang-kii's daughter.

Farther afield, **Ban Nam Chiaw** – about halfway to Laem Ngop (8km from Trat) – is a mostly Muslim village where one of the main industries is the handweaving of hemispherical straw hats called *ngôp*, the traditional Khmer rice farmer's hat.

Markets

Of Trat's several markets, the largest are the new municipal day market beneath the shopping centre off Sukhumvit Rd, the old day market off Tat Mai Rd and the day market next to the air-con bus office; the latter becomes a night market in the evening. Look for delicacies like deep-fried lizards.

Organised Tours

A few of Trat's guesthouses can arrange local day trips to gem markets, to the Trat River estuary or even to Ko Chang, if enough people are interested. The estuary trips leave by boat from the canal in town to the Trat estuary to gather clams (in season) for 100B or less per person for an all-day outing – though the price depends on the number of people.

Places to Stay

Trat The friendly *NP Guest House* (☎ 512-564) has moved from its former location on the outskirts of town to a more central spot at 1-3 Soi Luang Aet, Lak Meuang Rd (in a lane which is a south-west continuation of Tat Mai Rd); it's a short walk from the main day and night markets as well as local bus stops. It's basically an old wooden shophouse with a glassed-in downstairs; a bed in the clean three-bed dorm costs 50B or you can get a private room for 80/100B single/double with shared bath.

Foremost Guest House (☎ 511923), at 49 Thana Charoen Rd towards the canal, offers rooms upstairs in an old shophouse; bathrooms are shared but clean, and a hot shower is available. Rates are 60/80/100B for a single/double/triple. The same family runs the *Windy Guest House* across the road on the canal; here rooms are 40B dorm, 60/80B single/double. Bicycles and motorcycles are also available for rent for 20B and 180 to 250B per day. Ask about renting canoes for

exploring the canal (20B per day) – it depends on who's managing the guesthouse at the time and whether canoes are available.

Most of the hotels in Trat are along or just off Sukhumvit Rd. *Trat Inn* (☎ 511208) at 66-71 Sukhumvit Rd has rooms from 110 to 200B. *Thai Roong Roj (Rung Rot)* (☎ 511-141), in a lane off Sukhumvit Rd, has rooms with fan from 140B or with air-con from 250B. Then at 234 Sukhumvit Rd is *Sukhumvit Inn* (☎ 512151) with 140 to 180B rooms.

More comfortable is the renovated *Meuang Trat* (☎ 511091), off Sukhumvit Rd next to the market, which has standard fan rooms for 220 to 300B, air-con from 340B. This is the only hotel in town with a lift.

Eleven kilometres south-east of town at Laem Sok, the *Ban Pu Resort* (☎ /fax 512400) has opened adjacent to Suan Puu, a famous seafood restaurant/crab farm. Large, well-appointed wooden bungalows connected by a boardwalk surrounding a large crab pond start at 1200B for a one-bedroom unit with two beds; a larger one-bedroom unit with six beds costs 2600B. There are also deluxe two-bedroom bungalows with TV, VCR and stereo for 2400 to 3400B. It's a 20B, 15 minute mini-songthaew ride from town. Ban Pu can arrange speedboat transport to Ko Chang and other Trat islands.

Laem Ngop There's usually no reason to stay here, since most boats to the island leave in the morning and early afternoon and it's only 20km from Trat. If you must, however, there are a couple of good choices. A five minute walk from the harbour on the right is the *Chut Kaew Guest House*, which is run by a nurse, teacher and university student – local, somewhat dated information (including hiking info for Ko Chang) is available in thick notebooks compiled by guests. Rooms cost 60B per person and are quite clean. Food is available, as are bike rentals for 10B a day.

The next place on the right, about 100m from the road, is *PI Guest House*, a new, clean place with large rooms in a Thai house; it's usually closed during the June to November rainy season. All rooms have one double bed for 60/120B a single/double. The *Laem*

Ngop Inn (☎ 597044) is farther up again, but 300m from the road, with rooms with fan for 200B and air-con ones for 300 to 450B. The *Paradise Inn* (☎ 512831), near the police station, has similarly priced rooms.

At the Laem Ngop pier there are two good seafood restaurants. The *Saengchan Restaurant*, on the right in front of the pier, doesn't have great food but many travellers wait here for minibuses to Trat which connect with air-con buses to Bangkok.

A Bangkok development company is constructing a new pier and commercial site called Koh Chang Centre Point at Laem Ngop. Supposedly the large project will have its own waste-water treatment system to prevent pollution of the strait running between Ko Chang and the mainland.

Places to Eat

With all the markets in Trat, you're hardly ever more than 50m away from something good to eat. The indoor municipal market beneath the shopping centre has a food section with cheap, good noodle and rice dishes from early morning to early evening. Another good spot for a cheap breakfast is the ancient coffee stand in the old day market on Tat Mai Rd.

In the evenings, there's a good night market next to the air-con bus station. On the Trat River in the northern part of town is a small but atmospheric night market – a good choice for long, leisurely meals. Trat is a good city for seafood, which is cheaper here than in Bangkok or in more well-touristed cities around the country (it's not the international tourists who drive up the seafood prices but the Thais, who spend huge sums of money eating out).

Max & Tick Breakfast Cafe (☎ 520799), at 1-3 Soi Luang Aet, Lak Meuang Rd (in a lane which is a south-west continuation of Tat Mai Rd) offers good coffee and western breakfasts from 6.30 am till 11 am. This is also a good spot for local info; Max and Tick are a friendly young Thai couple who speak excellent English and they know the area well. Their collection of music tapes/CDs is one of the best around.

One of the longest running Thai-Chinese restaurants in town is the *Jiraporn*, a small cafe-style place a few doors up from the Meuang Trat Hotel where a small crowd of older regulars hang out over tea and coffee every morning. As it's mostly a breakfast place, the main menu offerings are toast and eggs with ham, jók and khâo tôm, but they can also do fried rice or noodles.

The *Nam Chok* outdoor restaurant on the corner of Soi Butnoi and Wiwatthana Rd is another local institution. Around lunchtime a good find is *Raan Joh* (no English sign) at 90 Lak Meuang Rd. The number is next to impossible to see, just look for the only place making khanŏm beûang, a Khmer vegie crepe prepared in a wok. They also do other local specialities – it's very inexpensive but open lunchtime only.

A good mid-range restaurant, the air-con *Sueng Fah* (☎ 511222) at 156-7 Sukhumvit Rd has a large menu with Thai specialities between 50 and 100B. The food is good, and there are plenty of seafood dishes. They also serve breakfast, when you might (or might not) want to try the house speciality – 'rice with curdled pig's blood'.

The best place in the whole province for seafood is *Suan Puu* (Crab Farm) in Ban Laem Hin, on the way to Laem Sok, 11km south-east of town (a 20B mini-songthaew ride each way). Tables are atmospherically arranged on wooden piers over Ao Meuang Trat (Trat Bay). All seafood is served fresh; crab, raised on the premises, is of course the house speciality and prices are moderate to medium high (still considerably cheaper than Bangkok). The menu is in Thai only, so bring along a Thai friend to translate.

Getting There & Away

Bangkok Buses to/from Bangkok cost 140B air-con or 80B ordinary and leave from the Eastern bus terminal. The trip takes five to six hours one way by air-con bus, or about eight hours by ordinary bus. Three bus companies operate a Trat to Bangkok service; Sahamit, on Sukhumvit Rd near the Trat Inn and night market, has the best and most frequent (12 a day) air-con buses to Bangkok.

EASTERN GULF COAST

Chanthaburi Ordinary buses between Chanthaburi and Trat are 22B and take about 1½ hours for the 66km trip.

You can also take the quicker share taxis between Trat and Chanthaburi for 40B per person – these take around 45 minutes. During the middle of the day, however, it may take up to an hour to gather the seven passengers necessary for a departure; try to schedule your departure between 7 and 9 am or 4 and 6 pm for the shortest wait.

Laem Ngop Share taxis to Laem Ngop leave Trat from a stand along Sukhumvit Rd next to the municipal market; these cost 10B per person shared or 100B to charter. They depart regularly throughout the day, but after dark you will have to charter.

Khlong Yai, Bo Rai & Hat Lek Songthaews and share taxis to Khlong Yai cost 25B per person and take about 45 minutes. The songthaew fare from Khlong Yai to Hat Lek is 10B for the 16km trip; these taxis leave from the back of the municipal market. Motorcycle taxis are also available between Khlong Yai and Hat Lek for 50B. A door-to-door minibus to Bo Rai is 35B.

Getting Around

Samlors around town should cost 10B per person. Small songthaews cost 5B per person on a share basis or 20B for the whole vehicle.

KO CHANG NATIONAL MARINE PARK

Forty-seven of the islands off Trat's coastline belong to a national park named for Ko Chang ('Elephant Island'), which at 492 sq km is the second-largest island in Thailand after Phuket. The park officially encompasses 192 sq km of land surface and 458 sq km of sea. Ko Chang itself is about 70% undisturbed island rainforest – the best preserved in Thailand, perhaps all of South-East Asia – with steep hills and cliffs reaching as high as 744m Khao Jom Prasat. Beach, forest and mangrove are also abundant.

Notable wildlife includes stump-tailed macaque, small Indian civet, Javan mongoose, monitor lizard, water monitor, Burmese and reticulated pythons, king cobra, barking deer and wild pig. Bird species (61 resident species, 12 migratory) include Pacific reef egret, nightjar, green imperial pigeon, white-winged tern, blue-winged pitta, hooded pitta and three hornbill species. An endemic amphibian, the Ko Chang frog *(Rana kohchang)* is also found here.

Other major islands in the park include Ko Kut and Ko Mak. Ko Chang is ringed with small bays and beaches, among them **Ao Khlong Son**, **Hat Sai Khao**, **Hat Khlong Phrao**, **Hat Kaibae**, **Ao Bang Bao** and **Ao Salak Phet**. Near each of these beaches are small villages, eg Ban Khlong Son, Ban Bang Bao and so on.

Until very recently there wasn't a single paved road on Ko Chang, only red dirt roads between Khlong Son and Hat Kaibae on the west coast of the island, and between Khlong Son and Ban Salak Phet on the east side, plus walking trails passable by motorcycle from Kaibae to Bang Bao and Salak Kok to Salak Phet. The road on the west side is being extended (a paved section now exists between Khlong Son/Ao Sapparot and Hat Sai Khao), and Trat authorities say the island will have a paved ring road – or at least the beginnings of one – within the next two or three years. The province has plans to 'civilise' the island further by stringing power lines above the paved road.

In 1995 the island received around 60,000 visitors, most of whom were Thai. Thai visitors tend to arrive on weekends and holidays only, stay for 24 hours or less, and stay in the more expensive accommodation. The average stay for non-Thai visitors is around five days; a small number of visitors take up residence for weeks on end.

A combination of steep terrain and year-round streams creates several scenic waterfalls. **Than Mayom Falls**, a series of three falls along the stream of Khlong Mayom in the interior of the island, can be reached via Tha Than Mayom or Ban Dan Mai on the east coast. The waterfall closest to the shore can be climbed in about 45 minutes via a well-marked footpath. The view from the top is quite good and there are two inscribed stones bearing the initials of Rama VI and Rama VII nearby. The second waterfall is about 500m farther east along Khlong Mayom and the third is about 3km from the first. At the third waterfall is another inscribed stone, this one with the initials of Rama V. At the lower levels are public picnic areas.

A smaller waterfall on the west coast, **Khlong Pliu Falls**, can be visited from Ao Khlong Phrao (45 minutes) or from Hat Kaibae (one hour) by following Khlong Phrao 2km inland. Or pedal a bicycle along the main dirt road until you see the sign on the eastern side of the road. Ride up to the restaurant near the falls, from where it is only a 15 minute walk. The pool beneath the falls is a good spot for a refreshing swim, and it is possible to stay in bungalows or camp here.

On **Ko Kut** you'll find beaches mostly along the west side, at Hat Tapho, Hat Khlong Chao and Hat Khlong Yai Kii. A dirt road runs between Ban Khlong Hin Dam, the island's main village on the west coast, and Ao Salat along the north-east shore. Other villages on the island include Ban Ta Poi, Bang Ao Salat, Ban Laem Kluai, Bang Khlong Phrao and Ban Lak Uan. The nearby small islands of Ko Rang and Ko Rayang have good coral in spots. Ko Kut is best reached from Khlong Yai on the mainland.

Ko Mak, the smallest of the three main islands, has a beach along the north-west bay and possibly others as yet undiscovered. Monsoon forest covers 30% of the island while coconut plantations take up another 60%. A few tractors or jeeps travel along the single paved road which leads from the pier to the main village. It is possible to rent motorbikes and organise diving trips from the resorts on the island.

Ko Wai has some of the best coral and is excellent for snorkelling and diving. The island has one bungalow operation. **Ko Kham** is also recommended for underwater explorations; accommodation is available.

Ko Lao-ya has natural attributes similar to those at Ko Wai, with one rather expensive place to stay.

The tiny **Ko Rang** archipelago, to the south-west of Ko Chang, is a primary nesting ground for the endangered hawksbill sea turtle.

As with other national marine parks in Thailand, park status versus resort development is a hot issue. On Ko Chang, so far, everyone seems to be in agreement about what is park land and what isn't. Any land that was planted before the conferral of park status in 1982 can be privately deeded, bought, sold and developed – this includes many beach areas used for coconut plantations, or about 15% of the island. The Forestry Department makes regular flights over the island to check for encroachment on the 85% belonging to the national park – mostly in the interior – and they are said to be very strict with interlopers.

Information

There is no bank on Ko Chang, but money-changers will change US dollars and travellers cheques at very unfavourable rates. The only post office is near the pier at Ban Khlong Son, where there is a telegram service but no international phones. On Hat Sai Khao and Hat Kaibae, a few places offer international telephone service at very high rates.

There is a health clinic at Khlong Son; the nearest hospital is in Laem Ngop on the mainland. A two-room jail at Ban Salak Phet sometimes holds visitors caught smoking dope on the island.

Walking on Ko Chang

In general the more interesting hikes can be found in the southern half of the island where there are fewer roads. At the northern end you can walk from Khlong Son to Hat Sai Khao in about 1½ to two hours, from Hat Sai Khao to Hat Khlong Phrao in about two hours, and from Hat Khlong Phrao to Hat Kaibae in about two hours. All three are straightforward walks along the main road. If you're looking for more grunt, just head into the interior – the steep, forested hills will have you sweating in no time. A footpath connects Khlong Phrao on the west coast

EASTERN GULF COAST

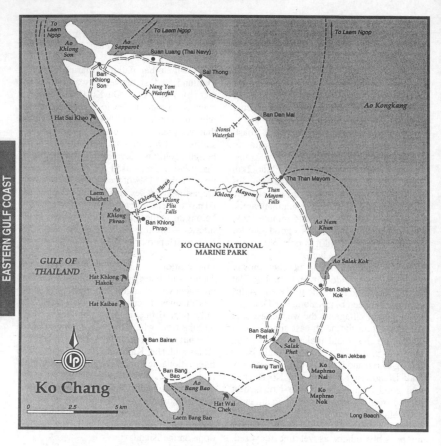

Ko Chang

with Khlong Mayom on the east, but this all-day cross-island route shouldn't be undertaken without a local guide.

Down south a challenging walk is to hike from **Kaibae to Ao Bang Bao** through coconut and rubber plantations – this takes three to four hours and is a bit more involved. You may have to ask directions from villagers along the way as there are several interconnecting trails.

Bang Bao to Salak Phet Don't try it unless you're an experienced tropical hiker with moderate orienteering skills – there's a lot of up-and-down and many interconnect-

ing trails. A Swede who hiked the entire perimeter of the island suggested that for this part of the island you carry a note in Thai reading 'I would like to go to Salak Phet. I like very much to walk in the jungle and have done it before. Please show me the start of this trail'. If you don't get lost, this hike will take four to six hours; should you decide to attempt it, carry enough food and water for an overnight, just in case. If you do get lost, climb the nearest hilltop and try to locate the sea or a stream to get a bearing on where you are. Following any stream will usually take you either to a village or to the sea. Then you can either follow the coast or ask directions. This advice is also good for hiking anywhere across the island, as it is very easy to get lost on the many intersecting, unmarked trails. At the south-east end of Ao Bang Bao, around a headland that leads to Ao Salak Phet, is a beautiful and secluded beach, **Hat Wai Chek**.

On the east side of the island it's a one hour walk between Dan Mai and Than Mayom, two hours between Dan Mai and Sai Thong (or between Khlong Son and Sai Thong). Salak Kok to Salak Phet is straightforward and takes around three hours. The **estuary** at Ao Salak Kok's western end boasts one of the best mangrove systems in Thailand, though like other coastal wetlands it's threatened by increased shrimp farming.

A hike around the entire island can be done at a comfortable pace in a week to 10 days. Remember to carry plenty of water and watch out for snakes – a few poisonous varieties live on the island.

Diving & Snorkelling

Ko Chang and its vicinity is a new frontier compared to other marine locales in Thailand. With regard to climate and visibility, November to April is the best diving season. The better dive sites are found at islets and seamounts off the southern tip of the island, stretching between Ko Chang and Ko Kut. In this area **Hin Luuk Bat** and **Hin Laap** are both coral-encrusted seamounts with depths of around 18 to 20m. A few kilometres farther south, the northern end of **Ko Rang Yai** gets scenic at 10 to 25 m, while **Hin Phrai Nam** (between Ko Wai and Ko Rang) has coral and whitetip reef sharks to around 20m. A small islet near Ko Rang Yai's northern tip, **Ko Kra**, has good snorkelling in depths of 4 or 5m near the islet's south end. The islets around Ko Rang are favoured nesting grounds for sea turtles – this is one of your better opportunities to see them in Thailand.

South-west of Ao Salak Phet, reef-fringed **Ko Wai** features a good variety of colourful hard and soft corals at depths of 6 to 15m.

Near the mouth of Ao Salak Phet, at the extreme south-eastern tip of the island, lies

the wreck of a **Thai warship** at a depth of 15m. The ship was supposedly sunk by the French in 1941 during a dispute over whether these islands belonged to Thailand or to French-colonised Cambodia. According to Thai history there should be a second wreck nearby but divers have yet to report on it. This site should not be dived without a guide.

Dive Services Ko Chang Divers at Haad Sai Khao Bungalows at Hat Sai Khao specialises in PADI certification for novice divers. Dive trips typically include two dives with all guiding, transport and equipment for 1200B; snorkellers are welcome to join for 250B per day. Ko Chang Divers offers a free half hour, one-tank introduction at beachside, or a full PADI course for 6000B; instructors speak German, English, French and Thai. The only other full-time dive guiding/instruction centre on the island so far is the Dive Centre at Hat Kaibae, between Nangnuan Bungalows and Porn's.

You can also hire your own boats from Ko Chang's western beaches for around 800 to 1000B a day, but there's no guarantee the boat pilots will be able to locate the dive sites described above. They may know the islands but not necessarily the best places for coral, or the best way to moor the boats near the coral.

Other Activities

Some of the guesthouses at Hat Sai Khao rent kayaks and sailboards. Rooks Ko Chang Resort at Ao Khlong Phrao offers water sport equipment and instruction, eg water-skiing for 1500B per hour or you can rent a mask and snorkel for 100B per hour. Mountain bikes can be rented at several places on the island, including Muk Hut Restaurant at Hat Sai Khao and Palm Beach Resort at Hat Kaibae.

Several bungalow operations along Ko Chang's west coast beaches offer boat trips to nearby islands, eg 150B per person to Ko Yuak or Ko Man; 300B to Ko Rang, Ko Wai, Ko Khlam or Ko Mak; and 1000B to Ko Kut.

Places to Stay

Ko Chang – West Coast Many beach huts on the island have only been open about five years and standards vary quite a bit. Some are only open during the dry season (November to May), but this may change as the island becomes more popular year-round and boat service becomes more regular. During the rainy season, boats usually only go as far as Ao Sapparot ('Pineapple Bay'), Dan Mai and Than Mayom – the surf farther south along the west coast can be impassable during heavy rains.

Even during dry months, the trend now is for boats to drop off at Ao Sapparot so that visitors can continue on to the beaches by songthaew. When boats ply the west coast, remember that you can ask the boat pilots to drop you off at almost any bungalow operation on any beach, so if you know where you are going ask the pilot in Laem Ngop. It is also possible to get picked up from any bungalow on any beach – skiffs or long-tail boats take people to the boat if there is no pier. At Hat Sai Khao the boatmen have been known to charge 5B per person to relay passengers from the ferry to the beach.

As the island's better beaches are along the west coast, this is where most of the beach accommodation is. Most huts and bungalows have one double mattress on the floor or on a raised platform. If you are staying longer than a few days all places will discount their rates, even in peak season. Most of the island has limited electricity or no electricity at all; on the popular beaches most restaurants use generators between 6 pm and midnight, otherwise sites are lit by kerosene or gas lanterns. Only a few places have music and, blessedly, even fewer have videos.

At the northern tip of the island is the largest village, Khlong Son, which has a network of piers at the mouth of the khlong, a wat, a school, several noodle shops, a health clinic and one basic friendly bungalow operation on stilts, *Manee Guest House* near the piers for just 40 to 70B a night. Few people stay here any more since most passenger boats now moor at the Ao Sapparot pier rather than in Khlong Son. A

few long-timers like staying here for village life, however.

It's 5km from Khlong Son to Hat Sai Khao ('White Sand Beach'). At the lower end of the beach, well off the road and separated from other Hat Sai Khao bungalow developments by a couple of small rocky points, is the nicely landscaped *White Sand Beach Resort* where solid huts go for 100/150B for singles/doubles, and more up-market ones with bath cost 300 to 400B; roofs are tarped so that they don't leak in the rain.

Next south are a couple of less isolated spots beginning with the *Rock Sand*, which has a few rustic wooden huts on a rocky outcrop surrounded by beach on both sides for 100B per hut and nicer ones up to 500B. The similarly priced grass mat huts at *KC* are better but the recent addition of electric power probably means this one is about to rebuild as a more upscale resort. *Yaka Bungalows* is a small place with inflatable kayaks for hire.

Farther south is a string of cheapies with basic huts for 100 to 200B (only 40 to 100B in the off season), more solid ones from 300B. All are very similar in style and layout; if you get off the boat anywhere along this beach, you can walk from one to the other before deciding. This is one of the island's more 'social' beaches, where long-termers stoke their bongs with Cambodian herb while watching the sun set. Starting from the north you'll find *Tantawan* and *Bamboo*, which – like several other bungalow operations along this coast – organise trips to other islands. A newer place, *Ban Rung Rong* (☎ 597184), offers flashier huts for 120 to 200B and nicer ones with bath for 300B; techno parties are another drawcard or turn-off, depending on your disposition. They also offer money exchange (5% commission) and rent mountain bikes for 120B per day. Next is *Cookie* with basic huts for 100B, and motorbike rental for 60B per hour or 400B per day. Then there is *Mac* and *Nut Hut* with nicer bungalows for 300 to 450B, including bath.

Next comes the well-run *Haad Sai Khao* with simple thatched huts from 100B along the back row, 120B middle rows, 150B front row, and a couple of flash bungalows with private bath facing the front for 900B; telephone and mail service are available. When it's full Haad Sai Khao rents tents for 100B. *Apple* and *Sunsai* finish off this stretch with decent huts in the 150 to 200B range.

The German-owned *Plaloma Cliff Resort* is a bit south of Sunsai on the other side of a rocky headland, spread over a rocky cliff. Large tile-and-cement bungalows – shades of Ko Samui – cost 600B and 900B per night. On the cliff's highest point Plaloma has some very nice bamboo-and-thatch huts with private bath for 250B a night; the interspersed coconut palms and sea views are additional pluses.

About 4km south of Hat Sai Khao (9km from Khlong Son) is Ao Khlong Phrao ('Coconut Bay'). It stretches south of Laem Chaichet and encompasses the canal Khlong Phrao as well as its namesake village Ban Khlong Phrao (12km from Khlong Son). On the north side of the canal is *Chaichet Bungalows* starting at 80 to 200B for separate bungalows with private bath. The bungalows are strung out along Laem Chaichet, a gently curving cape, though there's no beach to speak of. Also on the north bank of Khlong Phrao, *Klong Plow Resort* has modern wooden bungalows in a semi-circle around a lagoon for 700B. Near Ban Chaichet south of Ao Khlong Phrao is *Coconut Beach Bungalows*, where typical thatched-roof-style bungalows cost 100B for singles/doubles or you can pay 400B for bamboo or concrete bungalows with bath. The bungalows are well kept and the pleasant beach has its own pier. Chaichet shares a pier with Coconut Beach Bungalows.

About a 10 minute walk farther south along the beach is the pricey *Rooks Ko Chang Resort* (☎ (01) 329-0434, Bangkok ☎ (2) 277-5256). Up-market bungalows here cost from 1766 to 2943B and include all the usual comforts with air-con and colour TV. The majority of the guests are Thai business-people on vacation, many on incentive travel packages.

It is possible to cross the river in a long-tail boat but you need to call for one on the southern bank. If you are staying at the PSS huts the service is only 5B but if you're staying anywhere else it's 10B. The *PSS Bungalow* cost 120B. About a 10 minute walk farther south near Wat Ban Khlong Phrao is *KP Bungalows*, where basic thatched huts cost 60/100B, larger and nicer ones with bath cost 300B. The food here is good, but the restaurant closes at 8 pm and the lights are out by 9 pm. The service could be a little friendlier. It is closed during the rainy season.

About 700m past the turn-off for Khlong Pliu Falls, off the main road in Ban Khlong Phrao, is the secluded *Hobby Hut* (☎ (01) 213-7668). A favourite with Thais associated with the music business, Hobby Hut has only four simple but large wooden cottages that rent for 1500B per month (shorter rentals may be possible if there's a vacancy). It's 300m to the nearest beach; a small inland lagoon offers canoeing. There's live music Wednesday to Friday evenings.

Around another headland to the south are two beach areas separated by a canal – Hat Khlong Makok and Hat Kaibae (15km south of Khlong Son). These beaches tend to disappear during high tide but they're OK – lots of coconut palms. *Erawan* and *Magic* have bungalows for 80B but they're none too clean, while the better bungalows with bath cost from 150 to 300B. Magic has a pier, telephone service and scuba diving. The owner has a boat monopoly from Laem Ngop so is able to funnel many passengers directly to this beach. Magic's best feature is its restaurant built over the bay. Next door is *Good Luck (Chokdee)*, with cleaner, nicer thatched huts for 50B or concrete bungalows for 300B, set amid coconut palms – a drawback is that it has no beach to speak of.

Next south on Hat Kaibae proper (15km south of Khlong Son) is an area that has become quite developed, with a new pier and bungalows with generator-powered electricity (yes, this means more videos of Arnold firing large weapons or Van Damme kicking snot from people's faces). Starting in the north, the first place you come to is the German-run *Palm Beach Resort*, where basic huts start at 50B and go up to 350B for large bungalows. The food here is reportedly good; mountain bikes rent for 150B per day.

Coral Resort is set amid a bumper crop of coconut palms and costs 50B for basic huts or 450B for larger bungalows with private bath. They also have an international telephone service. A khlong separates the similar *Nang Nual Resort*; this area is a bit trashed out in places and the adjacent shrimp farm is a definite detraction.

Kaibae Hut, on the south side of the khlong, has a nicely laid out restaurant and fair bungalows, plus a bit of a beach even at high tide; rates are the usual 80B for basic huts and 200 to 250B for nicer bungalows with bath. It's quiet, too, and has a security gate that's locked at night.

There is more of a beach down towards the southern end of Hat Kaibae. *Porn's* has basic 80B huts while the large *Seaview Resort* has similar huts for 100B and nice large bungalows from 800B. Seaview Resort, which sits just opposite Ko Man Nai, charters boats from 150 to 5000B depending on the destination and trip length. A boat charter to Laem Ngop costs 3000B. The last place on the beach is the secluded and friendly *Siam Bay Resort* with huts for 80 to 100B and bungalows with private bath from 200B, more expensive fancier huts up to 1000B.

Ko Chang – South Coast None of the following south coast places is typically open during the rainy season, from May to November, when regular transport is difficult. Ao Bang Bao has the *Nice Beach Bang Bao* with average bungalows with attached bath for 250 to 300B, and the cheaper *Bang Bao Blue Wave* and *Bang Bao Lagoon* for 80 to 300B. You may also be able to rent rooms cheaply in the village (Ban Bang Bao). At the moment you can walk between Bang Bao and Hat Kaibae in about three hours; eventually a road will connect the two. During the rainy season the only way here is on foot.

The next bay along the coast, Ao Salak Phet, features the on-again, off-again *Ban Salakpetch Bungalow* with typical thatched

huts for 40 to 60B. A couple of as yet unnamed bungalow places rent huts for 50 to 100B a night near the fishing villages of Ruang Tan and Ban Salak Phet. As at Ao Bang Bao, you may be able to rent a room or house in Ban Salak Phet. Rumours that bungalows are under construction farther southeast along the bay at Ban Jekbae are yet to bear fruit.

The very secluded *Long Beach Bungalows*, near the end of the long cape to the south-east of Ao Salak Phet, has well-made huts with electricity for 100/120B a night. They are closed between July and December. Farther on, right at the tip of the cape, is the friendly *Tantawan House* on a rocky outcrop with only seven huts costing 70/100B. The beach is only a two minute swim away. To get here take a boat from Ao Salak Phet for 30B.

A dirt road leads from Ao Sapparot all the way to Ban Salak Phet; songthaews meet the Ao Sapparot boats. The village itself is very spread out; the main road terminates at Wat Salak Phet, from where there are smaller tracks along the southern coast. Power lines also terminate in Ban Salak Phet.

Ko Chang – East Coast There are a couple of mediocre places to stay near the nicely landscaped national park headquarters at Than Mayom. Privately managed, unnamed *bungalows* opposite the park offices cost 200B; they're not in very good condition and hardly anyone ever seems to stay here. A couple of kilometres north, *Thanmayom Resort* rents A-frame huts for 100B a night; there is a pier but no beach to speak of, and since the huts are on the other side of a dusty road from the sea, it's not very inviting. If you have camping gear, it might be better to hike up and camp near Than Mayom Falls.

The visitor centre contains faded photo displays with English labels and useful info. At the end of a small pier is a very casual restaurant with rice and noodle dishes.

Ko Kut At Hat Tapho on the west coast, the aptly named *First* has expensive bungalows for up to 1000B, plus a few basic huts for

100B, with outside bath. If this one's closed when you arrive, try village homes in nearby Ban Hin Dam.

Ko Mak On the west bay, amid a coconut and rubber plantation, is the Israeli-managed *Lazydays Resort* (Bangkok ☎ (2) 281-3412), where huts with verandas cost 100B a night. *Ao Kok Resort* (☎ 425263) offers comfortable bungalows with fan and private bath for 500B a night in the low season, 700B high season. *TK Huts*, a new place, reportedly has nice bungalows for 300B. Diving equipment and instruction are available from Ao Kok Resort. Boat fare from Laem Ngop is 150B.

Ko Kradat The *Ko Kradat* has air-con bungalows for 600B. Mr Chumpon in Bangkok (☎ (2) 311-3668) can arrange accommodation at Ko Kradat and transport to the island in advance.

Ko Kham *Ko Kham Resort*, run by a friendly ex-cop, offers bamboo bungalows for 80 to 120B. More upscale huts are available from 250B. A resort-sponsored boat leaves the main Laem Ngop pier daily at 1 pm, November to April only.

Places to Eat

Menus at all the bungalows on Ko Chang are pretty similar, with highest marks going to Kaibae Hut (Hat Kaibae), Sunsai Bungalows (Hat Sai Khao) and Tantawan (Hat Sai Khao).

Several small eateries have opened up along the east side of the main road in Hat Sai Khao. *AM/PM Restaurant*, an upstairs place where you sit on cushions, is good for Thai lunches and dinner and western breakfasts, while the *Muk Hut* next door does pizza and other western dishes. The latter also does moneychanging and mountain bike rental.

Sandalwood, off the road a bit further south opposite Sunsai Bungalows, is a larger indoor-outdoor place with Thai food, seafood barbecues and occasional live music. On opening night in 1996 Phii Surachai, lead composer/singer of the seminal Thai folk-rock band Caravan, performed here. Nearby,

Aloha Bakery is popular for items like banana bread and chocolate chip cookies.

The food is also quite good at *KP* on Ao Khlong Phrao and at the *Beach Restaurant* at Hat Kaibae.

Rim Saphan is a decent seafood restaurant on the Laem Ngop pier.

Getting There & Away

Ko Chang Take a songthaew (10B, 25 minutes) from Trat to Laem Ngop on the coast, then a ferry to Ko Chang. In Laem Ngop there are now two piers servicing Ko Chang, the main one at the end of the road from Trat, and a newer one called Ko Chang Centrepoint, which is operated by Rooks Ko Chang Resort.

At the first pier you have a choice of several ferries, depending on the destination and time of day. Only Ao Sapparot on Ko Chang is able to dock boats year-round; even in the dry season this is where most people disembark. There are several kinds of departures available; in many cases the same boat makes two or three stops. All times listed below are approximate and depend on weather, number of passengers and any number of other factors. You should check fares in advance – sometimes the boat crews overcharge farangs. During the wet season the boat service is erratic and most boats will only go to Ao Sapparot, where it will be necessary to go to the beaches by pickups or motorbike. Boat fares to Ao Sapparot usually include taxi fare on to one of the beaches, although you can insist on paying only the boat fare if you have your own transport waiting on the island. Otherwise it's simpler just to pay the whole thing; it's 70B with taxi, 40B without.

From the gleaming Ko Chang Centrepoint pier, 4km north-west of Ban Laem Ngop, there's so far only one boat per day at 7 am for 80B. The boat drops passengers off at Ao Sapparot and the fare includes a songthaew ride to one of the beaches. The problem with using the Centrepoint pier is that there's no accommodation or restaurants nearby, so the 7 am departure means an even earlier wakeup in Ban Laem Ngop or Trat.

If you get enough people together, the

Foremost Guest House in Trat can arrange boat trips from the canal in town all the way to Ko Chang (destination of choice, except in high swells when the west coast may be unnavigable) for 100B per person.

There are direct mini-vans from Khao San Rd in Bangkok to Laem Ngop for 250B per person. Although it's no longer the case that the mini-vans necessarily miss the last boat to Ko Chang, it's better to take a regular bus, spend the night in Trat or Laem Ngop and take your time choosing a boat the next day. Or start out earlier in the day by government tour bus to Trat from Bangkok's Eastern bus terminal, then in Trat catch a songthaew to Laem Ngop in time for the afternoon boats. You can make the last boat to Ko Chang at 3 pm if you catch the 140B air-con bus to Trat at 8.30 am from Bangkok's Eastern bus terminal. This will arrive in Trat around 1.30 pm, leaving plenty of time to get a songthaew to Laem Ngop in time for the boat.

Ko Kut Two or three fishing boats a week go to Ko Kut from the pier of Tha Chaloemphon on the Trat River towards the east side of Trat. They'll take passengers for 80B per person. Similar boats leave slightly less frequently (six to eight times a month) from Ban Nam Chiaw, a village about halfway between Trat and Laem Ngop. Departure frequency and times from either pier depend on the weather and the fishing season – it's best to enquire ahead of time. The boats take around six hours to reach Ko Kut.

Coconut boats go to Ko Kut once or twice a month from a pier next to the slaughterhouse in town – same fare and trip duration as the fishing boats.

If you want to charter a boat to Ko Kut, the best place to do so is from Ban Ta Neuk, near Km 68 south-east of Trat, about 6km before Khlong Yai off Hwy 318. A long-tail boat, capable of carrying up to 10 people, can be chartered here for 1000B. Travel time is about one hour. During the rainy season these boats may suspend service.

Ko Mak During the November to May dry season, boats to Ko Mak leave daily from the

Laem Ngop pier at 3 pm (7 to 7.30 am in the reverse direction); the fare is 150B per person and the trip takes around three to 3½ hours. During the rainy season the departure schedule is cut back to every other day – except in high surf when boats may be cancelled altogether for several days.

Coconut boats also go to Ko Mak from the pier near the slaughterhouse in Trat twice a month. The trip takes five hours and costs around 100B per person.

Other Islands Daily boats to Ko Kham depart from Laem Ngop around 3 pm (arriving at 6 pm) for 150B. A boat to Ko Wai from Laem Ngop leaves at 3 pm and arrives at 4.30 pm, costing 70B. Both boats return the next day at around 7.30 am.

Getting Around

To get from one part of Ko Chang to another you have a choice of motorbike taxi, Japanese pickup, jeep, boat and walking (see the earlier Walking on Ko Chang section).

Songthaew & Motorcycle Taxi Songthaews meeting the boats at Ao Sapparot charge about 30B per person to any beach along the west coast.

The motorcycle taxi mafia on the island charge 40B from Ao Sapparot to Hat Sai Khao, then from Sai Khao south it's 40B to Laem Chaichet and Khlong Phrao (or 70B from Ao Sapparot) and 60B to Hat Kaibae (100B from Khlong Son). The main motorcycle taxi stand is opposite the north end of Hat Sai Khao; you can also rent one of their motorcycles to drive yourself for 400B a day. Other bungalow operations in Khlong Son and Hat Sai Khao also charge 400 to 600B per day for motorbike hire; elsewhere on the island rental bikes are scarce. The owners claim they have to charge these rates because the island roads are so hard on the bikes.

Jeep Between Ao Salak Kok and Ao Salak Phet there's a daily jeep service that costs 10B per person. The jeep leaves Ao Salak Kok around 4.30 pm, returning from Ao Salak Phet the following day at 6 am.

Boat The regular boat to Ao Phrao and Hat Kaibae usually stops first at Hat Sai Khao and Ao Phrao; you can catch a ride from one area to the other along the west coast for 30B. Boat rides up Khlong Phrao to the falls cost 50B per person and can be arranged through most bungalows.

On the east coast, there is a daily boat between Than Mayom and Ao Salak Kok for 20B per person. On the southern end, you can charter a boat between Salak Phet and Long Beach Bungalows for around 150B.

Charter trips to nearby islands average 500B for a half-day, 800 to 1000B all day. Make sure that the charter includes all user 'fees' for the islands – sometimes the boatmen demand 200B on top of the charter fee for using the beach.

AROUND TRAT PROVINCE
Trat Beaches
The sliver of Trat Province that extends south-eastward along the Cambodia border is fringed by several Gulf of Thailand beaches. Hat Sai Ngoen ('Silver Sand Beach'), lies just north of Km 41 off Hwy 3; a billboard says a resort will be constructed here but so far there's no sign of development. Nearby at Km 42 is **Hat Sai Kaew** ('Crystal Sand Beach') and at Km 48 **Hat Thap Thim** ('Sapphire Beach'); neither quite lives up to its fanciful name, though they're OK places to walk along the water's edge or picnic in the shade of casuarina and eucalyptus trees.

The most promising beach is **Hat Ban Cheun**, a very long stretch of clean sand near Km 63. The partially paved, 6km road (currently being upgraded) that leads to the beach passes the leftover foundation pillars from a defunct Cambodian refugee camp. There are the usual casuarina and eucalyptus trees, a small restaurant and four unattractive huts (200B) set on swampy land behind the beach. Camping on the beach would be a far better choice; you could ask the restaurant owners to look after your valuables for you.

Khlong Yai
Khlong Yai consists of a cluster of older wooden buildings west of the highway, sur-

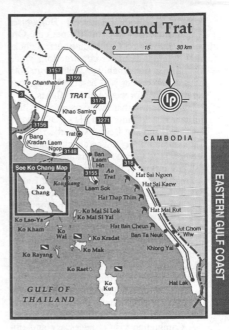

rounded by modern structures on both sides of the highway. There's a large market in the centre of town, as well as the moderately priced Suksamlan Hotel and two banks with foreign exchange services. Just south of town is a large shrimp farm.

The *Suksamlan Hotel*, an old-fashioned Thai-Chinese-style place on a street between the market and the highway, offers rooms with fan from 120B, or 250B with air-con. Out of town a bit off Hwy 3, *Bang In Villa* has nicer rooms but with less character starting at 150B.

See the Trat Getting There & Away section for information on public transport to Khlong Yai and Hat Lek.

Hat Lek to Cambodia
The small Thai border outpost of Hat Lek is the southernmost point on the Trat mainland. Untaxed goods ply between Cambodia and Thailand here; at the small market just before the border crossing itself, next to the pier for

boats to Cambodia, American Budweiser beer is often available for 20B per can. Opposite Hat Lek on Cambodian turf, a cockfighting arena is under construction; when it's finished, presumably residents from both sides of the border will be able to convene here visa-free for weekend cockfights.

Until recently there were as many as five military checkpoints along Hwy 3 between Trat town and Hat Lek to slow the flood of Cambodian refugees. The checkpoints have been reduced to two, but this areas still sees a steady inflow of illegal immigrants.

Small boats are available from Hat Lek to Pak Khlong on the island of Ko Kong – on the Cambodian side of the border – for 100B per person or 800B charter. If you plan to continue further, you can take a passenger ferry from Pak Khlong to Sao Thong for 10B, then change to a three hour speedboat ride (500B per boat) to Sihanoukville. From Sihanoukville it's a three hour, 40B share taxi ride to Phnom Penh. You may also be able to catch a once-daily bus all the way to Phnom Penh.

A Cambodian visa is necessary and obtainable in Bangkok, not at the border. As far as the Thai authorities are concerned this is semi-illegal and while in Cambodia, you are technically in Thailand! You need to do the trip with a valid Thai visa on which you can return to Thailand. Some expats in the Trat/Ko Chang area use the Trat-Cambodia route for Thai visa renewals. The Thai government has proposed upgrading Hat Lek to a formal international border crossing: if this happens foreigners will be able to use this border legally.

If this option is not available or you just feel like getting a taste of Cambodian border life, it's easy to visit Ko Kong, an island on the Cambodian side of the border, by boat as described above. Though not a particularly exciting destination in itself, Ko Kong is an important relay point for goods imported from Singapore into Cambodia, which is now Singapore's largest trade entrepôt in Indochina. Contact the Foremost or Windy guesthouses in Trat for the latest information about entering the country.

Warning While security conditions have improved in the border area, this doesn't mean it's entirely safe. Avoid solo treks to deserted beaches or other areas. If you're planning on crossing into Cambodia and continuing overland to Phnom Penh, bear in mind that you'll be going through a region that still sees armed battles between the government and the weakening (but still deadly) Khmer Rouge insurgents. Several foreigners travelling this route a few years ago were kidnapped and later murdered by Khmer Rouge forces, and theft and incidents of violence have been reported since.

Prime Minister Hun Sen's 1997 coup d'état also destabilised the country to a significant degree. If you choose to travel to Cambodia, do so with caution and research the current situation in advance.

North-Western Gulf Coast (Phetburi to Chumphon)

North-Western Gulf Coast Highlights

- Phetburi temples – spanning several centuries, this complex of wats is the perfect cultural stopover
- Khao Luang Caves – Phetburi's cave sanctuary is filled with old Buddha images, many of them put there by King Rama IV
- Cha-am – its long, casuarina tree-lined beach is virtually deserted during the week but lively during the weekends and holidays
- Khao Sam Roi Yot National Park – Fascinating wildlife and birdlife to seek out, stunning views from the top of Khao Krachom, beaches flanked by limestone hills and caves to explore

Heading south from Bangkok, the Gulf of Thailand's western coast undulates its way along the edges of four provinces (Samut Sakhon, Samut Songkhram, Phetburi and Prachuap Khiri Khan) in a south-westerly direction until it makes an abrupt turn to the north-east at the southern end of Chumphon Province. Just north of this geographically significant point lies the Isthmus of Kra, the shortest crossing between the gulf and Andaman coastlines, and the official beginning of the Thai-Malay peninsula.

This coastal section has seen little exploration by foreign tourists. There isn't much in the way of beaches until you pass south of Phetburi to the low-key seaside resorts of Cha-am, Hua Hin and Chumphon. Away from these small but slowly growing areas, most of the countryside is agricultural and rural; pineapple-growing and fishing are the mainstays of the local population. In terms of everyday costs for food, lodging and public transport, this is one of Thailand's least expensive seacoasts to visit. But in many ways this stretch requires more initiative, since the most interesting shorelines aren't necessarily signposted. Nor do any guided tours or easy-to-book Bangkok mini-vans reach the majority of them.

PHETBURI

• ☎ (32) • pop 35,000

Situated 160km south of Bangkok, Phetburi (or Phetchaburi, also known as Meuang Phet) is worth a visit for its many old temples spanning several centuries; it's a nice cultural stopover on the way to beaches at Cha-am or Hua Hin a bit farther south. Six or seven temples can be seen while taking a circular walk of two or three hours through the city: Wat Yai Suwannaram, Wat Trailok, Wat Kamphaeng Laeng, Wat Phra Suang, Wat Ko Kaew Sutharam and Wat Mahathat. These temples have made very few concessions to the 20th century and thus provide a glimpse of the traditional Siamese urban wat.

Also noteworthy is Khao Wang, just west of the city, which has the remains of a King Mongkut palace and several wats, plus a good aerial view of the city. The underground Buddhist shrine at the Khao Luang Caves is also worth seeing.

257

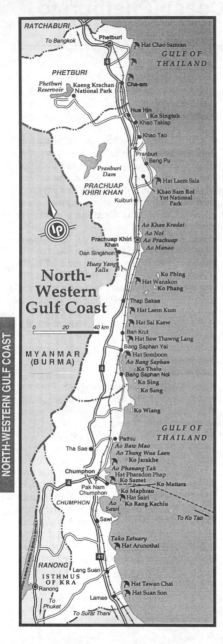

RATCHABURI
To Bangkok
Phetburi
Hat Chao Samran
GULF OF
THAILAND
PHETBURI
Phetburi
Reservoir
Kaeng Krachan
National Park
Cha-am
Hua Hin
Ko Singtoh
Khao Takiap
Khao Tao
Pranburi
Bang Pu
Pranburi
Dam
Hat Laem Sala
PRACHUAP
KHIRI KHAN
Khao Sam Roi
Yot National
Park
Kuiburi
Ao Khan Kradai
Ao Noi
Prachuap Khiri   Ao Prachuap
Khan
Ao Manao
Dan Singkhon
Huay Yang
Falls
North-
Western
Gulf Coast
Ko Phing
Hat Wanakon
Ko Phang
0   20   40 km
Thap Sakae
Hat Laem Kum
Hat Sai Kaew
Ban Krut
Hat Baw Thawng Lang
Bang Saphan Yai
MYANMAR
(BURMA)
Hat Somboon
Ao Bang Saphan
Ko Thalu
Bang Saphan Noi
Ko Sing
Ko Sang
Ko Wiang
GULF OF
THAILAND
Pathiu
Ao Baw Mao
Tha Sae
Ao Thung Wua Laen
Ko Jarakhe
Chumphon
Hat Pharadon Phap
Ko Samet
Pak Nam
Chumphon
Ko Maphrao
Ko Mattara
Hat Sairi
CHUMPHON
Ao
Sawi
Ko Rang Kachiu
Sawi
To Ko Tao
Tako Estuary
Hat Arunothai
RANONG
Lang Suan
ISTHMUS
OF KRA
Ranong
To
Phuket
Lamae
Hat Tawan Chai
Hat Suan Son
To Surat Thani

NORTH-WESTERN GULF COAST

Orientation

If you arrive at the train station, follow the road south-east of the tracks until you come to Ratchadamnoen Rd, then turn right. Follow Ratchadamnoen Rd south to the second major intersection and turn left towards central Phetburi to begin the walk. Or take a samlor from the train station to Chomrut Bridge (Saphaan Chomrut), for 10B. If you've come by bus, you'll be getting off very near Khao Wang, and will have to take a samlor into the centre of town.

Information

Money The Siam Commercial Bank has an exchange office at 2 Damnoen Kasem Rd, just south of the post office. Several other banks in the vicinity have foreign exchange and ATMs.

Post & Communications The post office is on the corner of Ratwithi and Damnoen Kasem Rds. An international telephone office, upstairs in the same building, is open daily from 7 am to 10 pm.

Khao Wang & Phra Nakhon Khiri Historical Park

Just west of the city, a 10B samlor ride from the bus station, is Khao Wang. Cobblestone paths lead up and around the hill, which is studded with wats and various components of King Mongkut's palace on Phra Nakhon Khiri (Holy City Hill). The views are great, especially at sunset. The walk up looks easy but is fairly strenuous. Fat monkeys loll about in the trees and on the walls along the main paths. In 1988 Phra Nakhon Khiri was declared a national historical park, so there is now an entry fee of 20B. A tram has been installed to save you walking up to the peak (15B per person one way). The park is open Monday to Friday from 8 am to 5.30 pm and on weekends till 6 pm.

Khao Luang Caves

Five kilometres north of Phetburi is the cave sanctuary of Khao Luang (Great Hill). Concrete steps lead down into an anteroom, then into the main cavern, which is filled with old

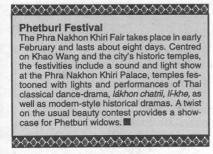

Phetburi Festival
The Phra Nakhon Khiri Fair takes place in early February and lasts about eight days. Centred on Khao Wang and the city's historic temples, the festivities include a sound and light show at the Phra Nakhon Khiri Palace, temples festooned with lights and performances of Thai classical dance-drama, *lákhon chatrii*, *lí-khe*, as well as modern-style historical dramas. A twist on the usual beauty contest provides a showcase for Phetburi widows. ■

Buddha images, many of them put in place by King Mongkut (Rama IV). Two holes in the chamber ceiling spray sunlight on the images, which are a favourite subject for photographers. To the rear of the main cavern is an entrance to a third, smaller chamber. On the right of the entrance is Wat Bunthawi, with a *sala* (open-sided shelter) designed by the abbot and a bòt with impressively carved wooden door panels.

Admission to the caves is free (though donations are accepted). A samlor from the city centre to Khao Luang costs 50B, a motorcycle taxi 25 to 30B.

Places to Stay
To the east of Chomrut Bridge, on the right bank of the Phetburi River, is the *Chom Klao Hotel* (☎ 425398), an ordinary, fairly clean Chinese hotel with friendly staff. It costs 100B for a room with fan and shared bath, or 130B with private bath.

The *Nam Chai Hotel* (no English sign) is a block farther east from Chomrut Bridge and the Chom Klao Hotel, and has rooms for 100B with shared bath, 140/150B with attached bath; but it is not as good value as the Chom Klao. Another cheapie is the *Ratanaphakdi Hotel* on Chise-In Rd, where a clean room with private bath costs 200B for a single/double.

Behind the Nam Chai is the *Phetburi Hotel* (☎ 425315), a divey sort of place, with grotty and overpriced rooms for 150B with fan and bath.

The *Khao Wang Hotel* (☎ 425167), opposite Khao Wang (the Hill Palace), has gone downhill a bit, but rooms are still fairly clean, and there are nice views of the city from the roof. Rooms with fan and bath cost 200/300B for one/two beds. Air-con rooms are 300/550B. Most rooms have TV.

The best hotel in town is the friendly and clean *Phetkasem Hotel* (☎ 425581), 86/1 Phetkasem Rd, on the highway north to Bangkok on the edge of town. Rooms range from 180 to 220B with fan and bath, 280 to 320B with air-con and 350 to 450B with hot water.

Places to Eat
There are several good restaurants in the Khao Wang area, with a range of standard Thai and Chinese dishes. A variety of cheap eats is available at the *night market* at the southern end of Surinleuchai Rd, under the digital clock tower.

Other good eating places can be found in the town centre along the main street towards the clock tower. Across from Wat Mahathat, *Lamiet* sells really good khanŏm mâw kaeng (egg custard) and făwy thawng (sweet shredded egg yolk) – which it ships to Bangkok. This shop also has a branch near Khao Wang, where there's a whole group of egg custard places.

Near Wat Yai Suwannaram on Phongsuriya Rd, the *Lotuacharaporn Food Center* is managed by a family who grow their own vegetables and breed their own animals without the use of chemicals. The menu covers a wide variety of Thai and Chinese dishes, none of them prepared with MSG.

The *Rabiang Rim Nam*, on the south side of Chise-In Rd near Chomrut Bridge and the river, features a Thai and English menu of over 100 items, including seafood and 30 kinds of yam; most non-seafood dishes cost around 25 to 50B, while seafood and some soups cost 70B or more.

Getting There & Away
Bus From Bangkok, buses leave regularly from the Southern bus terminal in Thonburi and cost 36B (ordinary) on the new road, 31B (ordinary) on the old road (via Ratchaburi and

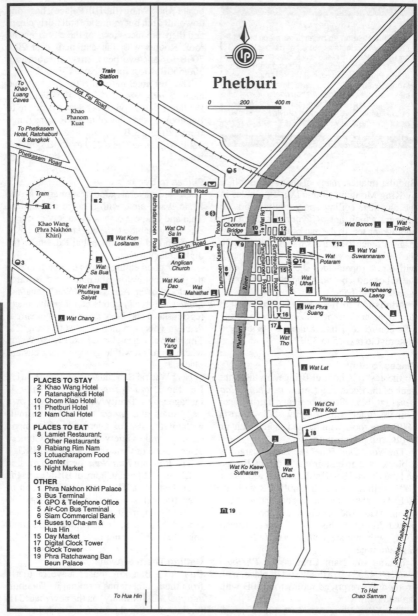

Phetburi

0   200   400 m

PLACES TO STAY
2 Khao Wang Hotel
7 Ratanaphakdi Hotel
10 Chom Klao Hotel
11 Phetburi Hotel
12 Nam Chai Hotel

PLACES TO EAT
8 Lamiet Restaurant;
   Other Restaurants
9 Rabiang Rim Nam
13 Lotuacharaporn Food
   Center
16 Night Market

OTHER
1 Phra Nakhon Khiri Palace
3 Bus Terminal
4 GPO & Telephone Office
5 Air-Con Bus Terminal
6 Siam Commercial Bank
14 Buses to Cha-am &
   Hua Hin
15 Day Market
17 Digital Clock Tower
18 Clock Tower
19 Phra Ratchawang Ban
   Beun Palace

Walking Tour – Phetburi Temples

Wat Yai Suwannaram
After you've crossed the Phetburi River by Chomrut Bridge (the second-northernmost bridge in Phetburi) heading east, and passed the Nam Chai Hotel on the left, walk about 300m farther until you see a big temple on the right. This is Wat Yai, built in the 17th century and renovated during the reign of King Chulalongkorn (1868-1910). The main *bòt* is surrounded by a cloister filled with sober Buddha images. The murals inside the bòt date to the 1730s and are in good condition. Next to the bòt, in the middle of a pond to keep insects at bay, is a beautifully designed old *haw trai*, or tripitaka library.

Wat Borom & Wat Trailok
These two wats are next to each other on the opposite side of the road from Wat Yai, a little to the east. They are distinctive for their monastic halls and long, graceful, wooden 'dormitories' on stilts. Turn right onto the road heading south from Wat Trailok and follow it down past a bamboo fence on the right to the entrance for Wat Kamphaeng Laeng.

Wat Kamphaeng Laeng
This is a very old (13th century) Khmer site with five *prangs* (towers) and part of the original wall still standing. The prang in front contains a Buddha footprint. Of the other four, two contain images dedicated to famous *lŭang phâw* (venerable elderly monks), one is in ruins (but is being restored) and the last has recently been uncovered from a mound of dirt. The Khmers built these as Hindu monuments, so the Buddhist symbols are late additions.

Wat Phra Suang & Wat Lat
Follow the road beside Wat Kamphaeng Laeng, heading west back towards the river until you pass Wat Phra Suang on the left, undistinguished except for one very nice Ayuthaya-style *prasat*. Turn left immediately after this wat, heading south again until you come to the clock tower at the southern edge of town. You'll have passed Wat Lat on the left side of the street along the way, but it's not worthy of breaking your momentum; this is a long walk.

Wat Ko Kaew Sutharam
Turn right at the clock tower and look for signs leading to the Ayuthaya-period Wat Ko. Two different sois on the left lead to the wat, which is behind the shops along the curving street. The bòt features early 18th century murals that are among the best conceived in Thailand. One mural panel features what appears to be a Jesuit priest wearing the robes of a Buddhist monk, while another shows other foreigners undergoing Buddhist conversions. There is also a large wooden monastic hall on stilts similar to the ones at Wat Borom and Wat Trailok but in much better condition.

Wat Mahathat
Follow the street in front of Wat Ko north (back towards central Phetburi) and walk over the first bridge you come to on the left, which leads to Wat Mahathat. Alternatively, you can cross the river at Wat Ko, near the clock tower, and take the street on the other side of the river around to Wat Mahathat. The large white prang of this wat can be seen from a distance – a typical late-Ayuthaya, early-Ratanakosin adaptation of the Khmer prangs of Lopburi and Phimai. This is obviously an important temple in Phetburi, judging by all the activity here. ■

Nakhon Pathom) or 65B air-con. The bus takes about 2½ hours.

Buses to Phetburi from Cha-am and Hua Hin cost 15 and 20B and take 60 and 90 minutes respectively. Other ordinary bus fares are: Ratchaburi, 15B (45 minutes); Nakhon Pathom, 25B (two hours); Prachuap Khiri Khan, 40B (three hours); and Phuket, 180B

(12 hours). The main bus terminal in Phetburi is just south-west of Khao Wang.

Train Trains leave Bangkok's Hualamphong station at 1.30 pm (rapid), 1.40 pm (ordinary 3rd class), 2.25 pm (special express), 3.15 pm (special express), 3.50 pm (rapid), 6.30 pm (rapid), 7.20 pm (express), 7.45 pm (rapid)

and 9.55 pm (special express). All of these trains have 1st and 2nd class seats (but no 3rd) and take about 3½ hours to reach Phetburi. Fares are 78B and 153B, not including rapid or express surcharges. The bus is cheaper and faster.

There is no longer an ordinary train between Hualamphong and Phetburi, but there are still two ordinary 3rd class trains daily from Thonburi's Bangkok Noi station at 7.20 am and 7.15 pm; the 3rd class fare is 34B.

Getting Around

Samlors go anywhere in the town centre for 10B; you can charter one for the whole day for 100B. Share mini-songthaews cost 5B around town, including to and from the train station.

CHA-AM

• ☎ (32) • pop 22,000

A tiny town 178km from Bangkok, 38km from Phetburi and 25km from Hua Hin, Cha-am is known for its long, casuarina-lined beach, good seafood and, on weekends and school holidays, its party atmosphere – sort of a Palm Beach or Fort Lauderdale for Thai students. During the week the beach is virtually deserted.

Like Ko Samet in the eastern gulf, Cha-am tends to stay relatively dry during the southwest monsoon compared with almost any other beach destination in Thailand. It receives virtually no rain during the northeast monsoon and is a particularly popular retreat for Bangkokians during the hot, dry months of March, April and May.

Beach umbrellas and sling chairs are available for hire. The emergence of jet-skis is a definite minus but they are not that common yet; if the local tourism promoters want to lure visitors away from fast-developing Hua Hin, the first thing they should do is get rid of the jet-skis. There are public bathhouses where you can bathe in fresh water for 5 to 7B.

Near the beach there's not much of a town to speak of – the old centre is on the opposite side of Phetkasem Hwy, where you'll find the post office, market, train station and

government offices. Inland from the beach (follow the signs) at **Wat Neranchararama** is a fat, white, six-armed Buddha statue; the six hands cover the nine bodily orifices in a symbolic gesture denying the senses.

Information

Tourist Office A TAT office (☎ 471502) has been established on Phetkasem Hwy just 500m south of town. The staff are very helpful; they distribute information on Cha-am, Phetburi and Hua Hin. The office is open daily from 6 am to 8 pm.

Money Several banks maintain foreign exchange booths along the beach strip, typically open 10 am to 8 pm. In the town centre, west of Route 4, are a number of banks with foreign exchange services and ATMs.

Places to Stay – bottom end & middle

Cha-am beach has three basic types of accommodation: charming, old-style, spacious wooden beach bungalows on stilts, set back from the road; tacky apartment-style hotels built from cheap materials with faulty plumbing, right on the beach road; and more expensive 'condotel' developments. New places are going up all the time at the northern and southern ends of town. Expect a 20% to 50% discount on posted rates weekdays, except during Chinese New Year (February or March) and Thai New Year (mid-April).

Narathip Rd is the main road leading to the beach area from the highway; if you turn right you'll find the places listed under South below, turn left and you'll see those listed under North.

South Near the air-conditioned bus terminal, a couple of *guesthouses* which change name from time to time can be found in a row of modern shophouses similar to the scourge of Pattaya, Hua Hin and Phuket's Patong beach – they all look the same. Rooms here run from 200B with fan and shared bath to 500B with air-con.

South of the air-con bus terminal, the *Anantachai Guest House* (☎ 433396) has nice rooms with a beach view, air-con, TV, shower

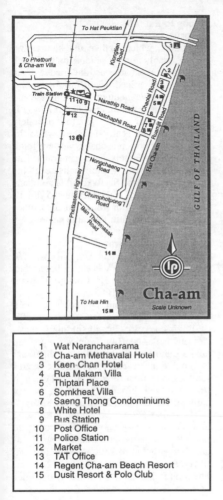

1	Wat Neranchararama
2	Cha-am Methavalai Hotel
3	Kaen-Chan Hotel
4	Rua Makam Villa
5	Thiptari Place
6	Somkheat Villa
7	Saeng Thong Condominiums
8	White Hotel
9	Bus Station
10	Post Office
11	Police Station
12	Market
13	TAT Office
14	Regent Cha-am Beach Resort
15	Dusit Resort & Polo Club

the early Cha-am-style wooden cottages and a newer, equally tasteful section. A room in a hotel-style section with bath is 300B with fan, 400B air-con. Larger two-bedroom cottages with bath and sitting area are 1000B, and it's 2000B for a three-bedroom, two-bath place. The *Nirandorn Resort* (☎ 471893) has similar cottages for 350B with fan, 500 to 700B with air-con.

Saeng Thong Condominiums (☎ 471466) costs 800 to 2000B per night, less in the rainy season. The *White Hotel* (☎ 471118), an air-con apartment-style place, costs 300 to 400B for a fan room with private bath, 500 to 600B with air-con, 700B for larger rooms with carpet, tub and TV.

North Moving north from the main intersecting road from the highway, *JJ Hotel* and *Somkheat Villa* (☎ 471229; fax 471229) are adjacent apartment-style hotels with rooms in the 300 to 600B and 500 to 800B range respectively.

Thiptari Place (☎/fax 471879) is fairly reasonable, with air-con rooms from 500 to 800B. Farther up, *Rua Makam Villa* (☎ 471-073) has old-style wooden cottages, spacious and off the road, for 400/700B single/double with fan, 600/1200B air-con. *Happy Home* has older-style wooden cottages from 250B with fan, and from 500B with air-con.

The *Kaen-Chan Hotel* (☎ 471314) has a variety of accommodation – bungalows are 200 to 250B with fan, 300 to 350B with air-con; air-con rooms in the hotel are 700 to 900B. There is a pool on the grounds.

The next cheapest places are the *Jitravee Resort* (☎ 471382) and the *Cha-am Villa* (☎ 471010/241), which will let you have rooms for 200B mid-week (300B on weekends); air-con rooms cost 400 to 500B. Better value yet is the new *Prathonchok House* (☎ 471215), which has clean fan rooms with shared facilities for 150B, air-con rooms with attached bath for 250B and fancier air-con rooms with TV and fridge for 400B.

Top House (☎ 433307) is a big place with 193 rooms for 400B with fan and private bath, 600 to 1200B with air-con, TV and hot water. *Jolly Jumper* (☎ 433887), operated by

and toilet for 500 to 800B. They also provide information about the area and have a cheap Thai restaurant.

Moving south, cheaper rooms are available at *Som's Guest House* (☎ 433753), where clean basic rooms with shared bath cost 200 to 250B.

Santisuk Bungalows & Beach Resort (☎ 471212) is a long-time favourite, with both a Dutch couple at 274/3 Ruamjit Rd, has fan rooms for 150 to 250B, plus air-con rooms for 450 to 600B.

At the northern end of the beach are the closely clustered bungalows of *Paradise Bungalow*, which cost from 250B with fan and from 600B with air-con and TV.

Inthira Plaza This complex off Narathip Rd is striving to become a Pattaya-style bar centre ('entertainment centre' in the jargon of the moment). A couple of the bars have apartment-style rooms upstairs for 250 to 300B with fan and bath, 350 to 400B with air-con. They could be noisy at night.

Places to Stay – top end

Many places in Cha-am call themselves 'resorts' but only two places in the central area come close to the term. First is *Cha-am Methavalai Hotel* (☎ 471580; fax 471590), which has well kept, modern rooms with flowers spilling from every balcony, plus a pool and a small beach area of its own in front. Walk-in rates are 2691B including tax but during the week an automatic 40% discount is given.

For roughly the same price, the seven storey *Novotel Gems Cha-am* (☎ 434003; fax 434002) is a resort-style hotel in which all 105 rooms have ocean views; rooms have all the amenities from satellite TV to IDD phones, and there's a business centre on the premises. Rates start at 2100/2300B per room plus tax and service.

Nearby *Long Beach Cha-am Hotel* (☎ 472-442; fax 472287) offers luxury rooms for 2600B weekends, 1530B weekdays.

South of town a bit, the *Regent Cha-am Beach Resort* (☎ 471480/91; fax 471491) has rooms starting at 3000B; they advertise a 30% to 40% discount for weekdays. Facilities include a swimming pool, squash and tennis courts and a fitness centre.

Also on the beach south of town is the posh *Dusit Resort & Polo Club* (☎ 520009; fax 520296), where rates start at 3872B. The Dusit has a fitness centre, mini-golf, horseback riding, pool, tennis and squash courts and, of course, polo.

Places to Eat

Opposite the beach are several good seafood restaurants, which, unlike the bungalows, are reasonably priced. Vendors on the beach sell all manner of barbecued and fried seafood.

Moderately priced *Khan Had Restaurant* has an extensive menu of Thai, Chinese and seafood dishes. *Anantachai Guest House* is a good place for inexpensive to moderately priced Thai and seafood dishes, while the *Jolly Jumper* does reasonable western food.

The luxury hotels have generally fine Thai, seafood and western cuisine at the standard hotel prices. Seafood and Thai cuisine are especially good at the Methavalai Hotel's *Sorndaeng Restaurant*, a branch of the famous Bangkok restaurant of the same name.

Getting There & Away

Buses from Phetburi and Hua Hin cost 15B. From Hua Hin, take a Phetburi-bound bus and ask to be let off at Hat Cha-am (Cha-am beach); the fare is 10B.

Ordinary buses from Bangkok's Southern bus terminal (Thonburi) to Cha-am cost 50B (92B air-con). In Cha-am ordinary buses stop on Phetkasem Hwy, from where you can take a motorbike-taxi (10B) or a share-taxi (5B) out to the beach. A few hundred metres south of the corner of Narathip and Ruamjit Rds, a private bus company operates six daily air-con buses to Bangkok for 83B.

The train station is on Narathip Rd, west of Phetkasem Hwy and a 10B motorcycle ride to/from the beach. Trains depart Hualamphong station at 9.25 am and 1.40 pm, and return at 6.25 am and 12.12 and 2.49 pm. The train is slower than the bus by one hour (it takes about four hours) and costs 36B.

Getting Around

Standard prices for motorbike taxis and public songthaews are 10B and 5B (30B to charter) respectively. You can also rent motorcycles yourself for 200 to 300B a day.

AROUND CHA-AM
Hat Peuktian

This sandy beach between Cha-am and Phetburi has the usual casuarina trees and food vendors favoured by Thai beach-goers, and hardly a farang in sight. Three rocky islets are within wading distance of shore, one with a sala for shade. Standing knee-deep just offshore is a 6m-high statue of Phi Seua Samut, the undersea female deity that terrorised the protagonist of the Thai classical epic *Phra Aphaimani*. A statue of the prince playing a flute sits on a nearby rock.

A tasteless two storey townhouse-style development has recently been built off the beach. Designed in the pseudo-classical style prevalent in modern city blocks all over Thailand, it looks rather incongruous with the natural beach surroundings.

HUA HIN
• ☎ (32) • *pop 34,500*

The beaches of Hua Hin first came to the country's attention in 1928, when King Rama VII built Klai Kangwon, a seafront summer palace just north of what was then a small fishing village. Rama VII learned of Thailand's first coup d'état in 1932 while playing golf at the Royal Hua Hin Golf Course. Once endorsed by the royal family, Hua Hin remained a traditional favourite among the Thais long after the beaches of Pattaya and Phuket had been taken over by foreign tourists. The palace is still used by the royal family from time to time.

Hua Hin's 5km-long sand beach is studded with large, smooth boulders, enough to give the beach a scenic appeal but not enough to hinder swimming. The surf is safe for swimming year-round, although jellyfish are an occasional problem during the rainy season (May to October). Water sports are limited to sailing and jet-skiing. Overall Hua Hin is still a fairly quiet, economical place to get away from it all, and is less than four hours by train from Bangkok.

Hua Hin, like Cha-am, has traditionally been the domain of domestic beach tourism. The renovation of the 1923-vintage, colonial-style Hua Hin Railway Beach Hotel by a major French hotel group in the late 80s attracted overseas attention. Now a number of cafes and bistros offer Spanish, French, Italian and German cuisine to an older poly-glot bunch who are enjoying two-week Thai beach holidays at bargain rates.

Perhaps the major sign that Hua Hin has arrived on the international beach scene is the recent construction of a high-rise property belonging to Spain's Meliá hotel chain. Still, most visitors – Thai or foreign – stay at the numerous smaller hotels, inns and guesthouses located a couple of blocks east of the beach. There is accommodation for every budget, and the area now attracts a mix of Thais and older farang tourists who are seeking a comfortable beach holiday close to Bangkok but don't want the sleaziness of Pattaya.

Unfortunately, Hua Hin may already be moving in that direction. Already appearing are a lot of the same kind of cheap, unsightly shophouse-apartment buildings with plumbing problems seen in Pattaya and Phuket's Patong beach, as well as a recent invasion of girlie bars. Hua Hin has almost entirely lost its fishing-village atmosphere – the fishing fleet is being moved out and the town's infamous squid-drying piers have been replaced by hotels.

On the bright side, a new sewage treatment plant and municipal sewer system have been constructed and the beach is cleaner than ever. The main swimming beach still has thatched umbrellas and long chairs; vendors from the nearby food stalls will bring loungers steamed crab, mussels, beer etc and there are pony rides for the kids. The Sofitel Central Hua Hin Hotel has successfully campaigned to have the vendors removed from the beach fronting the hotel – a minus for atmosphere but a plus for cleanliness. Vendors are now restricted to a small area near the public entrance to the beach, and to another short string south of the Sofitel. Beer, soft drinks and seafood are reasonably cheap and umbrellas and sling chairs are free if you order food.

Information

The home-grown *Hua Hin Observer*, an expat-published newsletter with short features in English and German, contains snippets on eating out, culture and entertainment.

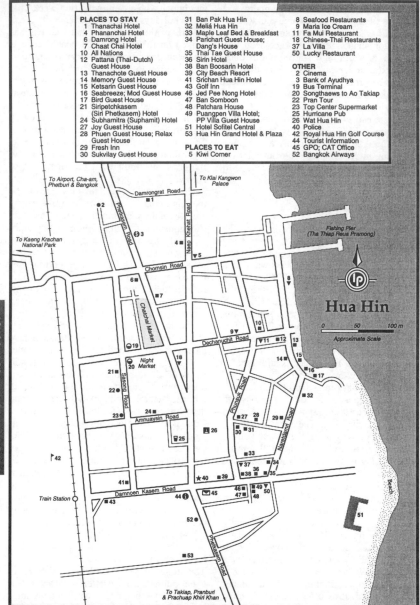

PLACES TO STAY
1 Thanachai Hotel
4 Phananchai Hotel
6 Damrong Hotel
7 Chaat Chai Hotel
10 All Nations
12 Pattana (Thai-Dutch)
 Guest House
13 Thanachote Guest House
14 Memory Guest House
15 Ketsarin Guest House
16 Seabreeze; Mod Guest House
17 Bird Guest House
21 Siripetchkasem
 (Siri Phetkasem) Hotel
24 Subhamitra (Suphamit) Hotel
27 Joy Guest House
28 Phuen Guest House; Relax
 Guest House
29 Fresh Inn
30 Sukvilay Guest House

31 Ban Pak Hua Hin
32 Meliá Hua Hin
33 Maple Leaf Bed & Breakfast
34 Parichart Guest House;
 Dang's House
35 Thai Tae Guest House
36 Sirin Hotel
38 Ban Boosarin Hotel
39 City Beach Resort
41 Srichan Hua Hin Hotel
43 Golf Inn
46 Jed Pee Nong Hotel
47 Ban Somboon
48 Patchara House
49 Puangpen Villa Hotel;
 PP Villa Guest House
51 Hotel Sofitel Central
53 Hua Hin Grand Hotel & Plaza

PLACES TO EAT
5 Kiwi Corner

8 Seafood Restaurants
9 Maria Ice Cream
11 Fa Mui Restaurant
18 Chinese-Thai Restaurants
37 La Villa
50 Lucky Restaurant

OTHER
2 Cinema
3 Bank of Ayudhya
19 Bus Terminal
20 Songthaews to Ao Takiap
22 Pran Tour
23 Top Center Supermarket
25 Hurricane Pub
26 Wat Hua Hin
40 Police
42 Royal Hua Hin Golf Course
44 Tourist Information
45 GPO; CAT Office
52 Bangkok Airways

Tourist Office Tourist information on Hua Hin and the surrounding area is available at the municipal office on the corner of Phetkasem and Damnoen Kasem Rds, a couple of hundred metres east of the train station. Its brochure *Welcome to Hua Hin* contains a lot of useful info on hotels, restaurants and transport. It's open daily from 8.30 am to 4.30 pm.

Money There are several banks around town. Most convenient to the beach is the Bank of Ayudhya's exchange booth on Naretdamri Rd, near the corner of Damnoen Kasem Rd.

Post & Communications The post office is on Damnoen Kasem Rd near the corner of Phetkasem Rd. The attached CAT office offers Home Direct international phone service daily from 6 am to 10 pm.

Beaches

Damnoen Kasem Rd leads east directly from the train station to the main beach, which runs about 2km along the southern half of town. The nicest stretch of sand lies in front of the Sofitel. Smooth granite boulders pierce the surfline – source of the town's name, which means 'Stone Head'.

Eight to 13km south of Hua Hin along Ao Takiap (Chopsticks Bay) are the beaches of **Hat Khao Takiap, Suan Son** and **Khao Tao**, all of which are undergoing resort development. Two hilltop temples can be visited here. **Wat Khao Thairalat** is well off the beach on a rocky hill and is nothing special. At the end of the bay is the more-well-endowed **Wat Khao Takiap**; climb the steps for a good bay view.

The southern end of Ao Takiap is now one big construction site as one high-rise after another goes up, blocking the sea view from all points inland. North along the bay, however, are several quiet, wooded spots with cabins and beach houses.

If you're driving, the turn-off for Ao Takiap is 4km south of Hua Hin. There are regular songthaews back and forth from town.

Places to Stay – bottom end

Prices are moving up quickly for places near the beach. Hotels in town are still reasonably priced and it's only a five or 10 minute walk to the beach from most of them.

Guesthouses Near – but not on – the beach, the cheapest places are found along or just off Naretdamri Rd. A room glut has kept rates low. Several small hotels and guesthouses in this area have rooms for 150 to 200B a night with fan and attached bath, 300 to 400B for larger rooms. Rooms at *Dang's House (Khun Daeng House)* on Naretdamri Rd cost 100 to 150B with private bath. Next to the more top-end Sirin Hotel, the *Thai Tae (Thae) Guest House* offers rooms with fan and bath for 200B. *Parichart Guest House* (☎ 513863), next to Dang's House, is a slightly more upmarket, multistorey place with rooms for 350B with fan and private bath, 450 to 550B with air-con. However, some travellers have complained that tiny rooms and constant traffic noise make this place a poor choice.

On the next block north, the Pakistani-run *Moti Mahal* (☎ 513769) at 152/1 Naretdamri costs 150B for clean, small rooms with bath and fan, 200B for larger rooms. Also on this block, the *Europa* (☎ 513235) at No 158 has rooms for 150B with bath, and a European restaurant downstairs. *Sunee Guest House* next door is an old wooden building with rooms for 150B with shared bath.

Along Soi Kanjanomai, off Naretdamri Rd just north of Damnoen Kasem Rd, is the comfortable-looking *Maple Leaf Bed & Breakfast* (☎ 533757). Rooms cost 120 to 180B, some rooms have bath, some don't. On the same soi are the similar *MP* and *SM* guesthouses.

Along the next soi north off Naretdamri Rd are a couple of charming old wooden guesthouses. *Phuen Guest House* is a fairly quiet place with a nice atmosphere and rates in the 150 to 200B range. *Relax Guest House* (☎ 513585), down an alley just before Phuen, charges 150B single/double for its four medium-size rooms with fan and bath in a private home. Farther along is the similar-looking *Sukvilay Guest House*, where fan rooms cost 150 to 180B and air-con rooms with hot-water showers are 380 to 400B. *Joy Guest House* (☎ 512967), on the opposite side of the soi, has similar charm and room rates of 150 to 200B. Also on this soi is the modern, apartment-style *Ban Pak Hua Hin*; it's quiet, exceptionally clean, and costs 200B with fan and bath, 300B with air-con.

Farther up Naretdamri Rd, where the old squid piers used to be, are a string of wooden motel-like places built on piers over the edge of the sea. *Mod (Mot) Guest House* has 29 rather small but otherwise OK rooms for 150 to 250B with fan, 350 to 450B with air-con and hot water, 650B with TV and fridge. The next-door *Seabreeze (Sirima)* costs 250B for rooms with fan and bath overlooking the water, or 160B for rooms closer to the road without bath. One problem here: during low tide the exposed beach beneath the piers emits a terrible smell, probably caused by inadequate waste disposal. A little south-east of here, down a soi that leads toward the beach, *Bird* (☎ 511630) is the best of the seaside guesthouses; it's well kept, well designed and charges 200 to 500B. In the opposite direction is the rather motel-like *Ketsarin Guest House* (☎ 513999), which combines a pier-style guesthouse with a seafood restaurant. The nearby *Thanachote Guest House* and *Karoon Hut* are similar. Both offer the same basic restaurant/guesthouse combo with fan rooms for 200 to 350B, and fancier rooms with air-con, fridge and TV for 400 to 700B.

Almost opposite Thanachote Guest House, in a long two storey white building, is the new *Memory Guest House* (☎ 511816). It's super-clean and also has a locked entrance gate; rates start at 200B.

Farther north along Naretdamri Rd on the same side of the street, an alley leads to the *Pattana (Thai-Dutch) Guest House*, a rambling collection of wooden buildings with decent rooms from 200B.

West off Naretdamri Rd on Dechanuchit Rd (just east of Phunsuk Rd), over an expat-managed pub, is the friendly and clean *All Nations*, where rooms cost 200 to 300B depending on the size. Each room in the tall,

narrow building comes with its own balcony and fan; each floor has a bathroom shared by two or three rooms.

Hotels To find hotels under 300B, you'll have to go up to Phetkasem Rd, the main north-south road through town. Just off Phetkasem Rd, behind the bank, is *Subhamitra* (Suphamit; ☎ 511208/487) with very clean rooms with fan and bath for 250B, air-con for 350 to 800B. Decaying, Thai-Chinese-style *Chaat Chai Hotel* (no English sign) at 59/1 Phetkasem Rd has rooms with fan and bath for 140 to 220B. Just past the market at 46 Phetkasem Rd is the *Damrong Hotel* (☎ 511574), where rooms with fan and bath are 120 to 150B, 350B with air-con; like the Chaat Chai, this one's fading fast.

Behind the Chatchai Market area on Sasong Rd, the *Siripetchkasem (Siri Phetkasem) Hotel* (☎ 511394) is similar to the hotels along Phetkasem Rd. Rooms with fan are 200B and air-con rooms are 400B. South of here on the same side of the road, the new *Srichan Hua Hin Hotel* (☎ 513130) charges 280B for cement-floor rooms with fan and private bath, 450B with carpet and air-con – a bit overpriced for this location.

Finally, in the town's north at 11 Damrongrat Rd, is *Thanachai* (☎ 511755), a good upper bottom-end place for 250B with fan and bath, 500B for air-con. The Thanachai accepts credit cards.

Places to Stay – middle

Hua Hin's middle-range places are typically small, sedate, modern hotels with air-con rooms and such luxuries as telephones. The forerunner of this trend, *Ban Boosarin* (☎ 512-076), is near the corner of Phunsuk and Damnoen Kasem Rds. It calls itself a 'mini-deluxe hotel' and although it's 670B a night, all rooms come with air-con, hot water, telephone, colour TV, fridge and private terrace. It's super-clean and rates don't rise on weekends. There's a 10% discount for stays of a week or more.

Along Soi Kasem Samphan next to the Jed Pee Nong Hotel are a couple of Ban Boosarin clones. *Patchara House* (☎ 511787) costs

300B for rooms with fan or 550/610B for singles/doubles with air-con, TV/video, telephone, hot water and fridge. Also on this soi is the similar *Ban Somboon*, where nicely decorated rooms are 300B with fan and hot showers, 550B with air-con; all rates include breakfast and there is a pleasant garden on the premises. On the corner of Soi Kasem Samphan and Damnoen Kasem Rd is the relatively new *Puangpen Villa Hotel* and *PP Villa Guest House* (☎ 533785; fax 511216), which share a garden and pool. Clean, air-con rooms cost 840B with hot water, TV and fridge in the former, 600B with hot water in the latter. These hotels, as well as the Jed Pee Nong and City Beach described below, are only a couple of hundred metres from the beach.

The popular *Jed Pee Nong* (☎ 512381) is on Damnoen Kasem Rd. Modern, clean but otherwise unimpressive rooms cost 400B with fan and bath, 500B with air-con or 600 to 800B for air-con rooms by the new swimming pool behind the hotel.

On Naretdamri Rd, the modern *Fresh Inn* (☎ 511389) has all air-con rooms for 700 to 875B. This pleasant tourist-class hotel would have had a sea view if not for the construction of the high-rise Meliá Hua Hin between it and the sea. Downstairs is an Italian restaurant called Lo Stivale.

Running north from Chomsin Rd (the road leading to the main pier) is Naep Khehat Rd. At No 73/5-7, the *Phananchai Hotel* (☎ 511707) has rooms for 350 to 600B. It's a bit of a walk from the swimming beaches but all rooms come with air-con, hot water, TV and telephone.

Places to Stay – top end

At the air-con *Sirin Hotel* (☎ 511150; fax 513571), on Damnoen Kasem Rd towards the beach, rooms are well kept and come with hot water and a fridge. The semi-outdoor restaurant area is pleasant. Double rooms are 850B during the week and 1200B on weekends and holidays.

Nearby, the old Hua Hin Raluk Hotel has been rebuilt and resurrected as the *City Beach Resort* (☎ 512870/75; fax 51244) at 16 Damnoen Kasem Rd. Quiet, semi-luxurious rooms with the usual service and extras cost from 1600B.

Near the train station, off Damnoen Kasem

Hua Hin Railway Hotel

In 1922 the State Railway of Thailand (then the Royal Thai Railway) extended the national rail network to Hua Hin to allow easier access to the Hua Hin summer palace. The area proved to be a popular vacation spot among non-royals too, so in the following year they built the Hua Hin Railway Hotel, a graceful colonial-style inn on the sea, with sweeping teak stairways and high-ceilinged rooms. In 1901, a double room was only 90B and the service was just as unhurried as it had been when I first stayed there in 1977. Back then, it probably hadn't changed much since 1923, except for the addition of electric lighting and screened doors and windows. Big-bladed ceiling fans stirred the humid sea air and in the dining room one ate using State Railway silverware and thick china from the 1920s. Unfortunately, when Bangkok's Central Department Store took over the management of the hotel they floundered in their attempt to upgrade the facilities, failing to take advantage of the hotel's original ambience.

In 1986 the French hotel chain Sofitel became part of a joint venture with Central and together they restored the hotel to most of its former glory. It now bears the awkward name *Hotel Sofitel Central Hua Hin*, but if you've been looking for a historic South-East Asian hotel to spend some money on, this could well be it. All the wood panelling and brass fixtures in the rooms and open hallways have been restored. While the old railway silverware and china have been retired to antique cabinet displays, the spacious, lazy ambience of a previous age still remains. Even if you don't want to spend the money to stay here, it's well worth a stroll through the grounds and open sitting areas for a little history. It's more interesting in terms of atmosphere than either the Raffles in Singapore or the Oriental in Bangkok (neither of which have 8 hectare grounds), and somewhere in between in terms of luxury.

Incidentally, in 1983 this hotel was used as Hotel Le Phnom for the filming of *The Killing Fields*. Also, the State Railway of Thailand still owns the hotel; Sofitel/Central are just leasing it. ∎

Rd near the Hua Hin golf course, is the *Golf Inn* (☎ 512473), where air-con rooms are 700 to 1290B.

Hua Hin also has several super-luxury hotels. The *Hotel Sofitel Central Hua Hin* (☎ 512021/40, Bangkok (2) 233-0974/0980), formerly the Hua Hin Railway Hotel, is a magnificent two storey colonial-style place on the beach at the end of Damnoen Kasem Rd. Rooms in the original L-shaped colonial wing cost 3100B; rooms in the new wing are more expensive. Across the road is the Sofitel's former Villa Wing, now called *Mercure Resort Hua Hin* (☎ 512036; fax 511014), a collection of charming one and two-bedroom wooden beach bungalows for 3100 to 5000B. From 20 December to 20 February there's a 700B peak-season supplement on all room charges at both the Mercure and the Sofitel.

The plush *Meliá Hua Hin* (☎ 512879; fax 511135, Bangkok ☎ (2) 271-0205), off Naretdamri Rd, is part of the Spanish-owned Meliá hotel chain and is Hua Hin's first high-rise (also the first to mar the skyline, unfortunately). Rooms with all the amenities cost 3700 to 4400B, more for suites. From 20 December to 10 January there's a 900B peak-season supplement on all room charges. There's not much of a beach in front of the hotel at high tide, but the adjacent free-form pool area is well designed to encompass sea views. Other facilities include two tennis courts, two air-con squash courts, a fitness centre, sauna and massage facilities.

Along Hua Hin's southern beach at 107/1 Phetkasem Beach Rd, the *Royal Garden Resort* (☎ 511881; fax 512422) offers 220 rooms and suites, all with sea views, in a modern high-rise style complex. Spacious rooms starts at 3400B and reach up to 13,000B for penthouse suites with jacuzzis and private rooftop gardens. The more laid-back *Royal Garden Village* (☎ 520250; fax 520259) at 41/1 Phetkasem Beach Rd north of town has 162 rooms and suites in Thai-style villas on 14 landscaped acres from 3600B. Both Royal Garden resorts have tennis courts and swimming pools, nearby golf course privileges, Thai massage services and

water sport activities; the Royal Garden Resort also has a golf driving range.

The US$26 million *Chiva-Som International Health Resort* (☎ 536536; fax 511154) at 74/4 Phetkasem Hwy has 40 ocean-view rooms and 17 Thai-style pavilions on seven beachside acres south of town (before Nong Khae and Ao Takiap). Chiva Som means 'Haven of Life' in Thai-Sanskrit. The staff of 200 fuses eastern and western approaches to health with planned nutrition, step and aqua aerobics, Thai, Swedish or underwater massage, t'ai chi, dance and the usual round of mudpacks, saunas (including a multi-level steam room), jacuzzis and hydrotherapy. Flotation tanks containing tepid salt water are on hand for sensory deprivation sessions. You can pick up a life-time membership with unlimited use of the facilities for US$18,000 (so far 250 members have signed up), or pay US$400 single, US$600 double per day, a rate that includes three meals (with wine only, and only at dinner) along with health and fitness consultations, massage and all other activities. One week, 10 day and two week packages are also available.

There are a few more top-end places on beaches just north and south of town. Some add peak-season (November to April) supplements, others offer 40% discounts in the off season:

Hua Hin Grand Hotel & Plaza – 222/2 Phetkasem Rd (☎ 511391, 511499; fax 511765, Bangkok ☎ (2) 254-7675); 1900 to 2800B
Hua Hin Sport Villa – 1085 Phetkasem Rd (☎ 511453); 1800B
Majestic Creek Country Club – Klai Kangwon Beach (☎ 520162; fax 520477); 3060B
Sailom Hotel – 29 Phetkasem Rd (☎ 511890/1; fax 512047, Bangkok ☎ (2) 258-0652); 1690 to 3500B

Places to Stay – Out of Town

In Hat Takiap, the *Fangkhlun Guest House* (☎ 512402) has five fan-cooled rooms from 500 to 600B. The *Ta-kiab Beach Resort* (☎ 512639; fax 515899) is south of Khao Takiap, and has air-con rooms and a pool from 1500B a night. The *Sri Pathum Guest House* (☎ 512339) is cheaper and has 11 rooms from 250B with fan, 350B air-con.

The *Vegas Hotel* (☎ 512290) has 32 rooms priced from 600B for a small room, 1000B for something larger.

In a forested area called Nong Khae at the north end of Ao Takiap are the quiet *Rung Arun Guest House* (☎ 511291), with cabins ranging from 200 to 700B, and the deluxe low-rise *Nern Chalet* (☎ 513588; fax 511288), with 14 air-con rooms for 1500B each. Between Nong Khae and Takiap, *Hua Hin Bluewave Beach Resort* (☎ 511036) is a condotel-style place with rooms for 1800 to 2000B; on the grounds are a pool and fitness centre.

In Hat Khao Tao, the *Nanthasuda Guesthouse (Nanthasuda Restaurant)* has rooms from 300B, while Hat Suan Son has the modern *Suan Son Padiphat* (☎ 511239) with fan-cooled rooms for 250B (600B on the sea) or air-con rooms for 500 to 1000B.

In low-key Pranburi, the *Pransiri Hotel* (☎ 621061) at 283 Phetkasem Rd and *Pranburi Hotel* (☎ 621942) at 283 Phetkasem Rd each have rooms starting at 150B. More expensive resort-style accommodation starting at around 1000B is found at *Club Aldiana* (☎ 611701, Bangkok (2) 233-3871) and *Bor Kaeo Resort* (☎ 621713, Bangkok (2) 246-5242).

Places to Eat

One of Hua Hin's major attractions has always been the colourful and inexpensive Chatchai seafood market in the centre of town, where vendors gather nightly to fry, steam, grill, parboil or bake fresh gulf seafood for hordes of hungry Thais. During the day many of these same vendors prepare seafood snacks on the beach; cracked crab and cold Singha beer can be ordered without leaving one's sling chair.

The best seafood to eat in Hua Hin is *plaa sāmlii* (cotton fish or kingfish), *plaa kapõng* (perch), *plaa mèuk* (squid), *hãwy malaeng phùu* (mussels) and *puu* (crab).

Fresh seafood in Hua Hin is found in three main areas. Firstly, there are some medium-priced restaurants along Damnoen Kasem Rd near the Jed Pee Nong and City Beach hotels, and off Damnoen Kasem Rd, on Phunsuk and Naretdamri Rds. Secondly, there's excellent and inexpensive food in the Chatchai night market, described above, off Phetkasem Rd on Dechanuchit Rd, and in nearby Chinese-Thai restaurants. The third area is next to Tha Thiap Reua Pramong, the big fishing pier at the end of Chomsin Rd. The fish is, of course, fresh off the boats but not necessarily the cheapest in town. One of the places near the pier, *Saeng Thai*, is the oldest seafood restaurant in Hua Hin and quite reliable if you know how to order. The best value for money can be found in the smaller eating places on and off Chomsin Rd and in the Chatchai night market. There is also a *night market* on Chomsin Rd.

Three Chinese-Thai seafood places along Phetkasem Rd include *Khuang Seng, Supharot* and *Thara Jan*, none of which bear English signs; all are fairly good value. The least expensive place to eat seafood is an out-of-the-way spot west of Phetkasem Hwy called *Phae Mai*. It's a very simple outdoor restaurant built over a pond, with a steady following among local Thais who can't afford the tourist places downtown. It's a 10B samlor ride from the centre of town; samlor drivers all know where it is. Virtually no English is spoken.

Chatchai Market is excellent for Thai breakfast – they sell very good jók and khâo tôm (rice soups). Fresh-fried paa-thông-kõ Hua Hin-style (small and crispy Chinese pastries, not oily) are 2B for three. A few vendors also serve hot soy milk in bowls (4B) – break a few paa-thông-kõ into the soy milk and drink free náam chaa (Chinese tea) – a very tasty and filling breakfast for 10B if you can eat nine paa-thông-kõ.

Gee Cuisine, next to the Jed Pee Nong, caters mostly to farangs but the Thai food is generally good. The nonstop video in the evenings, however, is a curse one hopes won't spread to other restaurants in town. *Lucky Restaurant*, next to PP Villa, is very similar to Gee Cuisine.

Moti Mahal Restaurant & Guest House on Naretdamri Rd serves decent Indian and Pakistani food; it's open daily 8 am to 11 pm.

Fa Mui, on Dechanuchit Rd near All Nations, is a cosy, atmospheric place serving

Thai and seafood cuisine to a hip crowd of local and visiting Thais; prices are inexpensive to moderate.

Phunsuk and Naretdamri Rds are becoming centres for farang-oriented eateries. On Naretdamri Rd the *Beergarden* is just what it sounds like – an outdoor pub with western food. The *Headrock Cafe* (not a misspelling but a pun on the name Hua Hin – 'head rock') is more of a drinking place, but also has Thai and western food. *Bob's German Bakery* at 120/2 Naretdamri Rd offers German rye bread, whole grain breads, pastries, cakes and cured meats. On the next street west, Phunsuk Rd, is the Italian *La Villa*, with pizza, spaghetti, lasagne and so on. The new *Le Paris Bangkok* restaurant at 54/2 Dechanuchit Rd specialises in French cuisine, with dishes starting from 100B. *Kiwi Corner* at 21 Chomsin Rd serves western breakfasts.

Maria Ice Cream at 54/2 Dechanuchit Rd offers fabulous home-made ice cream, including papaya, watermelon and coconut flavour.

Entertainment

Several farang bars under German, Swiss, Italian, French and New Zealand management can be found in and around Naretdamri and Phunsuk Rds. Most offer the familiar Thai hostess atmosphere. One that dares to be different is the *All Nations Bar* at 10-10/1 Dechanuchit Rd, which successfully recreates a pub atmosphere and has quite a collection of flags and other memorabilia from around the world. The owners may even set up an Internet link in the near future.

Stone Town, an old-west style pub next to Jed Pee Nong Hotel on Damnoen Kasem Rd, features live folk and country music nightly. For rock'n'roll, check out the semi-outdoor *Hurricane Pub* off Phetkasem Rd, where a live Thai band plays Thai and western pop nightly. There's no cover charge and drinks are no more expensive than at any of the town's farang bars.

Getting There & Away

Air Bangkok Airways (☎ 512083 in Hua Hin, (2) 253-8942 in Bangkok, (77) 420133 on Ko Samui) flies daily between Bangkok and Hua Hin (30 minutes, 900B). The Hua Hin airport is 10km north of the city. The Bangkok Airways office, on Phetkasem Rd a couple of blocks south of the tourist information office, is open daily 8 am to 5 pm.

Bus Buses from Bangkok's Southern bus terminal are 92B for air-con, 51B ordinary. The trip takes 3½ to four hours. Pran Tour on Sasong Rd near the Siripetchkasem Hotel runs air-con buses to Bangkok every half hour from 3 am to 9.20 pm. They cost 63B for 2nd class air-con or 92B for 1st class air-con. Pran Tour air-con buses to Phetburi are 60B.

MP Travel, at Nana Plaza Inn (2) 281-5954) on Khao San Rd in Bangkok, operates mini-vans to Hua Hin for 150B per person.

Ordinary buses for Hua Hin leave Phetburi regularly for 20B. The same bus can be picked up in Cha-am for 15B. Other ordinary buses from the main terminal o Sasong Rd go to/from Prachuap Khiri Khan (25B), Chumphon (66B), Surat Thani (112B), Phuket (163B, seven a day), Krabi (158B, two a day) and Hat Yai (178B, three a day).

Train In 1922 the Royal Railway of Siam (now the State Railway of Thailand) extended a rail link to Hua Hin and today the restored, dollhouse-like railway station is a minor attraction in itself. The same trains south apply here as those described under Phetburi's Getting There & Away section. The train trip takes 3¾ hours from Bangkok; 1st class fare is 182B (express only), 2nd class 92B (rapid and express only), 3rd class is 44B.

You can also come by train from any other station on the southern railway line, including Phetburi (3rd class, 13B), Nakhon Pathom (2nd/3rd class 52/33B), Prachuap Khiri Khan (3rd class, 19B), Surat Thani (2nd/3rd class, 116/74B) and Hat Yai (2nd/3rd class, 183/116B). The 1st and 2nd class fares do not include rapid or express surcharges.

Getting Around

Local buses/songthaews from Hua Hin to the beaches of Khao Takiap, Khao Tam and Suan Son cost 5B per person, though farangs are sometimes charged 10B. These buses run

MARK KIRBY

MARK KIRBY

Eastern Gulf Coast
Top: A brilliant sunset overlooking a fishing pier at Ko Samet: the perfect spot to seek solitude or share a peaceful moment.
Bottom: Painted wooden sea craft ply the waters between Ko Samet and Ban Phe on the mainland, ferrying locals, travellers and supplies back and forth.

RICHARD NEBESKY

RICHARD NEBESKY

RICHARD NEBESKY

Eastern & North-Western Gulf Coasts

Top: Houses lining the Chanthaburi River; Vietnamese-French influence has led to some interesting shophouse architecture.

Middle: Offshore islands seen from the scenic bay at Ao Manao, near Prachuap Khiri Khan.

Bottom: A traditional wooden canoe at Ko Chang's Hat Kaibae.

from around 6 am until 5.50 pm; the ones to Hat Takiap leave from opposite the main bus terminal on Sasong Rd, while the latter two leave from Chomsin Rd opposite the wat. Buses to Pranburi are 7B and leave from the same area on Chomsin Rd.

Samlor fares in Hua Hin have been set by the municipal authorities so there shouldn't be any haggling. Here are some sample fares: the train station to the beach, 20B; the bus terminal to the Naretdamri Rd, 20 to 25B; Chatchai Market to the fishing pier, 20 to 30B; the train station to the Royal Garden Resort, 40B.

Motorcycles and bicycles can be rented from a couple of places on Damnoen Kasem Rd near the Jed Pee Nong Hotel. Motorcycle rates are reasonable: 150 to 200B per day for 100cc, 200 to 300B for 125cc. Occasionally larger bikes – 400 to 750cc – are available for 500 to 600B a day. Bicycles are 30 to 70B per day.

At the fishing pier in Hua Hin you can hire boats out to Ko Singtoh for 800B a day. On Hat Takiap you can get boats for 700B.

KHAO SAM ROI YOT NATIONAL PARK

This 98 sq km park, meaning 'Three Hundred Peaks' (established 1966), has magnificent views of the gulf coastline if you can stand a little climbing. Khao Daeng is only about half an hours walk from the park headquarters, and from here you can see the ocean as well as some brackish lagoons. If you have the time and energy, climb the 605m Khao Krachom for even better views. If you're lucky, you may come across a serow (Asian goat-antelope) while hiking. The lagoons and coastal marshes are great places for bird watching. Along the coast you may see an occasional pod of Irrawaddy dolphins *(plaa lohmaa hŭa bàat)*.

Be sure to bring insect repellent for any park visits. King Rama IV (King Mongkut) and a large entourage of Thai and European guests convened here on 18 August 1868 to observe a total solar eclipse – predicted, so the story goes, by the monarch himself – and enjoy an elaborate feast prepared by a French chef. Two months later the king expired from malaria, contracted via mosquito bites inflicted here. The risk of malaria in the park is relatively low, but mosquitos can be quite pesky.

Fauna

Notable wildlife around Khao Sam Roi Yot (Three Hundred Peaks) includes the crab-eating macaque, dusky langur, barking deer, slow loris, Malayan pangolin, fishing cat, palm civet, otter, serow, Javan mongoose and monitor lizard. However, park officials admit that it's fairly uncommon to actually spot any wild animals, possibly due to the rise of tourism!

Because the park lies at the intersection of the east Asian and Australian flyways, as many as 300 migratory and resident bird species have been recorded, including the yellow bittern, cinnamon bittern, purple swamp hen, water rail, ruddy-breasted crake, bronze-winged jacana, grey heron, painted stork, whistling duck, spotted eagle and black-headed ibis. The park protects Thailand's largest freshwater marsh (along with mangroves and mudflats), and is one of only three places in the country where the purple heron breeds.

Waterfowl are most commonly seen in the cool season. Encroachment by shrimp farmers in the vicinity has sadly destroyed a substantial portion of mangroves and other wetlands, thus depriving the birds of an important habitat.

Beaches, Canals & Marshes

A sandy beach flanked on three sides by dry limestone hills and casuarinas, **Hat Laem Sala** has a small visitor centre, restaurant, bungalows and camping area. Boats which take up to 10 people can be hired from Bang Pu to the beach for 150B return. You can also reach the beach from Bang Pu via a steep trail, about a 20 minute walk.

Hat Sam Phraya, 5km south of Hat Laem Sala, is a kilometre-long beach with a restaurant and washrooms. The park headquarters is just past the village of Khao Daeng, about 4km south-west of Hat Sam Phraya. A larger visitor centre at the headquarters features well curated exhibits; there are also nature trails nearby. Binoculars or

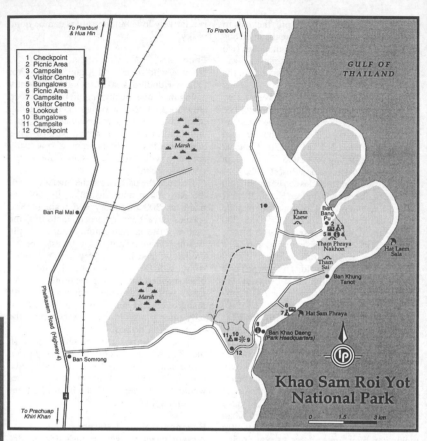

Khao Sam Roi Yot
National Park

0   1.5   3 km

NORTH-WESTERN GULF COAST

telescopes can be rented for bird watching; there are several bird blinds nearby. September to March are the best birding months for waterfowl.

A 4km canal trip in a 10 person boat along **Khlong Khao Daeng** can be arranged in Khao Daeng village for 200B. The trip lasts about 1½ hours and passes mangrove remnants and waterfowl habitats. The birds are most active in the early morning or late afternoon. You might also spot monitor lizards and monkeys. Before heading out, however, you may want to have a chat with your prospective guide.

After being offered a guide for a 20km canoe trip, I failed to enquire further. Bad idea. We ended up with a 'guide' who spoke no English and couldn't canoe. He turned out to be just a local man to whom we paid 300B to sit the middle of our boat – safely oarless – so he wouldn't dump us in the river, as he repeatedly did early in the trip. I now advocate asking about the expertise of purported 'guides'.

Brad Berthal

Caves

The other big attraction at Sam Roi Yot is Tham Kaew, Tham Sai and Tham Phraya Nakhon caves. **Tham Phraya Nakhon** is the most visited and can be reached by boat or foot. The boat trip takes only about half an hour there and back, while it's half an hour each way on foot along a steep, rocky trail. There are actually two large caverns, both with sinkholes that allow light in. In one cave is a royal sala built for King Chulalongkorn, who would stop off here when travelling back and forth between Bangkok and Nakhon Si Thammarat.

Tham Kaew, 2km from the Bang Pu turnoff, features a series of chambers connected by narrow passageways; you enter the first cavern by means of a permanent ladder. Stalactites and other limestone formations – some of which glitter with calcite crystals as if diamond-encrusted (hence the cave's name, 'Jewel Cave') – are plentiful. Lamps can be rented for 100B, but Tham Kaew is best visited in the company of a park guide because of the dangerous footing.

Tham Sai is ensconced in a hill near Ban Khrun Tanot, about 2.5km from the main road between Ale Sala and Sam Phraya beaches. Villagers rent lamps for around 30B at a shelter near the cave mouth. A 280m trail leads up the hillside to the cave, which features a large single cavern. Be careful of steep drop-offs in the cave.

Guides can be hired at the park office for 100B per hike; not much English is spoken but they're accustomed to leading non-Thai as well as Thai visitors.

Places to Stay & Eat

The Forestry Department hires out large bungalows near the park headquarters' visitor centre as well as at Hat Laem Sala for 500 to 1000B per night or 100B per person; they sleep eight to 20 people. Three-person tents are 40B a night to rent. You can also pitch your own tent for 10B per person at campsites at the park headquarters, Hat Laem Sala or Hat Sam Phraya. There are restaurants at all three places. Bring insect repellent along as the park is rife with mosquitos.

For accommodation reservations, contact the Royal Forest Department in Bangkok on ☎ (2) 561-4292, ext 747.

Getting There & Away

The park is 37km south of Pranburi. Catch a bus or train to Pranburi (8B or 7B from Hua Hin) and then a songthaew to Bang Pu for 20B – these run between 6 am and 4 pm. From Bang Pu you must charter a vehicle, hitch or walk.

You can save the hassle of finding a ride in Bang Pu by chartering a songthaew for 250B or a motorcycle taxi for 150B from Pranburi all the way to the park. Be sure to mention you want to go the national park (*ùthayaan hàeng châat*) rather than the village of Khao Sam Roi Yot.

Most convenient of all would be to rent a car or motorbike in Hua Hin. If you're coming by car or motorcycle from Hua Hin, it's about 25km to the park turn-off, then another 38km to park headquarters.

If you're coming straight from Bangkok, another option is to catch an air-con bus bound for Prachuap Khiri Khan, ask to get off at Ban Somrong (Km 286.5) and then hitch a ride 13km to the park headquarters at Ban Khao Daeng.

PRACHUAP KHIRI KHAN
• ☎ *(32)* • *pop 14,500*
Roughly 80km south of Hua Hin, Prachuap Khiri Khan serves as the capital of the province of the same name, though it is somewhat smaller than Hua Hin. There are no real swimming beaches in town, but the 8km-long bay of Ao Prachuap is pretty enough. Better beaches can be found north and south of town. The seafood here is fantastic, however, and cheaper than in Hua Hin. Fishing is still the mainstay of the local economy.

Information

Prachuap has its own city-run tourist office in the centre of town near the night market. The staff are very friendly and they have maps and photos of all the attractions in the area.

Things to See & Do

South of Ao Prachuap, around a small headland, is the scenic **Ao Manao**, a bay ringed by a clean white-sand beach with small islands offshore. Because a Thai air force base is near the bay, the beach was closed to the public until 1990, when the local authorities decided to open the area to day visitors. The beach is 2 or 3km from the base entrance. There are several salas along the beach, a hotel, one restaurant, toilets and a shower. Beach vendors offer chairs, umbrellas and inexpensive seafood and beverages. You must leave your passport at the gate and sign in; the beach closes at 6.30 pm except for military and guests at the hotel (see the Ao Manao section below).

Each year around late March/early April the Thai air force sponsors an international skydiving competition at Ao Manao – it's free and fun to watch.

At the northern end of Ao Prachuap is **Khao Chong Krajok** (Mirror Tunnel Mountain – named after the hole through the side of the mountain which appears to reflect the sky). At the top is **Wat Thammikaram**, established by King Rama VI. You can climb the hill for a view of the town and bay – and entertain the hordes of monkeys who live here. A metal ladder leads into the tunnel from the wat grounds. Note: this is a fairly sheer climb up a cliff face, and probably not a great idea for the faint-hearted or unfit visitor.

If you continue north from Prachuap Khiri Khan around Ao Prachuap to the headland you'll come to a small boat-building village on **Ao Bang Nang Lom** where they still make wooden fishing vessels using traditional Thai methods. It takes about two months to finish a 12m boat, which will sell for around 400,000B without an engine. West of the beach at Ao Bang Nang Lom is a canal, **Khlong Bang Nang Lom**, lined with picturesque mangroves.

A few kilometres north of Ao Prachuap is another bay, **Ao Noi**, the site of a small fishing village with a few rooms to let.

Organised Tours

Local resident Pinit Ounope has been recommended for his inexpensive day tours to Khao Sam Roi Yot, Dan Singkhon and nearby beaches, national parks and waterfalls. He lives at 144 Chai Thaleh Rd near the beach

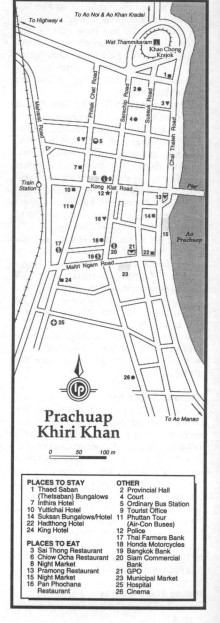

Prachuap Khiri Khan

PLACES TO STAY	OTHER
1 Thaed Saban	2 Provincial Hall
(Thetsaban) Bungalows	4 Court
7 Inthira Hotel	5 Ordinary Bus Station
10 Yuttichai Hotel	9 Tourist Office
14 Suksan Bungalows/Hotel	11 Phuttan Tour
22 Hadthong Hotel	(Air-Con Buses)
24 King Hotel	12 Police
	17 Thai Farmers Bank
PLACES TO EAT	18 Honda Motorcycles
3 Sai Thong Restaurant	19 Bangkok Bank
6 Chiow Ocha Restaurant	20 Siam Commercial
8 Night Market	Bank
13 Pramong Restaurant	21 GPO
15 Night Market	23 Municipal Market
16 Pan Phochana	25 Hospital
Restaurant	26 Cinema

NORTH-WESTERN GULF COAST

and invites travellers to visit him. His house is rather difficult to find, so take a tuk-tuk or a motorcycle taxi. The typical day tour is 200B for two people, plus 50B for each extra person.

Places to Stay
Prachuap Khiri Khan The *Yuttichai Hotel* (☎ 611055) at 35 Kong Kiat Rd has fair rooms with fan and shared bath for 100B/150B for one bed/two beds, or 150/200B with attached bath; the latter rooms are quieter since they're toward the back of the hotel. Around the corner on Phitak Chat Rd is the *Inthira Hotel* with similar rooms in the 100 to 200B range; it's currently under renovation so these rates may change. Both of these hotels are quite near the night market and tourist office.

The *King Hotel* (☎ 611170), farther south on Phitak Chat Rd, has larger fan-cooled rooms at 200 to 250B. Facing Ao Prachuap is the clean and quiet *Suksan* (☎ 611145), with fan-cooled rooms for 200 to 240B and air-con bungalows from 250 to 350B.

Also facing the bay, but farther north, are the plain but well kept *Thaed Saban Bungalows* (or Thetsaban Bungalows, meaning 'Municipal Bungalows' but also known as Mirror Mountain Bungalows), which are owned by the city. A one room bungalow (sleeps two) is 300B with fan and bath or 400B with air-con. A two room bungalow (sleeps four) is 600B; a three room (sleeps six) is 800B; and a four room (sleeps eight) is 1800B. There are also a couple of newer three-room bungalows for 1200B.

The slightly up-market *Hadthong Hotel* (☎ 601050; fax 601057), also next to the bay near Maitri Ngam Rd, has modern air-con rooms with balconies for 600B (mountain view) and 728B (sea view), plus a 200B surcharge from 20 December to 31 January. A pool is on the premises.

North of the city, on the road to Ao Noi, *Rimhad Bungalow* (☎ 601626) offers tiny fan-cooled rooms for 250B, larger rooms with air-con for 500B. The bungalows face scenic Khlong Bang Nang Lom and mangroves. *Happy Inn* nearby has the same prices and similar accommodation.

Ao Manao *Ahkan Sawadii Khan Wing 53* (☎ 611017) is a new place operated by the Thai air force in the middle of the beach. There are 92 units, each with a sea view; a room with TV, phone and private shower costs 500B single/double, while larger town-houses in a separate wing cost 1000B and include bathtubs and hot water.

Ao Noi In Ao Noi there are several rooms and small 'weekend inns', most catering to Thais. *Aow Noi Beach Bungalows* (☎ (2) 510-9790 in Bangkok) offers well kept cottages for 300 to 600B a night with breakfast; farangs – particularly Germans – make up a large percentage of the clientele. Facilities include a small bar and restaurant with Thai and western food, plus a clean, secluded beach.

Places to Eat
Because of its well deserved reputation for fine seafood, Prachuap has many restaurants for a town its size.

One of the seafood specialities of Prachuap Khiri Khan that you shouldn't miss is whole cottonfish that's sliced lengthways and left to dry in the sun for half a day, then fried quickly in a wok, called plaa sãmlii tàet dìaw. It's often served with mango salad on the side. It may sound awful, but the taste is sublime.

The best value place is the *night market* that convenes near the government offices in the middle of town. On Chai Thaleh Rd near the Hadthong and Suksan hotels is a smaller *night market* that's also quite good; tables set up along the sea wall sometimes get a good breeze.

Of the many seafood restaurants, the best are the *Pan Phochana* on Sarachip Rd and the *Sai Thong* on Chai Thaleh Rd near Thaed Saban Bungalows. Both have reasonable prices. The Pan Phochana is famous for its hàw mòk hãwy, ground fish curry steamed in mussels on the half-shell.

Just south of the Pan Phochana is a good night market with many seafood stalls.

Other good restaurants include the *Chiow Ocha* (a bit higher priced – this is where the Thai tour buses stop), the *Pramong* and the

Chao Reua. The *Phloen Samut Restaurant*, adjacent to Hadthong Hotel, is a good outdoor seafood place though it doesn't have everything listed on the menu.

Several good seafood restaurants can also be found along the road north of Ao Prachuap on the way to Ao Noi. *Rap Lom* (literally, 'Breeze-Receiving') is the most popular – look for the Green Spot sign.

The *Hadthong Hotel's* dining room offers a bargain Thai buffet lunch on weekdays for just 65B.

Across from the Inthira Hotel is a small *morning market* with tea stalls that serve cheap curries and noodles.

Getting There & Away

Bus From Bangkok, ordinary buses are 72B; they leave the Southern bus terminal frequently between 3 and 9.20 pm. Air-con buses cost 130B from the southern air-con terminal. In the opposite direction, air-con buses to Bangkok leave from Phuttan Tour (☎ 611411) on Phitak Chat Rd every two hours from 6.15 am to 6.30 pm. In either direction the trip takes four to five hours.

From Hua Hin, buses are 25B and leave from the bus station on Sasong Rd every 20 minutes from 7 am to 3 pm, taking 1½ to two hours.

From Prachuap Khiri Khan you can catch ordinary buses to Chumphon (50B), Surat Thani (100B), Nakhon Si Thammarat (125B), Krabi (140B) and Phuket (145B).

The air-con bus from Bangkok to Ko Samui stops on the highway in Prachuap at 12.30 am – if seats are available you can buy a through ticket to Ko Samui for 190B. It's a five minute, 10B motorcycle taxi ride from the town centre to the highway bus stop.

Train For departure details from Bangkok, see the Phetburi Getting There & Away section earlier in this chapter: the same services apply. Fares from Bangkok are 122B for 2nd class and 58B for 3rd class. Ordinary trains between Hua Hin and Prachuap are 19B; from Hua Hin they leave at 10.30 and 11.47 am and 6.25 pm, arriving in Prachuap 1½ hours later. There are also a couple of rapid trains between the two towns, but the time saved is only about 20 minutes.

A 3rd class ticket to Chumphon is 34B.

Getting Around

Prachuap is small enough to get around on foot, or you can hop on a tuk-tuk for 5B anywhere on the main roads.

A tuk-tuk to Ao Noi costs 25B. The Honda dealer on Sarachip Rd rents 100cc motorcycles for 200B a day.

A motorbike taxi to Ao Manao costs 20 to 25B. They aren't permitted past the gate, from where it is necessary to walk the 3km to the beach.

AROUND PRACHUAP KHIRI KHAN
Wat Khao Tham Khan Kradai

About 8km north of town, following the same road beyond Ao Noi, is a small cave wat at one end of lengthy **Ao Khan Kradai**. A trail at the base of the limestone hill leads up and around one side to a small cavern and then to a larger one which contains a reclining Buddha. If you have a torch you can proceed to a larger second chamber also containing Buddha images. From this trail you get a good view of Ao Khan Kradai (also known as Ao Khan Bandai), a long, beautiful bay that stretches out below. The beach here is suitable for swimming and is virtually deserted. It's not far from Ao Noi, so you could stay in Ao Noi and walk to this beach. Or you could stay in town, rent a motorcycle and make a day trip to Ao Khan Kradai.

Dan Singkhon

Just south of Prachuap is a road leading west to Dan Singkhon on the Myanmar (Burmese) border. This is the narrowest point between the Gulf of Thailand and Myanmar – only 12km across. The Burmese side changed from Karen to Yangon (Rangoon) control following skirmishes in 1988-9. The border is closed; on the Thai side is a small frontier village and a Thai police camp with wooden semi-underground bunkers built in a circle.

Off the road on the way to Dan Singkhon are a couple of small cave hermitages. The more famous one at **Khao Hin Thoen**, surrounded by a park of the same name, has some interesting rock formations and sculptures – but watch out for the dogs. The road to Khao Hin Thoen starts where the paved road to Dan Singkhon breaks left. **Khao Khan Hawk** (also known as Phutthakan Bang Kao) is a less well known cave nearby where elderly monk Luang Phaw Buaphan Chatimetho lives. Devotees from a local village bring him food each morning.

THAP SAKAE & BANG SAPHAN

These two districts lie south of Prachuap Khiri Khan and together they offer a string of fairly good beaches that receive hardly any tourists.

The town of Thap Sakae is set back from the coast and isn't much, but along the seashore there are a few places to stay (see next column). The beach opposite Thap Sakae isn't anything special either, but north and south of town are the white-sand beaches of **Hat Wanakon** and **Hat Laem Kum**. There is no private accommodation at these beaches at the moment, but you could ask permission to camp at Wat Laem Kum, which is on a prime spot right in the middle of Hat Laem Kum. Laem Kum is only 3.5km from Thap Sakae and at the northern end is the fishing village of Ban Don Sai, where you can buy food. Hat Wanakon was recently declared part of Hat Wanakon National Marine Park, which covers 22.6 sq km of coastline and 15.4 sq km of marine resources; it's primary use is as a training centre for park division staff.

Bang Saphan (Bang Saphan Yai) is no great shakes as a town either, but the long beaches here are beginning to attract some speculative development. In the vicinity of Bang Saphan you'll find the beaches of **Hat Sai Kaew, Hat Ban Krut, Hat Khiriwong, Hat Ban Nong Mongkon, Hat (Ao) Baw Thawng Lang, Hat Pha Daeng** and **Hat Bang Boet,** all of which are worth looking up. Getting around can be a problem as there isn't much public transport between these beaches.

There are also islands off the coast, including **Ko Thalu** and **Ko Sing**, where there is good snorkelling and diving from the end of January to mid-May.

Places to Stay & Eat

Thap Sakae The *Chaowarit (Chawalit),* right off the highway near the south end of town, has simple but clean rooms for 120B with shared bath, 150 to 200B with fan and bath – good value overall. Around the corner, less than 100m away from Chaowarit, the *Sukkasem* features very basic rooms for 70 to 120B.

Thap Sakae Hotel (☎ 671273), a new place at the north end of town on the highway, offers 10 clean fan rooms for 300/400B double, air-con for 400/500B.

On the coast opposite Thap Sakae are a couple of concrete block-style bungalows for 200 to 400B, eg *Chan Reua.* Much more congenial and economical – if it's open – is the *Talay Inn* (☎ 671417), a cluster of neglected bamboo huts on a lake fed by the Huay Yang waterfall, but back from the beach a bit in the fishing village. Accommodation in thatched bungalows costs 100B per person; there is also one new air-con bungalow for 300B. The place changed hands recently, so it may close or take new directions. It's about 1km east of the Thap Sakae train station, which is about 1.5km from Thap Sakae. Talay Inn is within easy walking distance of the sea.

Hat Sai Kaew Between Thap Sakae and Bang Saphan on the beach of Hat Kaew (Km 372, Route 4) is *Haad Kaeo Beach Resort.* It's actually just 200m from the Ban Koktahom train station, which can only be reached by ordinary train from the Hua Hin, Prachuap, Thap Sakae, Bang Saphan Yai or Chumphon terminals. Pretty, white, air-con bungalows with green roofs are 900 to 1200B per day on weekends, 20% less on weekdays.

Hat Ban Krut *Reun Chun Seaview* (☎ (01) 215-1857, Bangkok (2) 424-8364) has one bedroom bungalows for 800B, two-bedroom, two-bath ones for 1800B, all air-con – not bad for families. Nearby *Ban Rim Haad* (☎ (01) 216-7926) is similar.

The most economical place on this beach is *Long Samut* (☎ 695045), which rents air-con bungalows for 400B, larger ones for 500 to 1200B.

The new *Ban Klang Aow Beach Resort* (☎ 695086, Bangkok (2) 463-7908) is an up-market place on the beach with a nice pool. Standard bungalows costs 2000B, larger ones 3000B, all with air-con, TV and fridge. *Suan Ban Krut Resort* (☎ 695103, Bangkok (2) 576-0238) is a similar affair with 26 bungalows for 1250B as well as a number of beach homes for sale or rent.

Hat Khiriwong *Tawee Beach Resort* (also *Tawees*, *Tawee Sea*) has simple thatched bungalows with private scoop showers for 70/120B single/double, plus a few concrete bungalows with fans for 200/300B. Or you can pitch a tent for 10B.

Sai-Eak Beach Resort (☎ (01) 213-0317, Bangkok (2) 321-4543) opened in 1996 and is the nicest resort in the area. It's right on the beach, and features a variety of bungalows with satellite TV and fridge ranging from 2000 to 3000B – depending on whether they face pool or sea. Low season discounts of 30 to 50% are available from May to November.

Take a train or bus to the nearby town of Ban Krut, then a motorcycle taxi (30B daytime, 50B night) to Hat Khiriwong.

Bang Saphan Along the bay of Ao Bang Saphan are several beach hotels and bungalows. At Hat Somboon, the *Hat Somboon Sea View* is 480 to 580B per room with private hot-water bath and air-con. The cheaper *Boonsom Guest House* (☎ 691273) has rooms with fan for 200 and 300B. The *Van Veena Bungalows* (☎ 691251), also in this area, has rooms with fan for 200B or air-con for 550B, including TV and video. Bungalows are also available for 200B and 400B. The same management handles *Bangsaphan Resort* (☎ 691152/3), which has similarly priced rooms.

Karol L's (☎ 691058), operated by an American and his Thai wife, has 80B and 100B bungalows in the old Samui style 6km south of Bang Saphan Yai. If you call from the train or bus terminal, they'll provide free

transport. Recently they've had problems with their telephone, so if they don't answer you may need to find your own way there. Meals here are very reasonably priced as well. Karol L's can arrange trips to nearby islands and caves; they have lots of info about the area.

The new *Suan Luang Resort* (☎ (01) 212-5687; fax 691054) at 97 Muu 1 is 600m from the beach, just up from Karol L's. They will also pick up customers from the train station if you call. The resort is run by a friendly and helpful Thai-Italian couple, a combination also reflected in their dining-room menu. New and spacious bungalows with mosquito proofing cost 200B for wooden ones, 350B for concrete. There are discounts for longer stays. Camping is free if you have your own tent, and they have four motorbikes for rent as well as windsurfing, diving and sailing equipment. They can organise boat trips to nearby islands, or motorbike trips to surrounding areas, including Myanmar if the border is open.

The going rate for a half-day snorkel trip to Ko Sing is 300B, or full day to Ko Thalu 400B, including lunch. An overnight camping trip to Ko Thalu with meals included costs 1200B.

Bang Saphan Coral Hotel, under construction near Suan Luang, will offer two-bedroom suites for 1400B and single/double rooms for 970B.

The *Krua Klang Ao* restaurant, right near the centre of Ao Bang Saphan, is a good place for seafood. Because of an Italian-staffed development project nearby, many of the local hotel and restaurant staff speak a smattering of Italian.

Hat Bo Kaew Eight kilometres south of Hat Bang Saphan Yai (15km south of Bang Saphan town), this up and comer boasts two places to stay. *Suan Annan Resort* has 10 bungalows around 300m from the beach costing 500B a night with air-con, TV and fridge. Half a kilometre south, *Haad Boa Kaew* offers six fan-cooled bungalows for 300B and an air-con one for 600B; it's not as good a value as Suan Annan.

Getting There & Away

Buses from Prachuap Khiri Khan to Thap Sakae are 12B and from Thap Sakae to Bang Saphan Yai 8B. If you're coming from farther south, buses from Chumphon to Bang Saphan Yai are 25B.

You can also get 3rd class trains between Hua Hin, Prachuap Khiri Khan, Thap Sakae, Ban Koktahom, Ban Krut and Bang Saphan Yai for a few baht each leg, as all of them have train stations (the rapid and express lines do not stop in Thap Sakae, Ban Krut or Bang Saphan). Each of these train stations is around 4km from the beach, with motorcycle taxis the only form of public transport available. It's possible to rent 100cc motorbikes in Bang Saphan for 150B per day.

CHUMPHON
• ☎ (77) • pop 15,000

About 500km south of Bangkok and 184km from Prachuap Khiri Khan, Chumphon is the junction town where you turn west to Ranong and Phuket or continue south on the newer road to Surat Thani, Nakhon Si Thammarat and Songkhla. In reference to its function as a crossroads, the name derives from the Thai *chumnumphon*, which means 'meeting place'. The provincial capital is busy but of no particular interest, except that this is where southern Thailand really begins in terms of ethnic markers like dialect and religion.

Pak Nam, Chumphon's port, is 10km from Chumphon, and in this area there are a few beaches and a handful of islands with good reefs for diving. The best local beach is 4km-long Hat Thung Wua Laen (12km north of town), also known locally as 'Hat Cabana' because the long-running Chumphon Cabana Resort is here.

Pak Nam is a major departure point for boats to Ko Tao, a popular island north of Ko Samui and Ko Pha-Ngan. Hence many travellers bound for Ko Tao stop over for a night or two in Chumphon.

Nearer islands include Ko Samet, Ko Mattara, Ko Maphrao, Ko Rang Kachiu, Ko Ngam Yai and Ko Raet. Landing on Ko Rang Kachiu is restricted as this is where the precious swiftlet's nest is collected for the gour-

met market. If you want to visit there, you can request permission from the Laem Thong Bird Nest Company in Chumphon. For years now, rumour has abounded that the bird's nest island may open to tourism, but so far it hasn't happened. The other islands in the vicinity are uninhabited; the reefs around Ko Raet and Ko Mattara are the most colourful.

There are many other islands a bit farther out that are also suitable for diving – see Diving & Snorkelling under Around Chumphon below for details. Fishing is also popular around the islands – enquire at any of the hotels or guesthouses in town for information on organised fishing trips.

Information

Money Several banks in town offer foreign exchange services and ATMs; most are located along Sala Daeng Rd.

Post & Communications The GPO on Poramin Manka Rd is open weekdays from 8.30 am to 4.30 pm, weekends 9 am to noon. The CAT office on the 2nd floor of the same building is open for international telephone services daily from 8.30 am to 9 pm.

Books & Maps A new DK Book Store has been established opposite the Jansom Chumphon Hotel but so far it's predominantly Thai-oriented and carries only a few English-language titles. Maps of Chumphon may be purchased here, however.

Organised Tours

Several travel agents and guesthouses organise outdoor tours to the surrounding areas. Infinity Travel Service, one of the best, can arrange diving trips from 2000B per day. Tri Star Adventure Tours offers a series of interesting jungle treks, local cave trips and island tours lasting from two to five days and starting at 1250B per person. A one day cave exploration costs 400B and up, depending on the number of people. Tri Star can be contacted through any travel service or guesthouse.

PLACES TO STAY
2 Chumphon Guest House
3 Thai Prasert Hotel
6 Jansom Chumphon Hotel
7 Sooksamer Guest House
9 TC Super Mansion
10 Si Chumphon Hotel
12 Chumphon Suriwong Hotel
13 Paradorn Inn
15 Morakhot Hotel
17 Suriya Hotel
22 Infinity Travel Service
23 Mayaze's Resthouse
24 Tha Taphao Hotel
29 Si Taifa Hotel

PLACES TO EAT
1 Night Market
4 Curry Shops
11 Esan
14 Tiw Restaurant
25 Sarakrom Wine House
28 Night Market
31 Tang Soon Kee

OTHER
5 Shopping Centre
8 Provincial Hospital
16 Cinema
18 Bank
19 Buses to Ao Thung Wua Laen
20 Songthaews to Ko Tao Boat Pier
21 Minivans to Ranong
26 Bus Terminal
27 Chok Anan Tour
30 Cinema
32 Hospital
33 Market
34 GPO; CAT Office
35 Wat Suphannimit

Chumphon

0   100   200 m

Places to Stay – bottom end

Places continue to spring up as more people use Chumphon as a gateway to Ko Tao. North of the bus terminal, on the opposite side of the street, the *Infinity Travel Service* (☎ 501937) at 68/2 Tha Taphao Rd has three basic but clean rooms with shared bath in an attached guesthouse for 60B per person. They provide plenty of information on boats to Ko Tao and things to do in the area, and also allow travellers to shower while waiting for boat or bus transfers.

The *Sooksamer Guest House* (☎ 502430) at 118/4 Suksamoe Rd (also known as *Pat's Place*) is cosy, with clean, bright rooms in a home-like atmosphere for 120B. Pat, the English-speaking owner, cooks both Thai and European food and is happy for you to use the shower if you drop by to eat a meal on your way to Pak Nam for a Ko Tao boat. Information on Chumphon Province and Ko Tao is plentiful.

Chumphon Guest House (☎ 501242), also known as Miow House, is around the corner from Sooksamer on Krom Luang Chumphon Rd and has basic, clean rooms in an old house for 80 to 120B with shared facilities. The proprietors can arrange car and motorcycle rental as well as local tours.

Festivals

Sometime in March or April the city hosts a Chumphon Marine Festival, which features cultural and folk art exhibits, a windsurfing competition at Thung Wua Laem beach and a marathon.

The five day Lang Suan Buddha Image Parade and Boat Race Festival in October focuses on a procession of temple boats and a boat race on the Lang Suan River, about 60km south of the capital. ■

Mayaze's Resthouse (☎ 504452), down a soi connecting Sala Daeng and Tha Taphao Rds, offers five immaculate rooms for 150/200B single/double with fan, 250B single/double with air-con and 300B triple/quad with air-con. The shared bathroom facilities are equally immaculate.

Other cheaper hotels can be found along Sala Daeng Rd in the centre of town. The *Si Taifa Hotel* is a clean, old Chinese hotel built over a restaurant with large rooms for 140B with shared bath, 200B with shower and Thai-style toilet or 350B with air-con. Each floor has a terrace from which you can watch the sun set over the city. There's also the *Thai Prasert* at 202-204 Sala Daeng Rd, with rooms from 70 to 90B; and the rather drab *Suriya*, 125/24-26 Sala Daeng Rd, which costs a bit more – neither of them are particularly good.

Farther north on Sala Daeng Rd, *Si Chumphon Hotel* (☎ 511280) is a clean and efficient Chinese hotel with rooms for 200 to 350B with fan and bath, 350 to 500B for air-con. The almost identical *Chumphon Suriwong Hotel* charges 210B for a single/double fan room with bath, 280B for three or four people, and just 280/380B single/double for air-con.

The quiet, apartment-style *TC Super Mansion* on the east side of town near the provincial hospital offers decent rooms for 280B with fan, 330B with air-con.

Tha Yang & Pak Nam Near the piers for boats to/from Ko Tao the *Tha Yang Hotel* (☎ 521953) has clean air-con rooms for 315 to 490B.

At Pak Nam the *Siriphet Hotel* (☎ 521-304) has basic rooms from 80B.

Places to Stay – middle & top end
At the *Tha Taphao Hotel* (☎ 511479), at 66/1 Tha Taphao Rd near the bus terminal, comfortable rooms cost 290B for singles/doubles with fan and bath, 550B standard air-con, or 800B for a decked-out superior room. More expensive is the large *Paradorn Inn* (☎ 511-598) at 180/12 Paradorn Rd, where standard rooms with air-con and TV cost 500B or 640B with TV and fridge.

Though a bit newer, the *Jansom Chumphon Hotel* (☎ 502502; fax 502503) is already looking a bit run down. Air-con rooms start at 824B: it is not good value for the money.

Places to Eat
Food vendors line the south side of Krom Luang Chumphon Rd between Sala Daeng Rd and Suksamoe Rd nightly from around 6 pm to 10 or 11 pm.

The several *curry shops* along Sala Daeng Rd are proof that you are now in southern Thailand. Over on Tha Taphao Rd is a smaller *night market* and a very popular Chinese place called *Tang Soon Kee*. Up on Tawee Sinka Rd near the Chumphon Suriwong Hotel is the *Esan* with good north-eastern-style Thai food in the evenings. Several more *Isaan-style* places can be found along Krom Luang Chumphon Rd.

Sarakrom Wine House, opposite the Tha Taphao Hotel on Tha Taphao Rd, is a clean, slightly upscale restaurant serving Thai food from a menu printed in Thai, English and German. The wine list is dominated by wines from South Africa, along with some from Chile, France and Australia.

In Tha Yang, the indoor/outdoor *Reun Thai Restaurant*, next door to the Tha Yang Hotel and near the pier for boats to/from Ko Tao, has good seafood.

Chumphon Province is famous for klûay lép meu naang, 'princess fingernail bananas'. They're very tasty and cheap – 25B would buy around a hundred of these small, slender bananas.

Getting There & Away

Chumphon can be a difficult place to get away from, especially if you're trying to head north to Bangkok during the high season (December to April). If you're planning to use this place as a transport junction, consider the possibility that you may need to spend the night here: if you arrive in town late, trains and overnight buses to Bangkok may be all booked out.

Bus From Bangkok's Southern bus terminal ordinary buses cost 112B and depart at 3.30, 4, 6.05 and 6.50 am only. First class air-con buses are 202B and leave at 2, 9.40 and 10 pm; 2nd class costs 157B and leaves nightly at 9 pm. There is also a 9.40 pm VIP departure for 280B. In the reverse direction the air-con buses leave from Chok Anan Tour, which has an office just behind the main bus station. Departures are at 10 am, 2 pm and 10 pm.

Buses run regularly between Surat Thani and Chumphon for 60B (80B air-con, 3½ hours). To/from Ranong is 35B, Bang Saphan is 30B, Prachuap Khiri Khan is 45B and Phuket is 102B. In Chumphon the main terminal for these buses is on the west side of Tha Taphao Rd.

Air-con mini-vans run to/from Ranong daily every two hours between 8 am and 5.30 pm for 70B from Infinity Travel Service; other places do the same trip for 90B. There is also a mini-van to Bangkok which meets the Ko Tao boat at the Pak Nam pier, and leaves from Infinity Travel Service at noon and 5 pm, costing 300B. Others go to Surat Thani (90B, 2½ hours, several departures per day), Hat Yai and Phattalung (150B, four to five hours); these leave from the north side of Krom Luang Chumphon Rd.

Train Rapid and express trains from Bangkok take about 7½ hours to reach Chumphon and cost 172B for 2nd class, or 356B 1st class, not including rapid or express surcharges. There are only two ordinary trains to Chumphon, both of which originate at Thonburi (Bangkok Noi) station rather than Hualamphong; these cost 82B (3rd class only).

See the Phetburi Getting There & Away section earlier in this chapter for departure times.

There are several ordinary 3rd class trains daily to Prachuap Khiri Khan (34B), Surat Thani (34B) and Hat Yai (99B). Southbound rapid and express trains – the only trains with 1st and 2nd class service – are much less frequent and can be difficult to book out of Chumphon.

Boat to Ko Tao This small island north of Ko Samui and Ko Pha-Ngan (covered in the South-Western Gulf Coast chapter) can be reached by boat from Tha Reua Ko Tao (Ko Tao boat pier), 10km south-east of town. The regular daily boat leaves at midnight, costs 200B and takes about six hours to reach Ko Tao. From Ko Tao the boat usually leaves at 10 am and arrives at Tha Reua Ko Tao around 3.30 pm.

More expensive but faster is the speed boat from the Tha Yang pier, which takes only 2½ hours and costs 400B. Depending on the weather, it usually departs at 9.30 am daily (8 am in the reverse direction).

Songthaews run to both piers frequently between 6 am and 6 pm for 10B. After 6 pm, Infinity and most other travel services and guesthouses can send a van to the pier around 9.30 pm for 50B per person. Going later by van means you won't have to wait at the pier for six hours before the boat departs. The only other alternative is a 60B motorcycle taxi ride to the pier.

Regular air-con minibuses to/from Bangkok's Khao San Rd guesthouses and travel agencies also connect with the slow boat for 300B.

You can also charter a boat to Ko Tao from Pak Nam for around 2500B.

Getting Around

Motorcycle taxis around town cost a flat 10B per trip.

Songthaews to the port of Chumphon (Pak Nam Chumphon) are 13B per person. To Hat Sairi they cost 15B and to Thung Wua Laem, 13B. Buses to Tako Estuary (for Hat Arunothai) are 15B. A motorcycle taxi out to

Thung Wua Laem should be no more than 50B.

The Infinity Travel Service can arrange motorcycle and car rental.

AROUND CHUMPHON
• ☎ (77)

Meditation Temple
Around 48km south of town in Sawi district, Wat Tham Phan Meuang is a Thammayut monastery offering instruction in *vipassana*. There is one Thai monk who can speak English and translate.

Beaches
The best beaches in Chumphon Province are north of Chumphon at **Ao Phanang Tak, Ao Thung Wua Laem** and **Ao Baw Mao**. Nearer to town, in the vicinity of Pak Nam Chumphon, are the lesser beaches of **Hat Pharadon Phap** and **Hat Sairi**. About 40km south of Chumphon, past the town of Sawi, is the Tako Estuary and the fair beach of Hat Arunothai. Most of these beaches have at least one set of resort bungalows.

Diving & Snorkelling At Chumphon the Gulf of Thailand begins opening up more to the oceanic influences of the South China Sea and is less affected by freshwater river drainage than the upper gulf. This means more coral growth than at Pattaya, Ko Chang and other northern gulf dive sites. Because there is no airport nearby, only the more determined foreign divers seem to make it to Chumphon, which is an all-day bus ride from Bangkok, or 3½ hours from Surat Thani.

There are at least half a dozen small islands and seamounts off the Chumphon coast worth diving, most of them 15 to 35km east of the mainland. According to Seafari International, among the best are **Ko Ngam Yai** and **Ko Ngam Noi**, where there is abundant coral at depths of 5 to 20m and visibility of up to 15m or more in good conditions. Just off the north end of Ko Ngam Yai, **Hin Lak Ngam** (also known as Hin Phae) is also very good. All three spots are also suitable for snorkelling in good weather.

Diving conditions in this area tend to be best between May and November.

Seafari International (☎ 501880; fax 502-479), a branch of the similarly named dive operation in Pattaya, has an office at 66/5 Tha Taphao Rd near the Tha Taphao Hotel. Seafari offers dive trips, instruction and certification, equipment rental and repair, and airfills.

Chumphon's original dive shop, at Chumphon Cabana Resort (☎ 501990, Bangkok · (2) 224-1994) on Hat Thung Wua Laen (see Places to Stay & Eat further on), has 20 sets of rental diving equipment and offers instruction and airfills.

Both Seafari International and Chumphon Cabana can organise dive trips to Ko Tao, an island which is technically located in Chumphon Province although it's geographically closer to Surat Thani's Ko Samui archipelago. For Ko Tao diving, however, you're better off staying on Ko Tao itself as the island is three hours away from Chumphon by the fastest boats. Seafari can also arrange trips to the Ko Surin archipelago on the Andaman Sea side of the peninsula – not so far-fetched when you consider that most dive trips to the Surin Islands now operate out of Phuket, which is no closer. For more on the latter islands, see the Northern Andaman Coast chapter.

Places to Stay & Eat
The air-con *Porn Sawan Home Beach Resort* (☎ 521521) is at Pak Nam Chumphon on Pharadon Phap beach and has rooms starting at 840B. *Sai Ree Lodge* (☎ 521212) at nearby Hat Sairi has concrete bungalows with corrugated roofs for 950B with fan, 1150B with air-con. Farther north along Hat Sairi, *Sweet Guest House* (☎ 521324) offers fan rooms for 300B, air-con for 400 to 500B.

On Hat Thung Wua Laen (12km north of Chumphon) the well established *Chumphon Cabana Resort* (☎ 501990, Bangkok (2) 224-1994) has 26 well appointed bungalows and the oldest dive operation in the area. The nightly tariff is 500B with fan, or from 900B for air-con.

At the centre of the beach, *Chuanphun*

(☎ (01) 726-0049) has various rooms starting at 578B, all with air-con and hot water. Just north, the *Cleanwave* (☎ 503621) is the cheapest place on the beach with clean, motel-like rooms for 250B with fan and bath, air-con for 550B. Next door, the *View Seafood Resort* (☎ (01) 726-0293) rents wood-and-thatch A-frames for 300B/400B single/double with fan and bath, more solid concrete bungalows across the road for 600 to 800B. Two other similarly priced places on this beach, *Seabeach Bungalow* and *Khun Rim Lay*, are not as good value. The restaurant at View Seafood Resort is reasonably priced and is quite good. There are several other casual seafood restaurants along Hat Thung Wua Laen where you can dine on the beach.

A couple of kilometres north of Hat Thung Wua Laen is a newly developing beach area called Hat Sapli, where the friendly, well situated *Si Sanyalak* (☎ (01) 477-6602) features four rooms in a longhouse-style building with fan for 350B each, plus two separate bungalows with air-con, TV and fridge for 750B.

Chumphon Sunny Beach (☎ 541895) is at the Tako Estuary on Hat Arunothai, about 50km south of Chumphon. Bungalows are 400 to 450B with fan or 550B with air-con.

South-Western Gulf Coast (Surat Thani to Narathiwat)

South-Western Gulf Coast Highlights

- Chaiya – just north of Surat Thani, this is one of Thailand's oldest cities, featuring 9th century wat ruins, a famous Buddhist meditation centre and peninsular rainforest

- Khao Sok National Park – its native rainforest, waterfalls, limestone cliffs, streams and lakes are home to a plethora of wildlife, including the *Rafflesia*, the largest flower in the world

- Ko Samui – dive the offshore reefs, hike to stunning waterfalls, take a day trip to Ang Thong National Marine Park or relax by the beach

- Shadow puppetry – Nakhon Si Thammarat is one of the only places where traditional life-size buffalo-hide puppets are still made

- Culture of the south – soak up the distinctive pàk thâi way of life in Pattani, Narathiwat, Songkhla and Hat Yai, where Buddhism and Islam meet

South of Chumphon the Thai-Malay peninsula – the second longest peninsula in the world after the Kamchatka Peninsula in Russia – swells to its widest girth in Thailand.

Beyond the well known islands of Ko Samui, Ko Pha-Ngan and Ko Tao, few tourists are seen along this extensive coastline. From the perspective of industrial development there is relatively little agribusiness, aquaculture or manufacturing – in fact there's less development than anywhere else along either the gulf or the Andaman Sea shores.

The overall lack of tourism south of the Samui archipelago can only be explained by the fact that the South-Western Gulf's best season climatically runs from April to October, the exact opposite of Thailand's 'natural' tourist season (which coincides with the European and North American winter). Ko Samui's natural assets as a beautiful, remote island – coupled with the fact that the original Hainanese inhabitants of the island were quite open to foreign visitation and tourism development – counter this seasonal aspect. The mostly Muslim residents of the coastal provinces farther south have historically been more indifferent to tourism, so they haven't built beach huts, guesthouses and restaurants catering to the foreign tourist trade. This is all the better for those global wanderers seeking less trodden sands.

SURAT THANI
- ☎ (77) • pop 41,800

There is little of particular historical interest at Surat Thani, a busy commercial centre and port dealing in rubber and coconut, but the town's busy waterfront lends character nonetheless. It's 651km from Bangkok and the first point in a southbound journey towards Malaysia that really feels and looks like southern Thailand. For most people Surat Thani (often called simply Surat) is only a stop on the way to Ko Samui or Ko Pha-Ngan, luscious islands 32km off the coast – so the Talaat Kaset bus station in the Ban Don area of Surat and the ferry piers to the east become the centres of attention.

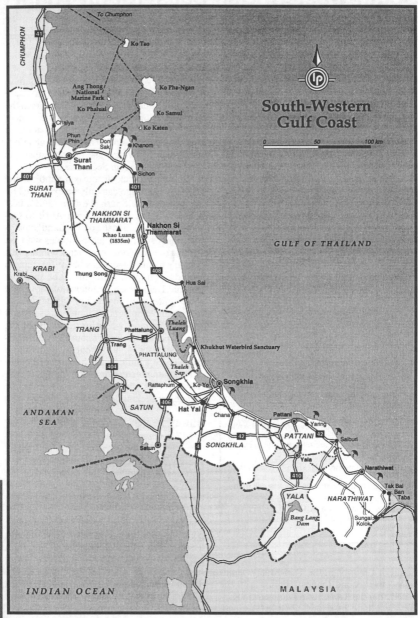

Festivals
In mid-October Chak Phra and Thawt Phaa Paa celebrations occur on the same day at the end of the Buddhist rains retreat (first day of the waning moon in the 11th lunar month) and are major events for Surat Thani. Thawt Phaa Paa, or 'Laying-Out of Forest Robes', begins at dawn with the offering of new monastic robes to the monks, while Chak Phra, or 'Pulling of the Buddha Image', takes place during the day and evening. During Chak Phra local lay devotees place sacred Buddha images on boats for a colourful procession along the Tapi River. A similar landborne procession uses trucks and hand-pulled carts. Lots of food stalls and musical performances, including *likeh*, or Thai folk opera, are set up for the occasion. ∎

Information

Tourist Office The friendly TAT office (☎ 288818), at 5 Talaat Mai Rd near the south-western end of town, distributes plenty of useful brochures and maps. It's open daily from 8.30 am to 4.30 pm.

Several travel agents in town handle travel to the islands or elsewhere in southern Thailand, including Phantip Travel (☎ 272230) at 442/24-5 Talaat Mai Rd and Songserm Travel (☎ 285124; fax 285127) at 30/2 Mu 3 Bangkoong Rd, with another office opposite the pier. Phantip is the most reliable travel agent in town; Songserm is notorious for its couldn't-care-less attitude because its parent company has a near monopoly on all boat transport to the islands.

Money There's a string of banks – one on every block for five blocks – along Na Meuang Rd south-west of Chonkasem Rd. All have ATMs and most offer foreign exchange. Bangkok Bank at 193 Na Meuang Rd has an exchange booth open daily from 8.30 am to 5 pm.

Post & Communications The GPO is on Na Meuang Rd. A new telecommunications centre on Don Nok Rd is the place to make international calls now. It's open daily from 7 am to 11 pm.

Places to Stay – bottom end

At many of Surat Thani's cheaper hotels, business consists largely of 'short-time' trade. This doesn't make them any less useable as regular hotels – it's just that there's likely to be rather more noise as guests arrive and depart with some frequency. In fact, if you're on a tight budget, it may be better to zip straight through Surat Thani via the night boat; you may even sleep better on the night boat than in a noisy hotel. If you arrive in Surat by train or bus in the morning you'll have no problem making a connection with one of the day express boats. Another alternative is to stay near the train station in Phun Phin (see under Places to Stay & Eat – Phun Phin later in this section).

All of the following places are within walking (or samlor) distance of the Ban Don boat pier:

The *Surat Hotel* (☎ 272243) on Na Meuang Rd, between the Grand City Hotel and the bus station, costs 150 to 300B for rooms with fan and bath. At the rear are some quiet, renovated rooms. Across the street from the Surat, the *Phanfa Hotel* has similar rooms for 120B.

The *Grand City Hotel* (☎ 272960) at 428 Na Meuang Rd has been renovated and has plain but clean rooms with fan and bath for 160/190B one bed/two beds, and air-con rooms for 330/500B.

Off Ban Don Rd, near the municipal pier, on a fairly quiet street off Si Chaiya Rd, is the *Seree (Seri) Hotel* (☎ 272279). You get adequate but somewhat airless rooms with fan and bath for 290B, air-con rooms for 330B.

One block from the night boat pier on Si Chaiya Rd is the *Thai Hotel* (☎ 272932), which is 140/180B for dingy but fairly quiet singles/doubles with fan and bath.

The best budget value in Surat is the *Ban Don Hotel* (☎ 272167) on Na Meuang Rd towards the morning market, with clean singles/doubles with fan and bath for 160/220B. You enter the hotel through a Chinese restaurant. The *Thai Rung Ruang Hotel* (☎ 273249), 191/199 Mitkasem Rd, off Na Meuang Rd, is also good, with rooms from 260/320B (fan) for one/two beds and 430/450B (air-con).

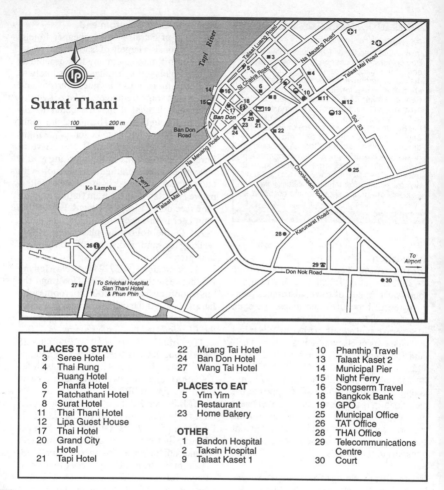

PLACES TO STAY
3 Seree Hotel
4 Thai Rung
   Ruang Hotel
6 Phanfa Hotel
7 Ratchathani Hotel
8 Surat Hotel
11 Thai Thani Hotel
12 Lipa Guest House
17 Thai Hotel
20 Grand City
   Hotel
21 Tapi Hotel

22 Muang Tai Hotel
24 Ban Don Hotel
27 Wang Tai Hotel

PLACES TO EAT
5 Yim Yim
   Restaurant
23 Home Bakery

OTHER
1 Bandon Hospital
2 Taksin Hospital
9 Talaat Kaset 1

10 Phanthip Travel
13 Talaat Kaset 2
14 Municipal Pier
15 Night Ferry
16 Songserm Travel
18 Bangkok Bank
19 GPO
25 Municipal Office
26 TAT Office
28 THAI Office
29 Telecommunications
   Centre
30 Court

On Na Meuang Rd near the Talaat Kaset 1 bus station is the scruffy, not-too-clean *Ratchathani Hotel* (☎ 272972/143), which starts at 230B for rooms with fan and bath and from 300B for air-con.

Places to Stay – middle
Popular with travelling businesspeople, the *Tapi Hotel* (☎ 272575) at 100 Chonkasem Rd has fan-cooled rooms for 250 to 370B, air-con for 500 to 670B. The similar but older *Muang Tai* (☎ 272367) at 390-392 Talaat Mai Rd has fan-cooled rooms from 200B and air-con rooms from 300B and has gotten good reviews from travellers. Although these two don't cost much more than the budget places mentioned, the facilities are considerably better.

Places to Stay – top end

Surat Thani also has a number of more expensive hotels, including the *Wang Tai* (☎ 283020/39; fax 281007) at 1 Talaat Mai Rd. It's a big hotel with nearly 300 rooms, a swimming pool and prices from 680B. The *Siam Thani* (☎ 273081) at 180 Surat Thani-Phun Phin Rd costs 840B (as low as 580B in low season) and has a swimming pool. There's a good restaurant on the premises. The *Siam Thara*, on Don Nok Rd near the Talaat Mai Rd intersection, has air-con rooms for 560 to 640B.

Places to Eat

The *Talaat Kaset market* area next to the bus terminal and the *morning market* (between Na Meuang and Si Chaiya Rds) are good food-hunting places. Many stalls near the bus station specialise in khâo kài òp, a marinated baked chicken on rice which is very tasty. During mango season, a lot of street vendors sell incredible khâo niăw mámûang, coconut-sweetened sticky rice with sliced ripe mango.

Yim Yim Restaurant on Talaat Luang Rd serves reasonably priced seafood, including Surat's celebrated large white oysters, served raw in a lime-garlic-chilli marinade. *Athit Restaurant*, opposite Sun Hiam Chinese Restaurant on the same street as the Thai Hotel, is an air-con beer house with snacks and ice cream. Just around the corner from Bangkok Bank, off Na Meuang Rd in an old wooden building, is an exemplary southern-style *khanŏm jiin* place.

J Home Bakery, around the corner from the Grand City Hotel, is a dark, poorly ventilated air-con place, but it has inexpensive western breakfasts and a few baked goods, plus Thai and Chinese dishes on a bilingual menu. Another good bakery is the *Valaisak Bakery* next to the Tapi Hotel. *Homeburger Restaurant*, next to the Phanfa Hotel, does hamburgers, pizza, steak and some Thai dishes.

Next door to J Home Bakery is the inexpensive and popular *Yong Hua Long*, a decent Chinese restaurant with roast duck and a large buffet table.

Places to Stay & Eat – Phun Phin

You may find yourself needing accommodation in Phun Phin (where the Surat Thani train station is actually located), either because you've become stranded due to booked-out trains or because you've come in from Ko Samui in the evening and plan to get an early morning train out of Surat before the Surat to Phun Phin bus service starts. If so, there are a couple of cheap, dilapidated hotels just across from the train station. The *Tai Fah* has rooms for 100B with shared bath, 120B with attached bath. At the same location but slightly better is the *Sri Thani*, also with rooms at 100B.

If you can afford a few baht more, around the corner on the road to Surat, but still quite close to the train station, is the better *Queen* (☎ 311003), where rooms cost 150 to 200B with fan and 250 to 300B with air-con.

Across from the Queen is a good night market with cheap eats. The *Tai Fah* and *Sri Thani* do Thai, Chinese and western food at reasonable prices. Opposite the north end of the train station, *Oum's Restaurant* has an English menu and serves good Thai coffee, western breakfasts and simple Thai dishes.

Getting There & Away

Air THAI flies to Surat Thani from Bangkok twice daily (75 minutes, 1785B). The THAI office (☎ 272610) in Surat is at 3/27-28 Karunarat Rd.

Orient Express Air (☎ 210071), a relatively new service, offers five weekly flights between Surat and Chiang Mai for 2450B each way; this flight continues on to Hat Yai for another 1150B.

A THAI shuttle van between Surat Thani and the airport costs 40B per person. THAI also runs a more expensive limo service for 150B.

Bus, Share Taxi & Mini-van First class air-con buses leave Bangkok's Southern bus terminal in Thonburi daily at 8, 8.20 and 8.30 pm, arriving in Surat 11 hours later; the fare is 285B. There is also one 2nd class air-con departure at 10 pm that costs 222B and one VIP departure at 8 pm for 350B. Private companies also run 'Super VIP' buses with only 30 seats for 450B.

Ordinary buses leave the Southern bus terminal at 9.20 and 11 pm for 158B.

Take care when booking private air-con and VIP buses out of Surat. A company called Harmony Tours has been known to sell tickets for VIP buses to Bangkok, then pile hapless travellers onto an ordinary air-con bus and refuse to refund the fare difference. If possible get a recommendation from another traveller or enquire at the TAT office. Also, check carefully if you decide to book a bus through Songserm Travel. Some travellers bound for Krabi were talked into taking the Songserm 'direct bus' and soon found themselves stranded at the Songserm bus depot, some 20km out of Surat, where they waited several hours for the bus, a little detail the travel agent somehow forgot to mention.

Public buses and share taxis run from the Talaat Kaset 1 and 2 markets. The Muang Tai bus company books air-con tickets to several destinations in southern Thailand from its desk in the lobby of the Surat Hotel, including VIP buses to Bangkok. Phantip Travel handles mini-van bookings.

Other fares to/from Surat are:

Destination	Fare (B)	Hours
Hat Yai	85	5
(air-con)	120	4
(share taxi or van)	150	3½
Krabi	51	4
(air-con)	91	3
(share taxi or van)	150	2
Nakhon Si Thammarat	36	2½
(air-con)	55	2
(share taxi)	60	2
Narathiwat	127	6
Phang-Nga	50	4
(air-con)	100	3
(share taxi)	80	2½
Phuket	77	6
(air-con)	112	5
(share taxi or van)	150	4
Ranong	70	5
(air-con)	80	4
(share taxi or van)	150	3½
Satun	76	4
Trang	50	3
(share taxi)	100	3
Yala	100	6

Buses from Phun Phin If you're taking the train to Surat Thani, but going on to the Andaman Coast rather than Ko Samui or Pha-Ngan, there are bus services operating out of Phun Phin (where the Surat train station is actually located). This saves you having to go into Surat Thani proper.

The main destinations served are Takua Pa (where you can get buses north to Ranong), Phuket, and Phang-Nga on the Andaman Coast. Nearly all services are by ordinary bus, except for two air-con services for Phuket, which leave at 7.30 and 10.30 am. Other buses leave every one to two hours from 6 am to 3.30 pm. The ordinary buses to Phuket run past Khao Sok National Park, Takua Pa and Hat Khao Lak; Takua Pa buses pass Khao Sok. Buses leave from next to a white building south of the train station: look for the bus schedule painted on the wall.

Train Trains for Surat Thani (which actually stop in Phun Phin, 14km west of town) leave Bangkok's Hualamphong terminal at 1.30 pm (rapid), 2.35 pm (special express), 3.15 pm (special express), 3.50 pm (rapid), 5.05 pm (rapid), 6.30 pm (rapid), 7.20 pm (express) and 7.45 pm (rapid), arriving 10½ to 11 hours later.

The 6.30 pm train (rapid No 41) is the most convenient, arriving at 5.44 am and giving you plenty of time to catch a boat to Ko Samui, if that's your destination. Fares are 470B in 1st class (available only on the 2.35 and 3.15 pm special express) and 224B in 2nd class, not including the rapid, express or special express surcharges or berths.

There are no direct 3rd class trains to Surat from Bangkok, but you can travel from Chumphon to Surat on the ordinary No 119 or No 149 for 25B.

In addition, there is the all-1st-class special express No 981 (formerly called *The Sprinter*), which leaves Bangkok daily at 10.35 pm and arrives in Phun Phin at 7.20 am for 370B. No sleeping berths are available on this train.

The Phun Phin train station has a 24 hour left-luggage room that charges 5B a day for the first five days, 10B a day thereafter. The advance ticket office is open daily from 6 to 11 am and noon to 6 pm.

It is sometimes quite difficult to book long-distance trains out of Phun Phin – for long-distance travel, it may be easier to take a bus, especially if heading south. The trains are often full and it's a drag to take the bus 14km from town to the Phun Phin train station without a reservation and be turned away. However, you could buy a 'standing room only' 3rd class ticket and stand for an hour or two until someone vacates a seat down the line.

Advance train reservations can be made, without going all the way out to Phun Phin station, at Phantip Travel on Talaat Mai Rd near the market/bus station. You might try making an onward reservation *before* boarding a boat for Ko Samui. Songserm Travel on Ko Samui can also assist travellers with reservations.

Here is a list of other train fares out of Surat (not including surcharges on rapid, express or air-con coaches):

Destination	Fare (B)		
	1st class	2nd class	3rd class
Bangkok	470	224	-
Chaiya	-	-	8
Chumphon	71	34	25
Hat Yai	228	114	55
Nakhon Si Thammarat (Thung Song)	103	54	26
Prachuap Khiri Khan	255	127	-

Train/Bus/Boat Combinations These days many travellers are buying tickets from the State Railway that go straight through to Ko Samui or Ko Pha-Ngan from Bangkok on a train, bus and boat combination. For example, a 2nd class air-con sleeper that includes bus to boat transfers through to Ko Samui costs 679B. See the Getting There & Away sections under each island for more details.

Getting Around

Buses to Surat from Phun Phin train station leave every 10 minutes or so from 5.15 am to 8 pm for 6B per person. Some of the buses go straight to the pier in Tha Thong (if they have enough tourists), while others will terminate at the Ban Don bus station, from where you must get another bus to Tha Thong if you're getting the ferry there or to the Ban Don ferry pier if you're getting the night ferry.

If you arrive in Phun Phin on one of the night trains, you might be able to get a free bus from the train station to the pier, courtesy of the boat service, for the morning boat departures. If your train arrives in Phun Phin when the courtesy and public buses aren't running, then you're out of luck and will have to hire a taxi to Surat for about 60 to 70B, or hang out in one of the Phun Phin street cafes until buses start running.

Orange buses run from Ban Don bus station to Phun Phin train station about every 10 minutes from 5 am to 7.30 pm for 6B per person. Buses also wait at Tha Thong for passengers arriving from Ko Samui on the express boat, ready to drive them directly to the train station or destinations farther afield.

Around town, share tuk-tuks cost 5B and samlors are 10B.

AROUND SURAT THANI

Two inland places near Surat are worth visiting if you're looking for a break from sea and sand. Chaiya is an important footnote in Thai history, and boasts one of Thailand's most famous Buddhist meditation centres, while Khao Sok National Park preserves a large chunk of peninsular rainforest.

Chaiya

Just north of Surat Thani and best visited as a day trip from there, Chaiya is one of the oldest cities in Thailand, dating back to the Srivijaya Empire. In fact, the name may be a contraction of Siwichaiya, the Thai pronunciation of the city that was a regional capital between the 8th and 10th centuries. Before this time the area was on the Indian trade route through South-East Asia. Many Srivijaya artefacts in the National Museum in Bangkok were found in Chaiya, including a famous Avalokitesvara Bodhisattva bronze that's considered a masterpiece of Buddhist art.

The Face of Peninsular Thailand

Although under Thai political domination for several centuries, the narrow pendant of land dangling between the Andaman Sea and Gulf of Thailand has always remained culturally apart from the other regions of Thailand. Historically, the peninsula has been linked to cultures in ancient Indonesia, particularly the Srivijaya Empire, which ruled a string of principalities in what is today Malaysia, southern Thailand and Indonesia. The Srivijaya Empire is thought to have been based in Sumatra, with a major satellite in Chaiya. Srivijaya – Siwichai to the Thais – lasted nearly 500 years from the 8th to 13th centuries. The influence of Malay-Indonesian culture is still apparent in the ethnicity, religion, art and language of the *Thai pàk tâi*, the southern Thais.

Geography & Economy

Bounded by water on two sides, the people of southern Thailand are by and large a seafaring lot. One consequence of this natural affinity with the ocean is the abundance of delectable seafood, prepared southern style. Brightly painted fishing boats, hanging nets and neat thatched huts add to the pàk tâi setting; travellers who do a stint in southern Thailand are likely to come face to face with more than a few visions of 'tropical paradise', whatever their expectations might be.

Three of Thailand's most important exports – rubber, tin and coconut – are produced in the south so that the standard of living is a bit higher than in other provincial regions. However, southern Thais claim that most of the wealth is in the hands of ethnic Chinese. Throughout the peninsula – in Malaysia as well as Thailand – the Chinese are concentrated in the urban provincial capitals while the poorer Muslims live in the rural areas. This urban concentration of Chinese is a fact of life throughout South-East Asia, becoming more noticeable in southern Thailand and the Islamic state of Malaysia because of religious-cultural differences.

As in Malaysia, higher concentrations of Muslims live on the eastern side of the peninsula than on the western side – a legacy of non-Muslim migration patterns during the 19th and early 20th century British colonial period when Phuket and Penang were important international trading centres. Although most Thais will vehemently deny that Britain ever ruled any part of the Thai half of the peninsula, the reality is that the British did claim dominion over parts of Narathiwat, Satun and Yala provinces before the Anglo-Siamese Treaty of 1909.

Culture & Language

Officially, as well as ethnolinguistically, southern Thailand is made up of 14 provinces: Chumphon, Krabi, Nakhon Si Thammarat, Narathiwat, Pattani, Phang-Nga, Phattalung, Phuket, Ranong, Satun, Songkhla, Surat Thani, Trang and Yala. The Thai pàk tâi dress differently, build their houses differently and eat differently from Thais in the north. Due to a common history with Malaysia to the region's immediate south, many southern Thais are followers of Islam, and in many areas mosques outnumber Buddhist wats. Local men often cover their heads with white-lace haji caps or black Nehru-style 'topis', and in rural areas they may favour the long Malay sarong over ordinary western-style trousers worn in the northern, central and north-eastern regions of Thailand. Muslim Thai women sport brightly coloured batik dresses and may wrap their hair in gauzy scarves.

These regional differences will become most visible to those who leave the coastal resort areas and explore inland towns and cities. In the larger southern cities a strong Chinese presence adds another element to the cultural mosaic, so that one can wander from Buddhist wat to Malay tea shop to Chinese joss house in the space of a few blocks. The Chinese influence can also be seen in old urban architecture and in the baggy Chinese pants worn by rural non-Muslims.

All pàk tâi speak a dialect common among southern Thais that confounds even other Thai speakers – diction is short and fast: *pai năi* (Where are you going?) becomes *p'nái*, and *tham arai* (What are you doing?) becomes *'rái*. The clipped tones fly into the outer regions of intelligibility, giving the aural impression of a tape played at the wrong speed. In the provinces nearest Malaysia – Yala, Pattani, Narathiwat and Satun – many Thai Muslims speak Yawi, an old Malay dialect with similarities to modern Bahasa Malaysia and Bahasa Indonesia.

You'll notice that 'Ao', 'Hat' and 'Ko' sometimes precede place names; *ao* means bay, *hàat* is beach and *kàw* is village.

Southern Thais are stereotypically regarded as rebellious folk, considering themselves reluctant subjects of Bangkok rule and Thai (central Thai) custom. Indeed, Thai Muslims (ethnic Malays) living in the provinces bordering on Malaysia complain of persecution by Thai government troops who police the area for insurgent activity. There has even been talk in some quarters of these provinces seceding from Thailand, an event that is unlikely to occur in the near future. ∎

Wat Phra Boromathat, Wat Kaew & Chaiya National Museum The restored Borom That Chaiya stupa at Wat Phra Boromathat, just outside of town, is a fine example of Srivijaya architecture. In the courtyard surrounding the revered chedi are several pieces of sculpture from the region, including an unusual two-sided yoni (the uterus-shaped pedestal that holds the Shivalingam), rishis performing yoga and several Buddha images.

A ruined stupa at nearby Wat Kaew (also known as Wat Long), also from the Srivijaya period, shows the influence of central Javanese architecture (or perhaps vice versa) as well as Cham (9th century South Vietnam) characteristics.

The national museum near the entrance to Wat Phra Boromathat displays prehistoric and historic artefacts of local provenance, as well as local handicrafts and a shadow puppet exhibit. Admission to the museum is 10B; it's open Wednesday to Sunday from 9 am to 4 pm.

Wat Suan Mokkhaphalaram Wat Suanmok (short for Wat Suan Mokkhaphalaram – literally, 'Garden of Liberation'), west of Wat Kaew, is a modern forest wat founded by Ajaan Buddhadasa Bhikkhu (Phutthathat), Thailand's most famous monk. Born in Chaiya in 1906, Buddhadasa ordained as a monk when he was 21, spent many years studying the Pali scriptures and then retired to the forest for six years of solitary meditation. Returning to ecclesiastical society, he was made abbot of Wat Phra Boromathat, a high distinction, but conceived of Suanmok as an alternative to orthodox Thai temples. His philosophy was ecumenical in nature, comprising Zen, Taoist and Christian elements as well as the traditional Theravada schemata. During Thailand's turbulent 1970s, he was branded a Communist because of his critiques of capitalism, which he saw as a catalyst for greed. Buddhadasa died in July 1993 after a long illness.

The hermitage is spread over 120 hectares of wooded hillside and features huts for up to 70 monks, a museum/library and a 'spiritual theatre'. This latter building has bas-reliefs on the outer walls which are facsimiles of sculptures at Sanchi, Bharhut and Amaravati in India. The interior walls feature modern Buddhist painting – eclectic to say the least – executed by the resident monks.

Places to Stay Travellers could stay in Surat Thani for visits to Chaiya or request permission from the monks to stay in the guest quarters at Wat Suanmok. *Udomlap Hotel*, an old Chinese-Thai hotel in Chaiya, has rooms for 80 to 100B.

Getting There & Away If you're going to Surat Thani by train from Bangkok, you can get off at the small Chaiya train station, then catch another train to Phun Phin, Surat's train station.

From Surat you can either take a songthaew from the Talaat Kaset 2 market in Ban Don (20B) or get a train going north from Phun Phin. The trains between Phun Phin and Chaiya may be full but you can always stand or squat in a 3rd class car for the short trip. The ordinary train costs 8B in 3rd class to Chaiya and takes about an hour. A songthaew takes around 45 minutes. Or you can take a share taxi to Chaiya from Surat for 30B per person; in Chaiya, the Surat-bound taxis leave from opposite the Chaiya train station.

To get to Wat Phra Boromathat, you can catch any songthaew heading west from the main intersection south of the Chaiya train station for 3B. This same songthaew route passes the turn-off for Wat Kaew, which is about half a kilometre before the turn-off for Boromathat. Wat Kaew is less than a half kilometre from this junction on the left, almost directly opposite Chaiya Witthaya School.

Wat Suanmok is about 7km outside Chaiya on the highway to Surat and Chumphon. Until late afternoon there are songthaews from the Chaiya train station to Wat Suanmok for 8B per person. From Chaiya you can also catch a Surat-bound bus from in front of the movie theatre on Chaiya's main street and ask to be let off at Wat Suanmok (turn right on the road in front of the train station). The fare to Wat Suanmok is 5B. If buses aren't running you can hire a motorcycle taxi for 20B anywhere along Chaiya's main street.

Khao Sok National Park

This 646 sq km park is in the western part of Surat Thani Province, off Route 401 about a third of the way from Takua Pa to Surat Thani. The park contains 65,000 hectares of thick native rainforest with waterfalls, limestone cliffs, numerous streams, an island-studded lake formed by the Chiaw Lan Dam and many trails, mostly along rivers. Connected to the Khlong Saen Wildlife Sanctuary and three smaller preserves (thus forming the largest contiguous nature preserve on the Thai peninsula), Khao Sok shelters a plethora of wildlife, including the wild elephant, leopard, serow, banteng, gaur, dusky langur, tiger and Malayan sun bear, as well as over 175 bird species. In 1986 Slorm's stork – a new species for Thailand – was confirmed.

One floral rarity found in the park is *Rafflesia kerri meyer*, known to the Thais as *bua phut*, or 'wild lotus', the largest flower in the world. Found only in Khao Sok and an adjacent wildlife sanctuary (different varieties of the same species are found in Malaysia and Indonesia), mature specimens reach 80cm in diameter. The flower has no roots or leaves of its own; instead it lives parasitically inside the roots of the liana, a jungle vine. Once a year buds burst forth from the liana root and swell to football size. When the bud blooms it emits a potent stench (said to resemble that of a rotting corpse) that attracts insects responsible for pollination.

A map of hiking trails within the park is available from park headquarters near the park entrance. Three trails lead to the waterfalls of Than Sawan (7km), Sip-Et Chan (4km) and Than Kloy (8km). Guesthouses near the park entrance can arrange guided hikes that include waterfalls, caves and river-running. Leeches are quite common in certain areas of the park, so take the usual precautions – wear closed shoes when hiking and apply plenty of repellent.

The park is 1.5km off Route 401 between Takua Pa and Surat Thani at Km 109. Besides the camping area at park headquarters, there are several private bungalow operations featuring 'tree-house-style' accommodation.

Entrance to the park is 3B; rangers lead jungle tours and/or rafting trips for 150B per day. Rainforest Safari (☎/fax (76) 330852) in Phuket arranges treks and elephant rides in Khao Sok for 2200 to 4000B.

Places to Stay & Eat Khao Sok has a camping area and several places to stay. The national park has a house with rooms for 350B. Tents can be rented for 50B per person. A small restaurant near the entrance serves inexpensive meals.

Several places just outside the park between the highway and the visitor centre have accommodation. *Khao Sok River Huts* (☎ (76) 421155/613, both ext 107), has six rooms with bath for 200/300B a single/double, or a tree-house with bath for 400B. Meals are 40 to 70B. *Bamboo House*, off the main road to the park, has seven rooms for 100/150B with shared bath, 170/250B with private bath, plus 120B extra for three meals a day.

Art's Riverview Jungle Lodge (☎ (76) 4212394), off the same road beyond the Bamboo House, about a kilometre from the park, has seven rooms for 200 to 300B, tree-houses for 400B and two large houses with rooms with private baths and decks for 600B. Meals cost 250B a day or you can order à la carte at breakfast and lunch and pay 80B for a set Thai dinner. All places have guides for jungle trips. Meals are available for 40 to 60B.

Past Art's and the Bamboo House is *Our Jungle House*, a more upscale spot run by the owners of the Similana Resort near Takua Pa. Nicely designed tree-houses with private bath cost around 800B depending on the season, and there are also smaller, less expensive rooms in the main house where the dining room is.

Under the same management as Dawn of Happiness in Krabi, *Khao Sok Rainforest*

Resort (☎ (01) 464-4362; fax 612914) offers sturdy cottages raised on stilts with large verandas overlooking the forest, and with attached showers and toilets, for 300 to 600B. A longhouse-style dorm is planned along with air-con luxury bungalows – rather out of place in what purports to be an eco-sensitive resort.

Getting There & Away From Phun Phin or Surat catch a bus bound for Takua and get off at Km 109 (the park's entrance) on Route 401 for 75B air-con, 28B ordinary. You can also come from the Phuket side of the peninsula by bus, but you'll have to take an ordinary bus; Surat-bound air-con buses from Phuket don't use Route 401 any more. Even with the ordinary bus, check to make sure it goes via Takua Pa and Route 401.

KO SAMUI
• ☎ *(77)* • *pop 35,000*

Ko Samui is the namesake of the island group off the coast of Surat Thani Province known to the Thais as Mu Ko Samui. The Ko Samui archipelago consists of around 80 islands, of which seven – Samui, Pha-Ngan, Tao, Ta Loy, Taen, Ma Ko and Ta Pao – are inhabited. So far the bulk of the tourist interest has focused on the three largest islands, Ko Samui, Ko Pha-Ngan and Ko Tao. Ko Samui is Thailand's third-largest island at 247 sq km.

Samui's first settlers were seafaring islanders from Hainan Island (now part of the People's Republic of China) who took up coconut farming here around 150 years ago. You can still see a map of Hainan on the *sǎan jâo* or Chinese spirit shrine near Siam City Bank in Na Thon, the oldest town on the island. Muslim families of Thai-Malay descent live in a few of the villages scattered around the island as well. Beginning around 20 years ago the island attained a somewhat legendary status among Asian travellers, but it wasn't until the late 80s that its popularity escalated to the proportions of other similar getaways found between Goa and Bali.

Perhaps due to the Hainanese influence, Samui culture differs from that of other islands in southern Thailand. Its inhabitants refer to themselves as *chao samǔi* (Samui folk) rather than Thais. They can be even friendlier than the average rural Thai and have a great sense of humour, although those who are in constant contact with tourists are often more jaded. Nowadays many of the larger resorts, restaurants, bars and other tourist enterprises are owned or operated by Bangkok Thais or Europeans, so you have to get into the villages to meet true chao samǔi.

The island has a distinctive cuisine, influenced by the omnipresent coconut, still the main source of income for chao samǔi, who have disproportionately less ownership in beach property than outsiders. Coconut palms blanket the island, from the hillocks right up to the beaches. The durian, rambutan and langsat fruits are also cultivated.

The population of Ko Samui is for the most part concentrated in the port town of Na Thon, on the western side of the island facing the mainland, and in 10 or 11 small villages scattered around the island. One road encircles the island with several side roads poking into the interior; this main road is now paved all the way around. About 90% of the island is still uninhabited though you wouldn't know it from looking at the coastline. Retirement homes owned by foreigners as well as Thais are beginning to appear in the interior. Condos start at half a million baht, with 100% ownership possible (in condo developments only) even for non-Thais.

Information
When to Go The best time to visit the Samui group of islands is during the hot and dry season, February to late June. From July to October (south-west monsoon) it can rain on and off, and from October to January (north-east monsoon) there are sometimes strong winds. However, many travellers have reported fine weather (and fewer crowds) in September and October. November tends to get some of the rain which also affects the east coast of Malaysia at this time. Prices tend to soar from December to July, whatever the weather.

Shifting Samui Sands

Since the advent of the Don Sak auto/bus ferry in the late 1980s and the opening of the airport, Ko Samui has been rapidly changing. During the high seasons, late December to February and July to August, it can be difficult to find a place to stay, even though most beaches are crowded with bungalows and resorts. The port town of Na Thon teems with farangs getting on and off the ferry boats, booking tickets onward and collecting mail at the post office. With nearly a dozen daily flights to Samui from Bangkok, the island is rushing headlong into top-end development.

However, Samui is still an enjoyable place to spend time, and more than a few people have been making regular visits for nearly 20 years. The island still has some of the best value accommodation in Thailand and a casual, do-as-you-please atmosphere that makes it quite attractive to would-be escapees from the international rat race. Even with an airport, it still has the advantage of being far from the mainland. Coconuts are still an important part of the local economy – up to two million are shipped to Bangkok each month.

But there's no going back to 1971, when the first two 'official' tourists arrived on a coconut boat from Bangkok, much to the surprise of a friend who had been living on the island for four years as a Peace Corps volunteer. A recent article in *Samui* magazine included photos by a Swiss journalist who claimed to have taken them in 1965; Samui appeared in a few German-language guidebooks of that era but nothing in the guidebook entries suggested that the authors had actually visited the island!

The main difference between then and now is that these days there is a much greater number and variety of accommodation available, most of it in the mid to high range by Thai standards. And of course, with this 'something for everyone' climate have come more people, more traffic, more noise and more rubbish, but so far not in intolerable proportions. Samui residents are beginning to formulate policies to deal with these social and environmental challenges and the prognosis is, tentatively, optimistic – only time will tell. One of the first controls to be established on the island is a ban on any construction that is more than 12m high. Of course there's always the very real possibility that this limit will be side-stepped via payoffs to the local Department of Construction. Bangkok's Central Department Store has already attempted to violate the ban by starting construction of a four storey hotel on Chaweng beach. ∎

Maps In Surat or on Ko Samui, you can pick up the TAT's helpful Surat Thani map, which has maps of Surat Thani Province, Ang Thong National Marine Park and Ko Samui, along with travel info. A couple of private companies now do good maps of Ko Samui, Pha-Ngan and Tao, which are available in tourist areas of Surat and on the islands for 35 to 40B. The most accurate and up-to-date is V Hongsombud's *Guide Map of Koh Samui, Koh Pha-Ngan & Koh Tao*.

Tourist Office A TAT office at the northern end of Na Thon, past the post office on the opposite side of the road, dispenses the usual handy brochures and maps. The TAT says this is a temporary office and that it is looking for a new location elsewhere in town. The office is open daily 8.30am to 4.30pm.

Samui Welcome, a home-grown, tourist-oriented newspaper with articles in German, English and Thai, comes out a couple of times a year and costs 15B. The much glossi-er, advertisement-packed *Samui* magazine, issued once a year, contains lots of photos of topless Caucasians on the beach and is the kind of magazine in which only the advertisers are marked on the maps; the articles, however, show respect for the island's history and environment.

Immigration Travellers have been able to extend their tourist visas at the Ko Samui immigration office in Na Thon, 6/9 Thawi Ratchaphakdi Rd, for 500B. Hours are 8.30 am to 3.30 pm weekdays.

Money Changing money isn't a problem in Na Thon, Chaweng or Lamai, where several banks and exchange booths offer daily exchange services.

Post & Communications The island's main post office is in Na Thon, but in other parts of the island there are privately run branches. Many bungalow operations also sell stamps and mail letters, but most charge a commission.

International telephone service is available on the 2nd floor of the CAT office, attached to the Na Thon GPO, daily 7 am to 10 pm. Many private phone offices around the island will make a connection for a surcharge over the usual TOT rates.

Travel Agencies Surat Thani travel agents Phantip (☎ 421221/2) and Songserm (☎ 421-288) have offices in Na Thon.

Internet Services The Internet Cafe at Chaweng beach offers online access at 300B per hour, allowing you to send and receive electronic mail and surf the Worldwide Web. The online address is: goin@samart.co.th.

Medical Services A new medical facility, Bandon International Hospital (☎ 425382/3; fax 425342), has recently opened in Bo Phut. Although we haven't yet received any feedback on the quality of the hospital's staff or facilities, emergency ambulance service is available 24 hours and credit cards are accepted for treatment fees.

Dangers & Annoyances Several travellers have written to say take care with local agents for train and bus bookings. Bookings sometimes don't get made at all, the bus turns out to be far inferior to what was expected or other hassles develop.

Take care with local boat trips to nearby islands. Visitors have reported boats getting swamped on windy days, and travellers sometimes being forced to spend the night stranded on an uninhabited island.

Environmental Message

Ko Samui's visitors and inhabitants produce over 50 tonnes of garbage a day, much of it plastic. Not all of it is properly disposed of, and quite a few plastic bottles end up in the sea, where they wreak havoc on marine life. Request glass water bottles instead of plastic, or try to fill your own water bottle from the guesthouse or hotel's large, reusable canisters kept in their restaurant. On Ko Tao the

TAT arranges monthly volunteer rubbish collections with half a dozen dive agencies, who offer discounts to customers who participate; ask at a Samui dive shop if a beach cleanup is planned.

Diving & Snorkelling

Reefs lie off many parts of the island but the better ones are found along the east side near the beaches of Chaweng and Lamai. These areas are OK for snorkelling but there is better diving to the north around Ko Pha-Ngan and especially Ko Tao.

Samui's many dive operators offer guided dives to the better underwater sites. Gear hired for beach dives costs around 500B per day. Dives from boats start at 1000B, and a four day certification course is about 5500B. An overnight dive trip to Ko Tao, including food and accommodation, costs around 3500B, or you can do a longer four day, three night trip for around 5000B.

The highest concentration of dive shops is found on Hat Chaweng. Among the more established are:

Chang Divers – Hat Chaweng & Hat Lamai (☎ 424-121)
The Dive Shop – Hat Chaweng (☎/fax 230232)
Matlang Divers – Na Thon & Hat Chaweng (☎ 442172)
Samui International Diving School – Na Thon & Hat Chaweng (☎ 421056; fax 421465)

Sea Kayaking

Sea Canoe Thailand (☎ 422037; fax 422401) at the Blue Lagoon Hotel on Hat Chaweng offers guided kayak trips to nearby islands – Ko Mat Lang off the coast of Hat Chaweng is a three hour paddle, while the trip to Mu Ko Ang Thong runs all day. From Christmas to August Sea Canoe Thailand also offers a three day Ang Thong kayaking/camping trip.

Waterfalls

Besides the beaches and rustic, thatched-roof bungalows, Samui has a couple of waterfalls. **Hin Lat Falls** is a worthwhile visit if you're waiting in town for a boat back to the mainland. If you're up for a long walk, you can

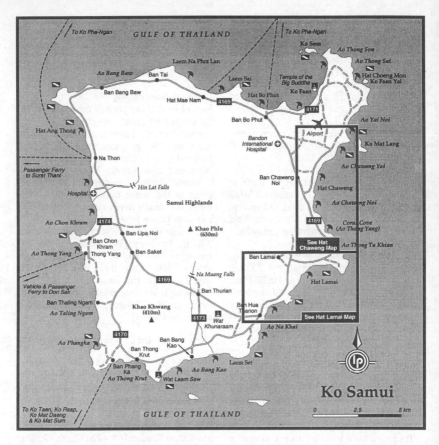

Ko Samui

SOUTH-WESTERN GULF COAST

get there on foot – walk 3km or so south of town on the main road, turning left at the road by the hospital. Go straight along this road for about 2km to arrive at the entrance to the waterfall. From here, it's about a half hour walk along a trail to the top of the waterfall.

Na Muang Falls, in the centre of the island about 12km from Na Thon, is more scenic and somewhat less frequented. A songthaew from Na Thon should cost about 20B; get off at the marked turn-off, then walk 2km to the falls. Songthaews can also be hired at Chaweng and Lamai beaches.

Temples

For temple enthusiasts, at the southern end of the island, near the village of Bang Kao, **Wat Laem Saw** features an interesting and highly venerated old Srivijaya-style chedi. At Samui's northern end, on a small rocky island joined to Samui by a causeway, is the so-called **Temple of the Big Buddha**, or Phra Yai. Erected in 1972, the modern image stands about 12m high and makes a nice silhouette against the tropical sky and sea behind it. The image is surrounded by *kutis* (meditation huts), mostly unoccupied. The monks like receiving visitors there, though a sign in English requests that proper attire (no shorts) be worn on temple premises. There is also an old semi-abandoned temple, **Wat Pang Ba**, near the northern end of Hat Chaweng where 10 day Vipassana courses are occasionally held; the courses are led by foreign monks from Wat Suanmok in Chaiya.

Near the car park at the entrance to Hin Lat Falls is another trail left to **Suan Dharmapala**, a meditation temple. Another wat attraction is the ghostly **Mummified Monk** at Wat Khunaraam, which is off Route 4169 between Ban Thurian and Ban Hua Thanon.

Ang Thong National Marine Park

This archipelago of around 40 small islands combines dense vegetation, sheer limestone cliffs, hidden lagoons and white sand beaches to provide a nearly postcard-perfect opportunity to enjoy gulf islands at their best. The park itself encompasses 18 sq km of islands, plus 84 sq km of marine environments. From Ko Samui, a couple of tour operators run day trips out to the Ang Thong archipelago, 31km to the north-west. A typical tour costs 350B per person, leaves Na Thon at 8.30 am and returns at 5.30 pm. Lunch is included, along with snorkelling in a sort of lagoon formed by one of the islands (from which Ang Thong, meaning 'Golden Jar,' gets its name) and a climb to the top of a 240m hill to view the whole island group. Some tours also visit Tham Bua Bok, a cavern containing lotus-shaped cave formations. Tours depart daily in the high season, less frequently in the rainy season. The tours are still getting rave reviews. Bring hiking shoes, snorkelling gear and plenty of sunscreen and drinking water.

At least once a month there's also an overnight tour, as there are bungalows on Ko Wua Ta Lap, site of the park headquarters. These cost 500B per person and include three meals. You may be able to book just the passage to the Ang Thong islands; enquire at Songserm Travel or Ko Samui Travel Centre in Na Thon.

You can also arrange to join a more active but more expensive Ang Thong kayak trip through Sea Canoe Thailand at the Blue Lagoon Hotel on Chaweng beach (see under Sea Kayaking earlier in this section). Yet another alternative would be to get a group together, charter your own boat and design your own Ang Thong itinerary. At the park headquarters on Ko Wua Ta Lap you can rent bungalows for 400B a night or tents for 50B. For reservations, call Ang Thong National Marine Park on ☎ (077) 283025.

Na Thon
• *pop 4000*
On the upper west side of Ko Samui, Na Thon (pronounced *nâa thâwn*) is the arrival point for express and night passenger ferries from the piers in Surat Thani. Car ferries from Don Sak and Khanom land at Thong Yang, about 10km south of Na Thon. If you're not travelling on a combination ticket you'll probably end up spending some time in Na Thon on your way in and/or out, waiting for the next ferry. Or if you're a long-term beachcomber, it makes a nice change to come into Na Thon once in a while for a little town life.

Although it's basically a tourist town now, Na Thon still sports a few old teak Chinese cafes along Ang Thong Rd where descendants of the island's original Hainanese immigrants gather.

At the northern end of Na Thon there's a Thai boxing ring with regular matches. Admission is around 100B for most fights. The quality of the mostly local contestants isn't exactly top-notch.

Places to Stay If you want or need to stay in Ko Samui's largest settlement there are seven places to choose from.

If you're looking for something inexpensive, check out the *Seaview Guest House* (☎ 420052) on Thawi Ratchaphakdi Rd, which has Khao San Rd-style rooms with fan and shared bath for 150B, fan and private bath for 180 to 200B, and air-con for 300B – none of the rooms actually have sea views.

The *Palace Hotel* (Thai name: *Chai Thaleh*) has clean, spacious rooms starting at 250 to 280B with fan or 350 to 400B with air-con. The *Win Hotel* farther down the road has

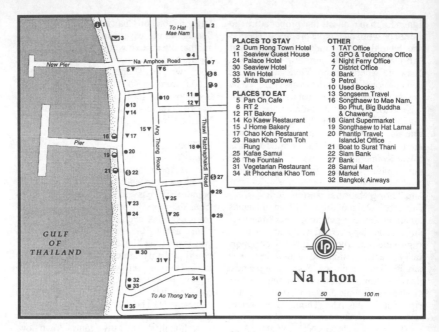

PLACES TO STAY
2 Dum Rong Town Hotel
11 Seaview Guest House
24 Palace Hotel
30 Seaview Hotel
33 Win Hotel
35 Jinta Bungalows

PLACES TO EAT
5 Pan On Cafe
6 RT 2
12 RT Bakery
14 Ko Kaew Restaurant
15 J Home Bakery
17 Chao Koh Restaurant
23 Raan Khao Tom Toh Rung
25 Kafae Samui
26 The Fountain
31 Vegetarian Restaurant
34 Jit Phochana Khao Tom

OTHER
1 TAT Office
3 GPO & Telephone Office
4 Night Ferry Office
7 District Office
8 Bank
9 Petrol
10 Used Books
13 Songserm Travel
16 Songthaew to Mae Nam,
   Bo Phut, Big Buddha
   & Chaweng
18 Giant Supermarket
19 Songthaew to Hat Lamai
20 Phantip Travel;
   IslandJet Office
21 Boat to Surat Thani
22 Siam Bank
27 Bank
28 Samui Mart
29 Market
32 Bangkok Airways

Na Thon

0   50   100 m

all air-con rooms with TV and telephone for 420B, plus a nice coffee shop downstairs. Around the corner from the Win Hotel is the similar four storey *Seaview Hotel* (☎ 421481) with rooms for 350/380B single/double with air-con, TV, phone and fridge.

On the main road north out of town is the *Dum Rong Town Hotel*, which charges 500B and up for rooms with fan and bath. *Chao Koh Bungalow*, just north of town nearer to the sea, is 300 to 800B. On the southern edge of town, the *Jinta Bungalows* has pretty basic rooms for 150 to 250B.

Places to Eat There are several good restaurants and cafes in Na Thon. On the road facing the harbour, the *Chao Koh Restaurant* is still serving good seafood and Thai standards at reasonable prices. *Ko Kaew* is a similar standby.

Farther down the road towards Thong Yang are the *Pha-Ngan* and *Sri Samui* restaurants, both quite good Thai seafood places.

Towards the Palace Hotel is a Thai rice and noodle place that's open all night, *Raan Khao Tom Toh Rung* (no English sign) – the cheapest place to eat on this strip. During the high season, many of these restaurants fill up at night with travellers waiting for the night ferry.

On the next street back from the harbour are *J Home Bakery* and a few old Chinese coffee shops, such as *Kafae Samui*. Farther south on this street is *The Fountain*, an Italian place specialising in pasta and pizza. At the intersection of Na Amphoe and Ang Thong Rds, you can't miss the popular bakery/cafe called *RT 2*, which has an extensive Thai menu (dishes 35B and up) as well as freshly baked goods. After midnight the only places open are the *Khao Tom Toh Rung* and the flashy Thai nightclub *Pan On Cafe*, which is rather expensive, dark and well chilled.

The third street back from the harbour has mostly travel agencies, photo shops and other small businesses. Two small supermarkets, Samui Mart and Giant Supermarket, are also here. The Charoen Laap day market is still thriving on this street as well. The *RT Bakery* on the same street is similar to the previously described RT 2.

One of the few places in town still serving Thai (and Chinese) food on a large scale is *Jit Phochana Khao Tom* on Thawi Ratchaphakdi Rd. A small *vegetarian restaurant* opens at night on the southern end of Ang Thong Rd.

Ko Samui Beaches

Samui has plenty of beaches to choose from, although the proliferation of new places seems to have stabilised a bit over the past three years – at last count the TAT had registered 250 places to stay on the island. Getting from beach to beach is usually no problem. The most crowded beaches for accommodation are Chaweng and Lamai, both on the eastern side of the island. Chaweng has more bungalow 'villages' – over 80 at last count – plus several recently built flashy tourist hotels. It is the longest beach, over twice the size of Lamai, and has the island of **Mat Lang** nearby. Both beaches have clear blue-green waters and OK coral reefs for snorkelling and underwater sightseeing. Both have open-air discos; Lamai has a higher concentration of bars.

There's a bit more to do in Hat Lamai because of its proximity to two villages – Ban Lamai and Ban Hua Thanon. At the wat in Ban Lamai is the **Ban Lamai Cultural Hall**, a sort of folk museum displaying local ceramics, household utensils, hunting weapons and musical instruments. The drawback to Lamai is the rather sleazy atmosphere of the strip of beer bars behind the beach; Chaweng's bar-and-disco strip is decidedly more sophisticated and more congenial for couples or single women.

Chaweng is the target of up-market development because of its long beach. Another factor is that only Chaweng beach (and the northern part of Lamai) has water deep enough for swimming from October to April; most other beaches on the island become very shallow during these months.

For more peace and quiet, try the beaches along the north, south and west coasts. Mae Nam, Bo Phut and Big Buddha are along the northern end; Bo Phut and Big Buddha are part of a bay that holds **Ko Faan** (the island with the 'big Buddha'), separated by a small headland. The water here is not quite as clear as at Chaweng or Lamai, but the feeling of seclusion is greater, and accommodation is cheaper.

Hat Thong Yang on the western side of the island is even more secluded (only a few sets of bungalows there), but the beach isn't very good by Samui standards. There is also Hat Ang Thong, just north of Na Thon, which is very rocky but with more local colour (eg fishing boats) than the others. The southern end of the island now has many bungalows as well, set in little out-of-the-way coves – worth seeking out. And then there's everywhere in-between – every bay, cove or cape with a strip of sand gets a bungalow nowadays, right around the island.

Accommodation & Food Prices vary considerably according to the time of year and occupancy rates. Some of the bungalow operators on Samui have a nasty habit of tripling room rates when rooms are scarce, so a hut that's 80 to 100B in June could be 200B in August. Rates given in this section can only serve as a guide – they could go lower if you bargain or higher if space is tight.

Everyone has his or her own idea of what the perfect beach bungalow is. At Ko Samui, the search could take a month or two, with more than 200 places to choose from. Most offer roughly the same service and accommodation for 100 to 400B, though some cost quite a bit more. The best thing to do is to go to the beach you think you want to stay at and pick one you like – look inside the huts, check out the restaurant, the menu, the guests. You can always move if you're not satisfied.

Beach accommodation around Samui now falls into four basic categories chronicling the evolution of places to stay on the island. The first phase consisted of simple bungalows with thatched roofs and walls of local, easily replaceable materials; the next phase brought concrete bathrooms attached to the old-style huts; then came a transition to the third phase of cement walls and tile roofs – the predominant style now, with more advanced facilities like fans and sometimes air-con. The latest wave is luxury rooms and bungalows indistinguishable from mainland inns and hotels.

Generally anything that costs less than 100B a night will mean a shared bath, which may be preferable when you remember that mosquitos breed in standing water. For a pretty basic bungalow with private bath, 100 to 150B is the minimum on Ko Samui.

Food is touch and go at all the beaches – one meal can be great, the next at the very same place not so great. Fresh seafood is usually what they do best and the cheapest way to eat it is to catch it yourself and have the bungalow cooks prepare it for you, or buy it in one of the many fishing villages around the island, direct from the fisherfolk themselves, or in the village markets. Good places to buy are in the relatively large Muslim fishing villages of Mae Nam, Bo Phut and Hua Thanon.

The ownership and management of various lodgings around the island change so frequently that it's difficult to name favourites. Cooks come and go, bungalows flourish and go bankrupt, owners are assassinated by competitors – you never can tell from season to season. Prices have remained fairly stable in recent years, but they are creeping up. It's easy to get from one beach to another, so you can always change bungalows. With the establishment of several places charging well over 3000B per night, the jetset seems to be discovering Samui. Finally, if Samui isn't to your liking, move islands! Think about Ko Pha-Ngan or Ko Tao.

What follows are some general comments on staying at Samui's various beaches, moving clockwise around the island from Na Thon.

Warning For several years now we have continued to receive reports of theft on Ko Samui. If you're staying in a beach bun-

galow, consider depositing your valuables with the management while off on excursions around the island or while you're swimming at the beach. Most of the theft reports have come from Chaweng, Lamai and Mae Nam beaches.

Ban Tai (Ao Bang Baw) Ban Tai is the first beach area north of Na Thon with accommodation; so far there are just a handful of places to stay here. The beach has fair snorkelling and swimming. The *Axolotl Village* (☎ 420017), run by an Italian-German partnership, caters to Europeans (the staff speaks English, Italian, German and French) with tastefully designed, mid-range rooms for 300B or bungalows for 400 to 600B. Meditation and massage rooms are available – a massage costs 150B per hour. A very pleasant restaurant area overlooking the beach has an inventive international menu.

Next door is the similar-looking and similarly priced *Blue River*, under Thai management. Also at Ban Tai is *Sunbeam*, a set of bungalows in a very nice setting. Huts are 250 to 300B, all with private bath.

Hat Mae Nam Hat Mae Nam is 14km from Na Thon and one of the main beaches for budget bungalow development – definitely still the cheapest area on the island.

At the headland (Laem Na Phra Lan) where Ban Tai ends and Mae Nam begins is the *Home Bay Bungalows* with basic huts for 80B and bungalows with bath for 200 to 400B. Next is *Coco Palm Village* (150 to 300B), followed by *Plant Inn*, also spelt *Phalarn*, with bungalows from 80 to 150B.

Also in this area are *Naplarn Villa*, *Harry's* and *OK Village* – all in the 100 to 400B range. The beach in front of Wat Na Phalaan is undeveloped and the locals hope it will stay that way – topless bathing is strongly discouraged here.

The next group of places east includes *Anong Villa*, *Shangrilah Bungalows* (many bad reports on this one), *Maenam Resort*, *Palm Point Village* (nice ambience) and *Shady Shack Bungalows*, where prices start at 100 to 150B. *Maenam Resort* (☎ 425116)

RICHARD NEBESKY

RICHARD NEBESKY

RICHARD NEBESKY

Southern Gulf Coast
Top: Sunrise at Hat Rin Nai, Ko Pha-Ngan.
Bottom Left: A 'fasting Buddha' image at Nakhon Si Thammarat, a city steeped in history and culture.
Bottom Right: Bungalows beneath towering coconut palms at Hat Lamai, Ko Samui.

RICHARD NEBESKY

RICHARD NEBESKY

JOE CUMMINGS

Southern Gulf Coast
Top: Design on a *reua kaw-lae*, the traditional painted fishing boats of southern Thailand.
Middle: Young Muslim boys from the provincial capital of Narathiwat.
Bottom: Ko Pha-Ngan is quieter and less expensive than Ko Samui; attractions include
four year-round waterfalls, live coral and several peaceful beaches.

is a good mid-range place with spacious bungalows for 250 to 700B, while *Seafan Resort* offers spacious air-con bungalows and a pool for 1200 to 3500B.

Ban Mae Nam's huge *Santiburi Dusit Resort* (☎ 425038, Bangkok (2) 238-4790) – complete with tennis courts, waterways, ponds, bakery and sports facilities – costs from 6000B a night.

Right in Ban Mae Nam, but without beach views, are *Lolita Bungalows* and *Suksom Villa*, both in the 200 to 500B range.

Down on Hat Mae Nam proper is *Friendly*, which has clean, well kept huts for 80B, or 100 to 200B with private bath. Also good are *New La Paz Villa* (150 to 200B, or up to 550 with air-con) and *Silent* (80 to 150B).

Moving towards Bo Phut you'll find *Moon Hut Bungalows*, *Rose Bungalows*, *Laem Sai Bungalows*, *Maenam Villa* and *Rainbow Bungalows*, all with old-style Samui huts for 80 to 150B a night.

There are at least 10 or 15 other bungalow operations between Laem Na Phra Lan and Laem Sai, where Ao Mae Nam ends. The *Ubon Villa* (100 to 150B) is one of the better ones.

Hat Bo Phut This beach has a reputation for peace and quiet, and those who come here regularly hope it will stay that way; this is not the place to show up looking for a party. The beach tends to be a little on the muddy side and the water can be too shallow for swimming during the dry season – a blessing wrapped in a curse which keeps development rather low-key and has preserved Bo Phut's village atmosphere.

Near Bo Phut village there's a string of bungalows in all price ranges, including the farthest north and budget-friendly *Sunny* and *Chalee Villa*, both 100 to 300B, followed by the *Bophut Guest House* (80 to 200B), *Sandy Resort* (400 to 800B), *World Resort* (150 to 1000B), *New Sala Thai* (100 to 200B), *Calm Beach Resort* (100B fan, up to 500B air-con) and the long-running, well run *Peace Bungalow* (150 to 350B). More money to spend? Go for semi-luxurious *Samui Palm Beach* (☎ 425494) at 1200 to 2200B or *Samui Euphoria* (☎ 425098; fax 425107), a posh

spot with rooms and bungalows for 2800B and up.

Proceeding east, a road off the main round-island road runs to the left and along the bay towards the village. One of the golden oldies here is *Ziggy Stardust* (☎ 425410), a clean, well landscaped and popular place with huts for 200 to 300 and a couple of nicer family bungalows for 500 to 1200B. Next to Ziggy's is the *Siam Sea Lodge*, a small hotel with rooms for 250B with fan, hot water and fridge, or 400B with ocean view. You'll find several more cheapies along this strip, including *Miami*, in the 120 to 200B range, and *Oasis* with huts in the 80 to 150B range. In the same vicinity on the inland side (no sea view), *Smile House* starts at 250B and offers the bonus of a large swimming pool.

Up the street from Smile House and facing the ocean is a newer place, *The Lodge* (☎ 425337; fax 425336), which features a two storey design reminiscent of old Samui architecture. Rooms with air-con and TV cost 800 to 1000B (200B less in the low season). Next door you'll find the original *Boon Bungalows*, still holding on with cheap, closely spaced huts for 50 to 100B a night.

If you continue through the village along the water, you'll find the isolated *Sand Blue* with huts for 150 to 400B, and *Sky Blue* in the 80 to 150B range. This area is sometimes called Hat Bang Rak.

The village has a couple of cheap local-style restaurants as well as French, German, Spanish and Italian restaurants. The Australian-managed *Boathouse* has good western and Thai food in a nice setting, and great cocktails. It is also an agent for a PADI diving school. *Bird in the Hand* next door to The Lodge serves good, reasonably priced Thai and western food in a rustic setting overlooking the water. A little farther east on Bo Phut's main street, *Ubon Waan Som Tam* serves cheap and tasty Isaan food.

Big Buddha Beach (Hat Phra Yai) This beach now has nearly 20 bungalow operations, including the moderately expensive air-con *Comfort Resort Nara Garden* (☎ 425-364), with rooms for 600 to 1500B and a swimming pool. *Family Village* gets good reviews and costs 200 to 700B. *Big Buddha Bungalows* (200 to 350B) is still OK. *Sun Set* is about the cheapest place, with simple huts at 80 to 300B. *Como's*, *Champ Resort*, *Beach House*, *Kinnaree* and *Number One* are in the 150 to 300B range. The Beach House also has huts for 200 to 400B, and has also gotten praise for its restaurant. *Niphon* has bungalows costing 200 to 650B.

Ao Thong Son & Ao Thong Sai The big cape between Big Buddha and Chaweng is actually a series of four capes and coves, the first of which is Ao Thong Son. The road to Thong Son is a bit on the hellish side, but that keeps this area quiet and secluded. *Samui Thongson Resort* has its own cove and bungalows for 200B with fan, 850 to 1200B with air-con; knock off about 25% from May to November. *Thongson Bay Bungalows* next door has old-style bungalows for 100 to 150B; farther on is the similar *Golden Pine* with 100 to 200B bungalows.

The next cove along is as yet undeveloped and there isn't even a dirt road yet. The third, Ao Thong Sai, has *Imperial Tongsai Bay* (☎ 425015), a heavily guarded resort with a private beach, swimming pool and tennis courts. Rates start at 4700B.

Hat Choeng Mon The largest cove following Ao Thong Sai has several names, but the beach is generally known as Hat Choeng Mon. It's clean, quiet and recommended for families or for those who don't need night life and a variety of restaurants (these can be found at nearby Chaweng anyway). At Choeng Mon you'll find the well run, popular *PS Villa* (200 to 400B), along with *Choeng Mon Bungalow Village* (150 to 650B), *Chat Kaew Resort* (200 to 1000B), *Island View* (100 to 300B) and the well-laid-out *Sun Sand Resort* (starting at 950B), which has sturdy thatched-roof bungalows connected by wooden walkways on a breezy hillside. Across from the beach is **Ko Faan Yai**, an island that can be reached on foot in low tide.

Between Choeng Mon Bungalow Village and PS Villa are two top-end places. The *Imperial Boat House Hotel* (☎ 425041, Bangkok fax (2) 2619533) has a three storey hotel plus separate two storey bungalows built to resemble rice barges; rates are 2200 to 6000B. Just north is *The White House* (☎ 245315), a collection of deluxe bungalows for 1200 to 2900B.

Next is a smaller bay called Ao Yai Noi, just before north Chaweng. This little bay is quite picturesque, with large boulders framing the white-sand beach. The secluded *IKK* bungalows are 200 to 500B and the *Coral Bay Resort* has larger, well spaced bungalows with air-con, set on grassy grounds, for 1500 to 2200B.

Hat Chaweng Hat Chaweng, Samui's longest beach, also has the island's highest concentration of bungalows and hotels. Prices are moving up-market fast; accommodation is now 60 to 80B at the cheapest places in the off season, and up to 8000B at the Central Samui Beach Resort. There is a commercial 'strip' behind the central beach which is jam-packed with restaurants, souvenir shops and discos. If there are a lot of vacant huts (there usually are during the low season) you can sometimes talk prices down to 80B for a basic hut. The beach is beautiful here, and local developers are finally cleaning up some of the trashy areas behind the bungalows that were becoming a problem in the 1980s.

The central area, Hat Chaweng proper, has the most bungalows and hotels. At the southern end of Chaweng beach, the elegant Imperial Samui Hotel offers a multi-level freshwater pool surrounded by whitewashed, Mediterranean-style rooms built into a hillside overlooking Chaweng Bay. At the other end of the beach – and a world away in terms of style – the notorious Reggae Pub has been expanded into a huge thatch-and-bamboo complex that encompasses a dance hall, pub, restaurant and accommodation catering to the younger party crowd. This is also where the strip behind the hotels and huts is centred, including restaurants (most with videos), bars, discos, video parlours, pool halls, tourist police, TAT mini-office, post office, mini-marts, one hour photo-developing labs, ago – some have just added the word 'resort' to their name.

One minus here are the irritating trucks mounted with loudspeakers that are driven up and down the strip announcing bullfight (bull-against-bull, Thai-style) matches at nearby stadiums; the noise of the loudspeakers drowns out all conversation and any music being played or performed in local bars and restaurants. Another blight on the scene is the ongoing construction of a multistorey hotel in the centre of the beach that obviously flaunts the island's 12m height restriction for beach structures. One hopes a group of honest Samui residents will take on the task of exposing the corruption in the local government department that presumably allowed this monstrosity to begin.

Chaweng has kilometre after kilometre of beach bungalows – perhaps 70 or more in all – so have a look around before deciding on a place. There are basically three sections: North Chaweng, Hat Chaweng proper and Chaweng Noi.

North Chaweng places are mostly in the 100 to 800B range, with simple bungalows with private bath at the northernmost end. Besides being less expensive than lodgings farther south, the north Chaweng places are out of earshot of central Chaweng's throbbing discos. *Papillon Resort* and *Samui Island Resort*, the northernmost of the hotels, offer concrete bungalows starting at 300B, though rates can be half as much in the low season. Friendly *Matlang Resort* (☎ 230468) has better-than-average bungalows for 150 to 400B, and the same can be said for *Marine Bungalows* and *Venus Resort* next door. In the same area, the most inexpensive place, *Blue Lagoon Bungalow*, charges 100 to 400B. After that you have the OK *Family* (150 to 300), *K John Resort* (100 to 400B) and the rather aggressively commercial *Moon* (200 to 300B).

At the end nearest to central Chaweng are a small group of up-market places starting at around 2000B or more: *Samui Villa Flora* (☎ 422272), *Chaweng Blue Lagoon Hotel* (☎ 422037; fax 422401) and *Amari Palm Reef Resort*. The Amari is the nicest of the

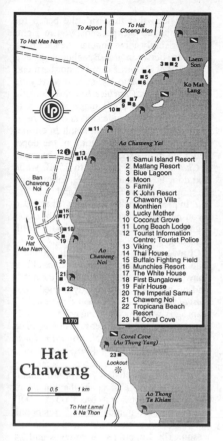

1 Samui Island Resort
2 Matlang Resort
3 Blue Lagoon
4 Moon
5 Family
6 K John Resort
7 Chaweng Villa
8 Monthien
9 Lucky Mother
10 Coconut Grove
11 Long Beach Lodge
12 Tourist Information Centre; Tourist Police
13 Viking
14 Thai House
15 Buffalo Fighting Field
16 Munchies Resort
17 The White House
18 First Bungalows
19 Fair House
20 The Imperial Samui
21 Chaweng Noi
22 Tropicana Beach Resort
23 Hi Coral Cove

tailors, souvenir shops and currency exchange booths.

Water sports are big here too, so you can hire sailboards, go diving, sail a catamaran, charter a junk and so on. Parasailing costs around 400B and water-skiing is 250 to 300B per hour. This area also has the island's highest average prices, not only because accommodation is more up-market but simply because this is/was the prettiest beach on the island. In general, the places get more expensive as you move south; many of these are owned by the same families who owned them under different names 10 or 15 years three, with individual two storey, Thai-style cottages and two swimming pools; it's also the most environmentally conscious luxury resort on the island, using filtered sea water for most first uses and recycling grey water for landscaping. Rooms and bungalows start at 2990/3220B for singles/doubles, 3680B for a mezzanine (two storey) cottage and up to 4485B for a terrace room or suite. The Chaweng Blue Lagoon costs 2200B per room but sometimes offers special rates of 1500B. The Blue Lagoon is home to Sea Canoe Thailand kayak trip operators (see under Sea Kayaking earlier in this section). There are also two mid-range places in the area, the *JR Palace* (400B to 1200B) and *The Island* (400 to 1500B); the latter has a very popular open-air restaurant.

Off the road that leads away from the beach toward the interior is the new *Novotel Ko Samui Resort* (☎ 422472; fax 422473, Bangkok ☎ (2) 267-0810). Novotel's 74 rooms and suites are built in stepped, two storey hotel wings built on a slight slope with sea as well as lagoon views. Rates start at 2200 for deluxe doubles and continue up to 4200B for suites.

Rather than listing all the places on **Chaweng central**, here's a selection across the price spectrum, starting in the north:

Charlie's Hut – 100 to 350B
Chaweng Garden Beach – (☎/fax 422265); 450 to 900B
Chaweng Villa – (☎/fax 422130); 600 to 1000B (air-con)
Coconut Grove – (☎ 422268); 100 to 300B
Joy Resort – 200 to 1000B
Long Beach Lodge – (☎ 422372); 200 to 750B
Lucky Mother – 100 to 300B
Montien House – (☎ 422169; fax 422145); 500B (fan) to 1000B (air-con)
Munchies Resort – 300 to 1500B
Poppies Samui – (☎ 422389; fax 422420); 2000 to 3000B
The Princess Village – (☎ 422216; fax 422382); 1200 to 3400B

The queen of the central Chaweng properties is *Central Samui Beach Resort* (☎ 230500; fax 422385), a huge neo-colonial-style place with rooms starting at 4200B. If you're get-

ting the idea that this isn't the beach for bottom-budget backpackers, you're right, but surprisingly a few popular cheapies have survived between the Beachcomber and Central Bay Resort. From the northern end is *Silver Sand* (300 to 400B), followed by the least expensive, *Charlie's Hut I*, with rustic huts in the 80 to 100B range. There have been complaints of rude staff and theft here, along with pot 'busts' that result in on-the-spot fines but no confiscation of the dope. Better but more expensive huts can be found at *Charlie's Hut II* for 150 to 250B, while next door *Viking* starts at 100B, followed by the similarly priced *Thai House* and *Charlie's Hut*. In peak season these places fill early, so if you're keen to save money it may be easier to go to another beach entirely – or try North Chaweng.

Chaweng Noi is off by itself around a headland at the southern end of central Hat Chaweng. One place that straddles the headland on both bays is the aptly named *First Bungalows* (the first built on this beach 17 years ago), with wooden bungalows for 600B and concrete-and-tile types for 700B up. The *New Star* starts at 350B. Nearby *Fair House* has fan-cooled rooms for 400B, air-con up to 1200B.

The plush, multistorey *Imperial Samui Hotel* is built on a slope in the middle of Chaweng Noi proper and costs 3000 to 5000B for air-con accommodation with telephone and colour TV – up to 40% less in the off-season. The Imperial's 56 cottages and 24 room hotel are built in a pseudo-Mediterranean style with a 700 sq metre saltwater swimming pool and a terrace restaurant with a view. The *Chaweng Noi*, at the southern end of the beach, is the only cheap place left – huts cost 100 to 150B. Finally there's the *Tropicana Beach Resort* with all air-con rooms for 650 to 1200B.

Entertainment The *Reggae Pub* has built a huge new zoo-like complex off the beach with several bars, an artificial waterfall and a huge open-air dance floor with high-tech equipment and trendy DJs who play music most of the night. Another popular dance place is the *Green Mango*, which stays open later. New clubs include *The Doors Pub*, a rock and roll place whose decor pays tribute to Jim Morrison et al; the *Santa Fe*, a huge place with an American southwest theme, beach entrance and state-of-the-art sound and lighting; and *Phra Chan Samui Club*, an enclosed air-con place that's open all night. A mellow alternative to the raging clubs is, oddly enough, the Club Bar.

The crowds tend to trek from bar to bar as the evening wears on: the Reggae Pub from 12 to 2 am, the Doors Pub or the Green Mango from 2 to 4 am and Santa Fe from 4 to 6 am. The order tends to shift around a bit, but don't be surprised if you find a place dead quiet at one time, and bursting at the seams just a few hours later.

Coral Cove (Ao Thong Yang) Another series of capes and coves starts at the end of Chaweng Noi, beginning with scenic Coral Cove. Somehow the Thais have managed to squeeze three places around the cove, plus one across the road. The only one with immediate beach access is *Coral Cove Resort*, where basic huts start at 150B and rise to 300B for a decent bungalow with fan, 500 to 850B with air-con. At the southern end of the cove is the new *Samui Yacht Club* (☎/fax 422400), with luxurious Thai-style bungalows for 3300 to 4300B (1000B less in the low season).

Hi Coral Cove, on a lovely, remote spot above the bay, costs 80 to 400B – good value if you don't mind walking to the beach. *Coral Mountain Chalets*, on the hill opposite the road, costs 350 to 500B.

Ao Thong Ta Khian This is another small, steep-sided cove, similar to Coral Cove and banked by huge boulders. The *Samui Silver Beach Resort* has bungalows overlooking the bay for 400B with fan or 850B with air-con, and a pleasant restaurant with a beach view. On the other side of the road is the *Little Mermaid* with bungalows for 200 and 350B. This is a good spot for fishing, and there are a couple of good seafood restaurants on the bay.

Hat Lamai After Chaweng, this is Samui's most popular beach for farangs. Hat Lamai rates are just a bit lower than at Chaweng beach overall, and there's none of the larger places like the Central Samui or the Imperial (yet) and fewer of the 500B-plus places. As at Chaweng, the bay has developed in sections, with a long central beach flanked by hilly areas. There continues to be reports of burglaries and muggings at Lamai. Take care with valuables – have them locked away in a guesthouse or hotel office if possible. Muggings mostly occur in dark lanes and along unlit parts of the beach at night.

Hotels at the north-eastern end of the beach are quieter and more moderately priced, though the beach is a bit thin on sand. At the top of the beach is the inexpensive *New Hut*, with 80B huts for two people; the proprietor here has been known to eject guests who don't eat in the restaurant and we've had complaints of rudeness. Farther south and almost as inexpensive is an oldie, *Thong Gaid Garden*, where huts are 150 to 250B. *Comfort Bungalow* has undergone a facelift and new ownership and now costs 500 to 1000B for all air-con rooms. There's also a pool.

Also on north Lamai, the semi-secluded *Royal Blue Lagoon Beach Resort* (☎ 424086; fax 424195) sounds fancier than its tariffs might indicate. Smallish bungalows are available for as low as 350B in the low season while larger, better-appointed beachside bungalows cost 1300 to 1800B. It also has a pool and a good restaurant in a nice setting. Less expensive are the *Island Resort* (200 to 250B), *Rose Garden* (150 to 450B) and *Suksamer* (150 to 300B). There are a sprinkling of others too that seem to come and go with the seasons.

One relatively new northern Lamai place that looks like it's here to stay is the American-run *Spa Resort* (☎ 230855; fax 424126), a New Age place that offers herbal sauna, massage, natural foods, meditation and yes, even colon cleansing. Bob Weir of Grateful Dead fame reportedly checked in for a few days in 1996. At the moment simple bungalows here cost 250 to 500B near the beach, 100 to 200B for smaller ones near the

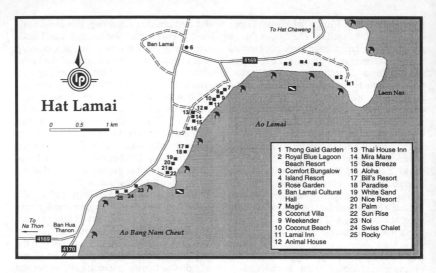

Hat Lamai

0   0.5   1 km

To Hat Chaweng
Ban Lamai ● 6
4169
■ 5 ■ 4 ■ 3
■ 2 ■ 1
Laem Nan
8 ■ 7 ■
10 ■ ■ 9
13 ■ 12 ■ ■ 11
■ 14
■ 15
■ 16

Ao Lamai

17 ■
18 ■
19 ■
20 ■
21 ■ ■ 22
23 ■
25 ■ 24 ■

To
Na Thon   Ban Hua
Thanon
4169
4170

Ao Bang Nam Cheut

1 Thong Gaid Garden	13 Thai House Inn
2 Royal Blue Lagoon	14 Mira Mare
Beach Resort	15 Sea Breeze
3 Comfort Bungalow	16 Aloha
4 Island Resort	17 Bill's Resort
5 Rose Garden	18 Paradise
6 Ban Lamai Cultural	19 White Sand
Hall	20 Nice Resort
7 Magic	21 Palm
8 Coconut Villa	22 Sun Rise
9 Weekender	23 Noi
10 Coconut Beach	24 Swiss Chalet
11 Lamai Inn	25 Rocky
12 Animal House	

road. The restaurant serves vegetarian and seafood. As lodgings alone, these huts are overpriced relative to the neighbourhood; fees for health services are extra. Other activities include t'ai chi, chi kung, yoga and mountain biking.

Down on the main section of Lamai is a string of places for 100 to 600B including *Mui*, *Utopia*, *Magic*, *Coconut Villa* and the *Weekender*. The Weekender has a wide variety of bungalows and activities to choose from, including a bit of a night life. Moving into the centre of Ao Lamai, you'll come across *Coconut Beach* (80 to 200B), *Animal House* (skip this one, it's attracted several complaints) and *Lamai Inn* (300 to 800B).

This is the part of the bay closest to Ban Lamai and the beginning of the Lamai 'scene'. Just about every kind of service is available here, including currency exchange, medical services, supermarkets, one hour photo labs, clothing shops, bike and jeep-rental, travel agencies with postal and international telephone services, restaurants (many with videos), discos, bars, bungy-jumping and food stalls. The girlie bar scene has invaded this part of the island, with several lanes lined with Pattaya-style out-door bars. By and large it's a farang male-dominated scene, but unlike Pattaya and other similar mainland places, where western males tend to take on Thai females as temporary appendages, you may see more than a few western women spending their holiday with Thai boys on Lamai.

Next comes a string of slightly up-market 100 to 600B places: *Thai House Inn*, *Marina Villa*, *Sawatdi*, *Mira Mare*, *Sea Breeze* and *Varinda Resort*. The *Aloha* (☎ 424014) is a two storey more up-market resort where bungalows start at 1050B, rooms at 2200B. All of these places have fairly elaborate dining areas; the Aloha has a good restaurant with seafood, Thai and European food. Also in this area is the *Galaxy Resort*, with fully loaded bungalows for 1400 to 1600B and more basic air-con ones for 400 to 450B, reasonable value. *Golden Sand* is still looking good at 450 to 800B for air-con bungalows.

Central Hat Lamai also has a mixture of places costing anywhere from 80 to 600B. *Paradise* has been here for 20 years, the second-longest-running place on the beach, with thatched huts from 100 to 150B and concrete bungalows for 400 to 600B. Standing apart in terms of providing high-quality, friendly service is *Bill's Resort* (☎ 233054; fax 424286), where bungalows are close together but spacious inside and cost 200 to 400B. The *White Sand* is another Lamai original and huts are now 80B and up. A flea market run by farangs is held here on Sundays – many travellers sell handmade jewellery. The long-standing *Palm* has bungalows in the 150 to 250B price range. The *Nice Resort* has huts for 150B up but they're really too close together. Finally, there's the *Sun Rise*, where acceptable huts go for 100 and 200B, new bungalows with fan for 400B or 700B with air-con.

At this point a headland interrupts Ao Lamai and the bay beyond is known as **Ao Bang Nam Cheut**, named after the freshwater stream that runs into the bay here. During the dry months the sea is too shallow for swimming, but in the late rainy season when the surf is too high elsewhere on the island's beaches, south Lamai is one of the best for swimming. Look for the well known, phallus-like 'Grandmother' and 'Grandfather' rock formations.

Closer to the road than the coast is *Samui Park*, a concrete block with rooms and a few bungalows from 650 to 1250B. Down farther, *Noi* offers huts starting at 80B and bungalows from 150B. Next is *Chinda House*, with air-con bungalows for 800 to 2000B. The *Swiss Chalet* has large bungalows overlooking the sea for 200B and the restaurant does Swiss as well as Thai food. Then comes the old-timer *Rocky*, with a few thatched huts for 150 to 250B, renovated and newer ones for 400 to 800B.

Entertainment Lamai has two large dance clubs, the older *Bauhaus Pub* and the newer *Mix Pub*, the most local dance venue on the island. Interspersed with DJ-ed music are short drag shows and Thai boxing demos.

Ao Na Khai & Laem Set Just beyond the village of Ban Hua Thanon at the southern end of Ao Na Khai is an area sometimes called Hat Na Thian. As at Lanai, the places along the southern end of the island are pretty rocky, which means good snorkelling (there's

a long reef here), but perhaps not such good swimming. Prices in this area seem fairly reasonable – 100B gets you what might cost 200B in Chaweng. The hard part is finding these places, since they're off the round-island road, down dirt tracks, and most don't have phones. You might try exploring this area on a motorcycle first. The *Cosy Resort* has 11 well spaced, simple huts for 100 to 200B. Next is the *Royal Resort* with bungalows for 350B with fan and up to 1200B with air-con. The cheaper *Wanna Samui Resort* has bungalows with fan for 250 and air-con for 950B.

Down a different road in the same area is the drab concrete *Samui Orchid Resort* (☎ 424017), which, with huts for 650 to 1200B and a swimming pool, makes an unsuccessful attempt to be up-market.

Turn right here, follow the coast and you'll come to the basic *Sonny View* (80B) and the nicely designed *Na Thian* (100 to 150B). At the end of the road, at the foot of Khao Thaleh, the secluded *Laem Set Inn* (☎ 424393; fax 424394) commands a pretty corner of sand-and-boulder beach. Some of the buildings here are old Samui-style homes that have been salvaged by the English owner from other parts of the island. Rustic but charming bungalows start at 1150B with veranda, hot-water shower and sea view. More contemporary air-con rooms facing the sea cost from 2500B. On the premises are a small art gallery and a good Thai restaurant (pricey, small portions according to one reader). At Laem Set you pay for atmosphere and ecological sensitivity more than for amenities; some people will find this just what they're looking for, while others may feel they can find better value on the more popular beaches.

Ao Bang Kao This bay is at the very south end of the island between Laem Set and Laem So (Saw). Again, you have to go off the round-island road a couple of kilometres to find these places: *River Garden* (60 to 150B), *Diamond Villa* (100 to 300B), *Samui Coral Beach* (150 to 400B) and *Waikiki* (300 to 400B).

Ao Thong Krut & Ko Taen Next to the village of Ban Thong Krut on Ao Thong Krut is, what else, *Thong Krut*, where huts with private bath are 150 to 250B (100B in low season).

Ban Thong Krut is also the jumping-off point for boat trips to four offshore islands: **Ko Taen, Ko Raap, Ko Mat Daeng** (best coral) and **Ko Mat Sum**. Ko Taen has three bungalow villages along the east-coast beach at Ao Awk: *Tan Village, Ko Tan Resort* and *Coral Beach*, all in the range of 80 to 250B a night. Ko Mat Sum has good beaches – some travellers have camped here. Lately rubbish has been a problem, though, perhaps because there are fewer bungalow proprietors to organise cleanups.

Boats to Ko Taen cost 50B each way. If you want to have a good look at the islands, you can charter a boat at the *Sunset Restaurant* in Thong Krut from 9 am to 4 pm for 900 to 1100B; the boats carry up to 10 people. The Sunset Restaurant has good seafood (best to arrange in advance) and delicious coconut shakes.

West Coast Several bays along Samui's western side have places to stay, including Thong Yang, where the Don Sak and Khanom ferries dock. The beaches here turn to mudflats during low tide, however, so they're more or less for people wanting to get away from the east coast scene, not for beach fanatics.

Ao Phangka Around Laem Hin Khom on the bottom of Samui's western side is this little bay, sometimes called Emerald Cove. The secluded *Emerald Cove* and *Sea Gull* have huts with rates from 80 to 300B – it's a nice setting and perfectly quiet. Between them are the newer and slightly cheaper *Gem House* and *Pearl Bay*. During the low season there are so few guests on this cove that the bungalow proprietors tend to let the rubbish pile up.

Ao Taling Ngam Dominating the north end of this shallow curving bay from its aerial perch atop a steep hill, *Baan Taling Ngam* (☎ 423019; fax 423220, Bangkok ☎ (2) 236-

0400) is Samui's most ultra-exclusive resort at the moment. Managed by the Mandarin Oriental hotel group, Baan Taling Ngam boasts tennis courts, two swimming pools, a fitness centre and a full complement of equipment and instructors for kayaking, windsurfing and diving. As it's not right on the beach, a shuttle service transports guests back and forth. Luxuriously appointed guest rooms containing custom-made Thai-style furnishings start at 4000B for a deluxe in the low season (April to December 14) and up to 10,000B for a cliff villa or deluxe suite in the high season, not including 17% tax and service.

Sharing the same bay just below Baan Taling Ngam, *Wiesenthal* (☎/fax 233165) offers nine bungalows well spaced amid a coconut grove costing 300B single/double, 800B for a family-size bungalow. The Swiss-managed restaurant serves good Thai and European food.

Ao Taling Ngam is a 15 to 20B songthaew ride from Na Thon or the vehicle ferry pier. Baan Taling Ngam of course provides airport/ferry transfers for all guests.

Ao Thong Yang The vehicle ferry jetty is in Thong Yang. Near the pier are *In Foo Palace* (100 to 400B), *Coco Cabana Beach Club* (350B and up) and the motel-like *Samui Ferry Inn* (400 to 900B). The Coco Cabana is the best of the lot.

The vehicle ferry jetty may be moved to another location in the near future or this one may remain and a second one built elsewhere along the coast. Either way the local accommodation will be affected by the change, possibly winding down and eventually closing.

Ao Chon Khram On the way to Na Thon is sweeping Ao Chon Khram, with the *Lipa Lodge* and *International*. The Lipa Lodge is especially nice, with a good site on the bay. Most huts are 100 to 150B, with a few as high as 650B. There is a good restaurant and bar here. On the other hand, the International is nothing special at 200 to 500B. Between them is the up-market *Rajapruek Samui*

Resort (1150 to 3500B), and farther north the isolated and slightly more expensive *The Siam Residence Resort*.

Getting There & Away

Air Bangkok Airways has some flights daily to Ko Samui from Bangkok. There is an office in Na Thon near the Win Hotel and another at the airport (☎ 425012). The fare is 2300B one way – no discount for a return ticket. The flight takes one hour and 20 minutes.

Bangkok Airways also offers daily flights to Samui from Phuket (1330B, 50 minutes) and U-Tapao, near Pattaya (1640B, one hour).

During the high season flights may be completely booked out as much as six weeks in advance, so be sure to plan accordingly. An alternative is to fly to Surat Thani on THAI and then catch a THAI bus from the airport directly to Ko Samui (via the Don Sak vehicle ferry) for 200B.

The Samui airport departure tax is 100B. Bangkok Airways has an air-con van service for 60B per person to/from its Na Thon office and the north/north-west beaches, 80B to/from Lamai. For other beaches you'll have to rely on songthaews or taxis. Chartered taxis from the airport cost 250B to anywhere on the island.

There is talk that the Samui airport may be expanded to accommodate international flights sometime within the next five years.

Bus The government bus/ferry combo fare from Bangkok's Northern air-con bus terminal is 327B. Most private buses from Bangkok charge around 350B for the same journey. From Khao San Rd in Bangkok it's possible to get bus/ferry combination tickets for as low as 220B, but service is substandard and theft is more frequent than on the more expensive buses.

Train The SRT also does train/bus/ferry tickets straight through to Samui from Bangkok. These save you only 10 or 20B on 2nd class seats, otherwise for the other classes a combo ticket actually costs around 50B more than separate train, bus (from the train station to piers) and boat tickets – which may be worth it to avoid the hassles of separate bookings/connections. See the Surat Thani Getting There & Away section for details on train travel.

Boat To sort out the ferry situation you have to understand that there are two ferry companies and three ferry piers on the Surat Thani coast (actually four but only three are in use at one time) and two on Ko Samui. Neither ferry company is going to tell you about the other. Songserm Travel runs express ferry boats from Tha Thong, 6km north-east of central Surat, and slow night boats from the Ban Don pier in town. These take passengers only. The express boats used to leave from the same pier in Ban Don as the night ferry – when the river is unusually high they may use this pier again.

Samui Ferry Co runs vehicle ferries from Don Sak (or Khanom when the sea is high). This is the company that gets most of the bus/boat and some of the train/bus/boat combination-ticket business.

Which boat you take will depend on what's available next when you arrive at the bus terminal in Surat or train station in Phun Phin – touts working for the two ferry companies will lead you to one or the other.

During the low season (ie any time except December to February or July/August), young Thais may throng the piers around departure time for the Ko Samui boats, inviting farangs to stay at this or that bungalow. This same tactic is employed at the Na Thon and Thong Yang piers upon arrival at Ko Samui. During the high tourist season, however, this isn't necessary as every place is just about booked out. Some of the more out-of-the-way places to stay put touts on the boats to pass around photo albums advertising their establishments.

Tha Thong – Express Boat From November to May three express boats go to Ko Samui (Na Thon) daily from Tha Thong. Each takes two to 2½ hours to reach the island. From November to May the departure times are usually 7.30 am, noon and 2.30 pm, though these change from time to time. From June to October there are only two express boats a day, at 7.30 am and 1.30 pm – the seas are usually too high in the late afternoon for a third trip in this direction during the rainy season. The express ferry boats have two decks, one with seats below and an upper deck that is really just a big luggage rack – good for sunbathing. Passage is 105B one way, 170B return, but this fare seesaws from season to season. If any rival companies appear on the scene (as has happened twice in the past four years), Songserm tends to drop its fares immediately to as low as 50B one way to drive the competition out of business.

From Na Thon back to Surat, there are departures at 7.15 am, noon and 2.45 pm from November to May, or 7.30 am and 2.45 pm from June to October. The 7.15 am boat includes a bus ride to the train station in Phun Phin; the afternoon boats include a bus to the train station and to the Talaat Kaset bus station in Ban Don.

Ban Don – Night Ferry There is also a slow boat for Samui that leaves the Ban Don pier in Surat Thani each night at 11 pm, reaching Na Thon around 5 am. This one costs 70B for the upper deck (includes pillows and mattresses), or 50B down below (straw mats only). The locals use this boat extensively and the craft itself is in better shape than some of the express boats. It's particularly recommended if you arrive in Surat Thani too late for the fast boat and don't want to stay in Ban Don. And it does give you more sun time on Samui, after all. The night ferry back to Samui leaves Na Thon at 9 pm, arriving at 3 am.

Don't leave your bags unattended on the night ferry, as theft can be a problem. Theft usually occurs after you drop your bags on the ferry well before departure and then go for a walk around the pier area. Most victims don't notice anything's missing until they unpack after arriving on Samui.

Don Sak – Vehicle Ferry Tour buses run directly from Bangkok to Ko Samui, via the

vehicle ferry from Don Sak in Surat Thani Province, for around 327B. Check with the big tour bus companies or any travel agency.

From Talaat Mai Rd in Surat Thani you can also get bus/ferry combination tickets straight through to Na Thon. These cost 70B for an ordinary bus, 90B for an air-con bus. Pedestrians or people in private vehicles can also take the ferry directly from Don Sak, which leaves at 8, 10 am, 2 and 5 pm, and takes one hour to reach the Thong Yang pier on Samui. In the opposite direction, ferries leave Thong Yang at 7.30 and 10 am, noon, 2 and 4 pm; in this direction the trip takes around an hour and 45 minutes.

Without bus fare included, the straight fare for pedestrians is 50B, for a motorcycle and driver 75B and for a car and driver 190B. Passengers in private vehicles pay the pedestrian fare. The ferry trip takes about 1½ hours to reach Don Sak, which is 60km from Surat Thani.

Buses between the Surat Thani bus station and Don Sak cost 14B and take 45 minutes to an hour to arrive at the ferry terminal. If you're coming north from Nakhon Si Thammarat, this might be the ferry to take, though from Surat Thani the Tha Thong ferry is definitely more convenient.

From Ko Samui, air-con buses to Bangkok leave from near the old pier in Na Thon at 1.30 and 3.30 pm daily, both arriving in Bangkok around 5 am due to a stopover in Surat. Other through bus services from Na Thon include Hat Yai (200B), Krabi (191B) and Phuket (193B); all of these buses leave Na Thon around 7 am, arriving at their respective destinations around six hours later. Check with the several travel agencies in Na Thon for the latest routes.

Getting Around
It is quite possible to hitch around the island, despite the fact that anyone on the island with a car is likely to want to boost their income by charging for rides.

Local Transport Songthaew fares are 15B from Na Thon to Lamai, 10B to Mae Nam or Bo Phut, 15B to Big Buddha, 20B to Chaweng or Choeng Mon. From the car-ferry landing in Thong Yang, rates are 20B for Lamai, Mae Nam and Bo Phut/Big Buddha, 25B for Chaweng, 30B for Choeng Mon. A few years ago official fares were posted for these routes but nowadays songthaew drivers like to overcharge newcomers, so take care. (Songthaew fares haven't changed for nearly four years, so they may be ready to rise by perhaps 5B.) Songthaews run regularly during daylight hours only. A regular bus between Thong Yang and Na Thon costs 10B. Note that if you're arriving in Thong Yang on a bus (via the vehicle ferry), your bus/boat fare includes a ride into Na Thon, but not elsewhere.

At night the songthaews transform themselves into taxis, and charge anywhere from 60B to 200B for a ride, depending on distance and your bargaining abilities.

Car & Motorcycle Rental Several places rent motorcycles in Na Thon and various bungalows around the island do too. The going rate is 150B per day for a 100cc bike, but for longer rentals you can get the price down (280B for two days, 400B for three days etc). Rates are generally lower in Na Thon and it makes more sense to rent them there if you're going back that way. Take it easy on the bikes; several farangs die or are seriously injured in motorcycle accidents every year on Samui, and, besides, the locals really don't like seeing their roads become race tracks.

Suzuki Caribian jeeps can be hired for around 700 to 800B per day from various Na Thon agencies as well as at Chaweng and Lamai beaches. Aside from all the small independents doing rentals, Hertz has branches at Samui airport (☎ 425011) and at the Baan Taling Ngam and Chaweng Blue Lagoon resorts.

KO PHA-NGAN
• *pop 10,000*
Ko Pha-Ngan, about a half hour boat ride north of Ko Samui, has become the island of choice for those who find Samui too crowded or too expensive. It started out as a sort of 'back-door escape' from Samui but is well established now, with a regular boat service and over 156 places to stay around the 190 sq km island. It's definitely worth a visit for its remaining deserted beaches (they haven't all been developed) and, if you like snorkelling, for its live-coral formations.

Diving & Snorkelling
As at Ko Samui, coral reefs can be found intermittently at various points around the island. The better bay reef spots are at the island's north-western tip and are very suitable for snorkelling. There are also some rock reefs of interest on the east side of the island.

An outstanding site for scuba divers, a pinnacle called **Hin Bai**, lies about 13.5km north of the island. According to Samui International Diving School (SIDS; at Tommy Resort on Hat Rin), an abundance of corals and tropical fish can be seen at depths of 10 to 30m; conditions are best from April to October, when divers sometimes enjoy visibility up to 20m or more. Hin Bai can also be reached from Ko Tao, although the boating distance from the latter adds 4 to 5km to the trip.

In addition to SIDS, other dive operations on the island include Thong Sala Divers at Siriphun Bungalows, Ao Wai Nok (about 2km north of Thong Sala) and the Dive Inn at Ao Chalok Lam.

Waterfalls
In the interior of this somewhat smaller island are four year-round waterfalls and a number of more seasonal ones. Boulders carved with the royal insignia of kings Rama V, Rama VII and Rama IX, all of whom have visited the falls, can be found at **Than Sadet Falls**, which cascades along Khlong Than Sadet in the north-eastern part of the island. **Phaeng Falls** is off the main road between Thong Sala and Chalok Lam, almost in the centre of the island. A third falls, **Than Praphat Falls**, is situated near the eastern shore in an area that can be reached by road or boat, while **Than Prawet Falls** is in the north-east near Ao Thong Nai Pan.

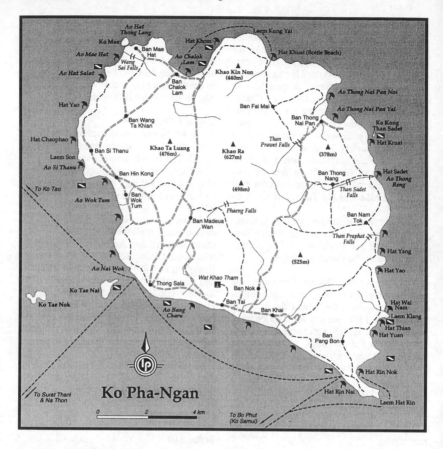

Ko Pha-Ngan

Although hordes of backpackers have discovered Ko Pha-Ngan, the lack of an airport and relative lack of paved roads has so far spared it from tourist-hotel and package-tour development. Compared with Samui, Ko Pha-Ngan has a lower concentration of bungalows, less crowded beaches and coves, and an overall less 'modern' atmosphere. Pha-Ngan aficionados say the seafood is fresher and cheaper than on Samui's beaches, but it really varies from place to place. As Samui becomes more expensive for both travellers and investors, more and more people will be drawn to Pha-Ngan. But for the time being,

overall living costs remain about half what you'd pay on Samui.

Except at the island's party capital, Hat Rin, the island hasn't yet been infested with video and blaring stereos.

Wat Khao Tham

This cave temple is beautifully situated on top of a hill near the little village of Ban Tai. An American monk lived here for over a decade and his ashes are interred on a cliff overlooking a field of palms below the wat. Actually it's not a true wat since there are only a couple of monks and a nun in residence

SOUTH-WESTERN GULF COAST

(among other requirements, a quorum of five monks is necessary for wat status), nor is it even a *sămnák sŏng* (monastic centre). It is rather a retreat centre for foreigners interested in learning something about Theravada Buddhist meditation. An American-Australian couple lead ten-day meditation retreats here during the latter half of most months. The cost is 1800B; write in advance to Khao Tham, Ko Pha-Ngan, Surat Thani, for information or register in person. A bulletin board at the temple also has information.

If you ride a motorcycle to Wat Khao Tham, it's best to leave the bike parked near the bottom of the narrow road that leads up the steep hill to the centre. The road is quite steep in places – too steep for many riders – and the engine noise could disturb the meditating residents.

Thong Sala

About half of Ko Pha-Ngan's population of 10,000 live in and around the small port town of Thong Sala. This is where the ferry boats from Surat and Samui (Na Thon) dock, although there are also smaller boats from Mae Nam and Bo Phut on Samui that moor at Hat Rin.

The town sports several restaurants, travel agents, banks, clothing shops and general stores. You can also rent motorcycles here for 150 to 250B per day.

Information Bovy Supermarket on the main street leading from the pier sells just about anything you might need – sunglasses, sunscreen, liquor, snorkelling gear, cereal, cosmetics, even frisbees.

Money If you're continuing on to other areas of the island and need to do some banking, this is the place to do it. Krung Thai Bank, Siam City Bank and Siam Commercial Bank buy and sell travellers cheques and can arrange money transfers and credit card cash advances; Siam Commercial generally has the best service. Foreign exchange services at Hat Rin are comparable to those in Thong Sala, though you can't wire money there.

Post & Communications The post office is at the southern end of town, in the direction of Hat Rin; it's open weekdays 8.30 am to noon and 1 pm to 4.30 pm, Saturday 9 am to noon. Cafe de la Poste, opposite the post office, sells stamps and offers a parcel/packaging service as well as phone service.

Medical Services The new Ko Pha-Ngan hospital, about 2.5km north of Thong Sala off the road to Chalok Lam, offers 24 hour emergency services. Anything that can wait until Bangkok should wait, as medical facilities are of higher quality.

Dangers & Annoyances While many travellers may like to sample some of the local herb, it may be wise to think twice. There are constant reports of travellers being offered and sold marijuana or other drugs by restaurant or bungalow owners, and then being promptly busted by policeman who *somehow* know exactly who, when and where to check. The result is often a steep fine (50,000B seems to be the standard fee) and in some cases, deportation. Not exactly the makings of a laid-back vacation.

Places to Stay & Eat Aside from a couple of local brothels, the only place to get a room in town nowadays is the *Pha-Ngan Central Hotel* (☎ 377068; fax 377032), on the bay about 150m south of the pier. All rooms have air-con and TV and cost 600B or 700B facing the sea.

Several cafes near the pier cater to farang tastes and also sell boat tickets. *Cafe de la Poste*, opposite the post office, offers imported cheeses, coffee, sandwiches, pizza, pasta and vegetarian dishes. There are a couple of karaoke bars in Thong Sala.

There are a few beach bungalows at Ao Nai Wok, a small bay a couple of kilometres north of the pier. Although the beach here isn't spectacular, it's a fairly nice area to while away a few days – especially if you need to be near Thong Sala. People waiting for an early boat back to Surat or on to Ko Tao may choose to stay here (or south of Thong Sala at Ao Bang Charu) since transport from other parts of the island can be unpredictable.

To get to Nai Wok turn left at the first main crossing from the pier, then walk straight until the road crosses a concrete bridge, and then turn left again when the road dead-ends at a T-junction. Soon you'll come to *Phangan* (60B with shared bath, up to 300B with bath), *Charn* (80 to 120B, all with bath), *Siriphun* (100 to 400B, all with bath) and *Tranquil Resort* (60B with shared bath, up to 200B with bath) – a distance of about 2km. Siriphun seems particularly good value and it still has the best kitchen locally; Siriphun also has some larger houses for long-term rent and has become the headquarters for Thong Sala Scuba Diving.

Ko Pha-Ngan Beaches

Beach bungalows are still mostly concentrated north and south of Thong Sala and especially on the southern end of the island at Hat Rin, but there are many other places to stay around the island as well. The few paved roads on Pha-Ngan means transport can be a bit of a problem, though the situation is improving as enterprising Thais set up taxi and boat services between the various beaches.

As a general rule of thumb, beaches on the east coast don't tend to disappear at high tide as much as those on the west. For the moment the island's best road runs north to south, so visitors tend to cluster at the northern and southern ends of the island. Hat Rin is by far the most developed beach area so far.

Many of the huts on Pha-Ngan have been established by entrepreneurs from Ko Samui with several years experience in the bungalow business. Huts with shared bathing facilities go for 60 to 100B on average and as low as 40B between May and October; many of these do not have electricity or running water. Some have generators which are only on for limited hours in the evening – the lights dim when they make a fruit shake. For many people, of course, this adds to Pha-Ngan's appeal. Other places are moving into the 100 to 300B range, which

almost always includes a private bath, and a few scattered spots on the west and southeast coasts have resort-like amenities – including 24 hour electricity – for 500B and up.

As travel to Pha-Ngan seems particularly seasonal, you should be able to talk bungalow rates down 30 to 40% when occupancy is low. During the peak months (December to February and July and August), there can be an acute shortage of rooms at the most popular beaches and even the boats coming to the island can be dangerously over-crowded.

Since many of the cheaper bungalows make the bulk of their profits from their restaurants rather than from renting huts, bungalow owners have been known to eject guests after a few days if they don't eat meals where they're staying. The only way to avoid this, besides patronising the restaurant, is to get a clear agreement beforehand on how many days you can stay. This seems to be a problem only at the cheaper (40 to 60B) places.

There are a number of beaches with accommodation on Pha-Ngan; the following are listed in an anti-clockwise direction starting at Thong Sala.

Ao Bang Charu South of Thong Sala, the shallow beach here is not one of the island's best, but it's close to town and so is popular with people waiting for boats or bank business.

Petchr Cottage, *Sundance*, *Pha-Ngan Villa* and *Moonlight* are all similar, basic thatched huts in the 60 to 120B range, with a few wood or concrete huts costing a bit more. If you follow a coconut grove to the south you'll find the distinctive high-pitched roofs of *Charm Beach Resort*, a nicely landscaped place starting in the same range and reaching 400B. *Chokkhana Resort* has big, solidly built hexagonal cottages in addition to more traditional huts, costing up to 500B. Charm Beach and Chokkhana Resort both have decent restaurants.

Farther south-east towards Ban Tai, past a school, *First Villa* offers cement-block, tiled-roof cottages but lacks atmosphere. A bit farther on, *First Bay Resort* has even more characterless concrete small huts.

Ban Tai & Ban Khai Between the villages of Ban Tai and Ban Khai unfold a series of sandy beaches with well spaced bungalows, mostly in the 50 to 100B range (a few also have 200B bungalows). Like other western shore beaches, these tend to become quite slim at high tide but many people like this area because it is quiet, yet close to village markets and cafes, and a short songthaew ride from Thong Sala.

Not all bungalows here are signed from the paved road; to really survey the area you must walk along the beach. *Dewshore* and *P Park* are accessed from a road in the centre of Ban Tai; Dewshore offers well constructed huts for 50 to 200, while the P Park couldn't be more dilapidated. Starting at the southern outskirts of Ban Tai you'll find *Birdville*, *Pink*, *Mac Bay Resort*, *Liberty*, *Jup*, *Sabai*, *Bay Hut*, *Lee's Garden*, *Baan Khai Bay*, *Pha-Ngan Rainbow*, *Green Peace*, *Pha-Ngan Island Resort* (300 to 450B) and *Golden Beach*.

In Ban Khai the locals also rent rooms to travellers, especially from December to February when just about everything is filled up. You can get a hut for a month at very low rates here. 'Dark moon parties' are held on the beach at Ban Khai on the day of the month when there's no moon as an alternative to Hat Rin's infamous 'full moon raves'.

Getting There & Away Long-tail boats to other parts of the island can be chartered from Ban Khai. At one time there was a regular boat service to/from Hat Rin but with the paving of the road all the way to Hat Rin it has stopped.

Songthaew taxis from Thong Sala to Ban Tai or Ban Khai cost 15B per person; a motorbike taxi is 20B.

Laem Hat Rin This long cape juts south-east and has beaches along both its westward and eastward sides. The eastward side has the best beach, Hat Rin Nok, a long sandy strip lined with coconut palms. The snorkelling here is pretty good, but between October and March the surf can be a little hairy. The western side of the cape more or less acts as an overflow for people who can't find a place to stay on the eastern side, as the beach is often too shallow for swimming. Some people prefer the west shore's relative quietude. Together these beaches have become the most popular on the island.

Across the ridge on the west side is Hat Rin Nai (Inner Rin beach), which overall is much quieter than Hat Rin Nok. Here you'll find long-runners *Palm Beach* (50 to 150B) and *Sunset Bay Resort* (80 to 200B), plus a string of places in the 70 to 250B range: *Dolphin*, *Charung*, *Haad Rin Village*, *Friendly* and *Family House*. The *Rin Beach Resort* has a few larger huts with private bath and fan from 300B as well as concrete air-con bungalows for 800B.

At the northern end of Hat Rin Nai, around a small headland, are the newer *Bang Son Villa*, *Blue Hill*, *Star*, *Bird*, *Sun Beach*, *Sandy*, *Sea Side*, *Rainbow*, *Coral*, *Sooksom* and *Laidback Shack*, all in the 50 to 100B range. For 80B, the nicest thatched bungalows are those at Blue Hill, situated on a hill above the beach.

Along the road that joins Hat Rin Nok and Hat Rin Nai, in the centre of the cape, you'll find the *Pooltrub (Phuntrap) Resort*, which has upgraded to the 100 to 300B range with solidly built bungalows on landscaped grounds. It's a short walk to Hat Rin Nai.

The eastern beach, or Hat Rin Nok (Outer Rin beach), has gradually become a more or less self-contained town, complete with travel agencies, moneychangers, mini-marts, restaurants, bars, tattoo parlours and two large commercial generators, which supply electric power to the area (at 8B per unit, twice the national average – one reason accommodation prices are higher here). Hat Rin Nok is famous for its monthly 'full moon raves' featuring all-night beach dancing and the ingestion of various illicit substances – forget about sleeping on these nights. Suan Saranrom ('Garden of Joys') psychiatric hospital in Surat Thani has had to take on extra staff during full moon periods to handle the number of farangs who freak out on magic mushrooms, acid or other abundantly available hallucinogens. There are plenty of other drugs available from the local drug mafia and drug-dependent visitors, and the police occasionally conduct raids (see Dangers & Annoyances earlier). Travellers should be careful of their personal safety at these parties, especially female travellers; assaults have occasionally been reported.

Lately the district authorities and the TAT have stepped in and tried to establish a more wholesome 'full moon party' featuring water sports and cultural events during the daytime, and keeping a close watch at night so things don't get out of hand. Word is that the infamous Hat Rin 'full moon party' is already toning down quite a bit. Still, even when the moon isn't full, several establishments blast dance music all night long – head for the western side if you prefer a quieter atmosphere.

The bungalows here are stacked rather closely together and are among the most expensive on the island. Starting from the south, *Paradise Bungalows* is one of the oldest establishments and offers a variety of cottages from near the beach to inland on the rocks, plus rooms in a motel-like structure perpendicular to the beach, starting at 150B. The newer *Beach Blue* continues the trend of renting motel-like rows of rooms extending away from the beach for 120B a night. Next are the slightly more up-market *Anant Bungalows* and *Haadrin Resort* with rooms in the 150 to 500B range. Nicely kept *Phangan Orchid Resort* is similar, while *Sea Garden Bungalows* is on the cheaper side with simple huts for 80 to 150B. *Sunrise Bungalows*, more or less in the middle of the beach, is another long-timer and is usually a good choice; huts made of local materials are priced from 60 to 300B depending on proximity to the beach and the current occupancy rate. It's often full December to August.

Pha-Ngan Bayshore Resort (☎ (01) 725-0430), Hat Rin's first semi-upscale establishment, occupies the middle section of

beach and charges around 400 to 500B a night. Next is *Tommy Resort*, another old-timer and home to Samui International Diving School; bungalows here run 100 to 300B. *Palita Lodge*, a large group of wooden bungalows next door, costs 80 to 200B and boasts one of the better beach restaurants. Toward the north end of the beach is the badly maintained *Seaview Haadrin Resort*, set amid trashy grounds; the usual bungalows cost 100 to 300B but consider this place only as last resort.

Built into the rocky headland at the north end of Hat Rin, *Mountain Sea Bungalows* shares a set of cement stairs (inundated by the surf at high tide) with *Serenity*. Each has huts with and without bath for 80 to 200B; an advantage to staying here is that it's relatively quiet here at night compared with places right on the beach.

Behind the main row of beach lodgings a second row of bungalows are appearing, including *Bumblebee Huts* and *Haad Rin Hill*, both in the 80 to 150B range. Bumblebee has gotten kudos for its food. Perched on the slopes of a hill in the centre of Hat Rin's southernmost point are the similarly priced *Leela Bungalows* and *Lighthouse*, plus one or two others that come and go with each high season.

On both sides of Hat Rin, hammers and saws are busy putting together new huts, so there may be quite a few more places by now. Not only are the cliffs on each side of the bay filling up, but a few one storey hotels are now under construction back from the beach due to the popularity of the area.

Places to Eat Restaurants here are getting almost as expensive as on Samui, but the seafood is good and fresh, particularly at *Sand* and *Crab*. The *Haadrin Bakery & Restaurant* offers a wide variety of cakes, rolls and other baked goods. On the road between the two beaches, *Namaste Chai Shop* serves Indian food.

Getting There & Away Songthaew taxis go back and forth between Hat Rin and Thong Sala for 40B. This road was paved with concrete in 1996 but, ironically, the steeper, windier passages are more dangerous now than before the paving as everyone drives faster and the smooth surface doesn't afford much braking traction. Motorcycles can be rented in Hat Rin Nok; take extra care when riding them on this road as lots of people wipe out on the steep downhill slopes; there is no shoulder on the road either, so watch out for passing vehicles.

East Coast Beaches Between Hat Rin and the village of Ban Nam Tok are several little coves with the white-sand beaches of **Hat Yuan** (2.5km north of Hat Rin), **Hat Thian** (3km) and **Hat Wai Nam** (3.5km). The beach at Hat Yuan has no places to stay but would be perfect for camping if you bring your own food; it's connected by an inland trail to Hat Rin.

Around a small headland at the north-eastern end of Hat Yuan, crescent-shaped Hat Thian has accommodation at *The Sanctuary*, a New Age-oriented spot built into boulders overlooking the beach. Bungalows with shared facilities cost 60 to 100B, with attached bathroom 100 to 300B; instruction in yoga, t'ai chi, meditation and massage is available. Nearby, the *Hadd Tien Resort* (☎ (01) 725-0919) has double-bed bungalows with mosquito nets and attached bath for 120 to 180B. North over a cape called Laem Klang and past another headland lies Hat Wai Nam, where a *hotel* is only open December to April.

Hat Yao (5km from Hat Rin) and **Hat Yang** (6km) are virtually deserted. A dirt track (traversable on foot but only partially accessible by motorcycle) runs along the coast from Hat Rin before heading inland to Ban Nam Tok and Than Sadet Falls. Then 2.5km north of Ban Nam Tok by a separate dirt track is the pretty double bay of **Ao Thong Reng**, where *bungalows* are 50B. Above the beach on the headland, *Than Wung Thong Resort* offers huts for 60 to 150B. North of the headland, a pretty cove ringed by Hat Sadet features a string of places whose names change regularly, all in the 50 to 80B range.

Getting There & Away Beaches between Hat Rin Nok and Hat Yang can be reached on foot via the above-mentioned dirt track, or by charter boat from Hat Rin Nok from April to September. Charter rates are negotiable, but it shouldn't cost more than 50B per boat as far as Hat Yuan or Hat Thian, 70B or so for Hat Wai Nam and Hat Yao, 80B to Hat Yang.

There is a rough dirt track from Thong Sala to Ao Thong Reng – the same track that goes to Than Sadet Falls, and traversing it is very much subject to weather conditions. A songthaew taxi should cost around 70 or 80B between Thong Sala and this cove. Boats to/from Thong Sala (70B) and Hat Rin (50B) make the trip by water every morning between September and April.

Ao Thong Nai Pan This bay is really made up of two bays, **Ao Thong Nai Pan Yai** and **Ao Thong Nai Pan Noi**. The latter is the best all-around swimming beach. On the beach at Thong Nai Pan Yai, south-east of Ban Thong Nai Pan village, are the *White Sand, AD View* and *Nice Beach*, all with huts from 60B with shared bath or up to 300B for nicer ones with attached bath. The other end of the beach features the similarly priced *Pen's* and *Pingjun Resort*, along with the more basic *Chanchit Dreamland* at 70B per hut.

Up on Thong Nai Pan Noi are the very nicely situated *Panviman Resort* (☎/fax 377048, Bangkok ☎ (2) 587 8491; fax 587 8593) and *Thong Ta Pan Resort*. Panviman sits on a cliff between two beaches and offers 40 rooms in wooden bungalows or in a two storey building for 300B with fan or up to 1500B with air-con, all with private bath. The more basic but clean Thong Ta Pan Resort, at the north end of the smaller bay, costs 80 to 150B. Between them is the similarly priced *Rocky Blue* and *Big Yogurst*. *Star Huts* (☎ 84280) at Thong Nai Pan Noi receives high marks for well maintained huts with fans for 100/150B single/double in high season, nicer huts for up to 300B.

Getting There & Away Songthaew taxis from Thong Sala to Thong Nai Pan cost 60B.

Panviman runs its own taxi service from the Thong Sala pier.

Hat Khuat & Chalok Lam These are two pretty bays with beaches at the northern end of Pha-Ngan. They are still largely undeveloped in regard to tourism because of their distance from major transport points to Samui and the mainland. Some of the island's least expensive accommodation is found here – hence it's popular with long-termers – but that means more likelihood of being evicted from your hut if you don't buy meals from the bungalow kitchens. Be sure to establish whether you'll be required to buy meals before taking a hut.

Hat Khuat (Bottle beach) is the smaller of the two and currently has four sets of bungalows, all in the 60 to 250B range – *Bottle Beach*, *Bottle Beach II*, *OD Bungalows* and *Sea Love*. West of Hat Khuat, 2.5km across Laem Kung Yai, is **Hat Khom**, where the *Coral Bay* rents standard huts for 40 and 50B. You can walk to Hat Khuat from Ban Chalok Lam but until they build a better bridge over Khlong Ok, no jeeps or motorcycles can access it – all the better for quiet days and nights.

The friendly fishing village of Ban Chalok Lam at the centre of Ao Chalok Lam features several small mom-and-pop grocery stores, laundry services and lots of fish drying at the side of the main street. The Dive Inn here offers scuba courses in English or German – this is Ko Pha-Ngan's closest dive operator to Hin Bai. Some shops rent bicycles.

Starting from the north-eastern corner of the village, *Mr Phol's* offers very basic huts with no beach to speak of for 50B a night. Farther on in this direction, *Fanta* is larger and a bit better, with several rows of huts starting at 40B per person and a fair chunk of beach frontage.

Across Khlong Ok via a rickety footbridge, *Try Tong Resort* offers largish wooden cabins facing the bay and canal for 50 to 200B. There's no beach at Try Thong save for a small scallop of sand with boulders at the surf line that all but disappears in high tide. Farther on toward Hat Khom is *Thai*

Life, with simple huts for 40B, plus better bungalows with more facilities for up to 200B.

At the other end of long Hat Chalok Lam, west of the village, is the slightly nicer *Wattana* with huts for 60 to 80B and bungalows with fan for 150 to 250B. The beach is better – wider and cleaner – here, too.

Places to Eat The food situation in the village Ban Chalok Lam has improved of late. Of the several simple restaurants on the main road parallel to the bay, the most reliable for quality are *Seaside* and *Porn*. There are also a few inexpensive noodle stands around.

Getting There & Away The road between Thong Sala and Ban Chalok Lam is paved all the way now, and songthaews do the route regularly for 25B per person, or you can do the same trip by motorcycle for 30B. These fares are really keyed to the old days when the road wasn't so good, so we can expect the fare to drop as the number of songthaews plying this route increases. Ao Chalok Lam is a good place to hire boats for explorations of the northern coast as many fishermen dock here (particularly between February and September). During this season boats run regularly from here to Hat Khuat twice a day for 20B per person. On some days the service may be cancelled due to high surf, so anyone electing to stay at Bottle beach should leave a couple of extra days for planned departure from the island just in case. A new concrete pier was recently completed in Ban Chalok Lam, so boat services may increase.

Ao Hat Thong Lang & Ao Mae Hat As you move west on Pha-Ngan, as on Samui, the sand gets browner and coarser. The secluded beach and cove at Ao Hat Thong Lang has no accommodation at the moment, though there was once a small bungalow operation here with huts at the usual 30 to 40B rate.

An all-weather road leads west from Chalok Lam to Ban Mae Hat, a small fishing village with a few bungalow resorts. The beach at Ao Mae Hat isn't fantastic, but there is a bit of coral offshore. Close by, a little inland via a well marked dirt track (200m off the road from Chalok Lam near Km 9), is Wang Sai Falls, also know as Paradise Falls. Toward the north-east end of the bay, *Maehaad Bungalows* has good, simple thatched huts for 50B plus wood-and-thatch huts with private bath for up to 150B, while the *Mae Hat Bay Resort* and *Crystal Island Garden* have small wooden huts in the same price range. Moving south-westward, the *Island View Cabana* offers good clapboard huts from 50 to 250B for nicer ones. The Island View also has a good restaurant.

Bang Sai Resort, at the south-western end of Mae Hat, offers nice-sized bungalows built among boulders on a hillside; all have views of beach and bay. Rates run 60 to 200B, depending on the position on the slope. An open-air restaurant is well away from the huts, down on the beach.

Opposite the beach on the islet of Ko Mae are five *huts* that go for just 40B.

The paved section of the road from Chalok Lam gives out at Km 10 (counting from Thong Sala), but a new road under construction will eventually link with Hat Yao to the south-west. Songthaew/motorcycle taxis from Thong Sala cost 25/30B.

Hat Salat & Hat Yao These coral-fringed beaches are fairly difficult to reach – the road from Ban Si Thanu to the south is very bad in spots, even for experienced dirt-bikers – come by boat if possible. Hat Yao is a very long, pretty beach with a reasonable drop-off that makes it one of the island's best swimming beaches.

Hat Salat has *My Way* with huts for 60B. Down at Hat Yao are the basic *Benjawan*, *Dream Hill*, *Blue Coral Beach*, *Sandy Bay*, *Ibiza*, *Bayview* and *Hat Thian*; the latter two are isolated on a beach north of Hat Yao around the headland; the road is very steep and rocky. All of these places offer basic 40 to 120B huts. Along the best section of beach is *Haad Yao Bungalows*, which sensibly charges extra for basic accommodation if

you don't eat here and also has 200 to 500B bungalows; its tall security fence, however, lends a definite air of paranoia and posted signs say it's for sale.

Around a small headland to the south to Hat Yao is *Rock Garden*, which lives up to its name with all manner of creative rock placements, including a steep rock path leading down to the bungalows from the road; tread carefully. Its isolation may appeal to those looking for a long-term hideaway.

Hat Chaophao & Ao Si Thanu Hat Chaophao is a rounded beach two headlands south of Hat Yao, while around a larger headland farther south is Ao Si Thanu. In these areas you begin to see the occasional mangrove along the coast. Inland there's a pretty lagoon at the south end of Hat Chaophao near Laem Son.

There are four places to stay along the beach at Hat Chaophao. The popular *Sea Flower, Sri Thanu* and *Great Bay* all have bungalows with private bath for 80 to 180B, and some without for 50 to 80B. We've heard complaints about sexual harassment of female travellers and general cheating (eg promising one room rate, than upping it when you check out) at Great Bay. *Hat Chaophao*, sandwiched between the others, has only 300B bungalows. At the south end of the bay, past curving Laem Niat, *Bovy Resort* has standard huts with attached bath for only 50 to 70B; it's owned by the same family who own Bovy Supermarket in Thong Sala, which means it's usually well stocked with food.

On the rounded, pine-studded cape of Laem Son, at the north end of Ao Si Thanu proper, lies *Laem Son Bungalows* with simple, quiet, shaded huts for 40 to 70B. South over a creek comes *Seaview Rainbow* with similar rates. Down towards the south end of the bay, *Lada* offers 200B bungalows with fan and bath.

Loy Fah and *Chai*, both sitting high on a point at the southern end of the bay on the cape of Laem Si Thanu, offer good views and sturdy huts. Nicely landscaped Loy Fah, the better run of the two, offers good-sized wooden cottages for 150B, cement for 200B, all with fan, mosquito net, toilet and shower. Loy Fah also has two large, 400B cottages at the bottom of the cliff on a private cove. In the low season you can knock 40% off these rates. Down at the southern base of the cliff is the similarly priced *Nantakarn*, but it's not as good value.

Ao Hin Kong/Ao Wok Tum This long bay – sometimes divided in two by a stream which feeds into the sea – is just a few kilometres north of Thong Sala but so far has hardly any development. In general this is the cheapest place to sleep on the island. At the centre of Hin Kong, not far from the village of Ban Hin Kong, is the basic *Lipstick Cabana* for the usual 40 to 150B. On the southern end of the village is the similarly priced *Hin Kong*. Down at the southern end of Ao Wok Tum on the cape between this bay and Ao Nai Wok are *Tuk* and *Kiat*, both in the 40 to 60B range. A little farther down around the cape that separates Ao Wok Tum from Ao Nai Wok are *OK*, *Darin*, *Sea Scene*, *Porn Sawan*, *Cookies* and *Beach*, most with simple 30 to 80B huts – Darin, Sea Scene and Porn Sawan also have bungalows with private bath in the 120 to 300B range.

See the earlier Thong Sala section for accommodation just north of Thong Sala at Ao Nai Wok.

Songthaews to this area cost 30B per person but you won't see them outside ferry departure/arrival times.

Getting There & Away

Ko Samui – Express Boat Songserm express boats to Ko Pha-Ngan leave from the Na Thon pier on Ko Samui every day from November to May at 10 am and 3 pm, the remainder of the year 10 am and 4 pm. The trip takes 50 minutes and costs 50B one way. Boats back to Samui leave Pha-Ngan's Thong Sala pier at 6.15 am and 1 pm daily; in this direction the fare is 60B.

Ko Samui – Other Boats A small boat goes direct from Samui's Bang Rak (near Bo Phut village) to Hat Rin on Ko Pha-Ngan for 50 to 60B. Depending on who's got the conces-

sion, the boat sometimes leaves from Bo Phut instead. This boat departs Bang Rak/Bo Phut just about every day at 10.30 am and 3.30 pm, depending on the weather and number of prospective passengers, and takes 40 to 45 minutes to reach the bay at Hat Rin. In the reverse direction it usually leaves at 9.30 am and 2.30 pm and takes 30 to 40 minutes.

From January to September there is also one boat a day from Hat Mae Nam on Samui to Ao Thong Nai Pan on Pha-Ngan, with a stop at Hat Rin. The fares are 120B to Ao Thong Nai Pan and 60B to Hat Rin. The boat usually leaves Mae Nam around 1 pm. In the reverse direction the boat leaves from Ao Thong Nai Pan around 8 am.

A new company called Rossarin Tour has 35-passenger speedboats that go between Samui's Hat Mae Nam and Thong Sala for 150B. This boat leaves at 1 pm and only takes about half an hour to reach Thong Sala.

Surat Thani – Night Ferry You can also take a slow night ferry direct to Pha-Ngan from the Ban Don pier in Surat. It leaves nightly at 11 pm, takes 6½ hours to arrive at Thong Sala, and costs 100B on the upper deck (includes pillows and mattresses), 60B on the lower (straw mats only). This is most convenient if you happen to arrive in Surat in the late afternoon or evening. Of course you'll also save a night's hotel tariff sleeping on the boat.

As with the night ferry to Samui, don't leave your bags unattended on the boat – there have been several reports of theft.

Surat Thani – Other Boats A couple of years ago a fast jet-boat and another express boat competed with Songserm for about a year, but Songserm immediately dropped its fares to a loss level and ran them out of business. With increasing tourism on the islands, it's only a matter of time before someone else steps in and gives Songserm a run for its money.

Ko Tao Subject to weather conditions, there are daily express boats between Thong Sala and Ko Tao, 47km north, at 2.30 pm. The trip takes 2½ hours and costs 150B one way.

A Rossarin Tour operates speedboats between Thong Sala and Ko Tao a couple of times a day for 350B per person; the crossing only takes about an hour.

Train/Bus/Boat Combinations At Bangkok's Hualamphong train station you can purchase train tickets that include a bus from the Surat Thani train station (Phun Phin) to the Ban Don pier and then a ferry to Ko Pha-Ngan. These generally cost around 30 to 50B more than buying each ticket separately yourself. Several travel agencies on the island can help book the journey back to Bangkok, though beware of places that offer you 'vouchers' rather than train tickets: these could turn out to be worthless. Reputable agents should have no problem supplying the actual tickets.

Getting Around
A couple of roads branch out from Thong Sala, primarily to the north and the south. One road goes north-west from Thong Sala a few kilometres along the shoreline to the villages of Ban Hin Kong and Ban Si Thanu. From Ban Si Thanu the road travels north-east across the island to Ban Chalok Lam. Another road goes straight north from Thong Sala to Chalok Lam. There is also a very poor dirt road along the west coast from Ban Si Thanu to Ao Hat Yao and Ao Hat Salat.

Hat Khuat (Bottle beach) can be reached on foot from Ban Fai Mai (2km) or Ban Chalok Lam (4km) or there are boats during certain months.

The road south from Thong Sala to Ban Khai passes an intersection where another road goes north to Ban Thong Nang and Ban Thong Nai Pan. The paved road to Hat Rin is now passable year-round, so there's regular transport between Thong Sala and Hat Rin. Even with the paving, only experienced motorbike riders should attempt the section between Ban Khai and Hat Rin. Steep grades, blind turns and a slippery road surface (which will only become more slippery with use) make it the most dangerous piece of road on the island, perhaps anywhere in southern Thailand.

Songthaews and motorcycle taxis handle all the public transport along island roads. Some places can only be reached by motorcycle; some places only by boat or foot.

You can rent motorcycles in Thong Sala for 150 to 250B a day.

Songthaew & Motorcycle Taxi From Thong Sala, songthaews to Hat Chaophao and Hat Yao are 30B and 40B per person respectively, while motorcycle taxis cost 40B and 50B. To Ban Khai, it's 15B by songthaew, or 20B by motorcycle; if you're only going as far as Wat Khao Tham or Ban Tai the fare remains the same for motorcycles but drops to 10B for a songthaew.

A songthaew from Thong Sala to Ban Chalok Lam is 25B, a motorcycle taxi 30B.

To get to Hat Rin from Thong Sala, a songthaew costs 50B one way while a motorbike is 70B. To get there by boat, see the following Boat section.

Thong Nai Pan can be reached from Thong Sala by songthaew (60B) or motorcycle (90B). See the following Boat section for water transport to Thong Nai Pan.

Boat There are daily boats from Ao Chalok Lam to Hat Khuat at noon and 4 pm (returning at 9 am and 3.30 pm) for 20 to 30B per person depending on the number of passengers. The service operates from January to September, depending on the weather.

Thong Nai Pan can be reached by boat from Hat Rin on south Pha-Ngan at noon for 60B, but these boats generally run only between January and September, depending on the weather. When the ferry arrives at the Thong Sala pier from Surat or Samui, there may be boats waiting to take passengers on to Hat Rin for 50B – it takes about 45 minutes, but with the road paved all the way to Hat Rin these boat services are fading.

Regular boat service between Ban Khai and Hat Rin has all but halted, though boat pilots will still take one to three persons for 50B each, four or more for 20B each. Although the boat is slower, it's a lot easier on the nerves than the Hat Rin's 'death highway'.

KO TAO

Ko Tao translates as 'Turtle Island', named for its hump-backed shape. It's only about 21 sq km in area and the population of 750 are mostly involved in fishing, growing coconuts and catering to tourism. Snorkelling and diving are particularly good here due to the relative abundance of coral, though most of the beaches are too shallow for swimming.

Since it takes three to five hours to get there from the mainland (from either Chumphon or Surat Thani via Ko Pha-Ngan), Ko Tao doesn't get people coming over for day trips or for quick overnights. Still, the island can become quite crowded during high season, when Mae Hat, Hat Sai Ri and Ao Chalok Ban Kao have people sleeping on the beach waiting for huts to vacate.

Ban Mae Hat, on the western side of the island, is where inter-island boats land. The only other villages on the island are **Ban Hat Sai Ri** in the centre of the west coast and **Ban Chalok Ban Kao** to the south. Less than a kilometre off the north-west shore of the island is **Ko Nang Yuan**, which is really three islands joined by a sand bar.

The granite promontory of **Laem Tato** at the southern tip of Ko Tao makes a nice hike from Ban Chalok Ban Kao.

Information

Ban Mae Hat, a one-street town with a busy pier, is the only commercial centre on the island. Here you'll find a police station, post and telephone office (open daily from 8.30 am to 4 pm), travel agents, dive shops, restaurants and general stores. There is no bank on the island, but several moneychangers offer exchange services below the usual bank rates.

Boat tickets can be purchased at a booking office by the harbour as well as from travel agents.

Diving & Snorkelling

Relative to its size, Ko Tao has a large number of diving shops, with some of Thailand's lowest prices for training and/or excursions. Underwater visibility can be very high and the water is cleaner than around most other

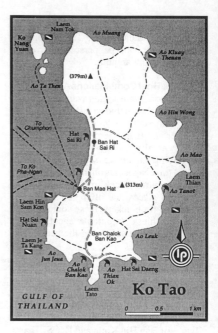

inhabited islands in the gulf. Because of the foreign presence, the best diving spots have English names, eg White Rock, Shark Island, Chumphon Pinnacle, Green Rock, North-West Pinnacle and South-West Pinnacle. Newer spots are being discovered all the time. March to October are generally the best diving months.

One of the closest good spots is **Hin Khao** (White Rock), which lies just south of Ko Nang Yuan – about half a kilometre off Ko Tao's north-west tip – and features lots of coral and fish at depths of 5 to 20m. Also easy to reach is **Kong Sai Daeng** (known among foreign divers as 'Shark Island'), which is a couple of hundred metres off the south-east end of the island. This one mixes colourful corals with rounded granite boulders, plenty of fish and fair to excellent visibility depending on weather conditions. Depths are suitable for snorkelling in spots. A bit farther afield, about 8km south-west of Ko Tao, **Kong Tungku** (commonly called 'Southwest

SOUTH-WESTERN GULF COAST

Pinnacle') is a large seamount with coral at depths of 6 to 28m and visibility that sometimes exceeds 20m.

You can also find fair coral at the rocky ends of several bays on the island, good fun for beach snorkelling.

Dive Shops At the time of writing there were 16 dive operations on the island, most charging basically the same dive rates. To support so many instructors, this means nearly every tourist who visits Ko Tao will be solicited for diving lessons/trips; most are directly affiliated with accommodation on the island for just this purpose. During high season you may have to sign up for diving or be refused accommodation.

Scuba Junction, opposite SP Cabana on Hat Sai Ri, has a very professional setup and good gear. It also runs an awareness program aimed at cleaning up reef areas, and has been recommended by several readers. Master Divers has friendly staff and offers good dive site information. Many of the other dive setups on the island seem to come and go with each tourist season. Rates typically run 500 to 600B per dive (including gear, boat, guide, food and beverages) or 350B if you bring your own gear. An all-inclusive introductory dive lesson costs 1500B while a four-day, open-water PADI certificate course goes for around 6500B – these rates include gear, boat, instructor, food and beverages. A snorkel mask and fins typically rent for 100B (or 50B separately) per day.

Places to Stay
With the steady transformation of Ko Tao into a diving resort, huts on Ko Tao have moved up-market relative to Ko Pha-Ngan – positioned sort of in between Samui and Pha-Ngan in terms of costs and amenities. Few bungalows are made with local materials any more, perhaps a boon to the environment. At last count there were about 650 huts in 48 locations around the island. At most places electricity is provided by generators from 6 pm to midnight. Simple thatched or wooden huts typically cost 80 to 150B per night, while larger wood, brick or concrete

bungalows with private bath range from 200 to 600B.

During the peak season (December to March) it can be difficult to find accommodation anywhere – no matter what the time of the day – and people end up sleeping on the beach or in restaurants for one or two nights until a hut becomes available. What is more common is that all the cheaper huts are occupied and only the places costing 250B or more are available. On arrival at Ban Mae it may be best to follow a tout who can find vacant huts, as your chances of finding a place on your own might be very slim.

Some bungalows with associated diving operations will refuse accommodation to visitors who don't sign up for a dive trip or instruction. Some of the cheaper operations – especially those at the north end of Hat Sai Ri and at Ao Tha Then – will give you the boot if you don't buy food at their restaurants; we still receive reports of visitors being locked out of their bungalows or being violently ejected. On the other hand in the off season it can be a problem finding a bungalow operation that hasn't closed down till next high season.

Ao Mae At Hat Ao Mae, just north of Ban Mae Hat, the shallow bay has plenty of coral – nothing to compare with the offshore dive sites but enough for casual snorkelling. *Crystal* offers basic plywood huts for 150B and concrete and wood bungalows with bath for 500 to 650B – the most expensive on the island and rather overpriced considering the lackadaisical staff. Friendly, quiet *Dam* has nice thatched huts with shared facilities and small verandas with hammocks for 100B to 150B; it's often full because it's one of the best value places on the west side of the island. On the headland overlooking the bay are *Queen Resort* (100 to 200B for standard bungalows) and *Tommy Resort* (80B for a room over the restaurant/office, and from 250 to 500B for a nicer bungalow). Just beyond Tommy, the *View Cliff Restaurant & Bungalows* offers basic huts with shared bath for 100B, larger huts with shower and toilet for 250 to 350B.

Hat Sai Ri Around the headland to the north is the longest beach on the island, with a string of bungalow and dive operations starting with *AC Resort I & II*, side-by-side places with sturdy bungalows with attached bath and nice landscaping in the 200 to 350B range. (Last we heard this place was running 'full moon raves' on the weekends, which can make for a noisy stay). *Haad Sai Ree Resort* and *Ko Tao Cabana* have similar accommodation at the same rates. Up next *SB Cabana* has clean wooden bungalows with attached toilet and shower for 200 to 250B. *Bing Bungalow*, on the other side of the road, has cheaper huts for 100B with shared bath, 200B with attached bath. *Big Fish Dive Resort* and *Ban's Diving Resort* each offer sturdy bungalows starting at 150B.

The air-con stucco cottages at *Sunset Bari Resort* have a Mediterranean look and are the poshest digs on the island so far. Rates start at 500B and there's a swimming pool on the premises. Farther north along Hat Sai Ri are four places in the 80 to 250B range: *Sai Ri Cottage*, *New Way*, *Haad Sai Ree Villa* and *O-Chai*. New Way is one of the places that locks guests out of their rooms if they don't purchase a sufficient amount of food.

North of the beach in an area sometimes called Ao Ta Then are several inexpensive bungalow operations with very basic huts – most off the beach and built high on the rocks – including *Golden Cape*, *Silver Cliff*, *Sun Sea*, *Sun Lord*, *Eden Resort* and *Mahana Bay* in the 50 to 150B range. Farther north, the lone *CFT* has basic huts for 70B and bungalows with attached bath for up to 300B.

Ao Muang & Ao Kluay Theuan On the northern and north-eastern tip of the island, accessible only by boat, are two coral-fringed coves without bungalow accommodation. As the pressure for places to stay increases, new operations should start appearing at both.

Ao Hin Wong South of Ao Kluay Theuan and 2km north-east of Ban Hat Sai Ri by trail, tranquil Ao Hin Wong has a handful of huts called *Hin Wong Bungalows* for 80 to 100B. Despite the lack of competition the restaurant serves good food.

Ao Mao, Laem Thian & Ao Tanot Continuing clockwise around the island, Ao Mao, connected by a 2km dirt trail with Ban Hat Sai Ri, is another cove with no beach accommodation so far. On the cape which juts out over the north end of Ao Tanot, *Laem Thian* has huts built among the rocks from 60B.

To the south, Ao Tanot is one of the island's best spots for beach snorkelling and features a good set of bungalow operations; the proprietors so far tend to cooperate to keep the beach clean, a major plus. The well landscaped *Tanote Bay Resort* charges 50 to 100B for simple but well maintained huts, while *Poseidon* has rather shabby huts for 50 to 80B. The friendly *Diamond Beach* offers huts from 50 to 100B. *Bamboo Hut*, a new place, has nice decked bungalows for 100B; the kitchen specialises in spicy southern Thai-style food.

Khao Mae Hat On the way to Ao Tanot from Mae Hat, a path forks off the main track and leads up the slope of 310m Khao Mae Hat in the centre of the island to *Two View Resort*, so named because it affords sunrise and sunset views of both sides of the island. It's a 15 minute walk up the path. There are only five bungalows, starting at 50B. Two View advertises three-day meditation retreats and five-day Thai massage courses.

Ao Leuk & Hat Sai Daeng Ao Leuk, connected by a 2.2km dirt road with Ban Mae Hat, has the lone *Ao Leuk Resort*, with huts from 60B. Another kilometre or so south is Hat Sai Daeng, where *Kiet* offers simple huts from 60B or nicer ones with private bath for up to 300B.

Ao Thian Ok & Laem Tato East of impressive Laem Tato is pretty Ao Thian Ok with *Rocky* at 80 to 300B. We continue to receive complaints from people who have been ejected from the place for not buying enough meals there.

Ao Chalok Ban Kao This nicely situated coral beach, 1.7km south of Ban Mae Hat by road, has become quite crowded. In peak season it can be very difficult to find a free hut here and travellers end up sleeping on the floor of a restaurant for a night or two until something becomes available.

On the hill overlooking the western part of the bay, you'll find *Laem Khlong* (100 to 500B, no beach) and *Viewpoint*, with lots of bungalows for 80 to 350B and a grumpy staff. Next is *Sunshine* with basic but clean bungalows for 150 to 400B, all with fan and attached bath. *Buddha View Dive Resort* next door has similar bungalows as well as rooms in a multistorey building for 200B; the restaurant is one of the best outside of Hat Sai Ri. Next are two cheaper places, the well run *Carabao* (50 to 80B) and the rather dilapidated *K See* (100 to 150B – with bath). Towards the eastern end of the bay, the friendly *Ko Tao Cottages* has the some of the island's most luxurious bungalows for 550 to 650B.

Around a couple of small points to the south along Laem Tato is a beach which can only be reached on foot and at low tide. Here *Tatoo Lagoon* offers basic huts for 60B, plus more elaborate ones with attached bath for up to 300B. Connected by a network of bridges and walkways, bungalows at the newish *Pond Resort* perch on rocks overlooking the bay and start at 200B. Also on the hillside are the more basic *Banana Rock* and *Aud Bungalow* for 100 to 200B.

South-West of Mae Hat As might be expected, beaches just south of town get better the farther south you go. A few hundred metres south-west of Mae Hat, across a stream and down a footpath, *Paew* has sturdy bungalows for 100 to 350B, while *Coral Beach* offers standard but clean huts with shared facilities for 80 to 100B, with attached bath for 150B. Between the two is the new, up-market *Sensi Paradise Resort* (☎/fax 377196) with solid cottages made from local materials for 350 to 700B depending on size, as well as a few larger places with sleeping lofts suitable for families for 1500B; none of the rooms have air-con.

A couple of kilometres farther south of Ban Mae Hat is a series of small beaches collectively known as **Hat Sai Nuan**, where you'll find *Siam Cookie* (80 to 250B) and *Cha* (60 to 80B).

Around at **Laem Je Ta Kang** (about 1.2km west of Ao Chalok Ban Kao) is another tiny beach with *Tao Thong Villa* (50 to 80B). South of Laem Je Ta Kang, by itself on **Ao Jun Jeua**, is *Sunset* (70 to 150B). The latter commands a beautiful point that juts out into the sea. The only way to get to these is to walk along the dirt track from Mae Hat or take long-tail boats.

Ko Nang Yuan This pretty little tripartite island is occupied by *Ko Nangyuan Dive Resort* (☎ (01) 726-0085), where as the name suggests the emphasis is on diving. Accommodation starts at 150B (100B long-term) for standard bungalows and go up to 1500B for air-con villas. Regular daily boats to Nang Yuan leave from the Ban Mae Hat pier daily at 10 am and return at 4 pm for 40B round trip. You can easily charter a ride there for 50B. Note that the management does not allow any plastic bottles on the island – these will be confiscated on arrival.

Places to Eat
In Ban Mae Hat there's a string of simple seafood restaurants south of the pier – *Mae Haad, Lucky, Neptune, Baan Yaay* – all with dining platforms built over the water's edge. The *Swiss Bakery* on the road that leads to the pier sells very good breads and pastries.

There are also several restaurants on Hat Sai Ri, most associated with bungalows. Back from the beach on a slight slope, *Chaba Restaurant* is an atmospheric place with a choice of outdoor or loft dining areas; the Thai seafood is very good here although the spices are toned down for western tastes.

Getting There & Away
Bangkok Bus/boat combination tickets from Bangkok cost 450 to 650B and are available from travel agents on Khao San Rd.

Beware of travel agents on Ko Tao selling boat/train combos. Usually this involves receiving a 'voucher' that you're supposed to be able to exchange for a train ticket in Surat Thani or Chumphon; more than a few travellers have found the vouchers to be worthless. If you make train reservations a few days (or more) in advance, any legitimate agency on Ko Tao should be able to deliver the train tickets themselves. It's same-day or day-before reservations that usually involve voucher problems.

Chumphon Two boats from the mainland – a slow boat and a 'speedboat' – leave daily from Chumphon to Ko Tao. Some weeks departures may be fewer if the swells are high. The slow boat leaves Chumphon at midnight, takes five or six hours to reach Ko Tao and costs 200B one way. In the opposite direction it departs from Ko Tao at 10 am. See the Chumphon section for more details.

The speedboat departs Chumphon at 8 am (from Ban Mae Hat at 11 am) and takes about one hour and 40 minutes. The speedboat fare is 400B. See the Chumphon section for more details.

Surat Thani Every third day, depending on the weather, a boat runs between Surat Thani (Tha Thong) and Ko Tao (Ban Mae), a seven to eight hour trip for 220B one way. Boats depart from Surat at 11 pm and from Ban Mae at 9 am.

Ko Pha-Ngan Depending on weather conditions, boats run daily between the Thong Sala pier on Ko Pha-Ngan and Ban Mae Hat on Ko Tao. The trip takes anywhere from 2½ to three hours and costs 150B per person. Boats leave Thong Sala around noon and return from Ko Tao at 9 am the next day. Twice a day – again depending on marine conditions – Rossarin Tour runs an 800hp, 35 passenger speedboat that costs 350B and does the trip in an hour.

Getting Around
The various pick-ups cost 20B per person to anywhere on the island during the day, but to charter one after hours costs whatever it takes

to motivate someone – usually 100B. Long-tail boats can also be chartered for 500 to 800B a day depending on the number of passengers carried.

Walking is an easy way to get around the island, but some trails aren't clearly marked and can be difficult to follow. You can walk around the whole island in a day, though the up-and-down, rocky paths make it challenging. The *Guide Map of Koh Samui, Koh Pha-Ngan & Koh Tao* by V Hongsombud offers a rough outline of the trails.

NAKHON SI THAMMARAT
• ☎ *(75)* • *pop 71,500*
Centuries before the 8th century Srivijaya Empire subjugated the peninsula, there was a city-state here called Ligor or Lagor, capital of the Tambralinga kingdom, which was well known throughout Oceania. Later, when Sri Lankan-ordained Buddhist monks established a cloister at the city, the name was changed to the Pali-Sanskrit *Nagara Sri Dhammaraja* (City of the Sacred Dharma-King), rendered in Thai phonetics as Nakhon Si Thammarat. An overland route between the western port of Trang and eastern port of Nakhon Si Thammarat functioned as a major trade link between Thailand and the rest of the world, and between the western and eastern worlds.

During the early development of the various Thai kingdoms, Nakhon Si Thammarat also became a very important centre of religion and culture. Thai shadow play (*nãng thalung*) and classical dance-drama (*lákhon* – Thai pronunciation of 'Lagor') were developed in Nakhon Si Thammarat; buffalo-hide shadow puppets and dance masks are still made here.

Today Nakhon Si Thammarat is also known for its nielloware (*khrêuang thõm*), a silver and black alloy/enamel jewellery technique borrowed from China many centuries ago. Another indigenous handicraft is *yaan lipao*, basketry woven from a hardy local grass into intricate contrasting designs. Yaan lipao handbags are a fashion staple among Thai women, so you should see lots for sale around town.

Much of the surrounding province is covered with rugged mountains and forests, which were, until recently, the last refuge of Thailand's Communist insurgents. The province's eastern border is formed by the Gulf of Thailand and much of the provincial economy is dependent on fishing and shrimp farming. Besides fishing, rural Nakhon residents earn a living by growing coffee, rice, rubber and fruit (especially *mongkhút*, or mangosteen).

Along the north coast are several nice beaches: **Ao Khanom, Nai Phlao, Tong Yi, Sichon** and **Hin Ngam** – see Around Nakhon Si Thammarat further on for details.

Orientation & Information

Nakhon Si Thammarat can be divided into two sections, the historic half south of the clock tower and the new city centre north of the clock tower and Khlong Na Meuang. The new city has all the hotels and most of the restaurants, as well as more movie theatres per sq km than any other city in Thailand.

A TAT office (☎ 346516) is housed in a 70-year-old building in the north-west corner of the Sanaam Naa Meuang (City Field) off Ratchadamnoen Rd, near the police station. They distribute the usual helpful information printed in English, and can also assist with any tourism-related problems.

The main post office is also on Ratchadamnoen Rd, along with an upstairs telephone office with international service (open from 8 am to 11 pm).

Suan Nang Seu Nakhon Bowonrat

The Suan Nang Seu, or Book Garden, at 116 Ratchadamnoen Rd next to Bovorn Bazaar and Siam Commercial Bank, is Nakhon's intellectual centre (look for the traditional water jar on a platform in front). Housed in an 80-year-old building that once served variously as a *sinsae* (Chinese doctor) clinic, opium den and hotel, this nonprofit bookshop specialises in books (mostly in Thai) on local history as well as national politics and religion. It also co-ordinates Dhamma lectures and sponsors local arts and craft exhibits.

Nakhon Si Thammarat National Museum

Since the Tampaling (or Tambralinga) kingdom traded with Indian, Arabic, Dvaravati and Champa states, much art from these places found its way to the Nakhon Si Thammarat area, and some is now on display in the national museum. Notable are Dong-Son bronze drums, Dvaravati Buddha images and Pallava (south Indian) Hindu sculpture. Locally produced art is also on display.

If you've already had your fill of the usual Thai art history surveys from Ban Chiang to Ayuthaya, go straight to the 'Art of Southern Thailand' exhibit in a room to the left of the foyer. Here you'll find many fine images of Nakhon Si Thammarat provenance, including Phutthasihing, U Thong and late Ayuthaya styles.

Admission to the museum is 10B and hours are Wednesday to Sunday from 9 am to 4 pm. The museum is well south of the principal wats on Ratchadamnoen Rd, across from Wat Thao Khot and Wat Phet Jarik, on the left – 2B by city bus or 3B by songthaew.

Wat Phra Mahathat

This is the biggest wat in the south, comparable to Wat Pho and other large Bangkok wats. If you like wats, this one is well worth a trip. Reputed to have been founded by Queen Hem Chala over a thousand years ago, and reconstructed in the mid-13th century, the huge complex features a 78m chedi, crowned by a solid gold spire weighing several hundred kilograms. Numerous smaller grey-black chedis surround the main chedi. The temple *bòt* contains one of Thailand's three identical Phra Singh Buddhas, one of which is supposed to have been originally cast in Sri Lanka before being brought to Sukhothai (through Nakhon Si Thammarat), Chiang Mai and later, Ayuthaya. The other images are at Wat Phra Singh in Chiang Mai and the National Museum in Bangkok – each is claimed to be the original.

Besides the distinctive bòt and chedi there are many intricately designed *wihãans* surrounding the chedi, several of which contain crowned Nakhon Si Thammarat/Ayuthaya-style Buddhas in glass cabinets. One wihãan

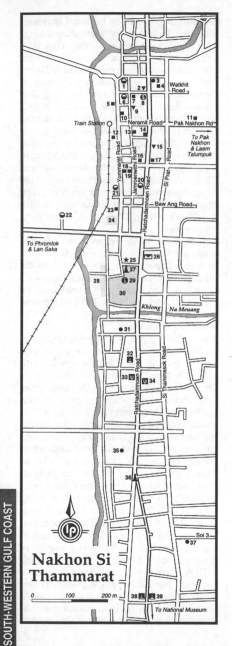

PLACES TO STAY
4   Taksin Hotel
5   Phetpailin Hotel
7   Thai Fa Hotel
10 Si Thong Hotel
11 Nakhon Garden Inn
12 Montien Hotel
13 Siam Hotel
14 Thai Hotel
16 Muang Thong Hotel
17 Thai Lee Hotel
18 Nakhon Hotel
19 Bue Loung (Bua Luang) Hotel
23 Laem Thong Hotel

PLACES TO EAT
2   Dam Kan Aeng
9   Yong Seng Restaurant
15 Bovorn Bazaar

OTHER
1   Taxis to Surat, Chumphon &
    Ranong
3   THAI Office
6   Mini-vans to Sichon &
    Khanom
8   Bangkok Bank
20 Songthaews to
    Khao Luang
21 Shared Taxi Stand
22 Bus Station
24 Market
25 Police Station
26 Main Post Office &
    Telephone Office
27 Lak Meuang (City Pillar)
28 Handicraft Shops
29 TAT Office
30 Sanaam Naa Meuang
    (City Field)
31 Prison
32 Wat Sema Muang
33 Shiva Shrine
34 Brahma Shrine
35 Provincial Offices
36 Clock Tower
37 Suchart's Shadow
    Puppet Workshop
38 Wat Phra Mahathat
39 Wat Na Phra Boromathat

Nakhon Si
Thammarat

0   100   200 m

houses a funky museum with carved wooden
kruts (garudas, Vishnu's mythical bird-
mount), old Siwichai votive tablets, Buddha
figures of every description including a
standing Dvaravati figure and a Siwichai
naga Buddha, inlaid-pearl alms bowls and
other oddities. A 12m whale skeleton lies in
the back of the complex under the north
cloister.

Wat Phra Mahathat's full name, Wat Phra Mahathat Woramahawihaan, is sometimes abbreviated as Wat Phra Boromathat. It's about 2km from the new town centre – hop on any bus or songthaew going down Ratchadamnoen Rd.

Wat Na Phra Boromathat
Across the road from Wat Phra Mahathat, this is the residence for monks serving at Mahathat. There is a nice Gandhara-style fasting Buddha in front of the bòt here.

Shadow Puppet Workshop
Traditionally, there are two styles of shadow puppets, năng thalung and năng yài; the former are similar in size to the typical Malay-Indonesian style puppets while the latter are nearly life-size and unique to Thailand. Both are intricately carved from buffalo-hide. Performances of Thai shadow theatre are rare nowadays (usually only during festivals), but there are two places in town where you can see the puppets being made.

The acknowledged master of shadow puppet craft – both manufacture and performance – is Suchart Subsin (Suchaat Sapsin), a Nakhon resident with a workshop at 110/18 Si Thammasok Soi 3, not far from Wat Phra Mahathat. Khun Suchart has received several awards for his mastery and preservation of the craft and has performed for the king. His workshop is open to the public; if enough people are assembled he may even be talked into providing a performance at his small outdoor studio. Puppets can be purchased here at reasonable prices – and here only, as he refuses to sell them through distributors. On some puppets the fur is left on the hide for additional effect – these cost a bit more as special care must be taken in tanning them.

Another craftsperson, Mesa Chotiphan, welcomes visitors to her workshop in the northern part of town. Mesa sells to distributors but will also sell direct at lower prices. Her house is at 558/4 Soi Rong Jeh, Ratchadamnoen Rd (☎ 343979). If you call she will pick you up from anywhere in the

Festivals
Every year in mid-October there is a southern-Thai festival called Chak Phra Pak Tai held in Songkhla, Surat Thani and Nakhon Si Thammarat. In Nakhon Si Thammarat the festival centres on Wat Phra Mahathat and includes performances of năng thalung and lákhon as well as the parading of Buddha images around the city to collect donations for local temples.

In the third lunar month (February to March) the city holds the colourful Hae Phaa Khun That, in which a lengthy cloth jataka painting is wrapped around the main chedi at Wat Phra Mahathat. ■

city. To get there on your own, go north from the city centre on Ratchadamnoen Rd and after about half a kilometre north of the sports field, take the soi opposite the Chinese cemetery (before reaching the golf course and military base).

Places to Stay – bottom end
Most of Nakhon Si Thammarat's hotels are near the train and bus stations. The best budget value in town is the friendly *Thai Lee Hotel* (☎ 356948) at 1130 Ratchadamnoen Rd, where clean rooms with ceiling fan, shower and toilet cost 120B with one bed, 200B with two.

On Yommarat (spelt 'Yammaraj' on some signs) Rd, almost across from the train station, is the *Si Thong Hotel* (☎ 356357), with adequate rooms for 120 to 180B with fan and bath. Also on Yommarat Rd is the *Nakhon Hotel* (☎ 356318), with similar rates and facilities as the Si Thong. Avoid the nearby *Yaowarat*, which is almost exclusively used as a brothel.

On Jamroenwithi Rd (walk straight down Neramit Rd opposite the train station two blocks and turn right into Jamroenwithi Rd) is the large *Siam Hotel* (☎ 356090); rooms with fan and bath cost from 130B. Farther south on this street is the *Muang Thong Hotel*, where 100B will get you a clean room with fan and bath. A block north of the Siam, on the same side of the street, is the *Thai Fa*

Hotel (☎ 356727), a small, two storey place with adequate rooms for 100 to 150B.

The *Laem Thong Hotel* (☎ 356478) at 1213/5-6 Yommarat Rd was recently closed for renovations; when it's open again it will probably cost somewhere around 200B a night.

Places to Stay – middle & top end

Once Nakhon Si Thammarat's flashiest hotel, the *Thai Hotel* (☎ 341509) on Ratchadamnoen Rd, two blocks from the train station, now seems rather ordinary with fan-cooled singles/doubles for 270/300B, and air-con rooms from 440 to 600B. The six storey *Taksin Hotel* (☎ 342790) stands off Si Prat Rd amid a string of massage places and costs 590B for all-air-con rooms with hot-water showers.

The *Bue Luong (Bua Luang) Hotel* (☎ 341-518), on Soi Luang Meuang off Jamroenwithi Rd, has large, clean singles and doubles with fan and bath for 170B, with air-con for 270B, or add TV and fridge for 340B.

On Yommarat Rd next to the train station, the fading, eight storey *Montien Hotel* (☎/fax 341908) has large rooms with fan and attached bath from 220B and air-con for 420B – a bit overpriced considering the low upkeep. The nearby *Phetpailin* (☎ 341896; fax 343283), a block north, is similar but costs 180B with fan, 380B with air-con,

The quiet *Nakhon Garden Inn* (☎ 344831; fax 342926) at 1/4 Pak Nakhon Rd, east of the centre, is more middle than top-end. It has 50 rooms with air-con and TV costing 500 to 600B.

Nakhon's top spot now is a place under construction on Pattanakan Kukwang Rd in the extreme south-eastern corner of town, the *Southern BM Hotel* (no telephone yet). It will have all the amenities expected by Bangkok business travellers and is projected to cost 1600B for a standard single/double room, 1800B for a deluxe room.

Places to Eat

There are lots of funky old Chinese restaurants along Yommarat and Jamroenwithi Rds. The latter street is the city's main culinary centre. At night the entire block running south from the Siam Hotel is lined with cheap food vendors – Muslim stands opposite the hotel sell delicious roti klûay (banana pancake), khâo mók (chicken biryani) and mátàbà (pancakes stuffed with chicken or vegetables) in the evening and by day there are plenty of rice and noodle shops. *Yong Seng* (no English sign) is a good, inexpensive Chinese restaurant on Jamroenwithi Rd.

To try some of Nakhon's excellent Thai coffee, stop by *Hao Coffee* at Bovorn Bazaar. Basically an update of an original Hokkien-style coffee shop once run by the owner's family in Nakhon, Hao Coffee serves international coffees as well as southern-Thai Hokkien-style coffee (listed as 'Hao coffee' on the menu) served with a tea chaser. Ask for fresh milk (nom sòt) if you abhor powdered non-dairy creamer.

Bovorn Bazaar offers several other culinary delights. Adjacent to Hao Coffee is *Khrua Nakhon*, a large open-air restaurant serving real Nakhon cuisine, including khâo yam (southern-style rice salad), kaeng tai plaa (spicy fish curry), khanŏm jiin (curry noodles served with a huge tray of vegies) and seafood. The restaurant also has egg-and-toast breakfasts; you can order Hao coffee from next door if you'd like. With a banyan tree in front and a modest display of southern-Thai folk art, the atmosphere is hard to beat. Get there early as it's only open from 7 am to 3 pm. Behind Khrua Nakhon is *Ban Lakhon*, in an old house, which is also very good for Thai food and is open for dinner.

On the corner of the alley leading into Bovorn Bazaar, *Ligor Home Bakery* bakes fresh European-style pastries daily. At night the bakery closes and Nakhon's most famous *roti vendors* set up along the alley. In Nakhon, roti klûay (banana roti or pancake) is a tradition – the vendors here use only fresh mashed bananas, no banana preserves or the like. Other offerings here include roti with curry (roti kaeng), with egg (roti khài) or as mátàbà (stuffed with meat and vegetables). They also do great khanŏm jìip, dumplings stuffed with a chicken-shrimp mixture, along with Nakhon coffee and better-than-average milk tea.

On the north-western corner of Ratchadamnoen and Watkhit Rds, the popular Thai-Chinese *Dam Kan Aeng* is packed with hungry customers every night.

Entertainment

Beyond the cinemas in town, there's not a lot of night life. *Rock 99% Bar & Grill*, an American roadhouse-style pub inside the Bovorn Bazaar, offers draft beer, cocktails and western pop music, as well as pizza, baked potatoes and sandwiches; this is where the few expats that live in NST hang out. It's open 6 pm to 2 am.

Getting There & Away

Air THAI has daily flights to/from Bangkok (two hours, 1770B). The THAI office (☎ 342-491) in Nakhon is at 1612 Ratchadamnoen Rd.

Bus & Mini-van Air-con buses bound for Nakhon Si Thammarat leave Bangkok's Southern bus terminal daily every 30 minutes or so from 5 to 8 pm, arriving 12 hours later, for 342B. Air-con buses in the reverse direction leave at about the same times. There are also two 2nd class air-con departures (266B) and one VIP departure (420B) nightly. Ordinary buses leave Bangkok at 6.40, 7 and 8.30 am, and 4.30, 5.30 and 6.30 pm for 190B.

Ordinary buses from Surat cost 37B and leave four times a day, while air-con departures are slightly less frequent and cost around 60B. Direct buses run from Songkhla via a bridge over the entrance to Thaleh Noi (the inland sea). Check with one of the tour-bus companies on Niphat Uthit 2 Rd in Hat Yai. Muang Tai Tours, on Jamroenwithi Rd in Nakhon Si Thammarat, does a 70B trip to Surat that includes a good meal and a video movie. There are a couple of other private bus companies on Jamroenwithi Rd in the vicinity of the Siam Hotel.

Hourly buses between Nakhon Si Thammarat and Krabi cost 50B per person (70B air-con) and take about three hours. Other routes include Trang (37B ordinary, 60B air-con), Phattalung (31B ordinary, 50B air-con), Phuket (92B ordinary, 130B air-con) and Hat Yai (53B ordinary, 60B air-con).

Mini-vans to Krabi leave from in front of the municipality office every half hour from 7 am to 3 pm for 71B; the trip takes 2½ hours; you can also catch mini-vans to Phuket (130B, five hours) and Hat Yai (80B, four hours). To Ko Samui (via Don Sak vehicle ferry) there's one air-con bus per day from the main terminal at 11.20 am (110B, four hours).

Share Taxi This seems to be the most popular form of intercity travel out of Nakhon. The huge share-taxi terminal on Yommarat Rd has taxis to Thung Song (25B), Khanom (40B), Sichon (30B), Krabi (80B), Hat Yai (80B), Trang (60B), Phuket (140B) and Phattalung (70B). A second, smaller stand on Thewarat Rd has taxis to Surat (60B), Chumphon (130B) and Ranong (180B).

Train Most southbound trains stop at the junction of Thung Song, about 40km west of Nakhon Si Thammarat, from where you must take a bus or taxi to the coast. However, two trains actually go all the way to Nakhon Si Thammarat (there is a branch line from Khao Chum Thong to Nakhon Si Thammarat): the rapid No 47, which leaves Bangkok's Hualamphong station at 7.45 pm, arriving in Nakhon Si Thammarat at 10.50 am, and the express No 15, which leaves Bangkok at 7.20 pm and arrives in Nakhon Si Thammarat at 10 am. Most travellers will not be booking a train directly to Nakhon Si Thammarat, but if you want to, 1st class costs 652B, 2nd class 308B, not including surcharges for rapid/express service or sleeping berths. There are no direct 3rd class trains to Nakhon Si Thammarat.

Getting Around

City buses run north-south along Ratchadamnoen and Si Thammasok Rds for 3B. Blue songthaews do similar routes for 4B during the day, 5B at night. Motorbike taxis cost 10B.

AROUND NAKHON SI THAMMARAT
Laem Talumpuk
This is a small scenic cape not far from Nakhon Si Thammarat. Take a bus from Neramit Rd going east to Pak Nakhon for 10B, then cross the inlet by ferry to Laem Talumpuk.

Hat Sa Bua
Sixteen kilometres north of Nakhon Si Thammarat in the Tha Sala district, off Route 401 to Surat Thani, are some semi-deserted white-sand beaches with few tourists. As yet accommodation isn't available, but there are some very reasonably priced restaurants here. Some travellers have found, however, that this beach seems to accumulate more than it's fair share of litter. It should cost about 11B to get here from Nakhon Si Thammarat by songthaew.

Hat Sichon & Hat Hin Ngam
Hat Sichon and Hat Hin Ngam are beautiful beaches 37km north of Nakhon Si Thammarat in Sichon district. Another good beach, **Hat Tong Yi**, is accessible only by boat and is hence almost always deserted – it's between Sichon and Hin Ngam (a chartered boat to Tong Yi from either beach costs 200 to 250B).

Get the bus for Hat Hin Ngam or Sichon from the Nakhon Si Thammarat bus station for 18B or take a share taxi for 30B. Hat Sichon is first; Hin Ngam is another 1.5km. Relaxing beach accommodation at Sichon is available at *Prasansuk Villa* (☎ 536299, 30 rooms, 280 to 420B), *Sailom Bungalow* (☎ 536299, 22 rooms, 120 to 500B) or on Hat Hin Ngam at *Hin Ngam Bungalow* (☎ 536204, six bungalows, 120B). The clientele at these places is almost entirely Thai.

Ao Khanom
About 25km from Sichon, 70km from Surat and 80km from Nakhon Si Thammarat is the bay of Ao Khanom. Not far from the vehicle-ferry landing for Ko Samui in Khanom is a string of four white-sand beaches – Hat Nai Praet, Hat Nai Phlao, Hat Na Dan and Hat Pak Nam. Most of the places to stay here offer five to 10 solid, plain bungalows with private bath for 500 to 800B a night; the lower end of this range may have fan only, while the upper end offers air-con. At Nai Phlao these include *Khanom Hill Resort* (☎ 529403), *GB Resort*, *Nai Phlao Bay Resort* (☎ 529039) and *Supa Villa* (☎ 529237). The eight bungalow *Fern Bay Resort* (☎ 528226) at Nai Phlao is a bit cheaper at 300 to 450B, while the *Khanab Nam Diamond Cliff Resort* (☎ 529144; fax 529111) handles the top end with 22 rooms for 500 to 3500B. The latter is the only place with a swimming pool, though the Nai Phlao Bay Resort is promising one by the end of 1997.

At Hat Na Dan, *Watanyoo Villa* (☎ 529224) has fan-cooled bungalows for 120 to 300B.

SONGKHLA
• ☎ (74) • *pop 85,000*
Songkhla, 950km from Bangkok, is another former Srivijaya satellite on the east coast. Not much is known about the pre-8th-century history of Songkhla, a name derived from the Yawi 'Singora' – a mutilated Sanskrit reference to a lion-shaped mountain (today called Khao Daeng) opposite the harbour. Originally the settlement lay at the foot of Khao Daeng, where two cemeteries and the ruins of a fort are among the oldest structural remains.

About 3km north of Khao Daeng village off the road to Nakhon Si Thammarat is the tomb of Suleiman (1592-1668), a Muslim trader who was largely responsible for Songkhla's commercial eminence during the 17th century. Just south of Suleiman's tomb, a Dutch graveyard testifies to a 17th century Dutch presence as well (look for large granite slabs in an overgrown area next to a Total warehouse). Suleiman's son Mustapha subsequently fell out of grace with Ayuthaya's King Narai, who burned the settlement to the ground in the following century.

Songkhla later moved across the harbour to its present site on a peninsula between the Thaleh Sap Songkhla (an inland sea) and the South China Sea (or Gulf of Thailand, depending on how you look at it). Today's inhabitants are a colourful mixture of Thais, Chinese and Muslims (ethnic Malays), and the local architecture and cuisine reflect the combination. Older southern Thais still refer to the city as Singora or Singkhon.

The seafood served along the white Hat Samila is excellent, though the beach itself is not that great for swimming, especially if you've just come from the Ko Samui archipelago. Beaches are not Songkhla's main attraction, even if the TAT promotes them as such, though the evergreen trees along Hat Samila give it a rather nice visual effect.

Offshore petroleum exploration projects commissioned through Unocal and Total – and the resultant influx of multinational oil company employees (particularly British and American) – have created a strong western presence in Songkhla. Several farang bars have opened around town to serve oil workers.

Orientation

The town has a split personality, with the charming older town west of Ramwithi Rd towards the waterfront, and the new town east of Ramwithi Rd – a modern mix of business and suburbia. If you are interested in seeing some traditional Songkhla architecture, walk along the back streets parallel to the inland sea waterfront – **Nang Ngam**, **Nakhon Nai** and **Nakhon Nawk Rds** all have some older Songkhla architecture showing Chinese, Portuguese and Malay influence, but it's disappearing fast.

Information

Consulates A Malaysian consulate (☎ 311-062, 311104) stands next to Khao Noi temple at 4 Sukhum Rd, near Hat Samila. There is also a Chinese consulate (☎ 311494) on Sadao Rd, not far from the Royal Crown Hotel.

Post & Communications The post office is opposite the department store/market on Vichianchom Rd; international calls can be made upstairs daily from 8 am to 8 pm.

Thaleh Sap Songkhla

Stretching north-west of the city is the huge brackish lake or 'inland sea' of Thaleh Sap Songkhla. Parts of the Thaleh Sap are heavily fished, the most sought-after catch being the famous black tiger prawn. Illegal gill-net

trawling for the prawn is now threatening the overall fish population; legal fishermen have begun organising against gill-net use.

The city's waterfront on the inland sea buzzes with activity: ice is loaded onto fishing boats on their way out to sea, baskets and baskets of fish are unloaded onto the pier from boats just arrived, fish markets are set up and disassembled, long-tail boats doing taxi business between the islands and mainland tool about. The fish smell along the piers is pretty powerful though: you have been warned.

National Museum

One of Thailand's most interesting provincial museums is housed in a 100-year-old building of southern Sino-Portuguese architecture, between Rong Meuang and Jana Rds (off Vichianchom Rd). It's a quiet, breezy building with a tranquil garden in front. The museum contains exhibits from all national art-style periods, particularly the Srivijaya, including a 7th to 9th century Shivalingam found in Pattani. Also on display are Thai and Chinese ceramics and sumptuous Chinese furniture owned by the local Chinese aristocracy. Hours are the usual 9 am to noon and 1 to 4 pm, Wednesday to Sunday; admission is 10B.

Temples & Chedis

On Saiburi Rd towards Hat Yai, **Wat Matchimawat** typifies the Sino-Thai temple architecture of 17th century Songkhla. One wihāan contains an old marble Buddha image and a small museum. Another temple with similar characteristics, **Wat Jaeng** on Ramwithi Rd, is currently under renovation.

There is a Sinhalese-style chedi and royal pavilion atop **Khao Tang Kuan**, a hill rising up at the northern end of the peninsula; to reach the top you'll have to climb 305 steps.

Beaches

Besides the strip of white sand along **Hat Samila**, there's the less frequented **Hat Son Awn** on a slender cape jutting out between the Gulf of Thailand and Thaleh Sap, north of Samila. Both beaches are lined with

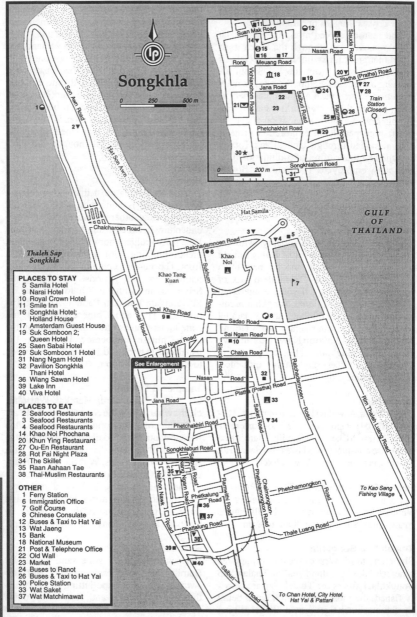

Songkhla

0   250   500 m

GULF
OF
THAILAND

Hat Samila

Thaleh Sap
Songkhla

PLACES TO STAY
5 Samila Hotel
9 Narai Hotel
10 Royal Crown Hotel
11 Smile Inn
16 Songkhla Hotel;
   Holland House
17 Amsterdam Guest House
19 Suk Somboon 2;
   Queen Hotel
25 Saen Sabai Hotel
29 Suk Somboon 1 Hotel
31 Nang Ngam Hotel
32 Pavilion Songkhla
   Thani Hotel
36 Wiang Sawan Hotel
39 Lake Inn
40 Viva Hotel

PLACES TO EAT
2 Seafood Restaurants
3 Seafood Restaurants
4 Seafood Restaurants
14 Khao Noi Phochana
20 Khun Ying Restaurant
27 Ou-En Restaurant
28 Rot Fai Night Plaza
34 The Skillet
35 Raan Aahaan Tae
38 Thai-Muslim Restaurants

OTHER
1 Ferry Station
6 Immigration Office
7 Golf Course
8 Chinese Consulate
12 Buses & Taxi to Hat Yai
13 Wat Jaeng
15 Bank
18 National Museum
21 Post & Telephone Office
22 Old Wall
23 Market
24 Buses to Ranot
26 Buses & Taxi to Hat Yai
30 Police Station
33 Wat Saket
37 Wat Matchimawat

Suan Mak Road
Nasan Road
Sisuda Road
Meuang Road
Rong
Vichianchom Road
Jana Road
Saibuti Road
Platha (Pratha) Road
Train
Station
(Closed)
Phetchakhiri Road
Ramwithi Road
Songkhlaburi Road

0   200 m

Chalcharoen Road
Khao
Noi
Khao Tang
Kuan
Ratchadamnoen Road
Sukhum Road
Chai Khao Road
Sadao Road
Sai Ngam Road
Sai Ngam Road
Chaiya Road
Lamai Road
Saibuti Road
Nasan Road
See Enlargement
Jana Road
Platha (Pratha) Road
Saket Road
Phetchakhiri Road
Songkhlaburi Road
Ratchadamnoen Road
Pim Thaleh Luang Road

Nakhon Nawk
Nang Ngam Road
Phetkalung Road
Phattalung Road
Ramwithi Road
Phetchamongkon Road
Chamongkon Road
Phetchamongkon Road
Thale Luang Road
To Kao Seng
Fishing Village
Saibuti Road
To Chan Hotel, City Hotel,
Hat Yai & Pattani

casuarina trees – a type of sea pine – rather than the usual palms. The water is clearest and calmest from April to October. At Samila, beach umbrellas and sling chairs can be used at no charge as long as you order something from one of the many food vendors.

Places to Stay – bottom end
The popular and clean *Amsterdam Guest House* at 15/3 Rong Meuang Rd has nice rooms with shared bath for 150 and 180B. It is run by a friendly Dutch woman. On the same street, near the corner of Vichianchom Rd, *Holland House* has clean rooms with shared facilities for 200B and an apartment for 350B; Dutch breakfasts are available.

One of the best deals in Songkhla is the *Narai Hotel* (☎ 311078) at 14 Chai Khao Rd, near the foot of Khao Tang Kuan. It's an older wooden hotel with clean, quiet singles/doubles with fan and shared bath (though each room comes with a washbasin) for 110B. A huge double room with bath is 200B.

The refurbished *Songkhla Hotel*, on Vichianchom Rd near the Rong Meuang Rd intersection, has good 140B rooms with shared bath, 180B with private bath. Just up the street from the Songkhla Hotel, the former Choke Dee has re-incarnated as the *Smile Inn* (☎ 311258), a clean place with medium-size rooms with ceiling fan and private cold-water shower for 280B, or identical rooms with air-con for 380B.

The *Suk Somboon 1* on Phetchakhiri Rd is not bad for 160/240B a single/double, although they're just wooden rooms off a large central area and you have to ask for that price – posted rates start at 180B. Rooms in the air-con wing next door are 380B.

The *Wiang Sawan*, in the middle of the block between Saiburi and Ramwithi Rds not far from Wat Matchimawat, has rooms from 200B, a bit overpriced for what you get.

Places to Stay – middle
The *Saen Sabai* (☎ 311090) at 1 Phetchakhiri Rd is well located and has clean, if small, rooms in an early Bangkok-style building for 150B with fan and shared bath, 270B with private bath, or 300B with air-con. Nearby is the *Suk Somboon 2* on Saiburi Rd, with fan-cooled singles/doubles for 160/300B. Next door is a new all-air-con wing with rooms costing 350B with TV, bathtub and fridge.

The *Queen* (☎ 311138) at 20 Saiburi Rd, next door to the Suk Somboon 2, has decent air-con rooms from 280/350B. The similarly priced *Charn (Chan)* (☎ 311903) is on the same road but on the outskirts of the central area on the way to Hat Yai.

The newish *Viva Hotel* (☎ 321033/7; fax 312608) at 547/2 Nakhon Nawk Rd has modern air-con rooms from 500B.

Places to Stay – top end
Catering mostly to visiting oil company employees and their families, the five storey *Royal Crown Hotel* (☎ 312174; fax 321027) on Sai Ngam Rd costs 1020 to 1288B for rooms with air-con, TV with in-house video, fridge and carpet; the tariff includes continental breakfast.

The newest and poshest place to stay is the nine storey, 180 room *Pavilion Songkhla Thani Hotel* (☎ 311355; fax 323716) at 17 Platha Rd, east of Ramwithi Rd. Large, luxurious rooms with wood panelling, air-con, IDD phones, satellite TV, carpeting and so on cost a bargain 900B during the hotel's soft opening in 1996 but will most likely rise to around 1800B in the future. The lobby is very swank compared with the Royal Crown's.

The popular *Lake Inn* (☎ 314240) is a rambling multistorey place with great views right on the Thaleh Sap. Rooms are 450B with air-con, carpet, hot water, TV minibar, 525B with the same plus a bathtub, or 600B with a balcony and lake view.

Places to Eat
There are lots of good restaurants in Songkhla but a few tend to overcharge foreign tourists. The best seafood place, according to locals, is the *Raan Aahaan Tae* on Nang Ngam Rd (off Songkhlaburi Rd and parallel to Saiburi Rd). Look for a brightly lit place just south of the cinema. The seafood on the beach is pretty good too – try the curried crab claws or spicy fried squid.

Competing with Tae for the best seafood title is *Buakaew* on Samila beach – there are several other seafood places in this vicinity. Fancier seafood places are found along Son Awn Rd near the beach – *Seven Sisters, Mark, Suda, Ying Muk, Smile Beach, Son Awn* – but these also tend to have hordes of young Thai hostesses, kept on to satisfy the Thai male penchant for chatting up áw-áw (young girls).

Along Nang Ngam Rd in the Chinese section are several cheap Chinese noodle and congee shops. At the end of Nang Ngam Rd along Phattalung Rd (near the mosque) are several modest Thai-Muslim restaurants, including *Sharif, Suda* and *Dawan*.

Khao Noi Phochana, on Vichianchom Rd near the Songkhla Hotel, has a very good lunchtime selection of Thai and Chinese rice dishes.

Auntie Bar & Restaurant and *Ty Brezh French Restaurant* on Sisuda Rd cater to expat tastes. Of the several expat pubs around town, *The Skillet* on Saket Rd has the cleanest kitchen and best food, including sandwiches, pizza, chilli, breakfast meals and steaks.

Farther south, along Sisuda Rd near the Chalerm Thong movie cinema and the old train station, is a hawker centre and night market called *Rot Fai Night Plaza*. In this section *Ou-en* is a very popular Chinese restaurant with outdoor tables; the house speciality is Peking duck. The very clean *Khun Ying*, next door to the Jazz Pub on Sisuda Rd near the Platha intersection, has inexpensive curries and khanŏm jiin during the day only.

Entertainment

The *Easy Pub, Lipstick, Cheeky* and *The Skillet* on Saket Rd next to Wat Saket cater to oil workers and other expats in town offering imported liquors, air-con and cable TV showing a mix of music videos and sports. The *Offshore* and *Anytime* on Sadao Rd are similar.

Thais tend to congregate at bars with live music in the vicinity of the Sisuda-Platha Rds intersection.

Getting There & Away

Air THAI operates several daily flights to/from nearby Hat Yai; see the Hat Yai Getting There & Away section later in this chapter for details. A taxi from Hat Yai airport to Songkhla costs 340B; in the reverse direction you should be able to find a car or songthaew to the airport for 150 to 200B.

Bus, Mini-van & Share Taxi Air-con public buses leave Bangkok's Southern bus terminal daily at 5, 6.45 and 7.30 pm, arriving in Songkhla 13 hours later for 425B. Ordinary buses are 236B from Bangkok, but there are only a couple of departures a day and the trip lasts at least 16 hours. The privately owned tour buses out of Bangkok (and there are several) are quicker but cost around 350B. VIP buses are available for 500 to 630B depending on the number of seats.

Air-con buses from Surat Thani to Songkhla and Hat Yai cost 120B one way. From Songkhla to Hat Yai, big green buses leave every 15 minutes (9B) from a spot on Saiburi Rd, or they can be flagged down anywhere along Vichianchom or Saiburi Rds.

Air-con mini-vans to Hat Yai cost 15B. These arrive and depart from a parking area in front of Wat Jaeng. Share taxis are 15B to Hat Yai if there are five other passengers, 90B if chartered; after 8 pm the rates go up to 20B and 120B respectively. Share taxis cost 50B to Pattani and 50B to Yala.

See the Hat Yai Getting There & Away section later in this chapter for more options, as Hat Yai is the main transport hub for Songkhla Province.

Train The old train spur to Songkhla no longer has a passenger service. See the Hat Yai Getting There & Away section later in this chapter for trains to/from nearby Hat Yai.

Getting Around

Red mini-songthaews circulate Songkhla and take passengers, for 5B, to any point on their route. Motorcycle taxis anywhere in town cost 10B.

KO YO

An island on the inland sea, Ko Yo (pronounced *kaw yaw*) is worth visiting just to see the cotton-weaving cottage industry there. The good-quality, distinctive *phâa kàw yaw* is hand-woven on rustic looms and available on the spot at 'wholesale' prices – meaning you still have to bargain but have a chance of undercutting the usual city price.

Many households around this thickly forested, sultry island are engaged in cotton-weaving, and there is a central market off the highway so you don't have to go from place to place comparing prices and fabric quality. At the market, prices for cloth and ready-made clothes are excellent if you bargain, and especially if you speak Thai. If you're more interested in observing the weaving process, take a walk down the road behind the market where virtually every other house has a loom or two – listen for the clacking sound made by the hand-operated wooden looms. As the island gradually gets taken over by condo and vacation home developments, the weaving villages may fade away.

There are also a couple of semi-interesting wats, Khao Bo and Thai Yaw, to visit. Along the main road through Ko Yo are several large seafood restaurants overlooking Thaleh Sap. *Pornthip* (about half a kilometre before the market) is reportedly the best.

Folklore Museum

At the northern end of the island at Ban Ao Sai, about 2km past the Ko Yo cloth market, is a large folklore museum run by the Institute of Southern Thai Studies, a division of Si Nakharinwirot University. The complex of Thai-style pavilions overlooking the Thaleh Sap Songkhla contain well curated collections (but unfortunately no English labels) of folk art as well as a library and souvenir shop. Displays include pottery, beads, shadow puppets, basketry, textiles, musical instruments, boats, religious art, weapons and various household, agricultural and fishing implements. Among these is a superb collection of coconut-grater seats carved into various animal and human shapes.

On the institute grounds are a series of small gardens, including one occasionally used for traditional shadow theatre performances, a medicinal herb garden and a bamboo culture garden.

Admission to the museum is 50B for foreigners, 30B for Thais.

Getting There & Away

From Hat Yai, direct Ko Yo buses – actually large wooden songthaews – leave from near the clock tower on Phetkasem Rd frequently throughout the day. The fare to Ko Yo is 8B; although the bus terminates on Ko Yai farther on, it will stop in front of the cloth market on Ko Yo (ask for *nâa talàat*, 'in front of the market'). To get off at the museum, about 2km past the market, ask for *phíphítaphan*. From Songkhla, buses to Ranot pass through Ko Yo for the same fare.

Nakhon Si Thammarat or Ranot-bound buses from Hat Yai also pass through Ko Yo via the new bridge system (part of Route 4146) and will stop at the market or museum. Another way to get there is to take a Hat Yai-Songkhla bus to the junction for Ko Yo (5B), then catch the Songkhla-Ranot bus (3B) to the market or museum.

HAT YAI

• ☎ *(74)* • *pop 139,400*

Hat Yai, 933km from Bangkok, is southern Thailand's commercial centre and one of the kingdom's largest cities, though it is only a district of Songkhla Province. A steady stream of customers from Malaysia keeps Hat Yai's central business district booming. Everything from dried fruit to stereos are sold in the shops along Niphat Uthit Rds Nos 1, 2 and 3, not far from the train station. The city is also a very important transport hub for southern Thailand. Many travellers stay in Hat Yai on their way to and from Malaysia.

Culturally, Hat Yai is very much a Chinese town at its centre, with loads of gold shops and Chinese restaurants. A substantial Muslim minority is concentrated in certain sections of the city, eg near the mosque off Niphat Songkhrao Rd.

Many travellers find Hat Yai unappealing,

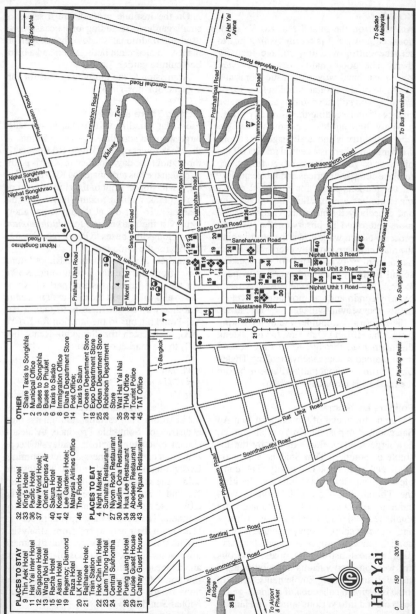

SOUTH-WESTERN GULF COAST

PLACES TO STAY

9 Thin Aek Hotel
11 Hat Yai Inter Hotel
12 Singapore Hotel
13 Wang Noi Hotel
15 Racha Hotel
16 Asian Hotel
19 Regency; Diamond
   Plaza Hotel
20 LK Hotel
21 Rajthanee Hotel;
   Train Station
22 Hok Chin Hin Hotel
23 Laem Thong Hotel
24 Central Sukhontha
   Hotel
26 Pueng Luang Hotel
29 Louise Guest House
31 Cathay Guest House

32 Montien Hotel
33 King's Hotel
36 Pacific Hotel
37 New World Hotel;
   Orient Express Air
40 Sakura Hotel
41 Kosit Hotel
42 Lee Gardens Hotel;
   Malaysia Airlines Office
46 The Florida

PLACES TO EAT

4 Night Market
7 Sumatra Restaurant
27 Niyom Rosh Restaurant
30 Muslim Ocha Restaurant
34 Hua Lee Restaurant
38 Abedeen Restaurant
43 Jeng Nguan Restaurant

OTHER

1 Share Taxis to Songkhla
2 Municipal Office
3 Buses to Songkhla
5 Buses to Phuket
6 Taxis to Sadao
8 Immigration Office
10 Diana Department Store
14 Post Office;
   Taxis to Satun
17 Ocean Department Store
18 Expo Department Store
25 Odean Department Store
28 Robinson Department
   Store
35 Wat Hat Yai Nai
39 THAI Office
44 Tourist Police
45 TAT Office

Hat Yai

0   150   300 m

but it's an important transport hub: almost any Thailand-Malaysia overland trip involves a stop here.

Information

Tourist Office The TAT Office (☎ 243747) is at 1/1 Soi 2 Niphat Uthit 3 Rd and is open daily from 8.30 am to 4.30 pm. The tourist police (☎ 1699 or 246733) can be found opposite the Florida Hotel.

Immigration The immigration office (☎ 243-019, 233760) is on Phetkasem Rd near the railway bridge. The nearest Malaysian consulate is in Songkhla.

Post & Communications Hat Yai's GPO is on Niphat Songkhrao 1 Rd just south of the stadium and is open from 8.30 am to 4.30 pm weekdays, 9 am to noon weekends. The adjacent telephone office is open from 7 am to 11 pm daily. For visitors staying downtown, there is a more convenient branch post office on Rattakan Rd, just north of the train station. A private packing service is available next door to this post office.

Money Hat Yai is loaded with banks. Several after-hours exchange windows can be found along Niphat Uthit 2 and 3 Rds near the Thamnoonvithi Rd (pronounced *thammanun-withi*) intersection.

Photography The Chia Colour Lab at 58-60 Suphasan Rangsan Rd, next to the Singapore Hotel, offers a good selection of films and quality processing. There are many other photo shops downtown.

Bullfighting

Bullfighting, involving two bulls in opposition rather than a person and a bull, takes place as a spectator sport twice monthly in Hat Yai. On the first Saturday of each month (or on the second Saturday if the first Saturday is a *wan phrá*, or Buddhist worship day, ie full or new moon). The venue changes from time to time, but lately they've been held at an arena at the Khlong Wat intersection about 5km out of town (50B by tuk-tuk).

Matches take place continuously from 10 am until 3pm and admission is 600 to 700B all day or 100 to 200B per round – although many hundred times that amount of money changes hands during the nonstop betting by Thai spectators.

Because the times and venues for these bullfights tend to change every other year or so, check with the TAT office for the latest.

Places to Stay – bottom end

Hat Yai has dozens of hotels within walking distance of the train station. During Chinese New Year most rooms rates at the lower end double.

Cheaper places nearby include the *Cathay Guest House* (☎ 243815), on the corner of Thamnoonvithi and Niphat Uthit 2 Rds three blocks from the station, with somewhat drab rooms ranging from 120 to 180B; there is also a 60B dorm. The Cathay has become a traveller centre in Hat Yai because of its good location, helpful staff and plentiful travel info for trips onward, including tips on travel in Malaysia. It has a laundry service and serves inexpensive breakfasts as well as other meals (they also don't mind if you buy takeaway food and eat it in the lounge). There is a reliable bus ticket agency downstairs with irregular opening hours.

Also inexpensive are some of the older Chinese hotels in the central area. Rooms are very basic but they're usually secure and service is OK – you can get towels and soap on request. The *Weng Aun* is an old Chinese hotel across from King's Hotel on Niphat Uthit 1 Rd, four doors down from the Muslim Ocha restaurant. Very basic singles start at 110B.

The friendly *Thin Aek Hotel* at 16 Duangchan Rd (behind Diana Department Store on Niphat Uthit 3 Rd) is another old Chinese relic; it's mostly a holding place for Bangladeshis trying to immigrate to Malaysia, but the owner caters to farang travellers as well. Rooms are 80B with shared bath, 100B with shower, 120B with shower and two large beds (four can sleep for 150B). The toilet is outside for all rooms.

Another bargain is the *Hok Chin Hin Hotel*

(☎ 243258) on Niphat Uthit 1 Rd, a couple of blocks from the train station. Very clean rooms with bath and fan cost 150B single, 240B double; there's a good coffee shop downstairs. Hat Yai used to have more hotels like this, but they're slowly closing down.

There's a rash of places in town calling themselves 'guesthouses' that are really small budget hotels. *Louise Guest House* (☎ 220966) at 21-23 Thamnoonvithi Rd is an apartment-style place with rooms for 200B with air-con, or 290B with air-con and hot water – not bad compared with some of the previously described places. *Lada Guest House* (☎ 220233) next to the Robinson Department Store complex near the train station is similar with rooms with fan from 160B and air-con from 250B. Near the Songkhla bus stand off Phetkasem Rd is *Sorasilp Guest House* (☎ 232635), where clean rooms with fan and bath are 150 to 300B.

Places to Stay – middle

For some reason hotels in Hat Yai take a disproportionate leap upward in quality once you go from 100 to 150B a night to 200B and above.

Very popular with Malaysian visitors as well as travellers is *King's Hotel* (☎ 234140) on Niphat Uthit 1 Rd. Rooms start at 350B with fan and bath, 410B with air-con and hot water. Not far from the train station on Thamnoonvithi Rd is the *Laem Thong Hotel* (☎ 352301) with fairly comfortable singles or doubles for 260B with fan and bath, or 350 to 600B with air-con.

The *OH Hotel* (Oriental; ☎ 230142) at 137-9 Niphat Uthit 3 Rd has very good fan-cooled singles/doubles in the old wing for 250B. In the new wing rooms with air-con, TV, phone and hot water cost 400/450B single/double. Beside the OH, the *Tawan Ok Hotel* (☎ 243071) at 131/1-3 Niphat Uthit Rd offers 32 clean rooms for a straight-forward 300B with fan, 400B with air-con.

The friendly *Pueng Luang (Pheung Luang) Hotel* (☎ 244548) at 241-5 Saeng Chan Rd has huge fan rooms with bath for 250B, plus a few smaller ones for 200B. Air-con

rooms go for just 350B. The *Wang Noi* (☎ 231024), 114/1 Saeng Chan Rd, has clean rooms for 200 to 220B with fan or 300 to 370B with air-con; it seems to be a relatively quiet location. Also good is the *Pacific Hotel* (☎ 244062) at 149/1 Niphat Uthit 2 Rd, with clean air-con rooms for 400B.

Another good spot is the *Singapore Hotel* (☎ 237478) at 62-66 Suphasan Rangsan Rd, which has clean rooms with fan and bath for 200B, air-con 350B, and air-con rooms with two beds, TV and hot water for 400B.

The *Montien Hotel* (☎ 234386; fax 230043) on Niphat Uthit 1 Rd is a large 180 room place that once occupied the city's top end; decent air-con doubles cost 330B, 370B with TV.

Places to Stay – top end

The top end in Hat Yai is mainly geared towards Malaysian weekenders, which keeps accommodation rates considerably lower than in Bangkok or Chiang Mai. The *Rajthanee* (☎ 232288; fax 232188), at the Hat Yai train station, couldn't be more convenient if you have an early morning train to catch or just like to be near the rails; good standard rooms with air-con, hot water, TV and phone cost 540B.

The nicest hotel in town is the 238 room *Central Sukhontha Hotel* (☎ 352222; fax 352223) at 3 Sanehanuson Rd, where spacious rooms with IDD phone, as well as use of all the top class amenities – including a swimming pool, 24 hour cafe, fitness centre, business centre and shopping mall (with a branch of Central Department Store) – cost 1800 to 2800B.

All of the following are fully air-con:

Asian Hotel – 55 Niphat Uthit 3 Rd (☎ 353400; fax 234890); 104 rooms, from 800B
Diamond Plaza – 62 Niphat Uthit 3 Rd (☎ 353147; fax 239824); 280 rooms, from 920B
The Florida – 8 Siphunawat Rd (☎ 234555/9; fax 234553); 119 rooms, from 715B
Hat Yai Central Hotel – 180 Niphat Uthit 3 Rd (☎ 230000/11; fax 230990); 250 rooms, 707B
Hat Yai Inter Hotel – 42-44 Niphat Uthit 3 Rd (☎ 231022; fax 232539); 210 rooms, doubles from 420B

Lee Gardens Hotel – 1 Lee Pattana Rd (☎ 234422; fax 231888); doubles from 690B

LK Hotel – 150 Saeng Chan Rd (☎ 235681; fax 238112); 196 rooms, doubles 850B including breakfast

New World – 144-158 Niphat Uthit 2 Rd (☎ 23100; fax 231105); 133 rooms, from 535B

Racha Hotel – 40-42 Niphat Uthit 1 Rd (☎ 230951/5; fax 234668); 65 rooms, from 453B

The Regency – 23 Prachathipat Rd (☎ 353333, 234102); 189 rooms, doubles from 798B

The Royal Hotel – 106 Prachathipat Rd (☎ 232162); 139 rooms, 470 to 1000B

Sakura Hotel – 185/1 Niphat Uthit 3 Rd (☎ 246688; fax 235936); 453B

Places to Eat

Hat Yai is southern Thailand's gourmet 'mecca', offering fresh seafood from both the Gulf of Thailand and the Andaman Sea, bird's nests, shark fins, Muslim roti and curries, Chinese noodles and dim sum. Lots of good, cheap restaurants can be found along the three Niphat Uthit Rds, in the markets off side streets between them, and also near the train station.

Chinese Start the day with inexpensive dim sum at *Shangrila* on Thamnoonvithi Rd near the Cathay Guest House. Specialities include khanŏm jìip (dumplings), salabao (Chinese buns) and khâo nâa pèt (roast duck on rice). In the evenings the Chinese-food action moves to *Hua Lee* on the corner of Niphat Uthit 3 and Thamnoonvithi Rds; it's open until the wee hours.

Jeng Nguan is an old feasting stand-by near the end of Niphat Uthit 1 Rd (turn right from the station; it's on a corner on the left-hand side). Try the tâo hûu thâwt kràwp (fried bean curd), hŭu chalăam (shark-fin soup), bàmìi plaa phàt (fried noodles with fish) or kíaw plaa (fish wonton). It's open from 9 am until late at night.

Malay & Indian The *Muslim-O-Cha* (Muslim Ocha), across from the King's Hotel, is still going strong, with roti kaeng (roti chanai in Malay) in the mornings and curries all day. This is one of the few Muslim cafes in town where women – even non-Muslim women – seem welcome. There are a couple of other Muslim restaurants near this one. *Makanan Muslim* at the corner of Saeng Chang and Prachathipat Rds is a clean open-air place with roti and mátàbà.

On Niyomrat Rd between Niphat Uthit 1 and 2 are *Abedeen*, *Sulaiman* and *Mustafa*, all specialising in Muslim food. Sulaiman has the best selection of dishes, including Indian paratha, dal, chapati, biryani, and various mutton, chicken, fish and vegie dishes. Abedeen is good for tôm yam kûng (spicy shrimp lemon-grass soup).

Sumatra Restaurant, next to the Pakistan Mosque near the Holiday Plaza Hotel, does Malay dishes like rojak (peanut-sauce salad) and nasi biryani (spiced rice plate).

Thai Although Chinese and Malay food is dominant in Hat Yai, there are a few Thai places as well. An old, established Thai restaurant is *Niyom Rot* (the English sign says 'Niyom Rosh') at 219-21 Thamnoonvithi Rd. The plaa krabàwk thâwt, whole sea mullet fried with eggs intact, is particularly prized here.

Although the name is Lao, the *Viang Chan* (no English sign) at 12 Niphat Uthit 2 Rd serves Thai and north-eastern Thai dishes along with Chinese. The food centre below the Tong Nam Hotel has both Thai and Chinese dishes.

A & A Food Centre on Niphat Uthit 2 Rd serves inexpensive Thai and Chinese food on the coupon system.

Night Markets The extensive night market along Montri 1 Rd specialises in fresh seafood; you can dine on three seafood dishes and one vegetable dish for less than 200B here if you speak Thai. There are smaller night markets along Suphasan Rangsan Rd and Siphunawat Rd.

Entertainment

Most of the many clubs and coffee shops in town cater to Malaysian clientele. The bigger hotels have discos; the most popular include *Disco Palace* (Emperor Hotel), the *Metro* (JB Hotel), the *Diana Club* (Lee Gardens

Hotel) and the *Inter* (Hat Yai Inter Hotel). Cover charges are 100 to 150B.

The *Post Laserdisc* on Thamnoonvithi Rd, a block east of the Cathay Guest House, is a music video/laserdisc restaurant/bar with an excellent sound system and well placed monitors. It has mostly western movies, and programs change nightly – the fairly up-to-date music videos are a filler between the films. It starts at 10 am and goes until 1 am – there's no admission charge and drink prices are only a little higher than at the average bar. Meals are served as well, including breakfast.

Opposite the Post Laserdisc, *Sugar Rock* is one of the more durable Hat Yai pubs, with good food, good prices and a low-key atmosphere.

Things to Buy

Shopping is Hat Yai's number-one drawcard, with most of the market action taking place along Niphat Uthit 2 and 3 Rds. Here you'll find Thai and Malaysian batik, cheap electronics and inexpensive clothing.

SMS Muslim Panich, 17 Niphat Uthit 1, has an excellent selection of south Indian sarongs, plus Thai, Malay and Indonesian batiks; although the markets are cheaper they don't compare to SMS for quality and selection.

DK Book House, about 50m from the train station on Thamnoonvithi Rd, carries English-language books and maps.

Hat Yai has three major department stores on Niphat Uthit 3 Rd (Diana, Ocean and Expo) and two on Thamnoonvithi Rd (World and Robinson), plus the newer Central Department Store next to the Central Sukhontha Hotel.

Getting There & Away – Within Thailand

Air THAI flies between Hat Yai and Bangkok five to six times daily. Flights take one hour and 25 minutes; the fare is 2280B one way. There are also THAI flights to Hat Yai from Phuket daily for 780B.

Newcomer Orient Express Air (☎ 335-771) flies to Hat Yai from Chiang Mai, with a stopover in Surat Thani, five times a week

for 2900B one way. Surat to Hat Yai costs 1150B one way. The OEA office is in the New World Hotel. THAI's office is at 166/4 Niphat Uthit 2 Rd.

Bus To Songkhla the green buses leave from outside the small clock tower on Phetkasem Rd. Share taxis leave from around the corner near the President Hotel.

Air-con buses from Bangkok are 428B (VIP 500 to 625B) and leave the Southern bus terminal at 7 am and 4, 5.30, 6, 6.15, 6.30, 7, 8 and 8.20 pm. The trip takes 14 hours. Private companies sometimes have fares as low as 300B. Ordinary government buses cost 227B and leave Bangkok at 9.45 and 10.50 pm.

There are lots of buses running between Phuket and Hat Yai; ordinary buses are 122B (eight hours) and air-con 197B (six hours). Air-con mini-vans to Nakhon Si Thammarat are available for 100B from the Rado Hotel on Sanehanuson Rd. Three daily buses go to Pak Bara (for Ko Tarutao) for 35B (three hours).

Magic Tour (☎ 234535), a travel agency downstairs from the Cathay Guest House, does express air-con buses and mini-vans to Phuket (200B), Krabi (130B), Ko Samui (250B) and Surat Thani (130B). Other buses from Hat Yai include:

Destination	Fare (B)	Hours
Bangkok	238	16
(air-con)	425	14
(VIP)	625	14
Ko Samui	200	7
Krabi	-	-
(air-con only)	125	4
Narathiwat	50	3
(air-con)	65	3
Padang Besar	18	1½
Pattani	35	2
(air-con)	43	1½
Phattalung	27	2
Satun	27	2
(air-con)	40	1
Sungai Kolok	-	-
(air-con only)	96	4
Surat Thani	86	6½
(air-con)	120	5½
Trang	40	2
Yala	35	2½

Agencies which arrange private intercity buses include:

Golden Way Travel – 132 Niphat Uthit 3 Rd (☎ 233917; fax 235083)

Hat Yai Swanthai Tours – 108 Thamnoonvithi Rd (☎ 246706)

Magic Tour – ground floor, Cathay Guest House (☎ 234535)

Pan Siam – 99 Niphat Uthit 2 Rd (☎ 237440)

Sunny Tour – Niphat Uthit 2 Rd (☎ 244156)

Universal On-Time Co – 147 Niphat Uthit 1 Rd (☎ 231609)

Share Taxi Share taxis are a good way to get from one province to another quickly in the south. There are seven share-taxi stands in Hat Yai, each specialising in certain destinations.

In general, a share taxi costs about the same as an air-con bus, but the taxis are about 30% faster. Share taxis also offer door-to-door drop-offs. The downside is that the drivers wait around for enough passengers (usually five minimum) for a departure. If you hit it right the taxi may leave immediately; otherwise you may have to wait for half an hour or more. The drivers also drive at hair-raising speeds – not a pleasant experience for highly strung passengers.

According to the TAT, the city may soon be establishing a single share-taxi stand on Siphunawat Rd. Whether or not it will work (each of the current share-taxi stands takes advantage of the quickest route out of the city towards its respective destination) remains to be seen; they've been promising this for at least two years.

Train Trains from Bangkok to Hat Yai leave Hualamphong station daily at 2.35 pm (special express No 19), 3.15 pm (special express No 11) and 4.02 pm (rapid No 43), arriving in Hat Yai at 6.34 am, 6.53 am and 8.29 am. The basic fare is 664B 1st class (express only), 313B 2nd class. To Bangkok you can take the 3.32 pm (rapid No 46), 4.50 pm (rapid No 44), 5.52 pm (special express No 12) and 6.24 pm (special express No 20), arriving in Bangkok at 8.35 am, 9.30 am, 10 am and 10.35 am.

Third class trains to Hat Yai start only as far north as Chumphon (99B) and Surat Thani (55B).

The advance booking office at Hat Yai station is open from 7 am to 5 pm daily. The station's Rajthanee Restaurant in the Rajthanee Hotel is good and not that expensive; there's a cheaper eating area on the platform. A left-luggage office (the sign reads 'Cloak Room') is open daily from 5.30 to 11 am and 1 to 7 pm. The cost is 5B per piece for the first five days, 10B thereafter.

Share Taxi Fares

Destination	Fare (B)	Hours	Taxi Stand
Songkhla	15	½	near the President Hotel off Phetkasem Rd
Phattalung	50	1¼	Suphasan Rangsan Rd near Wat Cheu Chang
Trang	60	2½	Suphasan Rangsan Rd near Wat Cheu Chang
Sungai Kolok	120	3½	Suphasan Rangsan Rd near Wat Cheu Chang
Betong	100	3½	Suphasan Rangsan Rd near Wat Cheu Chang
Nakhon Si Thammarat	70	2½	Suphasan Rangsan Rd near Wat Cheu Chang
Phuket	220	6	Duangchan Rd
Surat Thani	150	5	Duangchan Rd
Krabi	150	5	Duangchan Rd
Narathiwat	80	3	Niphat Uthit 1 Rd
Sadao	25	1	Siam Nakarin Department Store, Phetkasem Rd
Khukhut	25	1	Siam Nakarin Department Store, Phetkasem Rd
Ranot	30	2	Siam Nakarin Department Store, Phetkasem Rd
Yala	60	2	Niphat Uthit 2 Rd, near Cathay Guest House
Satun	35	1½	Rattakan Rd, near the post office
La-Ngu	50	1½	Rattakan Rd, near the post office

Getting There & Away – International
Air Both THAI and Malaysia Airlines fly from Penang; there are also Silk Air flights from Singapore.

THAI (☎ 243711) has offices in the centre of town at 166/4 Niphat Uthit 2 Rd (☎ 245851) and 190/6 Niphat Uthit 2 Rd (☎ 231272). Malaysia Airlines (☎ 245443) has its office in the Lee Gardens Hotel, with a separate entrance on Niphat Uthit 1 Rd.

Hat Yai international airport has a post office with an IDD telephone in the arrival area; it's open from 8.30 am to 4.30 pm weekdays, 9 am to noon Saturday, closed Sunday. Other airport facilities include the Sky Lounge Cafe & Restaurant on the ground floor near the domestic check-in, a less expensive coffee shop on the 2nd floor departure level and foreign-exchange booths.

Bus From Padang Besar on the Malaysian border, buses are 18B and take an hour and a half to reach Hat Yai. Bus services operate every 10 minutes between 6 am and 7.20 pm.

Magic Tour (☎ 234535), a travel agency downstairs from the Cathay Guest House, does express air-con buses and mini-vans to Penang (200B, five hours), Kuala Lumpur, Singapore and destinations within Thailand. Golden Way Travel (☎ 233917; fax 235083), 132 Niphat Uthit 3 Rd, runs VIP (30 reclining seats) buses to Singapore for 400B including all meals; super VIP (24 seats) costs 550B.

Other buses out of Hat Yai include:

Destination	Fare (B)	Hours
Butterworth (for Penang)	200	6
Kuala Lumpur*	250 to 350	12
Singapore*	300 to 550	15

* denotes private tour-bus companies; see the list on the previous page for contact details

Warning Care should be taken in selecting travel agencies to book bus trips into Malaysia. There are still reports of bus companies demanding 'visa fees' before crossing the border – since visas aren't required for most nationalities, this is a blatant rip-off. The offending company collects your passport on the bus and then asks for the fee – holding your passport hostage. Refuse all requests for visa or border-crossing fees – all services are supposed to be included in the ticket price. One Hat Yai company that has repeatedly perpetrated this scam is Chaw Weng Tours.

Share Taxi Share taxis are a popular way of travelling between Hat Yai and Penang in Malaysia. They're faster than the tour buses, although less comfortable and more expensive. Big old Thai-registered Chevys or Mercedes depart from Hat Yai around 9 am every morning. You'll find them at the train station or along Niphat Uthit 2 near the King's Hotel. In Penang you can find them around the cheap traveller hotels in Georgetown. They cost about 200B/M$20 – this is probably the fastest way of travelling between the two countries, and you cross the border with a minimum of fuss.

From Hat Yai the fare to Padang Besar is 25B for the one hour trip; taxis are on Duangchan Rd. For Penang the stand is on Niphat Uthit 1 Rd and the three hour trip costs 200B.

Getting Around
The Airport The THAI van costs 40B per person for transport to the city; there's also a private 150B THAI limo service. A regular taxi costs 150B from the airport to the city, about half that in the reverse direction.

Car Rental Hertz (☎ 751007) has an office at Hat Yai international airport. You may also be able to arrange car rental through travel agencies in town.

Songthaew The innumerable songthaews around Hat Yai cost 5B per person. Watch out when you cross the street or they'll mow you down.

AROUND HAT YAI
Ton Nga Chang Falls
'Elephant Tusk' Falls, 24km west of Hat Yai via Route 4 in Rattaphum district, is a 1200m

seven-tier cascade that falls in two streams (thus resembling two tusks). If you're staying over in Hat Yai, the falls make a nice break from the hustle and bustle of the city. The waterfall looks its best at the end of the rainy season, October to December.

To get to the falls take a Rattaphum-bound songthaew (10B) and ask to get off at the *náam tòk* (waterfall).

PATTANI
• ☎ *(73)* • *pop 41,000*
Unlike most provincial capitals in the deep south, which tend to function basically as trading posts operated by the Chinese for the benefit (or exploitation, depending on your perspective) of the surrounding Muslim villages, Pattani has more of a Muslim character. In the streets, you are more likely to hear Yawi, the traditional language of Java, Sumatra and the Malay peninsula (which when written uses the classic Arabic script plus five more letters), than any Thai dialect. The markets are visually quite similar to markets in Kota Baru in Malaysia.

Until the turn of the century Pattani was the centre of an independent principality that included Yala and Narathiwat. It was also one of the earliest kingdoms in Thailand to host international trade; the Portuguese established a trading post here in 1516, the Japanese in 1605, the Dutch in 1609 and the British in 1612. During WWII, Japanese troops landed in Pattani to launch attacks on Malaya and Singapore.

Although they can be somewhat difficult to reach, Pattani's beaches are among the most pristine in Thailand.

Orientation & Information
The centre of this mostly concrete town is at the intersection of Naklua Yarang Rd, the north-south road between Yala and Pattani harbour, and Ramkomud Rd, which runs east-west between Songkhla and Narathiwat. Intercity buses and taxis stop at this intersection. Ramkomud Rd becomes Rudee Rd after crossing Naklua Yarang Rd, and it is along Rudee Rd that you can see what is left of old Pattani architecture – the Sino-

---

Festivals
The tree that Ko Niaw hanged herself from has been enshrined at the **San Jao Leng Ju Kieng** (or San Jao Lim Ko Niaw), the site of an important Chinese-Muslim festival in late February or early March. During the festival a wooden image of Lim Ko Niaw is carried through the streets; additional rites include fire-walking and seven days of vegetarianism. The shrine is in the northern end of town towards the harbour.

Another festival fervently celebrated in Pattani is Hari Rayo, the Muslim month of fasting during the 10th lunar month. ■

Portuguese style that was once so prevalent in southern Thailand.

Pattani's main post office is on Pipit Rd, near the bridge. The attached CAT office provides overseas telephone service daily between 7 am and 10 pm.

Mosques
Thailand's second-largest mosque is the **Matsayit Klang**, a traditional structure of green hue, probably still the south's most important mosque. It was built in the early 1960s.

The oldest mosque in Pattani is the **Matsayit Kreu-Se**, built in 1578 by an immigrant Chinese named Lim To Khieng who had married a Pattani woman and converted to Islam. Actually, neither To Khieng, nor anyone else, ever completed the structure.

The story goes that To Khieng's sister, Lim Ko Niaw, sailed from China on a sampan to try and persuade her brother to abandon Islam and return to his homeland. To demonstrate the strength of his faith, he began building the Matsayit Kreu-Se. His sister then put a Chinese curse on the mosque, saying it would never be completed. Then, in a final attempt to dissuade To Khieng, she hanged herself from a nearby cashew-nut tree. In his grief, Khieng was unable to complete the mosque, and to this day it remains unfinished – supposedly every time someone tries to work on it, lightning strikes.

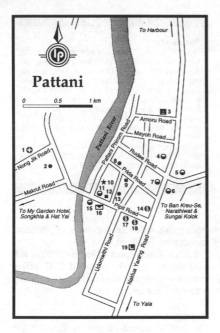

Pattani

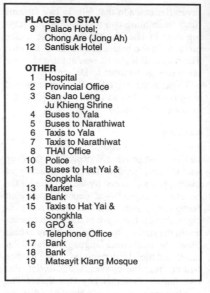

PLACES TO STAY
9 Palace Hotel;
   Chong Are (Jong Ah)
12 Santisuk Hotel

OTHER
1 Hospital
2 Provincial Office
3 San Jao Leng
   Ju Khieng Shrine
4 Buses to Yala
5 Buses to Narathiwat
6 Taxis to Yala
7 Taxis to Narathiwat
8 THAI Office
10 Police
11 Buses to Hat Yai &
   Songkhla
13 Market
14 Bank
15 Taxis to Hat Yai &
   Songkhla
16 GPO &
   Telephone Office
17 Bank
18 Bank
19 Matsayit Klang Mosque

The brick, Arab-style building has been left in its original semi-completed form, but the faithful keep up the surrounding grounds. The mosque is in the village of Ban Kreu-Se, about 7km east of Pattani next to Route 42 at Km 10; a gaudy Tiger Balm Gardens-style Chinese temple has been built next to it.

Beaches

The only beach near town is at **Laem Tachi**, a cape that juts out over the northern end of Ao Pattani. You must take a boat taxi to get there, either from the Pattani pier or from Yaring district at the mouth of the Pattani River. This white-sand beach is about 11km long, but is sometimes marred by refuse from Ao Pattani, depending on the time of year and the tides.

About 15km west of Pattani, **Hat Ratcha-daphisek** (or Hat Sai Maw) is a relaxing spot, with lots of sea pines for shade, but the water is a bit on the murky side. Then there's **Hat Talo Kapo**, 14km east of Pattani, near

Yaring district, a pretty beach that's also a harbour for *kaw-lae*, the traditional fishing boats of southern Thailand. A string of vendors at Talo Kapo sell fresh seafood; during the week it's practically deserted.

To the north of Pattani is **Hat Thepha**, near Khlong Pratu village at Km 96 near the junction of Routes 43 and 4085. Route 43 has replaced Route 4086 along this stretch and parallels the beach. Vendors with beach umbrellas set up on weekends. Places to stay at Hat Thepha are oriented towards middle-class Thais and include *Club Pacific* (☎ (01) 712-1020; 60 rooms, 600 to 1500B), *Leela Resort* (☎ (01) 712-0144; 38 rooms, 400B up), *Sakom Bay Resort* (☎ 238966; 23 rooms, 200B for fan to 600B with air-con) and *Sakom Cabana* (☎ (01) 213-0590; 14 air-con cabins, 700 to 1000B).

Other beaches can be found south-east of Pattani on the way to Narathiwat, especially in the Panare and Saiburi districts, where there are kilometres of virtually deserted beach. **Hat Chala Lai** is a broad white-sand beach 43km south-east of Pattani, near

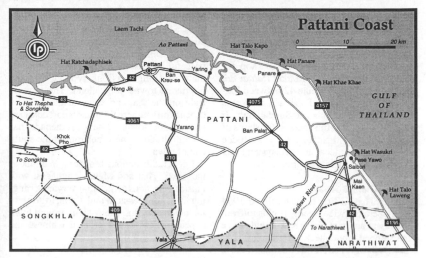

Panare. Eight kilometres farther on towards Narathiwat is **Hat Khae Khae**, a pretty beach studded with boulders. Three kilometres north of Panare is **Hat Panare**, which is another colourful kaw-lae harbour.

If you have your own wheels, follow Route 4136 along the coast south of where the broad Saiburi River empties into the gulf. Near Saiburi is **Hat Wasukri**, also called Chaihat Ban Patatimaw, a beautiful white-sand beach with shade. It's 53km from Pattani. You'll find miles of deserted beach starting at around Km 22, a few kilometres before you reach the Narathiwat provincial border. The cleanest and prettiest stretch, **Hat Talo Laweng**, is found near a Muslim cemetery just south of the tidy Muslim village of Laweng, where you could probably rent rooms from local villagers. The people here make their living from fishing and coconuts. Route 4136 veers off to Mai Kaen just before Laweng if you're heading north to Pattani. None of these beaches are signposted but you can't miss them if you're on Route 4136.

A good place to watch the building of kaw-lae is in the village of Pase Yawo (Ya-Waw), near the mouth of the Saiburi River.

It's a tradition that is slowly dying out as the kaw-lae is replaced by flat-sterned boats painted in the same style.

Places to Stay & Eat

The *Palace Hotel* (☎ 349171) at 38 Soi Talaat Tetiwat, off Prida Rd, is a decent place with rooms for 140B with fan and bath, 200B with two beds or air-con, plus another 50B if you want TV.

The *Santisuk* (☎ 349122), at 29 Pipit Rd, has OK rooms for 80B without a bath, 130 with private bath and 200 to 350B with air-con. As in Yala, Narathiwat, Satun and Trang, all street signs are in tortured English transliterations of Thai (better than no transliterations at all, for those who can't read Thai).

My Garden (☎ 331055; fax 348200) at 8/28 Chareonpradit Rd, about a kilometre outside town, is a good-value middle-range hotel – 275B for a large two-bed room with fan and bath, 440 to 495B for air-con, 660B with TV. The disco is very popular on weekends. Samlor or songthaew drivers may know it by its former name, the Dina.

The *Chong Are (Jong Ah)* restaurant, next to the Palace Hotel on Prida Rd, serves decent Thai and Chinese food.

Things to Buy

Thai Muslims in southern Thailand have their own traditional batik methods that are similar but not identical to the batik of north-east Malaysia. The best place to shop for local batik is at the Palat Market *(talàat nát paalát)*, which is off Route 42 between Pattani and Saiburi in Ban Palat. The market is held all day Wednesday and Sunday only. If you can't make it to this market, the shops of Muslim Phanit and Nadi Brothers on Rudee Rd in Pattani sell local and Malaysian batik at perhaps slightly higher prices.

Getting There & Away

Air Pattani has an airport and until mid-1994 THAI operated twice weekly flights to/from Narathiwat and Hat Yai. These flights have been stopped – but check at Pattani's THAI office (☎ 349149) on 9 Prida Rd to see if these or other flights out of Pattani have been re-instated.

Bus & Share Taxi Pattani is only 40km from Yala. Share taxis are 25B and take about half an hour; buses cost only 12B but take around an hour. From Narathiwat, a share taxi is 45B, a mini-van is 50B and a bus is 28B. From Hat Yai ordinary buses cost 35B and air-con 50B.

From Bangkok there is only one ordinary bus departure at 6.30 pm; the fare for the 17 hour trip is 258B. A 1st class air-con bus departs at 10 am for 464B. In the reverse direction these buses depart Pattani at 6.30 pm for the ordinary bus and 2 pm for the air-con.

Boat Reportedly certain boats between Songkhla and Pattani will take paying passengers – the fare depends on boat size.

Getting Around

Songthaews go anywhere in town for 5B per person.

NARATHIWAT

• ☎ *(73)* • *pop 40,500*

Narathiwat is a pleasant, even-tempered little town, one of Thailand's smallest provincial capitals, with a character all of its own.

Many of the buildings are old wooden structures, a hundred years old or more. The local businesses seem to be owned by both Muslims and Chinese, and nights are particularly peaceful because of the relative absence of male drinking sessions typical of most provincial towns in Thailand. The town is right on the sea, and some of the prettiest beaches on southern Thailand's east coast are just outside town. A new promenade has been built along the waterfront at the south end of town.

Local radio stations broadcast in a mix of the Yawi, Thai and Malay languages, with musical selections to match – everything ranging from north-eastern lûuk thûng to Arabic-melodied dangdut. Many signs around town appear in Yawi as well as Thai, Chinese and English.

Information

The GPO is at the southern end of Pichitbamrung Rd. An attached international phone office is open daily from 7 am to 10 pm.

Two batik factories close to town, M Famabatik (☎ 512452) and Saenghirun Batik (☎ 513151), sell batik direct to visitors.

Beaches

Just north of town is a small Thai-Muslim fishing village at the mouth of the Bang Nara River, lined with the large painted fishing boats called *reua kaw-lae* which are peculiar to Narathiwat and Pattani. Near the fishing village is **Hat Narathat**, a sandy beach 4 to 5km long, which serves as a kind of public park for locals, with outdoor seafood restaurants, tables and umbrellas etc. The constant breeze here is excellent for windsurfing, though only the occasional visiting Malaysian seems to take advantage of this. Shade is provided by a mixture of casuarinas and coco palms.

The beach is only 2km north of the town centre – you can easily walk there or take a samlor. This beach extends all the way north to Pattani, interrupted only by the occasional stream or river mouth; the farther north you go the cleaner and prettier the beach becomes.

Seven kilometres south of town, **Ao Manao**, is a pretty, curved bay lined with sea pines. Vendors on the beach offer food and drinks, along with umbrellas and sling chairs. The locals believe Ao Manao to be the province's prettiest, but it's not as nice as some stretches of sand farther north or south.

Almost the entire coastal stretch between Narathiwat and Malaysia, 40km south, is sandy beach as well – so remote that the beaches don't even have names yet. Unfortunately there is no direct public transport to any of them. Either you must have your own transport or you'll have to try your luck getting off along the highway on the way to Sungai Kolok, then walk to the coast – which is often no more than a couple of kilometres away.

Matsayit Klang (Central Mosque)

Toward the south end of Pichitbamrung Rd stands an old wooden mosque built in the Sumatran style. It was reportedly built by a prince of the former kingdom of Pattani over a hundred years ago. Today it's of secondary importance relative to the newer Arabian modernist-style provincial mosque at the north end of town but is architecturally more interesting.

Taksin Palace

About 7km south of town at the end of Ao Manao is Tanyongmat Hill, where Taksin Palace (Phra Taksin Ratchaniwet) is located. The royal couple stay here for about two months between August and October every year. When they're not in residence, the palace is open to the public daily from 8.30 am to noon and 1 to 4.30 pm. The buildings themselves are not that special, but there are gardens with the Bangsuriya palm, a rare fan-like palm named after the embroidered sunshades used by monks and royalty as a sign of rank. A small zoo and a ceramics workshop are also on the grounds.

A songthaew from the town to the palace area is 5B.

Wat Khao Kong

The tallest seated-Buddha image in Thailand is at Wat Khao Kong, 6km south-west on the way to the train station in Tanyongmat. Called Phra Phuttha Taksin Mingmongkon, the image is 25m high and made of bronze. The wat itself isn't much to see. A songthaew to Wat Khao Kong is 5B from the Narathiwat Hotel.

Narathiwat Fair

Every year during the third week of September, the Narathiwat Fair features kaw-lae boat racing, a singing dove contest judged by the queen, handicraft displays and silat martial arts exhibitions. Other highlights include performances of the local dance forms, *ram sam pen* and *ram ngeng*.

Places to Stay

The cheapest places to stay are all on Puphapugdee (Phupha Phakdi) Rd along the Bang Nara River. The best deal is the *Narathiwat Hotel* (☎ 511063), a funky wooden building that's quiet, breezy, clean and comfortable. Rooms on the waterfront cost 110B with shared bath; the downstairs rooms can sometimes get a bit noisy from the night trade – try to get an upstairs room. Mosquitos could be a problem – don't forget your repellent or mozzie coils.

Another OK place, a bit farther north on the same side of the street, is the quiet *Cathay Hotel* (☎ 511014) – signed in Yawi, English, Thai and Chinese – where spacious, clean, if somewhat cheerless, rooms with attached bath and ceiling fan cost 120B. The elderly Chinese owner speaks good English. There's a view of the river from the roof.

Across the street and next to the Si Ayuthaya Bank, is the *Bang Nara Hotel*, which is a barely disguised brothel with large rooms for 100B with shared bathroom.

The *Rex Hotel* (☎ 511134) at 6/1-3 Chamroonnara Rd is a fair place costing 170B for rooms with fan, 320B for air-con. Similar rooms with fan for 120 to 160B, 280 to 300B with air-con, are available at the *Yaowaraj Hotel* on the corner of Chamroonnara and Pichitbamrung Rds. Because of its busy location, it's not as quiet as the previously mentioned places.

SOUTH-WESTERN GULF COAST

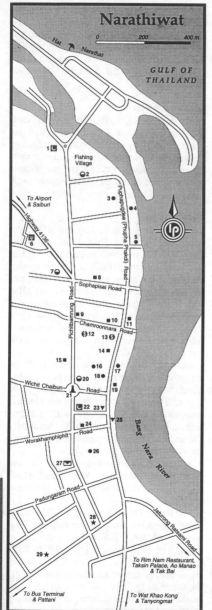

Narathiwat

0   200   400 m

GULF OF
THAILAND

Hat
Narathat

Fishing
Village

To Airport
& Saiburi

Highway 4136

Sophapisai Road

Chamroonnara Road

Wichit Chaibun
Road

Worakhamphiphit
Road

Padungaram Road

To Bus Terminal
& Pattani

Bang Nara River

To Rim Nam Restaurant,
Taksin Palace, Ao Manao
& Tak Bai

To Wat Khao Kong
& Tanyongmat

PLACES TO STAY
8   Tan Yong Hotel
9   Yaowaraj Hotel
10   Rex Hotel
11   Cathay Hotel
14   Bang Nara Hotel
15   Royal Princess Narathiwat
19   Narathiwat Hotel
24   Pacific Hotel

PLACES TO EAT
23   Khao Yam Seller
25   Mangkorn Tong Restaurant

OTHER
1   Provincial Mosque
2   Buses to Pattani
3   Market
4   Evening Fish Market
5   Customs
6   Chinese Shrine
7   Songthaews to Ban Thon
12   Siam Commercial Bank
13   Bangkok Bank
16   Municipal Market
17   Cinema
18   THAI Office
20   Bus Terminal
21   Clock Tower
22   Central Mosque
26   Provincial Office
27   GPO & International
     Telephone Office
28   Police
29   Police

The recently renovated *Pacific Hotel* (☎ 511076) costs 300B for large, clean rooms with fan and bath plus air-con for 330 to 410B.

The top end for the moment is the *Tan Yong Hotel* (☎ 511477), on Sophaphisai Rd, with air-con rooms from 500B. Most of the guests are Malaysians and Thai government officials.

A new upscale place is under construction off the west side Pichitbamrung Rd, the *Royal Princess Narathiwat* (☎ 511027). When completed it will offer 126 rooms in an eight storey building somewhere in the 1500 to 2000B range.

Seven kilometres south of town at Ao Manao, *Ao Manao Resort* features large but closely spaced cement cottages with fan and bath for 400 to 600B a night. It's back from the beach about 400m.

Places to Eat

The *night market* off Chamroonnara Rd behind the Bang Nara Hotel is good. There are also several inexpensive places along Chamroonnara Rd, especially the khâo kaeng place next to the Yaowaraj Hotel, for curries. A cluster of *food stalls* on Sophaphisai Rd at Puphapugdee Rd serve inexpensive noodle dishes.

On Puphapugdee Rd at the north-west corner of a soi leading to the back of the Central Mosque, an elderly couple operate a *small shop* (in a wooden building with a tile roof) selling delicious and inexpensive khâo yam. Malay-style fried rice noodles are served on the side with each order. Curries and rice are also available at this shop. Other places in town have khâo yam in the morning, but this one's best so go early before they run out. Farther south on the same side of the street is a *Muslim shop* with khâo mók and duck over rice. Along Wichit Chaibun Rd west of Puphapugdee Rd are several inexpensive Muslim food shops.

Mangkorn Tong Restaurant is a small seafood place on Puphapugdee Rd that has a floating dining section out back. The food's quite good and prices are reasonable.

The outdoor *Rim Nam* restaurant, on Jaturong Ratsami Rd a couple of kilometres south of town, has good medium-priced seafood and curries. South of Rim Nam is the similar but larger *Bang Nara*; both restaurants are popular with Malaysian tour groups these days.

Getting There & Away

Air THAI has daily flights between Narathiwat and Bangkok, via Phuket. The fare to Phuket is 990B, to Bangkok it's 2575B. The THAI office (☎ 511161) is at 322-5 Puphapugdee (Phupha Phakdi) Rd; a THAI van between Nara airport (12km north via Route 4136) and the THAI office costs 30B per person.

Bus & Share Taxi Share taxis between Yala and Narathiwat are 45B, buses 35B (with a change in Pattani). Buses cost 28B from Pattani. From Sungai Kolok, buses are 18B,

share taxis and mini-vans 40B. To Hat Yai it's 120B by share taxi or 100B by air-con mini-van; the latter leave several times a day from opposite the Rex Hotel for 100B per person.

To/from Tak Bai, the other border crossing, it is 10B by songthaew (catch one in front of the Narathiwat Hotel), 20B by taxi.

Train The train costs 13B for 3rd class seats to Tanyongmat, 20km west of Narathiwat, then it's either a 15B taxi to Narathiwat or 10B by songthaew.

Getting Around

Motorcycle taxis around town cost 10B. Wicker-chair samlors from Malaysia are mainly used for carrying goods back and forth to market; these cost from 10 to 25B depending on the distance and amount of cargo.

AROUND NARATHIWAT
Wadin Husen Mosque

One of the most interesting mosques in Thailand, the Wadin Husen was built in 1769 and mixes Thai, Chinese and Malay architectural styles to good effect. It's in the village of Lubosawo in Bajo (Ba-Jaw) district, about 15km north-west of Narathiwat off Route 42, about 8B by songthaew.

Wat Chonthara Sing-He

During the British colonisation of Malaysia (then called Malaya), the Brits tried to claim Narathiwat as part of their Malayan Empire. The Thais constructed Wat Chonthara Sing-He (also known as Wat Phitak Phaendin Thai) in Tak Bai district near the Malayan border to prove that Narathiwat was indeed part of Siam, and as a result the British relinquished their claim.

Today it's most notable because of the genuine southern-Thai architecture, rarely seen in a Buddhist temple – sort of the Thai-Buddhist equivalent of the Wadin Husen Mosque. A wooden wihãan here very much resembles a Sumatran-style mosque. An 1873 wihãan on the grounds contains a reclining Buddha decorated with Chinese ceramics from the Song Dynasty. Another wihãan on the spacious grounds contains murals painted by a famous Songkhla monk during the reign of King Mongkut. The murals are religious in message but also depict traditional southern-Thai life. There is also a larger, typical Thai wihãan.

Wat Chon is 34km south-east of Narathiwat in Tak Bai. It's probably not worth a trip from Narathiwat just to see this 100-year-old temple unless you're a real temple freak, but if you're killing time in Tak Bai or Sungai Kolok this is one of the prime local sights. It's next to the river and the quiet, expansive grounds provide a retreat from the busy border atmosphere.

To get there from Narathiwat, take a bus or songthaew bound for Ban Taba and get off in Tak Bai. The wat is on the river about 500m from the main Tak Bai intersection.

SUNGAI KOLOK & BAN TABA

These small towns in the south-east of Narathiwat Province are departure points for the east coast of Malaysia. There is a fair batik (*paa-té*) cottage industry in this district.

Be prepared for culture shock coming from Malaysia, warned one traveller. Not only are most signs in Thai script, but fewer people speak English in Thailand than in Malaysia.

Sungai Kolok

The Thai government once planned to move the border crossing from Sungai Kolok to Ban Taba in Tak Bai district, which is on the coast 32km east. The Taba crossing is now open and is a shorter and quicker route to Kota Baru, the first Malaysian town of any size, but it looks like Sungai Kolok will remain open as well for a long time. They're even building new hotels in Sungai Kolok and have established a TAT office next to the immigration post.

Still, as a town it's a bit of a mess; an estimated 3000 prostitutes form the town's second biggest industry. The rest of the economy is given over to Thai-Malaysia shipping; there's an entire district in the northeast part of town given over to warehouses which store goods moving back and forth between countries.

The border is open from 5 am to 5 pm (6 am to 6 pm Malaysian time). On slow days they may close the border as early as 4.30 pm.

Information The TAT office (☎ 612126), next to the immigration post, is open daily from 8.30 am to 5 pm. The post and telephone office is on Thetpathom Rd, while immigration is near the Merlin Hotel on Charoenkhet Rd.

Places to Stay & Eat According to the TAT there are 46 hotels in Sungai Kolok, most in operation to accommodate the weekend trips of Malaysian males and bearing names like *Marry, Come In, Honey, My Love* and *Hawaii*. Of the cheaper hotels, only a handful are under 150B and they're mainly for those crossing for only a couple of hours. So if you have to spend the night here it's best to pay a little more and get away from the short-time trade.

Most places in Sungai Kolok will accept Malaysian ringgit as well as Thai baht for food or accommodation.

The most inexpensive places are along Charoenkhet Rd. Here you can find the fairly clean *Thailiang Hotel* (☎ 611132) at No 12 for 150B, the *Savoy Hotel* (☎ 611093) at No 8/2 for 120 to 150B and the *Asia Hotel* (☎ 611101) at No 4-4/1 for 160B (fan and bath), or 200 to 250B with air-con. The *Pimarn Hotel* (☎ 611464) at No 76-4 is also quite good at 150B with fan and bath.

On the corner of Thetpathom and Waman Amnoey Rds is the pleasant *Valentine Hotel* (☎ 611229), with rooms for 180B with fan, 260 to 330B with air-con. There's a coffee shop downstairs.

Other reasonably decent hotels in the 100 to 200B range include the *An An Hotel* (☎ 611058) at 183/1-2 Prachawiwat Rd, the *Taksin 2* (☎ 611088) at 4 Prachasamran Rd, the *San Sabai 2* (☎ 611313) at 38 Waman Amnoey Rd, the cheaper *San Sabai 1* (☎ 612157) at 32/34 Bussayapan Rd and the *Nam Thai 2* (☎ 611163) at Soi Phuthon,

Charoenkhet Rd. Some of these hotels also offer air-con rooms for 200 to 360B.

Top-end hotels in Sungai Kolok include:

Genting Hotel – Asia 18 Rd (☎ 613231; fax 611259); from 600B
Grand Garden – 104 Arifmankha Rd (☎ 611219; fax 613501); from 550B
Intertower Hotel – Prachawiwat Rd (☎ 611192; fax 613400); from 399B
Marina Hotel – 173 Soi 3, Charoenkhet Rd (☎ 613-881; fax 613385); from 638B
Merlin Hotel – 40 Charoenkhet Rd (☎ 611003; fax 611431); from 410B
Plaza Hotel – off Bussayapan Rd (☎ 611875; fax 613402); from 374B
Tara Regent Hotel – Soi Phuthon, Charoenkhet Rd (☎ 611401; fax 611801); from 390B

The town has plenty of food stalls selling Thai, Chinese and Malaysian food. There's a good Chinese *vegetarian restaurant* between the Asia and Savoy hotels that's open daily from 7 am to 6 pm. A cluster of reliable Malay food vendors can be found at the market and in front of the train station.

Getting There & Away Air-con buses to/from Bangkok cost 533B, take 18 hours and depart from Bangkok at 6.30 pm and from Sungai Kolok at 12.30 pm. Standard bus fares are 296B, departing from Bangkok at 9 pm or from Sungai Kolok at 9 am – but you would have to be a dyed-in-the-wool masochist to do the entire 20 hour trip by ordinary bus. To Surat Thani standard buses are 143B (taking 10 hours), air-con 256B (9 hours).

Share taxis from Yala to Sungai Kolok cost 65B, from Narathiwat 40B; in Sungai Kolok the taxi stand is at the west end of Thetpathom Rd. There are also buses from Narathiwat for 18B (25B air-con). From Sungai Kolok taxis to Narathiwat leave from in front of the An An Hotel.

Air-con buses to Hat Yai cost 98B and leave from the Valentine Hotel at 7 and 9 am and 1 and 3 pm. From Hat Yai, departure times are the same. The trip takes about four hours. Share Taxis to Hat Yai cost 120B and leave from next to the Thailiang Hotel.

The border is about a kilometre from the centre of Sungai Kolok or the train station.

Transport around town is by motorcycle taxi – it's 10B for a ride to the border. Coming from Malaysia, just follow the old train tracks to your right, or, for the town, turn left at the first junction and head for the high-rises.

From Rantau Panjang (Malaysian side), a share taxi to Kota Baru costs M$4 per person (M$15 to charter the whole car) and takes about an hour. The regular yellow and orange bus to KB costs M$2.50.

The daily special express train No 19 to Sungai Kolok departs Bangkok at 2.35 pm and arrives at 10.20 am the next day. This train has 1st (808B) and 2nd class fares (378B), not including the special-express surcharge of 50B (and 1st or 2nd class sleeping berths if you so choose).

You can also get trains to Sungai Kolok from Yala and Tanyongmat (for Narathiwat), but buses are really faster and more convenient along these routes.

From Sungai Kolok to points farther north (via Yala), however, the train is a reasonable alternative. A train to Hat Yai takes about 4½ hours and costs 31B for a 3rd class seat, 65B 2nd class. Train Nos 124 and 132 leave Sungai Kolok at 6.30 and 9 am, arriving in Hat Yai at 11.37 am and 1.49 pm.

From Sungai Kolok special express No 20 leaves at 3 pm and arrives in Bangkok at 10.35 am the next day, with stops in Hat Yai (6.40 pm), Surat Thani (11.48 pm) and Hua Hin (6.42 am) among other towns along the way.

Ban Taba

Ban Taba, 5km south of bustling Tak Bai, is a blip of a town with a large market and a few hotels. Takbai Border House, a large Customs complex built in the hope of diverting traffic from Kolok, is underused and neglected. From the Customs and market area you can see Malaysia right across the Kolok River.

A few hundred metres north of the complex, **Hat Taba** is a beach park of sorts planted with casuarinas and bearing a few open-air shelters. You can change money at street vendors by the ferry on the Thai side.

A ferry across the river into Malaysia is

5B. The border crossing here is open the same hours as in Sungai Kolok. From the Malaysian side you can get buses direct to Kota Baru for M$1.50.

Places to Stay *Masaya Resort* (☎ 581125) has good rooms for 170 to 250B with fan and bath, 300B with air-con or 370B with air-con and TV. It's set back off the road leading from the Malaysian border and a bit difficult to find; take a motorcycle taxi there for 5B. The *Pornphet* (☎ 581331), a motel-like place near the beach north of Taba, isn't bad for 250 to 370B, all air-con.

Northern Andaman Coast (Ranong to Phuket)

Northern Andaman Coast Highlights

• **National Marine Parks** – the Similan and Surin Islands have Thailand's best coral colonies and are world-famous for their magnificent diving and snorkelling

• **Khao Lak/Lam Ru National Park** – sea cliffs, beaches, estuaries, forested valleys and an exotic array of wildlife, including the Asiatic black bear, drongos and tapirs

• **Phuket** – one of Thailand's most popular beach destinations, it also has world-class diving, yachting, a tantalising unique cuisine, lively markets and a cosmopolitan nightlife

• **Hot Mineral Springs** – friendly Ranong town boasts the Wat Tapotaram springs, where you can bathe in rustic rooms Thai style

Stretching from the Isthmus of Kra south to Ko Phuket and Ao Phang-Nga, Thailand's Northern Andaman Coast probably offers more geographic variety than any other coastal reach in the country. Pristine, little-visited mangrove forests in Ranong Province, the remote oceanic island groups of Surin and Similan, the quiet beaches around Khao Lak and the international jet-set destination of Phuket are all encompassed within this relatively compact area.

RANONG
• ☎ (77) • pop 18,000

The small capital and port of Ranong, separated from Myanmar (Burma) by only the Chan River, receives fairly few foreign visitors, unless you count the many Burmese residents from nearby Victoria Point who hop across to trade in Thailand or to work on fishing boats. Although there are no great cultural attractions in town, the buildings are architecturally interesting since this area was originally settled by Hokkien Chinese. Ranong also has a lively, friendly appeal that makes it easy to while away a day or two just strolling about, poking around the market and visiting a Hokkien coffee shop or two.

Beaches with tourist facilities include nearby Hat Chandamri and the coastal islands of Ko Chang and Ko Phayam; see the Around Ranong and Laem Son National Park sections further on for details.

Thai tourists are beginning to use Ranong as a gateway to Myanmar's Victoria Point and Thahtay Island. There are rumours that an international dive tour operator will soon open shop in Ranong in anticipation of leading dive trips to various islands and reefs off the southern tip of Myanmar, though at the time of writing nothing had yet transpired.

Information
Most of Ranong's banks are on Tha Meuang Rd (the road to the fishing pier), near the intersection with Ruangrat Rd. There is a post office with an attached international telephone office on Ruangrat Rd in the old town district.

Ranong Travel (☎ 833458; fax 833457) at 37 Ruangrat Rd, just south of the Asia Hotel,

359

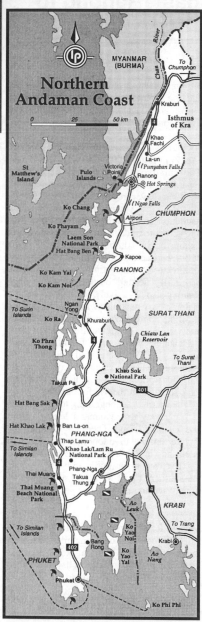

dispenses good travel info (the proprietor, Khun Nuansri, speaks excellent English) and arranges deep-sea fishing and diving jaunts, accommodation on Ko Chang, car and motorbike rentals and boat trips to the Ko Surin Islands. The office is open daily from 8 am to 6 pm and is on the 2nd floor at the back of a small bookshop: you'll see the sign outside.

Nai Khai Ranong

During the reign of King Rama V, a Hokkien named Koh Su Chiang became governor of Ranong (thus gaining the new name Phraya Damrong Na Ranong) and his former residence, Nai Khai Ranong, has become a clan house and shrine. It's on the northern edge of town and is worth a visit.

Of the three original buildings, one still stands and is filled with mementos of the Koh family glory days. The main gate and part of the original wall also remain. Koh Su Chiang's great-grandson Koh Sim Kong is the caretaker and he speaks some English. Several shophouses on Ruangrat Rd preserve the old Hokkien style, too. Koh Su Chiang's mausoleum is set into the side of a hill several kilometres farther north on the road to Hat Chandamri.

Hot Springs & Wat Hat Som Paen

About 1km east of the Jansom Thara Hotel is the Ranong Mineral Hot Springs at Wat Tapotaram. The water temperature hovers around 65°C, hot enough to boil eggs. You can bathe in rustic rooms (10B per person) where you scoop water from separate hot and cool water tanks and sluice the mixed water over your body Thai-style. Don't get inside the tanks and spoil the water. The Jansom Thara Hotel also pipes water from the springs into the hotel, where you can take a 42°C mineral bath in their large public jacuzzi for 100B.

If you continue on the same road past the hot springs for about 7km, you'll come to the village of Hat Som Paen, a former tin-mining community. At Wat Hat Som Paen, visitors feed fruit to the huge black carp (plaa phluang) in the temple stream. The faithful believe

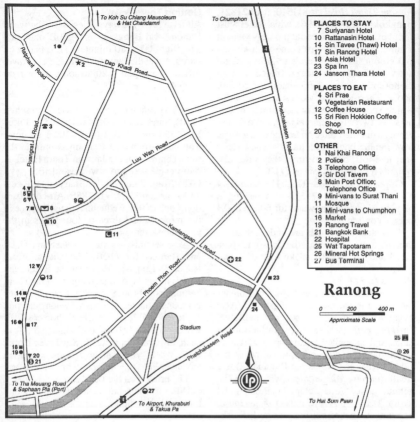

PLACES TO STAY
7   Suriyanan Hotel
10 Rattanasin Hotel
14 Sin Tavee (Thawi) Hotel
17 Sin Ranong Hotel
18 Asia Hotel
23 Spa Inn
24 Jansom Thara Hotel

PLACES TO EAT
4   Sri Prae
6   Vegetarian Restaurant
12 Coffee House
15 Sri Rien Hokkien Coffee
    Shop
20 Chaon Thong

OTHER
1   Nai Khai Ranong
2   Police
3   Telephone Office
5   Oir Dol Tavern
8   Main Post Office;
    Telephone Office
9   Mini-vans to Surat Thani
11 Mosque
13 Mini-vans to Chumphon
16 Market
19 Ranong Travel
21 Bangkok Bank
22 Hospital
25 Wat Tapotaram
26 Mineral Hot Springs
27 Bus Terminal

Ranong

0   200   400 m

Approximate Scale

these carp are actually *thewada*, a type of angel, and it's forbidden to catch and eat them. Legend has it that those who do will contract leprosy.

Places to Stay

The *Asia Hotel* (☎ 811113), at 39/9 Ruangrat Rd near the market, has fair rooms with fan and bath for 200 to 260B and air-con rooms for 550B. Across from the market is the *Sin Ranong Hotel* (☎ 811454) with adequate rooms with fan for 150/170B, air-con for 300/400B. North a bit, at No 81/1 Ruangrat Rd, the *Sin Tavee (Thawi) Hotel* (☎ 811213)

offers similar rooms for 160B, plus air-con rooms for 240/280B.

Farther up Ruangrat Rd are the *Rattanasin Hotel* on the right and the *Suriyanan Hotel* on the left across from the post office. The Rattanasin is a typical Thai-Chinese place that looks worse for wear despite a recent 'renovation'; rooms with fan and bath cost 150B single/double. The Suriyanan is dark and decaying, but the staff are friendly and claim they don't allow hookers in the hotel. A basic room is 80B with a fan, and 100B with fan and bath.

Outside the town centre, on Hwy 4 is the

Jansom Thara Hotel (☎ 811510; fax 821821, Bangkok ☎ (2) 448-6096), which offers just about everything you could possibly want in a hotel. Standard rooms come with air-con and colour TV and there's in-house video, hot-water bath with jacuzzi (piped in from the hot springs), and a refrigerator stocked with booze. There are also two restaurants, one of which specialises in Chinese dim sum and noodles, two large mineral jacuzzis, a fitness centre, a disco, a coffee house/cocktail lounge, a swimming pool and a travel agency. Rates start at 946B, but sometimes they offer discounted rooms for as low as 771B.

Opposite the Jansom Thara Hotel on Hwy 4, the *Spa Inn* (☎ 811715) is also cashing in on piped-in hot springwater for 600 to 800B per air-con room.

Two large new hotels are under construction in town, one near the Jansom Thara Hotel and the other by a lake west of town.

Places to Eat

For inexpensive Thai and Burmese breakfasts, try the *market* on Ruangrat Rd. Also along Ruangrat Rd are several traditional *Hokkien coffee shops* with marble-topped tables and enamelled metal teapots. Between the Rattanasin and Sin Tavee Hotels (same side of Ruangrat Rd as the Rattanasin) is a small *Burmese Muslim place* where you can get curry, rice, roti, pickled cucumbers and tea for 20B. Around here is also *Coffee House*, a tiny place that serves western-style breakfasts and light meals.

Just north of the cinema on Ruangrat Rd is a small *vegetarian restaurant* serving inexpensive Thai dishes; it's open Monday to Saturday from around 7 am to 6 pm. Nearby, the moderately priced *Sri Prae* at 313/2 Ruangrat is very popular with locals for stuffed crab and other seafood.

Chaon Thong at 8-10 Ruangrat Rd is a clean, air-con place with Thai food and western breakfasts. It's open from 6 am to 9.30 pm and is associated with Ranong Travel. A couple of kilometres north of town on the highway, between Caltex and PT petrol stations, the *Mandalay* specialises in Burmese and Thai-style seafood.

Getting There & Away

Air Bangkok Airways flies daily between Ranong and Bangkok for 1980B one way. The flight takes 80 minutes. Tickets can be purchased at the Jansom Thara Hotel's travel office. The airport is 20km south of town on Hwy 4.

Bus You can get to Ranong via Chumphon (35B), Surat Thani (60B, 80B air-con), Takua Pa (45B) and Phuket (80B, 100B air-con). The bus terminal in Ranong is outside the town centre, near the Jansom Thara Hotel. A motorcycle taxi into town costs 15B.

To/from Bangkok, ordinary buses cost 140B, air-con 250B, VIP 385B. Air-con buses don't depart that frequently, usually twice in the morning and three or four times in the afternoon/evening.

Air-con mini-vans run between Surat Thani and Ranong for 110B. They depart from Ranong's Luu Wan Rd (near the Rattanasin Hotel) around 8 am, arriving in Surat Thani around noon. From Surat Thani the van leaves at around 1 pm and returns to Ranong at 4 pm.

Air-con minibuses to Chumphon cost 70B and depart hourly between 7 am and 5.30 pm each day from opposite the Sin Tavee Hotel, from where you can also book a seat in advance. Vans to Chumphon have the letters 'CTR' printed on the back end.

Buses to Khuraburi cost 35B and take one hour and 20 minutes.

Getting Around

Songthaews ply the roads around Ranong and out to the hot springs and Hat Som Paen, Hat Chandamri, and also to Saphaan Plaa, from where you can get boats to Victoria Point, Myanmar. The fare is 5B to any of these places. Nearly all songthaews leave from in front of the market on Ruangrat Rd. Motorcycle taxis (look for the orange-vested drivers) will take you anywhere in town for 15B, or to the area around the Jansom Thara for 20B.

Mayline, a minimart next to the Jansom Thara, rents Honda Dreams for 200B per day. Ranong Travel can assist with motorcycle and car rentals.

AROUND RANONG
• ☎ (77)

Hat Chandamri

Touted as the nearest beach to Ranong, Hat Chandamri is really more of a mudflat, part of the Chan River estuary – known locally as 'Pak Chan' ('Mouth of the Chan'). A sister hotel to the Jansom Thara in Ranong, the *Jansom Thara Resort* (☎ 821611; fax 821821) has similarly equipped bungalows (but no jacuzzis) for 1400B (discounts to 900B frequently available). From the dining terrace overlooking the bay you can eat seafood and watch the sun set over Myanmar's Victoria Point. Past the resort on the road to Hat Chandamri, *Pak Nam Seafood* serves delicious and relatively inexpensive Thai seafood in a terraced dining area overlooking the seaside.

Hat Chandamri is 10km north-west of Ranong, about 50B by motorcycle taxi or 5B by songthaew.

Fishermen's Pier (Saphaan Pla)

The provincial fishing port, Tha Thiap Reua Pramong, is 8km south-west of Ranong. It's called Saphaan Pla ('Fish Bridge') for short and is always bustling with activity as fishing boats are loaded and unloaded with great cargoes of flapping fish. The fish traders buy from anyone who lands fish here, and about half the boats are Burmese. Boats can be chartered here for day trips to nearby islands. But the main reason most visitors come here is to catch a boat across to Victoria Point in Myanmar (see below). Songthaews to Saphaan Pla leave frequently from in front of the Ranong market on Ruangrat Rd.

Victoria Point (Kaw Thaung)

This lively, dusty port at the southernmost tip of mainland Myanmar (Burma) is only separated from Thailand by a broad estuary of the Chan River. To the British it was 'Victoria Point' and to the Thais it's 'Ko Sawng', which means 'Second Island' in Thai. The Burmese name, Kaw Thaung, is probably a variation on the latter.

The main business here is trade with Thailand, followed by fishing. The atmosphere is hectic, and shops are bursting with all manner of consumer goods. As you make your way through the crowds you can almost feel the money changing hands. Although only 30 minutes from Ranong, Victoria Point has much more of a third world border town feel than its Thai counterpart.

Many of the residents are bilingual in Thai and Burmese. Some people born and raised around Victoria Point, especially Muslims, also speak Pashu, a dialect that mixes Thai, Malay and Burmese. Among the Burmese, Victoria Point is perhaps best known for producing some of the country's best kickboxers. Nearby islands are inhabited by bands of nomadic Moken or 'sea gypsies'. Visits to islands further out, in the Mergui Archipelago, can be arranged through yacht operators in Phuket (see under Yachting in the Phuket section for details).

It's probably not worth making a special journey to Ranong just to visit Victoria Point, but if you're in the area it makes for an interesting day trip. It's a chaotic place, and even a few hours here can make Thailand seem sedate, organised and modern.

Visas & Currency Exchange Immediately as you exit the Victoria Point jetty there's a small immigration office on the right, where you must pay US$5 for a day permit. If you have no US currency it will cost you 200B. For the same rate you can stay up to three nights but then you're required to buy US$50 worth of Foreign Exchange Certificates. If you want to stay longer, you can extend your permit up to 29 days upon payment of US$36 and the exchange of US$300 into FECs.

Travelling further north may be possible if you already have a visa issued by an overseas Myanmar embassy, but even then it can be tricky. There are daily flights to Yangon (Rangoon) for 120FEC, but officially only tour groups can travel beyond Victoria Point. However, immigration officials at the head office in Victoria Point have been known to point travellers toward the Andaman Club on Thahtay Island, where they can 'join' a tour group. This loophole may get you the signature needed to buy a Yangon Airways ticket, though don't count on it.

To get to the main immigration office, walk straight out from the pier and turn left at the clock tower, taking the road leading uphill. The office is about 200m along on the right-hand side.

Organised Tours Jansom Thara Hotel in Ranong offers Victoria Point and island tours aboard four boats with capacities ranging from 15 to 200 people. A 'half-day tour' costing 600B per person sails from Ranong, visits a couple of pagodas in Victoria Point and returns to Ranong around 11 am. The 'full day tour' costing 850B goes to Pulau Besin for beach swimming and lunch and returns at 2 pm. Rates include immigration procedures on both sides, guide and boat; lunch is an extra 120B per person.

Ranong Travel arranges similar tours starting at 400B, but only for groups of 10 or more.

Places to Stay So far there are two places in Victoria Point itself approved to accept foreigners. Closest to the pier is the newly opened *Honey Bear Hotel,* which has all air-con rooms for US$45 or 700B: not a great deal. But then again, the other option is the shabby *Kawthaung Motel,* located about 300m beyond the main immigration office. For simple double rooms with private cold-water bath, Thais pay 400B, foreigners US$30, Burmese around 80B.

On nearby Thahtay Island, well-heeled Thai and Singaporean gamblers stay at the *Andaman Club* (☎ (01) 956-4354), a huge five-star hotel sporting a casino and Jack Nicklaus-designed, 18-hole golf course. All 191 rooms have sea views and start at 3000B. Guests with bookings are able to take a 125B boat direct from Jansom Thara Resort on Hat Chandamri, about 10km north-west of Ranong.

Getting There & Away Long-tail boats to Victoria Point leave from an incredibly jammed pier at Saphaan Pla. Boats leave when full, take 30 minutes to make the crossing and cost 30B per person. If you take a songthaew from Ranong, tell the driver you want to go to Victoria Point. You'll be dropped off near a small courtyard on the right-hand side. Walk through the courtyard and then through a row of buildings to reach the pier. There will probably be several touts to help you find the way.

Isthmus of Kra

About 60km north of Ranong, in Kraburi district, is the Isthmus of Kra, the narrowest point in Thailand. Barely 50km separates the Gulf of Thailand from the Indian Ocean at this point. Just off Hwy 4 is a monument commemorating this geographical wonder. At one time the Thai government had plans to construct the so-called Kra Canal here, but the latest word is that the canal – if it's built – will run east from Satun Province through Songkhla, about 500km farther south.

Waterfalls

Of the several well-known waterfalls in Ranong Province, **Ngao Falls** and **Punyaban Falls** are within walking distance of Hwy 4. Ngao is 13km south of Ranong while Punyaban is 15km north. Just ride a songthaew in either direction and ask to be let off at the *náam tòk* (waterfall).

Ko Chang

Don't confuse this island off the coast of Ranong with the much larger Ko Chang in Trat Province. As at many of the islands in this area, estuarial effluent from the Chan River inhibits clarity in the surrounding Andaman waters, but natural mangrove on the east coast and a hilly, forested interior are attraction enough for some. Birdlife includes hornbills, sea eagles and Andaman kites.

A couple of trails meander around the island and so far there are no motor vehicles or electricity – the few resorts on the island either do without or generate their own. Beaches are found along the western shore, and though they're not classic white-sand strands, regular visitors enjoy the laid-back atmosphere.

Bungalow operations on the island can arrange boat trips to Ko Phayam and other nearby islands for around 150B per person (including lunch) for groups of six or more.

Places to Stay & Eat Several beach places have opened up over the past couple of years, though for the most part they're only open November to April. Starting at the northern end of the island, *Rasta Baby* (Ranong ☎ (77) 833077) is a seven-bungalow spot run by a dreadlocked Thai and his American wife. You can choose from two price schemes: 200B for room, breakfast and dinner, or 100B per room only. Meals are often prepared and served communally.

Sharing the same small beach with Rasta Baby, *Ko Chang Contex* (Ranong ☎ (77) 812-730) is run by a Thai family with similar arrangements along with an à la carte restaurant menu.

Next south and west, the *Eden Bistro Cafe* offers two small bungalows with shared bath for 100B each, and one large bungalow with attached shower for 150B. Just down the beach from Eden, *Sunset* offers nicely built bungalows in a shady, breezy spot for 100B each.

Cashew Resort, the oldest and largest place on the island, charges 100B for simple huts with shared facilities. Service has slipped over the years, perhaps because the proprietors were the only game on the island for so long.

A few hundred metres past the pier for boats from the mainland are the friendly *Chang Thong* and *Pheung Thong*, side-by-side operations run by a brother and sister. Bamboo or plasterboard huts cost 80B here; Chang Thong's restaurant serves decent Thai food.

Nearby *Sabai Jai*, a well-run Swedish-Thai joint effort, has a six-bed dorm for 30B per bed as well as several thatched huts for 80 to 100B. Facilities are simple but clean and well maintained; the proprietors bake their own bread and the restaurant focuses on western food.

The rather unfriendly *Ko Chang Resort* sits on a section of rocky headlands. Huts with shared bath are 100B, with attached bath 150B. Monkeys are chained to table legs in the restaurant, not a good sign.

At the southern end of the island at Ao Lek ('Small Bay'), *N & X Bungalows* offers more of the same thatched huts for 100B each. At least three other bungalow operations are now under construction at this end of the island.

Getting There & Away From Ranong take a songthaew to Saphaan Pla, getting off by the petrol station toward the main pier. Look for signs advertising Ko Chang bungalows and follow them down a zigzag soi a couple of hundred metres, where you'll find long-tail boats that run to Ko Chang. If you have a heavy bag, a motorcycle taxi can bring you to this landing for 20B.

Depending on the tide, two or three boats leave every morning from November to April; turn up around 8 am to see when they're going as they don't usually leave before this hour; they return to the mainland in the early afternoon. The cost is negotiable depending on how many passengers board; if you book a bungalow through Ranong Travel in town, you may get a free boat ride along with a ride down to Saphaan Pla. Otherwise count on paying anywhere from 30 to 100B per person.

LAEM SON NATIONAL PARK

The Laem Son (Pine Cape) Wildlife & Forest Preserve stretches 315 sq km over the Kapoe district of Ranong and Khuraburi district in Phang-Nga. This area includes about 100km of Andaman Sea coastline – the longest protected shore in the country – as well as over 20 islands. Much of the coast here consists of mangrove swamps, home to various species of birds, fish, deer and monkeys, including crab-eating macaques, often seen while driving along the road to the park headquarters.

The best known and most accessible beach is **Hat Bang Ben**, where the main park offices, restaurant and bungalows are. This is a long, sandy beach backed by shady casuarina trees and it is said to be safe for swimming year-round. From Hat Bang Ben you can see several islands, including the nearby Ko Kam Yai, Ko Kam Noi, Mu Ko Yipun, Ko Kang Kao and, to the north, Ko Phayam. The park staff can arrange boat trips out to any of these islands for 800B per boat per day. During low tide you can walk to an island just a couple of hundred metres away from Hat Bang Ben.

Ko Phayam is inhabited by around 100 Thais, who mostly make their living fishing or growing cashews. There are good swimming beaches on Phayam and on the western side of some of the Kam islands, as well as some live coral. Although underwater visibility isn't great, it's a little better here than on Ko Chang as it's farther from the mouth of the Chan River. The beach on **Ko Kam Noi** has relatively clear water for swimming and snorkelling (April is the best month) plus the added bonus of fresh water year-round and plenty of grassy areas for camping. One island on the other side of Ko Kam Yai that can't be seen from the beach is **Ko Kam Tok** (also called Ko Ao Khao Khwai). It's only about 200m from Ko Kam Yai, and, like Ko Kam Noi, has a good beach, coral, fresh water and a camping area. **Ko Kam Yai** is 14km south-west of Hat Bang Ben.

About 3km north of Hat Bang Ben, across the canal, is another beach, **Hat Laem Son**, which is almost always deserted and is 'undeveloped' according to park authorities (which means they won't guarantee your safety). The only way to get there is to hike from Bang Ben. In the opposite direction, about 50km south of Hat Bang Ben, is **Hat Praphat**, very similar to Bang Ben with casuarina trees and a long beach. A second park office is here and this one can be reached by road via the Phetkasem Hwy (Hwy 4).

In the canals you ford coming into the park, you may notice large wooden racks which are used for raising oysters.

Places to Stay & Eat

Camping is allowed anywhere among the casuarina trees for 5B per person. *National park bungalows* have dorm-like wooden houses sleeping 10 or 16 for 700B and 900B respectively but individuals are allowed to stay for 100B per night. Similar park accommodation is also available on Ko Kam Yai but should be arranged in advance; call

Ranong ☎ (77) 823255 or Bangkok ☎ (2) 579-0529 in for information.

A few hundred metres before the park entrance (9.5km from the Hwy 4 junction) is the private *Wasana Resort*, a new place run by a Thai-Dutch couple. Clean bamboo bungalows with mosquito nets, fan and private bath cost 250B, larger concrete bungalows with verandas are 500B; discounts for long-term stays are available. The nearby *Andaman Peace Resort* (☎ 821796) offers five different styles of concrete bungalows for 600 to 1500B. Just outside the park entrance, the lacklustre *Komain Villa* offers small bungalows for 200B per night.

The food at the *park canteen* is quite reasonable, although *Wasana Resort* is the better choice.

Ko Phayam & Ko Chang There are only a few places to stay on Ko Phayam. On the west side of the island is a small beach with a couple of *bungalows* in the 100 to 150B range, plus a nicer, larger beach with five *bungalows* for 150B each. On the east side is the more expensive *Payam Island Resort* (☎ 812297; Bangkok (2) 390-2681) with bungalows from 400 to 2500B. There is also the *Thawon Resort* (☎ 811186) with bungalows for 100B and 150B.

On Ko Chang to the immediate north there are also several places to stay – see the earlier entry under Around Ranong.

Getting There & Away

The turn-off for Laem Son National Park is about 58km down the Phetkasem Hwy from Ranong, between Km 657 and 658. Any bus heading south from Ranong can drop you off here or you could hitch fairly easily – there is plenty of traffic along Hwy 4. Once you're off the highway, however, you'll have to wait a bit to flag down pickup trucks going to the village near Laem Son. If you can't get a ride all the way, it's a 2km walk from the village to the park. At the new police box at the junction you may be able to hire a motor-cycle taxi for 30B. The road is now paved all the way to the park, so if you're driving, it's a breeze.

Boats to Nearby Islands Boats going to Ko Phayam are irregular, unless you are willing to charter one for 2000B. Sometimes the Ko Chang boats continue to Ko Phayam – enquire at Ranong's Jansom Thara Hotel, Ranong Travel or at Saphaan Pla (see the Ranong section earlier in this chapter for contact details).

Boats out to the various islands can be chartered from the park's visitor centre; the cost is 800B per day. You can arrange to go as far as the Similan or Surin Islands (see the relevant sections further on) for 900B and 1200B per person respectively.

KHURABURI, TAKUA PA & THAI MUANG
• ☎ (76)

These districts of Phang-Nga Province are of some interest in themselves but are mainly used as departure points for other destinations, notably the Surin and Similan Islands. The exception is Takua Pa district, which has some quite nice beaches, the best of which is probably Hat Khao Lak.

From near **Khuraburi**, from the pier at Ngan Yong, you can reach the remote Surin Islands. Aside from this, there really isn't much around here besides farms and forest.

Takua Pa lies about halfway between Ranong and Phuket so buses often make rest stops here. Just off the highway is the *Extra Hotel* (☎ 421412) with rooms from 220B if you want to stop for the night (though it's only another hour by bus to Hat Khao Lak). From Takua Pa town you can head east to Khao Sok National Park and Surat Thani. **Hat Khao Lak** is about 30km south of Takua Pa along Route 4. A few kilometres further down is **Khao Lak/Lam Ru National Park**, which extends some 30km from the coast into tropical rainforest.

Not far past the park, in the district of Thai Muang, is **Thap Lamu** where you can get boats to the Similan Islands. Around 20km further south is **Hat Thai Muang National Park**, where sea turtles come to lay eggs between November and February.

The TAT has recently put out a revised, fairly accurate map of Phang-Nga Province

and also has glossy pamphlets listing sights, accommodation and restaurants. However, you'll probably need to go to the office in Phuket to get this information, though the head office in Bangkok may have some.

KO SURIN NATIONAL MARINE PARK
A national park since 1981, the Surin Islands are famous for excellent diving and snorkelling. The two main islands (there are five in all) of Ko Surin Neua and Ko Surin Tai ('North Surin Island' and 'South Surin Island') lie about 70km from Khuraburi and less than 5km from Thailand's marine border with Myanmar. The park office and visitor centre are on the south-west side of the north island at Ao Mae Yai, where boats anchor. Admission to the park is 40B. Some of the best diving is said to be in the channel between the two islands.

On the southern island is a village of sea gypsies (*chao leh* or *chao náam*). In April the chao náam hold a major ancestral worship ceremony, called Loi Reua, on Ko Surin Tai. The island may be off limits during that time, so check first at the park office. Long-tail boats can be hired at Ao Mae Yai to take you to the south island for around 100B per person for the day.

Compared with the Similan Islands to the south, Surin is more suited to visitors who are interested in hiking and exploring rather than diving. There are several hiking trails, especially on the northern island. Also, getting to some of the best reefs doesn't require scuba gear, another plus for non-divers. Snorkelling gear can be rented at the park office for 150B per day.

Most visitors to the islands are Thai tourists, who tend to arrive in large numbers on national holidays. There also seems to be a fairly steady flow of tour groups, again mostly Thai, visiting from December to March, though most only stay a night or two. The main advantage of going at this time, especially if you're not a diver, is that you can probably catch a ride on one of the tour boats for 1000B return: at other times the only way out to the islands is chartering your own boat (which is costly) or joining a diving

Surin Islands

0   2.5   5 km

To Burma Banks (Diving)

Ko Ree

Ko Surin Neua

Park Island Headquarters

Ao Mae Yai

Ko Klang

Ko Surin National Marine Park

Ko Surin Tai

To Ngan Yong

Ko Khai

Phuket. The three major banks, Roe, Silvertip and Rainbow, provide four to five-star class diving experiences, with fields of psychedelic coral laid over flat, underwater plateaux and loads of large oceanic as well as smaller reef marine species. Sharks – silvertip, reef, nurse, leopard and at least a half dozen other species – abound.

Many of the dive ops in Phuket have live-aboard diving excursions to the Surin archipelago. Because of the distances involved, Surin is the most expensive dive destination in Thailand; rates start at around 9000 to 10,000B for a minimum two night, three day trip.

Places to Stay & Eat
Accommodation at the park longhouses is 100B per person or you can rent six and eight-person bungalows for 1200B. At the campground, two-person tents cost 100B a night or you can use your own (or camp without a tent) for 20B per night per person. The park also offers three good meals a day (mostly seafood) for 300B or you can order meals separately. Electric power is generated from 6 to 11 pm. It's strongly recommended that you make bookings in advance by calling the park's mainland office (☎ (76) 491-378).

Should you get stuck in Khuraburi, the *Rungtawan* next to the bus stop has adequate rooms for 200B. If the attached sing-song cafe is too noisy, the only other possibility is *Tararain Resort*, 2km outside town, with three-person bungalows for 300 to 500B.

Getting There & Away
The mainland office of Ko Surin National Park is in the tiny village of Ngan Yong, from where boats to the islands depart. The road to Ngan Yong turns off Hwy 4 at Km 720, 6km north of Khuraburi and 109km south of Ranong. The park office, which is also where the pier is located, is about 2km down the road on the right hand side: from Hwy 4 a motorcycle taxi will take you there for about 10B.

Buses between Khuraburi and Ranong cost 35B and take about an hour and 20

trip. The disadvantage of course is that accommodation can easily get booked up.

Surrounding the Surin Islands are the most well-developed coral colonies in Thai seas, according to Piprell & Boyd's *Diving in Thailand*, though the Similans boast a richer variety of fish species. There are seven major dive sites in the immediate vicinity of the Surin Islands, of which the best are found at the south-eastern point of Surin Neua at **HQ Bay**; at **Ko Chi**, a small island off the north-eastern shore of Surin Neua; and at **Richelieu Rock**, a seamount about 14km south-east of Surin Tai. Whale sharks – the largest fish in the world – are reportedly spotted near Richelieu on 50% of dive trips, most commonly during the months of March and April. Snorkelling is excellent in many areas due to relatively shallow reef depths of 5 to 6m.

The little-explored **Burma Banks**, a system of submerged seamounts around 60km north-west of Mu Ko Surin, are so prized by Thai dive operations that the GPS coordinates are kept virtually secret. Actually the only way to visit the Burma Banks – unless you have your own boat – is by way of seven to 10-day live-aboard dive trips out of minutes; ask to be let off at Ngan Yong (saying Ko Surin should also work). To/from Phuket, buses cost 50B and take about three hours. From Khuraburi to Ngan Yong costs 30B by motorcycle taxi.

The cheapest way out to the island is to latch on to one of the tour group boats heading out there. To do this you'll need to call the Surin mainland office (☎ (76) 491378) to find out when and if any boats are making the trip. If so, park staff will try and book you seats: the price is usually 1000B per person return. Tour boats run from December to April, and the busiest time is between February and April.

You can charter a boat out to the Surin Islands from Ngan Yong through the park officers, who will serve as brokers/interpreters. A boat that takes up to 30 people can be chartered for 6000B return – it takes four to five hours each way. Ordinarily, boat travel is only considered safe between December and early May, between the two monsoons.

You can also get boats to the Surin Islands from Hat Patong in Phuket. A regular charter boat from Patong takes 10 hours, or you can get express boats during the diving season (December to April) which take only 3¼ hours. The fare for the latter usually runs around 1700B per person.

HAT BANG SAK

About 14km south of Takua Pa municipality, this beach stretches out for several kilometres, and is mainly a destination for locals out for a picnic or drinks and seafood at one of the little open-air places that line the shore. The beach itself is nice, offers good views of the coast to the south, and is lined with casuarina pines. But it's not regularly cleaned, so there's more litter here than further south at Hat Khao Lak. The areas inland are also cluttered and not too inviting. Still if you have time on your hands, it might be fun to do like the locals and come for a meal or a drink at sunset.

If you do decide it's worth more than that, there are two places to stay. *Bangsak Resort* is a modest place that has bungalows and

motel-style rooms for 250B with fan and bath. From the 'Bang Sak beach' turn-off from Hwy 4, it's about 2km north on the road running along the beach. Closer to the turn-off is the *New Bangsak Inn*. However, there's nothing new about this place. Rooms in a concrete block are grubby and mouldy and definitely not worth the 180B asking price. You'd do better sleeping on the beach.

Buses running between Takua Pa and Phuket will get you here; just ask to be let off at Hat Bang Sak.

HAT KHAO LAK

Though still pretty sleepy, this scenic beach is becoming increasingly popular, mainly with European visitors. It's easy to reach, quiet and, as yet, not overdeveloped: the kind of place you can imagine Phuket to have been 20 years ago. The beach is a pretty stretch of sand studded with smooth granite boulders. You can easily walk northward along the sand for many kilometres, almost as far as Hat Bang Sak. An offshore coral reef suitable for snorkelling lies 45 minutes away by long-tail boat, and some of the bungalow resorts here offer dive excursions to this reef as well as to the Similan and Surin Islands groups.

Hat Khao Lak is located about 30km south of Takua Pa municipality. It's actually located in a town called Ban La-on, but developers decided associating the beach with the nearby national park would sound more appealing.

The area immediately south of Hat Khao Lak is encompassed by the 125 sq km **Khao Lak/Lam Ru National Park**, a beautiful collection of sea cliffs, 1000m hills, beaches, estuaries, forested valleys and mangroves. Wildlife seen in the park includes hornbills, drongos, tapirs, gibbons, monkeys and Asiatic black bears. The visitor centre, just off Hwy 4, 2km south of Hat Khao Lak, has little in the way of maps or printed info, but there's a very nice open-air restaurant perched on a shady slope overlooking the sea, and a few basic bungalows as well.

Park ranger-guided treks along the coast or inland can be arranged through Poseidon

Bungalows (☎/fax (76) 443248), as well as long-tail boat trips up the scenic Khlong Thap Liang estuary. The latter affords an opportunity to view mangrove communities of crab-eating macaques.

Diving & Snorkelling

Live coral formations can be found just off Hat Khao Lak and along the west tip of the bay near Poseidon. Sea Dragon Dive Center (☎/fax (01) 723-1418), on Hwy 4 near the main entrance to Hat Khao Lak, is the main diving operation in the area. In addition to selling and renting diving/snorkelling equipment, they offer PADI-certified scuba instruction and dive trips to the Similan Islands. Sea Dragon's three day, two night Similan excursion costs 7800B for divers, including food, transport, accommodation and all equipment, or 5500B for non-divers. These are among the lowest rates available for dive excursions to the Similans; companies working out of Phuket typically charge more to cover the costs of the lengthy boat journey from Phuket. Local dive trips to nearby coral reefs cost 1000B per day including equipment and two tanks. The Swedish outfit Kon-Tiki International Diving has branched out from Phuket with a small office (☎ (01) 229-6767) on the grounds of the Khao Lak Laguna Resort. At the time of writing this branch only offered day dive trips and canoe tours; multi-day trips to the Similan and Surin Islands leave from Phuket.

Poseidon Bungalows offers three day, two night snorkelling-only trips to the Similan Islands for 3700B per person. These depart twice a week during the November to April dive season. These trips have gotten good reviews from travellers, no doubt in part because Poseidon's owners have been in business for nearly a decade and really do know their way around the area.

For both Poseidon and Sea Dragon, count on five hours one way to reach the islands; such trips operate only between October and April due to climatic conditions. For further information on getting to the Similans, see the Ko Similan National Marine Park section below.

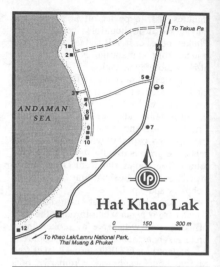

Hat Khao Lak

1	Khao Lak Bungalow
2	Garden Beach Resort
3	Seafood Restaurants; Open-air Bars
4	Nang Thong Bay Resort
5	Nang Thong Minimart
6	Bus Stop
7	Sea Dragon Dive Center
8	The Cocktail Bar
9	Tukta Bungalow
10	Nang Thong Bay Resort II
11	Khao Lak Laguna Resort
12	Khao Lak Sunset Resort

Places to Stay & Eat

Hat Khao Lak There is some reasonably priced accommodation at Hat Khao Lak, although the area seems to be moving steadily up-market. The two most recent additions, Khao Lak Laguna Resort and Khao Lak Sunset Resort, are both in the top-end bracket, and there's talk of two more such operations targeting this area.

At the north end of Hat Khao Lak is *Khao Lak Bungalow* (☎ (01) 723-1197), which has basic huts with mosquito nets and shared bath for 150B, and nicely designed Thai-style cottages with private bath and fan for 600B. There are also air-con rooms for 900B and up. The entire operation is set in a pleasant landscaped courtyard. This place is also referred to as 'Gerd & Noi Khao Lak Bungalow' in reference to the German-Thai couple who run it.

Next door is the *Garden Beach Resort* (☎ (01) 723-1179), which has clean, small huts with bath and fan for 200B. More spacious bungalows cost 300 or 400B depending on proximity to the beach. It's not quite as elegant as Khao Lak Bungalow, but it has a relaxed atmosphere and the restaurant is good. This place also rents motorbikes (200B per day) and Suzuki jeeps (900B).

Toward the centre of Hat Khao is the *Nang Thong Bay Resort* (☎ (01) 723-1181). This place is similar in style to the Garden Beach resort, with smaller bungalows (bath attached) away from the beach for 200B, larger ones for 300B and 550B for those closest to the beach. This is the only place in Khao Lak where you can change money (cash or travellers cheques). Motorbikes and jeeps are also available for rent here. Toward the southern end of the beach, *Nang Thong Bay Resort II* (☎ (01) 229-2727) has larger, more attractive cottages with bath and fan for 500B.

Dwarfed by Nang Thong Bay II is *Tukta Bungalow*, a tiny place owned by an affable European gentleman. There are three small but clean rooms with bath and fan for 250B, as well as more spacious apartments for longer-term stays. Tukta also has a very nice little restaurant sitting right on the beach.

Toward the south end of the beach the *Khao Lak Laguna Resort* (☎ (01) 723-1274) looks to be modelling itself after Westin or Shangri-La-style resorts, but wasn't quite making it, at least when we last checked. The accommodation looks fairly luxurious, and there is a swimming pool, but management seemed a bit lax, and the whole experience didn't seem worth 1800/2200B for fan/aircon bungalows. However, at the time of writing it had only been open for three months, so things may well improve.

About 1km further south along Hwy 4, *Khao Lak Sunset Resort* (☎ (76) 421807) is even more recently opened, and has upscale air-con hotel rooms with balcony and sea views for 1200 to 1500B.

A cluster of simple thatched-roof *beach restaurants* toward the centre of the beach (just north of Nang Thong Bay Resort) offer reasonably priced Thai dishes and tasty seafood, as well as a fine view of the sea and sunset.

National Park Environs Khao Lak/Lam Ru National Park has four simple *bungalows* for 200B per night at its headquarters, located 2km south of Hat Khao Lak. The restaurant nearby, in addition to its wonderful setting, has good food for pretty reasonable prices.

On the other side of the headland of Khao Lak/Lam Ru National Park, 5.5km south of Hat Khao Lak, is *Poseidon Bungalows* (☎ (76) 443258), one of the first bungalow operations in the area, and still one of the most beautiful places to stay. Sitting in a sheltered bay, it has basic thatched huts for 100B single/double with shared bath, larger huts with private bath for 350B or 450B for three people. The huts are non-intrusively dispersed among huge boulders and beach forest, affording quiet and privacy. The proprietors, who get high marks for their commitment to nature conservation, dispense information on the area and organise snorkelling trips to the local reef and to the Similan Islands. A beautiful little restaurant built on stilts over the sea serves Thai and European food.

North of Hat Khao Lak The beach just keeps going north from the Hat Khao Lak area, and there are a couple of places to stay around here that offer you still more solitude. *Chongfa Beach Resort* (☎ (01) 723-0253) has rooms in two storey, four-unit blocks for 500B: they're not the most architecturally appealing, but are new and quite clean. It's located 5km north of Hat Khao Lak.

If you're looking for a luxurious, aesthetic getaway, the only real choice in the whole Khao Lak area is *Similana Resort* (☎/fax (01) 723-1337, Bangkok ☎ (2) 379-4586). Sitting atop a headland 20km south of Takua Pa, it's a beautifully designed and landscaped grouping of all-wood bungalows and hotel rooms artfully hidden among the trees. Amenities include a swimming pool, although the beach around here looks so clean and secluded you may never touch the diving board. Of course none of this comes cheap: during the high-season (November to April) hotel rooms cost 1840B, and fan/air-con bungalows 2100/2500B. However, management will usually offer a discount of 25% unless it's a major public holiday. In the low season, rates drop by around 40%. Food at the restaurant (your only eating option within 10km) is good, but quite expensive. The resort has pickup and dropoff service (1000 to 1500B) to Surat Thani and Phuket, and jeeps and motorcycles are available for rent. Staff will also pick you up from Takua Pa free of charge if you ring them up.

Getting There & Away

Any bus running along Hwy 4 between Takua Pa and Phuket or Thai Muang will stop at Hat Khao Lak if asked. From the bus stop it's about 400m to the dirt road on which the accommodation is located. Buses will also stop near Chongfa beach, Khao Lak Laguna and Khao Lak Sunset resorts and the Khao Lak/Lam Ru National Park Headquarters.

If you're headed to Poseidon Bungalows, your best bet is to get off the bus at Thap Lamu and then take a motorcycle taxi from there for 30 to 40B. The turn-off for Poseidon is located between the 53 and 54 Km markers, but from there it's another 1.2km: a pretty hot and dusty walk if you have bags to carry.

KO SIMILAN NATIONAL MARINE PARK

The Similan Islands are world renowned among diving enthusiasts for incredible underwater sightseeing at depths ranging from 2 to 30m. Beside attractive sandy beaches, huge, smooth granite rock formations plunge into the sea and form seamounts, rock reefs and dive-throughs. As elsewhere in the Andaman Sea, the best diving months are December to May when the weather is good and the sea is at its clearest (and boat trips are much safer).

The Similans are also sometimes called Ko Kao, or Nine Islands, because there are nine of them – each has a number as well as

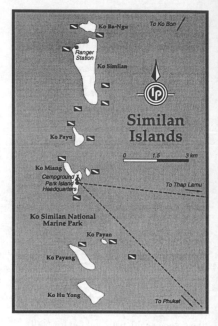

a name. The word 'Similan' in fact comes from the Malay word 'sembilan' meaning 'nine'. Counting in order from the north, they are Ko Bon, Ko Ba-Ngu, Ko Similan, Ko Payu, Ko Miang (which is actually two islands close together), Ko Payan, Ko Payang and Ko Hu Yong. Sometimes you see these listed in the reverse order. They're relatively small islands and uninhabited except for park officials and occasional tourist groups from Phuket.

Princess Chulabhorn, the present Thai monarch's youngest daughter, has a cottage on Ko Miang, a royal affinity that adds an extra layer of protection to the islands' national park status. The Thai navy operates a sea turtle preserve on Ko Ba-Ngu, yet another bonus for enforcement of park preservation.

While excellent scuba diving sites are all around the islands, snorkellers without access to boats or guides can also get to some fine coral from the beaches on the northern side of Ko Miang. There is not much in the way of hiking opportunities in this park; if that's what you're after, Surin or Khao Lak/Lam Ru are better bets. If you do set out snorkelling or hiking on your own, be alert and cautious: some of your natural neighbours will include stone fish, sting rays, fire coral and poisonous snakes. If you're camping, keep any food you have tightly sealed up against insects and wildlife.

The park office, visitor centre and accommodation is on Ko Miang (Island No 4). Admission to the park is 40B.

Ko Bon & Ko Kachai

These small islands lie approximately midway between the Similan and Surin archipelagos. Profuse hard corals appear at depths of 18 to 35m and, in good weather, visibility extends to 25m. Without a doubt these are two of the area's top dive sites, although they are hardly known outside Thailand.

Both islands are usually included in longer live-aboard dive trips that run between the Similan and Surin Islands.

Organised Tours

Thap Lamu Sea Dragon at Hat Khao Lak does three day/two night dive trips to the Similans for 7800B, while Poseidon Bungalows has a snorkelling trip for 3700B. Their boats depart from Thap Lamu; see the Hat Khao Lak section for more details.

Phuket Overnight diving excursions from Phuket are fairly reasonably priced – about 3500B a day including food, accommodation, diving equipment and underwater guides. Non-divers may be able to join these trips for around half the cost – snorkellers are welcome.

Package deals out of Phuket typically start at 9000B for a three day/two night dive trip, and go up to 37,000B for a seven day, seven night Similan and Burma Banks trip on Siam Diving Center's (☎ (76) 330608; fax 330608) live-aboard *MV Sai Mai*. The latter also offers longer, more exotic dive excursions such as a 10 day/10 night 'whale shark expedition' costing over 50,000B per person. Another

upscale option is the five day, six night cruise offered by Marina Divers (☎ (76) 330272). For 21,250B you get 'VIP' treatment on a luxury air-conditioned boat which takes a maximum of eight divers. A more affordable option is Kon Tiki Diving school's (☎ (76) 396312) five day, four night Similan trip for 14,600B.

Songserm Travel (☎ (76) 222570) in Phuket operates a one-day excursion trip to the Similans every Tuesday, Thursday and Saturday at 8 am for 1600B per person including lunch. Considering it takes 3½ hours each way, this doesn't leave a lot of time for island exploration. The Met Sine Tours office in Phuket (☎ (76) 223192) offers the same service.

Places to Stay & Eat

Accommodation, including camping, is only allowed on Ko Miang. The park has *hungalows* for 600B and four-bed rooms in a *longhouse* for 400B. If there are only one or two in your party, you may be able to get a per-person rate of 100B for the longhouse, but don't count on it. Tent rental costs 150B, and there's a 20B tent site fee if you bring your own. Bookings must be made in advance at the park's mainland office in Thap Lamu (☎ (76) 411914).

The only source of food is a privately run *restaurant* on Ko Miang. Prices here are ridiculously high (40B for a fried egg, for instance), and even then you need to let park staff know you're coming in advance if you want food to be there for you. Bringing your own food is strongly recommended, though occasional restrictions on open fires may force you to the restaurant at least a few times.

Getting There & Away

You can get boats to the Similans from the port at Thap Lamu (39km south of Takua Pa off Hwy 4, or 20km north of Thai Muang) and from Phuket. The park mainland office is also in Thap Lamu, about 1km from the pier.

From Thap Lamu the islands are 60km away, about three hours by boat. Met Sine

Tours (☎ (01) 723-0280), located near the pier, is the place to go for boat bookings. When we last checked, boats ran Wednesday, Friday and Sunday, departing Thap Lamu at 9 am and heading back from Ko Miang at 3.30 pm the same day. The return fare is 1600B. It would be best to call ahead just to make sure what's going on, as the situation seems rather fluid (there is at least one English speaker at Met Sine). Boats run to the Similans from November to May only; during the remainder of the year the seas are too rough. If the weather looks rough when you arrive give some thought as to how badly you want to go: there have been several incidents in recent years of boats operating out of Thap Lamu having foundered or becoming stranded, though no casualties have resulted.

AO PHANG-NGA
• ☎ *(76)* • *pop 9000*
Over 95km north-east of Phuket, this expansive, turquoise extension of the Andaman Sea is dotted with hundreds of islands, many mere limestone outcroppings that protrude from the sea. At some islands, partially submerged grottoes can be entered by small boat during low tide. Other islands are encircled by sandy coves where the only visible inhabitants are swiftlets who build their nests on high cliffs. Itinerant collectors farm the highly prized nests for use in the Chinese delicacy 'bird's nest soup', a broth made from the hardened bird saliva holding the nests together. Many of the islands are part of **Ao Phang-Nga National Marine Park** and can be explored by boat or canoe.

Very few of these islands receive overnight visitors. Ko Phi Phi, the most famous, is a dumbbell-shaped island ringed by coral reefs, caves and white-sand beaches; in this book it is covered in the Southern Andaman Coast chapter under Krabi Province.

Information
The TAT has a recently revised map of Phang-Nga Province that includes a separate map of Phang-Nga town, as well as pamphlets listing sights, accommodation and restaurants.

The most complete information is at the regional office in Phuket town, and you may be able to get some material in Bangkok.

In the centre of Phang-Nga town along Hwy 4 are several banks open during regular banking hours. The post and telephone office is about 2km from the bus station.

Things to See & Do
Along the northern shore of the bay is **Phang-Nga**, a small town wedged between verdant limestone cliffs. It is the capital of the province of the same name. Phang-Nga is the best – and least expensive – place to hire boats for exploring the northern half of the bay. The southern half of the bay is best approached from Phuket or Krabi.

In Phang-Nga itself there's little to see or do that isn't beachy unless you happen to be there during the annual Vegetarian Festival in October (see the Phuket section for information on this unusual event).

On the way to Phang-Nga, turn left off Hwy 4 at Km 31. Just 5km past the small town of Takua Thung is **Wat Tham Suwankhuha** ('Heaven Grotto Temple'), a cave shrine full of Buddha images. The shrine consists of two main caverns: a larger one containing a 15m reclining Buddha and tiled with *laikhram* and *benjarong*, two coloured patterns more common in pottery, and a smaller cavern displaying spirit flags and a *rishi* (hermit-sage) statue. Royal seals of several kings, including Rama V, Rama VII and Rama IX – as well those of lesser royalty – are inscribed on one wall of the latter cave.

Bay & Island Tours
Boat Trips Between Takua Thung and Phang-Nga is the road to **Tha Dan**, the Phang-Nga Customs pier. At an adjacent pier, boats can be hired to tour Ao Phang-Nga, with visits to a Muslim fishing village on stilts, half-submerged caves, and strangely shaped islands, including several which were used in the 1970s James Bond film *The Man with the Golden Gun*.

Tours from the pier vary from 150 to 400B; from Phuket they cost at least 300 to 600B per person. Sayan Tamtopol, a former postman from Ko Panyi (one of the islands in Ao Phang-Nga), has been organising overnight tours of Ao Phang-Nga for several years now and they continue to receive good reviews from travellers, though some have commented that service seems to have slipped a bit recently. The tour costs 300B per person and includes a boat tour of **Tham Lawt** (a large water cave), **Ko Phing Kan** ('Leaning Island'), **Ko Khao Tapu** ('Nail Mountain Island'), **Ko Maju, Tham Naga, Khao Khian** ('Drawing Cave', containing cave murals), a former mangrove charcoal factory and **Ko Panyi**, a mangrove swamp, as well as dinner, breakfast and accommodation in a Muslim fishing village on Ko Panyi. Sayan also leads morning (rainy season) and afternoon (dry season) trips for 150B; both trips include a seafood lunch.

The overnight trip is recommended over the day trips; the latter tend to be a bit rushed and sometimes you may not get to all the places on the itinerary. (You can pretty safely skip 'James Bond' island, where the scenery is now obscured by tacky stalls selling seashells and other trinkets.) Sayan Tour (☎ (76) 430348) now has an office next to the bus terminal in Phang-Nga or Sayan can be contacted at the Thawisuk Hotel there. Beware of touts posing as Sayan at Tha Dan.

You can also take a ferry to Ko Panyi on your own for 25B.

Whatever you do, try to avoid touring the bay in the middle of the day (10 am to 4 pm) when hundreds of package tourists crowd the islands. The Ko Panyi Muslim village is very commercialised during the day when hordes of tourist boats invade to eat lunch at the village's many overpriced seafood restaurants, and to buy tacky souvenirs at the many stalls. The village returns to its normal self after the boats depart. On Ko Panyi, always ask the price before eating as the restaurants often overcharge.

Canoe Tours A company based in Phuket, Sea Canoe Thailand (☎ (76) 212252; fax 212172, email @seacanoe.com), at 367/4 Yaowarat Rd, offers inflatable kayak excursions on the bay. The kayaks – a type of their

own design, called Sea Explorers – are able to enter semi-submerged caves inaccessible by long-tail boats. A day paddle costs 2675B per person and includes meals, beverages and equipment, while all-inclusive three or six day camping trips are 13,375B and 24,075B per person, respectively. The multi-day trips leave Wednesday and Sunday.

Many other companies in the area offer similar inflatable canoe trips for about half these prices, but Sea Canoe Thailand was the first and is still the most ecologically conscious in terms of the way in which they organise and operate their tours. Any travel agency can book their trips.

Places to Stay
Phang-Nga Phang-Nga has several small hotels. The *Thawisuk* (☎ 412100) is right in the middle of town, a bright blue building with the English sign 'Hotel'. Somewhat unkempt rooms upstairs go for 100 to 150B for one bed/two beds with fan and bath, plus towel and soap on request.

The *Lak Meuang* (☎ 412486), on Phetkasem Rd, just outside town towards Krabi, has rooms for 200B with fan and bath, 480B air-con, plus an OK restaurant downstairs. The *Rak Phang-Nga*, across the street from Thawisuk towards Phuket, is 80 to 120B but somewhat dirty and noisy.

Opposite the Rak Phang-Nga is the *Ratanapong Hotel* (☎ 411247), which has cleaned up its act and now offers OK one-bed rooms for 150B, two-bed rooms for 230B, three beds for 280B and 350B for four beds; air-con rooms are also available at 300/430B for one bed/two beds.

Farther down the road towards Phuket is the *Muang Thong* (☎ 412132), with clean, quiet singles/doubles for 120/180B with fan, 250 to 320B with air-con. Outside town, even farther towards Phuket, is *Lak Meuang II* (☎ 411500), with air-con rooms from 350B.

Tha Dan About 100m before the tour pier are the rustic *National Park Bungalows* (☎ 412188), which cost 350 to 750B a night. Farther on towards the town, before the Customs pier, the *Phang-Nga Bay Resort Hotel*

(☎ 412067/70) costs 1295B and up. All rooms come with TV, telephone and fridge.

Places to Eat

Duang Restaurant, next to Bangkok Bank on the main road, has a bilingual menu and a good selection of Thai and Chinese dishes, including southern Thai specialities. Prices have crept up a little higher than the standard of the food would indicate.

South-west of the market, not far from the bus terminal, the new and clean *Nawng James* ('Little Brother James') serves very good and inexpensive khâo man kài, wonton and noodles. Diagonally opposite Nawng James is the *Bismilla*, a tidy restaurant serving Muslim food.

Several *food stalls* on the main street of Phang-Nga sell cheap and delicious khanõm jiin with chicken curry, náam yaa (spicy ground-fish curry) or náam phrík (sweet and spicy peanut sauce). One vendor in front of the market (opposite Bangkok Bank) serves khanõm jiin with an amazing 12 varieties of free vegetable accompaniments – but only from 1 pm to 8 pm daily; an adjacent vendor does khâo mòk kài from 6 am to noon. Roti kaeng (flatbread and curry) is available in the *morning market* from around 5 am to 10 am. There are also the usual Chinese *khâo man kài* places around town.

Getting There & Away

Buses for Phang-Nga leave from the Phuket bus terminal hourly between 6 am and 6 pm. The trip to Phang-Nga takes two hours and the one way fare is 26B. Air-con buses leave about every two hours from 10 am to 4.30 pm and cost 50B.

Buses to/from Krabi cost 28B and take 1½ hours; to/from Surat Thani they cost 50B and take 3½ hours.

Ordinary buses to/from Bangkok cost 192B and take 14 hours, while air-con is 346B and VIP is 515B, both taking 13 hours.

Getting Around

Most of the town is easily accessible on foot. Sayan Tour at the bus terminal can assist with motorcycle rental.

Songthaews between Phang-Nga and Tha Dan (the Phang-Nga Customs pier) cost 10B.

AROUND PHANG-NGA
Ko Yao

Ko Yao Yai and Ko Yao Noi ('Big Long Island' and 'Little Long Island'), directly south of the provincial capital, in the middle of the bay between the provinces of Phuket and Krabi, together encompass 137 sq km of forest, beaches and rocky headlands with views of surrounding karst formations characteristic of Ao Phang-Nga. Contrary to first assumptions, Ko Yao Noi is the main population centre of the two, although even there fishing, coconuts and a little tourism sustains a relatively small group of year-rounders. **Hat Paa Sai** and **Hat Tha Khao**, both on Yao Noi, are the best beaches. Bring along a mountain bike if you want to explore the island's numerous dirt trails.

Ta Khai, the largest settlement on the island, is a subdistrict government seat and the source of minimal food and other supplies. Boat trips to neighbouring islands, bird-nest caves and sea gypsy funeral caves are possible. **Ko Bele**, a small island east of Ko Yai, features a large tidal lagoon, three whitesand beaches, and easily accessible caves and coral reefs around the entire island. A long-tail boat from Ko Yao Noi or from Ao Nang in Krabi can be chartered for around 500 to 1000B per day depending on the size of the boat.

Places to Stay On Ko Yao Noi, the only island with regular visitor lodgings, *Sabai Corner* is an environmentally sensitive resort associated with Sea Canoe Thailand (see the earlier Ao Phang-Nga Canoe Tours section for contact details), which arranges kayak trips here – self-paddles or guided trips – from November to August. Thatchand-wood bungalows cost 300 to 700B a night. *Long Beach Village* (☎/fax 381623, (01) 211-8647 on the island itself), has large wood-and-thatch bungalows for 500 to 1500B a night.

Getting There & Away Although both islands fall within Phang-Nga Province, the easiest places to find boat transport to Ko Yao Noi are Phuket (Phuket Province), Ao Leuk and Ao Nang (both in Krabi Province).

In Phuket city, catch a songthaew from in front of the Ranong Rd market to Bang Rong on Ao Paw for 20B. From the public pier at Ao Paw there are usually two mail boats a day to Ko Yao Noi, one between 8 and 9 am and another around noon. The fare is 40B per passenger and the trip takes about one hour. Between departures or after hours you can charter a long-tail boat out to the island for 500B one way. Coming back to Phuket from Yao Noi, there's one boat back that leaves between 6 and 7 am.

You can also get boats from Ko Yao Noi north-east across Ao Phang-Nga to Tha Laem Sak at Ao Leuk, Krabi. These cost around 40B on regular ferries, or 500B to charter. From Krabi's Ao Nang you can charter a boat for about 500B each way.

If you want to take a look around Ko Yao Yai, catch a shuttle boat from Ko Yao Noi's Tha Manaw pier (10B each way), or charter a long-tail boat or kayak from Sabai Corner.

Phuket Province

Dubbed 'Pearl of the South', by the tourist industry, Phuket (pronounced 'Poo get') is the country's largest, most populous and most visited island, a whirl of colour and cosmopolitanism that's literally a province unto itself. The coastal terrain of the 810 sq km island encompasses broad, sandy bays, rocky peninsulas, limestone cliffs, forested hills and tropical vegetation while the interior has rice paddies, rubber, cashew nut, cacao, pineapple and coconut plantations, as well as Phuket's last bit of island rainforest. Although Phuket is connected to Phang-Nga Province by a causeway, most visitors arrive via the island's international airport located near its northern tip.

Formerly called Ko Thalang and before that Junk Ceylon, Phuket has a culture all of its own, combining Chinese and Portuguese influences (like nearby western Malaysia) with that of the southern Thais, and the chao náam, a seafaring, semi-nomadic group that depend on fishing and boat building for their livelihood. Only about 35% of the island's population are Thai Muslims; even so, mosques slightly outnumber Buddhist wats, 38 to 37. This is Thailand's wealthiest province, and since the late 80s tourism has eclipsed tin mining as the island's largest source of income.

There is a lot to do in Phuket, and consequently, a lot to spend your money on. There are also more tourists in Phuket than on any other Thai island, though most flock to three beaches on the south-west side – Patong, Karon and Kata. Along the main roads here there seems to be a snake farm, bungy-jumping operation, gaudy billboard, half-built condo project, travel agency or tacky craft shop every half kilometre. The beach towns themselves are quite built up, and have all the amenities and entertainment one could wish for. If you're looking for a lively, action-filled vacation, this is the area to visit.

Beaches like Nai Han, near the southern tip, and Kamala, on the western coast, are relatively quiet, in spite of major tourist development at both, while Nai Thon, Nai Yang and Mai Khao to the north remain mostly untouched. In general the northern half of the island, both along the shore and in the interior, has not been swept up in the development wave, and thus offers quiet beach retreats and chances to explore rural inland areas.

The opening of the Club Méditerranée at Hat Kata, followed by the lavish Phuket Yacht Club on Nai Han and Le Meridien on Karon Noi marked an end to the decade-long era of cheap bungalows which started in the early 1970s with a 10B guesthouse attached to a laundry on Patong beach. Nowadays 100B is rock-bottom. Any remaining accommodation costing under 300B will probably be upgraded within the next couple of years to a minimum of 500B as Phuket completes the final stages of moving from rustic beach hideaway to full-fledged international resort.

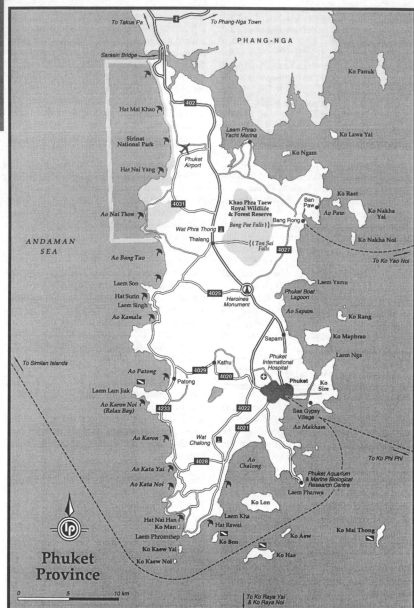

Phuket
Province

To some extent, the era of going for quick money regardless of the cost to the environment is also passing. Most beachside resorts are nowadays looking toward long-term, sustainable practices – not all of them, but a far greater percentage than on Ko Samui, Ko Phang-Ngan, Ko Tao, or even Trat's Ko Chang.

Diving & Snorkelling

Although there are many, many places to dive around Thailand, Phuket is indisputably the primary centre for the Thai scuba diving industry and one of the world's top 10 dive destinations. The island itself is ringed by good to excellent dive sites, including several small, uninhabited islands and islets to the south and east with hard corals – **Ko Hae, Ko Raya (Noi & Yai), Ko Yao (Noi & Yai), Hin Daeng** and **Shark Point** (a habitat for harmless leopard sharks) at the southern tip of the island – all of which make favourite day trips for novice and intermediate divers. Excursions further afield to the Ao Phang-Nga islands to the east, and to the world-famous Surin and Similan Islands to the north-west are also for the most part operated from Phuket.

Most Phuket diving operations are centred at Patong beach, with a sprinkling of branch offices at other beaches. Many companies stagger regularly scheduled dives throughout the week so that different dive groups don't bump into one another, eg South East Asia Divers might go to Ko Raya Yai on Monday and Shark Point Tuesday while Sea Hawk might do Shark Point Monday and Raya Yai Tuesday, and so on. Typical one day dive trips to nearby sites such as these cost around 1500B, including two dives, tanks and weights, transport, divemaster service, breakfast and lunch. Non-divers, including snorkellers, are often permitted to join such dive trips for 600 to 700B. PADI open-water certification courses cost 7000 to 7800B for four days of instruction and all equipment.

A few companies – generally the larger, more well-established ones – offer extended three to seven-day trips on live-aboard dive boats, costing from 10,000 to 20,000B, to Ko Phi Phi, Mu Ko Similan, Mu Ko Surin and the Burma Banks.

Most dive shops also rent the following equipment: regulator (250B a day), BCD (250B), mask, fins & snorkel (200B), wetsuit (150B).

Dive shops which have gotten good reviews from travellers and experienced divers include South East Asia Divers, (modern equipment, excellent dive boat, multilingual dive masters), and Sea Hawk Divers (well run, competent dive masters). Their contact information, and that of several other well-established dive companies on the island follow:

Andaman Divers, Patong beach (☎/fax 341126)
Calypso Divers, Kata-Karon beach (☎/fax 330869)
Dive Inn, Patong beach (☎ 341927; fax 342453)
Fantasea Divers, Patong beach (☎ 340088; fax 340309)
Marina Divers, Karon beach (☎ 330272, 330516)
PIDC Divers, Ao Chalong (☎ 280644; fax 381219)
Sea Bees Submarine Diving, Ao Chalong (☎/fax 381765)
Sea Hawk Divers, Patong beach (☎ 341179; fax 344151)
Siam Diving Center, Karon beach (☎ 330608; fax 330608)
South East Asia Divers, Patong beach (☎ 344022; fax 342530)

It's a good idea to make sure that the dive shop you pick is affiliated with Dive Safe Asia (☎ 342518) which operates a hyperbaric (decompression) chamber in Patong. This means the dive shop is insured should one of their customers need to use the chamber in an emergency. If a shop is not a member, and should you need Dive Safe Asia's services, you may ending up footing the bill (around US$3000).

As elsewhere in the Andaman Sea, the best diving months are December to May when the weather is good and the sea is at its clearest (and boat trips are much safer).

Yachting

Phuket is one of South-East Asia's main yacht destinations and you'll find all manner of craft anchored along its shores, from the

80-year-old wooden sloops that look like they can barely stay afloat to the latest in high-tech world motor cruisers. Marina-style facilities with year-round anchorage are available at three locations on the protected east side of the island: Laem Phrao Yacht Marina (☎/fax 327109) and Yacht Haven (☎ 206022/5; fax 206026) at Laem Phrao at the north-east tip; and Phuket Boat Lagoon (☎ 239055; fax 239056) at Ao Sapam, about 20km north of Phuket town on the east shore.

Phuket Boat Lagoon offers an enclosed marina with tidal channel access, serviced pontoon berths, 60 and 120 tonne travel lifts, hard-stand area, laundry, coffee shop, fuel, water, repairs and maintenance services. Laem Phrao has moorings and a jetty, workshop, sundries shop, ice, restaurant, fuel, water, showers and toilets. The Yacht Haven boasts 130 berths, condominiums, immigration facilities, restaurants and a health spa. In season (December to April) Ao Nai Han and Ao Chalong are popular anchorages with more limited services.

You may be able to travel by yacht between Phuket and Penang as a paying passenger or as crew. Ask around at these marinas or at Patong beach to see what's available. You may also find yachts going further afield, particularly to Sri Lanka. December and early January are the best months to look for them. The crossing takes about 10 to 15 days.

Some outfits are now beginning to offer cruises north to the nearly deserted islands of Myanmar's Mergui Archipelago. South East Asia Liveaboards has five-day cruises for US$500 per person, plus a US$80 surcharge, brought to you courtesy of the Myanmar government. The cost includes meals, scuba tanks and minibus transfers.

For information on yacht charters – both bareboat and crewed – yacht sales and yacht deliveries, contact the following:

Big A Yachting, Ao Chalong (☎ 381934; fax 381934)
Phuket Yacht Services, Laem Phrao Marina (☎ 224999)
Phuket Boating Association, Phuket Boat Lagoon (☎/fax 381322)

South East Asia Liveaboards, Patong beach (☎ 340406; fax 340586)
Sunsail Yacht Charters, Phuket Boat Lagoon (☎ 239-057; fax 238940)
Thai Marine Leisure, Patong beach (☎ 344261; fax 344262)
Thai Yachting, Patong beach (☎ 341153; fax 341154)

Charters aboard 32 to 44-foot yachts start at 9000B a day, while larger ones (39 to 85-foot yachts) start at 12,000B a day. Day trips usually include boat, crew, lunch and soft drinks, plus snorkelling and fishing gear.

Sea Canoeing

Several companies based in Phuket offer inflatable canoe tours of scenic Ao Phang-Nga; see the Ao Phang-Nga section earlier in this chapter for details.

Cycling

Tropical Trails (☎ 263239) offers fully supported half-day and full-day 'cycle safaris' around Phuket. Half-day trips range from 725 to 1150B, the latter including elephant and walking treks as well. Full-day rides cost 1450B. Rates include hotel pickup, van support, mountain bike and equipment, a guided hike, snorkelling, 'cultural break stops', lunch, insurance and a Thai massage. The owners are also looking at developing multi-day cycling tours of neighbouring areas like Phang-Nga and Krabi.

PHUKET
• ☎ (76) • *pop 60,000*

Centuries before Phuket began attracting sand-and-sea hedonists it was an important trade entrepôt for Arab, Indian, Malay, Chinese and Portuguese traders who exchanged goods from the world at large for tin and rubber. Francis Light, the British colonialist who made Penang the first of the British Straits Settlements, married a native of Phuket and tried unsuccessfully to pull this island into the colonial fold as well. Although this polyglot, multi-cultural heritage has all but disappeared from most of the island, a few vestiges can be seen and experienced in the province's *amphoe meuang* (provincial capital), Phuket.

In the older town centre you'll see plenty of Sino-Portuguese architecture, characterised by ornate two storey Chinese *haang tháew* or 'row companies' fronted by Romanesque arched porticoes with 'five-foot ways' that were a 19th century tradition in Malaysia, Singapore, Macau and Hainan Island (China). For a time it seemed this wonderful old architecture was all being torn down and replaced with modern structures but in recent years a preservation ethic has taken hold.

Information
Tourist Office & Tourist Police The TAT office (☎ 212213, 211036) at 73-75 Phuket Rd has maps, information brochures, a list of the standard songthaew fares out to the various beaches and also the recommended charter costs for a vehicle. Although it doesn't look like it, the tacky, advertisement-plastered A-O-A Phuket Map is probably the best one if you're going to do any driving around. It's more accurate than the other freebies available, and it has all the route numbers on it.

The TAT office is open daily from 8.30 am to 4.30 pm. The tourist police can be reached at ☎ 1699.

Money Several banks along Takua Pa, Phang-Nga and Phuket Rds offer exchange services and ATMs. Bank of Asia, opposite the TAT office on Phuket Rd, has an exchange window open from 8.30 am until 8 pm daily.

Post & Communications The main post office, housed in an architectural gem on Montri Rd, is open weekdays from 8.30 am to 4.30 pm, weekends 9 am to noon. However, the building has been undergoing renovation and until it reopens you'll have to go to the temporary location opposite the main bus terminal on Phang-Nga Rd.

Mail Boxes Etc (MBE; ☎ 256409; fax 256411) has a branch at 168/2 Phuket Rd, almost opposite The Books. MBE rents private mail boxes, sells packaging and mailing materials and offers laminating, binding, passport photo and business card services.

The Phuket Telecommunications Centre (☎ 216861), nearby on Phang-Nga Rd, of-fers Home Direct service and is open daily 8 am to midnight.

Bookshops Phuket has one decent, though pricey bookshop, The Books at 53-55 Phuket Rd, near the TAT office. The selection of English-language reading materials includes magazines, guidebooks and novels. There's a smaller branch at Robinson Ocean Plaza, off Ong Sim Phai Rd near the municipal market.

Magazines & Online Services The monthly English-language *Phuket Gazette* publishes lots of info on activities, events, dining and entertainment in town as well as around the island. The same publisher issues *Gazette Guide*, a 128-page listing of services and businesses on the island. Phuket Net is an Internet service (email info@phuket.net or Web address www.phuket.net) that provides tourism and business-oriented information on the islands. There is also a Phuket Bulletin Board (info@phuket.com).

Medical Services Western doctors rate the Phuket International Hospital (☎ 249400; emergency 210935), Airport Bypass Rd, as the best on the island. Bangkok Phuket Hospital (☎ 254421), Yongyok Uthit Rd, is reportedly the favourite with the locals, and is run by Bangkok General Hospital. Both hospitals are equipped with modern facilities, emergency rooms and outpatient care clinics.

Things to See & Do
For seeing historic **Sino-Portuguese architecture** your best bets are Thalang, Deebuk, Yaowarat, Ranong, Phang-Nga, Rasada and Krabi Rds. The most magnificent examples in town are the Standard Chartered Bank – Thailand's oldest foreign bank – on Phang-Nga Rd and the Thai Airways office on Ranong Rd, but there are lots of more modest buildings of interest along these streets.

Phuket's main **market** on Ranong Rd is fun to wander through and is a good place to buy Thai and Malay sarongs as well baggy

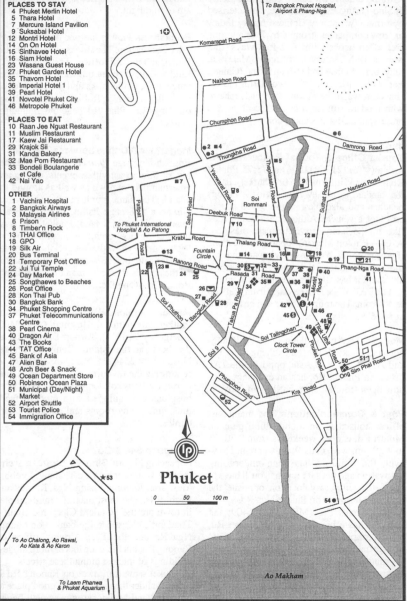

PLACES TO STAY
4 Phuket Merlin Hotel
5 Thara Hotel
7 Mercure Island Pavilion
9 Suksabai Hotel
12 Montri Hotel
14 On On Hotel
15 Sinthavee Hotel
16 Siam Hotel
23 Wasana Guest House
27 Phuket Garden Hotel
35 Thavorn Hotel
36 Imperial Hotel 1
39 Pearl Hotel
41 Novotel Phuket City
46 Metropole Phuket

PLACES TO EAT
10 Raan Jee Nguat Restaurant
11 Muslim Restaurant
17 Kaew Jai Restaurant
29 Krajok Sii
31 Kanda Bakery
32 Mae Porn Restaurant
33 Bondeli Boulangerie et Cafe
42 Nai Yao

OTHER
1 Vachira Hospital
2 Bangkok Airways
3 Malaysia Airlines
6 Prison
8 Timber'n Rock
13 THAI Office
18 GPO
19 Silk Air
20 Bus Terminal
21 Temporary Post Office
22 Jui Tui Temple
24 Day Market
25 Songthaews to Beaches
26 Post Office
28 Kon Thai Pub
30 Bangkok Bank
34 Phuket Shopping Centre
37 Phuket Telecommunications Centre
38 Pearl Cinema
40 Dragon Air
43 The Books
44 TAT Office
45 Bank of Asia
47 Alien Bar
48 Arch Beer & Snack
49 Ocean Department Store
50 Robinson Ocean Plaza
51 Municipal (Day/Night) Market
52 Airport Shuttle
53 Tourist Police
54 Immigration Office

Phuket

0   50   100 m

Ao Makham

fisherman pants. A few old **Chinese temples** can be found in this area.

Walk up **Khao Rang**, sometimes called Phuket Hill, north-west of town, for a nice view of the city, jungle and sea. If, as many people say, Phuket is a corruption of the Malay word *bukit* ('hill'), then this is probably its namesake.

Vegetarian Festival

Phuket's most important festival is the Vegetarian Festival, which takes place during the first nine days of the ninth lunar month of the Chinese calendar. This is usually late September or October. Basically, the festival celebrates the beginning of the month of 'Taoist Lent', when devout Chinese abstain from eating all meat and meat products. In Phuket, the festival activities are centred around five Chinese temples, with the Jui Tui temple on Ranong Rd the most important, followed by Bang Niaw and Sui Boon Tong temples. Events are also celebrated at temples in the nearby towns of Kathu (where the festival originated) and Ban Tha Reua.

The TAT office in Phuket prints a helpful schedule of events for the Vegetarian Festival each year. If you plan to attend the street processions, consider bringing earplugs to make the noise of the firecrackers more tolerable. The festival also takes place in Trang, Krabi and other southern Thai towns. See the boxed aside below for more details.

Places to Stay – bottom end

Near the centre of town, and close to the songthaew terminal for most outlying beaches, is the *On On Hotel* (☎ 211154) at 19 Phang-Nga Rd. This hotel's old Sino-Portuguese architecture (established 1929) gives it real character, though the rooms are basically just four walls and a bed. Rates are 100B for a single with ceiling fan and shared facilities, 150/220B single/double with fan and attached bath, 250/360B with air-con. The simple *Pengman* (☎ 211486, ext 169) nearby at 69 Phang-Nga Rd, above a Chinese restaurant, costs 100B single/double for basic but quite clean rooms with ceiling fan and shared bath.

The *Thara Hotel* (☎ 216208) on Thepkasatri Rd costs 120B with fan and bath. The nearby *Suksabai Hotel* (☎ 212287) is a bit better at 120B for similar but cleaner rooms, plus air-con for 280B. The dark *Siam Hotel*, 13-15 Phuket Rd, is basically a brothel with

---

Phuket's Vegetarian Festival

Besides abstention from meat, the Vegetarian Festival involves various processions, temple offerings and cultural performances and culminates in incredible acts of self-mortification – walking on hot coals, climbing knife-blade ladders, piercing the skin with sharp objects and so on. Shop owners along Phuket's central streets set up altars in front of their stores offering nine tiny cups of tea, incense, fruit, candles and flowers to the nine Emperor Gods invoked by the festival. Those participating as mediums bring the nine deities to earth for the festival by entering into a trance state and piercing their cheeks with all manner of objects – sharpened tree branches (with leaves still attached!), spears, trombones, daggers; some even hack their tongues continuously with saw or axe blades. During the street processions these mediums stop at the shopfront altars, where they pick up the offered fruit and either add it to the objects piercing their cheeks or pass it on to bystanders as a blessing. They also drink one of the nine cups of tea and grab some flowers to stick in their waistbands. The shopowners and their families stand by with their hands together in a *wai* gesture, out of respect for the mediums and for the deities by whom they are temporarily possessed.

Oddly enough, there is no record of this kind of activity associated with Taoist Lent in China. Some historians assume that the Chinese here were somehow influenced by the Hindu festival of Thaipusam in nearby Malaysia, which features similar acts of self-mortification. The local Chinese claim, however, that the festival was started by a theatre troupe from China who stopped off in nearby Kathu around 150 years ago. The story goes that the troupe was struck seriously ill and that they decided the illness had befallen them because they had failed to propitiate the nine 'Emperor Gods' of Taoism. The nine-day penance they performed included self-piercing, meditation and a strict vegetarian diet. ■

roach-ridden rooms for 150B: probably not worth it.

The *Wasana Guest House* (☎ 211754, 213-385), at 159 Ranong Rd (next to the market) has clean rooms for 180B with fan and bath or 280B with air-con.

Places to Stay – middle

The *Thavorn (Thawon) Hotel* (☎ 211333) at 74 Rasada Rd is a huge place consisting of an original, less expensive wing at the back and a flashier place up front. At the back, large rooms with ceiling fan and private bath cost 200/250B single/double while in the front all rooms come with TV, air-con, hot water and carpet and cost 500 to 600B. The cheaper rooms are better value. The *Montri Hotel* (☎ 212936), 12/6 Montri Rd, is similar and has gotten good reviews from some travellers: rooms cost 180B with fan, 320 to 480B with air-con.

The clean and friendly *Imperial Hotel 1* (☎ 212311), at 51 Phuket Rd, has good rooms for 250/300B with fan, 400/450B with air-con.

In the centre of town, at 81 Phang-Nga Rd, the *Sinthavee Hotel* (☎ 212153) offers comfortable air-con rooms in the old wing for 471/589B a single/double or 850/950B for deluxe rooms. All rooms come with carpeting, hot-water bath and refrigerators (add TV/video for deluxe); other facilities include 24 hour coffee shop, business centre and disco.

Places to Stay – top end

The island's original tourist-class place, the *Pearl Hotel* (☎ 211044), at 42 Montri Rd, has 212 rooms from 1400B, a rooftop restaurant, fitness centre, swimming pool and so on. By today's standards it's not a real standout but it's quite OK and has all the amenities. Another older tourist hotel, the *Phuket Merlin Hotel* (☎ 211866) at 158/1 Yaowarat Rd has 180 rooms for 1300B up and there's a swimming pool and fitness centre. In a similar class, the *Phuket Garden Hotel* (☎ 216900/8) on Bangkok Rd costs 1200 to 2400B with a pool and all the usual facilities.

One of the best located (though slightly frayed looking) top-enders is the plush, 248 room *Metropole Phuket* (☎ 215050; fax 215990), right in the centre of things on Montri Rd. 'Superior' rooms start at 2000B, deluxe from 3000B. Facilities include two Chinese restaurants, a coffee shop, three bars, swimming pool, fitness centre, business centre and airport shuttle service.

A short walk east of the Phuket Telecommunications Centre on Phang-Nga Rd is the towering 251 room *Novotel Phuket City* (☎ 233402; fax 233335), where state-of-the-art rooms start at 2900B.

Places to Eat

If there's one thing the town of Phuket is known for, it's good food – even if you're staying at the beach it's worth a trip into the city to sample authentic, Phuket-style cooking (a blend of Thai, Malay and Straits Chinese influences). Meals in the city tend to cost only half as much as meals at the beach.

One long-running local institution is *Raan Jee Nguat*, a Phuket-style restaurant run by Hokkien Chinese, across the street from the Siam Sport Club Building on the corner of historic Yaowarat and Deebuk Rds. Jee Nguat serves Phuket's most famous dish – delicious khanŏm jiin náam yaa phukèt – Chinese noodles in a puréed fish and curry sauce, Phuket-style, with fresh cucumbers, long green beans and other fresh vegetables on the side – for under 20B. Also good are khài plaa mòk, a Phuket version of hàw mòk (eggs, fish and curry paste steamed in banana leaves), and the kari mai fan, similar to Malaysian laksa, but using rice noodles. The curries are highly esteemed as well. Don't leave it too late, though; they open early in the morning but close around 2 pm.

A popular spot for travellers is *Mae Porn*, a restaurant on the corner of Phang-Nga Rd and Soi Pradit, close to the On On and Sinthavee hotels. There's an air-con room as well as outdoor tables. They sell curries, seafood, fruit shakes – you name it, Mae Porn has it – all at very reasonable prices. Another popular spot in town is *Kanda Bakery* on

JERRY ALEXANDER

JERRY ALEXANDER

Northern Andaman Coast
Top: A spirit house overlooks Hat Surin, Phuket, a beach popular with local Thais.
Bottom: A Thai Muslim fishing village on a quiet stretch of the ever-popular Phuket coastline.

MARK STRICKLAND/OCEANIC IMPRESSIONS

NICKO GONCHAROFF

RICHARD NEBESKY

Northern Andaman Coast
Top: Expansive sandy beaches dotted with huge smooth granite rock formations are a feature of Ko Similan National Marine Park.
Bottom Left: A tranquil stretch of beach at the Similans; offshore the magnificent corals are rated one of the world's top dive sites.
Bottom Right: Heading out on an open boat trip, Similan Islands.

Rasada Rd. It's open early in the morning with fresh-baked whole-wheat bread, baguettes, croissants, cakes and real brewed coffee; they also serve a variety of khâo tôm specialities any time of day.

Another good local discovery is the simple *Muslim restaurant* on the corner of Thepkasatri and Thalang Rds – look for the star and crescent. This friendly family-run place serves delicious and inexpensive mátsaman kài (chicken-potato curry), roti kaeng (flatbread and curry – in the morning only) and khâo mòk kài (chicken biryani – usually gone by 1 pm).

Fried rice and Thai pastry fans shouldn't miss *Kaew Jai* (no English sign), at 151 Phang-Nga Rd near Montri Rd. More basic than Kanda Bakery, this is the Thai idea of pastry heaven – especially the custard cake and cashew cake – even if the service is a bit surly. Among the highly varied fried rice dishes are khâo phàt náam phrík phâo (fried rice with roasted chilli paste), khâo phàt khreûang kaeng (rice fried in curry paste) and khâo phàt bai kà-phrao (with holy basil), each with a choice of chicken, pork, crab, shrimp or squid. In this same vicinity on Phang-Nga Rd are a two or three other inexpensive Phuket-style *ráan khâo kaeng* (rice-and-curry shops), including the *Aik Ocha*; try the tasty cashew-nut curry.

The venerable *Nai Yao* is still hanging on in an old wooden building with a tin roof near the Honda dealer on Phuket Rd. It features an excellent, inexpensive seafood menu (bilingual), cold beer and, at night, tables on the sidewalk. The house speciality is the unique and highly recommended tôm yam hâeng (dry tôm yam), which can be ordered with chicken, shrimp or squid.

Another Phuket institution, perfect for an intimate night out, is *Krajok Sii* (☎ 217903), in an old shophouse on Takua Pa Rd just south of Phang-Nga Rd on the west side of street. It's hard to spot as there's no romanised sign; look for the coloured glass transom (the restaurant's name means 'coloured glass') over the door. There aren't more than a dozen tables in the tastefully decorated dining room, but it's worth waiting for a table as the kitchen specialises in Phuket cuisine, including delicious *hàw mòk thaleh* (steamed seafood curry), green mango salad, shrimp toast and other delights. Prices are reasonable, but portions are small as befits traditional Thai cooking.

Kaw Yam (Khao Yam), on Thungkha Rd in front of the Phuket Merlin, has a clean, middle-class, indoor-outdoor atmosphere enjoyed by local office workers for breakfast and lunch. The kitchen serves very well-prepared khâo yam, the southern-Thai rice salad, as well as khanŏm jiin and many other Phuket specialities. Prices are inexpensive to moderate. Just as good for khanŏm jiin but cheaper is *Khwan Khanom Jiin* (no English sign) next door.

Next to the Robinson Ocean Plaza shopping complex off Ong Sim Phai Rd is Phuket's municipal market, around three sides of which an inexpensive *night market* convenes nightly.

Entertainment

The *Pearl Cinema*, on the corner of Phang-Nga and Montri Rds near the Pearl Hotel, occasionally shows English-language films. The *Alliance Française* (☎ 222988), at 3 Soi 1, Pattana Rd, shows French films (subtitled in English) weekly. They also have a TV with up-to-date news broadcasts and a library.

The major hotels have discos and/or karaoke clubs. The *Timber 'n Rock*, on the eastern side of Yaowarat Rd just south of Thungkha Rd, is a well-run pub with an attractive woodsy decor, lots of Phuket and Thai food and live music after 9 pm. Along the same lines is the *Kon Thai Pub*, on Bangkok Rd, which has a seven-piece band playing rock, folk and Thai pop tunes from 9.30 pm nightly.

To get a glimpse of what the hip young Thai crowd does on its night out, stroll up the little alley off of Tilok Uthit Rd, just south of the Metropole Phuket Hotel. The main drawcard here is *Alien*, a rock 'n roll bar that packs them in, especially on weekends. Drinks are a bit more expensive than average, and the place doesn't get started until around 10.30 pm, but it's a fun way to check out contemporary Thai night life. There are a couple of other pubs and clubs along this strip, as well as a pleasant outdoor bar, *Arch Beer & Snack*.

Things to Buy

Although there are loads of souvenir shops and clothing boutiques surrounding the beach resorts of Patong, Kata and Karon, the best bargains on the island are found in the provincial capital. There are two main markets, one off the south side of Ranong Rd near the centre of town, and a second off the north side of Ong Sim Phai Rd a bit southeast of the town centre. The Ranong Rd market traces its history back to the days when pirates, Indians, Chinese, Malays and Europeans traded in Phuket and offers a wide variety of sarongs and fabrics from Thailand, Malaysia, Indonesia and India. You'll also find inexpensive clothing and crafts here.

At the newer Ong Sim Phai Rd market the focus is on fresh produce. Adjacent to the market is the large Robinson Ocean Plaza, which contains Robinson Department Store as well as smaller shops with moderately priced clothing and housewares. Along Yaowarat Rd between Phang-Nga and Thalang Rds are a number of Indian-run tailor and fabric shops, while Chinese gold shops are lined up along Ranong Rd opposite the Ranong Rd market.

Getting There & Away

Air THAI operates nearly a dozen daily flights from Bangkok for 2000B one way. The flight takes just over an hour. There are also regular flights to and from Hat Yai for 780B. The airline office (☎ 211195) is at 78 Ranong Rd. Bangkok Airways (☎ 225033) flies between Ko Samui and Phuket daily for 1330B each way. The office is 158/2-3 Yaowarat Rd.

THAI flies between Phuket and several international destinations, including Penang, Langkawi, Kuala Lumpur, Singapore, Hong Kong, Taipei and Sydney. International airlines with offices in Phuket are: Dragon Air (☎ 217300), 37/52 Montri Rd; Malaysia Airlines (☎ 216675), 1/8-9 Thungkha Rd; and Silk Air (☎ 213891), 183/103 Phang-Nga Rd.

Southern Helicopter Service (☎ 327111; fax 327113) at the airport charters a Kawasaki BK117 helicopter, which carries up to seven passengers, for 48,000B per hour. The service covers all of Phuket and Ao Phang-Nga, including Ko Phi Phi. Southern Flying Group (☎ 247237) does small aeroplane charters.

Bus From Bangkok, one 1st class air-con bus leaves the Southern bus terminal at 6.50 pm for 368B. Buses leave Phuket for the return journey at 3 pm. Two VIP buses (570B) run daily from Bangkok (Southern bus terminal) at 5.30 pm and 6 pm. Departure time from Phuket is 4 pm. The trip takes 13 to 14 hours. Ordinary buses leave 10 times a day from 7.30 am until 10.30 pm for 210B; these buses take around 15 hours. The main bus terminal for government buses is off the north side of Phang-Nga Rd between the Phuket Telecommunications Centre and the Novotel Phuket City.

Several private tour buses run from Bangkok to Phuket regularly with fares of 378B one way or 700B return. Most have one bus a day which leaves at 6 or 7 pm.

From Phuket, most tour buses to Bangkok leave at 3 pm. Several agencies have their offices on Rasada and Phang-Nga Rds downtown.

Fares and trip durations for bus trips to and from Phuket's government terminal include:

Destination	Fare (B)	Hours
Hat Yai	112	8
(air-con)	192 to 202	7
Krabi	47	4½
(air-con)	85	4
Nakhon Si Thammarat	80 to 93	8
(air-con)	129	-
Phang-Nga	26	2½
(air-con)	50	1½
Surat Thani	77	6
(air-con)	139	-
Takua Pa	38	3
Trang	78	6
(air-con)	140	5

Taxi & Mini-van There are also share taxis between Phuket and other provincial capitals in the south; taxi fares are generally double the fare of an ordinary bus (Krabi 80B, Surat Thani 150B, Trang 120B). The taxi stand for Nakhon Si Thammarat, Surat Thani, Krabi, Trang and Hat Yai is on Phang-Nga Rd, near the Pearl Cinema.

Some companies run air-con mini-vans (rot tûu) with through tickets to Ko Samui from Phuket – it's part of a mini-van circuit that covers Phuket, Surat Thani, Krabi and Ranong. As with share taxis, fares are about double the public bus fares. You can also get vans to Hat Yai (220B), Krabi (150B), Penang (550B), Kuala Lumpur (650B) and Singapore (700B). Vans can be booked at the same intersection as the share taxis.

Getting Around

Phuket is a big island, and distances between the various beaches and sights are measured in kilometres. There is public transport, but only during the daytime, and in many cases you'll still need to take a taxi or tuk-tuk to get to some of the more out-of-the-way destinations, which will often cost 150B to 200B or more. Unless you're happy to stay rooted to one area of the island, you should seriously consider renting either a motorcycle or jeep, especially if there are several of you to share the cost.

The Airport There is a limousine service at the airport that will theoretically take you into town for 70B per person. However, if there aren't enough of you to fill the van, you'll most likely be directed toward a taxi. If you do get the shuttle bus, the dropoff point in town is a bit out of the way on a soi off Phunphon Rd. There's a similar service to Patong, Kata or Karon beaches for 100B, but again unless there are enough of you, you're probably out of luck.

Taxis ask 300B for the trip from the airport to the city, 400B to 450B to the beaches.

Songthaew Large, bus-size songthaews run regularly from Ranong Rd near the market to the various Phuket beaches for 10 to 30B per person – see the following Phuket beaches section for details. Beware of tales about the tourist office being 5km away, or

that the only way to reach the beaches is by taxi, or even that you'll need a taxi to get from the bus station to the town centre (the bus station is more or less in the town centre). Officially, beach songthaews run from 7 am to 5 pm; after that time you must charter your own mini-songthaew to the beaches.

Smaller songthaews or tuk-tuks around town cost a standard 10B.

Car Several agencies in town rent Suzuki jeeps for 900B per day, including insurance. If you rent for a week or more you can get the price down to 800B per day. Downtown your best choice is Pure Car Rent (☎ 211002) at 75 Rasada Rd. Avis charges a bit more (around 1100B a day) but has outlets around the island at Le Meridien, Phuket Arcadia, Dusit Laguna, Phuket Cabana, Club Med, Phuket Island Resort and the airport. Hertz is similar and has branches at the airport, Banyan Tree Resort and Holiday Inn.

In the bigger beach towns there are numerous stores, hotels and bungalows where you can rent jeeps, as well as motorcycles.

Motorcycle Motorcycle taxis around town are 10B. You can hire motorcycles (usually 100cc Japanese bikes) in Phuket along Rasada Rd between Phuket and Yaowarat Rds or from various places at the beaches. Costs are in the 150 to 200B per day range.

Take care when riding a bike, and use common sense. People who ride around in shorts, T-shirt, a pair of thongs and no helmet are asking for trouble.

Phuket has the highest injury and death rate for farangs in the country. In the high season 50 to 100 farangs are seen by Kathu Hospital staff each week. Even for experienced riders some of the winding roads through the mountain can be downright dangerous, especially if you are caught out by the rain.

Matt King

Phuket now has a helmet law that police claim will be enforced without exception: those caught not wearing one will be fined 500B. When we last visited there still seemed to be plenty of 'exceptions', but then again, it's just stupid to ride without a helmet.

Along with the standard sizes, bigger bikes (over 125cc) can be rented at a couple of shops at Patong and Karon beaches.

AROUND PHUKET TOWN
Ko Sire
This tiny islet, 4km east of the capital and connected to the main island by a bridge over a canal, is known for its chao náam (sea gypsy) village and a hilltop reclining Buddha.

In spite of frequent mentions in Phuket tourist literature, the sea gypsy community at Ko Sire is not really worth visiting as the indigenous traditions have been almost entirely obscured by outside influences. The nearest intact sea gypsy villages can be found on the slightly more remote Ko Lanta island group, roughly 90km south-east of Phuket (see the Ko Lanta section under Krabi Province in the Southern Andaman Coast chapter).

There are a couple of places to stay on Ko Sire, including *Madam Puye Bungalow* for 200B and *Siray Resort* for 300 to 500B.

AROUND PHUKET PROVINCE
• ☎ (76)
Warning
All of the western Phuket beaches, including Surin, Laem Singh and Kamala, have strong riptides during the monsoons. Take care when swimming, or don't go in the water at all if you're not a strong swimmer.

Patong
Fifteen kilometres west of Phuket, this large curved beach is the epicentre of the tourist earthquake that rattles Phuket throughout the high season (December to March). The town is saturated with hotels, up-market bungalows, foreign restaurants, expensive seafood places, pubs, go-go bars, shopping stalls and tour agencies. During peak periods both sidewalk and road traffic brings to mind scenes of Bangkok, except that there are far more foreigners (particularly Europeans) than locals.

Obviously, Patong is not the spot for those seeking to get away from it all. But if you want to get into the thick of it, there's no livelier spot on the island. You can find just about anything you need in terms of amenities, there are scores of restaurants and the night life goes on until sunrise. It's also a convenient spot to organise diving courses or boat charters (see the earlier Diving & Snorkelling and Yachting sections for more details).

Information Patong has many foreign exchange booths, plus a post and telephone office on the corner of Soi Phoemphong (Soi Post Office) and Thawiwong Rd.

Boat Trips Several companies on Patong do one day cruises to nearby islands. For excursions to the Similan and Surin Islands off the Andaman coast of Phang-Nga Province, see the sections on those islands earlier.

Hash House Harriers Phuket's chapter of the running-and-drinking HHH meets regularly at the Expat Hotel. Hashes (foot races) are held on Saturday afternoons; all interested people are welcome.

Places to Stay – bottom end Rates on Patong vary according to the season. During the high season (December to March, and August) you'll be doing very well to find something under 300B a night. On the beach there is nothing under 600B, but on and off Rat Uthit Rd, especially in the small sois, there are some nondescript guesthouses with rooms for around 250B. During off-season months some of the 600B places will drop as low as 400B or even 300B, but that's about it. Bottom-end places usually come with fan and shared bath; more expensive rooms in this category will have a private bath and perhaps air-con. The real low-end guesthouses tend to come and go, so be prepared to find that some of those listed below have either changed names or vanished. Prices can be similarly fluid.

During the rainy season, May to November, you may be able to knock 100B off the following rates:

Asia Guest House – Paradise Complex (☎ 340962); 400 to 700B

Best Guest House – Paradise Complex (☎ 340958); 300B

Boomerang Cafe & Inn – 77/57 Rat Uthit Rd (☎ 342182); 300 to 600B

Capricorn Villa – 82/29 Rat Uthit Rd (☎ 340390); 300 to 800B

Club Oasis – 86/4 Thawiwong Rd (☎ 293076); 300 to 600B

Duangjit Villas – 99/3 Thawiwong Rd (☎ 340778); 400 to 800B

888 Inn – Paradise Complex (☎ 341306); 400 to 800B

Expat Hotel – 89/14 Rat Uthit Rd (☎/fax 340300); 490 to 690B

K Hotel – 82/47 Rat Uthit Rd (☎ 340832); 500 to 900B

The Living Place – 38/6 Sawatdirak Rd (☎/fax 340121); 400 to 800B

Nordic Bungalow – 82/25 Bangla Rd (☎ 340284); 350 to 750B

PS II – 78/54 Rat Uthit Rd (☎ 342207/8); 250 to 650B

Shamrock Park Inn – 17/2 Rat Uthit Rd (☎ 340991); 500B

Places to Stay – middle The middle range at Patong beach runs roughly from 700 to 1800B, which always includes air-con and private bath; the more expensive ones will have hot water showers, lower-priced ones cold water only. Prices in this category can usually be negotiated downwards 100 to 200B during the rainy season.

Andaman Resortel – 65/21 Soi Saen Sabai (☎ 341516; fax 340847); 800 to 1600B

Casa Summer Breeze – 96/1 Muu 4, Soi Saen Sabai (☎ 340464; fax 340493); 600 to 1000B

Coconut Village Resort – 99/5 Thawiwong Rd (☎ 340146; fax 340144); 1000 to 1800B

Neptuna Hotel – Thawiwong Rd (☎ 340824; fax 340627); 750 to 1400B

Nilly's Marina Inn – 102/5 Thawiwong Rd (☎ 342197; fax 340616); 800 to 2700B

Patong Bed & Breakfast – 103/10 Thawiwong Rd (☎ 340819; fax 340818); 700 to 1500B

PS I – 50/2 Rat Uthit Rd (☎ 340184); 800 to 1250B

Safari Beach Hotel – 83/12 Thawiwong Rd (☎ 341170); from 800B

Seagull Cottage – 103 Thawiwong Rd (☎ 340238; 340259); 750 to 1400B

Sea Sun Sand Guesthouse – 64/27 Soi Kepsup, Thaiwiwong Rd (☎/fax 343047); from 800B

Tropica Bungalow – 94/4 Thaiwiwong Rd (☎ 340204; fax 340206); 600 to 1500B

The *Sky Inn* (☎ 342486) on the 9th floor of the Patong Condotel, caters to a primarily gay clientele and costs 900 to 1000B in high season and as low as 500B during the rainy season.

Places to Stay – top end At the lower end of the top price range, roughly around 2000 to 3000B, you'll find a number of all air-con places with swimming pools, modest room service, phones and other semi-luxury amenities. Most are located on Thawiwong Rd, which runs along the beach.

Ban Thai Beach Hotel – 89/71 Thawiwong Rd (☎ 340328; fax 340330); 1800 to 2700B

Beach Resortel – 96 Muu 3, Thawiwong Rd (☎ 340544; fax 340848); 1200 to 2500B

Casuarina Patong Garden Resort – 77/1 Thawiwong Rd (☎/fax 340123); 1800 to 3000B

Patong Bay Garden Resort – 61/13 Thawiwong Rd (☎ 340297/8; fax 340560); from 1710B

Patong Beach Bungalow – 96/1 Thawiwong Rd (☎ 340117; fax 340213); bungalows for 1500 to 3500B

Patong Beach Hotel – 94 Thawiwong Rd (☎ 340301; fax 340541); from 2500B

Patong Lodge Hotel – 61/7 Kalim beach (☎ 340286; fax 340287); 1600 to 1800B

Patong Merlin Hotel – 99/2 Muu 4, Thawiwong Rd (☎ 340037; fax 340394); 1500 to 3500B

Moving up a couple of notches to places with true world class standards, rates start at 3000B and reach epic proportions for large suites with the best bay views. Many top-end places add a 500 to 700B peak season surcharge between late December and mid-January.

Amari Coral Beach Resort – 104 Muu 4, Thawiwong Rd (☎ 340106; fax 340115); 3000B from 1 November to 31 March, 2000B the remainder of the year – add 500B for superior rooms, 2500B for suites

Club Andaman Beach – 77/1 Thawiwong Rd (☎ 340530; fax 340527); bungalows from 3708B

Diamond Cliff Resort – 61/9 Kalim beach (☎ 340501; fax 340507); from 3766B

Holiday Inn Resort Phuket – 86/11 Thawiwong Rd (☎ 340608/9; fax 340435); from 3200B

Patong Grand Condotel – 63 Rat Uthit Rd (☎ 341-043; fax 342205); 6500 to 10,000B

Phuket Cabana Resort – 94 Thawiwong Rd (☎ 340138; fax 340178); 2340 to 13,000B

NORTHERN ANDAMAN COAST

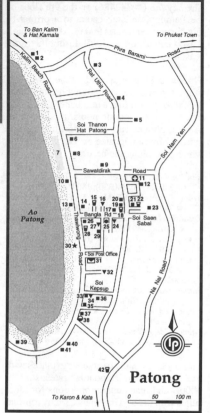

PLACES TO STAY
1 Patong Lodge Hotel
2 Diamond Cliff Resort
3 PS II Hotel
4 Shamrock Park Inn
5 Patong Grand Condotel
6 Club Andaman Beach
8 Casuarina Patong
   Garden Resort
9 The Living Place
10 Phuket Cabana Resort
12 Paradise Complex
13 Patong Bay Garden Resort
14 Safari Beach Hotel
17 Nordic Bungalow
19 K Hotel
20 Capricorn Villa
21 PS 1 Hotel
23 Expat Hotel
26 Tropica Bungalow
29 Patong Beach Hotel
33 Ban Thai Beach Hotel
35 Holiday Inn Resort Phuket
36 Sea Sun Sand Guesthouse
37 Patong Merlin Hotel
39 Amari Coral Beach Resort
40 Seagull Cottage
41 Nilly's Marina Inn

PLACES TO EAT
7 Seafood Vendors
16 Restaurant 4
24 Le Croissant
27 Noodle and Rice Stalls
32 Viva Mexico
34 Tandoor

OTHER
11 Kathu Hospital
15 UFO
18 Rock Hard
22 Soi Sunset Bars
25 Songserm Travel
28 Banana Discotheque
30 Police
31 Post & Telephone Office
38 Buses to Phuket
42 Simon Cabaret

Places to Eat Patong has stacks of restaurants, some of them quite good. Prices are usually a bit higher than average, and dishes tend to cater towards foreign palates; for authentic Thai food you may have to resort to the back alley rice and noodle stalls.

Seafood restaurants abound of course; *Restaurant 4* is among the best priced and is quite popular with both Asian and European tourists. Opposite Casuarina Patong Garden Resort is a string of inexpensive *seafood vendors*; you can dine right on the beach, sitting on sling chairs under the umbrellas provided. For inexpensive *noodle and rice*

vendors, check the soi near The Living Place, and the one next to the Songserm Travel office.

Around the intersection of Rat Uthit and Bangla Rds are a few inexpensive Thai and farang cafes worth trying. *Le Croissant*, on Bangla Rd, carries French pastries, French wines, sandwiches, salads, baguettes and imported cheeses. A couple of sois south of Soi Post Office, *Viva Mexico* does Mexican food.

An OK Indian restaurant, the *Tandoor*, can be found on Soi Kepsup near the Cosmos Inn.

Entertainment There are many bars around town, as well as a few cabarets and discos. *Banana Discotheque* at 96 Thawiwong Rd is still one of the more popular dance clubs, while *Rock Hard* on the corner of Bangla Rd and Rat Uthit Rd is one of the larger and more popular nightclub/bars. If you like transvestite shows, check out the *Simon Cabaret* at 100/6-8 Muu 4. This place has become an institution, complete with tour buses lined up in front at night. If you want something a little more grotty, try the similar performance at *UFO*, off Bangla Rd.

There is a string of bars located on Soi Sunset (near the intersection of Rat Uthit and Bangla Rds) that doesn't get started until around midnight, and rocks until about 6 am. The crowd consists mainly of western men and Thai women (many of whom will have just gotten off work), but it's still enough of a social scene that couples and female travellers can join in the partying with no problem.

Getting There & Away Songthaews to Patong from Phuket leave from Ranong Rd, near the day market and fountain circle; the fare is 15B. According to the TAT, the after-hours charter fare is 130B, but don't expect to pay any less than 200B. In the reverse direction, songthaews leave from Thawiwong Rd in Patong. You should be able to get after-hour charters for somewhat less in the Patong-Phuket direction, since most songthaews are based in Phuket and they'll need to get back there.

Getting Around Tuk-tuks circulate Patong for 10B per ride. There are numerous places to rent 125cc motorcycles and jeeps. Patong Big Bike on Rat Uthit Rd rents 250 to 750cc bikes.

Karon
Karon is a long, gently curving beach with small sand dunes and a few palms and casuarina trees. Sometimes it is referred to as two beaches: Karon Yai and Karon Noi. Karon Noi, also known as Relax Bay, can only be reached from Patong beach and is completely monopolised by Le Meridien Hotel. The main section of Karon now has a paved promenade with streetlights, and the entire area has blended with Kata beach to the south to produce a smaller, less frenetic version of Patong.

Karon is lined with multistorey inns and deluxe bungalows, along with a dwindling number of places with rooms or huts for under 400B. During the low season – May to November – you can often get a 400B room for as low as 200B, a 1000B room for 600B, and a 2000B room for 1000B.

Places to Stay Most of the places under 700B are located well off the beach, often on small hillocks to the east of the main road. To the north of the headland straddling Karon and Kata is the *Kata Tropicana* (☎ 330141), with well-maintained bungalows for 350 to 800B. At the northern end of the beach *Lume & Yai* (☎ 396096) has bungalows from 300 to 500B.

In the commercial centre of Karon, near the roundabout, the quiet *Karon Seaview Bungalow* (☎ 396912) offers OK concrete duplexes and row houses for 300 to 500B. On the main road away from the beach is the *Crystal Beach Hotel* (☎ 396580/5); it's good value at 300 to 400B for air-con rooms. Farther south and nearer the beach is the popular and friendly *My Friend Bungalow* (☎ 396344) with 45 rooms for 200 to 500B; the cafe out front is a plus. *Fantasy Hill Bungalow* (☎ 330106) closer to Kata, on a small hill off the main road, has good budget bungalows for 200 to 400B.

In the mid-range (averaging 500B and up) are *Karon Guest House* (☎ 396860), 500 to 800B; *Karon Village* (☎ 396431), 600 to 800B; *Phuket Ocean Resort* (☎ 396176), 1200 to 1400B; and *Ruam Thep Inn* (☎ 330281), 400 to 900B.

A large number of the options on Karon are new resort-type hotels with rooms starting at 1000B or above, with air-con, swimming

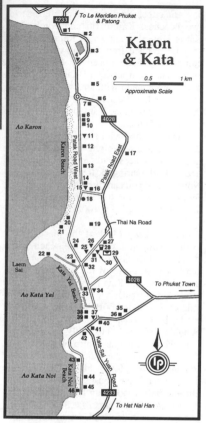

Karon & Kata

0   0.5   1 km
Approximate Scale

PLACES TO STAY
1   Felix Karon Swissotel
2   Lume & Yai Bungalows
3   Phuket Ocean Resort
5   The Islandia Travelodge Resort
6   Karon Guest House
7   Crystal Beach Hotel
8   My Friend Bungalow
9   South Sea Resort
10 Karon Villa; Karon Royal Wing
12 Karon Seaview Bungalow
13 Phuket Arcadia Hotel
14 Thavorn Palm Beach
16 Karon Inn
17 Karon Village
19 Kata Tropicana
20 Ruam Thep Inn
21 Marina Cottage
22 Laem Sai Village
23 Peach Hill Hotel
24 Fantasy Hill Bungalow
27 Lucky Guest House;
    Charlie's Guest House
31 Rose Inn
32 Smile Inn
33 Club Méditerranée
35 Bell Guest House
36 Sea Bees Bungalow
38 Chao Kohn Inn
39 The Boathouse
40 Friendship Bungalow
41 Cool Breeze
42 Pop Cottage
43 Kata Thani Amari Resort
44 Kata Noi Riviera
45 Kata Buri Resort
46 C Tapkaew Bungalows

PLACES TO EAT
4   Seafood Restaurants
11 Seafood Restaurants
15 Old Siam
25 Kampong-Kata Hill Restaurant
26 Siri's Kitchen
30 Bondeli Kata
34 Coconut Garden
37 Islander's

OTHER
18 Maxim Supermarket
28 Easy Rider's International Pub
29 Post Office

pools etc. Prices at most places have come down a bit over the last two years due to competition.

The top end includes:

Felix Karon Swissotel – (☎ 396666; fax 396853); 81 rooms, from 2200B
The Islandia Travelodge Resort – (☎ 396200; fax 396491); 128 rooms, 2000 to 4500B
Karon Beach Resort – (☎ 330006; fax 330529); 81 rooms, 2000 to 3500B
Karon Inn – (☎ 396519; fax 330529); 100 rooms, 1250 to 2300B
Karon Villa & Karon Royal Wing – (☎ 396139; fax 396122); 324 rooms, from 2700B

Le Meridien Phuket – (☎ 340480; fax 340479); 470 rooms, from 3800B
Phuket Arcadia Hotel – (☎ 396038; fax 396136); 225 rooms, from 3600B
South Sea Resort – (☎ 396611; fax 396618); 100 rooms, from 3500B
Thavorn Palm Beach Hotel – (☎ 396090; fax 396555); 210 rooms, 1700 to 4500B

Places to Eat As usual, almost every place to stay provides some food. The cheapest *Thai and seafood places* are off the roundabout near the commercial centre.

The Little Mermaid, 100m east of the traffic circle, has a long, inexpensive, mostly Scandinavian menu written in 12 languages; it's open 24 hours. Another cosy, inexpensive place with excellent food is *Sunset Restaurant*.

One of the better restaurants for Thai food is *Old Siam*, which has dishes from 100 to 240B. It's on Patak Rd West, near the southern end of the beach.

Kata

Just around a headland, south from Karon, Kata is a more interesting beach than Karon, and is divided into two – Ao Kata Yai ('Big Kata Bay') and Ao Kata Noi ('Little Kata Bay'). With around 30 hotels and bungalow resorts it can get a bit crowded, but it's still quieter than Karon or Patong. Kata Noi, separated from its larger northern brother by a headland, has a more secluded feel to it.

Along Thai Na Rd in Kata Yai, near the Rose Inn, is a Thai Farmers Bank (with exchange services) and a post office.

Places to Stay Rates range from 100 to 200B at *Bell Guest House*, quite a distance back from the beach toward the south end of Kata Yai, to more than 5000B at the classy The Boathouse, and the Club Méditerranée on Kata Yai. In general the less expensive places tend to be off the beach between Kata Yai (north) and Kata Noi (south) or well off the beach.

Friendship Bungalow (☎ 330499), a popular place off the beach at the headland between Kata Yai and Kata Noi, is 350 to 700B. Rooms at the *Cool Breeze* (☎ 330484) in Kata Noi's north start at 200B (certain huts only; others with toilet and shower are more expensive).

Coastline Bungalow (☎ 330498), just down from the Cool Breeze, has large, two storey brick cottages for a mere 350B, all with private bath. Two new budget apartment-style places worth checking out – both basic

but clean and friendly – are *Lucky Guest House* at 250 to 350B and *Charlie's Guest House* (☎ 330855) at 200 to 280B; both are found toward the back road that parallels the beach, north-east of Rose Inn and Bondeli Kata restaurant. All of the bungalows will give discounts during the May to October low season.

One of the best places in this area is *C Tapkaew Bungalow* (☎ 330433), down at the south end of Kata Noi beach. At 600B it's one of the few affordable spots that's right on the beach, and the bungalows are spacious and well maintained.

Recommended medium-range places (all air-con) are *Peach Hill Hotel* (☎ 330603; fax 330895), in a nice setting with a pool from 500 to 1000B; and *Smile Inn* (☎ 330926; fax 330925), a clean, friendly place with a nice open-air cafe and air-con rooms with hot water showers for 700B (800B including breakfast). Other mid-priced lodgings are available at *Pop Cottage* (☎ 330794), from 500 to 1000B, and the *Chao Khon Inn* (☎ 330403), 750 to 1500B.

Moving up in price a bit, one of the best ones at the lower edge of the top end is the long-running *Marina Cottage* (☎ 330517; fax 330516), a medium-scale, low-rise, low-density place on shady, palm-studded grounds near the beach. Marina Cottage doesn't accept tour groups and takes reservations only through selected travel agents, yet manages to keep rates for its comfortable, well-designed Thai-style bungalows in the 1400 to 3000B range.

The palatial, 202 room *Kata Thani Amari Resort* (☎ 330417; fax 330426) on the beach at Kata Noi has tastefully designed rooms and bungalows on very nicely landscaped grounds for 2000 to 4200B.

The Boathouse (☎ 330557; fax 330561, Bangkok ☎ (2) 438-1123), the brainchild of architect and Phuket resident ML Tri Devakul, is a 36 room boutique resort that manages to stay full year-round without resorting to off-season rates. In spite of rather ordinary-looking, if capacious rooms, the hotel hosts a steady influx of Thai politicos, pop stars, artists, celebrity authors (the hotel also hosts periodic poetry/fiction readings) and the ordinary rich on the strength of its stellar service and acclaimed restaurant, and because it commands a choice spot right on the south end of Kata Yai. Rooms start at 3700B.

And of course, there's the *Club Med* (☎ 330455; fax 330461), which occupies a large chunk of land near Kata Yai, as well as a fair swath of beachfront. Per-person rates range from around 2800 to 5000B.

Places to Eat Most of the restaurants in Kata offer standard tourist food and service. The best restaurant in the entire area, including Karon and Patong to the north, is the open-air *The Boathouse Wine & Grill*, which started out as a restaurant only but now has 36 rooms attached to its original location at the south end of Kata Yai (see Places to Stay above). The wine collection here has been cited for excellence by *Wine Spectator* magazine and the nightly seafood buffet is excellent. It's a pricey place but the atmosphere is casual and service is tops.

Another standout, though considerably less expensive, is the *Kampong-Kata Hill Restaurant*, a Thai-style place decorated with antiques and situated on a hill a bit inland from the beach. It's open only for dinner, from 5 pm till midnight. Dinner for two without drinks will probably cost around 500B. Nearby, *Siri's Kitchen* has the usual mix of Thai/western food, and always seems to draw a steady crowd. Just up the street the *Dive Café* serves multi-course Thai set dinners for 150 and 200B per person. *Bondeli Kata* serves fresh pastries, four kinds of coffee and nine teas.

The very large and mid-priced *Islander's* (☎ 330740) strives to provide something for everyone, including seafood, Italian, barbecue and fresh baked goods; if you call they'll provide free transport to/from your hotel. The Swiss-managed *Coconut Garden* also does Thai, Italian and seafood.

Getting There & Away Songthaews to both Kata and Karon leave frequently from the Ranong Rd market in Phuket from 7 am to 5 pm for 15B per person. After-hour charters cost 200B, despite what the TAT brochure may tell you. The main songthaew stop is in front of Kata Beach Resort.

Nai Han

A few kilometres south of Kata, this beach set around a picturesque bay is similar to Kata and Karon but, in spite of the 1986 construction of the Phuket Yacht Club, not as developed – thanks to the presence of Samnak Song Nai Han, a monastic centre in the middle of the beach that claims most of the beachfront land. To make up for the loss of saleable beachfront, developers started cutting away the forests on the hillsides overlooking the beach. Recently, however, the development seems to have reached a halt. This means that Nai Han is usually one of the least crowded beaches on the southern part of the island.

The TAT says Nai Han beach is a dangerous place to swim during the monsoon season (May to October), but it really varies according to daily or weekly weather changes – look for the red flag, which means dangerous swimming conditions.

Places to Stay Except for the Yacht Club, there's really not much accommodation available on or even near the beach. If you follow the road about 1km through and past the Yacht Club you'll come to the simple *Ao Sane Bungalows* (☎ 288306), which cost 200 to 400B depending on the season and condition of the huts. Farther on at the end of this road is the secluded *Jungle Beach Resort* (☎ 288264; fax 381108). The nicely done cottages are well-spaced along a naturally wooded slope with a small beach below, and there's even a small swimming pool. Low-season rates start at 400B for a sturdy hut without bath; high-season rates peak at 4000B for a large terraced cottage with private bath.

Well back from the beach, near the road into Nai Han and behind a small lagoon is the motel-like *Nai Han Resort* (☎ 381810), with decent rooms for 600 to 700B with fan, 900B for air-con. Near the other side of the lagoon, *Romsai Bungalows* (☎ 381338) has

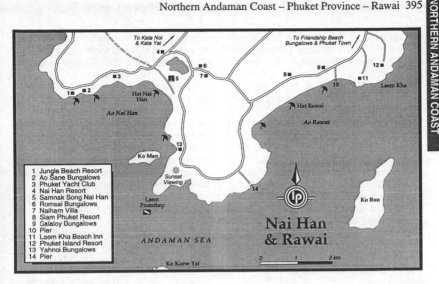

1 Jungle Beach Resort
2 Ao Sane Bungalows
3 Phuket Yacht Club
4 Nai Han Resort
5 Samnak Song Nai Han
6 Romsai Bungalows
7 Naiharn Villa
8 Siam Phuket Resort
9 Salaloy Bungalows
10 Pier
11 Laem Kha Beach Inn
12 Phuket Island Resort
13 Yahnoi Bungalows
14 Pier

Nai Han
& Rawai

ANDAMAN SEA

huts for around 400B in the December to April high season, and as low as 250B the remainder of the year.

The *Phuket Yacht Club* (☎ 381156; fax 381164) sits on the western end of Nai Han. Originally built at the astronomical cost of 145 million baht, the hotel has given up on the idea of becoming a true yacht club (apparently the bay currents aren't right for such an endeavour) with a mobile pier. The pier has gone but luxurious 'state rooms' are still available for 7768B a night and up.

On the other end of the bay from the Yacht Club is the newly opened *Yahnoi Bungalow* (☎ 288982). Simple huts cost 250B, there's a small restaurant, and the place enjoys a beautiful location with its own small beach. Getting there will pretty much require your own transport however.

Getting There & Away Nai Han is 18km from Phuket and a songthaew (leaving from the intersection of Bangkok Rd and the fountain circle) costs 20B per person. Tuk-tuk charters are, as usual, 200B one way.

Rawai

Rawai was one of the first coastal areas on Phuket to be developed, simply because it was near Phuket and there was already a rather large fishing community there. Once other, nicer beach areas like Patong and Karon were 'discovered', Rawai gradually began to lose popularity and today it is a rather spiritless place – but at least it's not crowded.

The beach is not great, but there is a lot happening in or near Rawai: there is a local sea gypsy village; Hat Laem Kha (better than Rawai) to the north; boats to the nearby islands of Ko Lon, Ko Hae, Ko Aew, Ko Phi and others; and good snorkelling off **Laem Phromthep** at the southern tip of Phuket island, easy to approach from Rawai. In fact, most of the visitors who stay at Rawai these days are divers who want to be near Phromthep and/or boat facilities for offshore diving trips.

Laem Phromthep is also a popular viewing point at sunset, when lots of shutterbugs gather to take the famous Phromthep shot. On a hill next to the viewpoint is a shrine to Phra Phrom (Brahma).

The diving around the offshore islands is not bad, especially at Kaew Yai/Kaew Noi, off Phromthep and at Ko Hae. It's a good idea to shop around for boat trips to these islands to find the least expensive passage – the larger the group, the cheaper the cost per person.

Places to Stay The long-running *Salaloy Bungalows*, at 52/2 Wiset Rd (☎ 381370), has bungalows for 300B with fan, up to 800B with air-con. Their well-patronised seafood restaurant is one of the better – and more moderately priced – ones in the area.

The relatively new *Siam Phuket Resort* (☎ 381346; fax 3812347) offers quite sturdy-looking bungalows in the 750 to 1300B range.

Round at Laem Kha, the well-managed *Phuket Island Resort* (☎ 381010/7; fax 381-018) has 290 air-con rooms from 2000B, a swimming pool and other mod-cons. The *Laem Kha Beach Inn* (☎ 381305) has 20 rooms starting at 450B, and reaching up to 1200B for larger ones.

About 2.5km north of Rawai, about halfway to the Ao Chalong traffic roundabout, is *Friendship Beach* (☎ 381281; fax 381034), a little self-contained bungalow complex that seems to cater to longer-term visitors. Aside from its own modest little beach, this place has a pool table, a useful bulletin board, universal gym, a video library, and second-hand shops for books, clothing and marine equipment. Perhaps most interesting, it hosts live music jam sessions every weekend (rock, R&B and blues on Saturday, jazz on Sunday).

Places to Eat Aside from the restaurants attached to the resorts in Rawai (Salaloy is the best), the only places to eat are the *seafood and noodle vendors* set up along the roadside near the beach.

Getting There & Away Rawai is about 16km from Phuket and getting there costs 15B by songthaew from the circle at Bangkok Rd. Tuk-tuk charters cost at least 150B from Phuket.

Laem Singh & Kamala

North of Ao Patong, 24km from Phuket, Laem Singh ('Cape Singh') is a beautiful little rock-dominated beach. You could camp here and eat at the rustic roadside seafood places at the north end of Singh or in Ban Kamala, a village farther south.

Hat Kamala is a lovely stretch of sand and sea south of Surin and Laem Singh. The north end, the nicest area, is shaded by casuarina trees and features a small thatch-roof snack bar with free sling chairs and umbrellas available. The middle of the beach is now dominated by resorts and seafood restaurants. Bangkok's Safari World has leased a 160 acre plot near the beach for the construction of a US$60 million entertainment park called Phuket Fantasea.

Places to Stay The up-market *Phuket Kamala Resort* (☎ 324396; fax 324399) dominates the centre of the beach and costs 1400 to 2000B.

Nearby, the quiet *Bird Beach Bungalows* offers small but solid cottages for 400 to 600B. In this same area are several laundry services and minimarts, evidence that Kamala is attracting long-termers.

In the village there are several small houses for rent starting at around 500B a night. At the southern end of the bay, over-looking but not on the beach, is *Kamala Beach Estate* (☎ 314111; fax 324115), where fully equipped, high-security, modern time-share apartments go for 1900 to 6400B a night. Around the headland further south, the similar *Kamala Bay Terrace Resort* (☎ 270801; fax 270818) has more luxurious apartments and time-shares for 2700 to 13,000B per night.

Surin

North of Hat Kamala and a little north of Laem Singh, Hat Surin has a long beach and sometimes fairly heavy surf. When the water is calm, there's fair snorkelling here. The beach has long been a popular place for local Thais to come and nibble at seafood snacks sold by vendors along the beach.

Places to Stay Surin's northern end has been dubbed 'Pansea beach' by developers and is claimed by the exclusive Amanpuri

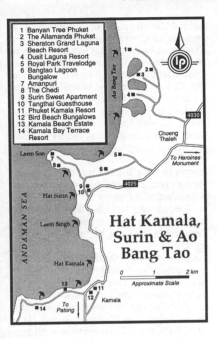

1 Banyan Tree Phuket
2 The Allamanda Phuket
3 Sheraton Grand Laguna
 Beach Resort
4 Dusit Laguna Resort
5 Royal Park Travelodge
6 Bangtao Lagoon
 Bungalow
7 Amanpuri
8 The Chedi
9 Surin Sweet Apartment
10 Tangthai Guesthouse
11 Phuket Kamala Resort
12 Bird Beach Bungalows
13 Kamala Beach Estate
14 Kamala Bay Terrace
 Resort

Hat Kamala, Surin & Ao Bang Tao

a haven for sailboarders; since 1992 the annual Siam World Cup windsurfing championships have been held here (formerly at Pattaya's Jomtien beach). A system of lagoons inland from the beach have been incorporated into the resorts and golf course, hence this is sometimes referred to as 'Laguna beach'.

Places to Stay With one exception, Bang Tao is strictly a haven for the well-to-do nowadays. Least expensive is the quiet and secluded *Bangtao Lagoon Bungalow* (☎ 324-260; fax 324168) at the south end of the bay, with small cottages for 500B, medium-sized ones for 1000B, or 1300 to 2500B for the largest.

Rooms at the plush *Dusit Laguna Resort* (☎ 324320; fax 324174) start at 4000B, with suites costing considerably more, not including tax. From 20 December to 20 February there is a 400B peak season surcharge. Another top-end place is the *Royal Park Travelodge Resort* (☎ 324021; fax 324243), where rooms start at 2600B in the low season, up to 3400B in the high.

Bringing yet more beachside luxury to the bay are the *Sheraton Grand Laguna Beach Resort* (☎ 324101; fax 324108) and the *Banyan Tree Phuket* (☎ 324374; fax 324375). The Sheraton has a sprawling 370 rooms starting at 4000B, while the more exclusive Banyan Tree has 86 villas (all with open-air sunken bathtubs, 34 with private pools) from 6350B. The Sheraton is the only place on this beach with a fitness centre. The Banyan Tree specialises in spiritual and physical spa treatments, including massage, seaweed packs and a three day 'Journey to Inner Wisdom' course for 6785B.

Finally, *The Allamanda Phuket* (☎ 324359; fax 324360) has 94 rooms for 2800 to 5600B, while the equally new *Laguna Beach Club* (☎ 324352; fax 324353) rivals the Sheraton and Dusit by providing 252 rooms for 4000 to 5000B.

Getting There & Away A songthaew from Phuket's Ranong Rd to Surin, Kamala or Bang Tao costs 15B. Tuk-tuk charters are

and The Chedi resorts. *Amanpuri Resort* (☎ 324333; fax 324100) plays host to Thailand's celebrity traffic, each of whom gets a 133 sq metre pavilion and a personal attendant; the staff to guest ratio is 3½ to one. It's owned by Indonesian Adrian Zecha and designed by the architect who designed the former Shah of Iran's Winter Palace. You can expect to pay 6900B and up per day for a room here.

The Chedi (☎ 324017; fax 324252) offers 110 rooms starting at 3000B and has its own golf course.

Toward the southern end of Hat Surin, *Surin Sweet Apartment* (☎ (01) 721-1153) and *Tangthai Guesthouse* offer simple but modern rooms in the 400 to 700B range.

Ao Bang Tao

North of Surin around Laem Son lies Ao Bang Tao, an 8km sandy beach with an 18-hole golf course that has attracted much upscale development. A steady breeze makes it

200B to Surin and Kamala, 170B to Bang Tao. A ride to Phuket town will probably cost you between 200 and 300B.

Nai Thon

Improved roads to Hat Nai Thon have brought only a small amount of development to this broad expanse of pristine sand backed by casuarina and pandanus trees. Swimming is quite good here except at the height of the monsoon, and there is some coral near the headlands at either end of the bay. Down on the beach, umbrellas and sling chairs are available.

Places to Stay The pleasant *Nai Thon Beach Resort* (☎ 214954; fax 214959), starts at 1000B a night for large, tastefully designed wooden cottages on the opposite side of the access road from the beach. Air-con cottages start at 1200B. Rates fall to 800B and 1000B respectively if you stay three days or more.

Getting There & Away Songthaews from Phuket cost 30B per person and run between 7 am and 5 pm only. A charter costs at least 250B; if you're coming straight from the airport it would be less trouble, less expensive and quicker to hire a taxi for 200B.

Nai Yang & Mai Khao

Both of these beaches are near Phuket airport, about 30km from Phuket town and are part of **Sirinat National Park**. The park encompasses 22 sq km of coastline, plus 68 sq km of sea, from the western Phang-Nga provincial border south to the headland that separates Nai Yang from Nai Thon.

Nai Yang is a fairly secluded area, especially the northern section which lies within the park and is favoured by Thais. The southern end of Nai Yang has been more developed, with a few hotels and a string of seafood restaurants. The crowd here is mostly foreign.

About 5km north of Nai Yang is Hat Mai Khao, Phuket's longest beach. Sea turtles lay their eggs on the beach here between November and February each year. This place is pretty much deserted, and there is no com-

mercial development or accommodation here. A new visitor centre with toilets, showers and picnic tables has recently been built at Mai Khao (replacing the old headquarters at the north end of Nai Yang). Hat Mai Khao is a stark, and beautiful, contrast to Phuket's other, developed beaches. Unfortunately, litter does get washed up on the sands, but only in some spots. Take care when swimming there, as there's a strong year-round undertow.

Places to Stay & Eat Camping is allowed on both Nai Yang and Mai Khao beaches. Sirinat National Park (☎ 327152) also rents out *bungalows* at Nai Yang for 400B. Check at the building opposite the visitor centre. Two-person tents can be rented for 60B a night.

Garden Cottage (☎/fax 327293) is actually on Route 4026, back from the southern end of Hat Nai Yang, but still within 10 minutes walk. Tidy cottages with air-con, fridge and private bath start at around 900B.

The fancy *Pearl Village Beach Hotel* (☎ 327006; fax 327338) commands 8.1 hectares at the southern end of Nai Yang, and seems geared mostly to European tour groups. Air-con rooms and cottages start at 3500B. Also at this end is the *Crown Nai Yang Suite Hotel* (☎ 317420), an ugly, multistorey place that rents modern boxes for 1500B and up.

Along the dirt road at the very southern end of the beach is a seemingly endless strip of *seafood restaurants* and, oddly enough, tailor shops. There is also a small shop near the entrance to the Pearl Village Beach Hotel.

Getting There & Away A songthaew from Phuket to Nai Yang costs 20B, while a tuk-tuk charter is 250 to 300B. There is no regular songthaew stop for Mai Khao but a tuk-tuk charter costs the same as for Nai Yang.

Khao Phra Taew Royal Wildlife & Forest Reserve

This mountain range in the northern interior of the island protects 2333 hectares of virgin island rainforest. There are some nice jungle hikes in this reserve, along with a couple of waterfalls, **Ton Sai** and **Bang Pae**. The falls are best seen in the rainy season between June and November. Because of its royal status, the reserve is better protected than the average Thai national park.

Near Bang Pae Falls, the **Phuket Gibbon Rehabilitation Centre** (☎ 381065, (01) 212-7824) is open to the public daily 10 am to 4 pm. Financed by donations, the centre adopts gibbons which have been kept in captivity and re-introduces them to the wild.

To get to Khao Phra Taew from the provincial capital, take Thepkasatri Rd north about 20km to the district of Thalang, and turn right at the intersection for Ton Sai Falls 3km down the road.

Also in Thalang district, just north of the crossroads near Thalang village, is **Wat Phra Thong**, Phuket's 'Temple of the Gold Buddha'. The image is half buried – those who have tried to excavate it have met with unfortunate consequences. Parts of the movie *Good Morning Vietnam* were filmed in Thalang.

Other Beaches & Islands

South-east of the capital on **Laem Phanwa** is the very plush *Cape Panwa Hotel* (☎ 391-123; fax 391177, Bangkok ☎ (2) 233-3433), where luxury digs start at 3500B, about half that from April to November.

On **Ko Hae**, an island a few kilometres south-west of Ao Chalong, the *Coral Island Resort* (☎ 281060; fax 381957) has up-market bungalows from 2300B with air-con.

Ko Hae is also referred to as Coral Island. It's a good spot for diving and snorkelling if you don't plan on going further a-sea.

Two islands about 1½ hours by boat south of Phuket, **Ko Raya Yai** and **Ko Raya Noi** (also known as Ko Racha Yai/Noi), are highly favoured by divers and snorkellers for their hard coral reefs. Because the coral is found in both shallow and deep waters, it's a good area for novice scuba divers and snorkellers as well as accomplished divers. Visibility can reach 15 to 30m. On Ko Raya Yai, accommodation is available at *Jungle Bungalow* (☎ 228550) or *Raya Resort* (☎ 327 803), starting at 400B for simple palm-thatch bungalows, and at *Raya Andaman Resort* (☎ 381710; fax 381713) from 900B for air-con digs.

For information on attractions and accommodation on the island of Ko Yao Noi and Ko Yao Yai, off Phuket's north-eastern shore, see the Around Phang-Nga section earlier in this chapter.

Getting There & Away Boats leave Ao Chalong for Ko Hae once daily at 9.30 am, take 30 minutes and cost 50B. Songserm Travel (☎ 222570) runs passenger boats to Ko Raya Yai from Phuket town port on Monday, Wednesday, Friday and Sunday at 8.30 am. The trip takes 1¼ hours and costs 300B one way or 550B return. Pal Travel Service (☎ 344920) runs a similar service on a daily basis. You can also charter a long-tail boat from Rawai or from Ao Chalong for 1500B.

Southern Andaman Coast (Krabi to Satun)

Southern Andaman Coast Highlights

BANGKOK

- Rock climbing – Krabi Province's world-class sites have become a mecca for the high-quality pocketed limestone surfaces and overhangs

- Wat Tham Seua – monastic cells are built into the cliffs and caves at this beautiful forest wat near Krabi town

- Beaches – stunning stretches of sand with magnificent scenery, coves and inlets at popular Ko Phi Phi as well as the less touristed Trang and Satun provinces and Ko Lanta archipelago

- Ko Tarutao National Marine Park – remote and virtually uninhabited, this park is one of the most pristine coastal areas in the country

South-east of Phuket, the southern reach of island-studded Ao Phang-Nga opens into the Andaman Sea, and Thailand's densest concentration of national marine parks begins to unfold, one after another all the way to the Malaysian border. The coastal provinces of Krabi, Trang and Satun represent the country's new frontier in terms of marine tourism; aside from intensive developments on Ko Phi Phi and along one small area of the mainland coast near Krabi's provincial capital, most of this stretch remains relatively undiscovered by international visitors.

Krabi Province

The coastal province of Krabi, 60km due east of Phuket, continues the scenic marine karst topography typical of Ao Phang-Nga. More than 200 islands offer excellent recreational opportunities; many of the islands belong to **Hat Noppharat Thara/Ko Phi Phi National Marine Park** or **Ko Lanta National Marine Park**. Many of Krabi's beaches feature shimmering stretches of sand lapped by calm, clear seas and backed by vine-choked limestone cliffs. Such cliffs have turned into a world-class rock-climbing mecca, and good reef diving is available at several offshore islets in the vicinity. Intact mangrove forests can be seen in several estuarial areas. Krabi is also a jumping off point for Ko Phi Phi, Ko Lanta and other islands in the area.

Hundreds of years ago, Krabi's waters were a favourite hideout for Asian pirates because of the abundance of islands and water caves. Latter-day pirates now steal islands or parts of islands for development: targets thus far include Phi Phi Don, Poda, Bubu, Jam (Pu), Po, Bilek (Hong), Kamyai and Kluang.

Beach accommodation is relatively inexpensive, but it is getting less so as more upscale places nudge out the cheapie bungalow outfits. From December to March, the hotels and bungalows along Krabi's beaches can fill up. The beaches of Krabi are nearly deserted in the rainy season, a good time to go if you're seeking solitude or low rates.

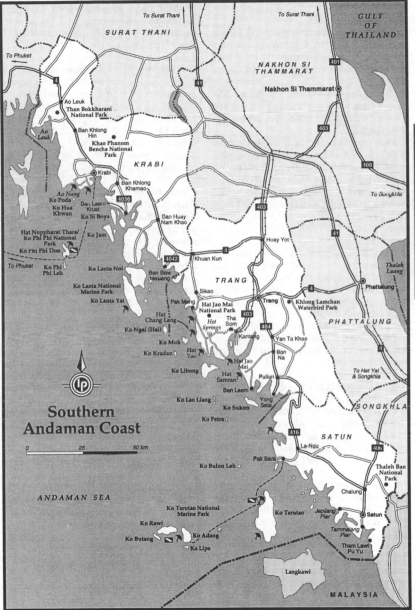

Southern Andaman Coast

KRABI (Capital)
• ☎ (75) • *pop 18,000*
Nearly 1000km from Bangkok and 180km from Phuket, this fast-developing provincial capital has friendly townspeople, good food and some good beaches nearby. The capital sits on the banks of the Krabi River right before it empties into the Andaman Sea. Across from town you can see Bird, Cat and Mouse Islands, limestone isles named for their shapes.

Most travellers breeze through town on their way to Ko Lanta to the south, Ko Phi Phi to the south-west or the beaches near Ao Nang to the west. But Krabi, with its pleasant riverside setting and good selection of restaurants, is also not a bad place to kick back for a day or two.

Information
Maps The *Guide Map of Krabi* put out by V Hongsombud is excellent, with detailed maps of both Krabi Province and city, Ao Nang, Ko Phi Phi and Ko Lanta, including hotels, sights and topographical references. It's well worth the 50B, and can be found at travel agents and bookshops in Krabi. *Krabi Holiday Guide*, a locally produced pamphlet, is also informative, though somewhat biased towards advertisers.

Tourist Office There is a small tourist information hut in the northern part of town, right along the river about 250m north of the Reuan Phae restaurant. It has maps and same basic info on sights and accommodation in the area. The tourist police also have an office here.

Post & Communications The post and telephone office is on Utarakit Rd past the turn-off for the Jao Fah pier. Home Direct international phone service is available here daily, 7 am to midnight.

Travel Agencies Krabi has dozens of fly-by-night travel agencies that will book accommodation at beaches and islands as well as tour-bus and boat tickets. Use these places with caution: few travellers have given any of these places glowing reports. One place that offers good service, and has received positive reviews from other travellers, is Frank Tour (☎ 611110).

Bookshops Several places sell and exchange used books. By far the most impressive collection is at a narrow little shop on Jao Fah Rd, near the intersection with Issara Rd. Prices are a bit steep, especially if you don't have a book to trade in, but the wide selection is perfect if you plan to spend several days or weeks lazing on the beach and reading the day away.

Places to Stay – bottom end & middle
Guesthouses The cheapest places to stay in Krabi are the many guesthouses, which seem to be everywhere. Some stay around only a season or two, others seem fairly stable. The ones situated in the business district feature closet-like rooms above modern shop buildings, often with faulty plumbing – OK for one night before heading to a nearby beach or island but not great for long-term stays.

The small *Riverside Guest House* (☎ 612-536) on Kongkha Rd near the Jao Fah pier and Customs House has decent 70B and 100B rooms with shared facilities and a restaurant with good vegetarian food. Next door to the Riverside, *S&R Guest House* (☎ 611930) has similar rooms for 100B.

On Maharat Soi 4 *Swallow Guest House* (☎ 611645) is a popular place with fairly clean and comfortable rooms for 80B (no window) and 100B (with window).

On Maharat Soi 2 are several other places with the usual upstairs rooms and slow plumbing, including the *KL* (☎ 612511) with rooms for 80/100B a single/double with shared bath. Around the corner on Maharat Rd is the *Seaside*, of similar ilk.

Better than either of these are the large, fairly clean rooms with private bath at *Grand Tower Hotel* (☎ 612713), over Grand Travel Center on Utarakit Rd. Rates here are 230/270B for singles/doubles; despite its name it has none of the facilities of a hotel and is run like a guesthouse. There are also a few rooms

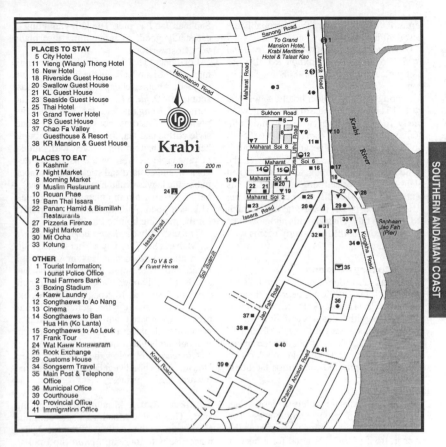

SOUTHERN ANDAMAN COAST

PLACES TO STAY
5 City Hotel
11 Vieng (Wiang) Thong Hotel
16 New Hotel
18 Riverside Guest House
20 Swallow Guest House
21 KL Guest House
23 Seaside Guest House
25 Thai Hotel
31 Grand Tower Hotel
32 PS Guest House
37 Chao Fa Valley
  Guesthouse & Resort
38 KR Mansion & Guest House

PLACES TO EAT
6 Kashmir
7 Night Market
8 Morning Market
9 Muslim Restaurant
10 Rouan Phae
19 Barn Thai Issara
22 Panan; Hamid & Bismillah
  Restaurants
27 Pizzeria Firenze
28 Night Market
30 Mit Ocha
33 Kotung

OTHER
1 Tourist Information;
  Tourist Police Office
2 Thai Farmers Bank
3 Boxing Stadium
4 Kaew Laundry
12 Songthaews to Ao Nang
13 Cinema
14 Songthaews to Ban
  Hua Hin (Ko Lanta)
15 Songthaews to Ao Leuk
17 Frank Tour
24 Wat Kaew Korawaram
26 Book Exchange
29 Customs House
34 Songserm Travel
35 Main Post & Telephone
  Office
36 Municipal Office
39 Courthouse
40 Provincial Office
41 Immigration Office

Krabi

with shared bath for 130/150B. Just down Utarakit Rd from here, *PS Guest House* has a few nicely maintained 80/100B rooms at the back of a travel agency.

Quieter and more comfortable are a few guesthouses in the southern part of town. On Jao Fah Rd the *Chao Fa Valley Guesthouse & Resort* (☎ 612499) has good-sized bamboo bungalows with fan for 150B. Next, on the same side of Jao Fah Rd, *KR Mansion & Guest House* (☎ 612761) offers 40 hotel-style rooms for 140B with fan and shared bath, 240B with private bath. The rooftop beer garden provides a 360 degree view of

Krabi – great for sunsets. The staff can arrange motorcycle rentals, local tours and boat tickets as well.

On the southern extension of Issara Rd, which is more or less parallel to Jao Fah Rd, the friendly *V&S Guest House* has a few rooms in an attractive old wooden house for 100B with shared bath.

Hotels The relatively new, well run *Grand Mansion Hotel* (☎ 611371; fax 611372) at 289/1 Utarakit Rd offers 58 comfortable, very clean fan-cooled rooms with hot-water shower for 300B, with air-con 480B. In terms of value for money, this is probably the best deal in town.

Closer to the centre of town, the *City Hotel* (☎ 611961) at 15/2-3 Sukhon Rd also has pretty clean rooms at 250/480B for fan/air-con.

Among the town's older hotels, *New Hotel* (☎ 611541) on Maharat Soi 6 has somewhat seedy rooms for 150B with fan and bath, 400B with air-con. The *Thai Hotel* (☎ 620560) on Issara Rd used to be good value, but it continues to raise the rates and lower the standards (stained carpets, cigarette-burned blankets). Overpriced single/double rooms with fan cost 300/330B, air-con 550B. *Vieng (Wiang) Thong* (☎ 611188/288) at 155 Utarakit Rd has also fallen in standards and now asks an outrageous 650B for mouldy rooms with stained carpets.

Places to Stay – top end
The swanky 221 room *Krabi Meritime Hotel* (☎ 620028; fax 612992) is near the river on the way to Talaat Kao. Rates for well decorated rooms with balconies and views of the river or mountains start at 1700/1900B single/double: not a bad deal considering the amenities, which include a swimming pool, nightclub, fitness centre and convention facilities.

Places to Eat
What Krabi lacks in hotels it more than makes up for in good eating places. The *Reuan Phae*, an old floating restaurant on the river in front of town, is good for a beer or rice whisky while watching the river rise and fall with the tide. Although the food at Reuan Phae is not amazing, certain dishes, including the fried shrimp cakes (thâwt man kûng) and spicy steamed curried fish (hàw mók tháleh), are well worth trying. Farther south down Utarakit Rd is a *night market* near the big pier (called Saphaan Jao Fah), with great seafood at low prices and a host of Thai dessert vendors. There's also another *night market* near the intersection of Maharat Rd and Maharat Soi 8.

One of the better and most reasonably priced restaurants in town for standard Thai dishes and local cuisine is the *Kotung* near

Saphaan Jao Fah pier. The tôm yam kûng is especially good, as is anything else made with fresh seafood.

For cheap Thai breakfasts, the morning market off Si Sawat Rd in the middle of town is good. Another cheap and tasty breakfast spot is *Mit Ocha*, a funky coffee shop on the corner of Kongkha and Jao Fah Rds, opposite the Customs house. Besides Thai-style coffee and tea, the old Chinese couple here serve khanŏm jiin (served with chunks of pineapple as well as the usual assorted vegies), and custard and sticky rice wrapped in banana leaves (khâo nĭaw sãngkha-yaa) – help yourself from the plates on the tables. This is a good place to hang out if waiting for the morning boat to Phi Phi.

The tastefully decorated *Barn Thai Issara* on Maharat Soi 2, run by a Thai man and his Australian wife, specialises in sourdough bread and wholesome western pastas and salads. It's only open 9 am to late afternoon. *Pizzeria Firenze* at 10 Kongkha Rd does excellent pizza, pasta, wine, gelati and Italian breads. Compared with Thai restaurants, prices at both places may be a bit higher, but you definitely get your money's worth.

Thammachart, below the Riverside Guest House, serves good vegetarian food oriented towards farang palates.

Southern Thai & Muslim Places serving spicy Thai-Malay Muslim cuisine continue to multiply as the earnings of the local populace rise with tourism. *Panan* (no English sign), on the corner of Maharat Soi 2 and Maharat Rd, has khâo mòk kài (chicken biryani) in the mornings, inexpensive curries and kũaytĭaw the rest of day. The roman-script sign reads 'Makanan Islam' (Malay for 'Muslim Food'). Next door are two other decent Muslim places, *Bismillah* and *Hamid*, signed in Thai/Yawi only.

Not far from the morning market, on Preusa Uthit Rd, the *Muslim Restaurant* serves roti kaeng, the Malaysian-style breakfast of flat bread and curry. Look for a sign that says 'Hot Roti Curry Service'. They have other Thai-Malay dishes as well. *Kashmir Restaurant*, nearby at the office of Waterfall

Resort, serves good Muslim food and caters to tourists as well as locals; in the morning the restaurant serves western breakfasts as well as roti kaeng.

Getting There & Away
Air When construction of the airport is complete, Bangkok Airways will operate regular flights to Krabi from Bangkok.

Bus, Share Taxi & Mini-van Government buses to/from Bangkok cost 193B ordinary, 368 to 377B air-con or 440B VIP (540B for super VIP – 24 seats). Air-con buses leave Bangkok's Southern bus terminal between 6 and 8 pm; in the reverse direction they leave Krabi between 4 and 5 pm.

Buses to/from Phuket leave hourly during daylight hours, cost 46B (85B with air-con) and take three to four hours. Share taxis to/from Phuket cost 70B; air-con mini-vans cost 170B.

Buses for Krabi leave Phang-Nga hourly throughout the day for 25B ordinary, 43B air-con. Most of these buses originate in Phuket and have Trang as their final destination.

Ordinary buses between Surat Thani and Krabi make the 4½ hour trip 13 times daily between 5 am and 2.30 pm for 60B. Air-con buses depart three times a day between 7 am and 3.30 pm for 150B and take around 3½ hours. Through various agencies in town you can pay 140 to 150B for a private air-con bus to Surat or 150B for an air-con mini-van. These agencies also arrange mini-vans to Hat Yai (150B) and Phuket (170B).

Government buses to/from Hat Yai cost 78B (127B air-con) and take five hours; departures are fairly frequent between 9 am and 3 pm. Buses to/from Trang cost 36B (66B air-con), take 2½ hours and leave hourly between 6 am and 4 pm. There are also share taxis running to/from Trang, Hat Yai and Satun; fares are roughly twice the ordinary bus fare.

Out-of-province buses to/from Krabi arrive at and depart from Talaat Kao, a junction about 4km north of Krabi on the highway between Phang-Nga and Trang. To get to the centre of Krabi, catch a songthaew for 5B or motorcycle taxi for 10B. Private air-con buses leave from Songserm Travel on Kongkha Rd.

Boat Krabi can be reached by sea from Ko Phi Phi and Ko Lanta. See the Ko Phi Phi and Ko Lanta sections further on in this chapter for details.

Getting Around
Any place in town can easily be reached on foot, but if you plan to do a lot of exploring out of town, renting a motorcycle might be a good idea. Several travel agencies and guesthouses can arrange motorcycle rentals for 200B to 250B a day, with discounts for multi-day rentals. Jeep rentals range from 800B (open-top) to 1200B (air-con) per day.

Songthaews to Ao Nang (20B) leave from near the intersection of Preusa Uthit Rd and Maharat Soi 6. They leave about every 15 minutes from 7 am to 6 pm during the high season (December to March), till 4 or 4.30 pm the remainder of the year. You might want to try catching one in front of the GPO: by this time they've usually finished their cruise through town to pick up passengers and are ready to roll (though you may not get a seat).

Songthaews to Ban Hua Hin (for Ko Lanta) also leave from Maharat Soi 6, with a second stop in Talaat Kao, for 30B. They leave about every half hour from 10 am to 2 pm and take 40 minutes to reach Ban Hua Hin. There are also more expensive air-con mini-vans available from Krabi travel agencies.

Boats to the islands and beaches mostly leave from Jao Fah pier. See the Ao Nang & Vicinity Getting There & Away section for boat details.

AROUND KRABI
You can hire boats at Saphaan Jao Fah pier for 100 to 200B per hour for a look at **mangrove swamps** just across the river. Two bird species that frequent mangrove areas include the sea eagle and ruddy kingfisher. In mud and shallow waters, keep an eye out for fiddler crabs and mudskippers.

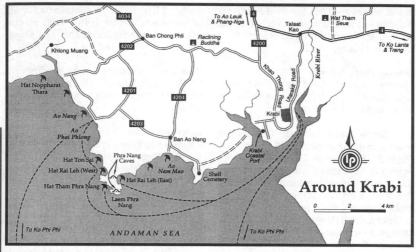

Around Krabi

0   2   4 km

ANDAMAN SEA

SOUTHERN ANDAMAN COAST

Wat Tham Seua

In the other direction, about 5km north and 2km east of town, is Wat Tham Seua (Tiger Cave Temple), one of southern Thailand's most famous forest wats. The main *wihãan* is built into a long, shallow limestone cave, on either side of which dozens of *kutis* (monastic cells) are built into the cliffs and caves.

The best part of the temple grounds is in a little valley behind the ridge where the *bòt* is. Follow the path past the main wat buildings, through a little village with nuns' quarters, until you come to some steep stairways on the left. The first leads to an arduous 30 minute climb to the top of a karst hill with a good view of the area.

The second stairway, next to a large statue of Kuan Yin (the Chinese goddess of mercy), leads over a gap in the ridge and into a valley of tall trees and limestone caves. Enter the caves on your left and look for light switches on the walls – the network of caves is wired so that you can light your way chamber by chamber through the labyrinth until you rejoin the path on the other side. There are several kutis in and around the caves, and it's interesting to see the differences in interior decorating – some are very spartan and

others are outfitted like oriental bachelor pads.

A path winds through a grove of trees surrounded by tall limestone cliffs covered with a patchwork of foliage. If you continue to follow the path you'll eventually end up where you started, at the bottom of the staircase.

Getting There & Away To get to Wat Tham Seua, take a songthaew from Utarakit Rd to the Talaat Kao junction for 5B, then catch any bus or songthaew east on Route 4 towards Trang and Hat Yai and get off at the road on the left just after Km 108 – if you tell the bus operators 'Wat Tham Seua', they'll let you off at the right place. It's a 2km walk straight up this road to the wat.

In the mornings there are a few songthaews from Maharat Soi 6 in town that pass the turn-off for Wat Tham Seua (10B) on their way to Ban Hua Hin. Also in the morning there is usually a songthaew or two going direct to Wat Tham Seua from Talaat Kao for around 6B.

Hat Nopparat Thara

Eighteen kilometres north-west of Krabi,

this beach used to be called Hat Khlong Haeng (Dry Canal beach) because the canal that flows into the Andaman Sea here is dry except during, and just after, the monsoon season. Field Marshal Sarit gave the beach its current Pali-Sanskrit name, which means 'Beach of the Nine-Gemmed Stream', as a tribute to its beauty. A couple of years ago the Thai navy cleared the forest backing the beach to make way for a new royal residence that is yet to be constructed.

The 2km-long beach, part of Hat Noppharat Thara/Ko Phi Phi National Marine Park, is a favourite spot for Thai picnickers. There are some government bungalows for rent and a visitor centre of sorts, with wall maps of the marine park.

Places to Stay *Government bungalows* at the park headquarters are 450 to 900B; they're quite OK, though on weekends the beach and visitor centre is thronged with local visitors. The park pier at the eastern end of Noppharat Thara has boats across the canal to Hat Khlong Muang, where the *Andaman Inn* (☎ 612728) has small huts with shared facilities for 50B, small huts with attached bath for 150B and larger huts with attached bath for 350B. Huts are well spaced and the grounds are well maintained. Down the beach are the similar but even more secluded *Emerald Bungalows* (150B shared bath, 350 to 500B attached bath), *Bamboo Bungalows* (100B with attached bath) and *Sara Cove* (300B with attached bath).

Long-tail boats ferry passengers across Khlong Muang from Hat Noppharat Thara to the Andaman Inn for free.

Getting There & Away Hat Noppharat Thara can be reached by songthaews that leave about every 15 minutes from 7 am to 6 pm (high season) or 4 pm (low season) from Maharat Soi 6 in Krabi town.

Ao Nang & Vicinity
South of Noppharat Thara is a series of bays where limestone cliffs and caves drop right into the sea. The water is quite clear and there are some coral reefs in the shallows. The longest beach runs along Ao Nang, a spot easily reached by road from Krabi. As a result this is the most developed beach in the area, and thus not as attractive as those at Hat Rai Leh, for example. But Ao Nang boasts the widest range of accommodation and restaurant options, and is not a bad base from which to explore the nearby beaches and islands.

Over the headlands to the south are the beaches of **Phai Phlong, Ton Sai** and **Rai Leh**, and then the cape of Laem Phra Nang, which encompasses **Hat Tham Phra Nang** (Princess Cave beach) on the western side, a beach facing east usually called **East Rai Leh** and another beach called **Hat Nam Mao**.

All these beaches are accessible either by hiking over the headland cliffs or by taking a boat from Ao Nang or Krabi.

Hat Tham Phra Nang This is perhaps the most beautiful beach in the area. At one end is a tall limestone cliff that contains **Tham Phra Nang Nok** (Outer Princess Cave), a cave that is said to be the home of a mythical sea princess. Local fisherfolk place carved wooden phalli in the cave as offerings to the princess so that she will provide plenty of fish for them. Inside the cliff is a hidden 'lagoon' called **Sa Phra Nang** (Princess Pool) that can be reached by following a cave trail into the side of the mountain. A rope guides hikers along the way and it takes about 45 minutes to reach the pool – guides are available from local guesthouses. If you turn left off the trail after 50m from the start, you can reach a 'window' in the cliff that affords a view of Rai Leh West and East beaches. It's also possible to climb to the top of the mountain from here (some rock climbing is involved) and get an aerial view of the entire cape and the islands of **Ko Poda** and **Ko Hua Khwan** (also known as Chicken Island) in the distance.

A second, larger cave on Laem Phra Nang was discovered only a few years ago. The entrance is in the middle of the peninsula near a batch of beach huts on East Rai Leh. This one is called **Tham Phra Nang Nai** (Inner Princess Cave) and consists of three caverns. All three contain some of the most beautiful limestone formations in the country, including a golden 'stone waterfall' of sparkling quartz. Local mythology now says that this cave is the 'grand palace' of the sea princess while Tham Phra Nang on the beach is her 'summer palace'. The cliffs around Hat Tham Phra Nang have become an internationally known destination for rock climbers and it's easy to arrange equipment, maps and/or instruction from beach bungalows on Hat Rai Leh.

The islands off Laem Phra Nang are good areas for snorkelling. Besides Ko Poda and Ko Hua Khwan there is the nearer island of **Ko Rang Nok** (Bird Nest Island) and, next to that, a larger, unnamed island (possibly part of the same island at low tide) with an undersea cave. Some of the bungalows do reasonably priced day trips to these as well as other islands in the area.

Rock Climbing Limestone cliffs on the huge headland between Hat Tham Phra Nang and Hat Rai Leh (East), and on nearby islands, offer practically endless rock-climbing opportunities. Most surfaces provide high-quality limestone with steep, pocketed walls, overhangs and the occasional hanging stalactite. Over 150 routes have been identified by zealous climbers, most in the mid to high difficulty level (grades 16 to 25). They bear names like Lord of the Thais, The King and I, Andaman Wall, One-Two-Three, Sleeping Indian Cliffs and Thaiwan Wall. Novices often begin with Muay Thai, a 50m wall with around 20 climbs in the 17 to 21 grade range at the south end of East Rai Leh. Certain areas are off limits because they're part of Hat Noppharat Thara/Ko Phi Phi National Marine Park, including the cliff next to the Dusit Resort.

Virtually any of the lodgings in this area can arrange guided climbs and/or rock-climbing instruction. A half-day climb with instruction and guidance generally costs around 400B, while an all-day is 700B, three days 2000B; all equipment is included. Equipment rental rates for a two person lead set are around 500B for a half-day, 800B for a full day. Tex Rock Climbing at Railay Bay

Bungalows and Phra Nang Rock Climbers near the Viewpoint Resort are the best equipped of the local outfits.

Diving & Snorkelling Baby Shark Divers at Railay Village, Phra Nang Diving School at Viewpoint Resort and Seafan's Divers next to Phranang Inn on Ao Nang beach do dive trips. Going rates are 1000 to 1800B for a day trip to nearby islands, while three to four-day certification courses cost 7200B. The most convenient local dive spots are Ko Poda Nai and Ko Poda Nawk. At nearby Ko Mae Urai, a kilometre west of Poda Nawk, two submarine tunnels lined with soft and hard corals offer lots of tropical fish and are suitable for all levels of divers. Another fairly interesting dive site is the sunken boat just south of Ko Rang Nok, a favoured fish habitat. Fun three-day snorkelling/camping trips – sometimes led by *chao náam* (sea gypsies) – can be arranged for 1000 to 1500B per person.

Sea Kayaking Touring the coast, islands and semi-submerged caves by inflatable canoe or kayak can be arranged through Sea Canoe Thailand (637170) near the Sea Breeze bungalows at Ao Nang or Sea Kayak Krabi (☎ 637359, Bangkok (2) 377086), also at Ao Nang. One of the best local paddles is the 'canyon river cruise', an estuary trip that cuts through 200m foliaged limestone cliffs, mangrove channels and tours through tidal lagoon tunnels (euphemistically called 'hongs', from the Thai word for 'room'). Sea Canoe Thailand generally charges 700B for half-day trips, 1200 for full-day excursions.

Places to Stay & Eat A large and growing number of bungalows and inns can be found along Ao Nang and nearby beaches. Most of the cheap places are being edged out, but there are still a few to be found in the 100 to 200B range. Also, when picking a place, scan around for an open-air bars in the area: these often go rather late and sound carries pretty easily: light sleepers take heed.

Ao Nang Because it's easily accessible by road, this beach has become fairly developed of late. The more expensive places usually have booking offices in Krabi town. The oldest resort in the area, *Krabi Resort* (☎ 612-160, Bangkok (2) 208-9165), at the northern end of Ao Nang, has luxury bungalows that cost 2367 to 5476B on the beach, 1415B away from the beach and 2047B in the new hotel wing. Most of the guests are with package tours or conferences. There are the usual resort amenities, including a swimming pool, bar and restaurant. Bookings can be made at the Krabi Resort office on Phattana Rd in Krabi and guests get free transport out to the resort.

Off Route 4203, on the road leading to the beach's north end, *Beach Terrace* (☎ 637180; fax 637184) has modern bungalows for 1340B with air-con, hot water, TV, fridge and complimentary breakfast. The *Ao Nang Ban Lae* (☎ 637078) next door has a cluster of simple but well maintained bungalows for 250B. On the opposite side of the road, *Ban Ao Nang* (☎ 637071) is a modern hotel with rooms for 850 to 1980B.

Down on the beach heading south you'll come to *Ao Nang Beach Bungalow, Wanna's Place* and *Sea Breeze*, all 100 to 200B for fairly simple huts. Wanna's Place, which seems

the best run of the lot, also offers air-con bungalows for 850B. Just a little farther down the road, *Gift's* (☎ 637166) has larger huts with bath for 350B. Next along the beach an obtrusive shopping centre called Ao Nang Tourist Centre is currently under construction.

The beach road intersects Route 4203 to Krabi just before you arrive at *Phranang Inn* (☎ 637130; fax 637134), a tastefully designed 'tropical hotel' with sweeping views of the bay and a small pool. Large air-con rooms start at 1776B a night in the high season (usually December to February), 1300B the remainder of the year. It has a good restaurant. A second, similarly designed annex recently opened across the road.

Next door is *Ao Nang Villa* (☎ 637270), with 90 upgraded cottages with all the amenities for 750 to 4500B. Right around the corner on Route 4203, the newer *Ao Nang Royal Resort* (☎ 637118) has decent bungalows for 700B with fan and private bath, up to 1200B with air-con.

Up Route 4203, 100 or so metres from the beach, is the small *BB Bungalow* (☎ 637147) with simple fan-equipped bungalows for 400B and air-con hotel accommodation for

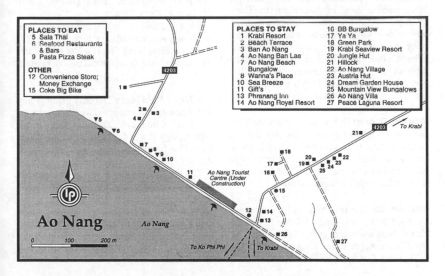

PLACES TO EAT
5 Sala Thai
6 Seafood Restaurants & Bars
9 Pasta Pizza Steak

OTHER
12 Convenience Store; Money Exchange
15 Coke Big Bike

PLACES TO STAY	
1 Krabi Resort	16 BB Bungalow
2 Beach Terrace	17 Ya Ya
3 Ban Ao Nang	18 Green Park
4 Ao Nang Ban Lae	19 Krabi Seaview Resort
7 Ao Nang Beach Bungalow	20 Jungle Hut
	21 Hillock
8 Wanna's Place	22 Ao Nang Village
10 Sea Breeze	23 Austria Hut
11 Gift's	24 Dream Garden House
13 Phranang Inn	25 Mountain View Bungalows
14 Ao Nang Royal Resort	26 Ao Nang Villa
	27 Peace Laguna Resort

Ao Nang

Ao Nang

To Ko Phi Phi To Krabi

1200B. *Ya Ya* (☎ 637176) next door (not to be confused with Ya Ya on East Hat Rai Leh) also charges 400B for its basic huts. Farther up the road, about 200m from the beach, the *Green Park* (☎ 637300) is one of the better cheapies with fairly well maintained huts for 100B with shared bath, 150B with attached bath – as low as 50B in the low season. Moving farther away from the beach, along Route 4203 is a string of bungalow operations:

Ao Nang Village – ☎ (637109); plain but serviceable huts for 100 to 200B
Austria Hut – more up-market rooms for 600 to 1000B
Dream Garden House – (☎ 637338); fairly upscale rooms from 600B
Hillock – motel-style rooms for 100B
Jungle Hut – (☎ 637301); rickety huts for 60/80B with shared bath, more solid ones with private bath for 150B
Krabi Seaview Resort – (☎ 637242); modern A-frames for 500/980B fan/air-con
Mountain View Bungalows – small huts for 150/250B, larger ones for 350B
Peace Laguna Resort – (☎ 637345); new fan huts 450B, air-con from 600B

At the north end of the beach, past where Route 4203 turns inland, is a short string of thatched-roof bars and restaurants. *Sala Thai* has earned a good reputation for its Thai-style seafood, while *Khon Thai* is a popular bar, no doubt in part due to its lengthy happy hour (5 pm to 10 pm). Squeezed in between Wanna's Place and Sea Breeze is a little place with no name, just a sign saying *'Pasta Pizza Steak'*: the chef worked with Italian cooks for 10 years and the food is excellent.

Ao Phai Phlong This peaceful, palm-studded cove is worth boating to for the day. At the moment there is no accommodation here. A few years back a hotel conglomerate was rumoured to have purchased land but so far there are no signs of construction.

Hat Ton Sai This beach can only be reached by boat from Ao Nang, Ao Nam Mao or Krabi. New management has taken over *Ton Sai Huts* here, providing accommodation for 80B (shared bath) to 350B (private bath).

Hat Rai Leh (West) At the centre of this pretty bay, *Railay Bay Bungalows* (☎ (01) 722-0112) packs in nearly a hundred huts right across the peninsula to East Hat Rai Leh. Rates range from 500 to 1000B depending on the size of the hut, number of beds and whether it has air-conditioning; rates can be negotiated down in the off season. Railay Bay Bungalows also has some tattered bungalows on the East Hat Rai Leh side, but you'll have to ask about these: staff won't volunteer any information on them.

The *Sand Sea* (☎ (01) 722-0114) next door features two rows of cottages facing each other, some thatched, some with plaster walls, for 580 to 800B for standard and 'deluxe' fan-equipped bungalows. Air-con will cost you 1400B, though all these rates should be lower in the off season. The similar *Railay Village* (☎ (01) 228-4366) has small cottages with glass fronts in two facing rows for about 600B (fan) and 1200B (air-con). All three have pleasant dining areas.

At the northern end of the beach is a private home development where it's possible to rent vacant beach homes from the caretakers for 400 to 4500B a night. Contact the caretakers at the site or phone/fax directly to ☎ (01) 464-4338; or write to Dick Balsamo, PO Box 8, Krabi 81000.

West Rai Leh can be reached by boat from Ao Nang, Ao Nam Mao or Krabi, or on foot from Hat Phra Nang and Hat Rai Leh (East) (but these must be approached by boat as well).

Hat Tham Phra Nang The only place to stay at this beautiful beach is the *Dusit Rayavadee* (☎ 620740, Bangkok (2) 238-0032), a tastefully designed and fairly unobtrusive resort with 179 luxurious rooms in cement-and-stucco or wooden cottages starting at 8000B.

The beach is not Dusit's exclusive domain – a wooden walkway has been left around the perimeter of the limestone bluff so that you can walk to Hat Tham Phra Nang from East Rai Leh. From West Rai Leh a footpath leads through the forest around to the beach.

Hat Tham Phra Nang is accessible by boat or foot only.

Hat Rai Leh (East) The beach along here tends towards mudflats during low tide, while the north-east end of the bay is vegetated with mangrove; most people who stay here walk over to Hat Tham Phra Nang or Hat Rai Leh (West) for beach activities.

Railay Bay Bungalows has another entrance on this side (see Hat Rai Leh (West)). *Ya-Ya* has some interesting bungalow designs, including some treehouse-style huts, though some of the rooms are fairly rustic. Rates range from 350B to 450B. The really cheap looking thatched towers are reserved for staff, but you may be able to get in there during the low season. Right next door, the newly opened *Sunrise Bay Bungalows* (☎ (01) 722-0236) has fairly solid looking cottages for 250 to 450B.

Coco Bungalows (☎ 612730), farther north-east towards the mangrove area, is set back from the shore and offers simple, quiet bungalows for 150B, and one of the better restaurants in the area.

A bit farther, near the Phra Nang Nai caves, the *Diamond Cave Bungalows* (☎ (01) 477-0933) enjoys a beautiful setting and has simple thatch bungalows for 200 to 250B and nicely done cottages for 400B; the latter seem the better deal for the money.

On a hill overlooking Rai Leh East and the mangrove, *Viewpoint Resort* (☎ (01) 722-0115) offers clean, well maintained two storey cottages for 400 to 500B, negotiable in the off season. Phra Nang Diving School, headquartered at Viewpoint, offers reasonable dive courses and excursions.

Ao Nam Mao This large bay, around a headland to the north-east of East Rai Leh about 1.5km from the Shell Cemetery, has a coastal environment similar to that of East Rai Leh – mangroves and shallow, muddy beaches.

Here you will find the environmentally friendly *Dawn of Happiness Beach Resort* (☎ 612730; fax 612251), where natural, locally sourced building materials are used wherever possible and no sewage or rubbish ends up in the bay. Thatched bungalows with private bath and mosquito nets cost 350 to 500B per night depending on the season. The

staff can arrange trips to nearby natural attractions.

Ao Nam Mao is accessible by road via Route 4204. If you phone from Krabi, the Dawn of Happiness will arrange free transport.

Getting There & Away Ao Nang can be reached by songthaews that leave about every 15 minutes from 7 am to 6 pm (high season) or 4 pm (low season) from Maharat Soi 6 Krabi town. The fare is 20B and the trip takes 30 to 40 minutes.

You can get boats to Ton Sai, West Rai Leh and Laem Phra Nang at several places. For Ton Sai, the best thing to do is get a songthaew out to Ao Nang, then a boat from Ao Nang to Ton Sai. It's 20B per person for two people or more, 40B if you don't want to wait for a second passenger to show up. You may have to bargain to get this fare. Boats also go between Ao Nang and Ko Phi Phi for 150B, October to April only.

For West Rai Leh or anywhere on Laem Phra Nang, you can get a boat direct from Krabi's Jao Fah pier for 40B. It takes about 45 minutes to reach Phra Nang. However, boats will only go all the way round the cape to West Rai Leh and Hat Phra Nang from October to April when the sea is tame enough. During the other half of the year they only go as far as East Rai Leh, but you can easily walk from here to West Rai Leh or Hat Phra Nang. You can also get boats from Ao Nang for 20B all year round, but in this case they only go as far as West Rai Leh and Hat Phra Nang (again, you can walk to East Rai Leh from here). From Ao Nang you'll have to pay 20B per person for two or more passengers, 40B for one.

Than Bokkharani National Park

In the Ao Leuk area in northern Krabi Province, Than Bokkharani National Park was established in 1991 and encompasses nine parks (as well as the former botanical gardens for which the park was named).

The park is best visited just after the monsoons – when it has been dry a long time the water level goes down. In the midst of the rains it can be a bit murky. In December Than Bokkharani looks like something cooked up by Walt Disney, but it's real and entirely natural. Emerald-green waters flow out of a narrow cave in a tall cliff and into a large lotus pool, which overflows steadily into a wide stream, itself dividing into many smaller streams in several stages. At each stage there's a pool and a little waterfall. Tall trees spread over 40 rai (6.4 sq km) provide plenty of cool shade. Thais from Ao Leuk come to bathe here on weekends and at that time it's full of laughing people playing in the streams and pools. During the week there are only a few people about, mostly kids doing a little fishing. Vendors sell noodles, roast chicken, delicious batter-fried squid and *sôm-tam* under a roofed area to one side. *Ao Leuk Bungalow*, on the highway half a kilometre before Than Bok, offers decent if overpriced cottages for 200B with private bath; you may be able to bargain for a lower rate if there are empty rooms. In nearby Ao Leuk Tai, the wooden *Thai Wiwat Hotel* next to the district office has plain rooms for 100B.

Than Bok, as the locals call it, is off Route 4 between Krabi and Phang-Nga, near the town of Ao Leuk, 1km south-west towards Laem Sak. To get there, take a songthaew from the intersection of Maharat Soi 6 and Preusa Uthit Rds in Krabi to Ao Leuk for 20B; get off just before town and it's an easy walk to the park entrance on the left.

Alternatively you may be able to arrange transport through one of the travel agencies in Krabi. Frank Tour runs day trips up to the **mangrove swamps** around Phang-Nga that also take in a visit to Than Bokkharani on the way back. The tours kick off at 8.15 am and cost 450B per person. You'll need to book one day in advance, and probably need several people in your group to make it feasible.

KO PHI PHI

Ko Phi Phi consists of two islands situated about 40km from Krabi, Phi Phi Leh and Phi Phi Don. Both are part of Hat Noppharat Thara/Ko Phi Phi National Marine Park, though this means little in the face of the rabid development that has taken place on Phi Phi Don.

Only parts of Phi Phi Don are actually under the administration of the National Parks Division of the Royal Thai Forestry Department. Phi Phi Leh and the western cliffs of Phi Phi Don are left to the nest collectors, and the parts of Phi Phi Don where the *chao náam* (sea gypsy) live are also not included in the park.

After Phuket this is probably the most popular tourist destination along the Andaman Coast, especially during the peak months from December to March, when hordes descend on the island and snatch up every room and bungalow on Phi Phi Don. Even so, the island still retains some of its original beauty, though to truly appreciate it usually means a fair hike to escape the crowds.

Ko Phi Phi Don

Phi Phi Don is the larger of the two islands, a sort of dumbbell-shaped island with scenic hills, awesome cliffs, long beaches, emerald waters and remarkable bird and sea life. The 'handle' in the middle has long, white-sand beaches on either side, only a few hundred metres apart. The beach on the southern side curves around **Ao Ton Sai**, where boats from Phuket and Krabi dock. There is also a Thai-Muslim village here. On the northern side of the handle is **Ao Lo Dalam**.

The uninhabited (except for beach huts) western section of the island is called Ko Nawk (Outer Island), and the eastern section, which is much larger, is Ko Nai (Inner Island). At the north of the eastern end is Laem Tong, where the island's chao náam population lives. The number of chao náam living here varies from time to time, as they are still a somewhat nomadic people, sailing from island to island, stopping off to repair their boats or fishing nets, but there are generally about 100. With stones tied to their waists as ballast, chao náam divers can reportedly descend up to 60m while breathing through an air hose held above the water surface. Like Pacific islanders of around 100 years ago, they tend to be very warm and friendly horizon-gazers.

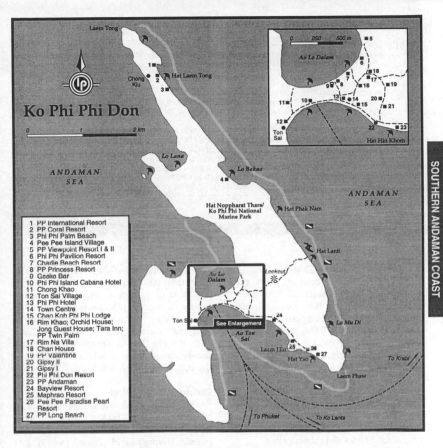

Ko Phi Phi Don

1 PP International Resort
2 PP Coral Resort
3 Phi Phi Palm Beach
4 Pee Pee Island Village
5 PP Viewpoint Resort I & II
6 Phi Phi Pavilion Resort
7 Charlie Beach Resort
8 PP Princess Resort
9 Gecko Bar
10 Phi Phi Island Cabana Hotel
11 Chong Khao
12 Ton Sai Village
13 Phi Phi Hotel
14 Town Centre
15 Chao Koh Phi Phi Lodge
16 Rim Khao; Orchid House;
   Jong Guest House; Tara Inn;
   PP Twin Palm
17 Rim Na Villa
18 Chan House
19 PP Valentine
20 Gipsy II
21 Gipsy I
22 Phi Phi Don Resort
23 PP Andaman
24 Bayview Resort
25 Maphrao Resort
26 Pee Pee Paradise Pearl
   Resort
27 PP Long Beach

Hat Yao (Long beach) faces south and has some of Phi Phi Don's best coral reefs. Ton Sai, Lo Dalam and Hat Yao all have beach bungalows. On the eastern coast of Phi Phi Don is another very beautiful beach, **Hat Lanti**, with good surf. For several years the locals wouldn't allow any bungalows to be built here out of respect for the large village mosque in a coconut grove above the beach – but money talked, and the chao náam walked. Farther north is the sizeable bay of **Lo Bakao**, where there is a small resort, and near the tip of Laem Tong are three luxury resorts.

Park administrators have allowed development on Phi Phi Don to continue unchecked, though it's doubtful they ever had the power or influence to stop the building, which finally seems to be slowing down. Beautiful Ao Ton Sai has become more of a boat basin than a beach, and more and more bungalows have been crowded onto this section of the island. For solitude and scenery, this place falls shorts. On the other hand, those travellers in search of a more lively social scene will be rewarded by a wide choice of restaurants, beachfront bars and up-market accommodation.

White Gold

On either side of the Thai-Malay peninsula – in Ao Phang-Nga, parts of the Andaman Sea near Phuket and the Gulf of Thailand near Chumphon – limestone caves and cliffs formed by marine karst topography (also known as 'drowned karst') are often home to swiftlets whose nests are a highly valued gourmet food item. These birds *(Collocalia esculenta)* like to build their nests high up in rocky hollows which can be very difficult to reach. Agile collectors build vine-and-bamboo scaffolding to get at the nests; the occasional misstep or loose grip can lead to serious injuries, even death, in precipitous falls. Before ascending the scaffolds, the collectors pray and make offerings of tobacco, incense and liquor to the cavern spirits.

Those who want to collect swiftlets nests must bid for a licence which gives them a franchise to harvest the nests for four years. In one year there are only three harvests, as the birds build seasonally, and the first harvest fetches the highest prices. The collectors sell the nests to intermediaries who then sell them to Chinese restaurants in Thailand and abroad. Known as 'white gold', premium teacup-sized nests sell for US$2000 per kilo – Hong Kong alone imports US$25 million worth every year.

The nests are actually made of saliva which the birds secrete – the saliva hardens when exposed to the air. When cooked in chicken broth, the nests soften and separate and look like bean thread noodles. The Chinese value the expensive bird secretions highly, believing them to be a medicinal food that imparts vigour. ■

Other parts of Phi Phi Don aren't as built-up, though the once-brilliant coral reefs around the island are suffering from anchor drag and runoff from large beach developments. The least disturbed parts of the island at present are those still belonging to the few chao náam who haven't cashed in.

Though development on Ko Phi Phi Don has slowed, there's still much room for improvement in terms of rubbish collection and waste disposal. Take a quick walk around the main town and bungalow area near Ton Sai: you can almost hear the island groaning under the weight of too many power generators, septic tanks and rubbish sites.

Money Near Ton Sai pier, Krung Thai Bank has an exchange booth open daily from 8.30 am to 3.30 pm. There's another booth farther on in the village, and many of the travel agents will also change money, though at predictably poor rates.

Phi Phi Leh

Phi Phi Leh is almost all sheer cliffs, with a few caves and a sea lake formed by a cleft between two cliffs that allows water to enter into a bowl-shaped canyon. The so-called **Viking Cave** contains prehistoric paintings of stylised human and animal figures along-side later paintings of ships (Asian junks) no more than 100 years old.

The cave is also a collection point for highly coveted swiftlet nests. No-one is allowed to stay on Phi Phi Leh because of the bird-nest business, but boats can be hired from Phi Phi Don for the short jaunt over to see the caves and to do a little snorkelling at the coral reefs in Ao Ma-Ya.

Diving & Snorkelling

Several places in Ton Sai village – around 20 at last count – can arrange diving and snorkelling trips around the island or to nearby islands. Diving near Phi Phi isn't world class but there are some good dives – at the islets of **Ko Bida Nai** and **Ko Bida Nok** just south of Ko Phi Phi Leh. Both are suitable for snorkelling as well as scuba diving, with coral at depths of 10 to 25m and visibility as great as 25m in good weather conditions. Although these islets can be dived all year round when the surf cooperates, conditions are usually best November to May.

The typical all day snorkelling trip includes lunch, water, fruit and equipment for 300B. Guided dive trips start at 700B for two dives. An open-water certification course costs around 7000B, a bit more expensive than elsewhere in Thailand, though generally cheaper than in Phuket. Mask, fins and snorkel can be rented for 50B a day.

Organised Tours & Boat Charters

From Ko Phi Phi Don, boats to Ko Phi Phi Leh can be chartered for 200B per trip. A half-day trip to Phi Phi Leh or Bamboo Island costs 500B, a full day 800B. Fishing trips average 1600B a day.

Places to Stay

During the high tourist months of December to February and July to August, nearly all accommodation on the island gets booked out. As elsewhere during these months, it's best to arrive early in the morning to stake out a room or bungalow. Latecomers sometimes wind up sleeping on the beach. At this time, prices are at their peak, but during the off season rooms free up and rates are negotiable.

Ao Ton Sai *Ton Sai Village* (☎ 612434; fax 612196) offers 30 very comfortable bungalows with air-con, hot water, TV and minibar for 1883B including breakfast; it's also a little removed from others on this beach so is a bit quieter. *Phi Phi Island Cabana Hotel* (☎ 620634; fax 612132), the oldest resort on the island, stretches across from Ton Sai across the Lo Dalam beach. Bungalows with fan start at 1200B while a standard room in the three storey hotel building are 2300 and up to 9300B for the Andaman Suite. Amenities include a swimming pool overlooking the beach surrounded by pseudo-Greek statues and a large fountain that looks like it's been brought in from Las Vegas.

Phi Phi Hotel (☎ (01) 712-0138; fax 611-233) has 64 rooms in a multistorey building off the beach near the pier. Rooms are 1800B with all the amenities but its proximity to the sometimes noisy pier, bars and restaurants is a minus.

Chong Khao is set inland with a path leading to both Lo Dalam and Ton Sai beaches. Fairly quiet rooms in a row house or bungalow range from 100 to 200B with shared facilities, 250B with attached bath. In the other direction, heading towards Hat Hin

Khom, *Chao Koh Phi Phi Lodge* (☎ 611313) consists of fairly basic but clean concrete bungalows with bath and fan for 300 to 500B, a bit off the beach.

Lo Dalam *PP Princess Resort* (☎/fax 620615) has large, well spaced upscale wooden bungalows with glass doors and windows for 1390 to 2990B. The bungalows feature nice deck areas and are connected by wooden walkways.

Charlie Beach Resort (☎ (01) 723-0495) has thatched-roof bungalows, a pleasant restaurant with amazingly lethargic service, and a beach bar in an atmospheric setting; there's live folk music at night. Rooms cost 350 to 750B, all with bath and fan, depending on size and position on the beach.

Phi Phi Pavilion Resort (☎ (75) 620633) is another thatched-roof place but in this case with air-con, most with sea views, from 900B.

Friendly *PP Viewpoint Resort I & II* (☎ (01) 722-0111) are situated on a hillside; No I overlooks Lo Dalam while No II doesn't have a bay view. Rates range from 450B for a room to 500 to 750B for a bungalow, depending on size and location. Monthly rentals for 4500B are also available. The bungalows are a bit rickety, but the ones with good views make a great spot for a sunset cocktail.

Just before the little bridge entrance to the Viewpoint, *Home Parklong Seasight* consists of five rooms in the home of a local entrepreneur for 550 to 750B a night, probably less in low season. Facilities are shared, so this is a bit pricey.

Hat Hin Khom This beach a little south-east of Ton Sai has become an alternate budget beach to Hat Yao, because it's not as crowded and the source of fresh water for showers is more constant. *Phi Phi Don Resort* (☎ (01) 722-0083) charges 500 to 800B for cement and stucco bungalows with tin roofs, all with fan and bath and 24 hour power. Many are right on the beachfront. *PP Andaman* has thatched huts – some in need of repair – for 200 to 250B, plus sturdier cement and stucco ones for 350B.

Bayview Resort (☎ (01) 723-1134) is an up-market place with modern-looking cottages geared to the Thai market, though plenty of farangs stay here as well. A cottage with fan and cold water shower costs 1200B, while one with air-con and hot water costs 1500 to 1800B.

Off by itself on a little cove at the southeast end of Hat Hin Khom, *Maphrao Resort* offers thatched A-frame huts in a natural setting for 150 to 380B. Showers are shared for the 150B bungalows, while 280B and 380B huts have attached showers; the latter also have large decks shaped like the prow of a ship, a unique touch. The restaurant is good and tables are arranged overlooking the beach rather than in the more typical large mess-hall style.

Hat Yao Bungalows on this beach are practically piled onto one another, with very little space in between. A shortage of fresh water means most showers employ salt water. The well-run *Pee Pee Paradise Pearl Resort* (☎ (01) 723-0484; fax 228-4370) has fully refurbished and new bungalows in all shapes and sizes, ranging from 400 to 800B. All have toilet, shower and fan. This one's a little tidier and more well spaced than others on Hat Yao.

PP Long Beach has huts starting at 100B on the hillside, 120B for better locations, 150B for newer huts, all with shared shower. For 200 to 300B you can get a hut with private bath and fan. The cheaper huts are quite rickety. Farther down the beach the *Coral Bay Resort* is out of action for the foreseeable future: only after building it did the developers realise it wasn't possible to get enough water up there to supply the operation's needs.

Lo Bakao *Pee Pee Island Village* (☎ (01) 2111907) is the only resort on this beautiful, secluded stretch of sand on the island's east coast. From November to April rooms start at 1400B and reach as high as 2100B. The remainder of the year they cost 800 to 1000B; air-con is available at the upper end of the price bracket.

Laem Tong Another nice beach, with pricey resorts and its own pier, Laem Tong is near Phi Phi Don's northern tip. *Phi Phi Palm Beach* (☎/fax (01) 723-0052) is only accessible by boat for a minimum charge of 200B or 100B per person. Top end cottages with everything start at 4173B; the premises are well landscaped and there's a good swimming pool. *PP Coral Resort* (☎ (01) 214056; fax 215455) offers wooden cottages on the beach for 1600 to 1800B high season, 1400 to 1600B low season. The 70 well appointed bungalows at *PP International Resort* (☎/fax (01) 723-1250) cost 2200/3200B single/double (add 350B peak season charge late December to late February). This one has the advantage of being at the end of the beach with a view of the next rocky cape.

Interior A little village of sorts has developed in the interior of the island near Ao Ton Sai and Hat Hin Khom. Amid the gift shops, scuba shops, bars and cafes there are several budget-oriented places to stay. This place is also home to several nightspots, so light sleepers may want to check what bars or pubs are nearby before choosing a place.

Tara Inn (☎ (01) 476-4830) has minimal rooms for 350/400B single/double with attached bath. *PP Twin Palm* (☎ (01) 4779251) is simply a few rooms in a house from 200 to 400B; *Jong Guest House* is similar. *Orchid House* continues the same theme for 150B; the proprietors seem friendly and helpful. *Rim Kao* and *Chan House* round out the offerings with motel-like rooms for 200 to 300B.

Gypsy I (☎ (01) 723-0674) offers solid concrete bungalows with tin roofs and attached toilet and shower for 400B, while *Gypsy II* has rather ill-repaired thatched bungalows for 150B with attached bath. Nearby, *PP Valentine* is one of the more promising budget places in this area, with sturdy thatched-roof huts with flowers growing around them for 250 to 350B. Friendly *Rim Na Villa* costs 350/550B for rooms with one/two beds, fan and attached bath. Unfortunately it looks as though a large hotel may be going up opposite here, which could rattle the peaceful atmosphere a bit.

MARK STRICKLAND/OCEANIC IMPRESSIONS

RICHARD NEBESKY

PAUL BEINSSEN

Southern Andaman Coast
Top: The 'handle' in the middle of dumbbell-shaped Ko Phi Phi Don has white-sand beaches and emerald waters on either side, and awesome overlooking cliffs.
Bottom Left: Krabi's coastline features scenic marine karst topography and limestone cliffs.
Bottom Right: The extra effort required to get to the Ko Tarutao archipelago, off Thailand's Southern Andaman Coast, has kept this national marine park pristine.

PAUL BEINSSEN

PAUL BEINSSEN

Southern Andaman Coast

Top: A *chao leh* (sea gypsy) boy at the beach on Ko Lipe, Ko Tarutao National Marine Park.
Bottom: Locals believe the Princess Cave, at one end of Krabi's Hat Tham Phra Nang, is
home to a mythical sea princess. Fisherfolk bring offerings to the cave so she will help
them catch many fish.

Rates for all of the above may drop as low as 50 to 100B a night between May and November, except in August.

Places to Eat

Most of the resorts, hotels and bungalows around the island have their own restaurants. Cheaper and sometimes better food is available at the restaurants and cafes in Ton Sai village. However virtually all of it is prepared for farang, not Thai, palates so the Thai dishes aren't usually very authentic. *PP Pizza* and *Mama Resto*, predictably, offer Italian food. The very popular *Garlic Restaurant* in the centre of the island has good but increasingly expensive seafood and some of the better Thai dishes on the island. *PP Bakery* prepares decent breakfasts, baked goods and sandwiches; prices are moderate.

For real Thai food, there's a great place just opposite the Columbus Bar, on the path leading towards Chao Koh Bungalows.

Entertainment

Phi Phi Don has numerous bars, most with trendy names like the Reggae Bar or the Rolling Stoned Bar. These and several others are located in the interior village. *Tintin Bar*, located near the Phi Phi Hotel (turn down the lane next to Barakuda Dive Shop), is one of the most popular spots, and the dancing and partying often goes on into the wee hours. If dancing and techno beats aren't your style, both *Charlie's Bar* (Charlie Beach Resort) and the *Gecko Bar*, near the PP Princess Resort, have live folk or rock music in the evening.

Getting There & Away

Ko Phi Phi is equidistant from Phuket and Krabi, though the latter is the most economical point of departure. Until recently, boats travelled only during the dry season, from late October to May, as the seas are often too rough during the monsoons for safe navigation.

Nowadays the boat operators risk sending boats out all year round – we've received several reports of boats losing power and drifting in heavy swells during the monsoons.

It all depends on the weather – some rainy season departures are quite safe, others are risky. If the weather looks chancy, keep in mind that there usually aren't enough life jackets to go around on these boats.

Another cautionary note regards the purchase of return-trip boat tickets. From Krabi there are currently two boat services and if you buy a return ticket from one company you must use that service in both directions. Neither service will recognise tickets from its competitor; not only that, they will refuse to sell you a new ticket back to Krabi if you hold a return ticket from the competitor. The advisable thing, then, is to buy one-way tickets only.

Boats moor at the pier at Ao Ton Sai, except for a few boats from Phuket which go to the pier at Laem Tong.

Krabi From Krabi's Jao Fah pier, there are usually four boats a day. Three regular boats depart at around 9 am, 1 pm and 3 pm for 125B per person and take about two hours. A faster air-con boat leaves at 9 am, costs 200B and takes an hour and 20 minutes. These fares are sometimes discounted by agents in town to as low as 100B. Departures are sometimes delayed because boats often wait for buses from Bangkok to arrive at the Krabi pier. From Ko Phi Phi back to Krabi the boats leave at similar times, but going in either direction you may find departure times change frequently, so check carefully.

Ao Nang You can also get boats from Ao Nang on the Krabi Province coast for 150B per person from October to April; there's usually only one departure a day, at around 9 am. The trip lasts an hour and 20 minutes. The boat from Krabi back to Ao Nang usually leaves between 3 and 4 pm.

Phuket A dozen different companies operate boats from various piers on Phuket, ranging from 250 to 450B depending on the speed of the boat – from 50 minutes to two hours. Any guesthouse or hotel on Phuket can arrange tickets; the more expensive fares include bus or van pickup from your hotel. Boats leave frequently between 8 am and 3.30 pm from May to September, usually from the port at Phuket city. Some boats dock at Ton Sai on Phi Phi, others at Laem Tong – if you have a preference be sure to ask in advance. Songserm Travel (☎ (76) 222570) runs the *Jet Cruise*, which leaves Phuket at 8.30 am (returning from Laem Tong at 2.30 pm) and takes 40 minutes.

Other Islands As Ko Lanta is becoming more touristed, there are now fairly regular boats between that island and Ko Phi Phi from October to April. Boats generally leave from the pier on Lanta Yai around 8 am, arriving at Phi Phi Don around 9.30 am. In the reverse direction boats usually leave around 11 am and 2 pm, but exact times tend to change a bit. Passage is 150B per person. It's also possible to get boats to/from Ko Jam; the same approximate departure time, fare and trip duration applies.

Getting Around

Fishing boats can be chartered at Ao Ton Sai for short hops around Phi Phi Don and Phi Phi Leh, but you'll have to do most of your getting around on foot. Touts meet boats from the mainland to load people onto long-tail boats going to Hat Yao (Long beach) for 20B per person. Other boat charters around the island from the pier at Ton Sai include Laem Tong (300B), Lo Bakao (200B) and Viking Cave on Ko Phi Phi Leh (200B).

KO JAM (KO PU) & KO SI BOYA

These large islands are inhabited by a small number of fishing families and are perfect for those seeking complete escape from the videos, farang restaurants, beach bars and so on. About the only entertainment is watching the local fishermen load or unload their boats, swimming or taking long walks on the beach. *Joy Resort* (☎ (01) 723-0502) on the south-western coast of Ko Jam offers spacious bungalows for 200 to 450B, though these prices may be negotiable. A bit farther south along the coast is *New Bungalow* (☎ (01) 464-4230), where rates range from 100 to

250B. Ko Jam's southern tip is occupied by a private residential development.

There is one set of bungalows on the western side of Ko Si Boya called *Jung Hut* for 100 to 200B per night.

Getting There & Away

Boats to both islands leave once or twice a day from Ban Laem Kruat, a village about 30km from Krabi, at the end of Route 4036, off Route 4. Passage is 15B to Si Boya, 20B to Ban Ko Jam.

You can also take boats bound for Ko Lanta from Krabi's Jao Fah pier and ask to be let off at Ko Jam. There are generally two boats daily which leave around 11 am and 2 pm; the fare is 130B as far as Ko Jam.

KO LANTA
• *pop 18,000*
Ko Lanta is a district of Krabi Province that consists of 52 islands. The geography here is typified by stretches of mangrove interrupted by coral-rimmed beaches, rugged hills and huge umbrella trees. Twelve of the islands are inhabited and, of these, three are easily accessible: **Ko Bubu, Ko Lanta Noi** and **Ko Lanta Yai**. You can reach the latter by ferry from either Ban Hua Hin, on the mainland across from Ko Lanta Noi, or from Baw Meuang, farther south.

Modest beach accommodation is available on the group's largest island, Ko Lanta Yai, a long, slender portion of sand and coral with low, forested hills down the middle; room and transport reservations are available through travel agencies in Krabi or Phuket. You can camp on any of the other islands – all have sources of fresh water. There are piers at **Ban Sala Dan**, at the northern tip of the island, and at the district capital **Ban Ko Lanta**, on the lower east coast.

The people living in this district are a mixture of Muslim Thais and chao náam who settled here long ago. Their main livelihoods are the cultivation of rubber, cashew and bananas, along with a little fishing on the side. The village of **Ban Sangka-U** on Lanta Yai's southern tip is a traditional Muslim fishing village and the people are friendly.

Ban Sala Dan at the northern end is the largest village on the island, with a few restaurants, tour outfits, dive shops and a Siam Commercial Bank exchange booth (open 8 am to 4 pm daily). Ban Ko Lanta town has a post office and long pier; there's not much to the town but the buildings are more solid-looking than those in Sala Dan and the ferry service accommodates larger vehicles.

An unpaved road goes around all but the south-eastern tip around Ban Sangka-U. In the centre of the island is **Tham Mai Kaew**, an intriguing five or six-cavern limestone cave complex.

Ko Lanta could become a model for environmentally conscious island tourism if the beach developers here cooperate to keep the island clean and noise-free. For now Ko Lanta Yai has been spared the sprawl of bars, souvenir shops and overpriced restaurants that have taken root on Phi Phi Don. This is definitely a place for those who want quiet, and aren't looking for a lot of entertainment options.

Ko Lanta National Marine Park

In 1990, 15 islands in the Lanta group (covering an area of 134 sq km) were declared part of the new Ko Lanta National Marine Park in an effort to protect the fragile coastal environment. **Ko Rok Nok** is especially beautiful, with a crescent-shaped bay featuring cliffs and a white-sand beach and a stand of banyan trees in the interior. The intact coral at **Ko Rok Nai** and limestone caves of **Ko Talang** are also worth seeing. Dive shops in Ban Sala Dan can arrange dives to these islands as well as **Ko Ha, Ko Bida, Hin Muang** and **Hin Daeng**.

Ko Lanta Yai itself is only partially protected since most of the island belongs to chao náam. As on Ko Phi Phi, many bungalows have been built on shorelands under the nominal protection of the Forestry Department. The interior of the island contains rubber, cashew and fruit plantations, with a few stands of original forest here and there, mostly in the hilly southern section of the island. It's not unusual to see metre-long monitor lizards in the interior.

The park headquarters is situated at the southern tip of Ko Lanta Yai.

Tham Mai Kaew Caves

A great break from the beach is a trip to this complex of caves in the centre of Ko Lanta Yai. Even the hike in, through original forest, is quite pleasant. But the real fun begins when you descend in through a small, indistinct hole in the rocks and enter the series of diverse caverns. Some sections are as large as church halls, other require you squeeze through on hands and knees. Sights en route include impressive stalactites and stalagmites, bats and even a cavern pool which you can swim in. The latter is not recommended for the faint-hearted, as access to the pool is via a long, slippery slope and a knotted rope that's almost as slimy: a bit of a challenge on the way back up.

A Muslim family that lives near the trailhead to the caves offers guide service for 50B per person. You really need a guide to find your way around, particularly inside the caves, and the service is definitely worth it. The family also runs a very basic restaurant where you can get snacks and drinks.

The caves are located off the lower of the two cross-island roads, down a narrow, 1.5km dirt track through a rubber plantation which ends up at the Muslim home. The best way to get there is by renting a motorcycle, though your bungalow may be willing to arrange transport.

Beaches

The western sides of all the islands have beaches, though in overall quality Lanta's beaches don't quite measure up to those found in Phuket or along Hat Tham Phra Nang. The best are along the north and south of Lanta Yai's west coast, with middle sections given over more to rocky shores and reefs. There are coral reefs along parts of the western side of Lanta Yai and along the Khaw Kwang (Deer Neck) cape at its northwestern tip. A hill on the cape gives a good aerial view of the island.

The little island between Ko Lanta Noi and Ko Klang has a nice beach called **Hat**

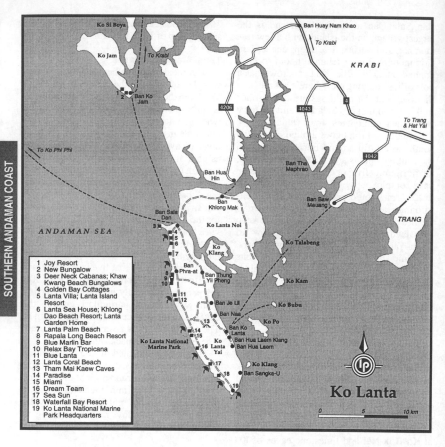

1 Joy Resort
2 New Bungalow
3 Deer Neck Cabanas; Khaw Kwang Beach Bungalows
4 Golden Bay Cottages
5 Lanta Villa; Lanta Island Resort
6 Lanta Sea House; Khlong Dao Beach Resort; Lanta Garden Home
7 Lanta Palm Beach
8 Rapala Long Beach Resort
9 Blue Marlin Bar
10 Relax Bay Tropicana
11 Blue Lanta
12 Lanta Coral Beach
13 Tham Mai Kaew Caves
14 Paradise
15 Miami
16 Dream Team
17 Sea Sun
18 Waterfall Bay Resort
19 Ko Lanta National Marine Park Headquarters

Ko Lanta

Thung Thaleh – hire a boat from Ko Klang. Also worth exploring is Ko Ngai (Hai) – see the Trang Province section further on for more details, as Ko Ngai is more accessible from that province.

Diving & Snorkelling

The uninhabited islands of **Ko Rok Nai**, **Ko Rok Yai** and **Ko Ha**, south of Ko Lanta Yai, offer plenty of coral along their western and south-western shores. According to Ko Lanta Dive Centre in Sala Dan, the undersea pinnacles of **Hin Muang** and **Hin Daeng** farther south-west are even better, with good-weather visibility of up to 30m, hard and soft corals, and plenty of large schooling fish such as sharks, tuna and manta ray. Whale sharks have also been spotted in the area.

In any given season there may be as many as four dive operations on Ko Lanta, all working out of Sala Dan but often bookable at beach bungalows. Rates for a one-day dive trip are around 1750B, including equipment hire. Two-day trips with six or seven dives start at around 3500B. Ko Lanta Divers and Aquarius Divers (☎ (76) 234201) have gotten some good reviews from travellers, and

Dive Zone also appears to be fairly well equipped. November to April is the best season for diving these areas.

Places to Stay

Ko Lanta Yai The best beach areas are along the north-west side of the island just south of Ban Sala Dan. This is where most of the development is concentrated, including the few upscale resort-style bungalows. Because it's long, wide and flat, this is a perfect beach for walking and jogging. Rates during the high season (November to May) range from 80B for bare-bones huts to 800B for air-con cottages. Prices drop dramatically after May, but slack business and flooded roads during the south-west monsoon means that only the northernmost beach bungalows usually stay open during low season.

At the northernmost section of the beach near Ban Sala Dan is the locally owned *Khaw Kwang Beach Bungalows* (☎ (01) 722-0106), the oldest of the beach places and still commanding the best stretch of sand. It's actually on the south-east side of the small peninsula of the same name that juts west from the island. Nicely separated thatched huts with private bath cost 100 to 300B depending on proximity to the beach; there are also some large VIP bungalows for 600B. The proprietors offer fishing and snorkelling trips to nearby islands. The adjacent *Deer Neck Cabanas* faces the western side of this tiny cape and is similar.

Starting about 2.5km south of Ban Sala Dan along the western side of the island are a cluster of places in varying price ranges. *Golden Bay Cottages* (☎ (01) 723-0879) is a very pleasant spot, with clean, sturdy bungalows with attached bath for 100 to 200B. *Lanta Villa* (☎ (75) 620629) is probably the most up-market choice on the island, with fan-equipped resort-style cottages for 400 to 600B, 800B with air-con. *Lanta Island Resort* (☎ (01) 212-4183), formerly the Lanta Royal Beach, has well built bungalows with fan for 300 and 400B, air-con ones cost 800B. The latter is popular with tour groups. This is followed by the similar *Lanta Sea House* with bungalows for 400 to 600B. *Khlong*

Dao Beach Resort and *Lanta Garden Home* nearby return to the budget theme with basic huts for 80 to 200B, though the latter also has more substantial cottages for 300B.

Just around a headland famous for a triple-trunked coconut palm, *Lanta Palm Beach*, has huts, some of which are in fairly poor shape, for 150 to 300B.

A couple of kilometres farther south along the beach is the *Rapala Long Beach Resort* (☎ (01) 722-0286) in the 150 to 350B range. The accommodation is actually quite nice, but you'll have to also contend with barbed wire fencing and consistently poor service. The nearby *Relax Bay Tropicana* features spacious bungalows with large decks for 200 to 600B; huts are perched around a rocky hillside overlooking the sea. The restaurant has a great deck for sunset drinks or dinners. The beach along this stretch – and for the next 2km – is nothing special.

Another kilometre or so south is *Lanta Coral Beach*, which has neatly kept huts for 150B.

Farther south another kilometre or so the beach begins improving again and the accommodation becomes cheaper. The *Paradise* offers OK bungalows with good beach frontage for 150 to 400B, while the *Miami* immediately south is a bit simpler and costs 80 to 200B.

Sitting by itself on a rather rocky stretch of beach is the beautifully landscaped *Dream Team* (☎ (01) 477-1626) with well kept, large, screened bungalows for 100 to 200B. A better sand beach is only about 10 minutes away on foot. Just before the road ends is the secluded *Sea Sun* with 80/100B cement bungalows.

Right at the end of the road, the well designed, eco-oriented *Waterfall Bay Resort* (☎ (01) 722-0014, Krabi (75) 612084) offers 18 well spaced wooden bungalows with thatched roofs overlooking a secluded bay. The bungalows cost 300 to 600B depending on their position relative to the beach. All have two rooms, one below and one above as a loft, making it very suitable for family stays. The namesake waterfall is a 30 to 40 minute walk, and boat trips to Ko Rok Nai and Ko Rok Nok can be arranged. As the Waterfall is often booked out when it's open (October to mid-June only) it's best to book in advance through its office in Krabi. A 4WD vehicle picks guests up from the pier in Sala Dan. From the resort a dirt track continues to the park headquarters and Ban Sangka-U. This is a good spot to stay if you're interested in hiking into the park interior.

Ko Bubu This tiny island has one bungalow village, *Boo Boo Island Resort*, with 13 huts. Rates are 100B per person in a dormitory, 200B in a bungalow with shared bath or 500B in a two bed bungalow with private bath.

To get to Bubu from Lanta you can charter a boat from Samsan pier (Ban Ko Lanta) for 150 to 200B. From Krabi the boat to Ban Sala Dan on Ko Lanta Yai continues on to Baw Meuang with a stop at Bubu. You can also get boats from Baw Meuang. More information is available at the Samsan pier on Ko Lanta or from Thammachart (☎ (75) 612536), on Kongkha Rd near the Jao Fah pier in Krabi.

Places to Eat

If you get tired of bungalow food there are a couple of basic places to eat in Ban Sala Dan at the northern end of Ko Lanta Yai. *Seaview* and *Seaside* are two small moderately priced restaurants over the water with Thai food and seafood. The *Swiss Bakery* next to the pier has good coffee and fine pastries. *Hans*, a German restaurant near Golden Bay Cottages, has received favourable reviews from German visitors: the fried potatoes are said to be especially good. Restaurants on the beach near Lanta Garden Home come and go with the seasons, usually offering Swiss, French or Italian food.

Entertainment

Between Relax Bay Tropicana and the Rapala Long Beach Resort is a great little bar, the *Blue Marlin*. The wood, stone and thatch building was constructed by owners Patrick and Tik, the setting is gorgeous and there's a happy hour from 5 pm to 8 pm. What more do you need?

Getting There & Away

Krabi At the time of writing there were a few mini-vans going to and from Krabi: this service may pick up in the future, though for most people the direct boat (see below) is probably a more pleasant trip. Bookings for the vans should be available at most of the bungalow outfits and in Sala Dan.

The slow way to get to Ko Lanta is to take a songthaew (30B) from Maharat Soi 6 in Krabi all the way to Ban Hua Hin, and then a vehicle ferry across the narrow channel to Ban Khlong Mak on Ko Lanta Noi. From there, get a motorcycle taxi (20B) across to another pier on the other side, then another vehicle ferry to Ban Sala Dan on Ko Lanta Yai. Both ferries cost 3B for pedestrians, 5B for a bicycle and one rider, 10B per motorcycle and 50B in a car or truck. Both ferries run frequently from 6 am to 6 pm, except on Fridays when they close at noon so that the Muslim pilots can visit local mosques.

Ban Hua Hin is 26km down Route 4206 from Ban Huay Nam Khao, which is about 44km from Krabi along Route 4. Songthaews from Krabi (Talaat Kao junction) to Ban Hua Hin run regularly until about 3 pm. Count on two hours to complete the trip, including ferry crossing. If you're travelling by private car or motorcycle, the turn-off for Route 4206 is near the village of Ban Huay Nam Khao (Km 64) on Route 4.

The quickest way to reach Ko Lanta from Krabi is to take a boat from Krabi's Jao Fah pier, only available October to April. Boats usually depart around 11 am and 2 pm and take one to 1½ hours to reach Ban Sala Dan; the fare is 150B. In the reverse direction boats leave at 8 am and 1 pm.

Ban Baw Meuang You can also take a boat from Ban Baw Meuang, which is about 35km from Ban Huay Nam Khao at the end of Route 4042 (about 80km total from Krabi). The turn-off for Route 4042 is at Km 46 near the village of Sai Khao. It's 13km from Ban Sai Khao to Ban Baw Meuang on this dirt road. The boats from Ban Baw Meuang are fairly large, holding up to 80 people, and they take an hour to reach Samsan pier on Lanta Yai's eastern shore. The ferry usually leaves Ban Ko Lanta between 7 and 8 am, and heads back in the other direction between 1 and 2 pm. The fare is 50B.

Ko Phi Phi During the dry season, October to April, there are two boats daily from Ko Phi Phi at around 11 am and 1 pm for 150B per person. They take about an hour and 20 minutes to reach Ban Sala Dan; in the opposite direction boats leave Ko Lanta at 8 am and 2 pm. There are also occasional boats to Lanta from Ko Jam.

Trang From Trang you can get a mini-van direct to Ko Lanta for 150B. Vans depart from opposite the Trang train station, usually at around 1 pm, and the ride takes two hours. Alternatively, you can take a bus from Trang to Ban Huay Nam Khao (25B), then transfer to a songthaew going south-west to the Ban Hua Hin pier.

Getting Around
Most of the bungalows on Ko Lanta will provide free transport to and from Ban Sala Dan. Motorcycle taxis are available from Ban Sala Dan to almost anywhere along the beaches for 10 to 40B depending on the distance. From Ban Ko Lanta, motorcycle taxi fares fall in the same range.

Motorcycles can be rented in Ban Sala Dan and from many bungalows. The rate is a fairly steep 250B a day, but this is by far the best option if you want to explore the island.

Trang Province

The province of Trang, as well as its southern neighbour Satun Province, bears a geography similar to that of Krabi and Phang-Nga, with islands and beaches along the coast and limestone-buttressed mountains inland. The area is much less frequented by tourists though. Caves and waterfalls are the major attractions in the interior.

Twenty kilometres north of Trang's pro-

vincial capital is a 3500 rai (5.6 sq km) provincial park, which preserves a tropical forest in its original state. In the park there are three waterfalls and government resthouses. To the north is **Thaleh Song Hong** (Sea of Two Rooms), a large lake surrounded by limestone hills. Hills in the middle of the lake nearly split it in half, hence the name.

Music & Dance
As in other southern provinces, public holidays and temple fairs feature performances of *Manohra*, the classical southern Thai dance-drama, and *năng thalung* (shadow play). But because of its early role as a trade centre, Trang has a unique Indian-influenced music and dance tradition as well as *lí-khe pàa* (also called *lí-khe bòk* and *lí-khe ram ma-naa*), a local folk opera with a storyline that depicts Indian merchants taking their Thai wives back to India for a visit. It's part farce, part drama, with Thais costumed as Indians with long beards and turbans.

Traditional funerals and Buddhist ordinations often feature a musical ensemble called *kaa-law*, which consists of four or five players sitting on a small stage under a temporary coconut-leaf roof or awning. The instruments include two long Indian drums, a *pii haw* (a large oboe similar to the Indian *shahnai*) and two gongs.

TRANG
• ☎ *(75)* • *pop 49,400*
Historically, Trang has played an important role as a centre of trade since at least the 1st century AD and was especially important between the 7th and 12th centuries, when it was a seaport for ocean-going sampans sailing between Trang and the Straits of Melaka. Nakhon Si Thammarat and Surat Thani were major commercial and cultural centres for the Srivijaya Empire at this time, and Trang served as a relay point for communications and shipping between the east coast of the Thai peninsula and Palembang, Sumatra. Trang was then known as Krung Thani and later as Trangkhapura (City of Waves) until the name was shortened during the early years of the Ratanakosin period.

During the Ayuthaya period, Trang was a common port of entry for seafaring western visitors, who continued by land to Nakhon Si Thammarat or Ayuthaya. The town was then located at the mouth of the Trang River, but King Mongkut later gave orders to move the city to its present location inland because of frequent flooding. Today Trang is still an important point of exit for rubber from the province's many plantations.

Trang's main attractions are the nearby beaches and islands, plus the fact that it can be reached by train. Among Thais, one of Trang's claims to fame is that it often wins awards for 'Cleanest City in Thailand' – its main rival in this regard is Yala. It may not seem that sparkling to the average visitor, but Trang does have a lively, trading town appeal that merits a stroll if you find yourself here overnight.

Information

Maps Outdated but useful maps of Trang, as well as English-language newspapers, are available at a small bookstore at the intersection of Visetkul (Wisetkun) and Phra Ram VI Rds.

Post & Communications The post & telephone office is on the corner of Phra Ram VI and Kantang Rds.

Travel Agents Trang Tour Service (☎ 214-564; fax 219280) is run by Chichamai, a friendly woman who is extremely knowledgeable about the area. She speaks English well, is happy to help out with queries, and can also arrange all sorts of interesting tours and treks to the sights around Trang, as well as book tickets and accommodation. Motorcycle and car rental is also available.

Places to Stay

A number of hotels are found along the city's two main thoroughfares, Phra Ram VI Rd and Visetkul (Wisetkun) Rd, which run from the clock tower. The long-running *Ko Teng* on Phra Ram VI Rd has large singles/doubles for a reasonable 160/250B, and a good restaurant downstairs. The *Wattana*

Festivals
At nearby Hat Jao Mai, a unique sailboat regatta is held on the first weekend of May. This one differs from the usual Phuket affair in that only wooden sailboats of traditional Andaman Sea type may enter. These boats feature square or triangular sails dyed with natural pigments from the *samèt* or cajeput tree. In addition to the races, events include live musical and theatrical performances, including lí-khe pàa and năng thalung.
   The Vegetarian Festival is celebrated fervently in Trang in September or October (see the Phuket section in the Northern Andaman Coast chapter for details). ■

Hotel (☎ 218184), on the same street, offers upgraded rooms for 280B with fan and bath or 480B with air-con.

Over on Ratchadamnoen Rd is the inexpensive *Phet Hotel* (☎ 218002), with fair rooms with fan and shared bath for 80B, or with attached bath for 120 to 170B. They also have a restaurant downstairs.

On Visetkul Rd are the *Queen Hotel* (☎ 218522), with large clean rooms with fan for 230B, or 360B with air-con, and the business-like *Trang Hotel* (☎ 218944), near the clock tower, with expansive fan-cooled rooms, some with balconies, for 480B or air-con for 540B.

The 10 storey *Thamrin* (☎ 211011; fax 218057) is an up-market place on Kantang Rd near the train and bus stations. Modern air-con rooms cost 600B standard, 900B deluxe, not including tax and service.

Kantang If you happen to become stranded in nearby Kantang waiting for a boat to Hat Jao Mao or the islands, there are three inexpensive places to stay. The *Siri Chai Hotel* (☎ 251172), on the main road leading to the port from the railway station, has small but fairly clean one bed rooms for 140B, two-bed rooms for 240B – or you can have a room for two hours for 100B!

Near the main market near the waterfront, *JT Hotel* (☎ 251755) has fan rooms for 200B, air-con for 300B. *Chula Pah Guest House*

SOUTHERN ANDAMAN COAST

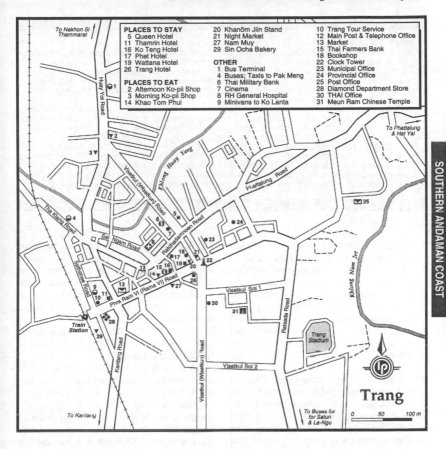

PLACES TO STAY
5 Queen Hotel
11 Thamrin Hotel
16 Ko Teng Hotel
17 Phet Hotel
19 Wattana Hotel
26 Trang Hotel

PLACES TO EAT
2 Afternoon Ko-pii Shop
3 Morning Ko-pii Shop
14 Khao Tom Phui

20 Khanŏm Jiin Stand
21 Night Market
27 Nam Muy
29 Sin Ocha Bakery

OTHER
1 Bus Terminal
4 Buses; Taxis to Pak Meng
6 Thai Military Bank
7 Cinema
8 RH General Hospital
9 Minivans to Ko Lanta

10 Trang Tour Service
12 Main Post & Telephone Office
13 Market
15 Thai Farmers Bank
18 Bookshop
22 Clock Tower
23 Municipal Office
24 Provincial Office
25 Post Office
28 Diamond Department Store
30 THAI Office
31 Meun Ram Chinese Temple

Trang

(☎ 251318), about a half kilometre north of the main intersection, near the harbour master station, costs 250B for a very clean fan room, 350B with air-con.

Places to Eat

Plenty of good restaurants can be found in the vicinity of the hotels. *Khao Tom Phui* on Phra Ram VI Rd serves all manner of Thai and Chinese standards in the evenings till 2 am, and has been honoured with the Shell Chuan Chim designation for its tôm yam (available with shrimp, fish or squid), sea bass in red sauce (plaa kraphõng náam daeng) and stir-fried greens in bean sauce (pûm pûy kha-náa fai daeng).

Next door to the Queen Hotel is the *Image Restaurant*, which has a very broad selection of rice and noodle dishes. *Nam Muy* is a large Chinese restaurant opposite the old Ko Teng Hotel; although it looks fancy, the menu is medium-priced.

The *Muslim Restaurant* opposite the Thamrin Hotel on Phra Ram VI serves inexpensive roti kaeng, curries and rice. *Diamond Department Store* on the nearby corner has a supermarket on the first floor, and a small hawker centre on the third.

Cuppa Ko-píi?

Trang is famous for its traditional *ráan kafae* or *ráan ko-píi* (coffee shops), which are easily identified by the charcoal-fired aluminium boilers with stubby smokestacks seen somewhere in the middle or back of the open-sided shops. Usually run by Hokkien Chinese, these shops serve real filtered coffee (called *kafae thūng* in the rest of the country) along with a variety of snacks, typically *paa-thông-kô*, *salabao* (Chinese buns), *khanŏm jĭip* (dumplings), Trang-style sweets, *mŭu yâang* (barbecued pork) and sometimes noodles and *jók* (thick rice soup).

When you order coffee in these places, be sure to use the Hokkien word *ko-píi* rather than the Thai *kafae*, otherwise you may end up with Nescafé or instant Khao Chong coffee – the proprietors often think this is what farangs want. Coffee is usually served with milk and sugar – ask for *ko-píi dam* for sweetened black coffee or *ko-píi dam, mâi sài náam-taan* for black coffee without sugar.

The best *ráan ko-píi* place in town is at Khao Ocha (open from 6 am to 8 pm) on Visetkul Rd Soi 5. There are also two good places near the intersection of Visetkul and Huay Yot Rds: one opens only in the morning, the other in the afternoon. Sin Ocha Bakery, next to the train station, was once the queen of Trang coffee shops (under its old name, Sin Jiaw), but has since been completely renovated into a modern cafe. Ko-píi is still available here, along with western pastries and breakfasts. ∎

At night the area around the intersection of Phra Ram VI and Visetkul Rds comes to life with *stalls* selling all types of noodles, curries, barbecued meats and sweets.

If you're longing for a fix of western food or beer, *Wunderbar*, next door to Trang Tour Service near the train station, serves good sandwiches and icy cold beers: not a bad place to wait for the overnight train to Bangkok.

Khanŏm Jiin Trang is famous for khanŏm jiin (Chinese noodles with curry). One of the of the best places to try it is at the tables set up on the corner of Visetkul and Phra Ram VI Rds. You have a choice of dousing your noodles in náam yaa (a spicy ground fish curry), náam phrík (a sweet and slightly spicy peanut sauce) or kaeng tai plaa (a very spicy mixture of green beans, fish, bamboo shoots and potato). To this you can add your choice of fresh grated papaya, pickled vegies, cucumber and bean sprouts – all for just 8B per bowl.

Getting There & Away

Air THAI operates daily flights from Bangkok to Trang (2005B). The Trang THAI office (☎ 218066) is at 199/2 Visetkul Rd. The airport is 4km south of Trang; THAI runs shuttle vans back and forth for 50B per person.

Bus & Share Taxi Buses for points north and east, including Krabi, Phuket, Hat Yai and Bangkok, leave from the bus terminal on Huay Yot Rd. First class air-con buses run to Krabi and Phuket approximately hourly between 7 am and 6 pm. To Krabi (three to four hours) the fare is 66B, to Phuket (six to seven hours) it's 140B. There are also ordinary buses to Krabi that do the journey in four to five hours and cost 35B.

Buses to Hat Yai leave every half hour from 6 am to 4 pm and cost 40B for ordinary and 48B for air-con (the 8B extra gets you a lot more comfort). Air-con buses to/from Bangkok are 375B (203B for an ordinary bus) or 565B for a VIP bus. Air-con buses leave at 4 pm, VIP buses at 5 pm; the trip takes about 12 hours.

Buses to Satun and La-Ngu (where you can change for transport to Pak Bara and Ko Tarutao National Marine Park) leave from a roadside stop in the southern section of town, on Ratsada road near the intersection with Visetkul Soi 7. The fare to Satun is 37B; to La-Ngu it's 30B. At the time of writing a regular mini-van service to Pak Bara was scheduled to start in March 1997, departing from in front of Trang Tour Service, near the railway station.

From Ban Huay Nam Khao, the junction for Route 4 and the road to Ko Lanta, a bus to Trang is 25B.

Train Only two trains go all the way from Bangkok to Trang, the rapid No 41, which leaves Hualamphong station at 6.30 pm, arriving in Trang at 9.55 am the next day and the express No 13, which leaves Bangkok at 5.05 pm and arrives in Trang at 7.35 am. In the reverse direction, rapid No 42 leaves Trang at 1.44 pm, express No 13 at 6.20 pm. The fare is 660B 1st class, 311B 2nd class, not including rapid or express surcharges. There are no direct 3rd class trains running to Trang; you must change in Thung Song, a rail junction town in Nakhon Si Thammarat Province. From Thung Song there are two trains daily to Trang, leaving at 9.30 am and 3.20 pm, arriving an hour and 45 minutes later.

If you want to continue on to Kantang on the coast, there is one daily ordinary train out of Trang at 5.02 pm which arrives in Kantang at 5.20 pm; the rapid No 41 also terminates in Kantang, arriving at 10.25 am. The fare from Trang to Kantang is 5B in 3rd class (5.02 pm train only) or 28B in 2nd class on the rapid No 41.

Getting Around

Samlors and motorcycle taxis around town cost 10B per trip. Honda 100cc motorbikes can be rented from Trang Tour Service from 250B per day. Trang Tours also rents cars, starting at 700B per day for local trips, more for long-distance journeys.

Big orange buses to the harbour at Kantang leave frequently from Kantang Rd in the vicinity of the train station for 10B. There are also air-con mini-vans which do the same trip every hour or so for 20B each; a motorcycle taxi will cost 60 to 70B, but this is really too long a jaunt for a comfortable pillion ride.

TRANG BEACHES
• ☎ (75)
Trang Province has several sandy beaches and coves along the coast, especially in the Sikao and Kantang districts. On Route 403 between Trang and Kantang is a turn-off west onto an unpaved road that leads down to the coast through some interesting Thai-Muslim villages. At the end, it splits north and south. The road south leads to Hat Yao, Hat Yong Ling and Hat Jao Mai. The road north leads to Hat Chang Lang and Hat Pak Meng.

Ko Ngai (Hai)
This island is actually part of Krabi Province to the north, but is most accessible from Trang. It's a fairly small island, covering about 3000 rai (4.8 sq km), but the beaches are fine white sand and the water is clear. The resorts on the island operate half-day boat tours of nearby islands, including Morakot Cave on Ko Muk, for around 200B per person.

Places to Stay Along the east shore of Ko Ngai are two 'resorts'. Towards the middle of the island is *Koh Hai Villa* (☎ 218029 in Trang, (2) 318-3107 in Bangkok), with fan-cooled bungalows for 300B a day and tents for 150B. The vapid food here is overpriced, and the staff can be surly.

At the southern end is *Ko Ngai Resort* (☎ 210496 in Trang, (2) 246-4399 in Bangkok), where one bed seaside huts cost 300B, two-bed rooms in large bungalows are 600 to 900B and a six bed bungalow is 1200B. Tents are also available for 150B.

You can book any of these through the Koh Hai Villa Travel Agency in Trang (☎ 210496, Bangkok (2) 246-4399) at 112 Phra Ram VI Rd. Each resort has its own office in the city, but this one is the most conveniently located if you're staying in the central business district.

Getting There & Away Four boats a day leave for Ko Ngai from the southern pier at Pak Meng for 50B per person or charter for 300 to 500B.

Ban Tung Laem Sai
At Ban Tung Laem Sai in Sikao district is an alternative homestay for visitors interested in ecotourism. Operated by Yat Fon, a local nonprofit organisation that promotes community development and environmental conservation, the staff educate visitors about

local mangroves, coral reefs, coastal resources and the Thai-Muslim way of life. No sunbathing or drinking is allowed in the vicinity. Contact Khun Suwit at Yat Fon, 105-107 Ban Pho Rd in Trang, for reservations and transport.

Hat Pak Meng

Thirty-nine kilometres from Trang in Sikao district is a long, broad, sand beach near the village of Ban Pak Meng. The water is usually shallow and calm, even in the rainy season. A couple of hundred metres offshore are several limestone rock formations, including a very large one with caves. Several vendors and a couple of restaurants sell fresh seafood. There are unnamed brick bungalows for rent at 200 to 300B a night, plus the *Relax Parkmeng Resort* (☎ 218940) with thatched bungalows in the 150 to 300B range and *Pakmeng Resort* (☎ 210321) for sturdier bungalows with fan and bath for 300 to 500B.

Around the beginning of November, locals flock to Hat Pak Meng to collect *hăwy taphao*, a delicious type of clam. The tide reaches its lowest this time of year, so it's relatively easy to pick up the shells.

About halfway between Pak Meng and Trang, off Route 4046, is the 20m-high **Ang Thong Falls**.

Getting There & Away Take a van (20B) or songthaew (15B) to Sikao from Trang, and then a songthaew (10B) to Hat Pak Meng. There are also one or two direct vans daily to Pak Meng from Trang for 30B. A paved road now connects Pak Meng with the other beaches south, so if you have your own wheels there's no need to backtrack through Sikao.

Hat Chang Lang

Hat Chang Lang is part of the Hat Jao Mai National Park, and this is where the park office is located. The beach is about 2km long and very flat and shallow. At the northern end is Khlong Chang Lang, a stream that empties into the sea.

Ko Muk & Ko Kradan

Ko Muk is nearly opposite Hat Chang Lang and can be reached by boat from Kantang or Pak Meng. The coral around Ko Muk is lively, and there are several small beaches on the island suitable for camping and swimming. The best beach, Hat Sai Yao, is on the opposite side of the island from the mainland and is nicknamed Hat Farang because it's 'owned' by a farang from Phuket.

Near the northern end is **Tham Morakot** (Emerald Cave), a beautiful limestone tunnel that can be entered by boat during low tide. At the southern end of the island is pretty Phangka Cove and the fishing village of Hua Laem.

Ko Kradan is the most beautiful of the islands that belong to Hat Jao Mai National Park. Actually, only five of six precincts on the island belong to the park: one is devoted to coconut and rubber plantations. There are fewer white-sand beaches on Ko Kradan than on Ko Muk, but the coral reef on the side facing Ko Muk is quite good for diving.

Places to Stay & Eat *Ko Muk Resort* (Trang office: 25/36 Sathanee Rd, next to the train station; ☎ 212613), on Ko Muk facing the mainland next to the Muslim fishing village of Hua Laem, has simple but nicely designed bungalows for 200B with shared bath, 250 to 300B with private bath. The beach in front tends towards mudflats during low tide; the beach in front of the nearby village is slightly better but modest dress is called for. The resort organises boats to nearby islands like Ko Ngai (Hai), Waen, Kradan and Lanta. The newer *Morning Calm Resort* (☎ (01) 979-1543) on the opposite side of the island offers 50 bungalows, all with fan and attached bath, for 200 to 800B depending on size.

Ko Kradan Resort (☎ 211391 in Trang, (2) 392-0635 in Bangkok) has OK bungalows and ugly cement shophouse-style rooms with fans and private bath for 700 to 900B a night and up. The beach isn't bad, but this resort still gets low marks for serving lousy, expensive food and for littering the area – a perfect example of the worst kind of beach resort development.

Getting There & Away The easiest place to get a boat to either Ko Muk or Ko Kradan is from Kantang. Songthaews or vans from Trang to Kantang leave regularly and cost 10B. Once in Kantang you must charter another songthaew to the ferry pier for 20B, where you can get a regular long-tail boat to Ko Muk for 50B (or charter for 300B), to Ko Kradan for 100B or to Ko Libong for 25B (noon daily).

You can also get to the islands from Hat Pak Meng. There are two piers, one at the northern end of the beach and one at the southern end. Boats are more frequent from the southern pier, especially during the rainy season. Boats costs 30 to 60B per person to Ko Muk (depending on the number of passengers), 120B to Ko Kradan.

Hat Jao Mai & Ko Libong

Both Hat Jao Mai and Ko Libong are in Kantang district, about 35km from Trang. The wide white-sand beach is 5km long and gets some of Thailand's biggest surf (probably the source of Trang's original unshortened name, City of Waves). Hat Jao Mai is backed by casuarina trees and limestone hills with caves, some of which contain prehistoric human skeletal remains. **Tham Jao Mai** is the most interesting of the caves, a large cavern with lots of stalactites and stalagmites. In their only known appearance on the Thai-Malay peninsula, rare black-necked storks frequent Jao Mai to feed on molluscs and crustaceans.

Hat Jao Mai is part of 231 sq km **Hat Jao Mai National Park**, which includes Hat Chang Lang farther north and the islands of Ko Muk, Ko Kradan, Ko Jao Mai, Ko Waen, Ko Cheuak, Ko Pling and Ko Meng. In this area the endangered dugong (also called a manatee or sea cow) can sometimes be spotted.

Camping is permitted on Jao Mai and there are a few bungalows for rent as well. *Sinchai's Chao Mao Resort* (☎ (01) 464-4140) offers a couple of two room wooden cottages with shared facilities for 200B. Cheaper but no bargain are three 100B dilapidated huts. Bathing is done at a well. *Ban Chaom Talay*

(☎ (01) 979-1540) near the pier for Ko Libong is being constructed by two Mahidol University professors who speak perfect English. They haven't set room rates yet but this will probably become a very good source of information on the area.

Off the coast here is **Ko Libong**, Trang's largest island. There are three fishing villages on the island, so boats from Kantang port are easy to get for the one hour trip. The Botanical Department maintains free shelters on Laem Ju-Hoi, a cape on the western tip of Ko Libong. On the south-western side of the island is a beach where camping is permitted. The *Libong Beach Resort* (☎ 214-676 in Trang) has A-frame thatched bungalows for 350 to 500B. About 1km from the pier on Libong is the *Tongkran Bungalow* with basic huts for 50B.

Getting There & Away The best way to reach Hat Jao Mai by public transport is to catch a bus, train or taxi from Trang to Kantang harbour, then hop one of the frequent ferries across to Tha Som on the opposite shore of the Trang River estuary. Tickets cost 1B for pedestrians, 5B for motorcycles, 12B for cars and 15B for pickups; the ferry operates daily 6 am to 8 pm. From Som Tha there are frequent songthaews to Hat Jao Mai.

A long-tail boat from the pier at Hat Jao Mai to Ko Libong costs just 20B.

Hat Yong Ling & Hat Yao

A few kilometres north of Hat Jao Mai are these two white-sand beaches separated by limestone cliffs. There is no accommodation here as yet.

Hat Samran & Ko Sukon

Hat Samran is a beautiful and shady white-sand beach in Palian district, about 40km south-west of Trang city. From the Customs pier at nearby Yong Sata you should be able to get a boat to Ko Sukon (also called Ko Muu), an island populated by Thai Muslims, where there are more beaches.

Sukon Island Resort (☎ 219679 in Trang, 211460 on the island) has bungalow accommodation for 200 to 500B a night.

TRANG CAVES

A limestone cave in the north-eastern district of Huay Yot, **Tham Phra Phut**, contains a large Ayuthaya-period reclining Buddha. When the cave was re-discovered earlier this century, a cache of royal-class silverwork, nielloware, pottery and lacquerware was found hidden behind the image – probably stashed there during the mid-18th century Burmese invasion.

Also in this district, near the village of Ban Huay Nang, is **Tham Tra** (Seal Cave), with mysterious red seals carved into the cave walls which have yet to be explained by archaeologists. Similar symbols have been found in the nearby cave temple of **Wat Khao Phra**.

More easily visited is **Tham Khao Pina**, off Route 4 between Krabi and Trang at Km 43, which contains a large, multilevel Buddhist shrine popular with Thai tourists. Another famous cave, **Tham Khao Chang Hai** near Na Meun Si village, in Nayong district, contains large caverns with impressive interior formations.

Satun Province

• ☎ (74)

Bordering Malaysia, Satun (or Satul) is the Andaman Coast's southernmost province. Besides offering a convenient crossing to Malaysia by land or sea, Satun is also home to the stunningly beautiful Ko Tarutao National Marine Park.

Eighty per cent of Satun's population – Thai, Malay and chao náam – profess Islam (some of the chao náam also practise animism). In fact throughout the entire province there are only 11 or 12 Buddhist temples, versus 117 mosques. Before 1813 Satun was in fact a district of the Malay state of Kedah; the name Satun comes from the Malay *setul*, a type of tree common in this area. At the time Kedah, along with Kelantan, Terengganu and Perlis, paid tribute to Siam. The Anglo-Siamese Treaty of 1909 released parts

of these states to Britain and they later became part of independent Malaysia.

As in Thailand's other three predominantly Muslim provinces (Yala, Pattani and Narathiwat), the Thai government has installed a loudspeaker system in the streets which broadcasts government programs at 6 am and 6 pm (beginning with a wake-up call to work and ending with the Thai national anthem, for which everyone must stop and stand in the streets), either to instil a sense of nationalism in the typically rebellious southern Thais, or perhaps to try and drown out the prayer calls and amplified sermons from local mosques. As in Pattani and Narathiwat, one hears a lot of Yawi spoken in the streets.

SATUN
• *pop 22,000*

The provincial capital of Satun itself is not that interesting, but you may enter or leave Thailand here by boat via Kuala Perlis in Malaysia. Sixty kilometres north-west of Satun is the small port of Pak Bara, the departure point for boats to Ko Tarutao.

Information

Immigration The relatively new Wang Prachan Customs complex at the Tammalang pier south of town contains an immigration office where anyone departing or arriving at Satun to/from Malaysia by boat will have their papers processed. You can also use this office for visa extensions.

Money If you are going to Kuala Perlis in Malaysia, remember that banks on the east coast of Malaysia are not open on Thursday afternoon or Friday, due to the observance of Islam. If you're heading south at either of these times, be sure to buy Malaysian ringgit on the Thai side first so you won't be caught short on the Muslim Sabbath.

Post & Communications The main post and telephone office is on the corner of Samanta Prasit and Satun Thani Rds.

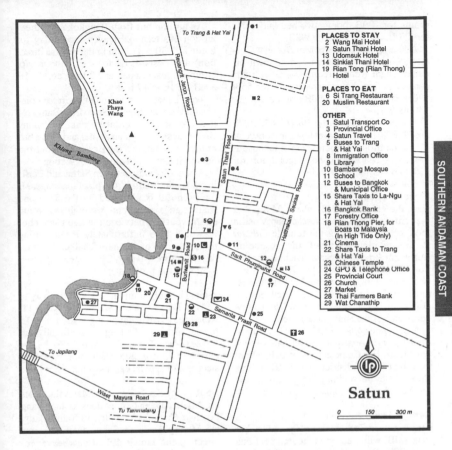

PLACES TO STAY
2 Wang Mai Hotel
7 Satun Thani Hotel
13 Udomsuk Hotel
14 Sinkiat Thani Hotel
19 Rian Tong (Rian Thong)
   Hotel

PLACES TO EAT
6 Si Trang Restaurant
20 Muslim Restaurant

OTHER
1 Satul Transport Co
3 Provincial Office
4 Satun Travel
5 Buses to Trang
   & Hat Yai
8 Immigration Office
9 Library
10 Bambang Mosque
11 School
12 Buses to Bangkok
   & Municipal Office
15 Share Taxis to La-Ngu
   & Hat Yai
16 Bangkok Bank
17 Forestry Office
18 Rian Thong Pier, for
   Boats to Malaysia
   (In High Tide Only)
21 Cinema
22 Share Taxis to Trang
   & Hat Yai
23 Chinese Temple
24 GPO & Telephone Office
25 Provincial Court
26 Church
27 Market
28 Thai Farmers Bank
29 Wat Chanathip

Satun

0   150   300 m

Khao Phaya Wang

If you find yourself with time to kill in Satun, you might consider a visit to the park along the western side of Khao Phaya Wang, a limestone outcropping next to Khlong Bambang. Steps lead up the vine-choked cliff on the khlong side of Khao Phaya Wang and at the top there are views of the winding green khlong, rice fields and coconut plantations. Pandan mats are available at the cool, bamboo-shaded picnic area next to the canal below. Vendors sell *sôm-tam, khâo niäw, kài thâwt, kûng thâwt* and *miang kham*.

Places to Stay

The *Rian Tong (Rian Thong) Hotel* is at the end of Samanta Prasit Rd, next to the Rian Thong pier, an embarkation point for boats to and from Malaysia. Large, clean rooms with ceiling fan and attached shower and toilet cost 120B. Near the municipal offices on Hatthakam Seuksa Rd is the two storey *Udomsuk Hotel* (☎ 711006), with reasonably clean rooms with ceiling fan and attached bath for 120B with one bed, 130B with two beds.

The *Satun Thani Hotel*, near the centre of town, is OK but noisy, with one-bed fan rooms for 190B rooms, two-bed fan rooms for 250B, air-con for 290/390B.

At the up-market *Wang Mai Hotel* (☎ 711-607/8), near the northern end of town off Satun Thani Rd, all rooms come with air-con, carpeting, hot water and TV for 550/590B single/double, 650B for deluxe, or 1300B VIP.

The new *Sinkiat Thani Hotel* (☎ 721055; fax 721059) in the centre of town on Buriwanit Rd has comfortable rooms similar to those at the Wang Mai but in better condition for 630B single/double.

Places to Eat

Near the gold-domed Bambang Mosque in the centre of town are several cheap Muslim food shops, including the reliable *Suhana Restaurant* almost opposite the mosque on Buriwanit Rd. Up on Satun Thani Rd across from the Satun Thani Hotel, *Si Trang* specialises in southern Thai curries but it isn't Muslim. Roti kaeng and Malay-style curries are also available at a clean *Muslim shop* a few doors east of the Rian Tong Hotel.

A no-name *coffee shop* next to the Udomsuk Hotel is a good spot for Thai and western breakfasts. For Chinese food, wander about the little Chinese district near the Rian Tong Hotel. They're nothing fancy, just a few noodle shops and small seafood places.

Getting There & Away

Bus & Share Taxi A share taxi to Hat Yai costs 40B, while a regular government bus costs 27B. Buses to Trang are 37B, share taxis 60B. Share taxis to Hat Yai park in two places in Satun, near the Sinkiat Thani Hotel and on Samanta Prasit Rd. The former stand also has taxis to La-Ngu for 25B, the latter to Trang for 40B.

Satul Transport Co, half a kilometre north of the Wang Mai Hotel on the same side of the road, sells THAI tickets (for flights out of Trang or Hat Yai), and also operates buses to Trang (37B) and Hat Yai (27B, 30B air-con) frequently from 6 am to 4.30 pm. With two days advance booking, the agency can also arrange rail tickets for the Hat Yai to Bangkok route.

An air-con bus from Bangkok's Southern air-con bus terminal leaves once a day for Satun at 7.30 pm (2 pm in the reverse direction) and costs 427B for the 15 hour trip. Ordinary buses depart at 7.30 pm, cost 234B and take 16 to 17 hours.

This is really too long a bus trip for comfort – if you want to get to Satun from Bangkok, it would be better to take a train to Padang Besar on the Malaysian border and then a bus or taxi to Satun. Padang Besar is 60km from Satun. See the following Train section.

A new highway between Satun and Perlis in Malaysia is still in the planning stages. If the proposal is approved by the Thai and Malaysian governments, the highway would cut travel time between the two towns but it would also unfortunately mean cutting through some of southern Thailand's dwindling rainforest – many Thais have organised to protest the proposal.

Train The only train that goes all the way to Padang Besar is the special express No 11, which leaves Hualamphong station at 3.15 pm and arrives in Padang Besar around 8 am the next day. The basic fare is 767B for 1st class, 360B for 2nd class, not including sleeper and special express surcharges.

Boat From Kuala Perlis in Malaysia, boats are M$4. All boats now dock at the Wang Prachan Customs complex in Tammalang, the estuary south of Satun. In the reverse direction the fare is 40B. Boats leave frequently in either direction between 9 am and 1 pm, then less frequently to around 4 pm, depending on marine conditions.

From Langkawi Island in Malaysia boats for Tammalang leave daily at 8 am, 11.30 am and 2 pm. The crossing takes 1½ to two hours and costs M$15 one way. Bring Thai money from Langkawi, as there are no money-changing facilities at Tammalang pier. In the reverse direction boats leave Tammalang for Langkawi at 8.30, 9.30 and 10.30 am and 1 and 3.30 pm and cost 180 to 190B, depending on the boat operator. For more information you can call Thai Ferry Centre (☎ 711453, 721959).

Getting Around

An orange songthaew to Tammalang pier (for boats to Malaysia) costs 10B from Satun. The songthaews run every 20 minutes between 8 am and 5 pm; catch one from opposite Wat Chanathip on Buriwanit Rd. A motorcycle taxi from the same area costs 20B.

PAK BARA

Pak Bara is the jumping-off point for the Ko Tarutao National Marine Park islands. There is not much of interest in the town itself but you may find yourself spending the night if you miss the boat to the islands.

Places to Stay & Eat

About 400m before the pier is the *Diamand Beach Bungalow*, with surprisingly nice bungalows for 150 and 200B with attached bath. The setting isn't anything special, but it's the closest place to the pier, and not bad for a night. Coming from La-Ngu into Pak Bara, Diamond Beach is on the left; there's a sign in English to direct you down a small dirt path to the entrance.

More attractive options can be found just over 1km from the pier, down a small road along the shore that runs parallel to the main road between La-Ngu and Pak Bara. Sitting among the casuarina trees, *Marina Bungalows* has a compound with narrow concrete huts costing 150B, larger plaster and bamboo cottages for 200 to 250B, and a fairly nice, though narrow, stretch of beach. Farther along the same road, in the direction of Pak Bara, *Krachomsai Bungalows* has basic A-frame huts in a well kept yard for 150B.

Another 500m along the main road towards La-Ngu is the *Ban Songtang Guesthouse*, a shabby affair with run-down huts for 150B. Opposite, and 200m down a small road, is the *Koh Klong Garden View Guesthouse*, a newly built, somewhat bizarre setup with clean motel-style rooms for 250B, including an upscale bathroom. It's a fair hike from the pier, however.

On rocky, palm-fringed Ko Kabeng (a 10 minute boat ride from Pak Bara), the quiet

Pak Nam Resort (☎ 781129) offers thatched A-frame bungalows for 180 to 260B. Transport to and from the resort is free, but you may have to book a room in Pak Bara with one of the dubious tour outfits to get this perk. Pak Nam Resort also arranges boat trips to other, more pristine islands in the area.

Pak Nam Resort and Marina Bungalows have the best food of all the Pak Bara lodgings. There are several food stalls near the Pak Bara pier that do fruit shakes and seafood.

Getting There & Away

To get to Pak Bara from Satun, you must take a share taxi or bus to La-Ngu, then a songthaew on to Pak Bara. Taxis to La-Ngu leave from near the Sinkiat Thani Hotel on Buriwanit Rd when there are enough people to fill a taxi for 25B per person. Buses leave frequently from in front of the public library along the same road and they cost 15B. From La-Ngu, songthaew rides to Pak Bara are 8B and terminate right at the harbour; you can take a motorcycle taxi this same distance for 20B.

From Hat Yai, there are three daily buses to La-Ngu and Pak Bara which cost 34B and take 2½ hours. If you miss one of the direct La-Ngu buses, you can also hop on any Satun-bound bus to the junction town of Chalung (20B, 1½ hours), which is about 15km short of Satun, then get a songthaew north on Route 4078 for the 10B, 45 minute trip to La-Ngu. Or take a share taxi from Hat Yao to La-Ngu for 50B; there is also a minivan service from Hat Yai for 50B, a better deal since it goes all the way to Pak Bara.

You can also travel to La-Ngu from Trang by bus for 30B, or by share taxi for 50B. A direct daily minibus service from Trang to Pak Bara was scheduled to start around the time of writing this guide. If this goes ahead, departure will be from in front of Trang Tour Service, opposite the train station.

For getting to the Ko Tarutao National Marine Park see that section's Getting There and Away information.

KO TARUTAO NATIONAL MARINE PARK

This park is actually a large archipelago of 51 islands, approximately 30km from Pak Bara in La-Ngu district, which is 60km north-west of Satun. Ko Tarutao, the biggest of the group, is only 5km from Langkawi Island in Malaysia. Only three of the islands (Tarutao, Adang and Lipe) have any kind of regular boat service to them, and therefore these are the ones generally visited by tourists. Access to the other islands, which offer excellent beaches and coral reefs, can only be arranged by chartering long-tail boats.

This park remains one of the most pristine and beautiful coastal areas in Thailand, in part because it requires a bit more effort to get there. Accommodation is fairly basic and transport slow and sometimes inconvenient. With any luck, it will remain this way, as park management has neither the staff nor the resources to handle a massive increase in visitors.

Ko Tarutao

The park's namesake covers around 151 sq km and features waterfalls, inland streams, beaches, caves and protected wildlife. Nobody lives on this island except for the employees of the Forestry Department. It was a place of exile for political prisoners between 1939 and 1947, and remains of the prisons can be seen near Ao Talo Udang, on the southern tip of the island, and at Ao Talo Wao, on the middle of the east coast. There is also a graveyard, charcoal furnaces and even fermentation tanks for making fish sauce. Wildlife on the island includes the dusky langur, mousedeer, dugong, wild pig, fishing cat, lobster and crab-eating macaque; dolphins and whales may be sighted offshore. Four varieties of sea turtles swim the surrounding waters – Pacific ridley, hawksbill, leatherback and green. All four lay eggs on the beaches between September and April.

Tarutao's largest stream, Khlong Phante Malaka, enters the sea at the north-west tip of the island at Ao Phante Malaka; the brackish waters flow out of **Tham Jara-Khe** (Crocodile Cave – the stream was once inhabited by ferocious crocodiles, which seem to have disappeared). The cave extends for at least a kilometre under a limestone mountain – no-one has yet followed the stream to

Treading Lightly in Tarutao

A remote location, small population and, more recently, near heroic efforts by Thailand's park service have kept Ko Tarutao National Marine Park one of the country's most pristine and beautiful areas. Not surprisingly it is drawing increasing numbers of tourists, both Thai and foreign, which poses a threat to the park's delicate environment. How you decide to visit it, therefore, may help stop it from going the way of Ko Phi Phi or Ko Samet.

While the park officials and staff are quite hospitable, they have limited time and resources to cater to foreign tourists. This is particularly true of Ko Adang, which has only basic facilities and accommodation (Ko Tarutao is better equipped and staffed). If the number of visitors demanding modern services grows too quickly, the National Parks Division of the Royal Thai Forestry Department may consider requests from private firms to build bungalows and hotels on park land to handle the load. If past history is any guide, this could ruin the park.

To help take the pressure off the park service, stay on Ko Lipe if you're seeking bungalows, restaurants and other services. Lipe is outside the park jurisdiction, and seems to have little trouble accommodating visitors. It's also the best place to charter boats for exploring the unspoiled coral in the park.

If you want to stay on Ko Adang, try to be fairly self-sufficient: bring a tent and your own food. Kitchen staff will happily prepare meals using visitors' food: it's a way for the cash-strapped operation to bring in a little extra revenue. But the restaurant's own food stocks are usually inadequate. The more visitors that show up prepared to look after themselves, the more confident park staff will be that the current setup can do the job. And the greater the chance that Ko Tarutao's gorgeous coral formations, pearl white beach and lush islands will remain intact. ■

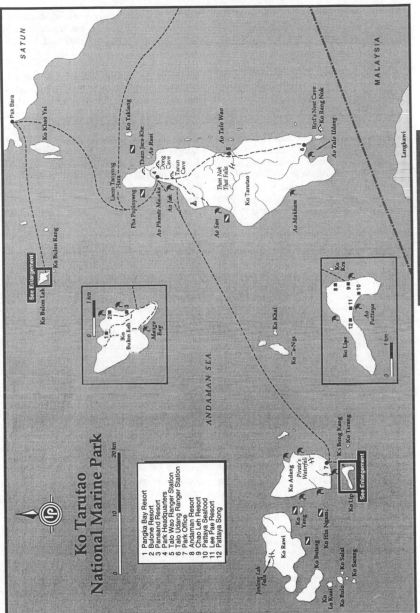

the cave's end. The mangrove-lined watercourse should not be navigated at high tide, when the mouth of the cave fills.

The park pier, headquarters and bungalows are also here at Ao Phante Malaka. A 50B park fee is payable on arrival. For a view of the bays, climb Topu Hill, 500m north of the park office.

The best camping is at the beaches of **Ao Jak** and **Ao San**, two bays south of park headquarters on the west coast. There is also camping at Ao Makham (Tamarind Bay), at the south-west end of the island, about 2.5km from another park office at Ao Talo Udang. Except for Ao Jak, these beaches are a long walk from park headquarters so you may want to consider hiring a long-tail to take you there: there are usually one or two boat operators snoozing in the shade near the information booth.

There is a road between Ao Phante Malaka, in the north, and Ao Talo Udang, in the south, of which 11km was constructed by political prisoners in the 1940s and 12km was more recently constructed by the park division. The road is, for the most part, overgrown, but park personnel have kept a path open to make it easier to get from north to south without having to climb over rocky headlands along the shore. The entire trek takes about eight hours, and while there are ranger stations to Talo Wao and Talo Udang, you'll need to bring a tent and your own supplies if you want to head down there.

Ko Rang Nok (Bird Nest Island), off Ao Talo Udang, is another treasure trove of the expensive swiftlet nests craved by Chinese throughout the world. Good coral reefs are at the north-west part of Ko Tarutao at **Pha Papinyong** (Papillon Cliffs), at Ao San and in the channel between Ko Tarutao and Ko Takiang (Ko Lela) off the north-east shore.

At the park headquarters, for 20B, you can pick up *Tarutao National Park: a Travellers Adventure Handbook*, a paper booklet that details the park's facilities, flora and fauna and hiking options. It's quite informative, and the history section in particular makes for interesting reading, complete with tales from the prison camps and accounts of gun battles between early park officials and angry locals opposed to having their home turf turned into protected parkland.

Ko Khai & Ko Klang

Between Ko Tarutao and Ko Adang and Rawi is a small cluster of three islands called **Mu Ko Klang** (Middle Island Group), where there is good snorkelling. One of the islands, Ko Khai, also has a good white-sand beach. Boats from Ko Tarutao take about 40 minutes to reach Ko Khai. You can also charter long-tails from Ko Lipe out to here: a full day's hire will cost around 600 to 700B.

Ko Adang & Ko Rawi

Ko Adang is 43km west of Tarutao, and about 80km from Pak Bara on the mainland. Ko Adang's 30 sq km are covered with forests and freshwater streams, which fortunately supply water year-round. Green sea turtles lay their eggs here between September and December. At **Laem Son** (Pine Cape), on the southern tip of the island where the pier and park office are located, visitors can stay in a thatched longhouse. Camping is also allowed. The restaurant is a little expensive considering the basic fare served – but then considering the transport problems, perhaps not. As on Tarutao, it's a good idea to bring some food from the mainland.

An interesting hike can be undertaken along the island's southern coast, past an old Customs house about 2km from the park station, and then up to Rattana Waterfall. On the east coast is the Pirate Waterfall, so named because it was once – perhaps still – used by passing pirate ships as a freshwater source, though it only really flows during the rainy season. Getting there will require clambering along the coast, as there is no inland trail. Farther up the east coast is the chao leh village of **Talo Puya**. The villagers are not keen on seeing tourists, so it's probably not a great spot to visit.

Ko Rawi is just east of Ko Adang, and a bit smaller. There are no facilities there at all. Off the west coast of Ko Adang, and the south-east coast of Ko Rawi, are coral reefs with many live species of coral and tropical fish. Other excellent snorkelling spots include the north side of **Ko Yang** and tiny **Ko Hing Ngam**. The latter is known for its beautiful smooth stones. However, you may not want to take one as a souvenir. Doing so is said to bring bad luck, and the visitor centre on Ko Tarutao has a basket of stones sent back by people who blamed the rocks for their subsequent misfortunes.

Through the efforts of park officials, many of these reefs have been spared degradation caused by dynamite fishing and other human activities. The park service has also recently set up around 40 mooring buoys in this area (used mainly by long-tails bringing snorkellers to the area) so that boat operators need not drop anchor in this ecologically delicate area. Try to make sure your boat uses one of the moorings. Long-tail boat operators on Ko Lipe generally charge around 600 to 700B to take groups out for a full day of snorkelling.

Ko Lipe

Ko Lipe is immediately south of Ko Adang and is inhabited by about 500 chao náam (*orang rawot* or *orang laut* in Malay), who are said to have originated on the Lanta islands in Krabi Province. They subsist on fishing and some cultivation of vegetables and rice on the flatter parts of the island. For some reason the chao náam on this island prefer to be called 'chao leh' – a term despised by other Moken on islands to the north, who prefer the term chao náam. In their own tongue, they refer to themselves as 'iraklahoi'. The chao leh village is in the island's northeast.

Ko Lipe is not under park control, and has thus become the main place to stay, given the limited facilities on Ko Adang. Several bungalow operations have been set up in the main village along the main coast and on Pattaya beach, on the southern side of this island. There are also one or two simple restaurants and shops in the main village. You can walk overland between the village and Pattaya beach in around 20 to 30 minutes, or take a long-tail for 20B.

Pattaya is the nicest of the two main beaches, as the one in front of the chao leh village is partially covered with boat moorings and some litter. However, the little island just opposite the village, **Ko Kra**, has some well preserved coral and makes for fine snorkelling. You can easily swim to there from the village beach.

Places to Stay & Eat

Officially, the Ko Tarutao National Park is only open from November to May. Visitors who show up on the islands during the monsoon season can stay in park accommodation, but they must transport their own food from the mainland unless staying with the chao náam on Ko Lipe.

Bungalows may be booked in advance at the park office in Pak Bara (☎ 711383, no English spoken) or through the Forestry Department (☎ (2) 579-0529) in Bangkok. For Ko Tarutao and/or Ko Adang, you may want to bring some food of your own from Satun or Pak Bara – the park restaurants are a bit expensive and nothing to write home about.

Ko Tarutao Park accommodation on Ko Tarutao, near park headquarters, costs 500B for a large 'deluxe' two room bungalow sleeping four, or 750B for cottages that sleep up to six people. A four bed room in a longhouse goes for 320B, or 80B per person. Full rates must be paid for the bungalows and cottages regardless of how many of you there are. Tents can be rented for 100B. If you have your own, the fee is 10B.

Staying at the park feels a bit like going back to youth camp: lights off at 10.30 pm, running water from 6 to 8 am and 6 to 10 pm only. But the buildings are clean and well maintained. One point worth noting: the longhouses have no screens or mosquito nets, so you may want to bring your own net, or at the very least some effective insect repellent.

Ko Adang Laem Son has longhouse accommodation similar to that on Ko Tarutao, and for the same rates. A small restaurant provides basic meals and sundries; it's closed in the rainy season. You can pitch your own tent for 10B.

Ko Lipe There are basically five places to stay on the island. Two are located in the chao leh village, on the north-east side of the island. At the northern side of the village the *Andaman Resort* (☎ 711313 in Satun) has newly built bungalows with attached bath for 200B and tents for 100B. You can also pitch your own tent here for 20B. At the other end of the village *Chao Leh Resort* has some pretty shaky thatch huts for 100B, more solid ones for 200B with attached bath, and wooden and thatch versions with glass windows that overlook the village backstreets for 250B. The beach is nicer in front of Andaman Resort than near Chao Leh Resort

On Pattaya beach, the biggest operation is the *Lee Pae Resort*, which has spacious thatch bungalows for 200 to 250B with attached bath and shower. Though it has more amenities than its competitors, this place also wins the prize for the least personality. Down at the western end of the beach *Pattaya Song* has simple huts on the beach with shared bath for 100B. On the adjacent hillside overlooking the bay are slightly fancier bungalows with attached bath for 200B.

On the other end of the beach *Pattaya Seafood* is mainly a restaurant, but the owner also has three decent bungalows with attached bath for 100B. This seems to be the only operation on the island that's actually run by an islander. Even if you don't stay, stop by for dinner: the food is excellent.

See the previous section for places to stay and eat in Pak Bara if you miss the boat.

Getting There & Away – Ko Tarutao

Pak Bara Boats to Tarutao leave regularly between November and April from the pier in Pak Bara, 60km north-west of Satun and 22km from Ko Tarutao. During the rest of the year boat service is irregular, since the park is supposedly closed. Satun Province officials have discussed constructing a new pier in Tan Yong Po district, nearer Satun, that will serve tourist boats to Tarutao and other islands, possibly on a year-round basis.

For now, boats leave Pak Bara for Tarutao in season daily at 10.30 am and 3 pm. The return fare is 200B, one way 100B, and it takes 1½ to two hours, depending on the boat. Departures back to Pak Bara are at 9 am and 1 pm.

If possible, it would be best to buy one way tickets for each leg of your journey, as this would allow a choice of routes back (say direct from Ko Lipe to Satun). Also, if the boat you have a ticket for doesn't make it to the islands due to bad weather or an engine mishap, you won't have to worry about getting a refund for both tickets. In practice it's nearly impossible. Staff at the local boat cartel, the La-Ngu Tour Boat Association, will refuse to sell any one way fares, and may give you some bullshit about not being able to buy tickets at Ko Tarutao or on board the boat. Ham-fisted tactics, but difficult to get around.

There are also occasional tour boats out to Tarutao, but these usually cost several hundred baht per person, as they include a guided tour, meals etc. Your final alternative is to charter a boat with a group of people. The cheapest are the long-tail boats, which can take eight to 10 people out from Pak Bara's commercial pier for 800B. On holidays, boats may travel back and forth to Tarutao every hour or so to accommodate the increased traffic.

Other Piers It is also possible to hire boats to Ko Tarutao from three different piers *(thâa reua)* on the coast near Satun. The nearest is the Ko Nok pier, 4km south of Satun (40km from Tarutao). Then there is the Tammalang pier, 9km from Satun, on the opposite side of the estuary from Ko Nok pier. Tammalang is 35km from Tarutao. Finally there's the Jepilang pier, 13km east of Satun (30km from Tarutao); this one seems most geared to boat charters.

Getting There & Away – Ko Adang & Ko Lipe

On Tuesday, Thursday and Saturday (November to May), a boat leaves Pak Bara at 10.30 am for Ko Adang and Ko Lipe, with a stop at Ko Tarutao along the way, for 300B each way. The boat continues on from Ko Tarutao at 1 pm, arriving between Ko Adang and Ko Lipe around 4 pm. From here you'll have to jump into a long-tail to the island of your choice, which will cost another 20 to 30B. The following day (Wednesday, Friday and Sunday), the boat heads back at 9 am, stops in Tarutao for lunch and wallows into Pak Bara around 3 pm. Long-tails between Ko Lipe and Ko Adang cost 20 to 40B per person, depending on the number of passengers and your bargaining skills.

Thai Ferry Centre (☎ 711453) recently started a direct service between Satun and Ko Lipe, running once daily Friday, Saturday and Sunday for 400B one way. The boats leave Satun's Tammalang pier at 9.30, and depart Ko Lipe at 4 pm. These times may change, however, as the service was still in a trial phase at the time of writing.

KO BULON LEH

This is a beautiful, laid-back island approximately 20km west of Pak Bara, and is the largest of the Ko Bulon island group. Though considerably smaller than the major islands of Ko Tarutao, Bulon Leh shares many of the same geographical characteristics, including sandy beaches and coral reefs. A fine white sand beach runs along the east and north shores of the island, and offshore are some fine coral sites that make for good snorkelling. There are a few tiny villages in the northern part of the island near Ao Pangka. Nearby Ko Bulon Don sports a chao leh village and some nice beaches, but no accommodation so far. Ko Bulon Mai Phai farther out is uninhabited and pristine.

Boat trips around the island and to nearby snorkelling sites can be easily arranged. The best place to check is at Bulone Resort, which has good contacts with some of the long-tail operators. You can also arrange passage direct between Bulon Leh and Ko Lipe in Ko Tarutao National Marine Park for around 300 to 400B per person if you can get a group of five or six together. Four to five-day island hopping trips out to Ko Tarutao are also available. Rates vary depending on the specific itinerary, but range between 2200B and 3000B and include accommodation, snorkelling and fishing gear, lunch and one barbecue dinner.

Places to Stay & Eat

Ko Bulon Leh has three accommodation options. The most up-market is the nicely designed *Pansand Resort* (☎ (01) 722-0279), which has basic huts with shared bath for 100B, A-frame fan-equipped bungalows for 200 and 250B, and solid brick and thatch cottages with deck and private bath for 650 to 800B. Two-person tents can be hired for 70B or you can pitch your own for 10B. For more information and reservations you can also contact First Andaman Travel in Trang (☎ (75) 218023; fax 211010) at 82-84 Visetkul Rd (opposite the Queen Hotel).

Bulone Resort, on the north-east shore close to Pansand, has simple bungalows with shared bath for 100 to 200B, and dorm beds in a longhouse for 70B. The huts are well spread out, giving guests a sense of privacy. Bulone Resort has no phone, but bookings can be made by writing to the Ongsara Family, Bulone Resort, 23 Muu 4, Tambon Paknam, Ampoe La-Ngu, Satun, Thailand 91110. Both Pansand and Bulone enjoy nice locations overlooking the island's best beach.

On the north side of the island, set near a rocky cove, is *Pangka Bay Resort*, which has fairly primitive bungalows for 150B. It's not really possible to go swimming around here: you'll need to hike about 15 minutes back to the main beach.

In between Pansand and Bulone is *Jeb's*, a small shop with basic necessities. The owner, Jeb, is in charge of renting out two government-owned bungalows with attached bath for 400B per night.

Although Ko Bulon Leh is still a sleepy place, it is getting increasingly popular, and in the high season both Pansand and Bulone resorts are often booked solid, though you can usually get a tent at Pansand. Reservations are highly recommended. You probably won't have trouble finding a free bungalow at Pangka Bay Resort due to its more remote location.

Bulone Resort probably has the best food of the three places, though Pansand's fare is good too. Jeb's also has a little side restaurant, where they serve dinners.

SOUTHERN ANDAMAN COAST

Getting There & Away

Incredibly slow boats to Ko Bulon Leh depart from the Pak Bara pier at 2 pm and cost 100B per person for the round trip. The trip takes two hours, and you'll have to transfer to a long-tail boat to actually get ashore, so it's best to be barefoot or in sandals upon arrival. On the return, boats usually leave Bulon Leh at 9 am.

Other Islands

A 10 minute boat ride from Pak Bara, **Ko Kabeng** is of mild interest. The beaches here are often littered and murky, so it's basically just a convenient place to stay in Pak Bara, but if you have time to kill, visit the charcoal factory at Khlong La-Ngu or check out the cashew orchards. If you speak enough Thai you could hire a fishing boat directly from Ko Kabeng's little harbour at the fishing village of Ban Jet Luk to other islands nearby.

Twenty-two islands stretching between Ko Kabeng and the boundaries of Mu Ko Tarutao belong to little-visited, 495 sq km **Ko Phetra National Marine Park**. Uninhabited **Ko Khao Yai**, the largest in the group, boasts several pristine beaches suitable for swimming and snorkelling. Crab-eating macaques are plentiful here (local Muslims don't hunt them). There's a castle-shaped rock formation on one shore; during low tide boats can pass beneath a natural arch in the formation. Nearby is **Ko Lidi**, which features a number of picturesque and unspoiled caves, coves, cliffs and beaches. There is a ranger station on the island, and camping facilities. Between Ko Lidi and Ko Khao Yai is a channel bay known as Ao Kam Pu, a tranquil passage with cascading waters during certain tidal changes and some coral at shallow depths.

The park headquarters is at Ao Nun, a small bay 3km south of Pak Bara, though it can sometimes be hard to find anyone on duty. There are several bungalows and a restaurant here as well. The road to Ao Nun is about 2km outside of Pak Bara, on the road to La-Ngu. Coming from the direction of La-Ngu there is a small sign in English a few hundred metres before the turn-off to the left.

Glossary

aahãan – food
aahãan pàa – jungle food
amphoe – district; next subdivision down from province; sometimes spelt *amphur*
amphoe meuang – provincial capital
ao – bay or gulf

ban – house or village; often spelt *bâan*
bai toey – pandanus leaf
bàw náam ráwn – hot springs
bòt – central sanctuary or chapel in a Thai temple; from the Pali *uposatha*

chaa – tea
chao náam (chao leh) – sea gypsies
chedi – stupa; monument erected to house a Buddha relic

dhammachakka – Buddhist wheel of law
doi – mountain peak

farang – foreigner of European descent

hat – beach; short for *chalhaat*; also *hàai*
hang yao – long-tailed boat
hãw trai – a *tripitaka* (Buddhist scripture) library
hâwng thaéw – Chinese shophouse

isãan – general term for north-eastern Thailand, from the Sanskrit name for the medieval kingdom Isana, which also encompassed parts of Cambodia

jataka – life-stories of the Buddha
jiin – Chinese

kâew – crystal, jewel, glass, or gem; also spelt *keo*
kafae thũng – filtered coffee, called *ko-pĩi* in southern Thailand
ka-toey – Thai transvestite
khão – hill or mountain
ko-pĩi – southern-style filtered coffee, particularly famous in Trang Province on the Southern Andaman Coast

khlong – canal
khõn – masked dance-drama based on stories from the *Ramakian*
ko – island; also spelt *koh*; pronounced *kàw*
kúay hâeng – Chinese-style work shirt
kuti – meditation hut

lâap – spicy mint salad with mint leaves
lãem – cape (in the geographical sense)
lákhon – classical Thai dance-drama
làk meuang – city pillar/phallus
lâo khão – white liquor
lâo thèuan – jungle liquor
lí-khe – Thai folk dance-drama

mãe chii – Thai Buddhist nun
mãe náam – river; literally 'mother water'
maha that – literally 'great element', from the Sanskrit-Pali *mahadhatu*; common name for temples which contain Buddha relics
mát-mii – tie-dye silk method
mâw hâwm – Thai work shirt
meuang/muang – city; pronounced *meu-ang*
mondòp – small square building in a *wat* complex generally used by laypeople, as opposed to monks; from the Sanskrit *mandapa*
muay thai – Thai boxing

náam – water
náam phrík – chilli sauce
náam plaa – fish sauce
náam tòk – waterfall
nakhon – city; from the Sanskrit-Pali *nagara*; also spelt *nakhorn*
nãng thalung/nãng yài – Thai shadow play
ngaan wát – temple fair
ngôp – traditional Khmer rice farmer's hat

pàak náam – estuary
paa-té – batik
pàk tâi – southern Thai
phâakhamãa – piece of cotton cloth worn as a wraparound by men
phâasîn – same as above for women
phrá – monk or Buddha image; an honorific term from the Pali *vara*, 'excellent'

phrá phum – earth spirits

pìi-phâat – classical Thai orchestra

prang – Khmer-style tower on temples

prasat – small ornate building with a cruciform ground plan and needle-like spire, used for religious purposes, located on wat grounds; from the Sanskrit term *prasada*

rai – one *rai* is equal to 1600 sq metres

reua hang yao – long-tail taxi boat

reua kaw-lae – traditional painted fishing boats of southern Thailand

reuan tháew – longhouse

reu-sǐi – a Hindu *rishi* or 'sage'

rót fai – train

rót thammadaa – ordinary bus (non air-con) or ordinary train (not rapid or express)

roti – round flatbread, common street food, particularly in the south

sǎalaa (sala) – an open-sided, covered meeting hall or resting place; from the Portuguese *sala* or 'room'

sala klang – provincial office

samlor – three-wheeled pedicab

sanùk – fun

sêua mâw hâwm – blue cotton farmer's shirt

sinsae – Chinese doctor

soi – lane or small street

sôm-tam – green papaya salad

sǒngkhran – Thai New Year, held in mid-April

songthaew – literally 'two rows'; common name for small pickup trucks with two benches in the back, used as buses/taxis

susǎan – cemetery

talàat náam – floating market

tambon – 'precinct', next subdivision below *amphoe*; also spelled *tambol*

thale sàap – inland sea or large lake

thanon – street/road/avenue

thêp – angel or divine being; from the Sanskrit *deva*

thewada – a kind of angel

tripitaka – Theravada Buddhist scriptures

tuk-tuk – motorised *samlor*

vipassana – Buddhist insight meditation

wâi – palms-together Thai greeting

wang – palace

wan phrá – Buddhist holy days (the full and new moons every fortnight)

wát – temple-monastery; from the Pali *avasa*, monk's dwelling

wihǎan – counterpart to *bòt* in Thai temple, containing Buddha images but not circumscribed by *sema* stones. Also spelt *wihan* or *viharn*; from the Sanskrit *vihara*

yàa dong – herbal liquor; also the herbs inserted in *lâo khǎo*

yam – Thai-style salad; usually made with meat or seafood

Index

Asides & Special Sections

Bangkok Traffic Alternatives 207
Changing the Image 218
Cuisine of Coastal Thailand 97-113
Cuppa Ko-pfi? 426
Emerald Buddha 167
Hazardous Marine Life 118-9
Hua Hin Railway Hotel 269
Jet-ski Request 235

Know Your Boats 209
Ko Samet: Environment or Economics? 234
Phuket's Vegetarian Festival 383
Shifting Samui Sands 298
Thai Art Styles
Thailand's Marine Environment 33-45
The Baht 79

The Face of Peninsular Thailand 294
The Problem of Pollution 219
Treading Lightly in Tarutao 434
Walking Tour – Phetburi Temples 261
Water Quality 219
White Gold 414

LONELY PLANET PHRASEBOOKS

Building bridges,
Breaking barriers,
Beyond babble-on

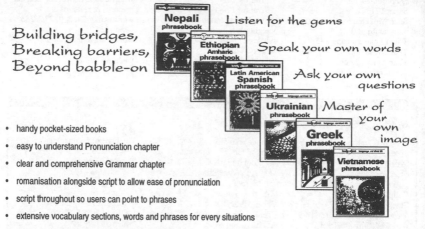

Listen for the gems

Speak your own words

Ask your own
questions

Master of
your
own
image

- handy pocket-sized books
- easy to understand Pronunciation chapter
- clear and comprehensive Grammar chapter
- romanisation alongside script to allow ease of pronunciation
- script throughout so users can point to phrases
- extensive vocabulary sections, words and phrases for every situations
- full of cultural information and tips for the traveller

'...vital for a real DIY spirit and attitude in language learning' – Backpacker

'the phrasebooks have good cultural backgrounders and offer solid advice for challenging situations in remote locations' – San Francisco Examiner

'...they are unbeatable for their coverage of the world's more obscure languages' – The Geographical Magazine

---

Arabic (Egyptian)
Arabic (Moroccan)
Australia
   Australian English, Aboriginal and Torres Strait languages
Baltic States
   Estonian, Latvian, Lithuanian
Bengali
Burmese
Brazilian
Cantonese
Central Europe
   Czech, French, German, Hungarian, Italian and Slovak
Eastern Europe
   Bulgarian, Czech, Hungarian, Polish, Romanian and Slovak
Egyptian Arabic
Ethiopian (Amharic)
Fijian
French
German
Greek
Hindi/Urdu
Indonesian

Italian
Japanese
Korean
Lao
Malay
Mandarin
Mediterranean Europe
   Albanian, Croatian, Greek, Italian, Macedonian, Maltese, Serbian, Slovene
Mongolian
Moroccan Arabic
Nepali
Papua New Guinea
Pilipino (Tagalog)
Quechua
Russian
Scandinavian Europe
   Danish, Finnish, Icelandic, Norwegian and Swedish
South-East Asia
   Burmese, Indonesian, Khmer, Lao, Malay, Tagalog (Pilipino), Thai and Vietnamese

Spanish (Castilian)
   Also includes Catalan, Galician and Basque
Spanish (Latin American)
Sri Lanka
Swahili
Thai
Thai Hill Tribes
Tibetan
Turkish
Ukrainian
USA
   US English, Vernacular Talk, Native American languages and Hawaiian
Vietnamese
Western Europe
   Basque, Catalan, Dutch, French, German, Greek, Irish, Italian, Portuguese, Scottish Gaelic, Spanish (Castilian) and Welsh

---

LONELY PLANET JOURNEYS

JOURNEYS is a unique collection of travel writing – published by the company that understands travel better than anyone else. It is a series for anyone who has ever experienced – or dreamed of – the magical moment when they encountered a strange culture or saw a place for the first time. They are tales to read while you're planning a trip, while you're on the road or while you're in an armchair, in front of a fire.

JOURNEYS books catch the spirit of a place, illuminate a culture, recount a crazy adventure, or introduce a fascinating way of life. They always entertain, and always enrich the experience of travel.

ISLANDS IN THE CLOUDS
Travels in the Highlands of New Guinea
Isabella Tree

Isabella Tree's remarkable journey takes us to the heart of the remote and beautiful Highlands of Papua New Guinea and Irian Jaya – one of the most extraordinary and dangerous regions on earth. Funny and tragic by turns, *Islands in the Clouds* is her moving story of the Highland people and the changes transforming their world.

Isabella Tree, who lives in England, has worked as a freelance journalist on a variety of newspapers and magazines, including a stint as senior travel correspondent for the *Evening Standard*. A fellow of the Royal Geographical Society, she has also written a biography of the Victorian ornithologist John Gould.

'One of the most accomplished travel writers to appear on the horizon for many years . . . the dialogue is brilliant' – Eric Newby

---

SEAN & DAVID'S LONG DRIVE
Sean Condon

Sean Condon is young, urban and a connoisseur of hair wax. He can't drive, and he doesn't really travel well. So when Sean and his friend David set out to explore Australia in a 1966 Ford Falcon, the result is a decidedly offbeat look at life on the road. Over 14,000 death-defying kilometres, our heroes check out the re-runs on tv, get fabulously drunk, listen to Neil Young cassettes and wonder why they ever left home.

Sean Condon lives in Melbourne. He played drums in several mediocre bands until he found his way into advertising and an above-average band called Boilersuit. *Sean & David's Long Drive* is his first book.

'Funny, pithy, kitsch and surreal . . . This book will do for Australia what Chernobyl did for Kiev, but hey you'll laugh as the stereotypes go boom'
– Time Out

LONELY PLANET TRAVEL ATLASES

Lonely Planet has long been famous for the number and quality of its guidebook maps. Now we've gone one step further and produced a handy companion series: Lonely Planet travel atlases – maps of a country produced in book form.

Unlike other maps, which look good but lead travellers astray, our travel atlases have been researched on the road by Lonely Planet's experienced team of writers. All details are carefully checked to ensure the atlas corresponds with the equivalent Lonely Planet guidebook.

The handy atlas format means no holes, wrinkles, torn sections or constant folding and unfolding. These atlases can survive long periods on the road, unlike cumbersome fold-out maps. The comprehensive index ensures easy reference.

- full-colour throughout
- maps researched and checked by Lonely Planet authors
- place names correspond with Lonely Planet guidebooks
  – no confusing spelling differences
- legend and travelling information in English, French, German,
  Japanese and Spanish
- size: 230 x 160 mm

Available now:
Chile & Easter Island • Egypt • India & Bangladesh • Israel & the Palestinian Territories •Jordan, Syria & Lebanon • Kenya • Laos • Portugal • South Africa, Lesotho & Swaziland • Thailand • Turkey • Vietnam • Zimbabwe, Botswana & Namibia

---

LONELY PLANET TV SERIES & VIDEOS

Lonely Planet travel guides have been brought to life on television screens around the world. Like our guides, the programmes are based on the joy of independent travel, and look honestly at some of the most exciting, picturesque and frustrating places in the world. Each show is presented by one of three travellers from Australia, England or the USA and combines an innovative mixture of video, Super-8 film, atmospheric soundscapes and original music.

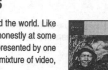

Videos of each episode – containing additional footage not shown on television – are available from good book and video shops, but the availability of individual videos varies with regional screening schedules.

Video destinations include: Alaska • American Rockies • Australia – The South-East • Baja California & the Copper Canyon • Brazil • Central Asia • Chile & Easter Island • Corsica, Sicily & Sardinia – The Mediterranean Islands • East Africa (Tanzania & Zanzibar) • Ecuador & the Galapagos Islands • Greenland & Iceland • Indonesia • Israel & the Sinai Desert • Jamaica • Japan • La Ruta Maya • Morocco • New York • North India • Pacific Islands (Fiji, Solomon Islands & Vanuatu) • South India • South West China • Turkey • Vietnam • West Africa • Zimbabwe, Botswana & Namibia

The Lonely Planet TV series is produced by:
Pilot Productions
The Old Studio
18 Middle Row
London W10 5AT UK

For video availability and ordering information contact your nearest Lonely Planet office.

Music from the TV series is available on CD & cassette.

PLANET TALK

Lonely Planet's FREE quarterly newsletter

We love hearing from you and think you'd like to hear from us.

When...is the right time to see reindeer in Finland?
Where...can you hear the best palm-wine music in Ghana?
How...do you get from Asunción to Areguá by steam train?
What...is the best way to see India?

For the answer to these and many other questions read PLANET TALK.

Every issue is packed with up-to-date travel news and advice including:

* a letter from Lonely Planet co-founders Tony and Maureen Wheeler
* go behind the scenes on the road with a Lonely Planet author
* feature article on an important and topical travel issue
* a selection of recent letters from travellers
* details on forthcoming Lonely Planet promotions
* complete list of Lonely Planet products

To join our mailing list contact any Lonely Planet office.

Also available: Lonely Planet T-shirts. 100% heavyweight cotton.

LONELY PLANET ONLINE

Get the latest travel information before you leave or while you're on the road

Whether you've just begun planning your next trip, or you're chasing down specific info on currency regulations or visa requirements, check out Lonely Planet Online for up-to-the minute travel information.

As well as travel profiles of your favourite destinations (including maps and photos), you'll find current reports from our researchers and other travellers, updates on health and visas, travel advisories, and discussion of the ecological and political issues you need to be aware of as you travel.

There's also an online travellers' forum where you can share your experience of life on the road, meet travel companions and ask other travellers for their recommendations and advice. We also have plenty of links to other online sites useful to independent travellers.

And of course we have a complete and up-to-date list of all Lonely Planet travel products including guides, phrasebooks, atlases, Journeys and videos and a simple online ordering facility if you can't find the book you want elsewhere.

www.lonelyplanet.com
or
AOL keyword: lp

ONELY PLANET PRODUCTS

nely Planet is known worldwide for publishing practical, reliable and no-nonsense travel information in our guides and on our web site. The Lonely Planet list covers just about every accessible part of the world. Currently there are eight series: *travel guides, shoestring guides, walking guides, city guides, phrasebooks, audio packs, travel atlases* and *Journeys* – a unique collection of travel writing.

EUROPE

Amsterdam • Austria • Baltic States phrasebook • Britain • Central Europe on a shoestring • Central Europe phrasebook • Czech & Slovak Republics • Denmark • Dublin • Eastern Europe on a shoestring • Eastern Europe phrasebook • Estonia, Latvia & Lithuania • Finland • France • French phrasebook • German phrasebook • Greece • Greek phrasebook • Hungary • Iceland, Greenland & the Faroe Islands • Ireland • Italian phrasebook • Italy • Mediterranean Europe on a shoestring • Mediterranean Europe phrasebook • Paris • Poland • Portugal • Portugal travel atlas • Prague • Russia, Ukraine & Belarus • Russian phrasebook • Scandinavian & Baltic Europe on a shoestring • Scandinavian Europe phrasebook • Slovenia • Spain • Spanish phrasebook • St Petersburg • Switzerland • Trekking in Greece • Trekking in Spain • Ukrainian phrasebook • Vienna • Walking in Britain • Walking in Switzerland • Western Europe on a shoestring • Western Europe phrasebook

Travel Literature: The Olive Grove: Travels in Greece

NORTH AMERICA

Alaska • Backpacking in Alaska • Baja California • California & Nevada • Canada • Florida • Hawaii • Honolulu • Los Angeles • Mexico • Miami • New England • New Orleans • New York City • New York, New Jersey & Pennsylvania • Pacific Northwest USA • Rocky Mountain States • San Francisco • Southwest USA • USA phrasebook • Washington, DC & the Capital Region

CENTRAL AMERICA & THE CARIBBEAN

Bermuda • Central America on a shoestring • Costa Rica • Cuba • Eastern Caribbean • Guatemala, Belize & Yucatán: La Ruta Maya • Jamaica

SOUTH AMERICA

Argentina, Uruguay & Paraguay • Bolivia • Brazil • Brazilian phrasebook • Buenos Aires • Chile & Easter Island • Chile & Easter Island travel atlas • Colombia • Ecuador & the Galápagos Islands • Latin American Spanish phrasebook • Peru • Quechua phrasebook • Rio de Janeiro • South America on a shoestring • Trekking in the Patagonian Andes • Venezuela

Travel Literature: Full Circle: A South American Journey

ANTARCTICA

Antarctica

ISLANDS OF THE INDIAN OCEAN

Madagascar & Comoros • Maldives• Mauritius, Réunion & Seychelles

AFRICA

Africa - the South • Africa on a shoestring • Arabic (Moroccan) phrasebook • Cape Town • Central Africa • East Africa • Egypt • Egypt travel atlas• Ethiopian (Amharic) phrasebook • Kenya • Kenya travel atlas • Malawi, Mozambique & Zambia • Morocco • North Africa • South Africa, Lesotho & Swaziland • South Africa, Lesotho & Swaziland travel atlas • Swahili phrasebook • Trekking in East Africa • West Africa • Zimbabwe, Botswana & Namibia • Zimbabwe, Botswana & Namibia travel atlas

Travel Literature: The Rainbird: A Central African Journey • Songs to an African Sunset: A Zimbabwean Story

MAIL ORDER

Lonely Planet products are distributed worldwide. They are also available by mail order from Lonely Planet, so if you have difficulty finding a title please write to us. North American and South American residents should write to Embarcadero West, 155 Filbert St, Suite 251, Oakland CA 94607, USA; European and African residents should write to 10 Barley Mow Passage, Chiswick, London W4 4PH; and residents of other countries to PO Box 617, Hawthorn, Victoria 3122, Australia.

NORTH-EAST ASIA

Beijing • Cantonese phrasebook • China • Hong Kong • Hong Kong, Macau & Guangzhou • Japan • Japanese phrasebook • Japanese audio pack • Korea • Korean phrasebook • Mandarin phrasebook • Mongolia • Mongolian phrasebook • North-East Asia on a shoestring • Seoul • Taiwan • Tibet • Tibet phrasebook • Tokyo

Travel Literature: Lost Japan

MIDDLE EAST & CENTRAL ASIA

Arab Gulf States • Arabic (Egyptian) phrasebook • Central Asia • Iran • Israel & the Palestinian Territories • Israel & the Palestinian Territories travel atlas • Istanbul • Jerusalem • Jordan & Syria • Jordan, Syria & Lebanon travel atlas • Middle East • Turkey • Turkish phrasebook • Turkey travel atlas • Yemen

Travel Literature: The Gates of Damascus • Kingdom of the Film Stars: Journey into Jordan

ALSO AVAILABLE:

Travel with Children • Traveller's Tales

INDIAN SUBCONTINENT

Bangladesh • Bengali phrasebook • Delhi • Hindi/Urdu phrasebook • India • India & Bangladesh travel atlas • Indian Himalaya • Karakoram Highway • Nepal • Nepali phrasebook • Pakistan • Rajasthan • Sri Lanka • Sri Lanka phrasebook • Trekking in the Indian Himalaya • Trekking in the Karakoram & Hindukush • Trekking In the Nepal Himalaya

Travel Literature: In Rajasthan • Shopping for Buddhas

SOUTH-EAST ASIA

Bali & Lombok • Bangkok • Burmese phrasebook • Cambodia • Ho Chi Minh City • Indonesia • Indonesian phrasebook • Indonesian audio pack • Jakarta • Java • Laos • Lao phrasebook • Laos travel atlas • Malay phrasebook • Malaysia, Singapore & Brunei • Myanmar (Burma) • Philippines • Pilipino phrasebook • Singapore • South-East Asia on a shoestring • South-East Asia phrasebook • Thailand • Thailand's Islands & Beaches • Thailand travel atlas • Thai phrasebook • Thai audio pack • Thai Hill Tribes phrasebook • Vietnam • Vietnamese phrasebook • Vietnam travel atlas

AUSTRALIA & THE PACIFIC

Australia • Australian phrasebook • Bushwalking in Australia • Bushwalking in Papua New Guinea • Fiji • Fijian phrasebook • Islands of Australia's Great Barrier Reef • Melbourne • Micronesia • New Caledonia • New South Wales & the ACT • New Zealand • Northern Territory • Outback Australia • Papua New Guinea • Papua New Guinea phrasebook • Queensland • Rarotonga & the Cook Islands • Samoa • Solomon Islands • South Australia • Sydney • Tahiti & French Polynesia • Tasmania • Tonga • Tramping in New Zealand • Vanuatu • Victoria • Western Australia

Travel Literature: Islands in the Clouds • Sean & David's Long Drive

THE LONELY PLANET STORY

Lonely Planet published its first book in 1973 in response to the numerous 'How did you do it?' questions Maureen and Tony Wheeler were asked after driving, bussing, hitching, sailing and railing their way from England to Australia.

Written at a kitchen table and hand collated, trimmed and stapled, *Across Asia on the Cheap* became an instant local bestseller, inspiring thoughts of another book.

Eighteen months in South-East Asia resulted in their second guide, *South-East Asia on a shoestring*, which they put together in a backstreet Chinese hotel in Singapore in 1975. The 'yellow bible', as it quickly became known to backpackers around the world, soon became *the* guide to the region. It has sold well over half a million copies and is now in its 9th edition, still retaining its familiar yellow cover.

Today there are over 240 titles, including travel guides, walking guides, language kits & phrasebooks, travel atlases and travel literature. The company is the largest independent travel publisher in the world. Although Lonely Planet initially specialised in guides to Asia, today there are few corners of the globe that have not been covered.

The emphasis continues to be on travel for independent travellers. Tony and Maureen still travel for several months of each year and play an active part in the writing, updating and quality control of Lonely Planet's guides.

They have been joined by over 70 authors and 170 staff at our offices in Melbourne (Australia), Oakland (USA), London (UK) and Paris (France). Travellers themselves also make a valuable contribution to the guides through the feedback we receive in thousands of letters each year and on our web site.

The people at Lonely Planet strongly believe that travellers can make a positive contribution to the countries they visit, both through their appreciation of the countries' culture, wildlife and natural features, and through the money they spend. In addition, the company makes a direct contribution to the countries and regions it covers. Since 1986 a percentage of the income from each book has been donated to ventures such as famine relief in Africa; aid projects in India; agricultural projects in Central America; Greenpeace's efforts to halt French nuclear testing in the Pacific; and Amnesty International.

'I hope we send people out with the right attitude about travel. You realise when you travel that there are so many different perspectives about the world, so we hope these books will make people more interested in what they see. Guidebooks can't really guide people. All you can do is point them in the right direction.'

– Tony Wheeler

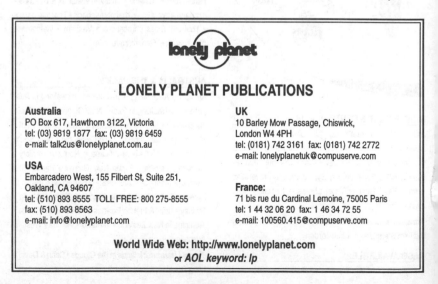

LONELY PLANET PUBLICATIONS

Australia
PO Box 617, Hawthorn 3122, Victoria
tel: (03) 9819 1877 fax: (03) 9819 6459
e-mail: talk2us@lonelyplanet.com.au

USA
Embarcadero West, 155 Filbert St, Suite 251,
Oakland, CA 94607
tel: (510) 893 8555 TOLL FREE: 800 275-8555
fax: (510) 893 8563
e-mail: info@lonelyplanet.com

UK
10 Barley Mow Passage, Chiswick,
London W4 4PH
tel: (0181) 742 3161 fax: (0181) 742 2772
e-mail: lonelyplanetuk@compuserve.com

France:
71 bis rue du Cardinal Lemoine, 75005 Paris
tel: 1 44 32 06 20 fax: 1 46 34 72 55
e-mail: 100560.415@compuserve.com

World Wide Web: http://www.lonelyplanet.com
or *AOL keyword: lp*